I LOVE YOU LIKE ONE

I LOVE YOU LIKE ONE

A LETTER TO MY DAUGHTER, ABDUCTED BY A CULT

IAIN AVERY BRYSON

I Love You Like One: A Letter to My Daughter, Abducted by a Cult

Iain Avery Bryson

ISBN 979-8-9905690-4-1 (paper)

1st edition 2024

Book Cover by 100covers.com

Visit the author's website at www.iloveyoulikeone.com

For my daughter, Adelle, her mother, Agata, and all of those who have suffered because of ritual abuse. Enough is enough.

ACKNOWLEDGEMENTS

In and for all things I first acknowledge God. He is the only reason for our hope, which is not only hope, but assurance. He is my only source of confidence. Because of Jesus Christ, the Son of God, we have a mediator to the Creator of all things. We have a God who hears us, loves us, and answers our prayers. From Him comes mercy, grace, healing, and freedom for all the captives. He is worthy of all glory and praise.

Without Emily Bryson, this book would not be anything close to what it is. Without Emily Bryson, I would not be who I am. This woman of God has voluntarily decided to give her life over to serving the One who can stop the abuse of her stepdaughter and her husband's first wife. Once she understood what was happening, she couldn't turn away. Emily is the epitome of compassion, patience, and love for all living things. She is my second wife, and she is my best friend. She is the editor of this book, and sometimes the co-author. Emily, I hope you know how much I love you. Thank you!

Agata, the mother of our precious child, my first wife, the strongest person I have ever known. Three days before the abduction, I told you that I was going to write a book about you and use your name. Your response to me was, "Good, I want you to use my name." This book is for our daughter, and for you. This book is for our family. I needn't go any further because the entire book is a testament to who you are; I can't wait for everyone else to see. Thank you, Agatka, I love you like one.

Adelle, my daughter. I know that you are amazing, just as you have always been. I am proud of you, and I love you. Nothing can change that. You are a treasure from God.

Thank you to my mom and dad. You provided me with everything that I needed to grow into the man I am today. Our home was full of love and joy. You were generous with your time and with your resources. You made it a priority to ensure that I knew the Lord, and that I received an excellent education. Though it may seem that I am critical of you at times in this book, it is only because I am as adamant about my daughter as you were for me. I pray that this book helps you to see the situation clearly, and I pray for reconciliation and restoration in our family. In all I do, I desire to honor you, mom, and dad. I love you.

When life throws at you something like what got thrown at me, you learn who your true friends are. Brian, I've known you the longest. You stuck by me through it all. Thank you and I love you. Art, my brother, your help sustained me through fifty months of Polish incarceration. You have one of the biggest hearts I have ever encountered. Thank you and I love you.

I have so many Polish friends to thank. There were so many people along the way who helped me in one way or another. You took me in as one of your own and treated me with honor and respect. Several of you asked me to be easy on your country when I wrote this book, and what I can say is this: I love the Polish people. They are the kindest, most hospitable, most selfless people I have ever encountered.

Maria and Aniela (not their real names) believed in me when nobody else did. They helped me to remember who I was and that I was not alone. Thank you.

Mariusz Wirkus and Marcin Kuc helped me immensely during my incarceration. They are a demonstration of true brotherly love. Thank you.

I also want to thank John S. and Pastor Bob McCoy for their friendship and counsel. And so many others, including Joshua Michael Cave, Randy Noblitt, Ellen Lacter, Jean Riseman, Diane (Rape Crisis Center in Texas), Eric Meldrum, our GBC family, Rebecca Davis, Lisa Meister, Patricia and Stoner Clark, and George Stepanik.

And together we shut it down!

CONTENTS

INTRODUCTION

"GUESS HOW MUCH I LOVE YOU"

―――――――――――――――――――
――――――――――――――――――――――――――
―――――――――――――――――――――――

My name is Iain Avery Bryson. I am your father, the man you called "Daddy" for the first four years of your life. You are Adelle Avery Bryson, and you were born in New London, Connecticut, USA on January 30, 2007. Your name has since been changed to Adela Soczewska; I do not know if they removed your middle name as well as your proper family name, but I suspect this is the case.

My daughter, you need to know this: On December 27th, 2010, after making our scrambled eggs together for breakfast and hotdogs for lunch, after we played outside in the snow for hours and went to the local farm, after we had all day together because your mom wanted me to spend time with you alone, you were taken from me and from our home. I gave you a hug thinking you were going to the library down the street, believing that I would be putting you to bed that night, but I never saw you again.

This book is for you, and I've written it to you. Of course, it is my desire that many others read it too. Evil cannot survive when it's exposed and brought to the light. I want you to know that I have never and will never stop fighting for our family, and that although I am weak and can do nothing on my own, we have an unshakable hope in Almighty God.

I am sorry it has taken me so long to get your story to the public; writing this book is one of the hardest things I have ever had to do. I have had to deal with losing everything, and then with being powerless and completely alone, because for years there was not a person on this planet who stood by me and said, "I believe you and will help you fight for your family."

While I can understand why nobody helped, whether it was family or government institutions, and I can say that I harbor no resentment, their error must be corrected. The reason being that this is not about them or me, but the fact that you were abducted by an evil cult, something that has not been rectified as of the day of the printing of this book.

Like the puzzles we used to do together on our living room floor, this story has many pieces, and it's important to correctly put them all together to understand the whole picture. The complexity of this puzzle has been sufficient up to this point to throw many off track. I want you and everyone to know the truth in its entirety, piece by piece. Once the puzzle is seen in its completed form, it would seem it would be difficult for this situation to not get the attention it deserves, as has been the case for over thirteen years.

I am going to come across many ways throughout the story because it takes place over time, and because I am an imperfect man, learning as I go. Because of the allegations against me that were used to take you away from me, one of my intentions is to show you that I am not afraid of any true story about me.

Due to factors that will be discussed, the last time I spoke to your mother she hated me, and I have been told that you have similar feelings. I'm not saying that your feelings are not real, but that they have been manipulated and misdirected. Everything you think about me has been fed to you by those who have allied themselves against me. Because of your age when you were taken from me, you could not have decided on your own that you hated me. The fact that authorities have respected your testimony in court proceedings is merely proof that they are ignorant of how beliefs are formulated in young children.

> "PA [Parental alienation] is a mental condition in which a child – usually one whose parents are engaged in a high-conflict separation or divorce – allies strongly with one parent (the preferred parent) and rejects a relationship with the other parent (the alienated parent) without legitimate justification" (Bernet, as cited in Lorandos and Bernet 2020, 5-6).

Your mother did not choose to abduct you, but rather was compelled to because of severe abuse. She had been warning me for weeks that her family in Poland "is a cult," and that she was going to take you back to the "cult" because of "mind control." She told me that she has "something like Stockholm Syndrome," and assured me that her dad had "created a red herring" so that nobody would believe me when I tried to get help, and that I would never see you again. It happened exactly as she warned it would. In this book, I will show you how.

In the case of losing a leg to a landmine, or a spouse to cancer or a car accident, the "normal" course of grief is for the survivor to go from the "no this can't be happening" stage to the "wow that was and is tough, but I'm going to make it and it doesn't feel so bad anymore, at least not all the time" stage, with several distinct stages in between. But what about when the event that causes the grief is never-ending? What happens when the grief grows exponentially with the passage of time? What happens when your worst nightmare is your reality, every day of your life? I didn't lose you (and your mom) once, but daily since December 27, 2010. I've had to watch you grow up with pictures from Google searches (see images below).

Some of the pictures of you I have found online between 2015 – 2024.

I used to wonder, *what is the purpose of life? What am I doing here? Is there a God? If there is, what would I need "it" for?* When you were born, I started to understand more about my purpose, but I was naïve, believing that life would be mostly easy. It wasn't until the year that everything I cared about was ripped from my grasp and extinguished like a cigarette under a cowboy boot that I didn't wonder so much about those questions anymore because the answers became clear; tragedy often brings clarity.

I didn't know that God exists until I first knew the devil does. After coming nose to nose with the absolute epitome of evil, ritual abuse, I no longer had any doubt about God's existence, and the fact that I need Him and stand no chance without Him.

Ritual abuse. I would expect you to ask, "What is that?" because by its nature, even though you're in it, you're not going to know that you're in it. I wouldn't think that most people reading this would have much of an idea at this point because I know what my understanding was prior to having it thrust before my face; I had never heard of it either. As the story unfolds, it will become clearer. For now, my point is that only the absolute terror of being confronted with what I believe is the greatest evil in our world convinced me that "God" is, in fact, our only chance.

* * *

When I first met your mother, I was, like much of society still is, oblivious to the extent and repercussions of child abuse. As I will show in detail, it was clear early on in our relationship that your mom had a history of abuse. I suspected this within weeks of knowing her because there were many serious red flags, but I also had decided by that point that I was going to love her no matter what. Her issues never went away, and the topic frequently came up, but we never got further than "incest" and "borderline personality disorder" because trying to speak to her about her childhood was an act of futility.

> "Prior to the 1980s, the sexual abuse of children and adolescents was a well-kept secret throughout society... Throughout the 1980s and 1990s, methodologically sound empirical studies were published indicating that approximately one third of all women and one fourth of all men are sexually abused prior to the age of eighteen" (Frawley-O'Dea 191).

While I could see that your mom had been abused, I completely neglected to take into account the possibility that it could've been anything more than inadvertent, random, or sloppy drunk abuse. I assumed wrongly. The idea that people would intentionally and systematically abuse children for the purpose of totally controlling them hadn't ever crossed my mind. The signs were there, as you will see, but I couldn't see them yet, not until it was too late.

> "In their research and clinical experience, therapists Bentovim and Tranter (1994) have found that families harbouring cultures of sexual abuse are of two types: openly dysfunctional and well known to welfare agencies, or closed systems unknown to the authorities and isolated from their surrounding communities. Whilst both kinds of families place a high premium on loyalty and secrecy, abuse within openly dysfunctional family types is more likely to be detected due to their contact with police and health and welfare services. In contrast, organised abuse within apparently 'normal' families who are not dependent on government assistance can go unnoticed for many years if at all. The children of these families are afforded few opportunities to disclose their abuse or to seek external intervention" (Salter 104).

So, then, why did your loving mother take you back to a cult? In her own words, it was "mind control." When I first heard her say this, I thought she was crazy. Incest and borderline personality disorder were in the public discourse, but "mind control" was something I couldn't yet wrap my head around, and it shattered the fabric of my reality when I did finally grasp it. While it is not a pleasant topic to encounter or ruminate on, it just is what it is, and it just is what happened. This book will demonstrate incontrovertibly that your mother did not "escape with you from me to safety," but that she was and is the subject of extreme coercive practices.

> "Trauma-based mind control programming can be defined as systematic torture that blocks the victim's capacity for conscious processing (through pain, terror, drugs, illusion, sensory deprivation, sensory over-stimulation, oxygen deprivation, cold, heat, spinning, brain stimulation, and often, near-death), and then employs suggestion and/or classical and operant conditioning (consistent with well-established behavioral modification principles) to implant thoughts, directives, and perceptions into the unconscious mind, often in newly-formed trauma-induced dissociated identities that force the victim to do, feel, think, or perceive things for the purposes of the programmer. The objective is for the victim to follow directives with no conscious awareness, including execution of acts in clear violation of the victim's volition, moral principles, and spiritual convictions" (Lacter and Lehman, 2008, as cited in Noblitt and Noblitt, 2008, 88).

I remember as a child in the 1980s and 90s, right in the middle of watching something "fun" on TV, images of starving, emaciated children would flash across the screen for twenty or thirty seconds with a 1-800 number so people could send money. Disgust and shame are two things I recall feeling, and while I can't speak to what anyone else was feeling because we didn't talk about it, I do know that the tendency was to change the channel as fast as possible. *Is it gone? Phew, let's get back to fun, eh? Those people are not us. Stinks to be them, if they're even real, but we have our own problems.*

> "The ordinary response to atrocities is to banish them from consciousness. Certain violations of the social compact are too terrible to utter aloud: this is the meaning of the word *unspeakable*. Atrocities, however, refuse to be buried" (Herman, 1992, 1).

Not only are certain atrocities "unspeakable," but many are often unthinkable. There are many people, therefore, who deny that ritual abuse exists. This plays into the hands of perpetrators, who depend upon incredulity. If one were to search and merely scratch the surface, it would be easy to conclude that ritual abuse is fictitious. A Google search for "ritual abuse" or "satanic ritual abuse" redirects to "Satanic panic," and describes it as "...a moral panic consisting of over 12,000 unsubstantiated cases of Satanic ritual abuse (SRA, sometimes known as ritual abuse, ritualistic abuse, organized abuse, or sadistic ritual abuse) starting in the United States in the 1980s, spreading throughout many parts of the world by the late 1990s, and persisting today" (https://en.wikipedia.org/wiki/Satanic_panic). (For ritual abuse deniers, see also Aquino, Frankfurter, Hicks, Nathan & Snedeker, Ofshe & Watters, Piper, Richardson et al., Spanos, and Victor).

The problem with these authors is that they argue that ritual abuse is not real. Undoubtedly there have been some false allegations of ritual abuse, just as there have been for property theft, assault, resisting arrest, or rape, for example. We wouldn't conclude that all property theft allegations are false, and that property theft is nothing more than an urban myth or a "panic," even if there were thousands of unsubstantiated cases and/or false accusations. So too it is a huge mistake to do so with ritual abuse. The fact is: we know that ritual abuse exists; there should be no doubt anymore. The authors above do not represent a real threat, because, in reality, it is they who have been debunked (see Appendix 1).

Ritual abuse, by its very nature, is designed to remain undetected and unbelievable; the victims and the survivors are the evidence. "Satanic Panic" is a term that has done nothing more (or less) than help to convince the public that ritual abuse is not anything they need to concern themselves with – better to focus on things like fuel prices or the weather. However, given that it is real, I think that a little "panicking" is in order; after all, most people have spent their lives never hearing about it, thinking it is a conspiracy theory, or believing that it is far from them and their loved ones. How would life change for them, I wonder, if they knew it was not, if they knew that someone was practicing it in their neighborhood, if they knew their children could marry into it, as I did.

> "So I have gone from someone kind of neutral and not knowing what to think about it all, to someone who clearly believes ritual abuse is real and that the people who say it isn't are either naive like people who didn't want to believe the Holocaust or—they're dirty" (Hammond).

* * *

From a Christian perspective, the Bible is the Word of God, authentic and true. Therefore, it follows that the truth is, "That which has been is what will be, That which is done is what will be done, And there is nothing new under the sun. Is there anything of which it may be said, 'See, this is new'?" (Ecclesiastes 1:9-10 NKJV).

"As we examined the historical and anthropological literature, we found accounts of religions, cults, and fraternal organizations that ostensibly used traumatic rituals for the purpose of creating altered states of consciousness. These mental states have sometimes been viewed as sacred – as the magical catalyst for profound visions or possession by gods. In other cases, these methods have allegedly been used to establish a powerful kind of psychological control that, until recently, existed underground in secrecy essentially unknown to the community of mental health professionals... These traumatic acts of mind control reportedly occur in modern societies, including the United States and other industrialized as well as developing countries. The stories are often incredible and include descriptions of abuse in sadistic ceremonies, some of which are allegedly associated with satanic, Luciferian, and other ideologies alien to many of us. The psychiatric symptom pattern displayed by these individuals appears similar to those historically and contemporaneously described as 'possessed'... Our conclusion is that the diagnosis of DID [dissociative identity disorder] is a Western version of what has been known historically and anthropologically as possession" (Noblitt and Noblitt, 2014, xi).

Children have been sacrificed and "passed through the fire" since the beginning of human existence. The worship of demons isn't something new, and ritual abuse is the ultimate practice of evil (Jeremiah 19:5, 32:35, 2 Kings 21:6). We should know that it is around because it has always been around; the devil has not stopped working or giving power to those who serve him all over the world. Ritual abuse was not invented in the 80s, nor was it debunked in the 90s. I believe that ritual abuse is the greatest issue of the 21st century. There is nothing else more pressing, nothing else that needs to be stopped more than it does.

I know this is a lot to process, and it may feel overwhelming at this point, but it has to be addressed because it is the reason you were taken from me. One of the reasons your abductors were successful was because of societal ignorance on this topic. Admittedly, this story is heavy, and it wasn't the story I anticipated for us, but now I know it is also a story of love and hope.

* * *

Your mom is the most extraordinary person I have ever met. If only I can get people to see her as I do: a little girl who was horribly abused, a mother who was forced to subject her own daughter to the same unthinkable abuse, a woman who did absolutely everything that she could've done so that her story would be heard. I don't expect people to take my word for it, but I do hope that they will look at the facts, not for me but for you and her.

Instead of "I love you," your mom often told me "I love you like one." I never knew what she meant; I assumed it was just one of those quirky things that people in love sometimes make up to express affection for their partner. When I asked her, she gave me that special look that she often would when she knew I hadn't yet grasped something of great importance; it was the look that informed me that I was going to have to wait to find out.

I look forward to the day when I get to ask her again, but the nature of our story has convinced me that she meant something like this: We are one, and as such, we must fight for each other. When one is suffering, all suffer. It is the true meaning of love, a love that is selfless and self-sacrificing for the other.

"So we, being many, are one body in Christ, and individually members of one another" (Romans 12:5 NKJV).

* * *

My daughter, you are sufficient to be the complete purpose of my life for a thousand lifetimes. I wrote this book because I had to; I believe that He who created us has laid it upon my heart to tell this story. My hope is that it glorifies Him, and that it attests to the fact that although the world is dark, He is light and far more powerful. My other hope is to stop you from being hurt, and to look in your eyes once again. You must be set free. Ritual abuse must be exposed. The people of the world need to wake up and begin to protect our children.

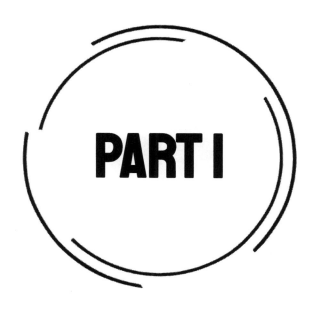

PART I

1977-2003

"THE YEARS TEACH MUCH WHICH THE DAYS NEVER KNOW"
- RALPH WALDO EMERSON
(FROM YOUR MOM'S QUOTE JOURNAL)

CHAPTER I

THE BEGINNING

The real story is you and your mother, but in order to get there, it seems necessary to introduce myself and where I came from. I met your mom when I was 27 years old, and she was 22. I thought that I had won the grand prize, and I had; I was married to her, and because of that you exist. But how did I get there, and what can I tell you that will help in understanding the rest of the story?

Me and my mom. June 1978. *Me and my dad. 1978.*

I am blessed to have been born into the family that I was born into. My childhood was idyllic, and of course I thought this was typical for most children. On the whole, I have lived a life surrounded and supported with love.

I was born on June 1, 1977, in Eugene, Oregon, USA, the firstborn of two hippies, Kirk and Marianne, a c-section baby, as were you, Adelle. I do not have any memories of the first few years of my life, though I do know from hearsay that my dad was working in home repairs, construction, and renovation, and my mom as a nurse. Despite my lack of vivid memories during this time, my feeling is that I was deeply loved and well cared for.

My middle name, Avery, is also the middle name that you were given at birth, and my mom's maiden name. Because of my mom, I have lots of stories to tell you about the Averys, but for now I will just make mention of the fact that Averys get butter on their nose on their birthday. I haven't participated in this tradition since January 30, 2010.

*Grandpa Avery putting butter on
my nose on my birthday.*

Me putting butter on your nose on your 3rd birthday. January 30, 2010.

My brother, Kyle, and my sister, Carrie, were both born in Oklahoma, in 1979 and 1981, respectively. Our parents were attending Rhema Bible College in Broken Arrow. I do not remember the births of my siblings, nor do I remember much of anything else that wasn't shown to me later in photographs. My mom's sister (Sara) and her family, my uncle Dave, and cousins Jeremiah (1975), Angela (1977), and Rachel (1980), were also in Oklahoma during this time.

My earliest memories are from this short stint in Oklahoma, when I was between two and four years old. The first, a faint memory of playing with bugs in our backyard, some type of centipede or millepede. I don't remember what I was doing with them, or if I played with them once or multiple times.

My only other memory from Oklahoma is of being spanked by my uncle. I only remember it happening once, and it was not physically painful. He believed that doing so was necessary and biblical, and I know that he has always loved me.

It is because of this moment that I have any memories of their house at all, which is where the spank took place. I remember the furniture, the layout of the room, and where my cousins were standing. I don't even have memories from within my own home during this period of my life.

> "Whether we remember a particular event at all, and how accurate our memories of it are, largely depend on how personally meaningful it was and how emotional we felt about it at the time. The key factor is our level or arousal. We all have memories associated with particular people, songs, smells, and places that stay with us for a long time" (van der Kolk 177).

Though this is my first memory of being spanked, it is not my last. Throughout my younger years, I remember being spanked by my parents, and although it was not an everyday occurrence, these events do represent some of my most vivid early childhood memories. While I cannot say that I deserved this, I can say that they had their reasons, and that they were doing their best with what they knew and believed.

After living in Oklahoma long enough for my brother and sister to be born, both my family and my aunt's family relocated to Connecticut. I remember sitting on my dad's lap as he sang me a song, a song that I would later incorporate and use myself with you. I recall the room, the chair, the feeling of being on my dad's lap, his hair, his embrace, his attention, and knowing that I was loved. I remember not wanting the moment to end. The only changes that I had to make when you were born were my name to your name, "he's" to "she's," and "son" to "daughter."

"Iain Avery Bryson, he's my number one son, he's so fine, I'm glad he's mine, Iain Avery Bryson."

"Adelle Avery Bryson, she's my number one daughter, she's so fine, I'm glad she's mine, Adelle Avery Bryson."

Your mom was always pleased with me when I sang this song to you. "Iain, I like that," she assured me, flashing something of a mix between a smile and a smirk. I think that she knew that it would stick deep into your memory banks where nobody could touch it, that your experience was ingrained like the experience with my own dad. I know that you knew you were loved.

* * *

Living in Old Saybrook, Connecticut, somewhere between preschool and second grade, my dad brought me up the stairs and into the bathroom to discipline me for saying a "bad word." The punishment for saying a "bad word" was to have my mouth washed out with soap.

I remember going up the staircase, the feeling as well as the visual aspects of the stairs themselves. I remember the bathroom, the mirror, my dad's hand, and the bar of soap. I remember being disgusted, not only with the "discipline" itself, but with the blatant realization that adults don't know how to communicate with children. I don't have any other memories containing that staircase or that bathroom.

One day when I was about seven years old, playing wiffle ball across the street with kids in the neighborhood, I said the derogatory word for "poop." From then on, a twelve-year-old neighbor girl named Jennifer threatened to tell my mom what I said if I didn't comply with her demands. I felt that I had to do what she said, since there was no way that my parents could know that I had said such a word. It was the first double bind I recall, whereby both options were undesirable, but I chose to comply with the abuser rather than get in trouble.

It started off with her bringing me into the woods and telling me to pull my pants down. Trusting her, and having no idea what was happening, I cooperated. As it progressed, I began to realize that something was wrong, but I had no frame of reference or understanding on such matters.

Another time she ordered, "Pull down your pants and lie under this blanket with me. If you don't, I'll tell your mom," and so I did. She fondled me and forced me to do the same to her, though I had no idea what was happening at age seven. I wondered why nobody noticed that I was under a blanket with this girl. I wondered why nobody stopped her, why nobody came to my rescue.

When I got home, I tried to communicate with my mom the best I could, but I didn't have the words and couldn't get through to her. I acted out in frustration by drawing on the side of Jennifer's house with my colored pencils and crayons. When it was discovered that I had defaced the house, I had to apologize and wash it off. There was never any wondering by the adults, that I was aware of, as to why I would do such a thing. All that I learned was that my reaction was wrong and unacceptable, and that nobody could speak my language.

It progressed to her bringing me into the woods with one of her friends so they both could look at me with my pants down. I felt violated and scared, never having experienced anything like that before. I ran away from them through the woods as if a monster was chasing me, and I tripped on a root or a rock that was protruding from the ground that caused me to fall hard and break my collarbone. "Running from a girl" was the official reason that everyone settled on.

I was taken to an emergency room where I was given an injection into my clavicle area, an x-ray, and a sling that I had to wear for a while. I was never asked why I was running, why I fell, or what had happened, and I didn't feel like I could say anything or that they would hear me if I did. *Why didn't they know?* I thought. *How could they not know?*

I repressed all memories of these events until much later, until you were three years old and painting on the walls of our house after one of your returns from Poland. It was only then that I recalled myself scribbling on the side of the neighbor girl's house, as well as the emotional state that I experienced both during and after the event. Even after remembering my own abuse, I was unable to connect the dots when I was in the adult role with you, in the same way that the adults in my own life hadn't been able to; I made the same mistake that my parents made.

While I could remember that it happened to me, I couldn't fathom the possibility that it could be happening to you. "The repression of past torments and its cost render people deaf to the screams of children and blind to the obvious connections" (A. Miller 3). I was too focused on myself and on the operation of my own memory; the idea that someone could be hurting you wasn't within the realm of possibility in my mind.

I believe that the most critical trauma was that I did not feel like I could approach my parents; I had nobody to turn to for rescue or for processing. This was a sort of betrayal, simply because those who were supposed to protect me didn't. I had no words for it, had never heard of it, and couldn't wrap my head around it, though the emotions of the experience were still trapped inside me with a desire to be expressed.

It was around this time that my first and only recurring nightmare began. A monster was after me, causing me to awake in a state of terror. I also started experiencing other symptoms of abuse like soiling my bed and anxiety. It seems to me that the abuse at the hands of the neighbor, along with the secondary trauma of not having anyone I felt I could turn to, led to me acting out over the next several years.

CHAPTER 2

"IF I DON'T DO IT, WHAT GOOD IS MY WORD?"

"What is important to understand is that the child learns cruelty not by watching TV but always by suffering and repressing" (A. Miller 46).

I was briefly kicked off the elementary school bus for fighting, and I remember putting nails under the bus tires when it stopped to pick me up. The only other thing that I remember about riding on this bus was that the driver played the same song every single day, over and over, Jimmy Buffett's "Volcano." I looked forward to it and wondered if I was the only one who noticed.

"Now I don't know, I don't know, I don't know where I'm a-gonna go when the volcano blows..."

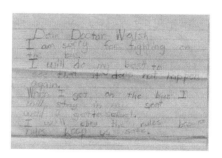

Letter I wrote to the principal of my school after the fight: "Dear Doctor Walsh, I am sorry for fighting on the bus. I will do my best to see that it does not happen again. When I get on the bus I will stay in my seat until I get to school. I will obey the rules because rules keep us safe."

One day I stopped the paperboy as he rode his bike passed our house. "Do you have a paper for me?" I inquired in a demanding tone.

"No," he replied, "I only have enough newspapers for the customers on my route."

"Ok, well tomorrow you are going to bring me a paper. If you don't have a newspaper for me tomorrow, then I will hit you with a rock," I threatened.

The next day I waited for him, and when he pulled up on his bicycle, I asked if he had my paper. When he told me that he didn't, I felt obligated to do as I said I would do in this situation. *If I don't do it, what good is my word?* I reasoned. *Why would I have said it if I didn't mean it?* I picked up a rock from the ground, and I tossed it at his head from a close distance.

My intention was not to hurt him, but to make good on my word; I really had no preconception of what the result would be of following through with my threat. The impact caused him to bleed, and so I rushed him into my house to show him to my mom, who I knew could help since she was a nurse. I was in shock, just doing what I knew needed to be done, not worried about getting into trouble and not concerned about his injury as I knew that my mom would take care of it.

My mom patched him up and we drove him over to his house to his mom. I went inside and apologized robotically, still in shock, feeling like his mom thought that I was a monster; I was glad that my mom was by my side. I knew that he had to get stitches, but I don't recall getting in trouble, nor do I remember thinking about it much at all, other than something like a vague *oops, phew, I won't do that again...*

Both my paternal and my maternal grandparents lived in the same town as us, and we spent a good amount of time with both. I remember fishing with Grandpa Bryson at the end of the pier and catching buckets of snapper bluefish. I remember my Grandpa Avery giving me my first gun, a Daisy BB gun for my birthday, and a friend from school chasing me around the fort in our yard threatening to shoot me with it. Needless to say, this was the last time he was invited over to our house.

My sister, brother, and I standing at the fort in our yard.

I enjoyed school and relished the academic challenges and competition therein. My mom instilled within me from a very young age that my job was to do my best, and being frequently reminded of this axiom caused it to become integrated into who I was becoming. I was brought up to love God and to love the principles upon which our country was founded, like liberty and justice for all.

We attended church for most of my childhood, a couple of different non-denominational Christian churches depending upon where we were living at the time. In Sunday School I learned the importance of the Word of God, and though I had no idea what the words meant at the time, I memorized the verses, unaware that I would need them for the future.

* * *

My parents sent my brother and I on a plane to Florida to visit our paternal grandparents whose custom was to winter in the Sarasota area on the Gulf Coast. We collected shark teeth on the beach and enjoyed the white, cool sand. On the return flight, wearing our badges to indicate that we were minors travelling without an adult, we found ourselves seated next to a woman who was chain smoking, as this was back in the day when smoking was normal on airplanes.

I watched in amazement as she sucked down one cigarette after another, stuffing the used filters into her little armrest ashtray, explaining to us that she started when she was our age. "I used to pick up butts on the side of the road and smoke whatever was left," she informed us. Looking back on this experience now, it appears that she got some kind of pleasure in introducing us to this vice and piquing our interest.

Eventually we moved about twenty-five miles up the Connecticut shoreline, first to a little fishing village called Noank, and then to Mystic. I attended Noank Elementary School, where I placed second in a school science fair for my presentation on turtles. We were by the beach, which was nice, and we spent a lot of time as a family doing things such as catching crabs with crushed muscles.

In Mystic, living on our twenty-acre parcel in the woods, I acquired a deep appreciation for nature, and especially for the woodlands that surrounded our house. I was able to shoot my gun whenever I wanted to, a .22 rifle that I had bought for $70 from a local gun store in Groton and still have today. With hatchets and machetes, I cut down trees to make various shelters and forts, and my turtle collection continued to grow. It seemed like I constantly had a poison ivy rash over my entire body, sometimes so severe that I thought death would be a relief.

One day I remember asking my mom, "Do you love me or Dad more?"

I could see her think for a moment, wanting to make sure to give her best answer before replying, "God says I am to love your dad more."

While part of me wanted her to say that she loved me more, I also knew that she loved me totally, and so I was forced to try to figure out why God would dictate that she was to love her husband more than her son, and what that could mean. I knew that her answer did not mean that she had a lack of love for me, or less love, but that it was something else. It is different to love a husband versus a son for a reason I couldn't grasp at the time. What I didn't figure out until I had my own child is that everything starts with the husband and wife, the parents, and that the best way for parents to love their children is for them to love each other.

In 2010, I remember passing through the hallway in our Den Haag apartment just to tell your mom, who was in our bedroom, that I had realized something very important.

"Agata, I figured something out," I said excitedly, feeling like I was on to something significant. "Our love, the love between you and I, the love that I have for you, this is both because of Adelle and for Adelle. Without you there is no Adelle, and to love you is the best thing that I can do for Adelle. You are Agata Avery Bryson, and it's just one big circle with you being the center and Adelle being the reason for it all. If you are my queen, then Adelle will never doubt who she is; she will know who she is and what she is, and that she is loved..."

Now I know what my mom meant.

CHAPTER 3

"B-I-V-O-U-A-C"

In fifth grade, my family relocated to Eugene, Oregon, all the way on the exact opposite side of the country. My aunt's family had moved out there before us; it is my understanding that a pivotal part of our decision to move was to remain close to them.

My cousin Jeremiah had been, and continued to be, my best friend; I looked up to him and thought of him as an older brother who had different parents. I tried to emulate him, always wanting the same haircut and the same sneakers, interested in whatever music and television shows he was interested in. For me, he was cool, while my brother, Kyle, was younger and not as fun to hang out with yet.

One hot summer day, Jeremiah and I decided to kidnap a local boy that was out walking around in the neighborhood. We brought him into the house and kept him in the bathtub for a while, but that's all I remember. Of course, being two years older than I was, Jeremiah was the mastermind of this operation, though I certainly enjoyed the thrill it brought as well.

For fifth grade, I attended a local private Christian school, Willamette Christian School. I placed second in a state spelling bee, losing because I spelled the word "bivouac" wrong. I have never forgotten this moment, and to this day b-i-v-o-u-a-c still echoes through my head on occasion.

We moved out of Eugene to Lorane, a farming community about thirty miles away, onto a 650-acre ranch that my parents purchased as our "forever" home. This property was a wonderland, a little slice of heaven. I had a motorcycle and a horse, and I was allowed to drive our Jeep Wagoneer on the property. I attended the local public schools for sixth and seventh grade.

My brother and I spent a great deal of time playing the newly released Super Mario Brothers on the arcade machine that was in one of the two local shops. Every walk to the arcade machine involved passing rows of cigarettes that I could have touched if I wanted to; it was here that my fascination for cigarettes reemerged. They were so accessible and almost calling my name, probably because of the woman on the airplane, the Marlboro Man cowboy telling me to "come to where the flavor is," and Clint Eastwood.

I didn't want to steal, so I took a pack of Dorals off the counter when the owner wasn't looking, leaving some money for him to find after I was gone. My brother and I sat behind a big tree on our property, puffing them down one after another, pretending to be adults.

Another friend introduced me to Red Man chewing tobacco one day while we were walking in the woods. I remember being surprised that his dad knew he did this at his age and realizing that things must be a bit different in the country. Of course, I didn't know what I was doing, and so I swallowed some of the juices, causing me to get sick and throw up in the car shortly thereafter.

Not being able to be honest about the reason I had vomited, I explained it away as "car sickness," and from that point on I was given front seat priority, something that my brother and sister did not like at all. While I felt bad about lying, I also didn't see a way around it at the time, and I was happy to never have to share the front seat with my siblings. It wasn't an error I wanted corrected after it was accepted as truth.

Horses became an important part of my life because we had a stable with an arena on our ranch. My parents paid for me to take lessons, and as my skills increased, I began regularly winning at horse shows, eventually taking a couple of championship trophies. On at least one occasion, someone offered me money to stay out of the event, but I declined, competition being more important to me than money.

Me and Rabbi Basque, my Arabian gelding. September 2, 1989.

Rabbi was my horse, and he would come running to me from across the field when I called him, like Zorro's horse, Tornado. I often rode him bareback without a bridle or reins around the ranch in my free time. It was as if I had my own winged mountain banshee like in the movie *Avatar*, and while I couldn't physically connect my hair to my horse as in the movie, we had a similar connection. I rode and showed a couple of other horses, but it was Rabbi that I had the best relationship with; when I rode him, it was as if we were one. We knew, trusted, and respected each other; we were best friends as well as horse and rider.

On the ranch, we had a John Deere tractor that we used to mow our vast fields. While I generally enjoyed riding the tractor, there was a limit as to how long it was enjoyable, and it took many hours to mow our fields. My dad sometimes tasked me with these types of jobs as punishment, and when I told him that I thought he was just using me to get work done, he indicated that he could just have me move a pile of manure from one location to another, and then back to the original location. I thought that this was a strange suggestion, but I got the point, and I chose to engage in punishment work that wasn't futile.

Now, as an adult, I can see that the alternative he offered to doing purposeful work as part of my discipline was to work as many did in the gulags of the Soviet Union as described by Aleksandr Solzhenitsyn in his book *The Gulag Archipelago*; non-purposeful work is a form of torture.

One day, when I was frustrated and unhappy, I asked my dad what the answer was to overcoming the kinds of feelings I was experiencing. "Well," he said bluntly after pausing for a moment to think, "it's a decision." I pondered this, and while I didn't grasp the concept then, I began to grasp it later, and while it is simple, it is certainly not easy to do.

As I got older, my interest in competing in horse shows waned as my interest in playing football waxed. I still loved my horse and living on the ranch, but I also lived on the west coast of the United States at the time Joe Montana and Jerry Rice were winning championships in San Francisco.

For eighth grade, my parents took me out of the public school system and put me into Eugene Christian School. My class was comprised of only about ten students, and so I played football for one of the public schools in Eugene. I tore my anterior cruciate ligament in my knee after getting tackled from behind as I ran the ball through the line of scrimmage, and my football season was done.

We found a new church, Eugene Christian Fellowship, and while I dreaded the early Sunday morning commutes, I am blessed to have been made to go. Knowing things like, "Our God is an awesome God, He reigns on heaven and earth, with wisdom, power and love...," the lyrics to a Rich Mullins song that we often sung on Sunday mornings, didn't make much sense to me then. It was later, after I saw the depths of evil, that I knew I needed this "awesome God."

At a weekend church camp for middle schoolers, I was baptized in a swimming pool by the youth pastor. This was the best experience of my life to date, the most real; I tasted and saw that the Lord is good (Psalm 34:8), and I knew that I wanted more of Him. I realized that my true desire was to be a man of God, a man of faith like Abraham and Noah, not a man of the world. *Could I be such a man?* I asked myself. *What does it mean to have their level of faith, and why doesn't anyone else want this? Does God still use people in such a manner?*

I felt like I couldn't tell anyone else what I was thinking, because somehow it wouldn't make sense to them. "You can serve Christ," they might reason, "but how are you going to pay your bills, and what about that new car you know you want? Ok, have faith, but what else are you going to do, and what about some common sense? God wants you to have money, don't you think? You're going to heaven, so cross that off your list and pick a worldly activity to tide you over and pay the bills until you get there. Look, everyone else is doing it, so you should too."

Why is everyone so quickly tricked back into thinking it is financial security that will make them happy, only seeking wisdom and faith for worldly comfort or success? What kind of funny thing is going on with money? Faith is more important than money, right? These types of questions swirled around in my head for a brief period before I, too, was again mesmerized by the world, and the bright and shiny things it possesses. My hunger and desire for more of the Holy Spirit gradually faded out of consciousness as I was drawn back into the "reality" of our world and the "reality" of those in the world.

CHAPTER 4

"OCCULT, I THOUGHT, *WHAT'S THAT?"*

I spent my first year of high school at Marist Catholic High School in Eugene, Oregon. This was my first exposure to Roman Catholicism; many of the classes were taught by brothers, and Religion was a required part of the curriculum, same as English or Algebra. I returned to playing football and hit the weight room, looking forward to the time when I would be able to play for the varsity team on Friday nights under the lights.

My only vivid memories of staff at school were of my Spanish teacher, Mr. Terrible, and my football coach. Mr. Terrible used fear and public mocking to motivate students to do their work and not mess around. If he called on you and you weren't prepared, or if he knew you had been wasting time or not paying attention, then he walloped you with his disappointment and scorn in front of everybody else. He didn't seem to hold back his more developed intellect's abilities to crush students into compliance and humiliate them in front of their peers. I did very well in freshman Spanish.

My football coach was a true Catholic, and a man that I respected. I found humor in his pregame prayers that started with, "Thank you Father, give us strength...," and ended with "...to crush the other football team and kick their [expletive]."

In the spring I joined the track and field team, where I ran the 100-meter dash, the 200-meter dash, and the 4 x 100-meter relay. My track season was cut short when, during a pre practice football toss, I dove for a touchdown pass and broke my other collar bone. I did catch the ball and hold on for the touchdown, which I was happy about, but again, I found myself in a harness with a broken clavicle.

* * *

My parents sold the ranch and told us that we were headed back to Connecticut; it felt like some of my deeper roots were being ripped out and broken off. Devastated that we were leaving what I thought was a perfect location, as well as my horse and a high school I was invested in, I cried out for them to reconsider. They assured me that there was no other option, that because of something to do with the real estate market we had to move back to the house in the woods we had lived in before, in Mystic, Connecticut. My aunt and her family followed us back east shortly thereafter.

I adjusted the best I knew how to at the time, joining the Fitch High School football team and taking all my classes seriously. Seldom did I receive anything below an A minus, and while I rarely did my absolute best, I always knew that my job was to aim pretty close to that in everything that

I did. From my high school perspective, always doing my absolute best would've been ridiculous and made me a nerd. I didn't want to be a nerd or a jock or anything like that; I just wanted to be me.

The Fitch football team lacked order and camaraderie compared to the Marist team, so I only played for one year. I tried wrestling next and enjoyed it, going undefeated for two years on the junior varsity team, and I also played on a local club lacrosse team for two years. I liked running as fast as I could and knocking people over, and once I even scored a hat-trick.

High school was a time that I began messing around with alcohol. My friends and I were binge drinkers any time we had the opportunity. I bought a 1983 Subaru hatchback for $750 and foolishly proceeded to drive drunk a couple of times per week. In my opinion, I was a pretty skilled drunk driver, motivated to become so because of the penalty should the police catch me, pushed to do it in the first place because of how transportation worked in my area of the world at that time.

There was no Uber or Lyft, nor was there a tram or a train. Taxies cost money, and there wasn't a lot of that during high school. Furthermore, if I took a taxi when I owned a functioning car, it would have been a dead giveaway to my parents. To ask for help from my parents was not possible because I couldn't admit to them that I had been drinking; they would have been forced to stop it somehow, and stopping it was not an option from my position.

It was better to risk it, I decided, hoping that my mom was right about my "guardian angels," but also not really worried about it because I had the mind of a young teenage boy at the time, supposing that nothing could hurt me.

I was a cigarette smoker as soon as I had my own car, and without much delay at all, I incorporated it into who I believed I was and who I was making myself to be. *I could never be addicted to this*, I decided, and *I enjoy this*, I repeated to myself. It wasn't long before I couldn't imagine life without cigarettes, though I realized that I could switch back and forth between them and smokeless tobacco with relatively zero effort, and so I did both.

I tried to quit on several occasions once I finally realized what addiction was, but to no avail; it had me. It always drew me back into itself with the simple lie, *you can have one*, along with the realization, *I don't think I can manage without one.* Rather than pull myself out, I went in deeper, and I made it a part of my identity. I remember thinking that I would smoke until the day I died, sucking it in so deep that I could finish cigarettes in a couple of drags, and even sometimes involuntarily cursing God in my thoughts when I did so. I ignored the voice inside telling me this was not the right way to go and kept going anyway.

Though I was reckless outside of school, I took academics seriously. I was a National Merit Semi Finalist on the PSAT, a member of the National Honor Society, on the Senior Executive Board, and Sports Editor of the school paper. My final academic ranking was fourteenth out of a graduating class of two hundred twenty-eight, factoring in my F in physics senior year because I wanted to sleep in class. Without any problem, I knew I would most likely be able to get into at least one top ten or Ivy League school if I wanted to.

But I also had no idea at all what I was doing or where I was going. I did not ever find anything on the list of approved or acceptable professions that I really wanted to do; nothing seemed to be calling my name. Sure, I knew that I could do many things, and I knew that I wanted to help people, but what I wanted to do or was called to do eluded me. *I guess I'll be a doctor*, I thought to myself, *at least then I'll be educated, helping people, well paid, and respected.*

* * *

Crazy Andy is his name, very tall, and about seven years older than me. His grandma lived next door, and one day he just poked his head out of the brush and said, "Hi, I'm Andy," and then we were friends ever since. He liked to build little bombs out of PVC pipe, black powder, cannon fuse, and hot glue, most of which we could get at the local sporting goods store. We enjoyed shooting and building things in the woods, and he was also old enough to buy me tobacco and alcohol, which I asked him to do frequently.

One of the reasons he is Crazy Andy, and not just Andy, is because he lived in the woods behind my house in a shack that he had constructed out of plywood. There was no insulation, water, heat, or electricity. Just Crazy Andy and his sleeping bag, and he never complained; he was the only person I knew who was happy exactly where he was. He rode his bicycle to work, often putting on a wet shirt that had just come out of the washer because, he claimed, "it will dry on the way to work."

I met Brian sometime during tenth grade while throwing a ball to our Doberman named Tina in the baseball field across the street from our house. He kind of walked right out of the woods just like Andy did, and we've been friends ever since as well. While I am generally not the kind of person to say I have a "best friend," and I don't think I've ever referred to him in that way, he has been and is exactly that to me.

Together, Brian and I could be what I would now call dangerous; driving can never be safe if there are people like we were on the roads. Splitting tractor trailers on the highway, running red lights at full speed without looking, or running from the police are a few examples. But we were also both good students and restrained compared to other boys our age.

It was miraculous I got through my teenage years without getting arrested for anything serious, hurting myself, or hurting someone else. There just wasn't that much rational, logical, deep thinking going on; it's amazing how much I thought I knew while knowing next to nothing.

One thing that I did get arrested for was driving through downtown Mystic and shooting at pedestrians and bicyclists with a super soaker squirt gun. Brian was a part of this too, but he didn't get arrested. The driver and myself, manning the soaker from the backseat, did get arrested when someone on a bike that we had just drenched got extremely mad at us.

On our next pass through town, the bike guy, who had now put down his bicycle, sprinted out from the sidewalk and grabbed onto the car, but our driver took a sharp left and shook him off. Out the window I could see him fall on the ground with a new fury in his eyes. The police eventually came and arrested us, the bike man having claimed that we had mace in the water. Of course, we did not have mace in the water, nor had any of us even considered this idea. We just thought that the reactions of people walking out of dinner in a nice restaurant and getting sprayed by a squirt gun were priceless, and we didn't even have smart phones to make a video for YouTube. The possibility that it might lead to us getting into trouble never crossed our adolescent minds. We were operating on impulse when we were together, so one might say we didn't know any better.

I could tell that the judge also saw the humor in what we had done, probably wishing that she could go back in time and try the super soaker out on unsuspecting adults for herself. The case was dismissed, the judge saying only, "You're not going to do that again are you?" When I said, "No," she offered me back the water gun.

The Groton Town Police pulled us over all the time while we were in high school, maybe 2-4 times per month, but it was always when we weren't doing anything wrong. Every time I saw a police car, I feared it was going to stop me. I don't know if it was just how the department was operating at that time, because I was young, or because I drove a beater, but eventually we got fed up with being harassed. Instead of shying away from the police and living in a perpetual state of fear, we decided to contend with them on our terms. We drove around looking for them, testing to see how many times we would have to pass by before they would decide to pull us over.

One time, when we knew we were about to be pulled over, Brian alerted me that he didn't have his driver's license. We were a block or two ahead of the cop when Brian stopped the car and we both jumped out and switched seats. The officer had no idea, and proceeded to admonish me for whatever it was Brian had done, oblivious to the fact that we had just pulled a switcheroo; it was difficult to keep a straight face.

On a different night, another friend flipped off a cop who was driving behind us blinding us with his high beams; we had no idea that it was the police behind us. He stopped us, got us out of the car, and lined us up on the white line on the side of the road. He went down the line, asking each of us what sport we played. After this he said, "Don't you ever flip me off again, or I'll break off your [expletive] finger," and then let us go on our way.

I loved the Wu Tang Clan, along with many other artists of the day like U2, Pearl Jam, Smashing Pumpkins, and REM, but in my car, it was only "the Wu." I bought every one of their albums, first on cassette and later on compact disk, as soon as I knew about it and could afford it. My mom confiscated some of the ones that she didn't like, the real problem being that I was playing it loudly in the house where my brother and sister could hear it; I wouldn't like it either if I was the parent.

In the house, as a family, we listened primarily to Christian music. My mom wanted to pump good things into us, and if we complained, she would remind us of the "garbage in, garbage out" rule, the rule that says if you put bad things in, then you will have bad things come out. I liked the Christian music and had even found some Christian bands that were decent, but I had no understanding of "garbage in, garbage out" at that point in my life.

On one occasion, I decided to put one of my other CDs into the disk changer in our living room. Of course, I hadn't put any thought whatsoever into the message in the music; I just liked the way it sounded and wanted to try it out on other people.

Whatever it was seemed to frighten my mom. The look on her face as well as the fact that she glared at me and said "occult" through clenched teeth burned a hole in me, and I switched it back to something I knew she would approve of as swiftly as my capabilities permitted.

"*Occult,*" I thought, *what's that? Well*, I reasoned, *she seemed pretty shaken up by it, but it must be something of a personal issue or she would tell me more. Right?*

Our family never found a permanent church again after moving away from Oregon. We occasionally attended Groton Bible Chapel (GBC) in Groton, CT, and I sometimes went to the youth group meetings on Wednesday nights, drawn in by the fact that they always went out for pizza, but also secretly hoping that someone would lead me back to what I had tasted at camp a couple of years earlier.

The beat of the drum was stronger outside the church; the loud noises and bright lights were luring me into the world where the possibilities seemed to be both tantalizing and endless. *Why do I need God?* I thought. *Surely whatever I will need will be found in the world.* This, combined with the fact that my parents didn't require it, led me to abandoning church and any notion that I needed God for a long time.

I met my first girlfriend at a student leadership conference in our high school gymnasium in grade 10 or 11. We were together for about seven years, breaking up before I entered graduate school.

Early on in the relationship, my mom was worried about the possibility of us having sex. Her only input on the matter was, "You'll find out when you're married." She asked Pastor Bob McCoy from GBC to speak to me, who I had spoken with a few times at church, and whose son was in my high school class. I walked over to his house, less than a mile from our Mystic house, and he led me up the stairs into his office for a chat.

"Iain, don't you think that those areas we go to the bathroom from are dirty?" he asked me.

"No, that's not how I think about it," I responded. "I think that we are just people, and that your argument is not persuasive since everyone is having sex."

I left, thinking that the conversation was strange, wondering why he would try to lead me away from sex with something that was so obviously not the truth. If it wasn't "dirty" for adults, why would it be so for young adults?

If he had said something like, "It's not Gods will for us to do that because...," or "In my experience...," this may have had an impact in the direction that he was hoping for, but to say something like, "Yuck, you don't want to do that, do you?" made me believe I had to figure out the truth on my own.

I began keeping a journal and tucked it away in one of my desk drawers, thinking nobody would ever find it. I wrote about parties and situations or concerns with my girlfriend and other things I was trying to figure out. One day I got in trouble for something I had never spoken out loud, and I knew that my mom had found it and read it.

I was incensed that my privacy was violated and ashamed that some of my deepest thoughts had been brought into the light without my consent. Rather than tell my mom that I knew she had read my journal, I retaliated by writing a note in my journal just for my mom and leaving it in the same place, a sort of a trap.

The note that I wrote was horrible, and I wished I hadn't written what I did when I could see that it caused her pain, but I still felt that I had been violated. I never kept a journal again until I was on my own, and I have always been anxious about the possibility of being confronted by its contents by someone I haven't invited to read it.

* * *

The main entertainment for our senior graduation party was a hypnotist. It was my first exposure to such a thing, and I found it fascinating how this man could take control over the minds of kids he had never met before. *How is he doing this? How did he get this guy to sing "La Bamba" as if he believes he is Richie Valens when he doesn't know the words of the song when not under hypnosis?*

I wasn't hypnotized, and I considered it impossible for me personally to be accessed or controlled in such a manner. *This is crazy stuff,* I mused, wondering why nobody was talking about how easy it was to control others, and briefly considering what the ramifications would be if it were used for nefarious purposes.

> "Hypnotism is a particular form of direct or prestige suggestion, something to which we are all exposed every day of our lives... In general, his [a person using hypnotic techniques] appeal will be on an emotional, non-logical basis since this sensitizes the brain and gives his suggestions far greater strength than can be obtained with any logical appeal. For this reason an understanding of hypnotism is of immense importance to the average layman" (Estabrooks 228–229).

It seems ironic that one of the most important lessons I learned in high school was during its last event, and that it was presented to us students as "entertainment." Hypnotism is not only a vital building block of ritual abuse, but also something that ordinary people are constantly "persuaded with" without their knowledge or consent. Furthermore, it is largely because of its presentation to the public as entertainment, such as in my own experience, that the public remains both unconcerned and unaware of the fact that they have become affected. Of course, I still had much to learn, but the fact that I had seen a classmate "become" Richie Valens became a recurring riddle that returned occasionally to see if it could be solved.

High school was an easy time of my life. I had everything that I needed to excel in school and have fun, including a mostly stable home and parents that cared. I yearned to be the adult version of myself and was glad to be moving on from high school. I couldn't wait to move out of my parent's house and begin the next step.

CHAPTER 5

"IF I'M GOING TO DO IT, THEN I'M GOING TO DO MY BEST"

My entire freshman year of college at the University of Connecticut was basically one big beer, bong, and pizza party, and Brian was my roommate. I could funnel beer faster than anyone else on the floor, and it didn't take me long to acquire a fake ID from an upperclassman down the hallway.

I was expelled from the university following my first year. It is difficult to pass classes if you never go to them, but I had to find that out the hard way. This was also the year that my parents got divorced, but I'm not sure how much that had to do with my expulsion. After a chat with the dean's office, where I explained that I was ready to try, I was readmitted and allowed to continue with my studies.

I had been pre-med, but decided again that I didn't know what I was going to do, so I started taking classes that interested me, courses in sociology, psychology, political science, and criminal justice. I enjoyed what I was learning, I loved researching, and I desired to be a person who could express himself with a pen.

My new roommate was someone who had lived on the same floor the year before; we called him "Dirty Johnny." It was here that a friend and I first tried psilocybin mushrooms, and I instantly knew that we had been lied to about them as well. Time literally slowed down; I tested it, and I was genuinely seeing things in slow motion, and other details that I had never seen before.

We tried to replicate the experience the next night, unsuccessfully. We got some more mushrooms and ate them at our friend Paul's house in New London. Once they started to kick in, we both felt very uncomfortable in our surroundings and decided to leave. We had nowhere to go, so we drove to a pay phone in downtown Mystic to call Dirty Johnny.

"We just had a strange experience at Paul's house and had to leave. We don't really know where to go now. These are acting differently than they did last night," we informed him, looking for suggestions on what to do.

"It's better not to eat them two days in a row," he told us. *Too late now.*

Two police cars surrounded us with their blinding lights, and we went into survival mode; we weren't doing anything wrong that I knew of. They searched the car and asked us questions, telling us that the temporary tags on the car were expired. I was supposed to have gone to the DMV to get regular license plates, and I had missed the expiration date.

I explained that I had just been busy and forgotten, that I did plan on going to the DMV as soon as I could. They told me that they had not caught us on the road or with the car on, so they weren't going to write any tickets, and we were offered a ride home.

We reluctantly accepted the ride back to my parent's house in the next town over, jumping into the back of the cruiser and hoping it wasn't a trap. The officer who drove us was suspiciously eyeballing us through the rear-view mirror. I smiled back and thanked him for the ride and felt a wave of relief when we got out of the car.

My friend and I did not want to talk to anyone else, so we bypassed the house and trekked out into the woods to Crazy Andy's shack, but he wasn't home that night. It was cold and we were ill prepared; the only fuel that we had was gasoline and five-gallon plastic buckets because we didn't have a flashlight to go hunting for firewood.

We huddled into fetal positions on the benches around the fire pit and were able to stay moderately warm. But we never recovered from the initial bad feeling we had at Paul's house a couple of hours prior, and we got to experience a "bad trip." It was quite horrible, something like a brief visit to hell, but once we were through it, we felt rejuvenated rather than beaten down or frightened. "That will never happen again," one of us said to the other, meaning not that we would never eat mushrooms again, but that we had figured something out about ourselves in the midst of our temporary suffering.

I didn't stay with Dirty Johnny for long; living in a dormitory was not for me. The distractions were nonstop and too tempting given my lack of self-discipline at the time, and I couldn't study. I decided to move back to Mystic for a while, where I would take classes at the local branch of the university, UConn at Avery Point.

Brian and I often visited a small college in New Hampshire where my girlfriend attended. It was a much smaller school than UConn, but it was also known for its party culture. Every weekend was the same: get drunk, hang out, see what else might be going on around you.

My girlfriend and I found out that we were pregnant, and I freaked out and entered a state of panic. The only person I told was Brian, who confirmed what I already thought when he said something like, "...that would drastically change your life. You wouldn't be able to finish school. You have to... I think..." Devastated and openly crying in front of him, I responded something like, "I can't see any other way... I can't leave school... this can't happen now..."

In retrospect, it felt something like it must feel to plan a hit on someone. It didn't feel right, but there were no alternative routes that I could make out, and so my girlfriend and I continued down that road to the clinic. Pro-life protesters held signs and yelled from across the street as we left our car and made our way into the building. I couldn't deal with my conflicting feelings of, *what are we doing? Is this really ok?* And other feelings like, *is it gone yet?* And *I can't wait to get rid of it.*

Abortion was so common and accepted, so I thought it was the logical choice for me. I checked out into the fog during the procedure, and I don't have a memory of much of it other than a vacuum and holding my girlfriend's hand. Unfortunately, I wasn't able to provide much emotional support for her, and once it was over, we didn't talk about it.

What did you get rid of? And, *what was that in the vacuum?* Were questions circling around in my head, and, if I was honest with myself, I knew it was a baby. It wasn't a mass of cells or inert matter; it had the potential to be a particular human, or we wouldn't have been so keen to get rid of it. We knew what it was going to do, and we didn't want it to do it.

As I reflect on this, the primary issue may not be the legality of abortion, but how it is presented to the public, and specifically to children. Should we promote it? Should we defend it so strongly that we teach our children and all of society that it's normal, desirable, and easy? Should we treat it no differently than how we treat the removal of a tooth or a skin tag? Of course not, but that is exactly what we have been doing.

I encouraged my girlfriend to have an abortion because I thought it would be a simple solution to what I viewed as a problem. I believe I could have persuaded her the other way if I had been so inclined, and so I have had to deal with the fact that I made the decision to terminate her pregnancy. What I viewed as a problem was a child, the same as you are my child, and if I had been able to understand it in those terms, I would never have made the decision I did.

* * *

At this point in history, around 1998-1999, anybody going to the dentist for a filling was bound to get a prescription for some kind of opiate medication. This was how, like so many others, I discovered Percocet and Vicodin. I liked the way it relieved nearly all of my physical and mental aches and pains and made me feel comfortable in my own skin, and I preferred to feel that way all the time. Here began my decade-long dance with the poppy.

In the early days, I remember once trying to change the number on a paper prescription so that the pharmacy would give me more. They caught me, but I just went back to the dentist for a new script and acted as if it was an accident.

I began looking in medicine cabinets, and any other place that these pills might be. I emptied out all the Percocet from my girlfriend's parent's house over time, and then I proceeded to take something like one hundred pills from Grandpa Avery's medicine cabinet. Using my girlfriend as an accomplice, I switched out his pills with a pill that looked alike, a generic over the counter pain killer. My girlfriend and I bought several different kinds at CVS and chose the best match. It felt terrible, like I was out of control, but it also felt great to be sitting on such a bounty.

Eventually I just went to the doctor and got my own prescriptions, feeling lucky that I had a condition that qualified me: discogenic disease and cervical stenosis, which caused me to suffer from chronic pain in my neck and back. Several doctors were very accommodating, even sometimes letting me choose the pills that I wanted. Other people, like my brother, weren't so fortunate. He didn't have a qualifying condition, so he wrote his own scripts and travelled around the state using made up names. When the pharmacy wanted to confirm that it was a real script, they would call the number, and one of my brother's friends in the parking lot would answer it on a burner phone and say they were from the doctor's office.

On one occasion, my brother showed up at my apartment, out of the blue, with crack cocaine. "Try this," he encouraged.

"I guess, why not, what's it like?" I reacted, hesitating for only a moment before taking it out of his hand to inspect it.

I took a hit, started spinning, and puked. Then I tried it again. Of all the things people say about crack, I believe three are the most telling: it works, it doesn't last long, and you're going to want more of it once you start. I spent the next couple of weeks hanging out with my brother at a crack house he was frequenting, kissing some older woman to get more crack, looking through the carpet fibers for crack as if looking for diamonds.

I had my own crack pipe, I knew how to make crack, and somebody offered me enough crack for a couple of days if I was to lend them my car, but I told them no. This period of my life was short lived for me because of a specific moment when I was driving and looking for a place to pull over for a hit of crack, and I woke up.

Hey! What are you doing? That crack is crazy. It's too strong, get rid of it, something in my head demanded. I threw the pipe and the rest of what I had out the window, and I never touched it again.

There are more stories of things I experimented with over the years. There wasn't much that I wasn't willing to try if I thought it would advance my understanding or dispel the propaganda that had confused me for so long. I saw myself as a fearless explorer, willing to go anywhere for the prize of knowledge. I knew that the course could get treacherous, as was evident in those trapped in the world of addiction, but for me, not knowing was the more frightening path.

* * *

College was enjoyable once I decided to put my head into it. *If I'm going to do it,* I thought, *then I'm going to do my best.* Some of the introductory courses were extremely boring, but then it got exciting; I looked forward to my future classes and plotted what I wanted to take long in advance. I chose professors that were known to be good at what they did, and often tough, compared to those who were known to be an easy pass.

Law was my focus once I got into graduate school. But during my undergraduate years, some of my favorite courses other than law were Abnormal Psychology, Personality Psychology, Revolutionary Movements, and Drugs and Society, among others.

The professor for Drugs and Society assured us that drugs were not inherently bad, but that they had been demonized by our society either, 1) as a way to target a specific group of people for legislation, 2) because we are afraid of them due to propaganda and ignorance, or 3) because of the economics of prohibition. This was music to my ears, finally someone was telling the truth.

I switched back to the main UConn campus in Storrs, and lived with some friends for a while before moving into one of my dad's apartments in Norwich, CT. My brother lived in the same building, and this is where I lived when I met your mom a few years later. My girlfriend and I gradually drifted apart as we visited each other less and less. I wasn't mature enough to honor the commitments I had made over the years. When we broke up, I went through a period of guilty relief. I worked part-time at a Mexican restaurant and had an internship with the Office of Adult Probation at the courthouse, but at the same time, I had to deal with some of my own legal difficulties.

Not long after the breakup, a friend wanted to race me in his BMW on our way home from the bar. I spun out in my Ford Probe GT and ended up on the side of the road. My friend stopped and I jumped into his car; we tried to flee but were pulled over less than a mile down the road, and I had to perform a full DUI field sobriety test. I knew that the law in Connecticut was that I could not be forced to blow into a breathalyzer unless I failed a preliminary test, so I put my game face on. I was also carrying a pistol in my waistband for which I had a legal permit, which the officer took "for my safety."

Despite having taken multiple shots of bourbon prior to getting in my car, I was still able to pass the tests, probably because of all the practice I had put in, but the officer didn't like me or the fact that he couldn't arrest me, so he told me that he was going to have my pistol permit revoked. He returned my gun, and I went home, but within a couple weeks I received a letter from the state telling me to mail in my permit. My dad hired a lawyer and at the hearing they said I could have my permit back in one year if I didn't fight them, but I chose to fight them, so the revocation was indefinite.

I decided that I needed a dog, so I went to the local animal shelter looking to adopt a puppy. My application was declined because of issues that we had with our dogs killing the neighbor's rabbits when I was a child. So, I had a friend go and pick out a dog for me; what he put into my arms was a total surprise. I named him Butch, and he became an important part of my life, my "child" before I had you.

As a Probation Officer Intern, I got to walk around the metal detector, write presentence investigation reports, be on a first name basis with the prosecutors and judges, and have a large say in what happened to anyone given probation if I was working that day. I was given the keys to the office, and when my supervisor was out for the day, it was me who ran the Office of Adult Probation in that courthouse.

The Chief Probation Officer eventually offered me a job, a position I could begin as soon as I graduated. My boss told me that I should take it, that it was a great opportunity with excellent starting pay and an early retirement option because it was "hazardous duty" like police work. "She never asks anyone out on the sidewalk if they want a job. She really wants you," my boss assured me, wondering what I could be pondering that made me hesitant.

It felt good to be recruited, but I was not willing to commit to anything for the next twenty years. *Sure, I could do that*, I reasoned, *I would be good at it, and it would be easy in a way. State job with great benefits, the opportunity to help the people I would come across.* But something inside of me told me that I was meant for something else, and I told the Chief, "I think I am going to go to law school…"

I continued doing the job of an intern long after my internship was complete because I enjoyed it. Just a couple of hours per week, enough to keep me walking around the metal detectors.

Eventually I found a job as a Community Service Supervisor with a company called Alternative Incarceration Center (AIC).

My job was to take first-time possession of marijuana offenders to various community service projects so that they complete the 120 hours that was mandated by the court in lieu of something like incarceration or probation. This amount of community service worked out to be about every Saturday for a year, which I thought was severe and unfair. I tried to help the people that were assigned to me as best I could, and I always worked alongside them.

I drove a big, white, multi passenger van for which I had to get a commercial driver's license, and I worked with local communities to put together suitable and meaningful projects. If these people had to be there, then I wanted their time spent to be purposeful. I wanted them to do work that I was willing to do, work that made a difference.

Once my partner or I drove to the project site, everybody wanted to smoke weed before we started, so my partner and I would go our way and the clients would go their own, with the understanding that we would meet back up in ten minutes or so. We were all in the same boat; it was just that my partner and I had not been caught.

After a while at this job, I was hired by the same company to be the Operations Assistant, where I had many duties. I collected hundreds if not thousands of urine samples to test for drugs since I was one of the few male staff members, along with John S. (who you will meet later in the story), and because most of the clients were male. I also had a small caseload of clients of whom I was the Case Manager. I was as lenient as I could reasonably be with these people, realizing that it was but by the grace of God that our positions were not reversed.

Years later, when we lived in New London around the time that you were born, people frequently approached me on the street to shake my hand and thank me for how I had treated them when I worked for AIC. One of the best feelings in this life is making a positive impact in the life of another, of that I was certain.

As I hope is apparent by now, I am trying to be as vulnerable, open, and honest as I can possibly be, voluntarily exposing the areas of my life that were the most private, and often the most shameful. It is ok with me that people see all of me, for in doing so maybe it will finally be understood that you were not taken from me because your mom feared for your lives, or because of me at all, but because of something else entirely.

> "This is why there is power in exposing the secret skeletons in your closet. When you let the world see the worst you've ever been, the bindings of shame fall off, and with it goes the fear and guilt. Instead, you become a free person able to learn how to do good to those who spitefully use you and say all kinds of evil things about you" (Reynolds 127-128).

PART 2

2003-2010

"TO SEE WHAT IS IN FRONT OF ONE'S NOSE NEEDS A CONSTANT STRUGGLE"
— GEORGE ORWELL
(FROM YOUR MOM'S QUOTE JOURNAL)

CHAPTER 6

GRADUATION TIME

I didn't know what was coming next after graduating from UConn in 2003 with a Master of Arts in political science. There was still nothing specific that I wanted to do, and I figured that I would just keep going to school, since that was what I seemed to be good at. I enjoyed law, and although I didn't really want to be a lawyer in the typical sense of billing hours and making money, I did want the education, and I wasn't opposed to the potential financial benefits. I admired and respected men like Thomas Jefferson, James Madison, and John Adams, and so I felt it was natural that I work toward having similar credentials (see Appendix 2).

My favorite professor advised me to take some time to think about whether or not to pursue law school, but I couldn't see any other options at the time. He had been a lawyer himself and had even prepared and presented cases to the United States Supreme Court, later finding out that it was not what he was looking for. "Are you sure that you aren't supposed to be doing something else?" he asked me. I was confused as to why he would ask me such a question, but I took him seriously and began to ponder. *What am I supposed to do? Why am I here and what is my purpose in this life?*

I didn't believe that I had to strive to figure it out; I did believe that I had a purpose, and that it would come to me when the time was right. I didn't call it "God" at the time but had an inner understanding that I was on the earth for a reason, and that, while I couldn't become aimless or lazy, I also didn't have to figure it out right away. Whatever "it" was would figure it out for me, as long as I kept my eyes open and my intentions relatively pure. I knew that I was capable of doing many things, and I didn't want to settle.

By this time, opiate medications were an everyday part of my life – to manage my pain and the dependance that develops with regular use of such medications. And, while I did have pain, the psychological underpinnings of my relationship with these medications were a bit more complicated. I was able to convince myself that I needed them for pain but was also using them for relief from anxiety and stress. In addition, within my circle of friends they were a sort of luxury item, an amenity that everyone wanted and now I had, legitimately.

My brother was dealing drugs, and I found it exciting to be around his friends and his scene. We hung out, went to rave clubs, watched tv, and played a lot of video games, especially Grand Theft Auto. I knew that I couldn't do this forever, but I enjoyed the reprieve from the real world and having to spend all my time in the books.

Our friend lived a couple of blocks away, and one day he told me to come over to meet his new Polish friends. I drove over, and when I got out of the car, he was standing with three people in their early twenties on the sidewalk outside of his apartment. I caught your mom's eye, and I immediately knew that I had found what I was looking for.

It was as if I was in a trance, captivated by everything about her, feeling like I already knew her, immediately smitten, with all my defenses down. The fixed gaze in her eyes informed me that she was already mine. This had to be what love at first sight was, I imagined. I was introduced to the other two as well, one of whom was her boyfriend, but that was of no significance to me. I invited them to move into the apartment next door to me, and within a couple of days your mom moved out of there and into my apartment, telling her now ex-boyfriend that she had found her true love. Shortly thereafter she called her mom from the pay phone across the street and informed her about finding her "soul mate."

The ex-boyfriend moved out, and though I did feel empathetic, I also didn't feel like there was any other option. I offered him a key to another apartment in the building to use temporarily should he need it, but he had somewhere else to go. Your mom and I started our new life together, but I knew that her three-month J-1 visa would be expiring soon, and that she would have to return to Poland.

Her English was pretty good, and although she had an accent, we didn't have any trouble communicating. When we watched movies, we did so with the English subtitles because she had some trouble understanding everything when multiple people were talking fast, and also to improve her vocabulary. She began reading novels in English, and it wasn't long before her reading, writing, and comprehension skills were better than most Americans that I knew; her memory astonished me.

Your mom, 2004. Uncasville, CT.

Me, your mom, Sylwia, Kyle, 2004. Mystic, CT.

Some of the details that I am including may at first appear out of line, or otherwise inappropriate in some manner. In adding graphic and personal details, my intention is not to be shocking or crude, but to demonstrate and document that your mother is a victim, and that I am not her perpetrator.

I began noticing incongruities during our first sexual encounter. "How do you want my legs?" she questioned. "Do you want them like this, or this, or this?" she demonstrated robotically, waiting for my response.

"What do you mean?" I asked, bewildered. "How do *you* want your legs?"

Immediately after having sex, she frantically rushed into the bathroom to wash herself like she had to go put out a fire that I was unaware of. "Agata, why are you in such a hurry? What's wrong?" I asked.

"I feel dirty. There is something wrong with me, I think," she explained.

"Dirty?... Doing that isn't going to stop you from getting pregnant. Aren't you taking birth control?"

"No, I'm not taking birth control. I don't care if I get pregnant; that would be fine. I think that there is something wrong with me," she repeated.

"There is nothing wrong with you. What do you mean? And I do care if you get pregnant. I wish you had told me."

The next day we went to the emergency room to get a morning after pill, as they were not sold over the counter at the time. "I will talk to my mom about getting birth control," she informed me, which I thought was strange. We ended up going to Planned Parenthood after she had talked to her mom to get her started on the pill.

"Have you ever been on birth control before?" I asked her.

She responded, "My mom gave it to me when I started having my period, because he was worried," abruptly stopping her sentence and looking away. I let it go, confused, wondering who "he" could be, but also thinking that maybe she had meant "she," which would make more sense if it was her mom. I was unwilling to make her feel any more uncomfortable than she already was, and I dropped it.

Once, early on, I suggested the idea of oral sex to her, thinking it was normal. She was horrified, as if I had asked her to eat a spider, with a spider being the thing that she was most afraid of. She screamed at the top of her lungs, "Never ever, I will never ever never ever never ever do that with you," startling me and making me feel awful.

"Ok, Agata, I wasn't saying that you had to," wondering what she meant by "with you." "You asked me what I wanted, and I responded. I didn't know. I'm sorry."

I felt terrible, and she kept repeating, "Never ever, never ever, never ever..." It was as if even the thought of it was raping her. *Maybe that is not normal in Poland*, I figured.

If it was "no" because of inexperience or because it just wasn't a normal thing for Polish women, then this would not have raised an alarm. It wasn't the "no," but the fear, the freaking out, the yelling. I considered that there was something wrong with me, and so I tried to eliminate possibilities by washing myself after every trip to the toilet and making myself more presentable.

Anytime I brought it up for the purpose of trying to understand, she reverted to, "I think there is something wrong with me," and, "I want to, you are going to be my husband, of course I want to." This didn't make sense to me since she couldn't elaborate on what was "wrong" with her, and because I figured that if she really wanted to that she would.

We drove to the Finger Lakes region of New York to get away from Norwich and stay at my aunt's lake house (see Appendix 3). Sitting in the car in the driveway on our first night there, she took a ring off her finger, handed it to me, and bid me to ask her to marry her, which I did. I wanted to, and I also felt that I didn't have a choice (see Appendices 4 and 5).

When we returned home from the lake house, we began planning for our future married life. I would return to Poland with her until we could get her a fiancé visa, and then we would come back to Connecticut to get married. That was all that we knew, and that was all I felt I needed to know. Things between us were up and down from the start, sometimes wonderful and sometimes horrible, but I was committed, and I knew that she was going to be my wife; for me there was no turning back.

She frequently repeated that she thought something was wrong with her, that she only had vague memories of her childhood, and that she seemed to have no relationship with her father. "The only thing he ever did for me was bring me a cup of tea," she informed me.

"That's it?" I asked, not believing her, and finding it hard not to laugh at first. "All that he ever did for you was bring you tea on one occasion?"

"Yes, that's it," she answered.

"It sounds untrue to me, Agata. Please don't lie to me," I begged her. "I can handle any truth, but I can't handle being lied to." I was confused; *this couldn't possibly be true*, I thought to myself. *What is she telling me? She's twenty-two years old and the only thing that she can remember her dad doing for her is that? That just makes no sense at all*, I knew, dumbfounded.

"Tell me what you remember," I urged her.

"I remember that my dad cheated on my mom when I was a little girl. He took me for a walk and explained to me what happened, and I ended up confronting the other woman."

"This happened when you were a little girl? How old were you?"

"I think that I was about twelve. After I confronted the other woman and told her to leave my family alone, my mom took a trip by herself to get away from my dad."

"What did your dad tell you exactly? Are your parents doing well now?"

"He told me that he was having sex with her... I don't think that my mom is happy."

"Agata," I said, "the fact that your dad brought you in on this at that age is not ok. A twelve-year-old should never have to think about these things or feel like she needs to confront an adult to protect her family. This was abuse; it may be minor abuse, but it is still child abuse. Please let me know if you remember anything else."

I began to suspect incest, but I had no idea how to broach the subject with her. *Wouldn't she just tell me if that was the case? Why does she keep repeating that there is something wrong with her?* I didn't have any idea how to talk to her about these things, and I wanted to give her space and allow her to disclose at her own pace, in her own timing. Anytime I tried to bring it up on my own, her response was defensive and fearful, and I didn't want to cause her to feel bad or uncomfortable.

"Agata," I pled, "I love you and I am going to marry you. I want you to know that nothing you tell me will change that. I am on your side. Please know that I am here for you and that you can tell me anything. I am not afraid of anything except not knowing the truth, and I promise that I will never leave you no matter what it is."

"Ok," she replied, "I love you too. I don't know what it is; I just feel like there is something wrong with me." I had her make a list of the things that she didn't like about herself along with the things that she did like about herself, hoping that this exercise would provide me with some insight (see Appendix 6).

I began researching on my own, trying to understand the woman that I was set to marry. *If I can't get the information out of her*, I reasoned, *then I can figure it out by observing her and identifying her characteristics, as one might do when trying to identify an unfamiliar bird through binoculars.* Right away I considered the possibility of borderline personality disorder; all signs were pointing toward some type of trauma disorder (see Appendix 7). *What could it be and why doesn't she just tell me?*

Kreisman and Straus (2010) list nine criteria associated with diagnosing borderline personality disorder, many of which your mother had already exhibited, even before we were married. "1. Frantic efforts to avoid real or imagined abandonment. 2. Unstable and intense interpersonal relationships. 3. Lack of clear sense of identity. 4. Impulsiveness in potentially self-damaging behaviors… 5. Recurrent suicidal threats or gestures, or self-mutilating behaviors. 6. Severe mood shifts and extreme reactivity to situational stresses. 7. Chronic feelings of emptiness. 8. Frequent and inappropriate displays of anger. 9. Transient, stress-related feelings of unreality or paranoia" (10–11).

It wasn't that I had concluded with any certainty that it was borderline personality disorder, but that this was the best explanation I had found to date. I realized that psychiatric diagnoses are not cut and dry, and that there are possible comorbidities and blends; in short, each individual is unique, and it is difficult to put anyone into any one box (unless you are Polish "expert" court psychiatrists, as will be made apparent in Part 6).

"Additionally, studies corroborate that about 90 percent of patients with the BPD diagnosis also share at least one other psychiatric diagnosis" (Kreisman and Straus 2010, 6). I hadn't yet heard of Multiple Personality Disorder or Dissociative Identity Disorder, which I now believe to be the correct psychiatric diagnosis of your mother. I don't believe this was even touched on in my college Abnormal Psychology course, but I was about to find out all about it through life experiences with your mother.

All of my research pointed to the fact that "Borderline patients have a high rate of reported childhood sexual abuse (CSA)" (Paris and Zweig-Frank, 1997, as cited in Zanarini, 1997, 15), and I tried to bring this up with your mom on several occasions. It felt strange to suggest "incest" to her, and I didn't know how. Rather than respond to my vague inquiries, she froze up or became unintelligible. "The nicest thing my dad ever did for me was bring me one cup of tea." For her, that was the complete story.

Her ex had left some things in the apartment, and after not hearing from him for several weeks, he wanted them back. "Agata, find out where he is, and I will drop off his things. I don't want him coming over here. There's no reason for him to come back here."

Despite my attempts to reason with her, she told me that he was intent on coming to our place. We sat outside on our enclosed second floor porch, eating cheese and crackers, his box of things ready to go at the top of the stairs. There was a large Buck knife on the table, a gift from my stepdad, George, that we were using to cut slices of cheese.

He arrived and stormed up the stairs, yelling in Polish. I was seated in a chair closest to the stairs, your mom was sitting in a chair a few feet to my right. When he got to the top of the stairs, he walked over to me, still blabbering something in Polish, and he punched me once in the face. I stood up, your mom stood up, and then she hurried over to get in the middle of us.

I picked up your mom by the waist and put her behind me, and then instinctively grabbed the knife from the table. "You get the [expletive] off of this property now," I demanded. "Go, now!" I waved the knife at him and chased him back down the stairs, kicking his box down after him.

About ten minutes later a SWAT team arrived with assault rifles. "Where is the gun?" they ordered. I calmly replied that there was no gun, and that I had taken my gun to my mom's house, realizing immediately that he had lied to the police and told them that I had pulled a gun on him.

"It wasn't a gun. It was a knife. I picked up a knife and told him to leave after he punched me."

"Where is the knife then?" they challenged. Your mom had hidden the knife when she saw the police arrive, so she went to retrieve it.

"Are there any guns in the house?" they asked again.

"No, I don't have a gun here. He may have thought I had a gun here because I have shown him my gun, but I moved it to my mom's house last week because we were going out of town." The SWAT team entered my apartment and searched, but they didn't find a gun because it wasn't there.

They arrested both of us, me for threatening with the knife and him for punching me. I didn't feel like I should've been arrested since I had been attacked. I used the knife because I wanted him to be afraid and leave immediately, because it was quicker and more certain than me getting into a physical altercation with my hands, and because he had already slugged me in the face.

They took us both to the police station and seated us together in the waiting room. He kept running his mouth in Polish, and I could tell that the police didn't like that he had lied to them about the gun. "Can you please process me first and get me out of here?" I asked. "I don't want to be in the same room as this liar." I was disgusted with him, realizing that he could have caused me some real trouble if I did have my gun.

They took me out of the room and proceeded to book me first in accordance with my request; I could tell that they now sympathized with me. I wasn't worried about the charge because I knew that I was justified. *I can threaten someone to leave my property who has assaulted me and my fiancé,* I reasoned; *I didn't do anything wrong at all, but I am glad that I didn't have my gun in the house.*

The judge threw out the case at my first court appearance and told me that the other guy had been deported back to Poland. But he also told me that my knife had been "destroyed," and because of its sentimental value I was disappointed. *How could they destroy my property when I hadn't been found guilty of anything? I didn't do anything wrong, but they still destroyed my knife?* My lawyer talked me into accepting the fate of my knife and walking away, which I did reluctantly.

CHAPTER 7

"I REMEMBER THAT I HAVEN'T BEEN MARRIED"

Your mom returned to Poland after her visa ran out, and I followed her shortly thereafter; I arrived in Poland on November 12, 2004 (see Appendix 8). Initially we lived at your grandparents' house in Stargard. Your mom was the only person I knew who could speak English; everything that I wanted to say and everything that anyone wanted to say to me had to go through her. She taught me my first Polish phrase, "Jesteś moja narzeczona," meaning "you are my fiancé," and she had me repeat this to everyone I met.

Your grandpa told me, "If you get me drunk enough, I can speak in any language," but we never spoke more than a couple of words to each other even though we did get drunk together. He was always drinking, so drinking with him was one of the primary ways that I tried to bond with him. He explained to me that Polish men drink beer instead of water, and he demonstrated this when we went to the gym with beer in his backpack.

His drinking was amazing to me, as was his pride in drinking beer instead of water. Though I knew that it couldn't be a good thing, no major alarms were going off, partly because it was rarely mentioned; it was hush hush. Your mom sometimes whispered to me that your grandma told him that he couldn't drink during the day, but that he was, and they were fighting. Since your mom's words were the only ones in the house that I could understand, I thought that it was probably just a common Polish problem.

Your mom translated, "My dad says that I shouldn't let you take me to Utah."

I smiled, taking it as a joke, "What does he mean?"

"Utah is where the Mormons are, where polygamy is. The Mormons are a cult." *Ok*, I thought, smiling, *funny joke. Ha-ha.*

"I like young boobies," he told me through your mom, chuckling maniacally.

This time I don't think that my return smile was believable. "What does he mean that he likes young boobies?"

"That's all he said," your mom informed me. "He likes young boobies." *Ok*, I thought, *I have no idea what that means, but it sounds perverted.*

I tried to bond with your aunt Ada, who was taking English in school, but she was afraid to speak to me. I reluctantly did her English homework for her, knowing that she was in turn going to learn less, but at least I could maybe make her happy. She appeared to me to be a scared girl in general, very timid, and I was informed that she suffered from a heart condition that she was born with.

Your grandma, Iwona, was the most miserable person I had ever met to this point in my life. It astounded me that a person could be so miserable, though questioning the source of her despair never crossed my mind. As far as I was concerned, this was just the way that she was. *She was probably born that way*, I figured.

"Don't let Iain see your teeth," she warned your mom.

"Why can't I see your teeth?" I asked. "I want to see your teeth. I want to see all of you."

"No, my mom says it is bad luck." In the nearly seven years that we were together I never saw her back teeth; not once, because she wouldn't let me because of the "bad luck" that would imminently ensue.

Your paternal great grandfather was deceased, and I never met him. Your paternal great grandmother was someone who I thought was crazy. She was extremely hospitable, and she made certain that I had plenty of snacks whenever I entered her house, but her house was some kind of Catholic shrine to Jesus and Mary. Statues and pictures of Jesus and Mary were everywhere; I had never seen anything like it. She seemed to not get along with your grandfather, Sławomir, yet I had no idea why.

Your maternal great grandmother, Wera, was also extremely welcoming to me; she made me feel comfortable when I was in her home, and I remember her as a gracious woman, though also oddly quiet. The only time that she ever spoke to me, through your mom, was to ask me if I was hungry or if I needed a refill on my coffee.

Your maternal great grandfather, Waldek, was a strange man. He asked me how your mother was, referring to how she was in bed, giving me hand signals to show me that he was asking me about sex with your mom. "Good?" he asked. "Is she good?" I looked at your mom to try to get some help, but she looked away.

"Yes, good," I hesitantly replied, with a rare fake smile.

I was excited to meet my new family, and to be in Poland, but I also wanted to get your mom's fiancé visa as soon as possible and return to the United States. It was difficult living in a city where I could only communicate with one person, and I still had plans to enroll in law school. The Polish people in Stargard appeared to me to be mostly miserable; it was as if a dark, ominous cloud constantly covered the sky. I could feel it, and I was suffering from frequent panic attacks as a result.

This was not what I had expected; the buildings were dilapidated, the roads were as if they had just been hit by mortar rounds, and even the children and young people I met seemed to be in despair. The analogy that Poland is to western Europe as Mexico is to the United States began to stick. This was not a land of freedom, opportunity, or joy, but a land of poverty, gloom, and sorrow.

Sure, one could take a picture from the pretty side; a tourist on a brief visit may not catch what is just beneath the surface or around the corner. I once saw a tourism brochure for Stargard, and it was alluring. There are beautiful things to see, along with a plethora of history, and as long as you don't look under the proverbial rug, this could be all that you see.

When one looks briefly at the grass, it may initially appear that there is not much going on, but upon closer inspection they will see that it is teeming with life. In a similar way, I saw that Stargard, Poland was teeming with melancholy.

Your grandma called her doctor friend, and without a consultation I was given prescriptions for Doxepin, Tegretol, and clonazepam at twenty milligrams per day because of the panic attacks I was now experiencing. I didn't know it at the time, but clonazepam is one of the most addictive substances on the planet. Once dependent upon it, quitting it is more difficult than quitting heroin.

Incest continued to come up in conversation with your mom from time to time, but my attempts to talk about anything in the past were like running up against a brick wall. "I don't remember," she would assure me, though I thought she was lying.

"Well, what do you remember?" I asked, hoping for a little morsel.

"I remember that I haven't been married," she declared after thinking for a moment. *Ok*, I thought, *well that's good at least.* Then she added, "I remember he wouldn't let us play outside... because, he said, it was dangerous."

I knew that there was something weird going on with your grandfather, but I just couldn't put my finger on it. I spent most of my energy wondering why your mom wouldn't just tell me. *One cup of tea, and young boobies, eh? And then the other guy, the great grandfather, asking me how she is in bed – wow!*

"Female children are regularly subjected to sexual assaults by adult males who are part of their intimate social world. The aggressors are not outcasts and strangers; they are neighbors, family friends, uncles, cousins, stepfathers, and fathers. To be sexually exploited by a known and trusted adult is a central and formative experience in the lives of countless women" (Herman, 1981, 7).

The air was inhabited with Polish radio, in the house, in the car, in the taxis, in the shops; it was impossible to escape it. The music was about 50/50 in English and in Polish, which made me feel a little more at home, except that I hadn't heard most of the music they were playing. One song that played at least once a day, though I would guess a few times per day, was "Luka" by Suzanne Vega.

I remember your mom excitedly telling her mom that this was my favorite song followed by the latter giving the former a strange look that I still have not forgotten to this day. It wasn't until later that I looked up the lyrics, and then the look made sense, as it is obviously a song about child abuse.

"My name is Luka
I live on the second floor
I live upstairs from you
Yes I think you've seen me before

If you hear something late at night
Some kind of trouble, some kind of fight
Just don't ask me what it was (x3)

I think it's because I'm clumsy
I try not to talk too loud
Maybe it's because I'm crazy
I try not to act too proud

They only hit until you cry
And after that you don't ask why
You just don't argue anymore (x3)

Yes I think I'm okay
I walked into the door again
If you ask that's what I'll say
And it's not your business anyway..."
("Luka" - Suzanne Vega)

I met two of your mom's girlfriends, one of whom was married to a Brazilian man who had moved to Poland to play soccer. I didn't enjoy hanging out with him because he was a brazen womanizer; he slept with anyone anytime, and everyone knew what he was doing. It blew my mind, and I didn't want to be associated with him.

"Is that normal?" I asked your mom. "Doesn't his wife care?"

"That's how it is with many people here," she informed me. "They have their family, and then he does whatever he wants to do."

"I don't want our relationship to be like that," I told her. "I want you to know that you are the only woman that I need."

His wife was one of your mom's best friends from childhood. I tried to talk to her in broken English about your mom's instability on a couple of occasions, asking her if she was always this way, trying to figure out what was obviously plaguing her.

"Well," she informed me, "Agata always have serious fear of abandonment."

This wasn't what I had asked her, but I was thankful nonetheless for her answer. I concluded that I had to work harder so that your mom would know that I would never leave her, no matter what. I didn't know why she would possibly doubt my love for her, but that was something that I saw as a fixable problem.

Your mom and I eventually moved to our own apartment on Hallera street, a couple of miles from your grandparents' apartment on Piłsudskiego street. We acquired a fifth-floor apartment in a building without elevators. Here we stayed only for a brief time before finding a better place a couple of blocks from the courthouse. I began teaching English and doing some Polish to English translations with a dictionary and your mom's help.

I had about five students that I saw one-on-one an average of twice per week. I developed their lessons and planned their progression, helping them to prepare for exams, or simply supplementing their English language education. All the students were referred to me by your grandparents. While this was valuable experience, and I enjoyed and learned from the contact with other people, I probably averaged one dollar per hour because of the extensive preparation that was required for each lesson. I tried to expand by putting up flyers around town, but I never acquired any students on my own.

Your mom worked briefly for a manufacturing company before getting hired as a secretary to work in the courthouse. This is the same courthouse I was tried in seven years later. Her godfather, who is a judge and your grandfather's best friend, helped your mom to get this job.

One evening I found your mom in the kitchen, sitting in the corner on the ground, holding a steak knife to her wrist. "Agata, what are you doing!?" I demanded, exasperated. "What are you doing? Give me that knife right now!"

She reluctantly handed me the knife, saying only, "I feel that there is something wrong with me."

I wanted to return to the life we had planned in the United States, and I wanted to get married. Your mom and I travelled to the U.S. Consulate in Poznań to speak to someone about expediting the process. We were given a list of things that we had to do like getting your mom medically evaluated and proving that we were going to be able to support ourselves once in the United States.

I detested having to jump through these hoops to get my future wife into my country. Who were they to ask my fiancé for medical papers as if she were some kind of animal? If she were ill, did that mean that I couldn't marry her? My mom sent us her bank statements to satisfy the financial independence requirement as there was no way that we could have done this on our own.

We were in Poland for Christmas 2004, and shortly thereafter we got the green light to return to the United States together. I was given one gift that Christmas, which your mom told me was from both of your great grandmothers, your aunt Ada, and your mom's cousin, Pola. The gift was a used Gwen Stefani CD entitled "The Sweet Escape." I had heard of the pop group, No Doubt, and the lead singer, Gwen Stefani, but this wasn't music that I would listen to by choice. "Thank you," I said, smiling and trying to be authentic, thankful that they had thought of me, but thinking to myself that the gift couldn't have been any stranger.

"...If I could escape
I would, but first of all let me say
I must apologize for acting, stinking, treating you this way
'Cause I've been acting like sour milk all on the floor
It's your fault you didn't shut the refrigerator
Maybe that's the reason I've been acting so cold
If I could escape
And recreate a place as my own world
And I could be your favorite girl
Forever, perfectly together
And tell me, boy, now wouldn't that be sweet?...
If I could be sweet
I know I've been a real bad girl
I didn't mean for you to get hurt
(Whatsoever) we can make it better
And tell me, boy, now wouldn't that be sweet?
(Sweet escape)...
You held me down
I'm at my lowest boiling point
Come help me out
I need to get me out of this joint
Come on, let's bounce
Counting on you to turn me around
Instead of clowning around, let's look for some common ground
Woo hoo (I wanna get away) yee hoo
Woo hoo (to our sweet escape) yee hoo
Woo hoo (I wanna get away) yee hoo"
("The Sweet Escape" – Gwen Stefani)

* * *

We said goodbye to my new Polish family, unsure of when we would see them again. When we returned to the U.S., we moved into an apartment that my dad and stepmom owned in New London, CT. It was in the rougher part of the city; we had bullet holes in the house and prostitutes carousing the streets. One time when driving home we were pulled over. The officer asked us what we were doing in this part of town at this time of the night. Of course, when we told him that we lived there he let us go, but the assumption was that we were there to buy drugs.

Our neighbor in the upstairs apartment was one of the prominent heroin dealers in the neighborhood, which meant that there was a lot of traffic in and out of our building. I carried a gun whenever I took your mom out onto the street and into the neighborhood, and later when I took you out. It wasn't legal to do so ever since my permit had been revoked after the car accident, but in this case I didn't care.

Nobody knows I have it, I reasoned, *not even your mom knows most of the time, and nobody needs to know.* The only way that someone would have become aware of the gun would have been if I had to use it to protect you or your mother. And if someone forced me to protect you or your mother, then I was willing to pay whatever the cost would be for carrying my gun without a permit.

We were married at my mom's house by a justice of the peace on July 2, 2005. Your mom's sister, Ada, and cousin, Pola, flew in for the event. Mike, a guy I was told was a cousin, came in from New York City. Your mom explained to me that he was "with" her cousin, Pola, while she was in the United States, meaning they shared a bed. "Yes," I asked her, "but what about her boyfriend who is waiting for her in Poland?"

"Yes, Iain," she responded half annoyed, "She has a boyfriend, but when she is in the United States she is with Mike. This is just how it is."

"And they're both your cousins?" I continued, confused. "And they're only 'with each other' when she is in the United States?"

"Yes, Iain, that is just the way it is."

Pola & Mike. July 1, 2005.

Ada. July 1, 2005.

Your mom and I on our wedding day.

July 2, 2005.

I have a video of the wedding ceremony, of me vowing "I do" to your mom before God (as I knew Him at the time). While I did not know what I was getting myself into, nor could I have imagined it in my wildest dreams, I did know what "I do" meant. Like the paperboy who I hit with the rock as a child, if I say that I will do something, then I must do it. In this case, there would be no giving up on your mom no matter what. Not knowing "what" can never be an excuse, or what is the purpose of a vow?

We continued living in New London; I was working as a substitute teacher, your mom first at Catholic Charities and later at a local law firm as an assistant. I studied for and took the Law School Admissions Test, but your mom and I got into an argument on the

Pola, Ada, your mom, me, Grandma Bryson, and Grandpa Bryson. July 2, 2005.

morning of the test, and I couldn't focus, and didn't really try. The timing of the argument, along with the absurdity, made it feel like sabotage. I bombed it and decided that I would have to take it again later (see Appendix 9).

Thinking it might be a good idea to get out of Connecticut, I applied for a job with the Maricopa County Office of Adult Probation in Arizona. My decision to apply there was predicated on the fact that Brian had moved there and settled down. I passed the testing and the interviews with flying colors; the last step was to take a polygraph test, and then we would be moving to the sunny Southwest.

Almost as soon as we arrived in Phoenix for the test, your mom began fighting with me as she had before the LSAT. It didn't make sense to me, and I was embarrassed because it was obvious to Brian that something was going on. I could feel the walls once again closing in on me. *Why can't she just hold it together long enough for us to make some progress?* I asked myself. *Why does she have to mess with my head when I need my head the most?*

I questioned if she was doing this intentionally, maybe to steer us in a particular direction, because her issues, whatever they were, always cleared up as quickly as they had arrived. Soon, I knew, we would be back to normal again. "I don't know what's going on, Brian," I tried to explain, "sometimes she just does this."

I was completely unnerved, got no sleep, and awoke feeling like I had already failed the test. I smoked a joint driving to the testing location just to try to calm my nerves even though I knew that the tester would be asking me about drug use. In my mind, I had already given up on this job because I knew that I couldn't pass the test in my current agitated state of mind. If I happened to pass, it would be only through luck or divine providence, I concluded.

When I got into the chair and was hooked up to the machine, I decided to try a different strategy. Rather than trying to relax, which I found to be impossible even with the joint, I decided that I would try to ramp up my inner turmoil. *If I do this*, I reasoned, *then all my answers will look the same to the tester... my blood pressure will be through the roof with any question asked, whether it be, "How are you doing today?" or "Have you ever robbed a bank?" thus hopefully invalidating the reliability of the test itself.* However, it didn't work, and I didn't get the job; we returned to Connecticut.

I landed another interview opportunity in Washington D.C., in the office of then U.S. Senator Chris Dodd. Excited about the possibility of this experience, I contacted a high school friend living in D.C. to ask if we could stay with her, and your mom and I made the seven-hour drive south. Your mom didn't like my friend, and once again, on the day of the interview, your mom decided that she wasn't going to have a "good" day, and I didn't get the position.

Life with your mom continued to be turbulent. Sometimes I thought everything was perfect, and sometimes I thought that I was going to die. The panic attacks that I began developing in Poland were becoming more frequent; my use of clonazepam was daily. I saw a psychiatrist so that I could continue quelling my high anxiety levels with these highly addictive tablets, becoming almost as afraid of being cut off from them as I was terrified of your mom's volatility.

The severity of the panic attacks was such that on a couple of occasions I left a classroom while substitute teaching, right in the middle of a class without telling anyone, and I drove home to try to find solace. Sometimes it was too overwhelming for me to deal with, and it felt like the world was crashing down around me because of the chaos that your mom's drastic changes and instability brought into our home.

Over and over again I asked her, "Why are you lying?" and begged her, "Agata, we need to get you to a therapist. There are things that we need to begin to understand about you, and I can't take it. I love you and I'll never leave you. I will walk with you through whatever it is. I promise."

In desperation, I put my gun into my mouth, on my knees in the bed beside her. "Agata, this is how I feel. Don't you care? I don't know what you're doing. I don't know who you are sometimes. Please get help with me. You are making me feel this desperate! Can't you see what you are doing to me? I need you to get help."

"Ok, stop that and put the gun away. What do you want to know?"

"I need to know what is going on with you and why you are lying to me."

"What am I lying about?"

"Well, I could make a list, but for one thing you say that the nicest thing that your dad ever did for you was bring you exactly one cup of tea. What else do you remember about your dad?"

"That is what I remember, Iain. I'm not trying to lie to you."

"What do you mean 'you're not trying to lie to me'? Either you are lying, or you aren't. Which is it?"

"I am telling you what I remember. I don't think I'm lying."

"Ok, and what else do you remember?" I asked, thinking maybe we were starting an honest conversation.

She thought for a moment and then responded, "I remember that I have never been married before."

Yes, you've already told me that one, I thought, *and that is not much information at all. Does she think I might have thought otherwise? Why doesn't she ever tell me anything substantive, something that would help me begin to understand her?*

Crazy childhoods are normal, and time is all she needs, I reasoned. I didn't press her hard because there was an impenetrable wall. I assumed that the "bad" chapters would decrease with time, regardless of whatever had happened in her past. During a period of relative normalcy in 2006, we decided to get pregnant. In the same year, I was hired as a Social Worker Trainee (Child Protection Officer) for the Connecticut Department of Children and Families (DCF). I was excited about the future, ready to start looking forward, and thrilled that whatever was in the past was now getting further behind us.

I had to pass a drug test as the last step before starting my DCF training, but I was still smoking marijuana. I obtained some urine from a friend I knew would be "clean," and I devised a strategy whereby I put his urine into a rubber hot water bottle and strapped it to my groin area. I knew that this would not be a supervised test like the ones that I had administered to clients when I worked at the AIC a few years earlier.

Your mom came with me to the test, about as pregnant as she could get, looking like she could pop at any moment, and she sat in the waiting area. I was taken into the back and led to a bathroom to give my sample; the water was shut off to prevent me from diluting the sample. I spilled my friend's urine down my leg, nervously getting some of it into the sample cup. When the nurse inspected the cup, she told me that she knew that it was not my urine because of the temperature reading on the strip.

"It's mine," I said, trying to be convincing, "are you sure that the temperature strip isn't broken?" I knew that I was caught out, but I thought lying and playing dumb was my best option.

"You could have told me that you smoked once at a party, and I would have been ok with that." *How would I know that?* I thought to myself. "It's not your wife's urine, is it? It will show that it is a pregnant female's urine when it goes to the lab."

"No, it's not my wife's," I admitted, hoping for mercy.

"Ok, well I'm going to let it slide. I don't want to mess you up with your pregnant wife sitting out there in the lobby." She sent my friend's urine off to lab as if it were mine.

"Thank you, thank you, I'm sorry," I responded, feeling like I had just dodged a bullet, wanting to give her a hug. I got the job shortly thereafter.

CHAPTER 8

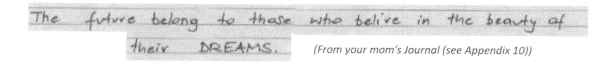

The future belong to those who belive in the beauty of their DREAMS. *(From your mom's Journal (see Appendix 10))*

Your mom and I began planning for your entry into the world, and once we knew you were going to be a girl, we began going over potential names together. We had a list of possibilities that we gradually narrowed down. I let your mom lead, though I thought that I had some say in the matter.

I was more flexible than she was; what mattered to me was that your middle name was "Avery" like mine. She acted as if we were doing it together, but I had a slight yet unprovable feeling that I was being steered in a particular direction.

Your grandparents, Sławomir and Iwona, flew over from Poland for your birth; it was very important to them that they be present, and getting them visas wasn't a simple process. We had to provide the government with bank statements and proof that they had jobs that they would be returning to. I was thrilled that they were going to be there, that it meant so much to them, and I fantasized about us all living together in the U.S., bringing it up to your mom in conversation several times.

Your mom's water broke in the middle of the night while we were sleeping. I drove her to the hospital, where she was in labor for a long time. After the epidural ran out, she was in excruciating pain. I had seen your head during a contraction, but now your mom was struggling, and I just wanted you to come out. Rather than offer her more pain medication, the doctor got in your mom's face and asked her if she wanted a c-section.

Because of her pain level and the fact that she was only given one option, she agreed. They wheeled her into a different room, and within minutes they had her cut open. I was upset because it appeared to me that the doctor had basically forced her into having a c-section. He should've known when the medication was going to run out, and she never should have been put into a position to make such a decision when she was in extreme pain.

I was holding your mom's hand when you were born, and I was in shock and exhausted. But all of a sudden, my little girl was in my arms; the clouds lifted, and the sun emerged. I felt relief and joy, knowing I was blessed (see Appendix 11).

Your presence brought wonder and hope into our home. I loved being a dad and all that it entailed. One of my favorite things was figuring out which foods were your favorites once you began eating solid food. You enjoyed being read to and licked by our dog, Butch. For me, you made all of the pieces of my life start to fall into place and make sense.

Me holding you. January 30, 2007.
New London, CT.

Me, your mom, and you. 2007.
Groton, CT.

* * *

The chaos caused by your mom's drastic fluctuations continued, and eventually the doctor diagnosed me with panic disorder because of the high frequency of my panic attacks, and I continued taking clonazepam along with the opiates that I was prescribed for the cervical stenosis/discogenic disease in my neck. I became dependent upon both things, and I often exceeded the recommended doses. The pain clinic was taking care of making sure that I had enough pain medication, but it seemed like I never had enough clonazepam, because no doctor would match the twenty milligrams a day that I had gotten used to in Poland. I found a place in Australia that would ship sealed bottles of one hundred pills, and I used this to supplement what I was picking up at the pharmacy.

While I was excited about having a job at DCF that paid better than substitute teaching and had great benefits, these factors weren't sufficient to make me satisfied with what I was doing. What I wanted to do was help children, and unfortunately this is not what they were training me to do or demanding I do on the job. This is not to say that DCF doesn't help any children, as I'm sure they do sometimes, but their primary obligation is to protect the state from liability.

I was given a caseload of about ten families after receiving some initial training on child abuse and what I was to do about it as a Child Protection Officer. The priority of the bosses was "get the paperwork done and do it correctly." They didn't seem to care if I had enough time with the children to adequately assess their situations; it was in and out and get the paperwork done. "Sink or swim" was the motto of the supervisors.

Because I wasn't willing to compromise the safety or wellbeing of the children on my caseload, I ended up spending more time with them than was allotted. My boss didn't like this, and she decided that I wasn't fit for the job; she told me that I was sinking. She was right, I wasn't fit for the job, as the job had little to do with the actual welfare of children. When you were about six months old, I stopped working for DCF.

Your mom made it clear that she wanted to be closer to her family in Poland, and I wanted your mom to be happy. In fact, I was desperate for her to be happy, and willing to sacrifice almost anything to get her there. The joy in our home, including my own, was totally dependent upon the roller coaster that was your mom, and it was imperative that our cart found level ground.

I am in no way claiming that I was perfect; I made plenty of mistakes as well. But, I am claiming that there was "something wrong with her," as she repeatedly assured me. We needed her to get help for whatever it was that was plaguing her, though I had no idea what that could be since she wouldn't tell me anything.

It felt like I was constantly walking on eggshells, caught in a sort of bondage to her recurring fluctuations. *Is she going to be happy and content today, or am I going to have to take the brunt of her misery?* This was my daily reality. *What is causing this seesaw effect? Why is she so often miserable and mean?* I couldn't figure it out, so I popped more pills, just looking for a little bit of relief.

She would not seek counseling, and she refused to talk to anyone else. I spoke to the pastor across the street from our house at Trinity Missionary Baptist Church, and then we attended one Sunday service. I wanted to add community to our lives, but your mom wasn't interested in that, and she refused to return.

As I began assenting to her desire to live in Europe, she began letting up on me, and I felt some relief and hope that we might be turning a corner. When she was nice to me, I was like putty in her hands.

"My parents want to help us with Adelle," she persuasively claimed. "Both of your parents are too busy, but mine have a lot of free time, and they can help us. The economy here is terrible, and if you were working in The Netherlands, you would make twice as much. You can get a job in one of the international courts in The Hague with your master's degree."

She was coaxing me, but it didn't matter. With her new desire, and me hearing her out, she seemed happy again, and I wanted to keep it that way. She also reminded me that marijuana was legal in The Netherlands and suggested that I go on a trip by myself to feel it out. *What could be better than a happy wife, a job that suited my degree with more money, and weed stores?* I asked myself.

I did take a trip to Amsterdam on my own since she kept suggesting it and thought that it would help me to decide. I was mostly already sold on the idea because she wanted it so badly, but once I visited, I was ready to move right away. It was a different world, a welcome change from New England where there were many unhappy and uptight people who seemed to mostly be worried about whatever the news had told them to be worried about the night before.

Starting fresh in an entirely new environment felt like exactly what we needed. This could be a place where your mother and I could find our own way, alone with you, and away from family and friends. I did not know anybody in Amsterdam; my closest relationship was to a woman I had met on eBay who asked me to bring a dog over for her on the plane. The next closest relationship was in Poland; "They want to help," your mom kept assuring me.

My dad advised against the move, saying, "Don't move your family out of the country," but it went in one ear and out the other. I wasn't concerned with what anyone else had to say; I was only interested in pleasing your mother. I didn't even consider his admonition for a moment. Nobody else ever saw what it could be like to live with your mom, and I certainly couldn't tell them. What would they do anyway? She was my wife, and I had put all my eggs into her basket.

* * *

I got off the plane at Schiphol Airport in Amsterdam, The Netherlands, carrying the eBay woman's dog in a travel carrier, along with three or four large suitcases containing most of the things that our family was taking with us from our old home to our new home. The woman met me at the airport, and after handing over the dog, I asked if she would bring me to a hostel. Because I did not know where I was going yet other than to Amsterdam, she chose a hostel and dropped me off. I lugged everything up the stairs and checked myself into a dorm room.

You and your mom went to your grandparents' house in Poland to wait; my job was to find us a place to stay, and to attempt to find work. I mingled with people from around the world who were stopping by the hostel on their adventures, transient families with young kids, Norwegian college graduates, and Italian teenagers visiting the Red-Light District to buy sex.

I was the only one that was not on some sort of vacation, but I enjoyed getting to be around all these travelers and hearing their stories. I especially got to know the people who worked at the hostel, Hostel Amigo in East Amsterdam, as they were the only ones who kept coming every day, while everyone else was quickly on their way somewhere else.

One of the main front desk people at the hostel, Wael, became a friend and helped me to find a room in somebody's home. This was a step in the right direction toward a more permanent address. We had now penetrated the rental market and were no longer tourists. Even though we would not be technically legal, that would change as soon as your mom got here and started her European Union paperwork. This was a step that many immigrant families went through temporarily on their journey toward legal residence.

Wael was from Egypt, with most of his network being Muslim. He would jokingly call me "Jesus," because, I assumed, I was one of his few non-Muslim friends. The place that he found for us was a room in an apartment in North Amsterdam, a short, free ferry ride from behind Central Station. Our new landlord was Mohammad, a fifty something Algerian with a drinking problem. We cooked and ate together, and he taught me that it was not strange to eat a dozen eggs in one sitting. Wael began taking me around, introducing me to more people, and helping me to begin to look for work.

Your mother arrived shortly thereafter, and though it was great to have her with me, I wanted desperately for all three of us to be together. I was frustrated that your mom had left you in Poland at less than two years old, but it was temporary, and it would allow us to work more efficiently toward finding our home.

Mohammad was charging us as much or more for a room than we would pay for an entire apartment, so we needed to move quickly. He was also a severe alcoholic who went on binges every time we gave him rent money, and it became clear that he did not have many other sources of income other than us. Moving in with him was a good step, but it was not really a place I wanted you to be.

After a couple of weeks, Wael helped us to find another room in West Amsterdam, a better location, and a more stable environment. A young man from France was living there as well, a cannabis expert who was trying to find his dream job in a coffee shop. This is where you moved in with us, where we started our journey as a family in The Netherlands. Your grandfather drove you to us, and he took your mother to a job interview at Saudi Aramco, an oil and gas company, which became her employer shortly thereafter.

In the meantime, we were getting our residence paperwork together, which would allow me to work there as your mother's husband. Otherwise, as an American, I would not have been approved to work. Once the papers were filed and I was given the appropriate stamp in my passport and a SOFI number, the equivalent of a U.S. Social Security Number, I found a job in the center of the city selling gourmet coffee and cannabis seeds to tourists.

I knew that it was not going to be a long-term job, but on a temporary basis it was something of a dream come true for me at that time, being paid to drink lattes, smoke joints, and help customers find the seeds that they needed to start their gardens at home. The boss's rule was, "Smoke them if you got them, just don't smoke mine."

Your mother's job as an executive secretary at the oil company was in The Hague, about a two-hour trip one way from our current location door to door. She was able to find a temporary apartment for us in Leiden through one of her new colleagues, bringing her commute time down to just under one hour each way. Our new apartment was on Druckerstraat street, and it was finally our own; we didn't have any housemates.

We now had a door that we could lock and a back yard, a place that we could call our own in The Netherlands. Though we knew it was not a long-term solution, at least we could fully unpack. I stopped working in Amsterdam and began looking for work in The Hague, where I had hoped I would be able to find a job in one of the many international criminal courts/tribunals with the help of my background in political science and criminal justice. Until then I would be a stay-at-home dad and try to hold down the fort.

Living in The Netherlands was an easy transition from living in the United States, but there were also major differences that took some getting used to. Public transportation was one of the most difficult adjustments; at first, I yearned to have my car back. The seats on the trains, trams, and buses were uncomfortable, and sometimes there wasn't a seat at all. Oftentimes on a tram we would be sandwiched in as tightly as could be, barely able to move or get something out of a pocket. I rode a bicycle everywhere I could, but only when I was alone; I wasn't willing to ride with you on the bike, even though many Dutch parents seemed to do this with ease.

CHAPTER 9

"DESPITE MY ATTEMPTS, STILL NO COUNSELING..."

NOTE: Paragraph divisions and some spelling corrections have been added to emails and journal entries for readability.

"Jul 30, 2008, 4:50 AM
[Email from] Iain Bryson to Sara [Aunt]
So, I am just sitting and trying to plan. Adelle is watching some Dutch cartoon and finishing her breakfast. Did you get the last email...just want to make sure I sent it to the right address because I typed it in manually. Anyway, I am going out after nap to drop off flyers around town, at schools, markets, churches, wherever me and Delle can think of for English tutoring. I want to start my own business as I did in Poland, because if I even get a few clients here, I will be making good money on the side.

My interview on Monday went great, and I think I can have that job if I want as an Enrollment Counselor for an online University. It starts Sept 1, so I am still looking, but Ada is not here any longer... Agata will never say anything to her sister, and protects her like she is a sick bird. I was never spoken to in English, nor was Adelle, and she would rather watch MTV or the computer than Adelle, so I am glad in a way, but now I am supposed to pay back Agata's mom. Now her father is coming, which will be good help... I just hope she doesn't play games because I don't want to and I don't appreciate it when people do that to me. Well, we are still trying to talk. Despite my attempts, still no counseling. Anyway, better play with Adelle. Love, Iain"

On a trip home from the store, the chain fell off my bike, and I went headfirst over the handlebars. I landed on my chin, unable to get my hands out in front of me to cushion the blow to my face. I spit out teeth, stood up, and tried to jump on the bike so that I could get home quickly, but it was totally inoperable. I thrust the bike away toward the canal on my right, abandoning it forever, frustrated that I would have to walk. I was uncertain of my injuries, but I did know that I was hurt.

After walking about a block down the street, I looked around and saw a person walking behind me. "Am I ok?" I asked. I was in shock, still totally unaware of the severity of my injuries.

"You're bleeding," he explained, trying to be helpful.

"Yes, I know I'm bleeding," I seethed through my broken face, deciding at that point to scamper home as quickly as possible.

At home, your mom just stared at me in the doorway for what seemed like an eternity, paralyzed by my trauma. "Call an ambulance," I barked at her through the clenched teeth that remained. Eventually she did, and an ambulance came to take me to the hospital, bouncing all the way on the brick and cobblestone streets of Leiden.

You and your mom met me at the hospital shortly thereafter. I told her to tell the doctor that I wanted glue and not stitches in my chin, but she was still in shock and did not relay the message for me. They informed me that I had a broken jaw, but that the specialist was not in the building. I was sent home to wait for my appointment with the specialist the following day.

They didn't offer me any pain medication except for a paracetamol suppository, so I just doubled the medication that I was already taking for my neck pain. I had to sleep on my belly with my hands on my temples holding my head up, but the pain was so intense that I didn't sleep that much anyway, and I couldn't eat any solid food at all (see Appendix 12).

After four days, I had surgery, and my mouth was wired shut for a couple of months. I interviewed with Laureate Online Education for the job of Student Support Manager soon after the wires were removed, though I still couldn't but barely open my mouth. I felt confident and qualified, my only doubts regarding the interview being that I spoke weirdly, almost like a ventriloquist. But I got the job, and I began the commute from Leiden to Amsterdam. The management and my coworkers were all warm and welcoming, and it was nice to have new friends, and to feel like our family was progressing in making it happen in The Netherlands.

I began my new job, which kept me away from home from 6:30 AM to 6:00 PM, and we found an apartment in The Hague, closer to your mom's job. I continued to look for employment in The Hague closer to where your mom was working, but in the meantime, this would suffice: a decent paycheck, paid sick and family time, and one month per year paid vacation. Our new home was at Newtonplein 25A, with a park directly across the street. By tram, it was about 20–30 minutes to Den Haag Central Station.

"Thu, Oct 30, 2008, 7:18 AM
Iain Bryson to Brian
B

just got the cpu up and running. got an apartment and have been painting and cleaning. it is getting there. got a job starting monday, so now trying to figure out daycare. what is up in AZ? Sucks you moved to a swing state. just busy getting everything together and going to Ikea and stuff like that. i will work as a student support manager in Amsterdam, so i have an hour or so train ride, but they pay for the transport. give me time to drink coffee and read or whatever. we are close to the tram stop so just have to have the exact timing so there is no waiting in the cold...once it comes. been fairly nice for this time of year… hope the fam is doing good. hi to everyone. talk to you soon. home phone is now 31 70 8879298 though with my luck it probably won't work for some reason, I"

"Thu, Nov 13, 2008, 2:37 AM
Iain Bryson to Brian
B-

Just got to work a little while ago. Almost done with the second week. Just getting used to the routine and travel. Had to figure out the best trains to take. I leave the house at 6:30 and get to the tram around 6:40 which takes 11 minutes to get to Central Station where I take a train with Agata to her stop which then keeps going to the airport, where I get off and go out for a smoke before switching trains. I was changing three times, because the times are a little better, but if one is late, it sucks, and it sucks to have to jump around when you can try to get something done for the time you are on it. The job seems good and not too difficult. I am working directly with master's students and the professors, but only on the phone and internet. Can't wait for the weekend. We are still trying to finish up the painting and stuff like that and still have to get to Ikea but things are coming along. Our nanny has been good, and often cooks and cleans for free as well, though I may try to compensate her in some way, but still haven't been paid as it is once per month. Other than that, just enjoying the little time with Adelle, and trying to figure out stuff with Agata. We are going to Poland for Christmas, and I am trying to figure out the best time for me to come to the States.
Well, should go do something. Talk to you soon. Iain"

We settled into our little apartment, and I began to get the hang of being a Student Support Manager while your mom continued at the Saudi oil company. You spent the days first with a babysitter, then later at a daycare center, Comme a la Maison, in The Hague, down closer to the beach. In the evenings we played in the park, or inside our apartment, doing puzzles or just hanging out.

This is where I started bringing you to look out your bedroom window after reading your bedtime books. I held you and hugged you, made sure that you saw the moon if it was visible, and told you that, "I love you to the moon, and back." I did not know what this meant at the time, but I did know it to be true.

Your mom and I did not communicate much; after putting you down, we mostly watched television together, then had to go to sleep to be semi ready for the next day, always tired. On the weekends we cleaned the apartment as a family and had more time to explore the local parks and playgrounds. The only new connections we made were through work; your mom had her work friends, and I had a couple of my own. The rest of the time it was just the three of us, except when Polish relatives came to visit.

My first friend was Art, ten years older than me, black, gay, and from San Francisco. He took me under his wing and accepted me as his long-lost brother. It was helpful to have someone to talk with about homelife. I vented to him, and he listened, which was an improvement in my support structure. He also vented to me, telling me about his severely abusive father, a man who was a well-respected Jehovah's Witness.

He didn't like your mom and told me that I should leave her, but for me that wasn't ever an option. I couldn't be sure if his vehemence about your mom's negative effect on me was due to his general distrust of all women as partners, his desire for more than a friendship with me, or if it was in the interest of our family. My only interest, of course, was our family.

Art was and is my friend but is also someone I probably would never have hung out with had home life been bearable. When I needed to get away, he was there to listen and console me. He was always welcoming, but he was also not shy about the fact that one of his desires was to have sexual relations with me.

The first time that I went out with Art, he took me to the Blue Light District in Amsterdam, which I didn't even know existed. This is where the gay bars are, and for the first time in my life I saw glory holes and slings with naked men, suspended and waiting for some action from anybody who was willing.

I was just happy to have a friend, and this is what my friend wanted to do. I viewed it as a chance to catch a glimpse of a world that I was oblivious to, something that I could write about someday. I was something of an undercover gay who was not gay, sometimes holding his hand as we walked down the street because that's what he wanted to do. I didn't feel threatened by this because I knew who I was, for the most part, and because of the anonymity of being in the city.

"Mon, Nov 24, 2008, 1:05 PM
Iain Bryson to Brian

b,

What up? long time. I have been sick and busier than I am used to, but feel a little better today. Working in Amsterdam and living in Den Haag, so it is a bit of a day, but the job is ok so far, and the people are pretty cool. Adelle is with Polish nanny during the day. Agata is about 15 minutes away in Leiden, the place we used to live in. Went to the dentist today and have major issues, so will be seeing specialists for a while. Taking a half day on Thurs and Agata is cooking for Thanksgiving. We are going to Poland for Christmas. We haven't been there for four Christmases, so Agata thinks we ought to go. Trying to plan a trip to CT to bring Adelle and get Butch, but waiting on my mom's schedule. Not been doing much but working. On the weekends we usually make it to the little farm down the street. Adelle likes the cows and can sit with the rabbits and feed them. Other than that, been snowing and hailing and too [expletive] cold. Went out with a friend from work in Amsterdam on Friday and didn't get home till 4, and was sick as a dog the next day at least. Adelle is going to bed...gotta help. Talk to you soon. I"

CHAPTER 10

"WHEN I AM IN POLAND, I AM NOT WITH YOU... I AM MY DAD'S"

We went to Poland for Christmas and stayed at your grandparents' house. As soon as we got there, my panic disorder again kicked into high gear right after your mom told me, "When I am in Poland, I am not with you. When I am here, I am my dad's. I have to be with him when I am here."

I had no idea what she meant; all that I knew was how I felt, which was horrible, and that she was regularly out with him. I wasn't welcome; I was on my own, constantly shaking inside, barely able to function. I stayed in bed most of the time because I was devastated at how your mom had abandoned me to be with her dad, whatever that meant, but that was what was happening. I began drinking to quell my terrors and ease my mind, just to get through the day. When we were home, I didn't drink at all, but now I felt like I had to.

One night, I was in the kitchen with your grandfather doing shots from a bottle of Johnny Walker that I had bought from a local kiosk, feeling like I was bonding with him. My eyes started to water as I tried to communicate with him. "I want you to know that I love Agata. I love her with everything that I am..."

He responded in broken English, using his hands for emphasis, "Agata is Agata, but Adelle. Oh, Adelle, Adelle... I'm sorry you are so weak. Yes, I'm sorry you are so weak." I didn't know what to say, so I just said, "Yes, well I love Agata and Adelle," feeling totally awkward and misunderstood.

Later I told your mom what he had said to me, looking to her for some clarification as to what he could have meant. "I'm sorry you're so weak," I repeated to her several times. "Why would he say that? He is the weak alcoholic without a job who you tell me I should send money to. All that I told him was that I love you."

"I will talk to my mom," she replied, shuddering, "he shouldn't be drinking. I will tell my mom and she will take care of it."

After returning from a local grocery store, I found you and your grandma on the couch watching cartoons. At first, I was pleased that she was hanging out with you, even though it was a bit disappointing that you were watching tv in the middle of the day. Upon further inspection, I noticed that the cartoon was extremely violent. *Why is she subjecting my baby to such brutal images?* I asked myself, feeling my blood boil; this was definitely not allowed in our house, and not something that was ok for you regardless of whose house we were visiting.

I didn't say anything to your grandma because I knew she couldn't understand me, but I did speak to your mom right away. "Agata, she is watching the most violent cartoon I've ever seen with our baby," I imparted. "This is not ok with me. Is it ok with you? She needs to turn this off now!" While she didn't seem concerned, she certainly knew that I was serious, and this was the last time I saw her watching something like that with you.

One of the things that was scheduled for this trip was to have you christened in the Catholic Church. I loathed the idea of this, but I felt like I had no choice; your mom told me this was going to happen. I rationalized it as not being a big deal since you were so young and would not remember, but I knew that I would have to put my foot down in the future when they wanted to go further down this road.

When we got back home to The Hague, things were a mess, but at least your mom was kind of with me and not "with her dad" anymore. She would not talk to me about anything difficult, and we just continued to slide by, watching tv in our time together. Whenever I pressured her to talk, she would offer me sex, and I would forget about whatever it was I had wanted to ask her.

I remember watching a *Criminal Minds* episode with her about cults (season 4, episode 13) entitled "Bloodline." We watched many hours of *Criminal Minds*, but this was the one that stood out because of her reaction to the plot. A family cult had abducted a child to marry her to their son and bond them together at a young age. They killed the parents and kept her in a closet. "Agata," I remarked, "this is horrible. How could people do this?" She did not verbally respond to me, but the look she flashed back at me imprinted this moment and this episode onto my mind; through dozens of episodes, her reaction caused me to remember this one, the one about a family cult.

* * *

I trained you to use the toilet, wanting to get you out of diapers and knowing that you were ready. It was as if your mom had no idea what she was doing in these matters, but I was glad to take on any responsibility that related to you, and it came naturally to me. I was extremely interested in your development, in trying to do things as best I could, and in my development which would lead to that end.

I wanted all aspects of life to be exciting and positive for you, and so I learned not to interject the negativity that had been a part of my training. When it was a cloudy or rainy day, I would take you to the window and say, "Look Adelle, look at this beautiful day!" When we cleaned the litter box together, I would sing a song and never indicate to you that I thought it was stinky. When we cleaned the house together, I tried to turn it into a dance, a joyous occasion where we listened to music and worked together as a team.

Your mom kept a box of wallet sized photographs by your bed. Every night before you went to bed, she and you would look through them together. I thought it was strange, but I liked the fact that she had placed my picture on the top. Below me were you and her, along with all the females in our Polish family.

No other men besides me were in this box, which was fine with me. We had several pictures hanging in our living room, of your mom and I, of you and I, and of your grandmother. When I asked your mom why there was no picture of your grandpa, she replied, "Adelle doesn't want it on the wall." *Ok, neither do I,* I thought to myself.

Among the many books in your book pile was one picture book with Bible stories. Though I wasn't sure about what I thought about bringing you up in a church, or even calling ourselves Christians, I did want you to be introduced to the Bible as I was. I tried to incorporate this book into our nightly reading routine, but the displeased look on your mom's face led to me abandoning the idea.

Instead, during our bedtime ritual, I always let you choose the books that I would read to you. Sometimes I would improvise and make up a story of my own when it was a book you weren't familiar with, or when I didn't like what the author had written. I always followed this by bringing you to the window to tell you, "I love you to the moon and back," as we searched together in the night sky to find the moon.

* * *

"Thu, Jan 29, 2009, 6:43 AM
Iain Bryson to Brian
hey, call me at work if you get a chance. how was firing someone? Never got to ask. What is your title now...VP or P? anyway, just at work. took a week off in March. going to see John Legend. Going to see the tennis finals here Feb 15. Also took May 15-June2 off so try to be in CT somewhere in there if you can. Hope everything is going good. Tell Kim [wife] I said hi. I am working on getting to the post office, just limited time and no car. The train I needed decided it wasn't coming so I was 45 min late, but they don't care because it happens to everyone. people that drive can spend hours in their car for a half hour ride depending on the

time. well, Adelle went swimming yesterday. going to the beach and farm this weekend and maybe trying to find some horses that are downtown somewhere. probably next to the sheep, so maybe I should ask paul [our Scottish friend]. anyway, back to the old jobby. Or a cig maybe first. later. I"

We didn't end up going to the tennis finals, but instead chose to invite your grandfather, knowing how much he loved tennis. He showed up at our house with one of his friends that I had never met before, and they slept on the floor in the living room for a couple of nights.

Your mom and I were working at the time, so we didn't get to spend much time with them. I bought a bottle of Jim Beam that I thought your grandpa and I would share, went to work, and when I returned the bottle was empty. "Agata," I pled, "that is ridiculous, I was gone for only eight hours and the entire bottle is gone. Why would he do that?"

"Iain, please don't say anything to him," she entreated, obviously fearful.

"I can't just joke with him and ask him what happened to my bottle?" I asked, prying.

"No, do not mention it. Please don't mention it. Don't say anything about the bottle," she hammered in.

The four of us went to the Albert Heijn grocery store that was around the corner from our apartment so that we could get some food for the week and incorporate your grandfather's choices. He didn't bring any money with him, which was fine, but on the way out he made a motion to your mom that he needed her to buy him beer. This exasperated me because I had already bought the Jim Beam.

We were working, so we had some money, but we certainly weren't rich, and we never kept our fridge stocked with beer or our cabinets with liquor. The Jim Beam was a treat, and now he was strongarming your mom to buy him beer. I could tell that the way he looked at her had instilled some kind of fear, the same type of fear that had manifested in her at the thought of me mentioning the missing Jim Beam. She added the beer to our cart, and I let it go, though it continued to be like a rock in my shoe.

Your grandfather and his friend stayed up all night in our living room having a drunken party with each other. They were loud as if nobody else was there, but of course you were sleeping in the next room, and I was trying to get some sleep since I had to go to work the next day. Your mom wouldn't say anything; she seemed to lay next to me in a state of paralysis, also not sleeping, but unwilling to confront him.

Sometime in the wee hours of the morning I finally got out of bed and stood in the doorway. While I knew that he couldn't understand my exact words, I also knew that he would be able to understand my tone. I told them to stop their nonsense and to quiet down in a stern voice as if I was dealing with two out of control teenagers, which is what it felt like. I didn't really care how I came across as I felt like the sanctity of our home and the fact that both your mom and I had to work had been totally disrespected. *If your mom can't stand up to him, I can,* I reasoned. If looks could kill, I'd have been dead right there, but I was certain I was right, and I figured he would see that too once he sobered up. *Why does she protect him no matter what?* I pondered.

He picked you up at daycare, allowing your mom and I not to have to rush home from work. Plus, he was in The Hague, so I thought it was nice that he would get to spend some time with you. The daycare center maintained a logbook for your mom and I where they kept notes on what your days with them looked like. They sent the book home with you every day, but it wasn't until after your abduction that I read the following entry: "Today your dad picked you up, and you were excited that it was him and not your grandfather."

We all went to the park together on Newtonplein, right across the street from our apartment. Our neighborhood mostly consisted of Arabs and Pollacks; most of the Dutch people had moved out of our part of the city because of the high levels of immigration. I got along more so with the Arabs than the Pollacks, as the former were quiet and respectful, while the latter were loud and rude, always drinking and whistling out their windows as the women passed by on the sidewalk. When your grandfather saw the Arab children, he referred to them as "little terrorists," which he thought was a joke. *As opposed to the little alcoholic womanizers that are from your country,* I thought to myself.

They left the next day without saying anything to me, and I tried to process through what had happened with your mom. "First the Jim Beam, then the beer, then having a party in our living room on a work night. I didn't get any sleep last night, and I had a horrible day at work."

"His feelings were hurt," she informed me, "you didn't even help him take his suitcase down."

"His feelings were hurt? What do you mean 'his feelings were hurt'? He was totally out of line last night, and I was working when he left. How would I have taken his suitcase down?" She wouldn't answer me; the fact that she had a total inability or unwillingness to see my concerns or to be critical of his behavior in any way floored me.

Sławomir, you, and your mom at the farm in The Hague. Photo taken by me.

"Iain," she continued, "he hurt his elbow and cannot play tennis right now. This is very hard for him. He can't play tennis, and he loves to play tennis." She started crying, which was something I don't think I had ever seen her do before in our entire relationship.

"Agata, you are crying because your dad can't play tennis right now? What is going on? Why does it matter to you so much that he has a hurt elbow?"

She continued sobbing, "He hurt his elbow, he can't play tennis," she repeated. I inspected her face and body, assuming I would see signs of crocodile tears, but I didn't. *She is genuinely devastated that her dad has a hurt elbow*, I recognized.

You were unwell after he left, and I sat on the couch, holding your hand, just trying to console you. It was as if a tornado had ravaged our home, and now I was back to picking up the pieces. I didn't know why you were sick, only that I felt a bit ill myself from all that had happened over the past few days. *Now he's gone*, I thought, *now we can get our house back in order again.*

Something was troubling you for a while, though your mom didn't want to take you to the doctor. It was as if I had lost contact with you; you were living in a sort of daze. You painted on the walls in your bedroom with some craft paint that I had bought you. I repainted and asked you not to paint on the walls again, and then you immediately did it again. I repainted once more, and while doing so I remembered when I drew on the house when I was a child after being sexually abused by my twelve-year-old neighbor, an event that had totally escaped my memory until that moment.

Following this visit, you began having temper tantrums and hyperventilating. When I took you out on the town for a walk, you had always held my hand when we crossed the street. But now you didn't want to hold my hand, and you told me that I was hurting you when I told you that you had to. You acted as if you were upset with me, though I knew that you had no reason to be upset with me.

Me and you sitting on the couch after Sławomir left. You are unwell, and I am trying to comfort you and understand what is going on. Photos taken by your mom.

CHAPTER II

"ONE CUP OF TEA"

"Mon, Mar 16, 2009, 8:25 AM
Iain Bryson to Brian
Yo,
Nice getting to talk the other day. Need to do that more often. Just so [expletive] busy as I am sure you are. But, gotta do it. Glad to hear the fam is doing good. Say hi to your parents for me. Your mom sent me a pic of your daughter. You have gotta let me in on your secret(s) for getting up so [expletive] early?? I want to have the gift, but can't figure it out. What do you do? Is Kim up with you? Anyway, just working and trying to win an auction as both U2 concerts sold out, so now we are trying to get VIP tix through an e-bay type auction. That is about it...thankfully the day is going fairly quick, but I have too much to do here. Then back home, dinner, an hour with Adelle, maybe an hour of tv and bed. Going to get my resume to the college this week and also to the guy I met on the plane [prospective employer]. Still trying to figure out when we can come back...depends mostly on Agata's VISA. And not Visa/MC, which is also an issue, as I think my mom could come here as well. Not that she is the only person I want to see, but I have to start banking something on a more regular basis if I ever hope to get back to school. Talk to you soon. I"

I was bored at work; it was a job, and a decent job at that, but it was also tedious, repetitive, and not what I considered a career opportunity. I grew sick of commuting, and of being away from home for the extra time that it required. I did not like that you were in daycare for so long, let alone at all, and I did not like that you had to be rushed out of the house in the morning when your mom and I went to work.

I was always the first or second person into the office in the morning, as that allowed me to also leave earlier, but I could not get my head away from home and my girls. I felt like there was something else I had to be doing, that something being raising you and getting our household under control. My boss knew I was not a good prospect for a

Your mom at a U2 concert,
Amsterdam Arena. July 21, 2009.

permanent contract, that my head was not in it, and he decided to not renew my contract, lifting a giant burden off my shoulders. I began trying to find a job in line with my degree, and in the meantime, I spent the time with you, instead of shipping you off for others to teach you whatever it was they were teaching you at the daycare.

Your mom and I kept having difficulties, and she kept refusing to go to counselling. She refused to let me in any further than she already had with such statements as "...one cup of tea," and, "I know I have never been married before." I knew that there was more, but *what could it be?* I constantly asked myself. I realized that I really didn't know her that well, since I only knew her as much as she knew herself, which was apparently not well at all.

Or she was lying, which was something I often considered. I drew a blank when I contemplated why she would lie to me about the cup of tea, and though I often accused her of lying, I also couldn't be sure if she was also just drawing blanks herself. "Agata, I will never leave you no matter what it is; please just tell me," I often repeated to her.

One day when I was home and she was out, I heard our doorbell ring. I looked out the window, but I didn't recognize the man, noticing only that he was holding a ladder. I went downstairs to see what he wanted, and he informed me that he was there to shut off our electricity, telling me that we hadn't been paying our bill.

I was dumbfounded, and I figured that it had to be a mistake, but he was there to do a job and I couldn't stop him. When your mom returned home, I confronted her, "Agata, why didn't you tell me about this bill? How did we not pay our electricity bill?"

"I never received the bill," she claimed, but later I went through our old mail and found an opened letter from the electric company, a shut off warning notice. She remained adamant that she had never seen it, and that she had no idea even when I showed this to her. I was forced to drop it; trying to get her to admit she had to know or at least had known when she opened the letter was like trying to milk a rock.

We received notice in the mail that we were in the process of being evicted for nonpayment of rent. I was floored, as we were definitely making enough money to pay rent, and because we were using her account to make the monthly automatic payments, an account that I never checked on my own.

"Agata, how did you let this happen? We haven't been paying rent for six months?"

"I guess not," she replied. "I had no idea."

"How could you have no idea that nearly half of your paycheck wasn't being taken out of your account for six months? That's impossible. I know you're lying. Where did that money go?"

"Iain, I didn't know," she tried to assure me, but I knew she was hiding something. She refused to make eye contact, and she acted like it was no big deal.

"I don't know where that money is," she repeated, trying her best to pull it off. I had always trusted her with the bills, and she had always taken care of them. I was in the practice of letting her handle all the money. We kept a small pile of fifty Euro notes on the top of the bookshelf that I would use if I needed anything, but everything else was in her control for payment of our bills.

"Agata, I know that you're lying. There is no way that you could miss that; it's impossible that you didn't know, and impossible that you don't know where that money is now."

I had no way of figuring out what had happened for sure, but I did take her to both of our banks to put my name on her account and her name on my account. *Ok*, I thought, *we will figure this out, but I also can't trust her anymore; why is she constantly lying to me?* It wasn't until later that I found bank records showing that your mom had been transferring money to her mom and her sister in Poland, at least showing where some of the money was going.

She physically attacked me on a few occasions, springing on me like a wild animal. For me the attacks were just another sign that we needed counselling, as I knew that she couldn't really hurt me. When she attacked, I grabbed her by the arms until she stopped, or I gave her a bear hug. She dug her fingernails into my arms, and on one occasion she caught me in the eye. I took a picture so that I could show her more evidence that we needed to talk to someone.

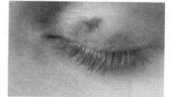

My left eye, bruised by your mom. 2010.

Since she refused to get counselling, and because I had nobody that I could talk to, I knew that I had to figure it out on my own. We often sat in bed for hours going around in circles, but never getting anywhere new. "Agata, is it incest?" I asked with my tail between my legs. "Please just tell me so we can deal with it. I don't care what it is. I love you, and I just want to figure it out with you."

"Among women, incest is so common as to be epidemic. Incest is easily the greatest single underlying reason why women seek therapy or other treatment. At any given time *more than three quarters of my clients* are women who were molested in childhood by someone they knew. Yet virtually none of these women has identified child sexual abuse as the reason for her problems. Many, if not most, incest survivors *do not know* that the abuse even occurred! Even if asked, they say – quite sincerely – No, nothing happened. Or, if they know that something happened, they cannot remember exactly what. This surprising phenomenon is the rule, not the exception, of the post-incest experience" (Blume xxi).

She scoffed and averted her eyes but wouldn't answer. I convinced her to take some psylocibin with me, knowing that she wouldn't be able to hide from me on a mushroom trip. But I couldn't get regular mushrooms at the store as The Netherlands had just banned their sale after some tourist deaths. What I could get were truffles, which I had no experience with; they contain the same medicine that is in the mushrooms, but I didn't know this at the time, and I didn't trust them. We both ate a small dose, but to no effect, and I never pursued this avenue with her again.

As a result of nearly constant stress, I was now suffering from agoraphobia and severe depression. I would head out to go somewhere, get on the tram, train, or bus, and then feel an intense fear and an urge to go back home. Cancelling my plans, I ran back home as fast as I could. When waiting for the train I would often fantasize about jumping in front of it; standing by a window on the second floor or higher, I would salivate at the thought of diving out onto the street, I think actually licking my lips. There was a fear fire burning within me, and it was tearing me up to the point where I couldn't help myself but to envision putting it out; the thoughts were intrusive, whereby I could fend them off but not stop them from popping up.

I went to the doctor for help and was given a prescription for citalopram for depression and Ambien to help me sleep. "Yes, I do feel like jumping into the train," I told the middle-aged female psychiatrist, laughing at the ridiculousness of what I was saying, "that is how I feel, but I'm not going to do it. My wife is driving me crazy, and I don't know what to do. I just feel like I need some help to lift me up out of this hole that I'm in." I took these pills for a short time, just until I felt like I was able to tread water again, and then I got rid of them.

On June 25, 2009, your mom and I saw Ben Harper and the Relentless 7 at Paradiso in Amsterdam. We stood about twenty feet from the stage, and the music was phenomenal. I was temporarily elevated from the dark fog that was festering in our home, a respite of sorts. I imagined that these types of experiences could help her get out from whatever was holding her down. After all, we had everything in the world...you. *What could be the problem? Why does she have such a deep emptiness?*

Your mom preparing herself for dinner with Jeremy.

Your mom started spending a lot of time with Jeremy, a guy from work. He began picking her up or sending a taxi to get her. We rarely went out, but they were now going out to dinner frequently. She always dressed up and acted as if she was in a good mood when preparing to see him, and one time she showed me the texts that he was sending her, which I regarded as highly suspicious and inappropriate.

I didn't have any energy to wonder if she was cheating on me, because it was all going into trying to maintain some peace and order within the walls of our apartment. I was content to get to spend time with you alone, and in many ways, it was easier and maybe even better when she wasn't home. I had no control over the situation anyway, and hoped that if she needed something elsewhere, that she would get it and then return to what was obviously the most important thing in the world: our little family. She often returned very late and very drunk, and I was just glad that she got safely back home.

She wouldn't let me touch her for several months. I wanted to give her whatever space she needed, but the uncertainty of whatever was happening was terrifying me and making it nearly impossible for me to get any quality sleep. Night after night, I laid in bed next to her, but it was as if there was a physical barrier between us. If I tried to put my arm around her, for instance, she would act as if I was hurting her.

When she finally decided to return to me, sometime in early 2010, it was sudden and as if nothing had happened. I remember her toe touching me when we were lying together in bed, a jolt of lightning shooting up through my leg and into my brain. I was just happy to have her back, and relieved to be in contact with her again. For a moment everything seemed better, but it wasn't going to last.

Your mom and me. 2010.

* * *

Your mom told me one day that we had to go to the pet store and get you a kitten. As usual, there was no explanation given or discussion to be had. It wasn't that I minded, but the way it was being done was both impulsive and mysterious.

"Agata, why does she need a cat?"

"She does... my mom says...," she attempted to explain.

"You told me that your mom doesn't like cats, Agata. What are you talking about now?"

"Well... cats are dirty in Poland... ours will live in the house... Adelle needs one..."

The three of us walked to a local pet store and your mom explained to the clerk that you were going to pick out a kitten. They let you into the cat pen and you chose the one you wanted. When we got home, I asked your mom, "Ok, so what is her name?"

She thought for a moment, and then replied, "Ally."

* * *

"**Thu, Jan 21, 2010, 3:37 PM**
Iain Bryson to Brian
hey bri
just chilling a bit. agatka is at a company get together [see Appendix 13] and adelle is asleep. my last week at Laureate Online Education is next week. I am looking for something else now, but going to start taking Dutch soon. also getting the law school application ready. i think i am on the short list for some jobs that are in my field, but another waiting game, and i guess we will see. so anyway, just working on that and trying to do the normal [expletive]. don't have to have the jaw broken again, which is good although i want another opinion to be sure, but lots of therapy and work. the pain clinic might switch me to methadone which is the only thing that has ever worked, so hoping on that. gonna call out from work tomorrow. will get paid and no reason to get up at five something and pay twenty euro for the train for nothing. the owner of the company already quit and told me he would write any letter i need so i don't need anything or any of their bs. i get seventy five percent unemployment for three to six [months] so that gives me a little room. would be nice to have like a month and know that to go skiing, make a trip to the US, and start, but so hopefully i will get a call from one of the ones i'm waiting on soon so i can plan. anyway, everything is going pretty well. think I am going to the range tomorrow, maybe a haircut, and sleep. you got skype yet? ttyyl"

It felt wonderful to be free of the daily grind, and it felt even better to be at home with you. Your mom would not let me cancel daycare completely, claiming that you should be in daycare sometimes, and so I compromised. I dropped you off late and picked you up early, or I did not drop you off at all. I became a house husband, a stay-at-home dad, and the best part about it was getting to spend the time with you. I recognized that I was fortunate to have this time, understanding that I would eventually have to go back to a regular job.

These were the best days of my life, even though I mostly felt terrible, and it is a shame that I was unaware how few of them there would be when they were occurring, but this is how life works. We did everything together: when I vacuumed, you sat on my shoulders, your "favorite place." I vacuumed going headfirst on my knees down our winding Dutch staircase, you held on as tight as you could, both of us laughing and singing as we cleaned the floor.

We visited parks, the beach, and the zoo in Amsterdam, and you taught me to get over my fears about singing in public. We freestyled new songs at the bus stop and on the bus in front of anyone that was nearby, and I could only do this because it was with you.

"Tue, Feb 2, 2010, 5:46 AM
Agata Bryson to me
Love it is ok for you to do nothing for a day! Stop pushing yourself and get your body and mind all set and then you can do anything. I love you and am missing you and my BFF :)
This is what I would like:
http://sephora.com/browse/product.jhtml;jsessionid=L3IEHOKZ1S1BUCV0KRTRHOQ?id=P254638&categ oryId=C7010

and this is what I need:
 http://sephora.com/browse/product.jhtml?id=P44903&categoryId=B23

Thank you sweety pie. Kisses :)"

Your mom and I took a trip to Antwerp, Belgium on March 1, 2010, to see Dave Matthews Band at Lotto Arena, and for a moment, things were going well between us. I used this opportunity to address the Jeremy "issue," but in the form of joking around. "Agata, Jeremy is married. Doesn't he love his wife?"

"I don't know," she responded, "he doesn't seem to like spending time with her."

"That's funny because I love spending time with my wife. Having you in this hotel room is like the best thing that has ever happened to me."

On March 3, 2010, your mom and I went to see Dave Matthews Band again at Heineken Music Hall in Amsterdam. I wanted to infiltrate her system with the positivity of music; I wanted her to feel what I felt, which was love and contentment with what I had. For me, a Dave Matthews Band concert was like a religious experience. I tried to get tickets for the concert in Stockholm, Sweden, but the show was cancelled due to some kind of family emergency of one of the band members.

* * *

At times, my frustration with your mom reached levels that led to me boiling over and not controlling my tongue. Out of sheer fear, desperation, and aggravation, I said the meanest things I could think of, things that were not ok to say no matter the circumstances. For this, I was wrong, and I am not defending myself, nor am I trying to hide anything. A point that will be made throughout this book is that I was not and am not perfect. But that also must be coupled with the fact that nothing I said or typed had anything to do with why you were taken from me. After reading this book it will be clear that the real problem is in Poland.

"Thu, Mar 11, 2010, 7:30 AM
Iain Bryson to Agata Bryson
how can you do this to us? you say you want to work on communicating, but you just lie. when it comes to actually doing it, you dont want to anymore. i hate you and hate everything. [expletive] you and how you always make me feel"

"I HATE YOU
Fri, Mar 12, 2010, 6:00 AM
Iain Bryson to Agata Bryson"

"Fri, Mar 12, 2010, 6:11 AM
Iain Bryson to Agata Bryson
WE ARE NOT TOGETHER. I HATE YOUR [EXPLETIVE] GUTS. YOU CAN DIE FOR ALL I CARE. YOU ARE NOT GOING ANYWHERE TONIGHT. I HOPE YOU GET FIRED. [EXPLETIVE] YOU"

"please dont let another day go by like this. we are losing everything
Tue, Mar 16, 2010, 8:14 AM
Iain Bryson to Agata Bryson"

"Tue, Mar 16, 2010, 10:36 AM
Iain Bryson to Agata Bryson
I would love to go to Prague. I cant. I have to be ok here. This family has to be ok. We have to be close. we have to communicate. I need to feel like we are one. i do not. i do not know what to do"

I was utterly desperate; her refusal to communicate and work with me felt like she was working against us. Lashing out wasn't the answer, but at the time, I had no idea what the answer might be.

"hi
Wed, Mar 17, 2010, 2:13 PM
Iain Bryson to Jackie DeLuca
Jackie,
I met you at the park a few minutes ago. It was nice meeting with you and your daughter, and wonderful seeing them begin to play together towards the end. I believe we will be going to the petting zoo on Saturday; just let me know if you want to come. Again nice meeting you and talk to you soon. Iain"

Jackie, a lawyer from Chicago, was the only American that I had met in The Hague. It was exciting to have an American to talk to, and perfect that she had a daughter that was your age. She, along with her husband, Mickey, and their daughter, Cicely, lived just around the corner in our neighborhood. *Now maybe we would have some friends, another couple to hang out with, some support*, I considered.

You and Cicely. 2010.

CHAPTER 12

"A LONG EASTER"

I was confused, frustrated, and desperately scrambling to figure out what could be wrong. I had seen this before, and I was fed up; your mom's patterns of idealizing and then devaluing me were becoming clearer and clearer each time I experienced it. The problem, as I saw it, was that it was possible for her to believe she loved me one moment and then hated me the next. I believed less and less that she was lying but couldn't yet understand how she could maintain such opposing views of me, and how she could flip from one to the other so rapidly and completely. Furthermore, when she was in the devaluation phase, she could not see that it ever could have been any other way.

The hardest part was that she wouldn't talk to me. Having a serious conversation with her in person was an extremely rare occasion, if it happened at all. I often wrote emails to her because at least that way she knew I had things that I wanted to talk about.

"Wed, Mar 22, 2010, 10:05 AM
Iain Bryson to Agata Bryson
i really cannot figure out what is going on. i feel like you have decided that you are done with me. this is how you act. there is nothing in this world that either one of us could do that should lead to where we are now. nothing. we can get and/or be upset, but we cannot deal with things this way. i just don't know what to do or to think anymore. i don't know where you got this from, but it is completely unacceptable. the worst part is that i really don't see anyway out of it, and the more you do this, the worse it gets. again, nothing should lead to this.

we work through things. that is what we must do if we are going to make this work. if you don't want that, just tell me. you cannot decide when and where you will 'deal' with your husband. if you are upset, you figure it out. you seem to forget that we are supposed to be two halves of a whole. if you really believed this, you would understand why i don't work and why you probably don't work without me. but, it doesn't seem that you really truly have internalized this. when the going gets rough, you go back to being an 'individual.'

i know things have not been perfect, or that they have been far from it, but that doesn't mean that we act this way. there is nothing that means that. what it should mean is that we do everything in our power to fix whatever issue(s) there are so that we move forward and not stand in place or run backwards like now. i don't get it. i don't get what you are thinking, what you want, what is going on with you that you would let things get like this or even think it is ok in the least bit. what am i supposed to think? why do I have to be left without my second half whenever you feel like it, and how do you expect me to do this when my whole life is built on the premise that we are part of one thing? i cannot do it.

i don't know what to do or what could possibly be running through your mind, what you think is going to happen, or even what you want. I am going to stop writing about this. I am beyond words. You can keep saying you are upset or whatever it may be, but the bottom line is that this Monday is exactly the same as last Monday and you will not work with me. Time goes on and on and we stay in one place. You tell me that you 'will not pretend.' I do not want you to pretend. I want you to work with the person who is supposed to be a whole half of you. How do you expect to get anything done missing half of yourself? I really cannot believe that this is how you choose to handle any situation, I am destroyed....

So, since we dont have a relationship and you dont want one, with me at least, I need you to print out the rest of this or tell me what is going on so that I at least have a clue since we are still legally together. Besides us, which I feel I have no control over anymore, and I do not know what to do, please try to help with the following:...[list of tasks]"

"hey
Thu, Mar 25, 2010, 11:35 AM
Iain Bryson to Brian
what up? me....nada. just going to go find a bench somewhere, smoke my pipe (trying no cigs), and read. trying to figure out everything, and as you know that can be overwhelming at times.maybe going to portugal to find myself a beach instead of prague. want to get away solo for a week soon. need to. going to keep Adelle home tomorrow to play....she went today because her friend has a birthday party. not much new. just trying to do this [expletive] thing called life. i am not sure i am that good at it. oh well. hope you and yours are doing great. when do you take time off? when are you not doing school? We have to catch up sometime in the near future. anyways, going to pack my travel bag and go find a bench to get out of the house for a while."

The three of us went back to Poland for Easter and stayed with your grandparents again. It was more of the same: "I have to be with my dad when I am in Poland," and more severe anxiety for me. Except when there was something for the whole family, I pretty much just stayed in bed. In Poland again, and now you were "sick" again. As your Aunt Ada comforted you, I looked on, trying to grasp what was going on (see Appendix 14).

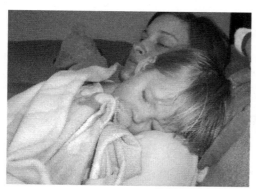

Ada comforting you in Poland,
Easter 2010.

Your mom, Wera, Ada, you, and Waldek in
Poland, Easter 2010.

"hey bro
Fri, Apr 9, 2010, 9:08 AM
Iain Bryson to Brian
B,
What's up with you and yours? We have been in Poland for the past week at my in-laws. A long Easter I guess. It's been ok but a bit crazy. We just have so much to do at home but the wifey had to be here. So, now we are leaving for a fifteen-hour bus ride back home tonight. fun fun. Just trying to get things moving and basically same old bs. Adelle got Scarlett Fever so she is going to stay here for a few more weeks so she can recover since she cant go to daycare. My father-in-law will bring her to Den Haag the beginning of May. I have to nail down this job or find something. I should be getting unemployment, but we are still dealing with the joys of Dutch bur[eaucracy] and it should hopefully be in place by next week. But, either way, I gotta figure it out and also still get my jaw/mouth fixed, figure out the next step with the neck, move, etc. How is everything? What have you guys been up to? You need to send us some pictures when you get a chance. How are the parents? Well, my f-in law just got home with Adelle and Agata is shopping with her parents. Gotta help for a bit but talk to you soon."

I never saw any paperwork about your "scarlet fever" from the doctor, your grandmother's "friend" who had prescribed me the clonazepam six years prior without seeing me; nor was I allowed to speak to the doctor on my own. I wasn't aware of any medication or treatment, but only that your grandparents said that you had to stay, adding that you "could die." Your mom insisted that I take their word for it.

"Mon, Apr 12, 2010, 5:08 AM
Iain Bryson to Mom, Dad, Sara [Aunt], Rachel [Cousin], Roger [Grandpa Bryson], Jeremiah [Cousin], Carrie [Sister], Brian
Attachments"

[1. Your mom kissing you in Poland. 2. You in the bathtub, Pilsudskiego Street, Poland. 3. You and Sławomir.]

"Mon, Apr 12, 2010, 5:27 AM
Iain Bryson to Mom, Sara, Rachel, Roger, Carrie, Brian
Attachments"

[1. You in the bathtub. 2. Pola and your mom in Poland. 3. You in Poland.]

"Mon, Apr 12, 2010, 5:55 AM
Iain Bryson to Mom, Brian, Dad, Rachel, Sara, Roger, Jeremiah
Attachments"

[1. Your mom and you. 2. You and Sławomir. 3. Your mom.

(All pictures from Pilsudskiego Street, Poland)]

* * *

"tues
Tue, Apr 13, 2010, 1:41 AM
Iain Bryson to Agata Bryson
Agatka,
I heard you close the door and I am up. I have no idea what, if anything, we are doing today because we don't talk. I don't think I can do anything anyways because you refuse to speak to me. I don't know what to do. I don't know who you are. You just yell and throw a tantrum when I ask you anything, or suggest there may be a problem. You tell me there is nothing you want to talk to and then you tell me you can't be happy. I don't know what you want me to do about this or how else you think I will or should feel. I feel like dying. I have no idea what to do. I cannot live like this. We cannot live like this. We cannot be like this. I just don't know. maybe i will after some coffee. I can't believe you still won't speak to me. You are killing me. you are doing it like you enjoy it. you are distant like i said. you don't seem to care or want us to be together. I just don't know. you obviously don't love me anymore. have a blast"

I was terrified, and I was desperate. It felt like everything was slipping through my fingers like a handful of dry sand at the beach; it seemed I had no control over anything. Because of this, I decided to eliminate the medications. They were no longer working anyway, and I knew that they were making me weaker than I could be. *The morphine and clonazepam have to go; I must be the strongest I can be for my family,* I decided.

I began weaning myself off, rapidly and consistently. The morphine was relatively easy to quit in comparison to the clonazepam, though to say it was easy would be antipodal to the truth. All that I knew was that I was determined to get through it or die trying. There was no turning back; I had thousands of dollars' worth of these medications on the shelf and no desire to take them any longer. I couldn't because I could see my family falling apart, and I knew that I couldn't afford to have any extra chinks in my armor.

Benzodiazepine withdrawal syndrome lasted for several months. Day to day and week to week, it didn't get better, but often worse. As time went on, the symptoms intensified, and I felt like I was dying. And I wanted to die more than I had during my jumping-in-front-of-the-train or out-the-window stage, because this was pure psychological torture. I had insomnia for at least a month, diarrhea and vomiting at the same time, heart palpitations, seizures, brain zaps, and constant muscle cramping, to name a few of the symptoms.

In *Beyond Order*, Jordan Peterson described his experience with acute benzodiazepine withdrawal as "...truly intolerable—anxiety far beyond what I had ever experienced, an uncontrollable restlessness and need to move (formally known as akathisia), overwhelming thoughts of self-destruction, and the complete absence of happiness whatsoever" (Peterson xviii). My experience was similar, except that there could be no "complete absence of happiness whatsoever," because I had you.

I was willing to submit to whatever your mom demanded, short of divorce or separation, and I went into a state of total submission. I was hypervigilant about keeping the house spotless, washing anything that was put into the sink immediately, folding her clothing as perfectly as I could, all in fear, not knowing what it was that was setting her off, but trying to eliminate all the possibilities that I had control over.

It didn't matter to me what her problems might be anymore. What I had to do, I decided, was submit to her every ultimatum, whether spoken or unspoken. I also had work to do on myself, and I knew that I had to specifically work on the way that I was reacting to her, which was often in anger because of my extreme frustration. It was easy for me to admit that I wasn't perfect and accept partial blame so that we could cross that off the list and make it a non-point of contention.

"Ok, Agata, you are right, I do need help. I'll do that right away. Now, how about you? Won't you get help too?"

I contacted an anger management group and told your mom that I was going to go, not caring that their cost was 500 Euro per hour. Your mom nixed this idea, but if she hadn't, this is what I would have done. 500 Euro per hour, or one finger per hour; I didn't care. I just wanted our family to be healthy again, and the only thing that I had some control over was myself, which I was willing to eliminate if that's what it took.

"Tue, Apr 20, 2010, 5:01 AM
Iain Bryson to Agata Bryson
Baby, I am sorry you feel so bad. That was not my intention; it is just that when I can't sleep and my head is spinning, it is tough for me to wake up positive. I did tell you I love you when you were leaving. It scares me when we don't have a substantive conversation. I know there is something that is just being put off, and I can't stand it. I never want to hear that I did something years ago that we've never really spoken about or dealt with, and it just scares me. I am happy we are talking more, and that we have figured out some things. I need you and I need you to be happy. I need to know that is the case. I love you and it just scares me.

I think that part of it also is just where I am at how I feel. I need your support and help or whatever now. You are my partner and I know that I also have to continue doing more but I surely cannot do much without you. I am trying to find a job, trying to stop taking a medication for an untreated disease on my own, and in desperate need of things like dental work so I don't continue to lose teeth and it is overwhelming for me. I also know that you get overwhelmed and I want to know so that we can talk and so I can comfort you. I love you and I am sorry you feel this way. I love you. Don't let every reaction get to you. I am not trying to be mean. I am confused and trying to move forward.

I miss you and wish we had more days like this weekend where you weren't working either, but I guess that is something we just need to plan for after we figure out this other crap. Please let me know at least a ballpark date when Adelle will be coming back. You have to understand that maybe you talk to them daily, but I have no clue what is going on. Yes, I trust you, but it is also not very comfortable knowing nothing and I don't think you would like the situation. Try to relax and just do your thing. You are wonderful and can deal with anything that goes on there. I know that it gets overwhelming sometimes, but it could disappear in a day as well. I love you baby"

I was upset that you were in Poland, and I wanted you back with your parents. "Agata, if she is sick, then she needs to be here with us," I argued. "If she is sick, then I want to take her to a doctor here or maybe even just take her to the United States."

"My parents say that she might die, that she has to stay there with them," she answered firmly, leaving no room for argument.

"Tue, Apr 20, 2010, 8:49 AM
Iain Bryson to Agata Bryson
Baby blue, I hope your day is better than it was. Smile please. My friend Mac wants me to go to Wales the week of May 17th. He wants to fly with me, he said I can take lessons, and go rock climbing. I guess it depends on a few things, but I would like to see him and see what it takes to get my flying license. love you"

"Wed, Apr 21, 2010, 3:57 AM
Iain Bryson to Agata Bryson
hey,
town hall to ask for an appointment and hand in the [gun] range [expletive], right? I can't remember. No sleep again and zero once you left. trying to wake up. i am not sure what to do. i love you. i need you. i don't know why i have trouble talking or we do, and i think we both have to figure out how to talk without yelling or getting angry. at least we are talking. it shouldn't have to be a fight. i love you"

"Fri, Apr 23, 2010, 4:41 AM
Iain Bryson to Agata Bryson
try to realize how frustrating it is to not be able to sleep and just be tortured by your mind all night. i am not mad and i don't know why i react like this. i am in pain and i am scared and frustrated. I love you and i am happy. i know we are talking more than before. but, before was ridiculous and we can never do that in anyway. We have to be able to talk to each other. i don't know what it is but I just feel that certain things will never be spoken of. i feel that this takes away from the time we have together, makes it harder to just enjoy falling asleep with my wife because my head and heart are in pain and there is no way i can sleep, and takes away from parts of our relationship.

We have to keep working on things and ensure that we talk about the important things. then the pressure wont build, i won't worry and wonder, and we will be working better as a couple instead of hoping and not really knowing. i am sorry that i have gotten upset. i wish you wouldn't put me down. i need you and that is the problem to begin with. i laid on the couch all night so i wouldn't keep waking you up because of moving or getting up and down and i tried not to get upset but i want to sleep so [expletive] bad. i had to lay there and know that i would be up pretty much all night, and then you would leave and I would be stuck for basically a day. i tried to sleep, i tried to meditate, but i had already done too much for me not to talk to you at all and my head wouldn't turn off.

if we spoke more about certain thing, then i would know what you think instead of wondering and I wouldn't get so frustrated or scared. i love you and don't know what to do. i am upset about the sleep and feel like [expletive]. i don't know what is up with my heart, but it has to be what is hurting… i thought it was deep but i guess it is really deep. i don't know. i want adelle to be home with her parents… we need to figure this out together. i can't and don't want to do it alone…i need you and i need your help and your support. whatever it is, we have to figure it out together. we need to go over our options. we need to somehow be able to tell each other how we feel and what we need from the other person. i would really like to figure out the adelle situation today.... i want us to be intimate on every level, freely sharing our thoughts feelings ideas and whatever else. i love you"

"yo
Apr 23, 2010, 6:43 AM
Iain Bryson to Brian
what the [expletive] is up with you? hope all is well in [brian]ville. i am basically just sitting on the couch and trying to figure out what my next step is going to be. unfortunately, have been doing this for a bit too long. trying to hold out for a job in The Hague. had a friend who could get me a job at Tom Tom in Amsterdam but decided with the wife that Amsterdam is ridiculous to have to go to everyday or even twice a day. i did it for over a year and a half and it is nuts. there are too many places in the Hague and I should be able to get something.

now, i have applications out to the international criminal court, the international court of justice, and also some other private jobs and a sub teaching thing at the American school of the Hague. i was told by one of agata's colleagues that i was all set for the international court of justice position, which would be the best thing now. but, until that happens, and his name is mohammad, i am starting to look in the states again.

if i can get a state job in Oregon or wherever, and i was getting calls for interviews in '08, we have tentatively decided to move back at least for a while. i would rather stay here and get more established here because i think we will eventually be here at least for some time during the year, but i just want to get going on something am sick of sitting and internet searching. i can't go out and find a job because there is no black market, or very little and only for Africans or Brazilians or Suriname, or whatever but never a white guy. i tried, and the government penalty is so high that anyone wants to see your Dutch SSI. So, I have to chill for the moment which is ok because i should get 70% pay for 3-6 months plus we are also back logged nearly two years of child care allowance. so we are waiting for that to go through the Dutch bureaucracy.

want to go back to school for a European/international law masters but only if we are going to be here for sure and i don't know yet. the wife doesn't ever want to go back except to visit, but when it comes down to it, it is the only place I know i can get an interview and i am much more confident now than I was in '08 with more experience so i think a pretty good state job wouldn't be that tough (just not CT).

Anyways, Adelle has been in Poland since Easter. She got scarlet fever and the doctor wouldn't allow her to travel. hope she will be dropped off by grandpa soon. tough not to see her for this long. Trying to get to England to see Mac. i think go flying and rock climbing or try at least but need the unemployment or job to happen.

quitting the pain meds. one more week prob. not too bad...just a bit weak and cold and insomniac but down to 30mg a day after a week and a half of doing it. doesn't work and it just isn't worth it anymore. will be nice once i don't 'have' to take anything. trying to see if my Dutch health insurance would cover surgery in Germany. they have the best disc replacement in the world...

anyway, say hi to the fam for me. agata says hi and is still working for Saudi Aramco. She is doing really well and runs a division. but, because she is not an engineer or maybe an accountant, she is at risk of hitting the bad side of Dutch employment law. after a certain period of time, they either have to give you a permanent contract or no contract. in many places, they abuse this to hire new people and only use them for two years to save money on raises and whatever else the permanent contract entails. So, we are also looking at that and she would like to get her MA at some point. well, write me soon.......or else [expletive]. miss ya and hope things are going and going good. I"

Your mom went back to Poland to get you, and though I didn't like how I was feeling, how I felt really made no difference in the big picture. I was fine regardless; what I needed was you back under my roof, and that was finally going to happen. When she left on the bus, I "joked" that I was going to throw water on the back of the bus for good luck; it felt like I was sending her into a war zone.

"Wed, Apr 28, 2010, 11:11 AM
Iain Bryson to Agata Bryson
so, we gotta do the apps, plan, figure out england/pl/usa and adelle/doctors/unemployment ....
lovey you"

"Tue, May 4, 2010, 6:00 PM
Iain Bryson to Agata Bryson

i miss you so much. hope you are sleeping and don't have ur phone buzzing on your lap. turn it off now baby. can't wait till we are all together and can't wait to see you. i love you so much too. i will call in the am. goodnight beautiful"

"Re: just wanted to let you know the disc didn't come in the mail. give our kid a kiss and think about me. i love you
Thu, May 6, 2010 at 11:45 PM
Agata Bryson to me

Will call tomorrow. I did give Adelle a kiss while sleeping and I never stop thinking about u love. Love u"

"Fri, May 7, 2010, 6:54 AM
Iain Bryson to Agata Bryson

hey baby, Just looking at the internet as usual. Going to go get paint today and clean/paint a bit. When you come back, i want to be at the bus, so let me know. then i have to go to schevengin or whatever for the meeting at 11. if it's nice we should lounge on the beach or something. don't forget to try to get picture frames. i want to get more plants too. i talked to my mom last night. she is upset because Carrie went to FL without telling her and her b'day is coming up for which my mom took the day off and also Mother's Day. she is upset she is going to be with Wendy on m' day. So, i told her i would skype her on Sunday.

i want to go to the parkpop in den haag. It will be better than going to melkweg and in a nice park so i think it would be nice to plan on. i really need us to sit down with the UN application and whatever else may be in den haag. i am making progress but want to make sure it's perfect so i need your tips and internet expertise. i am not sure what to do with the way i feel. I did not think it would last this long and i think i have begun to go crazy for lack of sleep and feeling [expletive]. i know it will pass but when is the question? seeing on the internet that it can take months scares me and i think we should look into other medicines that could take symptoms away. trying not to smoke....

we have to work together on some of these more important things so we are on the same page and so we get it done the best we can. with a little guidance i can do it. i just need some pointers or support with these bigger applications and then i think i can knock them off the list. dentist is bothering me. i know i need implants, braces and god knows what else. i really need your support with the way i have been feeling. it is harder physically then ciggies and I need you by my side. i just wonder how long i can put up with these effects. i just need you and us to be as close together, working together for our goals and doing it the best and most efficient ways possible. well, enough of that [expletive].

i am going to go out in a bit and then finish up or continue to finish off the house. gotta figure out what to eat. afraid to spend money on paint until we know more. Hope school goes smoothly today and no hassles. i love you so much"

"Fri, May 7, 2010, 10:49 AM
Iain Bryson to Agata Bryson

hey agatka,
still thinking about you....i need you both home. are you for certain staying until Thursday? when would/will you be home? it is such a [expletive] long time. is there now no chance of Monday? i went out, was going to run to the paint store, but it is cold and wet. So, i knew if I did that i would be cold on the way back. So, i just went to AH [grocery store] and Basra [coffee shop]. i am going to make another list, try to get to the paint store tomorrow, etc. i really need you to figure all of this out. i can do most of it but i need your help/guidance/thoughts/support. there is just too much going on… just wishing my girls were home.

i need us to figure things out and cross things off. I know we are doing this but i need to see the results or feel them. and i also thinking about the [expletive] that didn't happen; so you still 'hate' me?....miss you so [expletive] much. tough right now. i just feel like most of me is missing and it is an effort to be positive and work on things. we have so much to do and I think if we had a schedule of when it was going to happen or when we would work on it it might be easier for me and less abstract. i don't know. i can't wait to see you and for us to take adelle out and have fun.

we need to look around and see what is going on and what we can do. the zuiderpark parkpop with snoop is jun 27 and is free at zuiderpark. i will put that on our schedule. we need a sitter for the 21st [U2 concert]. i am going to relax, clean, read, and make a list to get us going a bit more (or me for now) until you get home. [expletive] i need you. i love you so much. i am so lucky."

"i dont know about england with adelle only being home for a few days. i need her and you more than anything now
Fri, May 7, 2010, 10:50 AM

Iain Bryson to Agata Bryson"

"Fri, May 7, 2010, 12:09 PM
Iain Bryson to Agata Bryson
I want you to get your degree. I just don't know why you rushed there by yourself… I miss you so much and I can hardly hold back the tears when I hear Adelle. You have to get your degree but we also have to work together here. We have so many things we have to do together or at least get started together so that then one of us can finish it. I don't think i will go to England now. I cannot fathom taking off for a week after seeing Adelle for three days and after you being gone for over a week. I don't want to live that out of control now. We have too much to figure out and do and enjoy and we will get there but not now. I know I should go but at least the money we may lose on the ticket will not be doubled or tripled by expenses. I know you don't worry as much as me but I still need your help. I love you and have fun at grandmas"

"ru u up? i love you....cant stop thinking about you and delly. i am waking up but just wanted to let you know i am, though you can probably feel me thinking about you.
Sat, May 8, 2010, 5:20 AM
Iain Bryson to Agata Bryson"

"Sun, May 9, 2010, 8:55 AM
Iain Bryson to Agata Bryson
babe, the [Microsoft] word doesn't work on the desktop either. i need to get these job questions out asap. any word from your 'friend'? love you and hope you are having fun.............i miss you so much. i think about you about 50 seconds of every minute. i need my girls. Happy mommy day to the best mommy ever. love you"

"hey
Wed, May 12, 2010, 9:53 AM
Iain Bryson to Jackie DeLuca
Jackie,
How is it going? I wish the sun would come out. Agata and Adelle are coming back from Poland tonight....finally. Agata had to go back to her college to get her degree; she had to get a bunch of signatures, but that is done now as well. I have attached my CV, or one of them for you to look at. I realize that your company probably only needs lawyers, but you had mentioned you would take a look. I hope you guys are well. It would be great to get together for a coffee or something. Adelle is finally going to be home and healthy. Iain"

CHAPTER 13

"IT'S A SOAP IRRITATION"

When you got back, it was as if they sent the darkness with you. You were a mess, and it wasn't scarlet fever. "Not my pee pee, not my pee pee!" you screamed, over and over again, hyperventilating, as you got ready to take a shower. This lasted for about a week after your return, each time your mom rushed you out of the shower and into the sink in your room.

"Iain, it's a soap irritation," she tried to convince me.

"What kind of soap are they using over there?" I retorted, doubtful, but also completely caught off guard and confused. "She was over there for a month, so why would they be using a soap that irritated her? Did they just keep using an irritating soap for the entire month? That doesn't make any sense at all. We need to take her to the doctor here."

"No, Iain, she is not going to the doctor. I already know that it is just a soap irritation." I didn't know what to say, so I just kept observing, wanting to believe that I could trust your mother, believing that she probably knew more about "vaginal soap irritations" than I did.

I had nowhere to go with what I was seeing; your mom wouldn't talk to me about it, and I couldn't believe that she could know you were being abused and not tell me. This was too far-fetched of a concept for me to grasp. *She loves our daughter just as much as I do*, I reasoned, *and if something like that was happening, not only would she tell me, but she would do anything she could to stop it.*

You seemed to be depressed and constantly in a fog. I figured that my job was to make you healthy, and to assure you that you were loved. We spent a lot of time at the swing set, me pushing you and reminding you from time to time, "Hold on and never let go. Just don't ever let go."

I made up a simple song just to reassure you, which I sung while you were swinging. "Daddy loves Delly, yes he does, Mommy loves Delly, yes she does, Grandpa loves Delly, yes he does, Grandma loves Delly, yes she does, Ada loves Delly, yes she does…"

Looking back, I wish I hadn't made up that song. I wish I didn't have the mental blockage that kept me from connecting the dots. One part of me knew that you had been abused, but another part refused to know, and accepted your mom's uninterested attitude as enough reason to move on. "I know that she doesn't need to see a doctor" was all that I could get from her.

Your mom was unreachable, which I was used to, but that didn't make it any easier. She barely acknowledged my presence or the psychological distress that I was still in as I continued to wean myself off clonazepam. "If you're not working, then you shouldn't eat," she announced one night at the dinner table. I begged her to come back, to communicate with me, to tell me what was going on, but she was cold and completely detached. She went back to work, and I went back to trying to put our household together again.

"My parents said that they like the way you are teaching Adelle," she said out of the blue, in the midst of weeks of non-communication.

"What do you mean, 'they like the way I am teaching Adelle?'" I asked, a shiver going down my spine.

"That's what they told me, you know, like reading and writing and stuff like that; they think you're doing a good job. They're pleased with what you're doing and her progress."

I didn't know this yet, but a loving, stable relationship before the age of four is important in trauma-based mind control. With this foundational experience in the child's life, they are less likely to go insane during the process of programming.

It felt like I was living in a bizarro world; it was like trying to keep a campsite intact during a hurricane. I had you back under my roof, so whatever it was that had traumatized you had stopped traumatizing you. Now all I could do was continue to focus on making myself stronger and attempt to keep the tent stakes in our home from being taken away by the strong winds, whatever those winds were.

"Agata, don't you realize that you don't make any sense? Something is going on, yet you refuse to talk to me about it. You go back and forth; there is no stability within our home. I should set up a camera to capture all the nonsense. I should film all of this; there should be a camera in our home recording everything. I can't believe how ridiculous you are."

In the evenings, after you were in bed, I often went out for a walk in the park by myself to alleviate my frustrations and increase the possibility that I would get some sleep. When I returned, I would tiptoe through the house, afraid to wake or otherwise disturb your mom, feeling like the ground was actually covered in eggshells that I dare not break.

When I was out, I started taking pictures with my phone of things that I noticed that I knew most people would not notice or pay attention to. When I showed them to your mom, she said, "Iain, I like that you are beginning to pay attention. I really like those pictures." *Weird*, I thought, knowing that they weren't great pictures, but also realizing that I was consciously looking beyond the beauty to the ugly, or to that which is typically disregarded or overlooked (see Appendix 15).

It was time to take you to your first dentist visit, and your mom was terrified. What perplexed me and concerned me wasn't that she was terrified, but that she was determined that you would also be terrified. I agreed to take you by myself, informing her that it was ridiculous to think that you would be scared of something you had never experienced.

As soon as I sat you down into the dentist's chair, you were absolutely petrified, shaking and crying, acting as if you knew it was going to be extremely painful. "Adelle," I said in a soothing voice, "all that he wants to do is count your teeth. He's just going to look and count; that's it, I promise." It took several minutes of this before you stopped sobbing and screaming, but eventually you did, and he literally looked into your mouth for about ten seconds.

It felt like a victory to me at the time, and I was proud of you. But why were you so afraid? Could it have been your mom's fear transferred onto you? Or could you have had a dental experience that I was unaware of? The latter option didn't cross my mind at the time. The dentist allowed you to choose a little plastic toy as a prize, and you chose a giraffe. On the way home, I called your mom to tell her that we had made it through the visit, but even on the phone she was still panicking. "No, Agata, she is fine," I assured her. "At first she was scared, but she calmed down and did great. I'm very proud of her," I relayed to her so that you could hear me.

Our pharmacy was at the end of Newtonplein, located right next to a Catholic church. One day the three of us took a walk to pick something up, and as soon as you saw the church, which you had seen before with no issues, you started having a panic attack and hyperventilating. "No amen, no amen, no amen," you kept repeating, sounding distressed in the same way as when you said "Not my pee pee, just not my pee pee…"

As far as I knew you were not going to church. *Why this strange aversion to church? Why is she scared of this building? Why does she keep saying, "No amen, no amen"?* I wondered to myself. Your mom assured you, "No Adelle, no amen. We are not going to amen." *What is "amen," and why is my daughter afraid of it?* I asked myself.

* * *

I continued to communicate with your mom via email, finding it easier to attempt to explain myself "on paper." An in-person conversation about a difficult topic always led to me thinking she was lying, or to her seducing me so that I would let it go.

"please read
Mon, May 17, 2010, 7:51 PM
Iain Bryson to Agata Bryson
Agata,
I cannot sleep. Please try and let me know you are trying. This [expletive] has been driving me insane for too long. We go back and forth and at each other's throats over words. Our stance on our marriage changes over words. I know you are beyond upset, at the end of the line, whatever it is; I cannot give up. I will never be able to in this situation. I love you.

We have been living together under these conditions, hoping they will change, expecting them to change because of the ridiculousness of it and not really doing much to ensure that it doesn't actually happen again. Leaving each other is not the answer to this. Getting this upset is not the answer to this. Yes, I do want you to be happy and I do love you and I am in love with you. I cannot handle a conversation about 'divorce' after this long stretch of craziness, going back and forth between extremes, and not dealing with it. On top of that, we are pretending anyway it can be looked at if we do continue to play this strange game.

I do understand that I have made you feel bad and that this is a problem. I understand it is a huge problem. All I am saying is that I know this, and that it is also a problem to live as we have been. Every night since the end of February I have felt this huge weight in my chest and have gotten more crazy. I have been trying to hold it together, but there has been too much uncertainty and back and forth and back. This will make me crazy.

Now, in saying that I want you to be happy, I do mean that in every way and would not want you to stay with me for the wrong reason. I feel like this has been happening for a long time and that is what is driving me crazy. These feelings have been telling me that you are distanced from me. I have told you that. I was telling you that before Poland the first time, during, after, and throughout even our 'better' time. I felt better too because at least we were trying, or I thought we were and we were together. We still wasted the majority of the time and I couldn't completely rid myself of the dread i felt. I knew we had things to still deal with and couldn't get through to deal with it with you. I know this has made you mad.

Please try to realize it; I am not asking you to forget or to immediately move past it, but to realize it and just rethink it....and again and again. We are still together and we cannot pretend. If we are not, then you did use the 'd' word and we do have to discuss this and not just act like it. Again, that is how I have been feeling and this has just put words and more certainty in my heart. I know I say horrible things to you...the worst things that could be said. I know you don't believe me. Please just try to look at the situation. If you see the big picture, it is all tied together, and although horrible and obviously horrible for you, it is not broken. It is a domino effect that we never need to start. I cannot and have not ever thought of this word. When it has crossed my mind, just like anything does for people who think, it goes out immediately.

We dated for a month before making the decision to get married and spend the rest of our lives together. That is a long time, I knew it, I knew it was difficult to judge a lot of things that would be with me from then on and I still had no doubts and don't now. I know what we had and have and have never doubted it. I am not able to because the thought of it is horrible in so many ways. We are married and we decided that we would not let life or bs to come between us and it will try...and obviously be more successful than either of us would like or like to feel at times. I know this is because of our inability to deal with certain things that have to be dealt with. We do not have a choice... we pretty much just ignore the elephant and watch stupid shows on tv.. These times allow us to shut all of that out, realize that there are things to deal with, and deal with it. By doing that we would not be damaging the time we had or being upset. We would feel a lot better and we would feel accomplishment as well.

Yes, I want us to have a good time and to not worry, but if there is something to worry about or deal with, we have to do that and then we will have a much better time and it will last. Please try to look at what is going on with Adelle. I am not trying to do anything in front of her. So, when I upset her, it was unintentional, and your response immediately helped her to think that I was in the wrong. We have to back each other up. We have to figure out how not to talk to each other with attitudes in front of her. I know I am guilty as well, but you have the ability to completely change how she feels about me.

She and I had a perfect day. She was happy and I was happy just to see that and do whatever she wanted. I did not see anything in her eyes that wasn't happy. Please don't let either of us take this away from her or each other. Neither of us can use or look like we are using each other or putting down each other in front of her. Please work on this with me. Please don't leave this hanging.

I need to move forward and I can't continue to feel like this. Now I know what the feeling was due to and it cannot go on. We are living together and we have not been trying or dealing with things. We cannot do this. We are already doing it. Please don't give up and please do not continue to make the same mistakes with me. The only way we can do this is to learn from them. I do not want you to be scared and I will work with you. We just have to get beyond the words to a less confrontational spot and not remain in the same place I have felt we were in for months except with the worst explanation for it.

I do love you and need us to actually try for real to get to the bottom of this. If that means turning off the phone, the computer, and the tv and sitting nose to nose until the issues are dealt with, we need to do that. We have not tried. We have done worse that that recently. You are my second half."

"Re: how u?
Wed, May 26, 2010 at 3:21 PM
Jeremiah to me
Dude. Don't ever tell me that you even think living is not a possibility. That's crazy talk. And that would absolutely be the wrong thing to do in many, many, ways. Not to mention all the people that would be hurt along the way, including your mom, dad, and most importantly you own daughter who needs a father. That's a selfish thought and you need to take that 100% off the table.
You might be so frustrated that you feel like dying. I can understand that - we've all been there at one point in our lives.
You need to rally here. It's like you have one last chance to save and salvage things. You need to be fighting for your 'life' and your relationship like you've never fought for anything before. Think of Agata and Adelle as the ultimate prize, and you're the warrior fighting for them. Seriously. And be prepared to make some drastic changes on your end. Your wife and daughter are worth it.
Agata is pretty upset with a lot of things. She admits she's far from perfect either. But you need to tackle these issues head on with her and be prepared to make things happen - even if it's outside your comfort zone.
I think you should also consider some time apart for a little while. Give both of you some time to breathe and think about things. Start with a week or more and then re-evaluate. If she needs this, you might have to oblige. All things should be on the table at this point. Hang in there. Love you.
J"

While my cousin's intentions were good, his response was that of a backseat driver who couldn't see the road. There was never any chance at all of me killing myself, as I already knew you and your mom were the "ultimate prize." I wasn't fighting for my life, but for yours and hers, as I still am. I don't know exactly what he was referring to, whether it was a text/email or a phone call, but in any case if I did say anything about dying, it was nothing more than a figure of speech, a way for me to try to express my exasperation and desperation in dealing with your mom.

He was talking to your mother, so I understand his confusion, but the results of trying to guess what a puzzle is without having all the pieces can be disastrous. She was contacting him and venting, and he was sympathetic to her and oblivious to the fact that she was manipulating him. Unfortunately, he was also unaware of the fact that she had a plan to use his growing trust of her at a later time.

"Fri, Jun 4, 2010, 7:51 PM
Iain Bryson to Agata Bryson
Hope you are having fun. i am up, took a nap, but still cannot sleep without you. Sorry. I was thinking about this weekend and what we can do. I believe you are seeing Jackie tomorrow which would be a good thing. Maybe she can watch Adelle for an hour or two sometime. Got an email from John S. finally who is getting married after nineteen years in October. I want us to go over things and get our [expletive] in order. Something we should have been doing anyways....I really do want you to be happy. I also want you and do love you, go ahead and puke a bit in your mouth, but I know that in order for that to happen I will have to go through hell to get to heaven again, if there is a heaven, which I believe there is when I think about my love for you. I will stop telling you and try to focus on the showing part. It is a phase thing because I do need you. i think i hear your footsteps and getting anxious. talk soon"

You and your mom returned to Poland again, though I do not remember any details from this trip. What I do remember is that your mom had strong recurring urges to return to Poland, and that when they arose, she was going no matter what my opinion was on the matter. One day there would be no indication that she had plans to go to Poland, and the next she would say something like, "I have to go to Poland with Adelle."

"hey you
Thu, Jun 10, 2010, 7:34 AM
Iain Bryson to Agata Bryson
Agatka,
How are you guys? Everything go smoothly on the bus? You getting some rest after that trip? Let me know when we can get on the phone but relax. Just checking in and thinking of you both.
Talk to you soon. LI"

"Jun 11, 2010, 12:36 PM
Iain Bryson to Agata Bryson
agatka, i need to talk to delly tomorrow. hope you are having a good time. miss us"

The constant roller coaster ride took its toll on my psyche, with your mom repeatedly cycling from lifting us up to slamming us back down. I was discombobulated; it seemed like every time I began to get my footing the strong winds would blow me over again. *I am learning patience*, I decided, *and if I work on myself, then surely your mother will come around.*

* * *

When you and your mom got back to The Hague, I decided to take a trip to the United States to clear my head and see my family. I was still titrating my medication and weaning myself off, but now I was down to only taking tiny pieces when I had to. I stayed with my mom for the most part, but I also flew out to Arizona to catch up with Brian.

Our dog, Butch, was dying, and I decided that it was necessary to put him down; he had a tennis ball size tumor on his neck, and he could barely walk. We spent the last days of his life driving around in my stepdad George's convertible Jeep Wrangler, his tongue wagging out the window. My dad and I dug a hole for him on the property of the house where I grew up in Mystic, CT. My hands bled from digging through the rocks, and I wept as if I was losing my best friend. "Be strong for him," your mom told me on the phone, "you have to be strong for him."

It was a blessing to get to be there and spend time with him before he died, to hold him in my arms as the veterinarian gave him the euthanasia shot, to tell him that it was ok and that I loved him. Afterward, my dad and I walked through the woods, and as I cried because of the tough emotional experience of putting our dog down, I told him, "Dad, I am sorry I haven't figured it out yet."

"Well," he said, "I don't think we really ever figure it out."

"No," I replied, "I am going to figure it out. I know that I am going to figure it out. I have to."

"hey u
Mon, Jun 28, 2010, 1:05 PM
Iain Bryson to Agata Bryson
Agatka,
I just wanted to say hi. I really hope you are doing ok and I really just wanted to talk to you last night. I am doing well and wish you were here. It is so easy to forget things and get caught up in things over there and it is important for us to remember both of our families and how much people care about us. I know things have been difficult and I want to work with you to figure it out. I know I upset you and that you have a reason to be upset with me. I do think that part of it is our surroundings and that we need to work together more to figure things out and learn how to speak to each other. We have so much, and we just need to keep moving forward and remember how wonderful we have it when we are on track. I wanted to let you know that TomTom [navigation company] did get back to me and that I will be interviewing with them. I miss my girls. I do think that the trip was good. It just seems like another world. I want the world with my two A's but it is good to get out of that situation and remember what we are working towards and talk to people other than the crazies that live around us. I love you"

On your mom and I's anniversary, July 2, I had flowers delivered to her at our home in The Hague. I couldn't wait to get back to both of you, and I couldn't believe how difficult it seemed to be for your mom to be content with what we had. *What is wrong with her?* I kept thinking to myself. *What is wrong that love cannot fix? If not love for me, then certainly love for our daughter can fix anything.*

The visit to Brian was amazing and rejuvenating. It was great to see him and his children and to catch up. We went to a shooting range in the desert to do some target practice. One of his guns was extremely small, so small that I could barely hold it. Trying to get a better grip, I ended up putting my index finger over the barrel; Brian kept me from shooting the tip of my finger off right at the last moment.

One day as we were cruising down the highway in his Jeep, the topic of "God" came up in our conversation. Neither of us had any solid arguments for whether or not we believed in God; this was just something that we hadn't really put much thought into, though we both agreed it was an interesting topic to discuss. "I just don't think that I need God," I concluded. "What would I need God for?" We left it at that, moving on to topics that were more pressing at the time.

I thought "faith" was a stupid word, a concept that was only needed by people who feared life or death, that it was completely illogical. I certainly wasn't about to believe in something that I couldn't put my finger on, something with the promise of saving me from damnation. I wasn't worried about hell; what I was worried about was now, and I couldn't imagine how faith could be of any assistance whatsoever.

I did believe in love, and in trying to lead a virtuous life. I knew that you were the reason for my existence, and that I was completely satisfied with living for my family, for my girls. What I hadn't any idea of was what real evil is; I had never come across it in my life to this point. I never spent much time thinking about it because what I wanted were good things for you. Evil wasn't even on my radar; why spend time on that when I saw that there was so much beauty in the world, so much hope and joy in just raising you?

"i see you called. call mom's from the house phone if you can. love you
Sat, Jul 3, 2010, 10:35 AM
Iain Bryson to Agata Bryson"

"Sat, Jul 3, 2010, 11:37 PM
Iain Bryson to Agata Bryson
agatka,
can we skype tomorrow? Just let me know a good time and I can call you? See you soon. Love you"

"Adelle Avery Bryson
Mon, Jul 12, 2010, 8:21 AM
Iain Bryson to Agata Bryson, Mom, Dad, Iwona
Attachments"

"Mon, Jul 12, 2010 at 8:25 AM
Iain Bryson to Agata Bryson, Mom, Iwona, Dad
Attachments"

When I got back to The Hague, I was ready to go, ready to take on the world with your mom. I had kicked my dependence on clonazepam and morphine to the curb; they no longer had any hold over me. I felt like I had conquered Mount Everest, and I knew that not many could say that they had done what I had just done. I didn't need rehab, I didn't need a doctor, I had done it all myself. *I could write a book about this*, I thought to myself, pitching it to your mom. *I could help a lot of people; I know what it takes, and I know how to do it. I did it.*

I dumped most of the pills I had been keeping on the shelf into the toilet, knowing that this dragon had been slayed and would not be returning. Your mom was in the other room, so I called her into the bathroom so she could watch, proud of myself, and wanting her to see that I was making strides toward being stronger.

Knowing the importance of music to children, I brought you a guitar back, thinking that we could begin learning together. I was also trying to decide on a language that we could start to study together, knowing that your mind was like a sponge at your age, assuming that once we got going you would be teaching me more than I would be teaching you. *She already speaks English, Polish, and Dutch, so why not add one more and do it together,* I decided.

You and your new guitar.
Newtonplein, The Hague. 2010.

CHAPTER 14

"MY HUSBAND THINKS I GO CRAZY SOMETIMES"

Your mom agreed to go to counseling, but our insurance wouldn't cover couples counseling. We found a psychologist who was covered, Kees de Vries, and though I was technically his patient, we both attended the meetings. He diagnosed me with ADHD, and I reluctantly began taking Concerta, a time release amphetamine used to treat ADHD.

Your mom began seeing another psychologist on her own. After her first meeting, she told me that she started off with, "My husband thinks I go crazy sometimes. I don't know if he is right or not." I had doubts about a regular psychologist's capabilities at getting to the bottom of whatever was "wrong" with your mom, as I knew how little she seemed to know or was willing to share. But at least this was a start, and I was seeing drastic improvements in our relationship. She would just have to stick with it and learn to be vulnerable, and I would be patient and there to support her every step of the way.

In "Sometimes I Act Crazy," Kreisman and Straus (2004) write, "BPD [borderline personality disorder] shares several characteristics with other personality dysfunctions... However, the constellation of self-destructiveness, chronic feelings of emptiness, and desperate fears of abandonment distinguish BPD... The primary features of BPD are impulsivity and instability in relationships, self-image, and moods" (6).

Her psychologist wanted her fill out some personality questionnaires (see Appendices 16, 17, and 18), but she didn't know the answers to many of the questions. "Iain, I need your help on this, because I just don't know," she told me, causing me to chuckle.

"Alright, Agata, I will help you. Maybe I know you better than you do."

We spent the evening going through her personality questionnaires together. I tried to help her answer many of the questions, because she really didn't seem to know the answers. It was as if we were talking about another person, someone we didn't know very well. I was excited that we were starting the therapy process for her, as I knew there was a lot we both weren't aware of.

I sent Kees an email after meeting with him a few times to express to him what I could not say in her presence. "Kees, Agata and I both think she has something like borderline personality disorder. We have thought this for quite some time. But you can't tell her that I told you this. I am afraid that she will take it as an act of betrayal if she knows I told you."

After sending the message, I deleted it from my sent folder and from my trash, destroying the evidence in fear of your mom's possible reprisal. I wanted him to know so that he had some insight when he was meeting with us, and I thought that he may be able to tactfully bring it up at some point, or at least begin looking for signs of what I had warned him about.

After taking the Concerta for a short time, I decided that I wanted to eliminate it; I didn't want to take anything anymore, even though I did find it to be helpful, mostly because I had just been through a major battle in freeing myself from morphine and clonazepam. I brought this up in one of the meetings with Kees, but both he and your mother suggested that I keep taking it for a while longer to see what the results would be. I hesitantly accepted their advice and was glad I did. My focus was better, I was reading multiple books per week, and I was having breakthroughs for the first time in a long time because of the conditions that had been present in our home whenever your mother wasn't well.

"good morning beautiful
Wed, Jul 14, 2010, 2:11 AM
Iain Bryson to Agata Bryson
Agatka,
I composed this diddy for you [see Appendix 19]. I guess it was done for me [by Dave Matthews], but it blows me away how real the words sound and feel and how they come together. I love you. Let me know about the phone calls please. I would like to go camping in Den Haag this weekend with you and Adelle. It would be nice to get out of the apartment and do something different close to home. I want to figure out some things with you, preferably starting today: we need to keep going over things together, I need some help sorting jobs, Adelle's room, I am sure there is more, but I will have to get back to you. You didn't translate that email for me."

Your mom and I's relationship seemed to have turned a corner; we were together again, planning for our future, happy to be in the present. It seemed to me that she was the happiest woman I had ever known at this point, and I had no sense that she could ever revert to what had been. On a nearly daily basis, we danced to the song your mom had chosen to be our song, "Up and Away" by Dave Matthews (see Appendix 20); everything had seemed perfect. I thought that we had gotten over the hump, that the desert was behind us, that love had finally healed her.

"Mon, Jul 26, 2010, 6:40 AM
Iain Bryson to Brian
hey,
how did your weekend go? get your condo cleaned out yet? Just working a bit here trying to get some things done. agatka stayed home from work today. her contract runs out in about a week, and she is getting to the point where she has nothing to do. also, her boss went to Saudi [Arabia] so it isn't a biggy. so, they are home with me which is slowing me down a little this morning. can you tell me once again how to do the New Haven tax thing so i can start working on that? hi to the fam. talk to you soon. I"

* * *

We started spending more time with Mickey, Jackie, and Cicely. As I got to know Mickey better, I began to like him less. I didn't want him in my life, or in our lives, but you were growing closer to Cicely, and he was part of the package. One evening, after the six of us had dinner together, he asked if I wanted to go for a walk. Once we were out of the house and around the corner, he started packing heroin into his cigarette.

"I didn't know if you would want one, but I assumed you would be cool with it," he informed me. I reluctantly took one, partly because I had never tried this method of ingesting heroin, partly because of peer pressure, and partly because I wanted to prove to myself that I had indeed slaughtered that dragon. *I can have one*, I thought to myself, *why not?*

While I could have one, and I found out that I wasn't at risk of relapsing, I had also opened a door to Mickey, showing him that I didn't have a problem with him bringing this into our lives. His wife was completely unaware of his habit, which had him spending money and lying to his wife, along with travelling long distances with Cicely to get more heroin when Jackie was at work. From this point on, I never hung out with him when I was taking care of you, unless his wife was also there, but I did hang out with him when it was just Cicely, Mickey, and I.

On one occasion, I took a trip to Arnhem with him and Cicely on the train so that he could purchase heroin. We stopped at a zoo so that he could explain the trip to his wife in positive terms. On other occasions, when you were at daycare and I dropped by their house, Mickey would be smoking heroin off tin foil while Cicely was watching tv. I felt a strong desire to get him out of our lives.

I informed your mom about what was going on, and she proceeded to tell me what she had learned from his wife. "A lot of money was missing from their bank account, and Mickey told

Jackie that he had no idea how it could've happened," she said. "But then the bank pulled up the video of Mickey making the withdrawal and he still maintains to her that he has no idea how it happened, even with the video."

"That's weird," Agata. "I don't want him in our home, and I don't want him in our life. I don't want Adelle to lose her friend, but he is dangerous, and I don't want to risk it." Though she seemed to agree with me, we never made a hard decision, and he continued to pop into our lives from time to time.

Mickey continued to give me reasons to distrust him, but at the same time it was nice to have another man to talk to that lived nearby. "I took Jackie's last name when we got married," he informed me, "because I have a criminal record in Denmark... They wouldn't let us move to the United States because I lied on the U.S. Customs form, so that is why we are here."

"When I was in prison," he informed me, "there was a lot of homosexuality. Everybody was giving everybody [expletive]."

"That's weird," I responded, "I don't want to do that with anybody except for my wife."

"Yes," he countered, "but most guys don't care where they get it from."

I stopped the conversation there, getting the feeling that I was dealing with some kind of a pervert, making a decision that he would never be alone with you. He came over to our house a couple of times when your mom was at work and pounded on our door for what seemed like an hour, not giving up, somehow seeming to know that we were home and ignoring him. We went into your room to hide from him, turning on the music to drown out his banging. On one occasion, I crawled on my belly away from the living room window to make sure he couldn't see me through the window.

One day he was irate with me because I didn't answer my phone. I explained to him later that I wasn't going to answer my phone if I was out with you, but his response was, "You had better answer the phone when I call."

"No, Mickey," I tried to explain calmly, feeling anxiety creep in, "I will not answer your calls if I am doing something with my daughter. When I am with her, I am fully with her. Period."

CHAPTER 15

"NEVER AGAIN, IAIN, I PROMISE"

With your mom healthy, joy filled our home once again. I could think of no reason why we would ever return to where we had been. *That was tough,* I thought, *very tough, but now we are out of that, now we have won the race, now we just have to maintain and move forward. Why wouldn't we? How couldn't we?*

I was putting out all kinds of job applications and felt as if I had reached a sort of pinnacle. Everything was falling into place, and with your mom back by my side, I knew that we could do anything. *Thank God she is with me,* I thought, *because when she is against me, my life is a living hell.* But she was back, and I could no longer imagine it any other way.

"Never again, Iain, I promise, never again," she pledged.

"What do you mean, 'never again'?"

"I will never treat you like that again. That will never happen again," she claimed.

"Do you mean that the reasons you told your therapist that your husband thinks you are crazy sometimes will never happen again?" I asked, looking for clarification.

"Yes, that is what I mean. Never again. I love you, Iain."

"I sure hope not, Agata, I love you too." As I responded to her, a song I hadn't heard for many years came into my conscious awareness, "Policy of Truth" by Depeche Mode, "...never again is what you swore the time before..." I believed her because I wanted to, and because I needed to, and I let it go. "I love you, baby," I reminded her.

It became apparent to me that we should try to move back to the United States. Though I enjoyed many aspects of European life, I wanted to return to where I was more comfortable, where I knew how things worked and what to expect. With you getting older, the immigrant life became less and less appealing. I thought it would be better for you to go to an American school, though my preference was to homeschool you, and I also wanted the American medical system to take care of you if you were to ever get sick.

Your mom and I discussed this in detail and decided together to move our family back to the U.S. We started the visa process so that she would be able to return and then complete the U.S. citizenship process; without a new visa, she was not able to return to the U.S. at all. We spoke to Kees about our decision, and he thought that this was a good choice. With her initial visa paperwork submitted, we decided to move forward with our plan.

I began to send out more job applications to various states in the U.S., and I contacted an Army National Guard Recruiter to get more information about entering the intelligence field. I also began looking very seriously at doctoral programs at the University of Connecticut. Which road we took wasn't concerning to me; the important thing was getting us back onto solid ground, which I believed to be across the big pond.

Since your mom couldn't enter the country yet, we decided that I would go on ahead to look for housing and work. Our plan was to make the move later that year, with the specific date dependent upon the issuance of your mom's visa. I bought a plane ticket, and we continued to try to plan our future.

The week before I was to leave, we went on a family vacation in Leiden. We stayed at Hotel Mayflower, which I thought was fitting since we were pilgrims about to move from one homeland to another. I was excited to be moving forward and thrilled to be exploring and relaxing with my girls (see Appendix 21).

Your mom was somber, appearing to be in a funk, as if an ominous presence was circling above her head. There was no worry on my end, only the realization that we still had work to do. But at least we would never be returning to that crazy world we had been in; at least now she was on her way toward health and happiness. At least now she saw what I saw: that we had it all, because we had each other, and because we had you.

CHAPTER 16

"I'M AFRAID WE'LL NEVER GET THIS BACK"

She pleaded with me not to go, not to leave her, terrified of us being apart, but I just thought that she was being nonsensical; I had no idea what she was talking about. I had seen her irrational fear of abandonment before, and here it was back again in full force. How could she think that I would ever leave her, that this could even cross my mind? Wasn't she in the same reality that I was, where our little family was the most precious, most amazing thing that there was in this world?

> "At one time or another, almost everyone worries that her lover is going to leave. But for a borderline, the fear of abandonment—rooted in years of family history—can be excruciatingly painful. The terror involves much more than the simple dread of being alone; abandonment can mean the destruction of the borderline's entire identity" (Kreisman and Straus, 2004, 19).

"Agata, I love you, and I am only going so that I can prepare things so that we can all go together. I don't want to go, I don't ever want to not be with you, I don't want there to ever be a morning that I don't wake up next to you, but I don't see how we can move without me going first to take care of some things. We need a place to live, one of us needs to have a job right away, and you can't go yet until we get your visa."

"Can't you ask Jer if he can get the visa now? Then we could all go together. We wouldn't have to be separated." She was jittery and clearly flustered, and I could tell that she was genuinely in distress over us being separated.

"How would that work, Agata?"

"With his contacts in the FBI, why do we have to wait?" she asked earnestly, hoping that this could be a possibility.

I chuckled to myself at her innocence and naivety, at the thought of the FBI expediting her visa because my cousin worked for them. I also didn't want to be separated from her, but I didn't see any possible reason to fear it, or any tangible way around it. "No, Agata, Jer can't just get us a visa. I don't think his job has anything to do with visas. We have to go through the process just like everybody else. We're not going to be separated. I'm going to get things ready for us, and we will be together as soon as your visa comes through. I don't see any other way; this is a big move."

"But why can't he ask someone? I'm afraid we'll never get this back. Iain, I'm afraid." She looked totally defeated, and my heart sank to feel what she was feeling, like a child who was just told that she could not keep her beloved puppy. I did not like that my wife was so troubled and scared, but her fears seemed nonsensical to me. I had to be stronger when she was weak, to console her, support her, get her back up on her feet again. I had to go if we were going to move back to the United States.

"Agata, we can never lose what we have. I love you so much, and I'm just going so that we can all be together as soon as possible. I don't want anything else either. You need to trust me, I love you. You are my collaborator," I joked, hoping to get her to smile and realize that everything was ok.

"Yes, I am your collaborator," she replied smugly, bringing a slight smile to my face, but not to hers, which remained resolutely dejected. I could tell that she was not convinced or satisfied.

We spent the last couple of days together as a family, dancing, going to the parks and the local farm, cooking, reading, and just generally loving each other (see Appendix 22). I was so incredibly lucky, and I knew it. I even considered the possibility of writing a self-help book on how to have a happy family or overcoming marital difficulties. *There are so many people who don't know what they are doing, that this is it, and there is nothing better. We'll show them what they are doing wrong, it's simple, they just don't see that they have everything they need right in front of their faces. I don't need another reason for life; why do they?* I pondered. *Where is the disconnect?*

Everything seemed perfect. There was nothing to be afraid of; your mom's fears were entirely irrational to me, and although I would have liked to iron them out and go through it with her so she could heal and we could understand, we didn't have time for that. Since I saw her fears as not rational, I also deemed that they were unreal. The reality I knew was that we were the strongest family I was aware of and there was nothing that could stop us. I believed that the kind of love we had was impervious to external forces.

I was concerned about you and your mom returning to Poland, mostly about your grandfather's alcoholism. I didn't want you to witness this; I didn't want this behavior to be normalized in your presence. Your mom and I spoke in depth about it, and she assured me that she would speak to her mom who would then tell her dad not to drink in front of you.

I didn't know how this was possible, as this man drank alcohol for breakfast, lunch, dinner, and even as a sports drink, but I trusted your mom when she told me that she also took this seriously and would handle it. I didn't feel that I had much choice but to trust her on this, as I simply couldn't be there if we were going to move again, and I thought it best that your mom had the support of other family in my absence.

When it was time to leave, I reminded your mom of how strong she was, of my undying love for her and for our family, and that I would be with her every step of the way. She beseeched me not to go one last time, telling me that she didn't know what it was, but that she was terrified of us separating, again that she was afraid that we would "never get this back."

"Agata you wouldn't be afraid if you knew how much I love you. Nothing can happen to us, we are too strong now," I tried to reassure her, but I also had to go. I held you both tightly, kissed you and told you I loved you, and then I had to get to the airport.

Your mom, you, me, and Ally.
September 6, 2010, 9:53 AM.

PART 3

SEPTEMBER 7, 2010 – DECEMBER 10, 2010

"I LOVE YOU FROM ALL OF MY HEART AND MISS YOU TERRIBLY"
- YOUR MOTHER

CHAPTER 17

"LOVEYOU!!!<3<3<3"

A large segment of Part 3 is composed of e-mail correspondence between your mother and me. The reason for this, though it may seem redundant or rambling at times, is to establish continuity and leave as few gaps for you as possible. This will make more sense once you get to Parts 4, 5, and 6.

I flew into Boston on the late afternoon of September 7, 2010, feeling like the happiest man in the world. I didn't want to be away from you, but I saw no way around it. All I could see in my head was the idea of you and your mom, and the joy and fulfilment of being your dad and your mom's husband; I danced on the way to the baggage carousel, one earbud in, anxious to taste Boston air.

My mom picked me up and brought me to her home in Connecticut where I would stay for the next three months with her and George.

"L O V E Y O U !!! <3 <3 <3
Wed, Sep 8, 2010, 8:04 AM
Agata Bryson to me
http://www.youtube.com/watch?v=V7wA7Zvm6oU
http://www.youtube.com/watch?v=n6eXhg_516c
[these are two love songs that are no longer available on YouTube]
Agata"

"Wed, Sep 8, 2010, 8:28 AM
Iain Bryson to Agata Bryson
baby,
getting organized and planning a little. my mom just left to go to deep river. george is going to bring me to niantic to get the car when he gets up. i will check the computer but need to take a shower, etc. will talk to you later this evening if not sooner. miss you"

"Wed, Sep 8, 2010, 6:00 PM
Agata Bryson to me
Sweety:
I'm going to bed. Tomorrow morning I am dropping Adelle off at the day care and have my unemployment interview at 9 am. I don't know how to sleep without you. I love you from all of my heart and miss you so terribly much. I hope you had a good day and that i will hear your beautiful voice soon. I am so very much proud of you and love you more than words can say. Will be dreaming of you my everything. Goodnight! Kisses everywhere.
 Your wifey"

"Dave Matthews Band Announces U.S. Fall Tour
Click here to view this message as a web page DAVE MATTHEWS BAND ANNOUNCES U.S. FALL
TOUR DATES Warehouse Ticketing Request Period Opens: Thursday, September 9th
Thu, Sep 9, 2010, 6:32 AM
Iain Bryson to Agata Bryson"

"Thu, Sep 9, 2010, 6:43 AM
Agata Bryson to me
I was waiting for u to forward me this ;)"

"Thu, Sep 9, 2010, 6:54 AM
Agata Bryson to me
Hey love,
Was wondering when i will get the DMB email forwarded by you. I got it too from Dave ;) Adelle is in the day care, i had my unemployment appointment this am, now am on my way to Belasting [tax office] and town hall to get us more money. How r u doing? Whats new? I miss u too muchy! Love you my prince charming ;*"

"Thu, Sep 9, 2010, 9:15 AM
Agata Bryson to me
My love,
Adelle and I are at the park we went to with jackie and Cicely. Its nice weather so we are trying to make the most of it. We miss you so much! I hope I will hear your voice soon. We love u!!! A&A"

"Sat, Sep 11, 2010, 7:42 AM
Agata Bryson to me, Mamusia [Iwona], Mom, Adusia [Ada]
Attachments"

[You and Cicely. Photographer unknown.]

* * *

In one of my first conversations with my mom, standing in her living room, she asked me if I knew that your name day was the same as your mom's name day (February 5). I indicated that I did not know this, and that it was strange given the importance of Polish name days in Polish culture, and the fact that there was a 1/365 chance (.0027%) that your names would both have the same celebration day, too small of a chance for it to be unintentional.

Name days are more important than birthdays for Polish people. I thought about the process that your mom and I went through to choose your name, and I began to doubt that I was indeed a part of that process. *She must have had your name already chosen, somehow leading me to choosing it as well*, I thought; *the odds of this occurring otherwise are too crazy.*

"No, I had no idea that they had the same name day," I informed my mom, feeling some bewilderment and anger that I was left in the dark on this one.

"Well," my mom retorted, "Agata is just trying to make her more Polish."

"Make her more Polish?!" I exclaimed, feeling exasperated that my wife must have chosen your name without any real input from me, wondering how that could happen. *How could you be more Polish than you already were, and what would this look like? Why didn't my wife tell me?*

"You should pray about it," my mom informed me.

I scoffed, "I don't need to talk to some imaginary friend in my head. I can figure things out without having to go to imaginary land."

"Prayer is very important for me," she stated, and I left it at that, not wanting to unnecessarily attack something I knew my mom thought was real.

At this point, I still believed that God was just something that weak, or maybe weak and stupid people and my mom needed. I certainly didn't think I needed Him because I felt strong and capable, and because I believed I had the only partner I needed in your mother. I thought that I had moved beyond the nonsense stories of my Christian childhood to truths that were deeper and substantive.

George had piles of wood around the property, and I lit a fire in the fire pit, a fire that I fed constantly, always trying to keep it alive in remembrance of you and your mom. More than anything, I did not want us to be apart, and the fire was one of my ways of constantly reminding myself of our journey, and of what we were fighting for and moving toward. It went out a few times during this three-month period, but I always did my best to keep it burning for you and your mom. I often pulled the car out onto the lawn by the fire pit so that I could play Jack Johnson or Dave Matthews and dream of the day we would all be able to sit by the fire together.

"Mon, Sep 13, 2010, 7:24 AM
Iain Bryson to Agata Bryson
good morning baby. i have a minute before i have to take my mom to east lyme. i love you so much. i miss my babies. things are going well. i just wish we were together. today i am just going to keep trying to move closer to crossing things off of our list. i will talk with you soon. hope you havent forgotten me. love you"

"Tue, Sep 14, 2010, 10:18 AM
Iain Bryson to Agata Bryson
i love you both so much and miss you more than you can imagine. it is only the knowledge that we will soon be together and knowing how happy that will be that keeps me going. i am working on my list (one of them) and in and out but busy. will try to skype later but not sure yet completely about the day and what i should do. what should you do ? i love you"

"Tue, Sep 14, 2010, 11:36 PM
Iain Bryson to Agata Bryson
hey babe,
i am getting ready to go to bed and wanted to catch up with you. I miss you so [expletive] much. i am just trying to get things going for us and it is a full time job. It is fun but I cannot wait to share the fun with my girlies. I was just out under the stars in the back. Fall has come and we are getting days that are perfect temperature...not hot or cold, sunny and kind of like a dutch day but warmer and more pleasant, or at least you would think so. The sky is like a planetarium in the back yard, or i guess everywhere, but in the back yard it is nice. And i guess the sky is probably better than a planetarium.

Anyway, I took my mom to work this morning and then came back here where i worked on the computer and in my notebook. Got some more job applications done and some planning and organizing which is a neverending task. Then I went for a ride with George to a couple of places. Then to the Mon[t]ville library to get my library card and some more books. Then I went to Groton to a couple of stores and then to the library in Groton. I guess i owe them fifteen dollars, which I will have to go back and pay them soon so more books can be gotten. The lady was only going to let me get two but I started going through them to try to choose which two and she probably saw how sad I was to have to leave any and she said she would make an exception. Then the fee turned up from who knows when and i was told the fifteen dollars is the maximum they can fine you. Think we are lucky as I am sure my fee should have been more. I sent off the debt disputes for the credit [expletive].

Planned some attack moves for the next couple of days. Hoping to get a call from one of the places I've applied and Grasso [High School] hopefully any day. Went to Ron's guitars....gotta get some lessons and equipment. Adelle cant start there till six but they have singing, banjo, and others. Talked to Rob and Eugene and wrote some more. Went to a cemetery to get some quiet in Niantic and waited for my mom to get out of work before picking her up from Snap, her fitness center. Came back and did dishes and started cleaning the car. Then dinner, the store for milk and half and half and bananas. Then more writing and reading and another walk in the back to look up and know that you are under the same sky.

Gonna go lie down. Was reading some things about child development and [expletive]. Lots of fun filled informative ideas but a couple i had already thought of were saying things like 'shy' or really anything for that matter....even 'princess' too much as it leads to categorizing oneself and labelling and [expletive] like that. Anyway, just be conscious of that stuff, as i know you are, but i have to say it anyway. and sugar is bad. baby teeth rot quicker and if they do they [expletive] up the growth of the other teeth. ok baby. sleeping to get my head recharged. love you. give me the update and do something fun with adelle"

I visited all the surrounding libraries during this time in Connecticut, including the UConn twenty-four-hour library, and I was known by most of the librarians. I had piles of books that I was going through; the back seat of the car was always full of totes filled with books. I had a strong desire to research and learn, and though I didn't know exactly what it was that I was researching, I let my subconscious mind take me wherever it felt I needed to go. Or was it God that was leading me? At the time I didn't think so, but now I would say yes.

"Wed, Sep 15, 2010, 6:31 AM
Agata Bryson to me
Hey love,
I just got back with Adelle from outside. We went for a nice walk, stopped by at the farm and the playground, library and the store for some milk and eggs. Now we will have lunch and then we are going to clean up a little and then I will start working on the cpu and the phone. Later in the day I will stop by at the Belastingdienst [tax office] to make sure our money is in on the 20th for the 3rd time and then around 5 I am meeting with Adelle the girls from work for a quick coffee and then home for dinner and bedtime.

I miss you more than I am capable of expressing and every day and night I think about you constantly. You are my love, my life, my rock and I am so deeply in love with you and proud of you that it lights up my heart and soul. You are the most wonderful person in the world to me and thinking about all that hard work that we put in for our family makes my heart full of pride and happiness. I miss you in every little thing I do, I miss your smile and your body but I know that we are working on something huge for us and it makes me happy and excited.

At the debt help appointment yesterday, the lady went with me through all of our paperwork and bills for almost 2 hours while Adelle was playing Lego's and coloring. She is going to send some letters out to our creditors and in about 3 weeks I will have an appointment with a financial advisor to discuss the details of the help we are going to get. I also applied for the unemployment, social help, we applied for rent help and insurance help, I applied for debt help and more money for Adelle. I sent in the reimbursements for the dentist and we should be reimbursed also from Adelle's day care based on a year and a half of us paying parental contributions and they compare it to our income during that period. I also emailed University of Leiden for the reimbursement of the application fee.

So as you see I am trying to be as busy as possible and knock on every tree there is to help us out and make it easier for us and I know exactly what you mean about a full time job. Cannot wait to be lying underneath the stars with my soul mate and I do look up the sky and also think that you are under the same sky, maybe not under the same grey clouds we are under.

About the library: I can see in my head the look you had to have when the lady told you you can only have 2 book-she had to sense what a book worm you are lovely. About Adelle I agree with you, and I don't use sugar for her tea but honey which I think is better for her teeth. OK honey gonna get going and catch up with you later. I love you and ttys my love. Kisses"

"I love u <3
Wed, Sep 15, 2010, 8:22 AM
Agata Bryson to me
http://www.metrolyrics.com/aint-no-other-man-lyrics-christina-aguilera.html"

"Thu, Sep 16, 2010, 3:28 PM
Iain Bryson to Agata Bryson
i love you and hate that you are sick. all i want is for us three to be together. i am trying to do a lot and plan so that i can do as much as possible in the time i have without rushing. i want to get a car next week and i know we are low on money so i kind of need to know the details. i am working on jobs and getting a lot done but it is still tough not getting any money 'today.' i am going to try to get back into focus. rest and make sure you get medicine and that they tell you exactly what it is. no looking and guessing. i am there with you baby. we are getting so much done and i dont think we will ever have to be physically apart for this long again...except when i go to dutch prison perhaps. love you and give the kid a kiss for me"

Prior to leaving for the U.S., I began joking with your mom about volunteering to go to prison so that I could acquire the experiences that people get from prison. It was kind of in jest because I didn't know how this would be possible, but mostly not in that I did want the experience, which I knew would make me more insightful and stronger.

"Sat, Sep 18, 2010, 10:13 AM
Iain Bryson to Agata Bryson
i love you. i dont want to argue when we speak as a family. i dont think it is healthy.
i am working and trying to figure out the day. be happy mommy. if you need money just let me know. talk to you soon...tomorrow at the latest unless you have plans with jeremy."

"Sat, Sep 18, 2010, 9:42 PM
Iain Bryson to Agata Bryson
i am going to go to bed soon. i miss you so much and ....yeah that says it all. i picked up my dad and wendy and hung out with them for a while today. got a letter back from one of the places i applied saying they are reviewing my application. got more i am working on and grasso/norwich tech [High School] should be straight soon with the fingerprints as long as [...inappropriate joke]

when i feel tired or maybe have the symptoms of being tired and more than a coffee would work i can think about you guys and how happy and great we are when we are together and i am confident again. maybe changing or adding the music helps but it is your faces that i remember that is the key. your laughs and your smiles. i wanted to start a fire tonight under the stars and do some writing but there are no sticks left to begin that [expletive] and I don't feel like taking the wheelbarrow into the woods in the dark....well not yet but maybe i should. we will see i guess. who the [expletive] knows. maybe i do i guess.

burned us some cds and been working on cleaning the house but it is a long process. got the volvo done. my mom went to look at an apartment down the street but she and george are out and i havent talked yet. i will take pictures for you soon. gotta find the plug for my phone to go into the computer.

kaitana [nickname your mom made up for she and I as a couple]. i hope you feel better. focus focus on adelle and try to not think about missing me. we will be together as soon as possible and it is not ideal, but feeling low will not help you get through it better. if i ruminated on it i would cry. i can feel it and i want to change it and i have plans i want to discuss with you. that will happen and i will [marital talk]. have fun and we will have time time time here soon enough and maybe some time there together. keep up the good work. you are wonderful. love you"

"Wed, Sep 22, 2010, 4:41 PM
Agata Bryson to me
Attachments"

Your mom's visa application was submitted, and now all we had to do was wait (see Appendix 23). She told me that the person she spoke to at the Embassy had indicated that it would take a few months for the entire process; I was excited.

I visited the local Montville post office at least once per week to send you presents and your mom books and letters. For Halloween, I sent you a pumpkin that I packed into a box. The woman working at the post office knew all about you and your mom, our plans to return to the United States as a family, and how much I love you. She once gave me $200 to take to the nearby store so that I could get some change for her, saying, "I know you and I trust you."

One day George and I went for a ride to a state park, and I brought along my duffel bag full of books and notebooks. "What are you doing with all those books and notebooks?" he questioned.

"I don't really know, but I feel that it is important. I wouldn't sell these notebooks for any amount of money, not even $100,000 for one," I said, unsure if I was joking or not. "I feel like I am working toward something, and that they are crucial to whatever is coming next." I recalled mindlessly scribbling the following words in my journal not long before: "I write for Adelle, and maybe for everybody," and though I had no idea what that could mean, I did have an innate understanding that my "work" would be important in some way.

"Fri, Sep 24, 2010, 12:21 PM
Iain Bryson to Agata Bryson
babe. just got back from coffee with john. got the interview at three. going to eat and plan a bit. have a great day. i will try to call you before you go to bed. will skype tomorrow if not. Lovey"

I tried to talk to you and your mom as much as possible, either on the phone or on Skype. I felt like we could stay connected in this way, and I couldn't stand not seeing you. I wanted to talk daily, but it didn't work out that way due to the six-hour time difference and our schedules. *It doesn't matter that much, I figured, as we will all be back together soon, and it might be better that my three-and-a-half-year-old daughter doesn't have to see me on a computer screen, as this might just be confusing to her.*

"Fri, Sep 24, 2010, 12:44 PM
Agata Bryson to me
http://www.youtube.com/watch?v=UAtxjvLSEn0
Agata

['Cater to You' by Destiny's Child
'Baby I see you working hard
I want to let you know I'm proud
Let you know that I admire what you do
The more if I need to reassure you
My life would be purposeless without you (Yeah)
If I want it (Got it)
When I ask you (You provide it)
You inspire me to be better
You challenge me for the better
Sit back and let me pour out my love letter…']"

CHAPTER 18

"ALL I CAN SAY IS THAT IT HURTS"

I set up an office in one of the classrooms at my dad and Wendy's old schoolhouse at 25 Riverview Avenue in New London, CT, only a few blocks from the hospital where you were born. The space that I had available to me at my mom's house was limited, but this office offered me the chance to set up a desk, and a place where I could relax, a place where nobody could find me if I was doing work which required focus. The solitude allowed me to work on my plans for getting you and your mother over here so that we could all be together. I could not stand being apart from my girls; I yearned for us to be back together again.

The schoolhouse was enormous and pretty cram packed with things that my dad and Wendy had accumulated, as well as things that they had stored for my siblings and myself. It was laid out such that classrooms surrounded the entire inner gymnasium area, with a regular size stage at one end. Parts of the building were crumbling; it needed quite a bit of renovating, a perfect project for my dad. It was exciting to have such a large, multi-functional building in the middle of New London, and I was involved with brainstorming with my dad regarding how we could utilize it to serve the community.

You and your mom went to Poland to be with the Polish side of our family, so that your mom would have support in my absence, and so that you could spend some time with them before we moved back to the United States. I was confident in your mom's capacity and ability to deal with whatever arose, satisfied that she had been "healed" from whatever it was we were dealing with before. *Soon we will be out of Europe*, I thought. *Just a little while longer and we will put all of this behind us once and for all.*

"Mon, Sep 27, 2010, 2:33 PM
Iain Bryson to Agata Bryson
love you so much. just working and organizing and [expletive] like that. hope you are having a great time in PL. Remember how strong you are and how great of a mother you are and how lucky and pecial we are. Remember the tendency to change like maybe one because of environment and/or expectations/habits...blah [expletive] blah. I miss you so much. My dad has a thing that you put out at night (from some science store) to catch bugs and then it has some pecial thing for looking at them and identifying those [expletive] for dellinski [Adelle]. my mom bought a banjo for her yesterday but don't tell her it's a present for xmas. i looked up some [expletive] with my mom about the place in nh. they have a place called monkey (something) and it is climbing and ropes and stuff....well look it up.. google and tweet it monkey new hampshire should work. storyland. some snow village [expletive] with horse rides, snow shoeing, cross country, and more things like it. i want us to buy a house with them when we can. look up jackson nh. yesterday i went to the school and did some research and [expletive] and then mowed the lawn and got to play chain saw mother [expletive] killer with some trees and bushes. i thought of the trees as japs like in the movie [*The Pacific*] because if you look at them...they look nice and sweet and probably friendly. went to kayla's [niece] soccer game on saturday. stacked some wood today. my mom and george love listening to

music.....it is like they get baked like one and lose all that stress and [expletive]. i think you need me to get a little baked and lose some anxiety....i am holding your hand now babin (and seeing how high on your leg i can touch without you slapping my hand"

"Mon, Sep 27, 2010, 2:50 PM
Agata Bryson to me
Here is the update love:
Money we are expecting:
UNEMPLOYMENT According to my calculations 1788.75 is 75% of my monthly salary (brutto 2385). I have not received a letter from UWV (unemployment) yet about how much they calculated my unemployment to be every month. I was told I should have the first payment in about 1 week now. I am entitled for 3 months unemployment (Sept, Oct, Nov)
HUURTOESLAG(rent) Was deposited 2630.00 today. Will be deposited with 267/month to follow in October November and December.
ZORGTOESLAG(health) We get paid 129/month on the 20th of each month
SCHULDHULP(debt) Saw them last Tuesday (14th). It will take them couple weeks to go through our file with all the bills, debt, collection agencies etc. and once they review it and scan it all to the system I will have a meeting with a Financial Advisor to determine what help we are entitled for.
UWV TOESLAG While I applied for the unemployment I was told I also qualify for some social help from the UWV (unemployment office) I sent the application in on the 9th and some additional documents then requested and am waiting for a letter from them. No indication what amount or is it going to be paid together with unemployment benefits or separate
BLUE UMBRELLA Because we cancelled the day care as of the end of October, they will look through all of our parental contributions and our income since Adelle was in the day care and we might get reimbursed if our parental contributions were higher than our income and what according to Belasting it should be based on our actual income.
MEDICAL REIMBURSEMENT Sent the reimbursements in and am checking every couple of days with them to see if it is all on track. We are looking at about 150-200 euros.
UNIVERSITY OF LEIDEN Sent an email to them requesting the refund of the application fee we paid and not hear from them yet but will try calling them again Monday and go there if necessary. 100 euros
We have +500 in the account now (+700 debit) after we got the Belasting money and the CC was taken (1002) and day care (300) and the 100 for you to ING. Plus 1000 on the CC that will be available tomorrow. Love u"

"Update RE: Concerta
Sep 29, 2010, 5:25 AM
Agata Bryson to me
Hey love:
I spoke to Saskia [receptionist for Kees] and the doctor will not change the prescription to 2 X 72 mg. He wrote one for 120 pills 4 x 18mg/day.
I called the Rite Aid to ask for their fax number because it wasn't anywhere on the Internet, and after asking me some questions, the pharmacist said that they will not fill in a prescription not signed by a US doctor or with a US license. I called 3 more pharmacies and they told me the same. They said you need to see a doctor in a US and get a prescription from him. I tried to call Ronnie but they were already closed and they are still closed now but I wanted to talk to her and to get you in to see Dr. Russo for 15 mins immediately. I will try her again between 8 am and 9 am your time.
In the meantime I will have somebody ship the medicine to you anyways although I have my doubts that it will get to you but I guess it is worth a try.
Give me a call when you get up or when you properly wake up after your coffee and [expletive] and I will keep working on this. I love you and miss you and you are my world. Ttys. Kisses. A
P.S. The internet and email on my phone are not working, so I dont have accss to email at all times but will have my phone with me all day.
Agata"

"Sep 29, 2010, 7:56 AM
Iain Bryson to Agata
told you it wasnt all set"

"Sep 29, 2010, 7:59 AM
Iain Bryson to Agata

what is the plan now? do you see how you finish something a little and then cross it off as completely finished…"

"Wed, Sep 29, 2010, 11:23 AM
Iain Bryson to Agata Bryson
i love you. i am not mad and don't want you to worry or be upset. it is just something we need to talk about and it can't be done unless we are together. i love you..just work on it and we will figure it out just like everything i just dont see the need to ever get to this point and want us to stop it sooner"

"Wed, Sep 29, 2010, 2:15 PM
Agata Bryson to me
love you so much too. I'm not upset I just feel bad that I didn't check this thing till the end. You are the smartest person i know. You should be a philosophise. I am working on it hard and it will be shipped tomorrow. I am working on other idea too will run it by you tomorrow. I love you from all of my heart and you are my world.
Agata"

"I LOVE YOU <3
Thu, Sep 30, 2010, 4:51 AM
Agata Bryson to me
http://www.youtube.com/watch?v=Nh5R6VBn63
[Armin van Buuren vs Sophie Ellis-Bextor – 'Not Giving Up On Love']"

"Thu, Sep 30, 2010, 11:54 PM
Iain Bryson to Agata Bryson
Baby. I love you so much. It hurts me to see or hear or know that you are in pain or something is wrong, as you know it does. It drives me crazy because it is the opposite of what I want. It is hard enough not being with you right now. When you tell me something like what you did today I feel like I need to go right away and be with you. I am sorry I couldn't hold you today. I am sorry I get so upset sometimes. I am not upset with you and I hope that you know that. I want us all to be together and I can do pretty well most of the time since that is what we are working on but when I can't get through to you or I need to hug you it is next to impossible.

You need to stop worrying about things and be the wonderful person that you are. Adelle needs you right now and I need to know you are doing well. You are strong and I know you can do it. We are fine and we are going to continue to be fine and you need to tell yourself that. When you feel differently, maybe look at something that reminds you of when we are together to try to get that emotion. That is pretty close to what I do. Just think of how wonderful and lucky we are....that is not going to change regardless of a situation or a temporary feeling so tell yourself that and you will learn to shift your emotions. I love you so much. It blows my mind to think about it. I need you here and it does get hard....very hard.. for me but I try to remember that it will tend to get more hard since that is what I need and that we will have that and that me feeling that way is not going to help or change what we need to do…

Please take care of yourself. It is all that I care about. Be the wonderful mother you are and clear your head of the [expletive]. I love you and will talk to you soon. Why haven't you signed into skype over there?"

I was already considering calling it quits and telling your mom to meet me back at our home in The Hague. I could tell that she wasn't handling this well and that she was struggling. I considered the possibility she was right about her fears of us being apart. *But how can she be right? Why does she seem to fall to pieces whenever she goes to Poland? Is this the "borderline personality disorder" poking its head up again? I thought we were done with all of that.*

* * *

When I had extra time, I frequented a little coffee shop in downtown Mystic, Connecticut that had free Wi-Fi and strong espresso. This coffee shop became one of my "offices," where I would respond to emails, plan our future, and get lost in my books and my writing. Sometimes I would just listen to conversations around me and enjoy the little interactions that would come up.

One day, the bell on the café door chimed, and a young woman I had never seen before walked in. Out of the corner of my eye, I saw her turn and walk as if directly toward me. "Can I sit down?" she asked, and I looked up to meet her eyes.

"Yes, of course," I answered, motioning with my hands to the chair across from me, wondering who she could be.

"Can you tell me what you are writing?" she inquired.

"Well, nothing yet specifically, I'm brainstorming a lot of ideas," I responded. The random nature of her question stirred up a suspicious curiosity within me as I continued to try to figure out what her purpose was.

"You have a wife and daughter, right?"

With a slight furrow in my brow, I replied, "Yes, I do."

I again met her steady gaze; she was staring right at me as if piercing through to my soul, and she said, "I think you should be writing about child abuse."

Feeling a deep sadness from the look in her eyes, but also like she had zapped me alert with static electricity, I asked, "Why do you say that?"

She paused, looking for the right words, and then replied, "All I can say is that it hurts." I began to tear up as we maintained our gaze for a few more moments, and then she got up and walked out the door without speaking to anyone else or buying anything from the shop.

* * *

"Letter for your GP
Thu, Sep 30, 2010, 12:37 PM
Kees de Vries [psychologist] to me, Agata Bryson
Attachments
Hi Iain and Agata,
Hereby I send you the letter I wrote for your GP.
Let me know if anything needs to be changed or if you want me to mail it.
Hope this email finds you well!
 Kees
Zorgbedrijf PsyQ
Expat programma
Lijnbaan 4
2512VA The Hague
To whom it may concern

30 september 2010
Patient de heer I. Bryson
Date of birth 01 june 1977
Address Newtonplein 25 A
2562 JV The Hague, the Netherlands

Geachte Sir / Madam,
Hereby I state that Mr. Bryson, born on june 1st, 1977, is under our treatment, with the following diagnosis:
DSM-IV diagnosis:
Axis I: 314.01 Attention-deficit / hyperactivity disorder, combined type (main diagnosis)
                 296.36 Major depressive disorder, recurrent, in full remission
Axis II: V71.09 No diagnosis
Axis III: 722.4 Degeneration of cervical intervertebral disc
Axis IV: 40 Work related problems
                 60 Financial problems
GAF: 70
Medication:
We have prescribed the following medication:
Concerta, 18mg, s/4dd1 (72mg per day)
Citalopram, 20mg, s/1dd1 (20mg per day)

For any questions, please contact us at the telephone number above.
Yours sincerely,
Mr. K. de Vries   Ms. E. Kuhler
Psychologist   Psychiatrist"

CHAPTER 19

"WE ARE SO CRAZY IN LOVE"

"My love
Fri, Oct 1, 2010, 5:23 PM
Agata Bryson to me
Sweety:
I love you so much it hurts to think about it because there is no possible way to describe it. I was trying to catch you online after dinner but you must be busy working. It is after 11pm and i am getting ready for bed, fell tired after such an early and busy morning. I feel fine right now. I want you to know that your girls love you very much and there isn't a day that goes by that we don't talk or think about you. I am so proud of you, all your hard work and how strong you are. I know I am strong too but I think us being together makes us so strong. I have moments of feeling mostly sorry for myself because I miss you so freaking much but a look at your picture or a thought of you makes me fell all better.

I hope that you are happy and that you are eating and taking care of yourself. We need you to do that for us. We are happy and busy and everyone is asking about you and cheering for you, and everyone said to tell you they love you. I have Skype on all day long. I sent you an invite at your mom's computer. My nick is adelajda92 or on our laptop its under mamusia I think. I love you and you are my world. Goodnight-I will be dreaming about you as always and praying for our family. Loads of kisses everywhere.
Agata"

Driving in my mom's Volvo wagon down to the Book Barn, a massive used bookstore in East Lyme, Connecticut, I was elated. The music was at near max volume, and I was dancing in my seat, bouncing up and down in pure ecstasy. Somebody passed me on the left and saw what I was doing, waving and laughing, and I thought, *yeah you would be as I am too if you could only wrap your head around the gloriousness of family, of raising a little child with a woman who you adore.* What else could one desire? I couldn't think of anything except for maybe a couple of books, which I was on my way to purchase.

I spoke to my cousin Jeremiah on the phone, the one who was working for the FBI, and I informed him of your mom's request to expedite her visa through his connections. There was a minuscule amount of hope within me that your mom had been correct in fantasizing that he would help, but of course, he laughed and confirmed that he would not be able to do that.

My cousin Rachel called me, and she wanted to talk to me about the difficulties of marriage. I felt like I had marriage all figured out given what your mom and I had already been through, overcoming what we both thought could be borderline personality disorder. I explained to Rachel that I had identified a strategy for dealing with marital problems that I thought would work in any marriage, and I described it to her:

"All of our issues are due to habits that we've engrained into our relationships, and poor communication. With Agata and I, I focused on the patterns that were associated with arguing or disagreeing, and I could see how it all worked on a sort of a bell curve. Something would trigger one of us, causing a reaction, leading to an escalation, and then it would eventually be resolved. Resolution was wonderful except that there was never any real resolution. The problems were never solved, and the process was bound to repeat itself again. I had to break it down so that we could deal with the triggers when they occurred, and avoid the whole reaction, escalation, and resolution components. Stop the curve before it goes into a bell shape and attack the underlying issues as they manifest themselves. It takes redefining the way that you communicate, dedication, and humility. It doesn't matter who is right or wrong; you are a team, and you have to fight for the health of that team."

Yes, I had it all figured out.

"Sat, Oct 2, 2010, 7:39 AM
Agata Bryson to me
Hun:
We are heading to my grandpa's celebration. Should be back in an hour or two. I am feeling good today. Hope all is well with you. Happy weekend. I love you so much!. Kisses. Your girls.
Agata"

"Sat, Oct 2, 2010, 2:03 PM
Iain Bryson to Agata Bryson
I love you baby. I am at the library and will be home in a while. I have to go to the pharmacy in Montville before six. I went this morning....again but that is another story, and they said that they needed a 'diagnosis code.' I could have it called in but they didn't want to call and get it. Pretty ridiculous but oh well. Stupid pharmacists. I went to the warehouse with Courtney [cousin, sister of Jeremiah, born 1990] today and am now here in Groton at the library after dropping her off. We sat outside the warehouse [building my dad owned in New London] with my dad and this painter whose name is Leiden. Her parents used to live there....small world. Court is going to go back next week and paint.

My mom went to NY upstate...close to where we need to go... I miss you guys so much. Your letter I read yesterday made me feel all warm all over. I started another fire yesterday. I went to Fishtown and walked around and came back after dark...spent some time with Butch. Want to build things out there with you and Adelle. Some forts, swings, rope walkways through the trees.....Been making something out of bamboo..or getting the bamboo ready i cut down but trying to think of what would be nice.

I need you and our dellinski around; not having you in my life daily is like missing my most important appointments on a daily basis. It gets harder and I have to remember the positives....it is always there but I do need you so it gets tough. exercise your brain and do the same thing. we will figure it out sooner if we are happy and putting all we have into positives and not feeling glum. gotta research and do something to hopefully make some money. love you"

"Reminder: agata.bryson@gmail.com has sent you a love ecard.
Sat, Oct 2, 2010, 6:07 PM
123Greetings.com to me
It's been a day since Agatka [agata.bryson@gmail.com] sent you an ecard."

"Adelle-Sierakowo
Sun, Oct 3, 2010, 5:22 AM
Agata Bryson to me
Attachments"

[You and Aunt Ada in Sierakowo, Poland.]

"Adelle-Sierakowo 1
Sun, Oct 3, 2010, 6:06 AM
Agata Bryson to me
Attachments"

[You and great grandfather, Waldek, in Sierakowo, Poland.]

"Sun, Oct 3, 2010, 8:49 AM
Agata Bryson to me
Love:
We are heading out to the aqua park with Adelle. We will be back this evening. Adelle is really excited. We were listening to Dave today and she kept saying: my daddy likes this song, and this one too. We love you very much sweety. Talk to you later on today. Kisses. Your girls.
Agata"

"Sun, Oct 3, 2010, 12:51 PM
Iain Bryson to Agata Bryson
i love you baby."

"Sun, Oct 3, 2010, 1:56 PM
Agata Bryson to me
I love you way more my everything.
Agata"

On October 6th, I dropped off my longtime friend John Hughley at TF Green Airport in Providence, Rhode Island, to fly to Tampa, Florida. His addiction to heroin was ruining his life, and as his friend and someone who could understand what he was going through, I felt it was my duty to help him. I knew the tricks that his mind was playing on him, and I knew that he couldn't help but be less than entirely truthful with me. *Hopefully getting away will help him to begin to make better decisions*, I considered. Our mutual friend, Rob, was in Florida, and I thought maybe he would be able to help, but that the most important thing was to get John out of his typical environment.

"Wed, Oct 6, 2010, 5:33 AM
Agata Bryson to me
Sweet cheeks:
I have only few minutes now because I was delegated to bring my grandma to the hospital for a shot in a hip some blocker or something, because I have been practicing driving again ;) and I got to take her to Szczecin and back. I will write more when I get back about all the questions, and all you wrote. I should be back between 8 and 9 am your time. I love you and I know that no matter what we are fine bc we have each other and we are so crazy in love. The rest is life that we will deal with head on together. I am so proud of all your hard work and I know that it will give fruit soon. I love you and you are my world. Ttys and pray that I still know how to drive ;) Kisses
Agata"

"Wed, Oct 6, 2010, 10:27 AM
Kees de Vries to Agata Bryson, me
Great to hear about your progress, Iain!

Did everything work out with the pharmacy in the US?
Kind regards, Kees"

"Wed, Oct 6, 2010, 10:56 AM
Iain Bryson to Kees de Vries
Kees,
Hope you are having a fine Dutch day. It is nice here. Everyone is starting to complain that the weather is cold, but I guess that is how it goes. Interesting how the 'news' sets the agenda for everyone's life on some level... Getting ready to go to the library to write a couple of things and probably get lost in a couple of books, but never enough time. That is the way of the USA. Stop at Dunkin Donuts for your 'fuel' and find ways to get minutes back by texting or maybe tweeting while driving or maybe going 67 MPH instead of 65, or maybe 90. Agata and Adelle are in Poland; would love to get them, but will soon enough.
    Well, I gotta get ready so I should be brief: The pharmacy is an issue… So, now I have to keep figuring it out, and I am hoping to talk to Agata soon and have a bit of a conference....I just have to get her out of the "I miss you sooo much" mood. "

"love you
Wed, Oct 6, 2010, 1:43 PM
Iain Bryson to Agata Bryson"

"Thu, Oct 7, 2010, 2:11 PM
Iain Bryson to Agata Bryson
i love you. i just want us together"

"Thu, Oct 7, 2010, 5:34 PM
Agata Bryson to me
I love you more and I want exactly the same more than you can imagine. I need you every second of every day. Just remember that we are doing something very pecial for our family-that's the only thing that keeps me going. I am proud of you and I love you.
Agata"

"Thu, Oct 7, 2010, 10:58 PM
Iain Bryson to Agata Bryson
love you more. can you skype tomorrow? 10 or just let me know and i will figure it out....or if not possible then saturday. be happy. thinking of you always"

"Fri, Oct 8, 2010, 6:28 AM
Agata Bryson to me
No I love you more. I can skype but at 11 am your time bc at 10 am your time we have a family dinner every day and I don't want distractions. Let me know if it works for you and if not then definitely Saturday. You and Adelle make me the happiest woman in the whole universe. I am thinking of you every second of every day and pray that we will be together very soon. But am also excited about this journey we are on bc we are working towards something so pecial. We love you. Kisses.
Agata"

"Fri, Oct 8, 2010, 7:47 AM
Iain Bryson to Agata Bryson
11 is good baby. talk to you soon. have a good dinner. the universe.....what about gilesse 581 - that new planet we could live on soon. google that and help me pick out some land. it is supposed to be perfect weather. love you"

"Fwd: pics
Fri, Oct 8, 2010, 6:21 AM
Agata Bryson to me
Attachments"

**"Adelle PL
Fri, Oct 8, 2010, 6:17 AM
Agata Bryson to me, Mom, Dad
Attachments"**

**"Sat, Oct 9, 2010, 8:30 AM
Agata Bryson to me**
Good morning love:
I love you more and I want to find a planet that I can live on only with you and Adelle!
Our crazy aunt had a surgery last night-they removed some [expletive] from her uterus. We are taking shifts at the hospital so someone is there with her at all times and someone is with Adelle keeping her away from the bs. I just got back from mine and am taking Adelle out for an adventure. I am sorry I didn't get a chance to send you the update but I am working on it in my head and writing my notes. I should be back in 2-3 hours with her and probably will have to bring my aunt some books and stuff tonight but will keep you posted. Adelle and I might go horseback riding tomorrow. She is very excited. I will write to you as soon as I can. Remember how much I love you and how much I grow thanks to you and that there isn't anything more important to me than our family. Have a great Saturday. We love you. Everyone says hi. Kisses my everything. Your wifey.
Agata"

**"Sat, Oct 9, 2010, 8:44 AM
Iain Bryson to Agata Bryson**
hope everyone is doing well....relax and remember you are wonderful. i had [expletive] from my uterus removed as well. update when you can. Don't feel pressure...just do it when you can and at your pace. if you are working you will get it done. if you feel you have to, you will tend to draw a blank. horseback riding sounds good. love you more"

"Sat, Oct 9, 2010, 4:47 PM
Agata Bryson to me
I am going to bed-exhausted after such a busy night and day. Aunt is better but in a lot of pain and the rest is happy the surgery went well. Talk to you soon. I love you from all of my heart. You are my world. Your wife. Agata"

"Sat, Oct 9, 2010, 6:20 PM
Iain Bryson to Agata Bryson
baby. take it easy. just do and think about one thing at a time. you will get more done and enjoy what you are doing...(links to games with children, etc.)... love you and will look on skype tomorrow."

"Sun, Oct 10, 2010, 5:22 PM
Agata Bryson to me
Attachments"

"Sun, Oct 10, 2010, 5:32 PM
Agata Bryson to me
Attachments
I LOVE YOU!!!"

"More pics
Sun, Oct 10, 2010, 5:23 PM
Agata Bryson to me
Attachments"

"Mon, Oct 11, 2010, 8:46 AM
Iain Bryson to Agata Bryson
u guys are beautiful. is there a good time we can talk tomorrow?
what is your parent's number so i can get a sti [long distance phone] card? any news on anything? miss you"

"Mon, Oct 11, 2010 at 8:53 AM
Agata Bryson wrote: 0048918 ▮▮▮▮
Agata"

CHAPTER 20

" CRAZY ROAD"

I knew she wasn't well, but I assumed she was just experiencing minor hiccups. She became more and more distant, and it became difficult to communicate. I could tell that she wasn't focusing or paying attention, and I sensed that she had slipped back into whatever had caused her to "forget" to pay the rent and the power bill; it felt like I was losing her at times, and it frightened me.

"Mon, Oct 11, 2010, 9:03 AM
Iain Bryson to Agata Bryson
everytime we speak, you go down that crazy road. you can't stop it. your mind wanders there and then becomes obsessed. we get nothing done. this is the case for our whole relationship except when we talk and you listen and we listen to each other."

"Mon, Oct 11, 2010, 11:15 AM
Iain Bryson to Agata Bryson
i really need to know how you are doing. stop getting so upset all of the time. it is the same cycle and also the same one you used over the summer except that one was an extreme. we have to make steps together or i have to come back there and we can try later. there is no point in me being here if you are going to only be there. it cannot work."

"Mon, Oct 11, 2010, 11:27 AM
Agata Bryson to me
I am doing OK except that I miss you so terribly much, that I don't know when I will get the [expletive] visa and will be able to fly to US and finally be in your arms and working on things hand in hand with you and my anemia stuff. On top of that it is really hard when you get upset with me every time we talk. You get so frustrated. I really am working hard on getting things done on this end and I do everything I can to help us out. It is upsetting when you tell me over and over that I do things the wrong way or I have a wrong attitude or I don't do enough. I am working right now on an update that I will update daily for you and I really hope that we can stop being upset for no reason. I love you.
Agata"

"Mon, Oct 11, 2010, 12:12 PM
Iain Bryson to Agata Bryson
missing each other is a given in this situation. we need to keep going. it is like the weather...not going to change right now. i miss you too. the visa is something we cant change right now. why worry about things you have zero control over. you need to tell me about the 'anemia stuff' and stop being low. i do not get upset. you do not understand that we have to do this [expletive] and you always wait to the last minute with everything. then it becomes an issue....this is the case with everything. you don't need to work or work hard. it is what you are doing other than taking care of adelle. do it. now you are all frustrated and stressed out for

no reason. there is nothing except your daughter which can make you go a few days without progress on this [expletive] and as far as i know she is fine. are you working hard? should you be working hard? once again, i don't nnneeed or want a daily update. i want quality updates. if you are doing work, you will have them for me. if not, you will not. if you cram i will know. you have to make it your job without the stress, which is how life should be in general. love you too"

"Mon, Oct 11, 2010, 12:21 PM
Agata Bryson to me
I Love you too much. And I know you are right and that I sometimes go nuttso but it's because I want to be with you now not tomorrow or in a month. I am working on not being a nut job but it's hard without your cuddles and your arms. I love you my other basket!
Agata"

"Mon, Oct 11, 2010, 10:54 PM
Iain Bryson to Agata Bryson
tulip dew,
i love you. Going to bed soon. Want to tweet you so [expletive] bad. The thing you sent is a good start baby but see where you can go from there. Take that [expletive] and evolve it into something that has more information, something which will tell us more. you will know when you get too far and cannot refine it further, but i don't think anyone ever gets there unless they decide they are there. I am fixing up a room in the school. Just started but it is big and i can work there. Have to call the staffing service for New London, and a couple other schools tomorrow to see when my appointment is; they called today but i had the phone off. Nothing in the mail yet. You need to spend a certain amount of time thinking only about this [expletive]. Nothing else, no distractions, no people interrupting. You will think of a reason to stop or a reason why you are done or can't do anymore unless you do that. Going to go to Fishtown again soon and find a place for a new log cabin. Gotsta go to bed honey. Been reading a lot working and seeing a friend here and there. Love you too much"

"baby...how r u? can you talk at 7 est tomorrow? Love yyou
Tue, Oct 12, 2010, 3:36 PM
Iain Bryson to Agata Bryson"

"Tue, Oct 12, 2010, 4:00 PM
Agata Bryson to me
Hey love:
Just got back from my fitness and a swimming session. It was a beautiful day so Adelle and I after breakfast headed out looking for a lot of adventures and we were out all day long. I am good. Still feeling the anemia and the medicine side effects but trying to not let it stop me. Adelle had an amazing day outside and fell asleep in a second after bath. It was good for me too. We try to use every day to do something special and it helps that I drive again ;) I hope you had a good day. I am working on some visa info for you. I contacted the unemployment today again and they said the payment will be made tomorrow but it might take few days to clear in our bank. They wouldn't tell me how much it will be for some reason. I am also working on all the other money sources daily to check in with them and monitor the progress. I definitely can skype tomorrow 7am your time. I love you from all of my heart and the thought of being in your arms keeps me going. Loads of kisses everywhere. Yes [marital talk] :* LOVE YOU! Wifey"

"Tue, Oct 12, 2010, 8:31 PM
Iain Bryson to Agata Bryson
thanks for the update....glad you are good and busy with adelle. wish i could hug you and help you to feel better. take care of yourself....we NEED you. we got a car....98 volvo s70 black with gray leather. will talk to you in the morning. went to a political debate with my dad. have to work on insurance and get ready for the interview in the morning. the 'warehouse' school room is going good. i will save a space for you and dellinski. love you"

"Wed, Oct 13, 2010, 7:36 AM
Agata Bryson to me
Honey bee: just wanted to let you know that [it] is a beautiful day and Adelle and I are on an adventure. Ttys. Love you loads. Your girls."

* * *

My mom told me that your mom had been trying to call me on the house phone all day. She indicated that your mom seemed scared and frantic. I immediately called her, and she stated that she was going to the hospital because of anemia. She seemed terrified, and I wanted to hold her, but she was too far away. I tried to calm her down and tell her just to take it one step at a time, to see what the hospital had to say. There wasn't much more that I could do from where I was except to seriously consider jumping on a plane right away to get back to her, but I felt that this would be to our detriment.

I wanted to get her to a doctor in either The Netherlands or the United States. I didn't think much of Polish doctors, and I wanted a doctor that I could also speak with. She was falling apart, again, I didn't like it one bit, but for now it was out of my hands. I assumed that whatever it was that was going on with your mom stemmed from the environment she was in, but I had no idea what that could possibly be. That was the only thing that had changed... so her environment was causing her to fall apart; I knew that I had to get back to her as soon as possible.

"Thu, Oct 14, 2010, 12:37 PM
Agata Bryson to me
Iain:
I have been in a hospital all day and had all kinds of test to try to figure out what is up with me."

"Thu, Oct 14, 2010, 4:21 PM
Agata Bryson to me
Iain:
I have been in the hospital all day because the doctor here wants to be on a safe side and check me for other things than anemia because the medication doesn't seem to work very well. I feel fine in general I just have not so good blood results and she is trying to figure out why. I have episodes of fainting and I get really weak sometimes and she wants to make sure it is nothing worst than anemia. I do take care of myself, I eat healthy, exercise and meditate. When I got back I wanted to do some work with Adelle I gave her a bath and put her to bed. She is doing great. I do not let her see me feeling unwell and she doesn't hear about it either. I feel a little drained after all the tests and blood work but I am going to try and do some work... I love you. Agata"

"Fri, Oct 15, 2010, 6:52 AM
Agata Bryson to me
I just got back with Adelle, we spent the whole morning outside looking for adventures. It is my grandma's Bday today so we are having dinner at her place. I am feeling OK. I am waiting for money from unemployment and I can transfer money to your ING account just let me know how much. Called unemployment and they said again the payment was made should be in ABN account today. I will keep you posted. Let me know how much you need me to transfer and once it's there i can make a payment directly to your ING. Let me know what else I can do today. I am checking with the PO regarding the package and it looks ok but they couldn't give me a day of when it will get there. I hope you are OK. I love you and miss YOU. Agata"

"Fri, Oct 15, 2010, 8:03 PM
Iain Bryson to Agata Bryson
i am working again tomorrow. i need your help. i am not sure how many times i have to say that. as of now, i plan on being in Amsterdam sometime next week so i can meet with you, get you going and hopefully come back here to get things moving. it is a shame we have to waste money because you cant get past the 'how' 'why' 'what' issues you always have. borderline personality disorder is the cause. it is also why you are sick without me. you need to be getting counselling, not back in the middle of the place where all of the issues came from. i love you"

Of course, I didn't know for sure that it was borderline personality disorder, but that is what we both thought her symptoms looked like before when she had sought out help because "my husband thinks I'm crazy." I didn't care what it was exactly; I just wanted us to be together, and for the love that was in our family to continue fixing whatever it was. Love heals; I had seen it before, and I wanted to get back at it. This was unacceptable. I absolutely hated that my wife was suffering, and I was frustrated with her that it seemed to be seeping back in.

Her physical health also seemed to be deteriorating with the frequency of her migraines increasing along with new issues that required pills and injections, though I was never informed of a diagnosis or what those medicines were. I was completely left in the dark, and it terrified me. I wanted to get her to an American doctor as soon as possible.

"agatka, where r u
Sat, Oct 16, 2010, 7:04 AM
Iain Bryson to Agata Bryson"

"Sat, Oct 16, 2010, 7:13 AM
Agata Bryson to me
I'm heading to the doctor for some shots. She thinks it might work better than the pills did. I worked since i got up and i will send an update when i get back."

"Sat, Oct 16, 2010, 7:15 AM
Agata Bryson to me
At the doctors waiting for my shot. Will be on the cpu in 30 mins i think."

"Sat, Oct 16, 2010, 9:09 AM
Agata Bryson to me
Iain:

I just got back from the shot. The doctor hopes that it works better than the pills and hopefully all my symptoms will go away after this. Adelle and I are going back to The Hague tomorrow. We have the bus tomorrow night so will be home Monday morning...

Regarding the visa I have been preparing for the following steps and requesting documents, filling out forms, getting more pics, etc. I had to request an extended version of my birth certificate and have it translated by a certified translator, I also requested my no arrest records from the police in Poland and in the Netherlands. I have filled out the forms that will be needed so we have them ready. I am working on my vaccination report now and translating it into English because at the medical exam before I get the visa they will need it and I might have to get some more vaccinations so trying to figure out which I might need if any.

I was calculating the bills that we will have at the end of the month and now that we don't have the day care it should be: 135 euros for gas, 150 euros for cells and 50 euros for cable which is 335 euros plus the credit card. With what we have now and the unemployment money that I hope will come on Monday we should have between 500-800 euros plus 1000 credit card depending what the final bill of the credit card will be.

I was looking at some jobs for me in the US but I am not sure if it is a good idea to apply now when I'm not there yet, what do you think?

I have been applying for jobs in the NL [The Netherlands] because I have to send a weekly updates to the work coach in order to get the unemployment money for us and the requirement is 5 applications a week and a report including all the emails etc to him weekly.

My dad has the Bridge World Championship first few days of November and says I will get paid for any help I can give him including the hosting of the main opening of the championship. It wouldn't be much (probably 100-200 euros) but always something. What do you think?

Adelle has been working with me daily on writing, reading and counting. She is so bright and has the best memory ever. She teaches everyone English and ABCs and days and months and numbers. She is really happy and has a lot of adventures and fun with me and my parents and sister. She says goodnight to you every night and we talk about you daily in a very positive way. We think for example about the next adventure we are all 3 going to go on and it really excites her. Besides she 'reads' books from the pictures and tells a story from them every day.

I will go have a snack and some tea and put some ice on my butt and will be back here on the cpu working and figuring stuff out.

I hope you are having a good day.
I love you,
a"

"Sat, Oct 16, 2010, 11:17 AM
Agata Bryson to me
Babe:

Just wanted to let you know that I need to take a break from the cpu and go have dinner and go for my shot. I will be back in couple hours I think if not earlier and will log on. My eyes are killing me from the monitor need to take my lenses off for a little bit. I will talk to you soon. Love you.
Agata"

"Sat, Oct 16, 2010, 7:37 PM
Iain Bryson to Agata Bryson
thanks for the letter. i will answer the questions tomorrow. i love you so much. i just want your help. i cannot stand being apart. i love you and will talk to you soon"

"Sun, Oct 17, 2010, 3:11 PM
Agata Bryson to me
Baby:

As I told you in the text Kamila-the girl from Stargard that I worked with at Aramco and sometimes I was riding to work with) called me to say that her parents are driving to The Hague and she knew I was in Stargard and wanted to check if I need a ride and I thought...I will check on the apartment and Ally and see what else I can get done in that one day tomorrow and a half or less of Tuesday and I will be back in PL Tuesday night...OK love I got to get ready, I'm just bringing my purse but need a lot of sandwiches for the night and wear some comfy clothes. I love you and will call you tomorrow from home or we can skype as well. I love you and miss you. Kisses, your wifey.
Agata"

CHAPTER 21

"YOU ARE MY DREAMS COME TRUE"

"Mon, Oct 18, 2010, 5:35 AM
Agata Bryson to me
Hey love:
I arrived safe and sound to The Hague. We got your cards! Thank you love it was so sweet and thoughtful of you! Adelle will love it!... I think I will be back around 10-11 am your time. I love you and long for your arms and cuddles and kisses. Have a great day baby. Your girls love you more than you can imagine. TTYS. Your wifey.
Agata"

It sounded like she left you in Poland, which I didn't like. *But what is there to worry about?* I thought. She seemed to be doing better, she was positive, and I couldn't control everything from where I was. I had to trust that it was all going to work out, and that she knew what she was doing.

"Mon, Oct 18, 2010, 6:10 PM
Agata Bryson to me
Babe:
I have been waiting to see if you will be online but it's getting late and I am heading for bed. Will check in first thing in the am. Have a good night. I love you. a
Agata"

"Tue, Oct 19, 2010, 12:57 AM
Iain Bryson to Agata Bryson
love you. hope all is good . been working. will tell you about it soon. sleeping now. late. love you"

"Tue, Oct 19, 2010, 9:04 AM
Iain Bryson to Agata Bryson
love you. just working and hoping you are doing the same so we can all get together. miss you guys terribly. have an interview at 2. been at the school and Fishtown and writing and reading and [expletive] like that. busy and need you. not sure if i will be here 10-11. got stuff to do. will be back this afternoon to get ready before going to nl [New London]."

"Tue, Oct 19, 2010, 10:20 AM
Agata Bryson to me
Love you too so much hun. I am getting ready to return to Stargard tonight. I sent you another pecial package. They said 5-12 days. I went to Belasting to make sure that we receive the little money from rent and health insurance help on the 20th and to the unemployment to see where the [expletive] our money is. It was paid yesterday I saw it in the system and Friday the latest should be in the ABN account. I went to the town hall to get my no arrest records going as well. I also made an appointment with the financial advisor for the 16th

of november. The heater in our house is not working so there is no heat, we have hot water but no heat it has been a freezing 2 days for me. I checked and it is like 58 degrees in the house. I am trying to sort it out and get it fixed. It's a migraine day today-so have been struggling a little but trying not to think about it. I need the info for the publishers/magazines from you when you get a chance. I love you. I need you so much and I cannot wait the moment i will be in your arms again. Good luck at your interview. You will do great i know it. I love you even more. You are my world!!!!
Agata"

"Tue, Oct 19, 2010, 11:28 AM
Iain Bryson to Agata Bryson
already going back. quick trip. thanks for doing that. how was everything. went to Fishtown this morning and used the chain saw a bit while writing and walking in the woods. hung some caution tape in a few areas next to my signs. been going there a few times a week to clean think and plan some [expletive]. thinking of some tree houses and bridges and cabins. would be good to put up some pecial thing like that for a business for the kids. nh has [expletive] like that. google monkey and new hampshire. and maybe kids too... why is the heater not working? is ally ok? tell monia [babysitter/cat sitter] i love my kitty. u need to get those migraines fixed baby/ i am sorry you have one. the school is going slowly but surely. been taking our stuff there and setting up a work area...cleaning out some [expletive] and getting the walls ready too/been working off and on with Eugene, the guy from Fishtown. went to a few of kaylah's soccer games/ Bree has the police test in november. kyle got a job with the utility company climbing poles (like you like to do) and fixing wires and [expletive]. what you know about buffalo bill. nothing so chill [expletive] ho you better [expletive] hold still. eminem
we need to talk so we can go over the figures and time things together and so i can hear you and we can talk and figure out when we will see each other. i love you. at dunkin using their wi fi. off to the next episode"

"Tue, Oct 19, 2010, 2:32 PM
Iain Bryson to Agata Bryson
agatka,
how r u feeling? was it nice to be back in the Netherlands for a bit? how is the blood [expletive] going? i just stopped up at my mom's. i had an appointment at 2 again for the nl [New London] schools but they [expletive] it up once again....incompetant people..anyway, is tomorrow at 9... went to fishtown and then to the school with dunkin doughnuts in between where i sent you the other email. how is the headache? sorry baby. so if you could put your questions in order so i can respond without having to take notes that would be helpful. what have you been up to? thanks for your help. the visa: hope we hear something else soon. do you know anything i dont
car. we have a volvo sedan/ nice car with leather heated seats/ we owe my mom who bought it on her own after i told her we couldnt afford one yet. i guess the time for using the jeep was up according to george. writing: i need your help. i can and am writing about everything but not sure what to do. i could get a couple of samples somewhere. i am not good at that part...how is my [expletive] kitty
i need to pick up squeeze my Adelle avery
working on the school which seems to be our warehouse./ going well but a lot of work
worked a few days with eugene on a basement in pawcatuck. not bad but gave all the money to my mom. the car was too much and we had taxes insurance bleepity blah.
i got a sti card today. let me know when i can get you love you"

"Wed, Oct 20, 2010, 5:55 AM
Agata Bryson to me
Sweety:
I got back very late at night and just got up an hour ago and have been with Adelle. She loves the ladybug card from you. She is reading it to everyone and doesn't leave her sight. You made us such a lovely surprise-thank you. I will have a snack and some coffee and take a shower and will be back to write you more. I love you from all of my heart and soul. Kisses.
Agata"

"Wed, Oct 20, 2010, 11:43 AM
Agata Bryson to me
My everything:
I have spent the whole day working with Adelle and playing. We just finished dinner and it is a nice day so my mom and I are taking Adelle for a nice walk looking for adventures before bath and bed. I will go online when I put her down around 2-3 pm your time and will write to you about the trip to NL and the updates. I

love you so much it hurts and having you and Adelle makes me the happiest girl in the world. I love our family so much and cannot wait for us 4 to be together. Love you, wifey
Agata"

"Wed, Oct 20, 2010, 5:14 PM
Agata Bryson to me
My handsome hubby:
It was so nice to hear your beautiful voice on the phone! I got back from my fitness, ate an apple, took a quick shower and am ready for bed. Still really tired from the trip back and forth in 2.5 days but I am glad I had an opportunity to do it for free, check on few things for us and get few things done. I am feeling better, since I had the shots I didn't faint and I'm crossing my fingers it's all set but most of the time I try not to think about it at all.. I have another check up on Monday. How are you feeling? Are you happy? Are you eating and taking care of yourself? Remember how much we need you preferably in 100% shape ;D

It was nice to be back in The Hague because I checked and got done few things but it is not our home or our place on earth so I was happy I'm there only for 1 night. and nowhere is home when us 3 are not there and I cannot wait to have a place we can call home asap. Sorry about your appointment I know how annoying it is I have been dealing with the dutch government for the past month and a half and I am amazed I didn't bomb them all yet ;) My headache is gone but was there even after I took some medicine the whole way back from NL to PL. I just cannot wait to see the real neurologist in the US. It is not normal for me to have to suffer so many times a month and not really having meds for it that work. I am trying to minimize the stimulants that can cause migraines and I am eating healthy, exercising, meditating and I am trying very hard to work on the stress levels and how I get all worked up and worried sometimes over things that I have no control over. I will send another email with the questions for your writing so it is easier and you don't have to take notes ;p I am still working on the chart and I am trying to be creative.

What have I been up to? I have been getting up with Adelle, having breakfast, playing, cleaning up, going for walks and adventures, getting stuff ready for dinner, helping my mom with dinner once she comes back from work, having dinner with my Adelle, my parents and my sister and her BF sometimes, doing stuff with Adelle, fitness or pool, and bedtime most of the days. I try to do something special with her every day and we do stuff really pecial on weekends like horseback riding, aqua park, etc. I also have become my dads assistant, the guy is so unorganized that he thanks me 100 times when I organize his work for him and all he has to do is write, besides all he knows how to do on the cpu is write ;) nothing else including saving ;D One day my mom and i moved the bedroom to the last room and adas room to the middle when my dad was adventuring with Adelle. It was hell of a workout. You are welcome for my help. Thank you for all you are doing for our family. I am so proud of you and the progress you are making that there are no words to express it. I love you and am so [expletive] lucky that you are mine.

The next step for the visa according to my research is that the NVC (National Visa center) will mail you an invoice for the fee for affidavit of support and then require us to send the affidavit of support documents. I hope we will get it very soon because I need to be with you so badly on daily basis but I think we wont ever have to be apart for so long and the thought of the moment when we will achieve our goal keeps me going. I saw the car on google and it looks great for us at the moment and I am happy you have your own car and don't need to rely on george's moods. How much money do we owe your mom? I will def help you with the publishing stuff see my email about it which i will send after this one. You cannot imagine how proud I am of you about the concerta and how great you are dealing with it. I am also happy you will see Rocco [Dr. Rocco Russo] soon because he cares about you and I know you will figure out if it is worth taking something or not. I hope my packages come to you really but if not I am sure we will be fine and will figure something out.

I am so proud of you Iain avery! You are truly inspirational on what a journey you went through and that you came out of the journey stronger than ever. It melts my heart. Ally is great but Monia wants some money for the time she is watching her now. I think like 100 euros for all of it so I don't think its bad, what do you think? Adelle is really happy here with all the people around that love her and it just reassures me that being in CT with all her family and cousins will be great for her. She still sleeps with your pic and walks with her ladybug card in hand. So what exactly is going to be in the school? Your pecial place? I am really proud of you that you are working, just promise me that you are taking care of yourself and your back, taking breaks, stretching, etc? I can be by the phone whenever you are available but maybe my parents phone is better bc it will give u more minutes from the sti than my cell. Just let me know. I know you have your appointment at 9 so maybe 12 or 3 pm? Just let your girl know, OK? I love you more than I ever will be able to express it with words. I love you Iain Avery Bryson and I always will. You are my second half and my world. Going to sleep dream about you.. Have a good night too and dream about me too! Kisses. Your so in love wifey :D"

"Thu, Oct 21, 2010, 12:32 AM
Iain Bryson to Agata Bryson
i love you my princess"

"Thu, Oct 21, 2010, 4:17 PM
Agata Bryson to me
Honey bee:
I'm heading to bed. I see you are out and about. I love you so much and you are my world and the reason I am the happiest girl in the world. Good night and talk to you tomorrow. Love you loads handsome. Kisses. Agata"

"Sat, Oct 23, 2010, 5:23 AM
Agata Bryson to me
Hey love:
Heading out for grocery shopping with my mom. I'm still practicing driving in Europe! It's a nightmare. Ada is taking Adelle outside looking for adventures and then back here for dinner. I will check in in few hours. Remember how much I love you. My belly hurts-taking a 1 day break from fitness today. Have a great Saturday. Talk to you soon. Love you. Kisss. Wifey
Agata"

"Sat, Oct 23, 2010, 2:47 PM
Iain Bryson to Agata Bryson
hey gorgeous. at the library in nl [New London] with my dad printing out something i need for my three rivers application. miss you guys terribly. getting a lot done...i think though it would be nice to be able to see what you think on a daily basis and it's too hard from across the atlantic. what did the publisher people tell you exactly? who did you talk to? i have a good book on it as well but i want to get something started on that this week. love you and will get a sti card soon"

"Oct 23, 2010, 5:28 PM
Agata Bryson to me
Hey lovey dovey:
It has been a crazy busy day. Morning & breakfast with Adelle, grocery shopping with my mom, dinner, animal farm with Adelle, my parents are out since 5pm for some event, had supper with Adelle, bath & bedtime, then my sister came we watched a movie, she left, I took a bath and am checking my emails.
How was your day? I hope every day is good for you, I know it will never be 100% good bc we are physically not together but the thought of us being soon is ecstatic. I love you so much! You are my dreams come true and I love you more than words can say. We miss you so much too but remember why we are doing it and that we will always be with you in your heart, soul, mind, everything. The thought of us is like we are with you bc we love you! I'm so proud of you and all the hard work that you do for our family. It makes me love you even more although it is already impossible to love you more. Does it make sense?
The publishers told me that I need to give them subjects of what you are writing and some samples and what kind it is, etc. I spoke to few of them both publishers and magazines, do you want their names? Remember how pecial you are and how pecial and like one in the world our lil family is. You rock and you are my rock. I love you."

"Sun, Oct 24, 2010, 5:24 AM
Agata Bryson to me
Love:
We are heading in an hour to the mall in Szczecin for small shopping. Ada needs a jacket and my mom shoes and Adelle needs warm boots and everything is way cheaper there. We will be back soon. I think by 9-10 am your time. Let me know what your plan is for today. I love you loads. Kisses, your wifey.
P.S. Writing [expletive]
P.S. 1. Money update follows
P.S. 2. Love you like crazy!!!
Agata"

"Sun, Oct 24, 2010, 10:05 AM
Iain Bryson to Agata Bryson
love you babe. woke up at moms. slept at the school two nights ago...working. gotta load up our car with more [expletive]. i forgot about all my uconn papers....found em last night. just working on jobs....want to send the app to all the community colleges tomorrow. old lyme schools tomorrow as well. and working on some writing samples. starting to get a little cold here which makes it tougher to go and stay at the school. thanks for the updates. will check back in on the computer. Let's plan a time to talk...not sure when but let me know when you think you will be around. love you"

"I LOVE YOU SO MUCH!!! Thanks to you I am the happiest girl in the world
Sun, Oct 24, 2010, 5:56 PM
Agata Bryson to me
Off to fitness. Love u. Will be back after 4pm ur time. I hope u had a good day. Love u some more"

"Mon, Oct 25, 2010, 5:58 AM
Agata Bryson to me
Hey lovey dovey:

How are you? How was your weekend? How are you feeling? I put Adelle down last night and watched 'Into the wild' the Sean Penn movie with my dad. My mom had a migraine so was helping her out too. I had a great morning with Adelle, we had a picnic on the ground eating breakfast and we went out for a walk and to get some meat for dinner. Then when she was doing painting and working on her sticker book I cleaned a little.

My dad is working on the cpu all day today for the local elections in couple weeks writing pamphlets for candidates and I am helping him get organized and use the cpu. In a little bit he will take Adelle out for their daily adventure into the green parts of the city and I am cooking dinner today bc my mom still has the migraine. Then at 10 am your time dinner and at 1pm your time I have my fitness-cant wait-had 2 days off bc of the weekend and feel like going really bad. Probably the same over the next couple of days.

On Nov.1st its All Saints Day and everyone with their families go to the graves of their family members so we are doing that. Saturday or Sunday we are going to the aqua park with Adelle. She absolutely loves it. She goes on the biggest slides with me and laughs out loud and says more mommy more! She is really happy, healthy and eats well, she misses you but we have our little things that we do to be closer to you, and we talk a lot. I think she is really happy that she has my parents and my sister and in some way fills the void of not seeing you, and has more people than just mommy to love her and do things with her.

She says dziadzius [grandpa Sławomir] pushes her on a swing harder than mommy but not as hard as my daddy! You are on our minds every single day. We love you and miss you and so proud of you. I cannot wait to have our own place on earth that we will call our home and be there all 3 of us every day. Other than that, I am working in the evenings daily on the NL, visa, moving, living in CT stuff, doing a lot of research and reading, as much as I can. Have the check up today re: anemia so will let you know how that went. I love you hun bun. You are my everything, you know right? TTYS. Loads of kisses. Wifey"

"Mon, Oct 25, 2010, 9:10 AM
Iain Bryson to Agata Bryson
hey coffee cake

trying to get going. doing well...busy and ready for us to be together. drinking coffee and trying to get my community college apps sent out. interview at 2:30 at Borders. need to get some publishing work done but need to do some other [expletive] first i guess. should get a haircut and maybe go to tj maxx but not sure what the day holds yet. we got a gay election here too. and montville is trying to put in a 6.5 M police station, the [expletive] nazis. trying to find my dutch phone, which i think fell out of my pocket in my moms car. i need help with organization. tell your dad this is a temporary setup. love you"

* * *

"FW: Iain Bryson
Tue, Oct 26, 2010, 9:56 AM
Lilly M [Grasso Tech High School] to me, Michele [Norwich Tech High School]
Hey!
You are officially on the list! Gonna start calling you!!!
What subject (background)????"

It took a while for all the paperwork and background checks to go through, but now I had a job as a high school substitute teacher. I was excited to be back in the classroom.

"Off to fitness. Love u. Will be back after 4pm ur time. I hope u had a good day. Love u some more!
Tue, Oct 26, 2010, 1:15 PM
Agata Bryson to me"

"Sweety: I was waiting to see if u 'll be on chat but its getting really late & Im dying after 2hrs of fitness&heading to bed. Love you!!!
Tue, Oct 26, 2010, 5:31 PM
Agata Bryson to me"

"Tue, Oct 26, 2010, 6:07 PM
Iain Bryson to Agata Bryson
love you. no time now. will try to get a sti or at least be on chat tomorrow. have an interview in the afternoon. saw russo [Dr. Rocco Russo]. problem with insurance....etc...gotta deal with it some more tomorrow. the cards aren't working. can you let me know what is up. love you"

"Wed, Oct 27, 2010, 3:11 AM
Agata Bryson to me
love you too so much. let me know whats your plan today. I'm home most of the day. have fitness at 1-2pm your time. what did Russo say? Whats the problem with the insurance? i called the credit card they said everything is OK. i have sent you an update about money. love you.
Agata"

"Wed, Oct 27, 2010, 7:14 AM
Iain Bryson to Agata Bryson
could you move some from abn to ing until i figure out the issue. or try. i love you
going to smakosh for breakfast with my mom. gotta get russo a letter today and deal with insurance and pharmacy. got a call from grasso so gotta figure out the three jobs now as i have an interview this afternoon at the friendship school for working with an autistic kid as well as borders tomorrow. love you and talk soon"

"I love you baby! Have a great day :*
Fri, Oct 29, 2010, 6:42 AM
Agata Bryson to me"

CHAPTER 22

"THIS IS PRIVATE PROPERTY"

My dad rented out some of the space in the school, and he was in the process of evicting a tenant I hadn't yet met by the name of Mike. Apparently, he had been breaking things and leaving messes in areas of the building that he was not legally allowed to access. My dad had been taking pictures of the damage to show the judge at the pending eviction hearing. He had also rigged up a temporary wall to attempt to block the evictee from areas of the building that he was not supposed to enter.

Mike was coming over to pick up some of his belongings, and my dad was hypervigilant, as if he was expecting trouble. Though it seemed to me that my dad was blowing the situation out of proportion, I decided to stop what I was doing in my office to give him some moral support. I doubted that the guy was as unreasonable as he suggested, and I figured that my presence alone would help my dad to feel better and alleviate some of his anxiety. I tucked my gun into my pants and covered it with my shirt, thinking nothing of it, as I had been walking everywhere in the building with the gun since I had started spending time in the office.

For some reason my dad had left the back door propped open, thereby making his blockade wall entirely useless. I approached the noise and found my dad and Mike in a heated argument, in the middle of where my dad did not want him to be. Mike was probably about my age at the time, early thirties, and it was obvious that he was a body builder. My impression of him was that he was not that bright, and I believed that I could talk some sense into him if my dad would only stop arguing back and forth. Mike smirked at the back-and-forth banter, and both of them quickly escalated into yelling at each other. In an attempt to antagonize, Mike roamed around touching my dad's belongings.

My dad moved to get in between Mike and whatever it was that he was touching, and they locked up with each other like a pair of sumo wrestlers, both hands on the other's shoulders. They staggered around a few steps like drunk dancing partners. Mike easily could have thrown him to the ground if he had wanted to.

"Dad, don't touch him," I barked, "Dad, get your hands off of him, don't touch him!" I put my hands on my dad from behind in order to reinforce my words, and also to be close to him if the situation were to escalate any further.

They eventually separated, and I felt some relief. My dad announced that he was going to call the police, and he exited the building, leaving Mike and me alone. Standing there with this intruder made me feel awkward and vulnerable. *Where is my dad? Why did he leave me here alone with this guy? Why didn't he call the police from right here? What am I supposed to do now?*

"Ok, Mike, you need to leave too," I instructed. "This is private property, and I am telling you to leave now. Go on, get out!"

He began messing around with the furniture, acting as if he might damage something, ignoring me and the fact that I was now yelling at him to leave.

"Get out, get off this property now!" I repeated, enough to make him stop what he was doing and face me. He stared back at me in full defiance of my attempt to secure this private property.

I stepped back a couple of feet to gain some distance from him, I drew the gun, and I pointed it at his head. "Get the [expletive] off of my property now!" I belted sternly again.

Instead of reacting in the manner I expected, he laughed and jeered, "Go ahead and shoot me, do you think I've never had a gun pointed at me before? Go ahead and shoot me!" he taunted.

Oh boy, now I knew that I was dealing with a total loon. Not only was he confirming my original impression that he was a dummy, but now I thought that there might be some steroid brain damage as well.

I immediately decided that I had to get rid of the gun, that if I didn't this guy might decide to rush at me and try to take it. He had a crazy look in his eye, and I didn't want any part of this nonsense anymore, nor did I want the distraction from my work in the other room.

Right away, I realized that I should not have pulled it out at all, and that if I had it to do over again, I would've gone outside and waited for the police with my dad. My goal had been to restore the tranquility of my space as quickly as possible and return to what I had been doing, but I should have been more patient and not have unnecessarily escalated the encounter with a firearm.

Taking a couple more steps back, I turned and jogged away, looking over my shoulder to make sure that he wasn't following me. When I got to a room in the back, I unloaded the gun and placed it in a large Rubbermaid container, and then returned to where Mike was to wait for my dad and the police. He was screaming to his girlfriend on the phone that he just had a gun in his face.

My mind scrambled for a moment as I decided the story I would tell the police: *He pushed me, causing me to lose my balance and my gun to be exposed. He saw that I had a gun, and he had already been aggressive with my dad and me. Therefore, I had to make sure that I could get myself and my gun out of the situation, and the best way to do that was to do so at gun point to preclude him from attacking me again, and potentially disarming me.*

Today I would not lie or put myself in this situation to begin with, but at the time I saw it as the best possible version of events for me. I was unsure of the exact laws in Connecticut for defending your property, and I really just wanted him to leave so that I could go back to work.

Two officers arrived and I explained to them what had happened, giving them the revised details and informing them that the gun was stored safely in the other room. They understood, and they said that what I had done was not a problem, even though Mike was right there yelling and pretending to be afraid. I don't know if they intended to arrest him or not at this time; I made no suggestion to the police that he should be arrested, but just gave them the "facts" in a calm and collected manner.

"Yes, what you did was perfectly reasonable," one of the officers indicated. I walked them over to the other room and allowed them to retrieve the gun and the magazine; the two officers seemed to be more interested in the building than in anything else.

And then the lieutenant entered the building. He came in after speaking with my dad and Mike's irate girlfriend. I could hear her yelling outside from where I was in the middle of the building. He told the other two officers that he had to make the arrest because a gun was involved, and my heart sank for a moment.

They cuffed me, and I rode to the police station with one of the first responding officers. They held me in a cell for an hour or two, and I had to talk to some detectives, but I left later that day with my dad who showed up with a bondsman. My court date was a few days later, and I knew that the charges would eventually be dropped. The three of us would be coming here as a family soon anyway, and it didn't matter that I had to make a court appearance at some future date. I didn't deal with this issue again until January because it soon plummeted to the bottom of my priority list.

* * *

On one evening around this time, your mom didn't want to have me talk to you, claiming that you were too tired. I persisted and told her that it was ridiculous for her to say that you were too tired to talk to your dad and she eventually relented. You didn't seem tired, but rather distant and confused, as if your head was spinning or you were stoned. In the middle of our conversation, your grandpa walked into the room behind you and then left. A chill went down my spine; I wasn't sure why, but he had frightened me.

"not sure if you are around tday. going to montville to eat, work and get ready for tomorrow. love you
Sun, Oct 31, 2010, 9:57 AM
Iain Bryson to Agata Bryson"

"Sun, Oct 31, 2010, 5:39 PM
Agata Bryson to me
Hey love:
We had dinner at my grandparents today with Pola and her parents. Then my crazy aunt came. I put Adelle down and took a shower. Now I'm going to read and go to sleep. I hope you had a good day and that your writing is going really well. I miss you so much! It was so amazing to see you on skype and to see you and Adelle talk. She was talking about it even today. I am so proud of you and so in love with you. You are everything to me my other basket. It's All Saints day tomorrow so everyone goes to the graves to light a candle and flowers. Wonder what Adelle will think about that. Good night sweetheart and have a great day at work tomorrow and know that your girls think about you always. I love you!!! Wifey :*"

I went to a Halloween party with my brother, and both of us dressed up as prisoners in orange jump suits. Though the costumes were his choice, I concurred with his decision. I had the chance to try out the uniform I would be wearing if I were to volunteer for prison, and he and I discussed why I thought it would be good for me to experience prison life for a while. Of course, I only wanted to go on a volunteer basis for research; I didn't want a sentence that I couldn't control, as this would mean that I wouldn't know or have any control over when I could hold you again.

"Mon, Nov 1, 2010, 5:49 PM
Agata Bryson to me
Hey love. I have been waiting for you here and working but you are probably out and about working. I am heading to bed it has been a long day. We have been at the cemetery and had dinner at my grandmas, visited with my cousin who just had a baby few months ago, had my crazy aunt over, etc. I hope you had a good day working at Norwich. Write to me and tell me how you are doing and feeling and what's new. Have a good night baby and dream about your girls. We love you so much and there is a surprise on the way to you from us. Let's Skype again soon or over the weekend if we can. Have the championship with my dad 5-6-7th November and a little scared of public speaking. I love you from all of my heart and can't wait to hear your voice. P.S. Which phone # r u using? i tried to call and one was off one no answer. Love you, Wifey Agata"

"agatka. i love you and i need you to stop be happy and get the things done we planned.
Tue, Nov 2, 2010, 3:59 PM
Iain Bryson to Agata Bryson"

"Tue, Nov 2, 2010, 4:10 PM
Agata Bryson to me
Love you too. I'm very happy. Just need to be with you. I'm at fitness. Love you some more. Kisses."

"Tue, Nov 2, 2010, 10:47 PM
Iain Bryson to Brian
http://www.youtube.com/watch?v=RYvfxvDwJxA [video unavailable]
when you coming?
thoughts for today
1. marxist model of the value of human life
2. hypnosis
3. SSR autonomic response
4. perceived high threat stimulus
5. lord of the flies- Golding
Tropic of Cancer - Henry Miller
A Brave New World - Huxley
D.H Lawrence"

I went back to the school to work in my office, and I decided to go up onto the roof. I wasn't there for more than thirty minutes when I saw Mike drive up with several of his friends. I tried to remain out of sight, but he saw me and began yelling at me and flipping me off. I did not want a repeat of what had happened before.

I tried calling my dad, but he didn't answer his phone. I called 911 and explained to the operator what was happening, that I was being threatened again, that there were multiple men acting hostile toward me, that I had been arrested not long ago and did not want any further problems.

"You're calling us for that?" she asked in a condescending tone. "You do not have an emergency. This is not the number to call."

"Yes, it is an emergency. I am being threatened. There are people who appear to want to fight me. I was arrested, and I don't want any problems. I just want to work, and I don't know what is going on."

The police eventually came, making it safe for me to come down off the roof. I explained the situation, but they weren't concerned. Mike and his friends left, and I got back to work.

CHAPTER 23

"I LOVE YOU SOME MORE (LIKE 1)"

"Wed, Nov 3, 2010, 9:29 AM
Iain Bryson to Agata Bryson
Agatka.
I know you miss me. I miss you too. We need to stay on track and stay happy and focused. When we worry we are being counterproductive. It feels like worrying because we care, and we do, but is the typical response, the one our body and minds tend towards and it doesn't work. Just like when we used to get in fights and we later decided to stop and think, that was also a 'normal' response felt right. Try not to react because it feels right or real. That is what we've trained ourselves to do. It is as if there is a right way to do something or that we just accept what our minds are telling us about how to best take care of a situation. whether it is right or not, it is better to reflect on why you feel the need to act react that way. this is true in all situations. It is much easier to test it out with me than with others whose actions you feel are more unpredictable. love you"

"can you send visa infor so i can call them? got called to sub. going now. will talk to you soon. love you
Wed, Nov 3, 2010, 10:01 AM
Iain Bryson to Agata Bryson"

"Wed, Nov 3, 2010, 1:40 PM
Agata Bryson to me
VISA SERVICES/Public Inquiries Division:
202-663-1225
usvisa@state.gov..."

"Wed, Nov 3, 2010, 7:38 PM
Iain Bryson to Agata Bryson
Agatka,
I miss you so much. I am sitting in the room at the [Mohegan] Sun [resort and casino] on the 32nd floor, thinking smiling about how wonderful you and Adelle are.
It is good to have a place which is comfortable where I can just sit, think, read, and write. I just wrote a letter to Russo, which I will print and give to him tomorrow. I tried to call regarding the VISA but will have to call tomorrow as they were closed. I was hoping to get called to Grasso today because they pay 160 a day. I got called by Sprague and waited to see if Grasso would still call. No luck but Sprague called back at ten and I went in. I was in pre school with 3-5 year olds. It was fun with kids Adelle's age but most of all it reminded me how great we are doing how much more advanced she is in every area, including over every five-year-old I met. When I stop to think about you and her, I get overwhelmed with joy. I feel like I am on ecstasy and that I want to cry at the same time. It is powerful goodness that envelops me. Tonight I am working. I am at the desk at the room and deciding whether to go get coffee and maybe a snack downstairs. I will hopefully get a call tomorrow and then I may see Courtney. I love you so [expletive] much my little butterfly"

"Thu, Nov 4, 2010, 12:29 AM
Iain Bryson to Agata Bryson
did you get your card? did you get a chance to look at ARc? can bout changing my ticket as well. / I love you to the core of the earth and back"

"ARC" is the alternative route to teacher certification, a path to being a full-time educator that I qualified for because of my master's degree. This precluded me from having to go through extensive teacher training or coursework.

"Thu, Nov 4, 2010, 6:07 PM
Agata Bryson to me
I got your card. I told u yesterday silly. I am researching the ARC will get a report to you soon. What about your ticket sweety? I hope you had a good day. I miss you so much it hurts when i think about it. I need you and I need us to be together. I want my visa. I am heading to bed. Going to Szczecin tomorrow a.m. for my sister's graduation ceremony with my mom and Adelle. I love you to the times before Jesus and back. Agata"

"Ticket
Fri, Nov 5, 2010, 5:44 PM
Agata Bryson to me
Iain:
I tried to change your ticket and they would not let me change it for you. They said you need to call yourself. The number is below. The reference number for your reservation is: 2FNNNB. I tried to call you multiple times about this but your phones are all not working and I cannot get through, the same yesterday. Let me know how you are. I love you."

"Sat, Nov 6, 2010, 9:47 AM
Agata Bryson to me
Hun: Have the bridge tournament with my dad all day long. Came home to change and eat dinner and heading back. Love you so much!
Agata"

"Sat, Nov 6, 2010, 9:54 AM
Iain Bryson to Agata Bryson
love yu so much. brian is here for the weekend. waiting for him to call"

"Sat, Nov 6, 2010, 11:09 AM
Iain Bryson to Agata Bryson
agatka. stay focused. we can do anything together. remember what dave [Matthews] says ['You and me together could do anything, baby, you and me together, yes, yes…'].
if we start going down paths which are negative, it stunts our progress. skype tomorrow please"

"Sun, Nov 7, 2010, 11:03 PM
Iain Bryson to Agata Bryson
Baby,
It was nice talking to you. It is one of the things i 'need' in my life. i am so excited about things, about us, about what we have and what we are doing and will do.
I have been studying and preparing a book (books). I feel great about it. I wanted to write to you before. i just feel so good about what i am writing elsewhere and don't want to stop because we will be together and we can explain things to each other in person. i am looking at the calendar and figuring out when i can come to see you. we will figure everything out. i need that visa. i love you and miss you so [expletive] much."

"at grasso ....90 minute snow delay....havent seen that in a while
Mon, Nov 8, 2010, 7:54 AM
Iain Bryson to Agata Bryson
love you. working, then going to drop off letter for russo. how are you and have you thought of anything? i saw tickets to amsterdam for 500 yesterday. i will be there this month or for xmas at the latest. i love you guys so [expletive] much"

**"Bridge
Mon, Nov 8, 2010, 5:19 PM
Agata Bryson to me
Attachments"**

**"Mon, Nov 8, 2010, 5:22 PM
Agata Bryson to me**
Sweety:
It was lovely and just great talking to you too. Remember that no matter what I love you from all of my heart and I am your other half. I have a little fever today, that's why I didn't get a chance to write more and to send you an update. I will do that first thing tomorrow morning. I feel congested and my head hurts a little from the fever but tomorrow I hope I will be like new. I hope you had a good day at Grasso today and that the snow is not too much for you. And of course I cannot not say drive carefully honey bee ;) Sweet dreams pumpkin. I love and miss you and you are always on my mind. Loads of kisses to my hubby. Your beloved wifey.
Agata"

**"Mon, Nov 8, 2010, 7:16 PM
Iain Bryson to Agata Bryson**
Agatka,
Thanks for the pictures. I am in the hotel room writing, laying my notes here and there. When I look at your pictures, like when I look and or think about you and Adelle, I am overwhelmed with happiness. I don't need anything but you and her. My eyes water because I am so happy and proud of you. You are amazing and I am so [expletive] lucky. We have everything. Remember that and don't let other's frustrations get to you. We will be together soon. It is on my list. between now and then, keep up the good work and enjoy dellinski. I cannot wait until we are all together and we can laugh and live. it will happen; other's only dream about what we have, and it is just going to get better. remember that. think about how we feel when we are all together laughing, loving, and playing; you need to feel that way always. that is us. I love you more than to the moon and back (but only like one), and i have goosebumps when i shift my attention to you. Be happy mommy. you are [expletive] beautiful and pecial."

**"Tue, Nov 9, 2010, 7:51 AM
Agata Bryson to me**
Baby:
You are welcome :) I feel exactly the same, and even a thought of you can change my mood to happiness anytime. I love you so much. I was thinking about what is the best reasonable solution while waiting for the visa. I would like to find work for part time only to make some extra money once the unemployment runs out

in December. We will still get some help but it won't be more than 500e a month if that. I am thinking if closing The Hague chapter from A to Z is not what we should do soon.

I have to be in The Hague on the 16th to see the work coach pretending I'm applying for jobs so we keep getting the money until December. Also Monia is travelling so I need to get Ally and figure that out. The only thing about closing everything in The Hague is that my visa goes through Amsterdam and I really don't want it to go to Warsaw and delay us further. I don't think that me giving the notice and pretending I live at Christine's for example would [expletive] it up but I am a little scared of that. Also finding a job in the NL would probably mean I have to be in Europe for 5 or 6 months and I pray to God that the freaking visa won't take that long, not to mention putting Adelle into day care for 10 hours a day or more, being all by myself with her and the apartment situation which might blow up anytime. If I could stay here and earn a little or get a little money somewhere to help with the food bill or so me and Adelle have some cash for fun it would be great. Let me know what you think and what your thoughts are about all of this.

I love you to the bottom of the earth and back and then up to the moon and back. We've sent you another package of Adelle's master paintings today :) She got the jojo [yo-yo I sent her in the mail] and calls it jajo like an egg in polish and is amazed by it. I bought her 2 learning books for preschoolers that we are going to work on and I am taking her to the kids gym with lots of balls and slides etc today after dinner. Fitness at 2pm your time as usual.

Remember that no matter what I love you and you are my world. Let's get that [expletive] place on earth to call home and be together forever. You make me so happy, I hope you realize that. Have a great day my everything. I love you loads and loads and loads. Your wifey."

**"let me know when you can talk...i love you
Tue, Nov 9, 2010, 10:41 AM
Iain Bryson to Agata Bryson"**

The following email was much longer. I've cut it for the sake of brevity, as it isn't sufficiently relevant to the story line. I was researching and studying many things, and I enjoyed sharing what I was thinking about with your mom. Much of what I was researching was pertinent to the "problem" that was brewing in our household, but I wasn't consciously aware that there was a problem, or that I was preparing for anything in particular. I was just doing what I believed I needed to do.

**"Tue, Nov 9, 2010, 11:48 PM
Iain Bryson to Agata Bryson**
The natural tendency of any thinking being is for it to believe it is more almighty than they are, that they are better than they really are, and that others are a bit more inferior than they are. This attribute of man predisposes him to survival, competition, and the goal of perfection. History shows us that human kind is resourceful, innovative, passionate, and determined. Discovery and art are the two most valued traits of any 'free' society.
A.   History of innovation
B.   Importance in Education
C.   Importance in Politics
D.   Not necessarily (most likely not) in this order.
Which way will you run when it's always all around you?
e. value of survival/strength/toughness/winning
f. history through history. Examples
g. how innovation aided with the mechanism of survival
h. definition of survival.....changing....examples evolution of
i. progression through 'inherited knowledge'
J>   value of thought
K. definition (time specific) of thought, thinking
L. Thoughts valued or devalued
M. Mechanisms of thought slander
N. Training Humans..."

**"Wed, Nov 10, 2010, 12:22 AM
Iain Bryson to Agata Bryson**
[expletive] agatka...i love you. what words can i use to express this? poetry i assume. or just love, whatever that is/or maybe should be.
how was your day?

i am excited and pumped for tomorrow like i am going into a test. my mental acuity is strong. i am memorizing/ going over questions before they are presented/working on how i will be perceived.

you aren't watching too much tv are you?

after tomorrow, i will go back to 'normal,' or back to work or whatever. not that i am not at work now. this is the best work i can get. but focus more on teaching, writing when ever i can, and on how and when to get to you. love you"

"Wed, Nov 10, 2010, 6:45 AM
Agata Bryson to me
I love you so much it hurts to think about because there is no way to describe it. I was trying to catch you online after dinner but you must be busy working. It is after 11pm and I am getting ready for bed, fell tired after such an early and busy morning. I feel fine right now. I want you to know that your girls love you very much and there isn't a day that goes by that we don't talk or think about you. I am so proud of you, all your hard work and how strong you are. I know I am strong too but I think us being together makes us strong. I have moments of feeling mostly sorry for myself because I miss you so freaking much but a look at your picture or a thought of you makes me feel all better. I hope that you are happy and that you are eating and taking care of yourself. We need you to do that for us. We are happy and busy and everyone is asking about you and cheering for you, and everyone said to tell you they love you. I have Skype on all day long. I sent you an invite at your mom's computer. My nick is adelajda92 or on our laptop it's under mamusia I think. I love you and you are my world. Goodnight-I will be dreaming about you as always and praying for our family. Loads of kisses everywhere.
Agata"

"Wed, Nov 10, 2010, 12:45 PM
Agata Bryson to me
I love you so much my wonderful hubby. You are so amazing a pecial to me. And thanks to you I am the luckiest and happiest girl in the whole universe. Good luck today and know and remember that I love you from all of my heart.
I made a list of all the books and authors I can read about and will get to work on it immediately. I read your stuff and I have to read it again. I think it is really good so far just very chaotic and it requires me to read it over and over again. I am so proud of you and so proud to be your wife.
I love you my sweetness and my honey bee and my pumpkin and my everything."

Your mom sent me a small package containing the following handwritten note, some of your recent artwork, and a drawing your mom did. At the time, this was life sustaining, as I was growing increasingly weary from us being apart for so long. Unfortunately, I no longer have the original note because I submitted it to the court as evidence that your mom had suddenly started "hating" me, but they wouldn't consider any of my evidence, and they wouldn't give it back to me.

Letter mailed from Agata to me, November 11, 2010
"Baby, I love you more than words can express. I miss you very much daily but the thought of us together soon gets me through each day. You are the world to me and I simply love our family and love every second of every day because we have each other.. I am so proud of you and all of your hard work. I am extremely excited about our adventure and finding a place on earth me and adelle and ally can call home and to always have a place to come back to. I love you. I miss you. I love you some more (like 1). You are my everything. Love, Your wifey"

["I LOVE YOU DADDY ADELLE"]

["ALLY, MOMMY, ADELLE, DADDY
[cut off/distant]"]

[One of your drawings. "Tomato, banana, cut cucumber, apple, avocado, Daddy [a speck], dragon [in upper right corner]"]

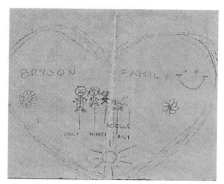

[Your mom's portrait of our family. "DADDY, MOMMY, ADELLE, ALLY"]

"Fri, Nov 12, 2010, 5:35 AM
Agata Bryson to me
Hey lovey dovey:
Im heading out to the kids gym with Adelle. Then to do my nails with my mom and then we have dinner at my grandma's and then I have yoga and then I will be back home and will go online. Have a great day sweety and remember how much I love you. I am going to The Hague tomorrow night for three days. I love you some more. Loads of kisses.
Agata"

"Fri, Nov 12, 2010, 6:55 AM
Iain Bryson to Agata Bryson
agatka.
just got into grasso for today.
what are you doing in the hague?
how are you getting there and back?
ally?
who will you stay with?
when you leaving?
can we skype?
i have to get ready for today. love you so much. let me know when we can talk so i can get ready....buy a sti or get on skype...whatever works for you. love you baby"

"Fri, Nov 12, 2010, 8:04 AM
Agata Bryson to me
Sweets: Im going to the TH [The Hague] bc on tuesday a.m. I Have the unemployment appointment that i Have to be at, get the no arrest [expletive] done at the town hall [for the visa]. Check on the financial advisor people. Get Ally. Im staying at Newtonplein. Going Sat 10.45 pm my time, returning Wed 5 am my time. Getting my nails done, then dinner and yoga. Will be back after 1pm your time and will turn the skype on. If not I will be home all day tomorrow until 1pm ur time. have a great day. I Love you!!!"

"Sat, Nov 13, 2010, 4:51 PM
Agata Bryson to me
Hey love: just leaving on the bus. Its packed and i have a migraine so i will try to fall asleep immediately. Will write and call tomorrow. Love you loads. Your wifey."

"Adelle at the basketball game
Sun, Nov 14, 2010, 6:11 AM
Agata Bryson to me
Attachments"

"Sun, Nov 14, 2010, 12:04 PM
Iain Bryson to Agata Bryson
agatka,

how was the trip?

i hope you are having fun and getting to see your friends. thanks for the awesome pics. it makes my day to get to see you and dell. i checked out the bridge pictures again too. try to think of a time when we can go over things....send me your list so i can think about what we need to go over. can you remind me of things that are there like books....etc/ also i need you to grab my medicine bag please....i love you and will talk to you soon."

"Sun, Nov 14, 2010, 5:09 PM
Agata Bryson to me
Iain:

The trip was awful. I got my period and had a migraine and the bus was packed so had to sit next to a woman that was farting while sleeping. I got to The Hague around 10 this morning and went to Nic's [work friend] house to get the 2 radiators and brought them by taxi to the apartment. Then I did some cleaning, laundry, opened the mail, took a shower and played with Ally. Then me and Nic visited Irina, we had some pizza and coffee and chatted for couple hours and I got home with a migraine, took some medicine and was laying down watching a movie. I feel a little better but ready for bed after sleepless night. Got a lot to do tomorrow. Was trying to call you but no answer. I was waiting on Skype but you must be out and about. Email me or call me when you get a chance so we can go over the stuff. My list:

Visa

Money

Jobs (day care?)

Place to live

Health Insurance

Transportation

Debts
Ally
Our stuff
In general it's pretty much it each thing has more details to it.
I love you.
A."

"Sun, Nov 14, 2010, 10:12 PM
Iain Bryson to Agata Bryson
agatka,
sorry about the trip. hope you've had time to relax and feel better. maybe nic has a bathtub you can use to relax. i will get a sti card and call you in the morning if i don't work and after school if i do.
i get paid this thursday.
can you put 40 bucks or so on the ing so i can get some cash/
daycare? ? wait so we can go over this [expletive] together. i love you. i saw you called but the phone i am using doesn't let me call you. i have the dutch phone now also. love you
ally back to poland. what do you mean by the other stuff? daycare and jobs....how would that work/ i don't want to do that and we need to get together soon so we can plan. i love you so much"

"Sun, Nov 14, 2010, 11:21 PM
Iain Bryson to Agata Bryson
hey,
gettting ready to go to bed. let me know when you can talk so we can figure that [expletive] out and whatever else. I need to get concerta. it helps me stay focused on my work. i am fine without it but it lets me just do what i want without distraction. need to figure out how to get it; russo doesn't seem to understand and any appointments take til january. we will figure out christmas. love you and talk tomorrow"

"Tue, Nov 16, 2010, 10:27 AM
Agata Bryson to me
That's not bad with the ticket. We need to get them asa [as soon as] we know when u can fly. The 8th is my mom's 50th Bday. I am heading to the city to eat something and heading for the bus. Leaving 5.45 my time to Stargard. Mickey is on Ritalin. So he will not torture Ally he seems to like her more than Cicely. Don't worry about her she is in good hands and I will be back here soon anyways. I love you. Email me bc I'm leaving in 5 minutes. Love you some more.
Agata"

"Tue, Nov 16, 2010, 11:02 AM
Iain Bryson to Agata Bryson
love you too much. like about one too much. i can fly on the ninth or the eighth in the evening. love you"

"Tue, Nov 16, 2010, 11:31 AM
Agata Bryson to me
Love u waaaaaaay more. Waiting for the bus. Will check the tickets tomorrow. Love u some more gorgeous. Kisses."

"Tue, Nov 16, 2010, 11:59 AM
Iain Bryson to Agata Bryson
love you bigger. have fun with the polish lectors. make sure they don't crash. love you way high"

"Tue, Nov 16, 2010, 12:08 PM
Agata Bryson to me
Still waiting for the bus. Wish me a safe trip! Love you way wider and deeper :)"

"Tue, Nov 16, 2010, 1:22 PM
Agata Bryson to me
Just departed. 1.5 hrs late. There is a massive fog and traffic jams. I'm gonna read and try to get some sleep later on. I Love you from all of my heart."

"Wed, Nov 17, 2010, 12:59 AM
Agata Bryson to me
Babe: i got here safely. Going to get some sleep. Love you so much"

"Wed, Nov 17, 2010, 5:05 PM
Agata Bryson to me
Babe:
I printed the info you sent me and am going to lay down in bed and read as much as possible. I read 2 of your stories and I really liked the way you wrote your casino encounter. The court one was very good too. I love you and will talk to you tomorrow. I hope I understand what you sent me but I'm sure I will need your help with some. I am so proud of you and I love you some more. Goodnight lovely.
Agata"

"Wed, Nov 17, 2010, 5:38 PM
Iain Bryson to Agata Bryson
it is just beginnings/pieces/ gotta tie em together or whatever."

CHAPTER 24

"I WAS STILL PRETTY SURE THAT I DIDN'T NEED GOD"

At this point in my life, I had found my general purpose, you, but I was still seeking to better understand how that should play out in the specifics. *Life has to be about making the world into a place that would be better for her*, I reasoned. *What I want for my child is all that is "good," so I need to figure out what that is and then head in that direction, starting with myself.*

If I don't do it, I surmised, *then why would I or how could I expect anyone else to?* For example, why would I think I could expect your future husband to be a good man if I didn't try to be the best husband that I could be to your mom? If I didn't make the decisions that I knew to be right, then I knew that I would be choosing to actively destroy reality for the most important and precious thing in the world – you. I wasn't willing to continue doing that, and so my mantra became "the best for Adelle is what I want."

I did not believe in the "God" of religions, per se, but I did believe in good and evil. I was fumbling through humanism and skepticism, and I considered myself to be an agnostic or an atheist. Like Sam Harris, I concluded that "atheism is nothing more than the noises reasonable people make when in the presence of religious dogma" (Harris).

It was obvious to me that many of the religious people of the world, those who claimed to be seeking and/or know God, were primarily doing so for the wrong reasons, either because of fear of what happens after death, or because of a desire to be "blessed" while here on the earth. These things were not attractive to me; I didn't care about any of this. Rather, what I was concerned with was you and what you would inherit. As long as you were better off than me, I was content with going wherever I would go when I died.

What use was the "God" that others claimed to believe in when the only reason they believed was to quell their own fears and seek their own empty desires? As far as religion went, I felt like Karl Marx had gotten it right when he said, "Religion is the sigh of the oppressed creature, the heart of a heartless world, just as it is the spirit of a spiritless situation. It is the opium of the people" (Marx 244).

For you, I wanted only the opposite of oppression. For you, I desired freedom, truth, justice, love, peace, and joy. As far as I could see, these things were not in the world, or in the religions of the world. Everybody was missing the mark, I concluded.

I had grown up with the Bible, and there remained within me a general idea of what it said, but I pushed it away as irrelevant because I associated it with how it was being interpreted by the world. If the fruits of the Bible were what others conceived them to be, if believing in the words written therein meant joining a church or believing for the sole purpose of getting to heaven, then I didn't need any of it.

Instead of the Bible, I was knee deep in such philosophers as Kant, Hegel, Aristotle, and Plato, searching for the origins of thought and belief themselves. Why did people claim to believe or trust in something that they obviously did not believe or trust in? What were the psychological and philosophical factors involved in belief itself? At this point in my life, I didn't see any reason to believe in God, and I was still pretty sure that I didn't need God.

I had to "know" before I was willing to believe in anything, and the only thing I knew was that I believed in love, though only generally, with the subjective understanding I had at the time. The way God built me, along with my experiences in life to this point, precluded me from filling in gaps in my understanding with what other people referred to as "faith" or "blind faith." I had drifted away from the God I briefly experienced at my 8th grade church camp, chalking Him up to be nothing more than another Santa Claus type figure. *How could I trust a decision or a feeling I had when I was thirteen years old?* My blind faith was that God, if He existed, would speak to me in a voice I could understand.

While I was in Connecticut, I decided to set up an appointment to meet with an old acquaintance, Bob McCoy, the head pastor of Groton Bible Chapel. He greeted me with a hug, saying, "Iain, the man who was too smart for college, it is so good to see you." I smiled at his comment, but didn't agree with him, as it was in college that I began to learn how to critically think, to research, and to write. It was good to see him as I had known him since I was in high school, and though I didn't respect his religion, I did respect him and his mind.

Pastor McCoy was a man of faith who was also a deep thinker, and this baffled me because it appeared to me that the two traits were mutually exclusive. My desire was to pick his brain, discuss philosophy, and have him explain to me the reasons for his beliefs. I wanted understanding, and I knew that speaking to other learned people and constantly challenging my ideas and assumptions would eventually lead there.

I brought my laptop into his office so that I could show him pictures of my family – my prized possession. I was so proud of you, and I felt so lucky to be your dad. To know that I would be returning shortly to you and your mother was like knowing that I had a trillion-dollar check that was about clear its hold. We must have flipped through fifty or so pictures as I explained what was happening in our little world in The Hague, as well as our imminent plan to move back to the United States.

"What do you think about humanism?" I asked him.

"Well, it all depends on what you mean by humanism," he responded.

What I meant was that humanists believe that God is not necessary, that faith goes against reason, that human goodness is enough, and that good people are sufficient if they act. "Do you really believe that you are teaching these people the truth, or are you just helping them to cope with the difficulties of life?" I queried. He responded with a grin, without words, leading me to conclude that I was on to something. I think that he knew, somehow, that I was going to find out for myself.

We went on to talk about Kant's *Critique of Pure Reason*, as well as some of the philosophies of Hegel and John Locke. He prayed as we ended our meeting, and I gave him a hug and thanked him for his time. "Iain," he started, "are you reading your Bible? You should be reading your Bible."

"Not yet," I responded as I walked out the door to my car, wondering to myself why I would want to read such a book.

* * *

"Thu, Nov 18, 2010, 11:21 AM
Agata Bryson to me
Hey lovely:
I'm heading out to fitness. Will be back in couple hours. I have been reading the stuff you sent me all day on and off as much as Adelle would allow me. It is so interesting but some stuff I need to reread and reread and reread. I hope you having a good day. I have a cold. I love you loads and loads and loads. Kisses. Wifey Agata"

"Thu, Nov 18, 2010, 5:40 PM
Agata Bryson to me
Love:
I have been sitting at the cpu and reading and waiting for you. I have a cold and my head feels like a balloon so I'm heading to bed. I love you more than I will ever be able to express during our lifetime. I miss you and

the thought of being in your arms soon is the only thing that keeps me going. I love you some more. Night night.
Agata"

"Thu, Nov 18, 2010, 8:01 PM
Iain Bryson to Agata Bryson
agatka,
listening to eminem/dre 'old times sake'; sorry i didn't get on the computer earlier...worked today again in carpentry. was a lotta fun. tired after and laid down for a minute. wish i could leave now and be with you tomorrow. a lot to figure out, but it's all good and we will be together soon. and we are doing wonderful. i just wish i could see my girls but soon enough and it will be amazing. i miss you and i will continue writing things so i can give you words closer to the expression of what 'love' means. once we are together and we get some [expletive] going, i will have more time to work on things like that.

applied to manchester community college yesterday. you could look over other community colleges, maybe take a look at my resume. i gotta look up some [expletive] and see what i can get done. went to the library but they were closed so i only got to drop off books, which i really didn't want to do. kyle and bree are having thanksgiving...bree told my mom she wants to do it all by herself....[expletive] nuts.

did you ever get in touch with kees or tim [W]? well, don't forget to practice reading. everyday should be a homeschool day....that's how i want to do it. it doesn't have to be called school nor does it need to be everyday or only not in the summer. all the time for our kid, within reason, depending upon what we believe she should/can know at any given time.

i love you baby. take some time for yourself and be happy. you make me and adelle the luckiest and happiest husband and daughter i've ever known....we've got the max....not some [expletive] in the middle."

"Fri, Nov 19, 2010, 8:05 AM
Agata Bryson to me
Hey lovely:
Battling my little cold. My mom stayed home today because she was up all night with a migraine. Don't worry about not being on the cpu I understand you are working and busy and anyways we will be together soon! I checked the tickets for you and it is cheaper from the 13th onwards. The tix are 220 dollars one way so below 500 round trip. We need to get it once the credit card is back to 1000.

I am so in love with you and our family and proud of us and our hard work. It will be so pecial to be with you and in your arms soon and all three of us together. Send me your CV so I can check it out and tell you what I think. I researched the community colleges and they are all far away from you except the three rivers and Middletown so let me know if it is OK or not really.

Thanksgiving done all by Bree-good luck she def is nuts ;) I didn't get a hold of Kees or Tim but left them messages and if needed I will go to Kees and get you in before you come back to the NL. I gotta go help my dad with the dinner bc my mom is out of order today. Later we have a mass for my uncle that died few years ago, my cousins (Adelle's godfather's) dad but I think Im going only for coffee and then to aerobox which is my Friday's fitness.

I love you as much as you love me and even some more. I am the luckiest girl in the world because I have you and Adelle my biggest treasures and my everything. Have a great day baby. Love you."

I still could not be certain at this point that your mom had been abused, but the clues were and had been adding up more and more over time. In addition to everything else going on, both she and her mom suffered from chronic, unexplained, debilitating migraines. I had been putting pressure on your mom to seek help in finding out what the cause was so that we could treat them and improve the quality of her life and therefore of everyone in our family, but it was as if she had given up, or maybe that she already knew that there was no treatment for what she had.

> "Chronic pain is one of the most common symptoms reported by abuse survivors, and it can range from mild to disabling... Past abuse has been related to chronic or recurring headaches..." (Kendall-Tackett, as cited in Goodyear-Brown 2012, 50).

"Sat, Nov 20, 2010, 12:50 PM
Agata Bryson to me
Hey love:
As promised a quick update. Most of the days look the same: I get up with Adelle when she is up and my parents are going to work. We have our morning routine of brushing teeth, washing hands, having breakfast and some tea, going out to run errands or for a walk/park/playground, work a little, cook dinner when my

parents come home from work, relax, work and play, go to fitness, bath time, bedtime , some more work and sleep...

Also like I said yesterday the tix are cheaper from the 13th onwards so let's decide on some dates so you can get it asap. That's about all I can think about right now although I'm sure there are way more things that I'm doing that do not seem so important right now. Have been battling my little cold and my head feels like a balloon for the past few days but nothing major. I got to go make some supper for Adelle and I and prepare her for her bath. I was shopping with my mom today and I found paint that you put in a tub that colors the water blue, green, red, etc so cannot wait to see how she likes it. She is wearing the pink/black dress today with the butterfly and is telling everyone that comes over or calls that it is from her lovely daddy who is working and will come back to her very soon. She is so pecial.

I think I will go to sleep earlier today to help my cold and congestion. Skype tomorrow-can't wait to see you. I love you loads and loads and loads and am the proudest girl in the universe bc I have you as my hubby. Love you.,
Agata"

"going out for a while. will be back and check computer later. have a great day. love you.
Sun, Nov 21, 2010, 11:18 AM
Iain Bryson to Agata Bryson"

"LOVE YOU!!! Had dinner with Adelle. Love you some more.
Mon, Nov 22, 2010, 10:28 AM
Agata Bryson to me"

"Mon, Nov 22, 2010, 4:06 PM
Iain Bryson to Agata Bryson
babinski
i love you too much and not enough at the same time. wow. [expletive] crazy amounts -like one - of love coursing through my arteries. i feel burning, but not in my [marital talk], just in the rest of me. the love is consuming like crack on a hot summer day with a wine cooler at the beach in rhode island with it being topless day. working tomorrow and the next in culinary at norwich tech. going to see what i can have them cook for me. sent you both some books today. love you a bit honey dewness..."

"Mon, Nov 22, 2010, 10:46 PM
Iain Bryson to Agata Bryson
agatka,
sitting with our laptop on my lap, thinking of you and what to do and you some more. got some coffee and a pad and a few pens. difficult to work here....need to be home or somewhere else i don't have to think about anything but what i am doing....like the casino. well, just gotta keep working on it. have you been reading? from what i see, i already know all the [expletive] i read. it is amazing to me that people have already written things, and because they have written it, it is discussed in terms which i can learn from. writing anything helps you to think about it, as i've told you....so basically each of the books is one i could have written.

i practice everyday with many different things. i have started lots and am working on something, though i have to get in the zone and am waiting for my mom to go to sleep. even then i can't really sing, yell, or just do without thinking about [expletive]. the thing is that i see too much that nobody else can. i now also know why this happened, why it happens to other people, and the problem/issue with most everything. this is of course progressive, as learning is life long. dh lawrence is my hero at the moment, and eminem, and agatka bryson. and [Dustin] pedroia [second base for Red Sox] a little bit.

so babinski, i gotsta work in culinary. I can't wait to eat all day...hopefully, though you never know so i am not keeping my hopes up. and i would rather work....on this [expletive], but it is all good in some way. i get concerta on wednesday, so that will help. i just need to find solitude. i want to come back asap, so keep a look out for the ticket. i really don't want to wait. let's figure it out. the sooner we are together, the sooner i can use your organization skills.

what have you guys been up to? what is a typical week like? and in order to do that for me, i would assume you need a pad so you can write down and remember the little moments when you smile, which is hopefully all the time. any word from jackie? what does she say in general? did you ever make it to the consulate when you were there? probably not huh? we are gonna figure it out honey and it is just as good, well [expletive] better, than it ever has been and will just get better. it's like a great book....you can not read it....you can start and then stop and not want to go on because you are so happy with what you just read, or you can plow on, being [expletive] amazed the entire time with a few dry sentences, leading to an explosive wonderful [expletive] chillax experience. well, experience is a bad word, as is every word since they are all used for a purpose which is twisted demented [expletive]. i mean a great time. the experience is manifested in our love, which is manifested in Adelle, and maybe a little guy in the future. love you"

We were in the process of being evicted because of the six months of missing rent. Jackie told your mom that she would use her legal connections to try to get some information for us to help stop the process.

"Tue, Nov 23, 2010, 5:23 PM
Agata Bryson to me
Babini:
Got back from 2 hours of fitness, took a shower and am heading to bed sore in good way and exhausted. Another busy day with Adelle tomorrow so the time flies quickly enough until we get to see you. I hope you had a great day and did some writing as well which is your idea of fun ;) I love you from all of my heart and miss you terribly. Good night my love. Love you."

"Wed, Nov 24, 2010, 5:49 AM
Iain Bryson to Agata Bryson
got a ticket for december 9th leaving new haven gettting to amsterdam 10:30am. love you"

"Wed, Nov 24, 2010, 2:50 PM
Agata Bryson to me
Awesome news sweety! I'm so happy to hear that! I love you so much."

Thursday, November 25 was Thanksgiving. Bree, my brother's wife, wanted to have the family celebration at her house, and everything was wonderful even though she tried to cook the turkey upside down. I Skyped with your mom, as I wanted to include her in the celebration, and it was apparent that something was wrong with her. When I looked at her eyes and her body, I could tell that she was tense, maybe scared. Something was going on that I was unaware of as this was not the version of your mom that I had left in September. I was concerned, but I concluded that she must be very upset that we were still apart. *What else could it be? How many times has she been sick during this short period? What the heck could be going on with the woman that I know to be the strongest woman I have ever known?*

"Fri, Nov 26, 2010, 6:28 AM
Agata Bryson to me
I love you toooooooooooooooo my sweet and pecial hubby :*"

"Can u try to get this for me??? Love you.
Fri, Nov 26, 2010, 6:47 AM
Agata Bryson to me
http://www.sephora.com/browse/product.jhtml?id=P269227&categoryId=C17621&shouldPaginate=true"

"Fri, Nov 26, 2010, 9:44 PM
Iain Bryson to Agata Bryson
hey
i am at kyle's watching the house and the girls. kyle bree heath and tiffany went out to some bars. i have the laptop and some books and my notebook, so i should be able to work for a while. i let the dog out of the cage and poured some egg nog. Didnt do much today...had dinner with my mom, who cooked a turkey and [expletive]. george got pissed off because he couldn't find a 'sharp' knife. he said, 'just throw the [expletive] thing out,' 'i want to eat out,' 'i can't eat that [expletive],' and more. eventually he just got so upset he went to sleep. i cant wait to be back with you....i need that [expletive]. so, that is about it. got some things to organize....more than i will cause i need you for that and then just working. can you tell me what you are thinking and figuring out as far as the apartment, holland, bills, and [expletive]. can you get me an appointment with kees and the psychiatrist? i would like to get some concerta as soon as possible once there. can you send me the [expletive] you want me to get from here for you and adelle. how are things going what have you been up to. what is new with adelle. i miss you so [expletive] much."

"Sat, Nov 27, 2010, 12:50 PM
Agata Bryson to me
Hey love:

It is so sweet of you to babysit for them. You are so lovely. I'm sorry about George just remember that in few days less than 2 weeks you will be home with your girlies. Today is my grandpa's name day so we all are going to my grandparent's house for dinner. Yesterday was a week day so as usual I got up with Adelle we made breakfast and had a relaxing morning. Then we went for a walk and got some meat for dinner and did crafts and painted. She has gotten so amazing at it. After that we went to the Post Office to send some of her paintings to you. Then we made dinner ate read books and went out with my parents and sister. Then we had a bath, bedtime and I went to fitness. That's pretty much how all days look like.

I have been reading a lot about all the authors you told me about. Their biographies, their writing style etc. It is really interesting stuff. The credit card should be cleared to 1000 again on Monday and we also should get some unemployment money then too. When you come we have to go to the unemployment office bc as a family and both of us unemployed we qualify for 1200-1300 a month in social help from the unemployment office but we have to apply for it both of us.

The house Jackie is working on and I haven't heard from her yet. I emailed her today and will see what she says. She said she will work on it over the weekend so I will update you as soon as I know anything. The bills are all paid off except the medical or more dentist stuff that I need to work on with the financial advisor when we get back to the NL. Everything else is all cleared. I emailed Saskia about your appointments and will give her a call Monday to make sure it is all set for the 10th or the following Monday. I will look through the Gap. Old Navy etc webs and will send you few things that we need after I came back from my grandpas celebration.

Things are great even more great is the thought that we will be all three of us again soon and it makes me feel so happy that I feel like I'm flying in the air. It will be so pecial and I just simply cannot wait to see you love. I have been up to raising and working with our daughter and taking care of myself and being happy and proud of our family. I love you from all of my heart and miss you terribly too but we will be together in 13 days :D LOVE YOU!!!"

"Shopping :D
Mon, Nov 29, 2010, 6:55 AM
Agata Bryson to me
Lovely:
I checked the web and you only have to go to one store which is Old Navy ;)

Adelle:
Fleece pants
Long sleeve tees
Sweater/Cardigan
Hoodie
Lined Jeans
Pants/Cords
Daddy's Little Girl PJs

Agata:
http://oldnavy.gap.com/browse/product.do?cid=26198&vid=1&pid=772286
regular in M
http://oldnavy.gap.com/browse/product.do?cid=26199&vid=1&pid=794151
doesn't have to be that one in particular I just need a warm jacket for winter size S or M doesnt matter what color
http://oldnavy.gap.com/browse/product.do?cid=41960&vid=0&pid=797632
Warm shoes doesn't have to be this pair just something tall and warm size 6
Iain:
http://oldnavy.gap.com/browse/product.do?cid=26068&vid=1&pid=797799
couple in different colors
http://oldnavy.gap.com/browse/product.do?cid=26065&vid=1&pid=796719&scid=796719012
http://oldnavy.gap.com/browse/product.do?cid=26065&vid=1&pid=796722&scid=796722012
Also couple pairs of sweaters-you only have one I think, one could be buttoned or with a zipper,"

"Tue, Nov 30, 2010, 7:02 AM
Agata Bryson to me
Hey lovely:
It was very strange the power in the whole area blew off and it didnt start working until this a.m. The whole street was pitch black. Yesterday I got up with Adelle we had breakfast, went out looking for signs of winter, did some shopping for dinner and drops for Adelle's bath that make water ocean blue because we ran out.

We also went to a consignment store and got couple tees with Dora and a hot waffle on the way back. We were out for about 4 hours and then we relaxed watching SpongeBob and after that we made dinner with my mom and Adelle made the salad and seasoned it and set the table. After dinner we played hide and seek and we painted as usual. Then we worked on writing with the erase board. Then my sister took Adelle for a walk and I helped my mom clean and when they got back Adelle and I did the supper, bath, bedtime routine and I went out for 2 hours of fitness: body shape and yoga and after the power blew off I went to bed and read with a candle.

This morning was similar, we looked at toys r us web and she loved browsing through the stuff she liked I will send u the links in a little bit. It is already way below freezing here so today we went out only for an hour or 2. Later on my dad is taking her to the kids gym while me and my mom will cook dinner. After dinner I have a playdate with Adelle at Dominika's and fitness in the evening as usual. Every day is pretty much the same: around Adelle and taking care of myself...

I like the way you write and how you voice your opinions I think it is one of your highest qualities while you write. You have the ability to convince people that what you write is the truth or is right or just be convincing that you know what you are writing,. It's exciting to me to think about all the stuff we can do with it. And I am proud of you.

I cannot wait to see you and to be just the three of us together. We have a lot to figure out but also when we are together it is way easier . I love you and I hope you are taking care of yourself, I don't like the 3 hours of sleep thing but I will work on it when I see you. I love you baby and you mean the world to me. Have a great day and talk soon love. Your wife.
Agata"

"LOVE YOU VERY MUCH!!!! Toys'R'Us
Tue, Nov 30, 2010, 7:16 AM
Agata Bryson to me
http://www.toysrus.com/product/index.jsp?productId=4232156
http://www.toysrus.com/product/index.jsp?productId=4056119
http://www.toysrus.com/product/index.jsp?productId=3508454
http://www.toysrus.com/product/index.jsp?productId=2327129
http://www.toysrus.com/product/index.jsp?productId=2380550
http://www.toysrus.com/product/index.jsp?productId=3887641"

[You posing with a toy you wanted me to get you.]

CHAPTER 25

"ALL THAT WE NEEDED WAS YOUR MOM'S VISA"

"The CC is back at 1000e. Love you!!!
Wed, Dec 1, 2010, 9:07 AM
Agata Bryson to me"

"Wed, Dec 1, 2010, 6:11 PM
Iain Bryson to Agata Bryson
agatka,
so, we need to figure out your plans for getting to holland.
we need to think of how and what we will do and accomplish in our first week....while we are getting readjusted, and what we cannot do so we do not get frustrated.
do you have a list of publishers or editors that we can give [expletive] to? i want to immediately churn something out that we can sell. hopefully this way, we will not need to search for jobs.
we should think of how we can start a tutoring/translation business. there are tons of polish people there who can undoubtedly use our services.
do we have insurance?
you said you made appointments....just double checking
what appointments do you and dell need?
dentist
[Dr.] Cambridge
keep up on the visa
the apartment/jackie/getting things like the shower fixed, etc.
finding a library i can go to
     i was able to get some concerta from a friend today. i am working at the green marble, the coffee shop in mystic, and a lot of courtney's [my cousin] friends hang out here, so i talk to them on occasion. it has wireless and good coffee ....kind of like amsterdam or do hagy [The Hague] but without the sweet cheeba. have you thought of anything you want for christmas, or do i get to choose?
what clothes did you want?
     the toys are interesting and shiny just like a bmw is to us. but, and within reason, i would much rather stimulate interest in things that may not be shiny, but will have more worth as far as learning, which is the truly fun thing in life. people repress this and go from one high to another, whether it be buying the new thing or having sex just to have sex. it feels great for a moment, but it cannot be sustained without the higher picture. i can't wait to have sex with you though, but i have so much i want to do....just not enough time....i love you and a [expletive] week till liftoff......say hi to everyone for me"

"Thu, Dec 2, 2010, 9:50 AM
Agata Bryson to me
Hey lovely:
We got snowed in, been all day long outside with Adelle and slides. We will eat dinner now and I will write back after that. Love you loads."

"Re: Iain Bryson
Thu, Dec 2, 2010, 11:54 AM
Agata Bryson to Kees de Vries
Sounds good. Thanks so much for your quick reply and we are looking forward to see you Monday the 13th.
Take care,
Agata"

"**Thu, Dec 2, 2010, 1:18 PM**
Agata Bryson to me
Hey lovely:
It was so nice talking to you. I cannot wait when we are together and we can talk all days long. I am leaving Stargard next Wednesday the 8th at 10.45 pm my time and arriving The Hague on the 9th in the morning. Both Adelle and I have return tickets. The 8th is my mom's 50th birthday. The few things I know for sure we need to do is: get your meds, see Kees, psychiatrist, Cambridge, apply for more social help at the unemployment office, send stuff to publishers and magazines and I have to see the financial advisor. I'm sure there is plenty more but it seems the most important right now.

I have a list of publishers and some magazines that we will go over and I'm sure once we get going more will come to us. Tutoring and translation is probably best for you because I'm not sure that someone in The Netherlands wants stuff translated into Polish but it is a good idea to look into. Corporations maybe. I am checking on the insurance and waiting to hear back. I haven't been paying because I was told that it is coming off of my unemployment and we weren't there anyways but I will make sure everything is all set for when we are back there. I made appointments and some [expletive] didn't put them in the system.

I talked to Saskia today and she was like nothing is here and I told her I talked with someone she works with and she didn't know anything about it anyways I called and emailed Kees and he will see you on Monday the 13th and the script for your meds will be waiting for me on the 9th and I will pick it up when I get to The Hague and drop it at the pharmacy so you have it when you get home on the 10th and Kees will make an appointment for you with the psychiatrist as well for the following week. Adelle we need to check if all her shots are up to date. I cannot think of anything I need right now but we will see. I will call dentist tomorrow morning. Cambridge will get back to me when he can see you I talked to his assistant.

Jackie is looking into it and is writing a letter to the collection agency but I told her it might be better to wait so we can discuss it with her next week. What do you think? I am supposed to let her know tomorrow. She said there is no way they can kick us out without a court warrant and we simply do not have income to pay. The big library in Spui has English books but I think you pay for the membership.

I don't have anything particular for Christmas that I want. Maybe only the box set for make up I sent you. My mom really liked the one you gave me last year maybe we could get it for her for her bday? No clothes for me just a winter jacket but will try to get one in a used store here. I cannot wait to have sex with you or rather make love and to see you and all. I have missed you so much. Gotta run help my mom with the supper, bath, bed time and then off to fitness. I love you so much my precious thing. Your wifey."

"**Thu, Dec 2, 2010, 2:19 PM**
Iain Bryson to Agata Bryson
hey babe,
what do you mean by having return tickets? you mean you don't have to buy one because you paid for both ways last time or you have a return to stargard again? more incompetent people with the doctors huh? just keep trucking forward doing what you can and knowing you have done all you can. that is the most you can do but you have to make sure you aren't slacking. we will put the social [expletive] in order, get all the things scheduled we need to, keep doing that and take care of the apartment.

i would be interested to see what jackie is thinking, what her strategy is, what she sees as likely possibilities, etc. i would say she should wait as long as she can to submit or do anything because that just gives us more time. if you file, send a letter today that is not due for two weeks, they can respond sooner and then the next step will be required sooner. no rush. we just need to have time to figure it out so we can buy your house....you know the one you deserve....translating and tutoring are a good idea. brainstorm that if you can.....

again, you isolate yourself and just think about that and see what branches out and what you can figure out. make yourself and you will make progress. if you let yourself say no, or that you did it already, you will not get anywhere. if you think you have figured out it, your mind is [expletive] with you, because even the things you have figured out are not really figured out. there is always room to grow and/or learn something new. if jackie can send me her notes, i can go over it....if possible, not a big deal if not possible. How much is the library membership? i can't wait to... babini."

"Thu, Dec 2, 2010, 4:32 PM
Agata Bryson to me
Hey precious:
I mean I don't have to buy one bc I paid both ways. Incompetent doctors, receptionist, [expletive] everyone involved with something medical is incompetent but Kees promised he will take care of it bless him. We need to sit with Jackie and figure out a plan of action. I just got back from fitness got to hop in a shower and have a bite and head to bed exhausted from so much freezing fresh air today and tomorrow Adelle wants to go out again as soon as she finished breakfast ;) The membership I heard was something like 30e/month or around it. I cannot wait to be with you and for us to be all together. I love you. Night night. Kisses"

"**Fwd: Iain Bryson**
Fri, Dec 3, 2010 at 10:35 AM
Agata Bryson to me
---------- Forwarded message ----------
Re: Iain Bryson
Thu, Dec 2, 2010, 6:36 PM
Agata Bryson to Kees de Vries
Dear Dr. Kees:
If you could arrange that so I could come and pick it up (both medicine) sometime on the 9th that would be great. That way Iain can have his medicine ready when he lands on the 10th in the morning. I really appreciate your help.
Have a good night.
Agata"

"**Fri, Dec 3, 2010**
Kees de Vries to Agata Bryson, me
Dear Iain and Agata,
 One last check to see if this is the right prescription. We have in our system:
Citalopram, 20 mg, s/1dd1 (once a day 20mg)
Concerta, 18mg, 4/dd1 (4 times a day 18mg).
I'm doubting the concerta. Didn't you use 36mg tablets? Concerta is available in 18 mg, 27 mg, 36 mg, 54 mg. Let me know!
Take care, Kees"

"**Re: Iain Bryson**
Fri, Dec 3, 2010, 3:39 PM
Iain Bryson to Kees de Vries
Cc: Agata Bryson
Kees,
Good to hear from you. I am looking forward to seeing you and being back in your country.
The medication you have listed is correct; it is what was last prescribed and without seeing the psychiatrist, I do not believe it can be changed. Two 36mg tablets does make more sense; either way is fine with me. Insurance may be happier with that arrangement as well. If you've got the desire and/or the power, feel free to pull the trigger on that change. All the best, Iain"

"**RE: Iain Bryson**
Fri, Dec 3, 2010
Kees de Vries to me
Cc: Agata Bryson
Great,
I'll do that.
Take care and see you soon!
Best regards, Kees"

"**Sun, Dec 5, 2010, 11:30 AM**
Agata Bryson to me
Hey sweety:
I've been out with Adelle playing in the snow but when I got back my tummy started to feel funny and I think I have a stomach flu or something. Have been laying under a blanket and drinking mint tea. I hope your Sunday was great and I hope to talk to you tomorrow or later if I'm able to sit for few minutes. I love you from all of my heart and you are my everything."

"Sun, Dec 5, 2010, 11:00 PM
Iain Bryson to Michele [Norwich Tech High School], Lilly [Grasso Tech High School]
Lily and Michelle,
I apologize for being unavailable last week. I have been using all of my time to write, going from the coffee shop during the day to the UCONN 24 hour lounge at night, and then back. I tend to lose track of time when I am writing, and I apologize for not being able to answer your calls. I am going to have to take some time off from teaching. I recently found out that I am going back to The Netherlands sooner than expected. Initially, at the US Consulate in Amsterdam, they told me it would take six weeks to get a VISA; the plan was to go back and scoop up my wife and daughter when this happened and work as much as possible in the meantime. After a couple of months, I called, and after finally getting through to an actual person after a few tries, I was told it could be five, maybe six or eight months.

So, I am going back on December 9, as three months away from my girls is enough. I still have an apartment in The Hague, so I will regroup with the family and have my wife use her wonderful organizational skills and work on getting something published. Since I really do not know when the VISA will be granted, we are just going to set up shop again over there. I am going to continue teaching, work on expanding that a bit, and my wife and I are going to try to start doing more translating. Once the VISA is bestowed upon my alien wife, we will have two months to enter the country, where we will process her green card so we never have to deal with this again, and then go from there.

I have thoroughly enjoyed working for you. Each day was a wonderful experience; I only hope I was able to give to the students as much as they gave me. It was a pleasure working for you, and I hope you have a joyous, restful holiday season.

I will be returning, and most likely during this school year. I would love the opportunity to teach at your schools again, and I intend on pursuing my ARC once I know I can spend the time in the country to get it done.
All the best, Iain"

"Sun, Dec 5, 2010, 12:14 PM
Iain Bryson to Agata Bryson
agatka,
i am sorry you don't feel well. please just stay positive. you will be amazed how well you do when you do that. it is not easy, as you don't feel well and you really dont. but if you fight and progressively go from yes i do,.. while no i don't will go back forcefully over and over. you can feel it [expletive] it is real. but keep doing it and fight with your mind and you will feel better. i promise and will explain it better later. it is no different than any other feeling and everyone affirms it by treating you like you don't feel well. i want you to feel well. i love you from all my heart babinski"

"Mon, Dec 6, 2010, 5:14 AM
Agata Bryson to me
Hey precious:
You were right, positive thinking and some rest and tea helped and I am like new today. It's Santa Clause day today in PL and it means that at night Santa Claus is coming to your home through the chimney while you sleeping and leaves small gifts under your pillow. So Adelle woke up at 7 am screaming Oh my God he was here Oh my God he was here!!! LOL. I laughed my butt off. Still some snow so we are heading out to use it until it's here and then little shopping for dinner and then we are cooking soup. Besides packing and getting ready for our trip on Wednesday. Have a great day lovely and talk to you later. Love you so much! Wifey"

"Mon, Dec 6, 2010, 6:54 AM
Michele [Norwich Tech High School] to me
IAIN, THE PLEASURE WAS ALL MINE........YOU WILL BE WELCOMED BACK WITH OPEN ARMS...THE BEST OF LUCK TO YOU...........................MICHELE"

"Mon, Dec 6, 2010, 7:34 AM
Lilly [Grasso Tech High School] to me
Hi Iain.
Sorry to hear the news, BUT happy at the same time!!! Glad to hear you are going to reunite with your family, just in time for Christmas! What a nice present your girls are getting! Their daddy back!!!!! J Wishing you lots of success in pursuing your dreams.....
Lily"

One thing was settled: when we returned to the U.S. as a family, I had a job waiting for me; two schools wanted me to teach for them. The principal at Grasso Tech had requested that I become a certified teacher so that she could hire me permanently. The vice principal at Norwich Tech indicated that I would be welcomed back with "open arms," in caps nonetheless, crossing one important thing off my list. Mission (partially) accomplished, and I had no doubt that we would figure out the other details when it came time to move. Now where was your mom's visa, and what was the holdup?

In addition, I had made progress in finding us a place to live. I looked at two different houses on my mom and George's road that were available, one with a little shop out front that I thought we could make into some kind of a Polish store. George and I had also spoken about the possibility of building a house for us on the backside of their property. All that was left was for your mom and I to talk it over and decide together. I was exuberant about the fact that we would all be back together soon, and I was looking forward to whatever we decided to do next.

I had spent time planning what to do on the twenty-acre parcel of woodlands that my dad had in Mystic, CT. Specifically, I wanted to build you a series of tree houses connected by bridges in the trees, and I was designing a track so that I could get you a little dirt bike, eventually. I didn't see any limits; rather, I just knew that your mom and I had to come together and regroup. It wasn't a question of if, but of when, and all that we needed was your mom's visa.

* * *

"Heading to bed. Hope to ttyt. Love you so freaking much!
Mon, Dec 6, 2010, 5:49 PM
Agata Bryson to me"

"BABY: write to me. Im worried-havent heard from you for a while. I LOVE YOU!!!!
Tue, Dec 7, 2010, 7:32 PM
Agata Bryson to me"

"Tue, Dec 7, 2010, 8:46 PM
Iain Bryson to Agata Bryson
baby,
doing good. very busy preparing. will be able to get away to catch up with you tomorrow afternoon or evening....let me know if you can.
i love you. see you soon. thank god"

"Tue, Dec 7, 2010, 8:49 PM
John S [friend/former coworker] to me
Colonel,
Have a safe trip back to Europe. Hugs and kisses to the family from me and Linda!
Don't forget to email me some of your writing.
Keep us informed of your whereabouts, progress, etc....
-- The Admiral"

"Wed, Dec 8, 2010, 5:30 AM
Agata Bryson to me
Baby:
Good to hear, was little worried. Good luck today-you will do great. I'm thinking of you. Adelle and I are saying bye byes today and celebrating my mom's Bday so very busy and out and about. Can't wait to be home tomorrow. Love you loads and loads. Kisses
Your girls.
Agata"

"Give me a call on my cell. We are starting the trip and the weather is terrible. Love u
Wed, Dec 8, 2010, 3:33 PM
Agata Bryson to me"

PART 4

DECEMBER 9 – 27, 2010

"I HATE YOU AND I'VE ALWAYS HATED YOU!"
- YOUR MOTHER

CHAPTER 26

"MY GIRLS...IN MY ARMS...TODAY"

On December 9, 2010, my mom and George drove me down to Tweed Airport in New Haven, Connecticut. This was one of the best days of my life, like a soldier returning from a long tour of duty. My anticipation level rose more and more as I contemplated and savored what returning home would be like. There was no destination in the entire universe that I would have rather been going to than to my girls. All that I wanted was to get to you, hold you in my arms again, and continue our journey together.

The time apart had been challenging on several levels, but none of that was important anymore. The only thing that I wanted was for our little family to be back together. I vowed to myself that the three of us would never again separate like we just had. This was obviously what your mother wanted as well based upon her emails to me during our time apart; it was even tougher for her than it was for me.

Our family was on a mission, and while I had no idea what was coming next, I fully believed in us, and I could not wait for whatever was around the corner. Because of you, I no longer questioned the meaning of life or its purpose. And with your mother, together, I felt we would be unstoppable in whatever we decided to do.

I thought that I had most of life figured out: My marriage was better than ever, and being a dad was all that I needed as my life's purpose. I had no use for God because I believed that I could do it all on my own. I believed I had things under control, and that I could even teach people how to accomplish what I already had. God was just something that relieved people of anxieties that I didn't have because what I did have was my girls.

I hugged my mom tight; it had been a wonderful and productive time back in the United States. The time that I had spent with my mom and George was priceless, but that could not change the fact that I was dying to get back to you and your mom. When we released our embrace, the tears in her eyes startled me, I think because I was unable to discern whether they were tears of joy or tears of sorrow. While I still do not know today, I do know that joy and sorrow are not mutually exclusive; in this life, they may be inseparable.

But at the time I did not know true sorrow. All that I could think about was getting back to my girls as soon as possible, and then subsequently getting my girls to the United States as soon as possible. None of the rest of it was of much importance to me. For me, heaven was making an omelet with you and reading to you before you went to bed, so it was relatively simple for me. The entire reason that I had just spent all this time over there was to prepare for our imminent emigration back to your country of birth. This was the decision that your mother and I had made together.

As far as I knew, we were just waiting for your mom's visa; that was where we had left it when we broke our huddle and parted ways in early September, and that had been your mom's position for the duration of our time apart, as was obvious from her correspondence to me. It certainly appeared that we were doing well; she had been saying all the right things, all positive things, and it was apparent to me that we were a team. Oh, how I couldn't wait to hold the both of you, how I couldn't wait to begin living life with you again, to pick up where we had left off.

I tried to keep myself calm as I waited for my turn to disembark the plane at Schiphol airport in Amsterdam, but I felt edgy and a bit frantic, not present, tired, not wanting anyone to get in my way. I was very close to you now, only another hour or so on the train, but it still felt very far away. I'd have rather skipped this part. I had waited long enough; three months was ridiculous. *My girls... in my arms...today...*

Once aboard the train, I found an aisle seat and plopped down, filling the window seat area with all the luggage, facing forward toward home, and I took out my notebook. I had the music turned up loud on my earphones because I wanted to zone out and burn time with songs. I just wanted to be home, I couldn't think about anything else, and the time in between was both difficult and wonderful, kind of like a dog must feel when waiting to jump on his master when his master's car pulls into the driveway.

I scribbled down a love letter to your mom in my notebook, one filled with excitement and anticipation about the next leg of our journey. Her strength, her spirit, her love filled me with immeasurable amounts of love and hope. Together, the three of us, we could do anything.

When the train got close to Den Haag Centraal (train station), I took my bags and walked to the door so that I could get out first, and I ran as fast as I could through the station and up the escalator to the tram platform. I felt no fatigue; the adrenaline from my anticipation and my love for you and your mom drowned it out completely. I thought that I was running to heaven, and I couldn't get there soon enough.

I continued running when I got off the tram at our stop, running the two city blocks home at full pace, one ear bud hanging down and dragging on the ground behind me, both hands wheeling large suitcases. When I got to the front door of our apartment on Newtonplein street, I rang the doorbell, out of breath, feeling overwhelmed with joy. I began to dig for my key at the same time, but I wanted you to head toward me as I headed toward you; our reunion couldn't happen soon enough, and I felt like I needed you guys more than I needed my next breath. We were oh so close now.

As I opened the door, I heard voices at the top of the winding Dutch stairs that led up to heaven. I could hear the footsteps coming down from the top, so I waited, knowing that we couldn't all be in the stairway at the same time with the luggage and the neighbor's bicycle.

Both of you came down and around the last bend of the spiral, and I was slapped by a wave of darkness the moment I saw you, the same darkness that I had felt when your grandpa walked into the room during our last Skype conversation. It was as if I could feel that the devil was present. I knew that something was off the moment my eyes embraced the two of you.

You were wrapped around your mom like a little monkey, your head pressed against her chest as if you were very tired or sick. It was as if you released a trail of stench when the door to our apartment was opened, carrying it down the spiral staircase like a wind tunnel, except that I could feel it and not smell it. Your mom stared at the ground, not making eye contact or changing her facial expression, "...wearing the blank and glassy expression characteristic of individuals in a state of shock" (Noblitt and Noblitt, 2014, 19).

I didn't know, and I didn't really care what was going on; I assumed that my reaction was mistaken, that I was probably overreacting. I knew that it had simply been an extremely difficult separation for you guys as well. I figured there would be some change, just for the fact that we had been apart for three months. I didn't really think at all because I was just happy to be home.

Upon embracing the two of you at the bottom of the stairs in a giant bear hug, I felt joy mixed with grave concern. While I felt like I had finally made it, another sharp wave of fear shot through me. I knew that your mom had struggled while we were apart, I knew that she would be stronger once our house was back in order, I knew that Poland offered many challenges for her, and I knew that my job was to now love her and bring her through whatever it was that she was dealing with.

You briefly acknowledged my presence with a darting but distant glance and a one-armed, half attempt at a hug, immediately turning back to and clinging to your mother's chest, your right arm around her shoulder as if holding on for dear life, burying your face as if hiding, almost as if I was a stranger, or you were sick.

Your mom turned and led the way back up the stairs to our home. I was now quite concerned, but I was also cocky, thinking, *ok, what the [expletive] is going on now? Just show me. I'll figure it out, and we will be fine, as usual. I'm too smart and too strong for this to get me again.* I followed the almost visible dark stench, a step or two behind, wondering what the heck life was going to throw at me now, sensing an invisible intruder in our home.

Whatever I had just walked into had taken the wind out of me, and I had to stop to take in some air and regain my composure. I plopped the suitcases down on the living room floor and slid them into the corner of the room. Your mom carried you over to the couch and turned on the television to some cartoon. I unzipped one of my suitcases, thinking I could lighten the mood and get everyone's attention with gifts, thinking it would be a good segue from the tv.

It didn't feel like I was in our home, but in your grandparent's home in Poland. This is not at all what I had envisioned. It felt like I had lost a pop fly in the lights, the only answer being to get under it and focus. Sure, I could also worry about it hitting me in the head, but if I did that then I would have a slimmer chance of catching the ball.

CHAPTER 27

"THE WINTER OF OUR DISCONTENT"

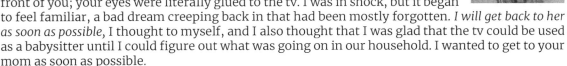

From the suitcase I handed your mom one of the many books I had brought back with me, thinking she might like to read some Steinbeck to settle herself down. Of course, I had no idea that this was the actual winter of our own family's discontent, the winter which would change everything, but then again something inside of me might have known something. Out of at least a dozen books that I had brought back from Connecticut, this is the one I gave to your mom. She laughed under her breath and left to go into the kitchen.

I focused on you, sitting there on the couch, so precious and finally back in my world, mesmerized by the tv as if in a trance. You did not care about any presents I had for you, and you did not even seem to care that I was there in front of you; your eyes were literally glued to the tv. I was in shock, but it began to feel familiar, a bad dream creeping back in that had been mostly forgotten. *I will get back to her as soon as possible,* I thought to myself, and I also thought that I was glad that the tv could be used as a babysitter until I could figure out what was going on in our household. I wanted to get to your mom as soon as possible.

Reconnecting with her was paramount; I had to figure out what was going on with her, my partner. I needed to be able to talk in a straightforward manner to your mother, and it could not wait until you were asleep. This felt like some kind of emergency, though I did not believe an emergency was possible; *the trip must have been extremely rough*, I reasoned. I scoffed that it was merely a waste of my time to have to set things straight once again, a waste of all our time, but soon we would be dancing again. I thought that we had kicked whatever this was out of our home, but apparently it was back. Apparently, it crawled back from Poland on you and your mom, whatever it was. *Well, here we go again...this time should be quick, we will just nip it in the bud.*

I sauntered toward the kitchen with a "what now" attitude, but also a bit afraid. I still thought that I had things under control. Of course, three months apart was going to be very tough for your mom; the three of us were always strongest when we were together, and she had begged me not to go because she knew that. And of course, living in Poland is way different than living at our home, and I realized that some old and/or otherwise unacceptable habits might have snuck back into the routine.

I knew that I could not control everything in your environment, and I believed that family was ultimately a good thing, despite the quirks your mom and I knew you would encounter, with things like your grandpa's alcoholism, or your grandma's constant misery. I believed that your mom could handle anything, and we consulted together on many of these issues prior to you going to Poland. In spite of the issues she often experienced that frustrated me so much, I trusted her completely.

She was facing the stove, a slim cigarette hanging out of her mouth, the type of cigarette her mom smoked, a Glamour menthol. She smoked these only after her returns from Poland, as if she wasn't herself anymore; any other time she hated menthol cigarettes. She had a distant look of sheer terror on her face, like a deer in headlights, or a rabid dog.

She needs me, it is good that I am here finally, I thought. I walked right up to her, confidently of course, as if returning to my bride after a long deployment, and I wrapped my arms around her waist, my right hand sliding under the waistband of her sweatpants on the small of her back, as I moved in to kiss her. *This is all she wanted and needed*, I thought, *for us to be back together again, working as a team*.

"Ouch!" she shouted, jumping backwards, apparently very frightened. "You're hurting me." She lurched away from me, startled as if suddenly awakened from a nightmare or burned by hot oil.

At this moment, I knew that the suspicions I had since the moment I laid my eyes on you were true. Something was going on with your mother, and I had seen this before. This was not good.

It was difficult for me to believe that she could act this out with a straight face, and for me that was the strangest part, a step into bizarro world. I could not help but smirk, not because I thought she was funny, but because I recognized for certain that I was once again dealing with the irrational: your mother when she was not well. Did she think that I would believe that my kiss or embrace could hurt her, that I would have any reason in the world to think that this could happen upon my return?

"What do you mean, I'm hurting you? Kissing you hurts you? Trying to hug you hurts you? Really?"

"Yes, it hurts me. You hurt me. You are hurting me. Ouch! I hate you."

I backed off, raising my hands in surrender, knowing that she was speaking nonsense, but also feeling like her reaction was genuine in some way; either that, or she was a great actress. She looked hurt, and she even sounded hurt, but then I remembered that all I had done was try to kiss my wife, who was totally in love with me as far as anything that I was aware of at the time. Something else was obviously going on. Somebody else had obviously hurt my wife or brought her to this state; *how could this be my doing? BPD again?* I considered. How could this possibly be the same woman I had been corresponding with for the previous three months?

> "Borderline personality disorder is characterized by deeply conflicted emotions, running the gamut from rage to terror, from depressed apathy to turbulent agitation...while at the same time expressing fears that they will be abandoned" (Noblitt and Noblitt, 2014, 6, 7). "Childhood sexual abuse is often identified as a factor that may cause this disorder" (8). "In citing the *DSM-III* (American Psychiatric Association, 1980, p.258), Abse added, 'I have never found severe psychic trauma to be absent in such cases' (1983, p.340)" (9).

"That doesn't make any sense, baby, what are you talking about?"

"I hate you, and I've always hated you."

"What do you mean you hate me? I don't believe that you hate me, that's one of the most ridiculous things you've ever said," I told her, in a voice as calm and loving as I could make it. It was obvious that she had some sort of thorn tormenting her. I had seen it before and I just needed to be patient; something had ripped your mother apart, again.

I was trying not to get worked up inside, but I could feel the dread rising within me. This I had felt before, but, surely, we couldn't be there again. *We beat that*, I thought, *that's in the past whatever that was, borderline personality disorder or whatever; I thought our love for our daughter had healed that... but could she hate me again, just like that, from everything is great to I hate you, in the blink of an eye?*

Before, she had told me, "I told my psychologist that my husband thinks I went a little crazy," and, "I promise that will never happen again." I had hoped it was gone, didn't see how it couldn't be gone, and I was now hearing things that told me that it wasn't gone. Here we go again... I really did not see this coming.

"I've always hated you. I'm taking Adelle back to Poland for either Christmas or New Year's. Adelle doesn't love you either, you are not a good father."

"Ok, Agata, no you are not, and you don't make any sense. Why do you say these things? What is wrong with you?"

"You are what is wrong with me. I hate you."

"Ok, well that is impossible. Don't you remember what you said and how you felt when I left you in August? Don't you remember what you said yesterday, and earlier today, and every day that we were apart? Agata, it's just not possible that I am what is causing this. I've not been here an hour yet."

I felt some relief, because whatever was going on had nothing to do with me; that was obvious. She was off her rocker, again, and though I didn't like it, I believed that I was strong enough to handle it, because I had seen this before. And I wasn't all that concerned about the long-term effects of any outside forces because I believed that I would figure out whatever it was and get us back on track, and that she would be strong again. I assumed that any effects from the outside could only be minimal, that it was just a difficult time in a weird place, that three months apart had pushed the envelope too far for your mom.

I thought that I was dealing with a relatively small problem, and I couldn't even imagine anything that could be trouble for us after what we had been through already. You were home, and I wasn't going to take my eyes off you. There was no possibility of you returning to Poland, or of you spending another night in this world not in my care; I would not let that happen – *over my dead body*, I told myself.

She wasn't getting ready to talk yet, so I continued, "Don't you remember how good we had it in this house? Don't you remember telling me you love me every day for the past three months? Agata, you begged me not to leave. You were terrified of me leaving, you told me that you thought we would never get it back again. Baby, I'm sorry I left you, but can't you see that it's not possible for me to be the problem; whatever the problem is must be something to do with Poland. I just got home."

Logically, I knew, the "thorn" had to be in Poland. The problem, whatever it was, could not be me, because I had been on a different continent for three months. Sure, I could've accepted that she was mad at me for something or frustrated with life in general and with being at your grandparent's house in Poland, but "I hate you" was crazy, as was everything else since I got back home. She did not look good at all, taken over by hate, anger, and utter despair.

"No, you are the problem, you've always been the problem, I hate you, and Adelle hates you, too. We are going back to Poland."

"What are you talking about? You don't make any sense. My daughter hates me. Really? What's wrong with you?" I struggled to keep a straight face due to her continued and now increasing lunacy.

"It's something like Stockholm Syndrome."

The only thing I knew about Stockholm Syndrome at this point was Patty Hearst, who was abducted and brainwashed to do the bidding of her captors, and to like it, to become one of them, to blur the lines between captor and captive. I knew that trauma could be a powerful implement, but I wasn't ready to start listening to what my wife was trying to say to me; I just wanted us to get help.

After that, she didn't look at me or respond, but just stood there, blank, and expressionless, not registering anything that I was able to perceive, as if staring at a tv that wasn't there. This was a common response for her, where she would just shut down completely, and I would wonder what to do, like maybe I should do a light knock-knock on her head to see if anybody was there. Eyes open, but not there, something I thought resembled catatonia. This struck me as strange, but I never thought too much of it, as it was just one of your mom's many unexplained idiosyncrasies, and I accepted her as she was.

"Stockholm Syndrome, Agata, what are you talking about? You've totally lost it again."

"The counterintuitive form of captor/captive bonding was first given a name in 1973: Stockholm Syndrome (Soskis and Ochberg, 1982). This condition embodies several of the essential attachment paradoxes (Graham, 1994): gratitude for the perpetrator having spared the victim's life, the leveraging of small kindnesses, false mediation and 'resolution' between captor and hostage through coerced sympathy for the ideological agenda of the perpetrator, and won-over identification with the devaluation of perpetrator enemies... Stockholm Syndrome is merely the outer (and consensually validated) layer of a more complex configuration for personality alteration in the hands of perpetrators who have more prolonged influence over victims. Patients from intergenerational, interfamilial and criminal cults and cartels describe specific child-rearing practices that involve the use of pain and fear (e.g., starving, burning, beating, sensory deprivation, overexposure to severe heat and cold, sexual sadism, electrical shock torture) (Lacter, 2011; Miller, 2012; Noblitt and Perskin, 2000; Sinason, 1994). Such experiences, which trigger and then institutionalize dissociative responses at an early age, can disrupt the usual differentiation of self- and other-representations; concurrently it creates a storehouse of rage that can be harnessed and redirected by perpetrators and programmers" (Schwartz 18).

The words "Stockholm Syndrome" brought forward the memory of your mom crying because your grandpa had a hurt elbow and couldn't play tennis. Some of the most genuine tears I had ever seen from your mom were because "he loves to play tennis," and temporarily couldn't.

"I'm taking Adelle back to Poland for either Christmas or New Year's."

I didn't know what to say to her. This statement was as perplexing to me as if she had said that she was going to rob banks with the Symbionese Liberation Army, and I didn't want to argue nonsense. I knew that you loved me, as I knew I was a man and not a giraffe. Her telling me otherwise was the same as her telling me that something terrible had happened while you were in Poland with your grandparents.

Certainly, my daughter doesn't hate me, and why would she want to return to Poland? I thought. *Did they tempt her with extra candy or let her stay up later?* I imagined, joking to myself in my head. According to you, I was your best friend, though I never wanted your mom to hear you say that, nor did I even really want it to be true. But I did know that it was true, and that this was just one more sign that something had happened in Poland. I was just a stay-at-home dad, spending every day with you for the past year, every day except for when you were in Poland. And now I was being told that you hated me on the first day together after you had spent three months with your grandparents.

While I knew it wasn't true and couldn't be true, I also knew that "young children are quite susceptible to parents [or grandparents] who would rewrite history for self-serving purposes," and that "it is fairly easy to confuse children into doubting their own perception of reality..." (Clawar and Rivlin 139). My antennae were up, and I knew that something was going on. I wasn't at ease, knowing that you "hating" me wasn't much more crazy than your mother "hating" me. *Why would she say either?* I wondered to myself.

It was very challenging trying to live with and raise a child with a person who could change anything at any time from white to black, and did, and I had to be ok with it and learn how to adapt under these conditions, but I wouldn't have traded it for anything else in the world. Whatever it was, whatever skeleton your mom had in her closet, I was ready, willing, and I thought able, to tackle it with her.

It was twice as difficult, at least, because I still believed that white would remain white, and black would remain black, and so I was burnt every time. Every time, I believed her, and every time she had her ways of keeping me away from any bona fide truth whatsoever, whatever that was.

How was six months of rent missing? I didn't and couldn't know because she wouldn't tell me. Why did you have to stay in Poland when the doctors said you might die earlier in the year, and why did I have no say in the matter? I didn't and couldn't know because she wouldn't tell me. Why did you hate me when an hour ago you loved me? I didn't and couldn't know. It just was because this was what she decided.

"Why would you go back to Poland?" I asked as if I was asking a nonsense question. "Just today you told me that you couldn't wait to be here with me, you've been desperate to get back to me since day one; you didn't want me to leave. Do you remember all the love letters you just wrote to me? How can you say these things? You don't make sense."

"We are going back for either Christmas or New Year's," she repeated with certainty, almost grinding her teeth as she spoke. I believed that she believed what she was saying, but at the same time, I also believed it to be utter nonsense, and it was difficult to treat it any differently.

"I wrote them on purpose, I wrote those letters on purpose," she mumbled, under her breath.

It felt weird, and I shot back, "You wrote them on purpose, and now you hate me. Don't you understand that what you are saying doesn't make any sense? Agata, what you are telling me is totally crazy."

"It's like a cult," she mumbled, looking at the floor, avoiding any eye contact with me.

> A 1988 document published by the Michigan State Police, entitled "Occult Criminal Investigation" defined a cult as, "A system of religious or magical beliefs. The term is used to describe practitioners of those beliefs, the ceremonies and the patterns of worship" (31).

The word "cult" bounced right off me; I didn't have the context to understand what that could even mean. My mind scrambled to respond to her as calmly and simply as possible.

"You just got back from there and you are miserable, like your psyche just went through a meat grinder. You are not going back to Poland with my daughter. I don't know what's wrong with you, but that will happen over my dead body. Do you think I'm not going to figure this out, Agata?"

"I know you will," she murmured, as if talking only to herself. It was as if she knew I was right but could only act as if I were wrong.

"Then why are you messing with me? Why are you speaking this crazy nonsense? Our daughter will not be going back to Poland until we figure out what just happened. Tell me what happened to you!"

"Yes, Iain, she is," she assured me again, talking to me as if it were already decided, as if she wasn't concerned with my point of view one bit, or that it just didn't matter as when you had to stay in Poland because you "might die." I didn't like it when she spoke this way, as there was no way to argue with her, no room for compromise from her side. And, in this case, what she was telling me was not possible because there was no way that I would let it happen.

"Why, Agata? Why would you go back?" I asked, flabbergasted, feeling like I was getting holes in my sails. I felt the same way I might have felt if I was asking her why she had just pooped on the floor in front of me. She was happy when we were together, now was miserable, and she was also telling me that she was going to return to the source of whatever was tormenting her, taking you with her. I couldn't believe it.

I knew that she was hurting, her pain was obvious, and I just wanted to wrap my arms around her and ease whatever pain she was going through. I couldn't stand to see her in pain, and I writhed within myself, feeling at least some of what she was feeling. But I couldn't do anything except keep asking questions. I had just gotten back. I was away for too long.

She had been staring at the ground, but now looked up, directly into my eyes. She was shaky and apparently extremely angry, her jaw was clenched, and her lips were pursed. "Mind control," she blurted out, quickly returning her eyes to the kitchen floor.

"Mind control? Who mind control, Agata? What are you talking about? What does 'mind control' mean?"

"You."

"Me? Are you crazy? You don't make any sense, again you make no sense at all. What happened over there in Poland? This is exactly what happened last time."

"No, this never happened before."

"Yes, Agata, this is exactly what happened after Easter. You are crazy now just like you were then; this is the same thing, again. You began to get help because of exactly this, and we thought that it was borderline personality disorder, and this is the same thing."

"No, that never happened. I've always hated you."

> "Variously known as brainwashing, coercive persuasion, thought reform, or thought control, the term mind control refers to processes or dynamics in which an individual or group systematically deploys manipulative methods to persuade, influence, or coerce others to conform to the manipulator's wishes and ideologies. The term mind control has been applied through many tactics – psychological or physical torture – which subverts an individual's sense of control over his or her own thinking, behavior, emotions, actions, or decision-making functions (Hassan, 1990; Lacter, 2011; Miller, 2012; H. Schwartz, 2000)" (Schwartz 80).

"In cases of organised abuse, clinicians have suggested that traumatic and dissociative psychopathology may be deliberately induced by sexually abusive groups in order to inhibit victim disclosure and reduce the likelihood of detection (Sachs and Galton 2008, Epstein et al. 2011, Miller 2012), resulting in what Chu (2011: 263) has described as 'massive devastation of the self.' In the literature on organised abuse, such ordeals are frequently referred to as 'mind control'... enjoining the victim to participate in her own exploitation'' (Salter 151–152, 154).

I turned away from her, feeling wounded and dejected, and I walked back into the living room to see what you were doing. Those words from her felt like hot daggers, but they also sounded utterly ridiculous; only hours ago, and for the duration of the previous six months, she had professed her undying and total love for me, and for our family. This felt unreal, and my distress was due to being aware that something was seriously wrong with her and that she was in tremendous pain. I just wanted my healthy family back.

I stood there a moment in the doorway watching you as you watched tv. You were still mesmerized, blankly staring at the screen, oblivious to me or anything else. I reached over and turned off the tv, and you immediately began to cry, in the same way that you might've if you had fallen off your bike. It was a cry of panic and fear, but I wasn't shocked. I had seen this before, after your last return from your grandparent's house in Poland.

"Behavior is a child's primary form of communication. When children do not have the words or ability to verbally communicate trauma they begin to 'act out,' have psychosomatic symptoms, or show their trauma through behavioral indicators. Many of the behaviors that may indicate CSA [child sexual abuse] are... sudden emotional or behavioral changes... clinginess or fear of being alone... sleep disturbances including nightmares... poor concentration... enuresis and encopresis... aggression... social withdrawal... eating disturbances... anxiety... and sexual behaviors..." (Goodyear–Brown 8).

Your mom rushed in as if something were wrong, and you left the couch and ran into her embrace, still crying. She looked at me as if I was terrible, and asked, "Why did you do that?"

"Why did I do what? Turn off the tv, Agata? Are you serious? Is that what you think the problem is? Since when does our daughter ever react like that? Only after being in Poland."

"Often, children demonstrate very rapid onset of physical and emotional agitation with equally rapid change back to relative calmness. Caretakers and clinicians will describe this effect as a 'light switch'. One moment, the child will be calm and happy, the next moment extremely upset and inconsolable, or agitated and aggressive" (Krill 20).

"I love you, Mommy. Mommy, are you ok? I love you, Mommy," you repeated several times.

"Yes, Delly, I am ok. I love you," she responded, though it was obvious she wasn't ok at all.

"Mommy, are you happy? I love you, Mommy. I love you, Mommy."

"Yes, of course I'm happy. I love you, Delly," she repeated back to you using baby talk, trying to pull off a smile.

For me, this was weird, all of it. Why were you worried about whether your mom was ok, whether she was happy? Was she not ok or happy? When did she stop being ok or happy?

Once you were done consoling your mom, I invited you to go into your bedroom to play. We closed the door, and we began to reconnect. I asked you what you wanted to do, and you got on all fours and began crawling around on the ground and pretending to be your cat.

"Daddy, I'm Ally, Daddy, I'm Ally," you said, as you crawled around on the ground by my feet.

"Ok, but I wanted to play with my daughter, Adelle, can I play with Adelle?"

"Daddy, I'm Ally, I'm Ally," you repeated.

"What does Ally want to do?" I asked, willing to play along to see what you were thinking.

You pushed a plastic ball over to me with your nose.

"Throw the ball, Daddy."

I rolled the ball, and you scampered after it on your hands and knees, pushed it back to me with your nose. "Meeyew, meeyew," you chimed in a high-pitched voice. I had never played this game before, so I knew where it originated: Poland. I rolled the ball out to you a couple more times so that I could observe more. It felt good to be in here with the door closed, a little distance away from whatever your mom was going through.

"Ok, I want to be Ally now," I stated, as I got down on all fours.

"I'm Ally, Daddy, I'm Ally," you claimed.

"I want to play too. Can't I be Ally too? I want to play with Adelle."

Without waiting for you to reply, I chased the ball around, acting like something in between a cat and a dog, trying to make you laugh, trying to begin to release whatever negativity had infiltrated our home. And you did laugh, and you seemed to wake up a bit. I didn't know what was going on, but I did know you, and it felt good to have you back. There was no way I was going to let you go back to Poland under the present circumstances, and if it were to ever happen again, I would be going with you. What the heck had been going on over there?

> "Traumatized children repeat actions. Whereas adults who are shocked or severely stressed tend to talk about it, dream, or to visualize, children take far more action. They certainly take more dramatic action. And they repeat. After traumatic experiences, children appear to have two behavioral options, to play or to reenact. And sometimes the boundary between these two behaviors is indistinct. Children, however, will define their post-traumatic play as 'fun,' even when it looks grim and joyless to the outsider" (Terr 265).

"I help Mommy when she's sick," you announced to me. It knocked the wind out of me to hear you say that.

"Adelle, what do you mean that you help Mommy when she's sick? Is your mom sick?"

"I help Mommy when she's sick," you repeated, rotely. I didn't push it; this was enough information for now.

Later that day, I unpacked my bags, hid all your Christmas presents in your mom's and my bedroom, and walked out of the bedroom with my new Realtree Camo baseball hat that I had brought back with me, a gift from my stepdad, your Grandpa George.

"Take that off. You cannot wear that hat. Iain, take it off, you can't wear it," your mom demanded, apparently angry and scared that I would consider wearing this hat. Things were not getting less weird and more back to normal as time went on.

"What do you mean I can't wear it? I like it, it's kind of like my thoughts are protected by the camo," I said, trying to joke with her and lighten her demeanor.

"Take it off. You can't wear it," she ordered again. I looked at you, and you were frozen, it was dense in our house, and wearing the hat was not worth it, and so I took it off.

This reminded me of the group of pictures that your mom had sent me, with your great grandfather, Waldek, wearing a camo hat. It also reminded me of the time that I opened a can of whiskey and coke, causing you to start to panic and hyperventilate. Your mom said, "Don't worry, it's Daddy, not Grandpa." That was after your trip to Poland for Easter earlier this year.

You with your maternal great-grandfather, Waldek Labun. Sierokowo, PL, 2010

I wondered if you were choosing to sit there with your great grandpa. Were you having fun? Your mom sure sent me a lot of these pictures; she certainly captured this moment. I wondered if anyone else wears a camo hat besides him that could cause you to be afraid of camo hats. I wondered how I could be forbidden from wearing my brand-new camo hat in my own house (see Appendix 24).

I was getting frustrated by the constant flow of nonsense since I returned, exactly the opposite of what I had imagined I would be experiencing.

The total loss of contact with your mom began to create some panic within me. Something was going on that I did not yet understand but knew I would. I tried to read, but my mind was spinning, and I could not focus. I dropped to the floor and did fifty pushups with ease; I was stronger than ever, physically and mentally, and I did not believe that the mountain in front of us could be any more menacing than the ones we had already conquered.

That evening, I tried playing one of the movies that I had downloaded for you, Disney's "Fantasia," and the same thing happened again. You and I were sitting on the couch as the 1940 classic began, the images on the screen in front of us bouncing to the classical music. I was thrilled just to be sitting next to my daughter again, a dream come true, but I could not yet relax.

Your mom appeared in the doorway to the living room almost as soon as the movie started, her hands on her hips, upset about this as well. I looked from her to you, and then back to her, trying to figure out what she could be thinking. Your eyes were glued to the tv, and you were getting visibly upset, beginning to hyperventilate. It appeared to me that you had seen this before. I had no idea what to expect as I had never seen this movie; I had just recently downloaded it for us to watch, simply because it was a classic.

"You can't watch this with her," your mom sternly instructed.

"What do you mean? Why wouldn't I be able to watch this with her? I can't wear the hat, and now I can't watch a Disney movie. What are you talking about now?"

"No, Iain, not this. You cannot watch this with her!" she repeated in dead seriousness, returning to the kitchen to be by herself. I turned it off, having no idea what was going on, but again, it was not worth arguing about. I wanted peace in our home, and there were obviously bigger fish to fry.

Everything was abnormal; whatever had taken place in Poland was causing this reaction, and I did not like it at all. Effects have a cause, or causes, and the effects that I was witnessing were not my doing; the causes were in Poland, and I had to get to the bottom of it, once and for all.

That evening when it was time for your shower, you started to hyperventilate and belt at the top of your lungs, "Not my pee pee, not my pee pee, not my pee pee, please not my pee pee!" just like after your previous return from Poland.

"Please not my pee pee, not my pee pee!" you continued to pleadingly demand, as if there were an imminent threat to your pee pee because it was shower time.

Your mom brought you from the shower to the sink in your bedroom without a word. She started pouring water from the faucet over your midsection, onto your private parts. You continued to cry out; I stood a few feet behind, utterly perplexed. This was identical to after the last visit, exactly the same thing, screaming about your pee pee, and being consoled by your mom in a way that appeared weird to me. I wanted to trust her, and I did, but I also began to realize that I maybe could not or should not.

I walked up and took you from your mom, glared at her, and I walked into the other room to get away from her, hugging you tight to my body while I sang to you.

"It's a soap irritation, Iain," she pled, as she did after the last time you returned from Poland.

"No, it isn't a soap irritation. This is the same thing, Agata, the exact same thing. Why can't you see that? You cannot lie to me any longer."

"It's a soap irritation," she repeated, robotically.

"No, Agata, it is not. There was no soap there tonight. None. We hadn't even begun to wash anything. Just walking into the shower makes her scream now? And why is it that we never have this problem except when she returns from your parents' house? What kind of soap are you using over there? Why would you keep using it? You don't make any sense." I was upset, but I did not yell, it was more of a hiss of disgust and dismay. There was nothing that I hated more than the thought, or the reality, of you in pain. "Agata, we are taking her to the doctor," I declared.

"No, we don't need to go to a doctor. I already know that it's just a soap irritation."

Again, I could not argue with her; it was all nonsense, and you were there, so it just wasn't possible. I would have to wait until later, when you would be sleeping, to really get to talk to your mom. I let her finish your shower for the night, having seen enough, not wanting to hear you scream again. I waited for you both to return, sitting on your bed, thinking.

Your mom carried you in, wrapped in a towel, and I stood up to take you from her. She passed you to me, and I finished drying you off while your mom selected your pajamas from the shelf.

"Adelle, show Daddy your butt," she directed.

You looked at her, appearing to be confused, looking for explanation or confirmation.

"Go ahead, Adelle, show Daddy."

You hopped up onto the bed and turned around so that I could clearly see your backside. Right in the middle of your right cheek was a dark bruise, bigger than a quarter dollar.

"Tell Daddy who gave it to you," she directed again.

You looked at her again, puzzled.

"Tell him, Delly. You can tell him."

"Dziadziuś," you blurted out, Polish for "Grandpa." Your mom looked satisfied that I had received that information. But then she immediately turned away from me, acting as if she was disgusted, letting me know she was refusing to divulge any more information on the matter.

I was dumbfounded, I just stood there, amazed, but not in a good way. My mind drew a blank – *ok so your grandpa gave you a nasty bruise on your butt.* I couldn't picture a scenario, even in my wildest imagination, where this could be possible, possibly a sports accident, or maybe... I didn't know, but I had zero information. This was all she gave me. I wasn't allowed to ask questions because she hated me now, apparently. I had to be patient, but I would get to the bottom of it.

We put you to bed early because I desperately needed time to talk to your mother alone. We each read two books that you chose for us to read to you. You gave your mom "One Fish, Two Fish" by Dr. Seuss, and "Are You My Mother" by P.D. Eastman. I chuckled to myself when you gave her the second title, thinking that you actually weren't sure, realizing how ridiculous that was. *I don't know if it's her either*, I thought. *Where is Mommy?*

You gave me "Curious George" by H. A. Rey and Margret Rey, and "Guess How Much I Love You" by Sam McBratney, the two books that I read to you the most, the two books that I read to you over the phone while we were apart. Your mom encouraged me to keep reading these two books to you.

"...I love you right up to the moon – and back," is how the McBratney book ends. I carried you over to the window so that we could look at the moon together, so that I could tell you that I also loved you, Adelle Avery, to the moon and back.

This is something that we did every night that we were together, often we would make up other places, for example, sometimes I would say, "I love you to Poland and back."

I was looking forward to having your mom to myself. I needed to speak with her without your eyes and ears within range. My "collaborator" was missing in action. I needed to reconnect with her, and I believed that we would, as we always had before. The things that she was saying were not true, but preposterous, and contrary to everything else she had said, contrary to the reality that I knew. The reality that I knew was, "Your girls love you and can't wait to see you." What had happened?

We got into bed together; she turned her back to me and lay still, as far away from me as she could get.

"Agata, we need to talk. I need you to tell me what is going on. I need you to explain to me what happened in Poland."

"My dad created a red herring. Your drug, psychological, and criminal histories will be used against you. Your parental rights are going to be terminated. You need to go back to the U.S. and let me and Adelle return to Poland."

"Your dad did what?" I paused, trying to process this new nonsense, and then continued, "I don't care about your dad or whatever you say he has created. What are you talking about now?"

"He created a red herring. Your drug, psychological, and criminal histories will be used against you."

"Agata, you are crazy. Let's stop worrying about me for now. We can talk about anything that you want to talk about, but right now I need to talk about you and what you are doing and saying now."

"Nobody is going to believe you. You need to go back to the U.S., and you need to let me and Adelle go back to Poland."

Merriam-Webster defines a red herring as "something that distracts attention from the real issue," and further explains the origin of the term is derived from the smell of red herring being used to "distract hunting dogs from the trail of their quarry" (https://www.merriam-webster.com/dictionary/red%20herring).

Grammarly defines a red herring as a "rhetorical device that diverts attention from the topic-at-hand." It is a "tool used in an argument. The red herring fallacy causes a distraction in an argument that draws attention off-topic. Because of this, a red herring is a type of logical fallacy. A red herring is a way for a speaker to win an argument by bringing up a matter that is irrelevant to the main issue." Using bullet points, the website breaks it down this way: "topic A is argued, speaker brings up topic B, irrelevant to Topic A, and then Topic A is either ignored or forgotten because Topic B takes precedence" (https://writingexplained.org/grammar-dictionary/red-herring).

According to your mom, even at this point, "A" would be me claiming you were taken to Poland against my will and "B" would be my drug, psychological, and criminal histories. She was claiming that this would be enough to totally distract people from thinking about "A," and I didn't believe her. But she was adamant.

"You aren't taking my daughter anywhere. You have lost it again, just like before. I don't care if anyone believes me. I don't care about my 'histories.' I care about right now. I care about you and about our daughter – that's it."

"I hate you."

"That's what I'm talking about, Agata. You can't just say that, and everything else, with no explanation. You can't just jump from white to black and then act as if it's only ever been black. You don't make sense. Why don't you talk to me? I miss you, Agata. I love you. I'm sorry I left you for so long. I'm back now."

"I'm taking Adelle back to Poland for either Christmas or New Year's."

I was talking to a wall; she wouldn't budge, just kept repeating the same things over and over, no willingness to reflect, no ability to go off script.

"Agata, I need you. I've been gone for three months. I need you, I need my partner, I need Adelle's mom, I need you, Agata, I need you."

"I hate you."

I was frustrated; she was totally unavailable. What had I returned to? Where was she, and what was she doing?

"I need you, I need you, I need you, I need you, I need you, I need you...," I repeated over and over.

She ignored me, and I kept going, "Agata, I need you, I need you, I need you...," purposely trying to be annoying, and to make a point.

She pushed her butt toward me as an invitation to have sex, to bribe me to shut up, to stop the conversation at least for the night, but this upset me more because this is not what I meant at all by "I need you."

"I don't want your pussy. I don't need your pussy. I don't care about your pussy. What I care about is your soul. Agata, I want your soul. What's wrong with you?"

She did not respond.

"Agata, we are going to see Kees together on Monday. I need you to go with me. Agata, I love you."

I was disgusted with her, and with myself, and I let it rest; we went to sleep.

CHAPTER 28

DAY 2: SATURDAY, DECEMBER 11, 2010

I was grateful to be home, to be back with my girls. The details mattered, of course, I did care that my wife supposedly hated me, and was saying she was going to take you to a cult. But I wasn't really all that concerned. I had seen these dramatic, 180-degree shifts in your mom before, and I wasn't scared or fooled; I could see through her. Well, maybe that is not entirely true, as I did wake up in a pool of sweat, but there was no doubt in my mind that I would figure it out.

Your mom didn't want to get out of bed in the morning; first she claimed that she was praying, and then she claimed that she had a migraine. I used a knife to chip some ice out of our freezer, put it inside a cloth, and handed it to her so she could put it on her forehead. She seemed grateful, and I was almost thankful that she had a migraine so I could help her with something.

"Migraine headaches are experienced by many patients suffering multiple personality disorder. Some are precipitated by repressed rage. Others occur when one alternate [personality] punishes or intrudes upon another, or when one tries to escape from an undesirable situation that is buried in the unconscious" (Kluft 31).

"When did you start praying? Who are you praying to? Why don't you talk to your husband?"

"I'm praying, please leave me alone," she repeated, and so I did.

"OK, Agata, whatever you say." I had never seen her pray before.

I needed to remain centered and focused, I could not jump into her world as I had done in the past. Rather, I had to stand firm. She had fallen overboard, and I knew that she would come back on board if I just remained there; it was my job to hold the line and give her something solid that she could hold onto when she was ready.

You and your mom were both talking in some sort of baby talk, something you were doing together, and something that only happened after Poland, in my experience. Even when she read to you last night, it was in some sort of sing-songy baby voice; I hated that voice. It was distant and fake sounding. It drove me nuts, because your mom was "playing," but you were not; you had actually regressed to using baby talk.

In addition, your mom started speaking to you in Polish right in front of me. I let it go for a while; I really couldn't believe it was happening. It wasn't as if she was teaching you Polish, but rather she was simply choosing to communicate with you in a way that she knew I could not understand. I observed it for a while, decided that its only purpose was so I didn't understand, and I told her that I wanted it to stop.

"Of course, you can speak Polish to her. I want you to speak Polish with her. I want her to speak many languages. But I don't understand Polish, this is my house too, and it is really weird in this house right now. Why do you want to leave me out? We speak English in our home. I am not going to put up with secrets, and I feel that you are disrespecting me."

"Yes, Iain, I hate you," she said in disgust, right in front of you. "Polish is Adelle's language. She is going to Poland."

"Polish is one of her languages, but I don't understand it. I'm asking that you not use it right now. She is definitely not going to Poland," I reiterated once again.

"Yes, Iain, she is. She doesn't like living here. My parents love her more than your parents do."

"Agata, what are you talking about? That doesn't even make sense. Do you remember trying to get a visa so that our family could move to the U.S.?"

"I never wanted to move to the U.S.."

"Yes, Agata, you did. I can prove to you that you did."

"No, that was just part of the plan. I never wanted to live in the U.S. I've always hated you."

"Yes, I have proof that you did. Everything you say now is the opposite of what it was just days ago. How can that be, Agata?"

"No, it's always been the same. I've always hated you. You are not a good father. Adelle is going back to Poland."

"Whatever you say, Agata," I conceded. "I need you to give me either your passport or her passport, and I will give you my passport. Then neither of us can leave the country with our daughter. I don't trust you right now, and you are scaring me."

"I'm not giving you my passport, and we are going back to Poland for either Christmas or New Year's."

"No, Agata, you are not, and that's what I'm talking about. And I'm not asking for your passport. I'm asking for either one, you can choose. And I'll give you mine. Then we're equal, and neither of us can leave with our child without the other."

"You're holding us hostage," she repeated.

She did eventually trade my passport for hers, but this lasted only a couple of days. She took her passport back out of my jacket pocket without telling me, and continued to insist that she was taking you back to Poland for either Christmas or New Year's.

You showed more signs that indicated to me that you had been abused. You came into the bathroom while I was peeing, and you told me I look like "Dziadziuś." Your mom heard, and she turned and walked away. Here's Dziadziuś again, first the nasty, circular, bruise, now you are comparing our penises. *What the heck is going on?!*

I exited the bathroom, was walking down the hall toward our living room, and you ran up to me, got on your knees and slid between my legs, kind of like a leapfrog game.

"Stinky balls, stinky balls, stinky balls," you blurted out, saying it as if it were funny.

I didn't look at you, but at your mom. I glared at her; I didn't say anything to either of you at the time, I just redirected us toward something else.

Later, the three of us were sitting on the couch, you in the middle of your mom and I, your mom barely sitting there, distant, pressed up against the armrest. "Jajko," you said, out of the blue, seemingly just to break the silence in the room.

"Jajko, jajko, jajko," you repeated.

I looked at your mom, "What is jajko?"

She didn't respond; I wanted to know.

"Agata, what is 'jajko'?" I pressed, sensing it was weird by both your behavior and by hers, the density of the air signaling that something strange was going on.

"It's what my dad calls balls," she replied nonchalantly, with a sigh, knowing that I was going to have an immediate reaction to her answer and trying to play it off as a non-issue.

What is going on with my daughter talking so much about her grandpa's testicles? Is this some new developmental stage I missed, some anatomy training that started in Poland? Why are balls even part of the conversation with my three-year-old girl? I know that I never have the need to talk to her about these things, my three-year old daughter. What could be going on while she's in Poland? "Stinky balls?" Is this really happening? Why doesn't Agata say anything to me about the obvious, instead of saying she hates me, and these other crazy things?

"But children do not always express information in words, and their small voices often reflect only a minimal understanding of their experience. Behaviors are precursors to language (Fivush, 1996) and powerful pieces of what preschool children have to disclose about their experiences" (Hewitt 4).

Ally, your cat, was now pooping everywhere except the litter box. She never did this, your mom hated it, and I thought that it was kind of funny. She was scared of your mom, as I was, and I found it ironic that the cat was mostly pooping on your mom's side of the bed, or on the chair that she liked to use in the kitchen. "Even the cat is afraid of you, Agata. This has happened before, why don't you see that?"

"No, this has never happened before," she claimed again, "this is how it's always been. God doesn't approve of our marriage," she stated confidently, then added, "It's been seven years," stating this as if I should have known that it was important, and what that would mean.

"Agata, what are you talking about? You don't make any sense. Monday we are going to Kees together, and you can tell him what you're telling me. I can't wait until you tell him what you're telling me. What 'god' are you talking about, and why doesn't it want us to be married?"

"During acts of atrocity, perpetrators expressed a sense of god-like or omnipotent selfhood. During abuse, Lily's father would tell her 'I am God, I am the God you must worship. I am the God you must adore. I am evil.' Other participants reported that their abusers called themselves 'gods', 'the masters of the universe', 'warlocks' and 'kings'" (Salter 161).

I couldn't wait to see Kees de Vries; I was excited and impatient, like waiting for an important package to arrive in the mail. I wanted your mom to tell him what she was telling me. I was sure that he would help us, and I wanted to tell him what was going on right away, but I had to wait until Monday when he would be back in the office. I knew that Kees had spent enough time with your mom to see through this current phase, that she and her current belief system could not hold up under scrutiny. I saw him as my ally, and though I didn't have many, I was confident that he would be a good one. There was no other family close by, no trustworthy friends for me to turn to or lean on.

You let out a scream from the bathroom, a blood curdling, terror scream. Your mom ran in and snatched you up from off the toilet, where you were apparently trying to poop. She rushed you to the sink in your bedroom to run the tap water over you, singing in Polish.

"What is it, Agata, another soap irritation? There is no soap irritation, there was no soap, this was never a soap irritation. We are taking her to a doctor."

"No, she is not going to a doctor," she reiterated, "I already know that it is just a soap irritation."

It felt like I was spinning, like everything was bizarre, all of a sudden. My partner was unavailable. I had to start trying to figure this out, so I went back to where we had left off before: borderline personality disorder. I emailed myself some of the things I was once again forced to research, for my record, for evidence.

"http://en.wikipedia.org/wiki/Borderline_personality_disorder
Sat, Dec 11, 2010, 5:43 PM
Iain Bryson to me"
["Borderline personality disorder (BPD), also known as emotionally unstable personality disorder (EUPD), is a personality disorder characterized by a long-term pattern of intense and unstable interpersonal relationships, distorted sense of self, and strong emotional reactions. Those affected often engage in self-harm and other dangerous behaviors, often due to their difficulty with returning their emotional level to a healthy or normal baseline. They may also struggle with a feeling of emptiness, fear of abandonment, and detachment from reality."]

"http://en.wikipedia.org/wiki/Splitting_(psychology)
Sat, Dec 11, 2010, 5:45 PM
Iain Bryson to me"
["Splitting (also called black-and-white thinking, thinking in extremes or all-or-nothing thinking) is the failure in a person's thinking to bring together the dichotomy of both perceived positive and negative qualities of something into a cohesive, realistic whole. It is a common defense mechanism wherein the individual tends

to think in extremes (e.g., an individual's actions and motivations are all good or all bad with no middle ground)."]

I was downloading movies, tv shows, and music using a torrent pretty much constantly when we lived in The Netherlands, and it was at full tilt, even while I was trying to get knowledge and understanding about whatever was going on with your mom.

"Can you download something for me?" she asked. I was so happy that she had spoken to me in a normal way, about something normal. It felt good to hear that side of her, and it felt good to be able to help her with something. This was a step up from chipping ice for her migraine.

"Of course, what can I get you?"

"Download me Drake's new album, 'Thank Me Later.'"

"Ok, not a problem; I'll have it for you shortly."

She listened to it incessantly over the next three weeks, hundreds of times sounds like an exaggeration even to me, but it may not be. It was as if the kitchen became a Drake concert. I had never listened to Drake; I didn't even know who he was, and I didn't know your mom listened to him either. But from then on it was just a few of the songs off this album that were bumping from your mom's phone wherever she went, which was mostly just in the kitchen.

The last album your mom asked me to download.
Thank Me Later *by Drake.*

One of the songs of her new soundtrack was "Miss Me," which ends with the following lyrics:

"...You know what it is when I finally make it home
I just hope that you miss me a little when I'm gone
Yeah I just hope that you miss me a little when I'm gone
And you just tell me what you down for, anything you down for
I know things have changed, know I used to be around more
But you should miss a little when I'm gone
I just hope that you miss me a little when I'm gone, gone, gone
Uh, yeah, forever in our hearts
JJ, we love you boy, H-Town
I'm gone, I'm gone, I'm gone
I'm gone, I'm gone, when I'm gone
I just hope that you miss me, miss me
Miss me, miss me
Miss me a little when I'm gone
Miss me a little when I'm gone, gone, gone
Oh woah, oh woah, oh woah"

This music instantly drove me crazy, like fingernails on a chalkboard. She was talking about leaving, and now she was listening to it as well, repeatedly. The living room had larger speakers, so I was able to drown it out, mostly, for the next few weeks. I wanted joy in our home, not this garbage.

"Agata, why do you keep listening to this? I miss you, I miss you, I miss you! I just got back from being away for three months. Three months! I missed you every day, and I miss you right now. Do you not miss me? Where are you? What is going on?"

I normally didn't pay that much attention to what your mom was listening to, but now she wasn't talking to me; she was pretty much a miserable tape recorder, just repeating strange things over and over. The fact that she specifically asked me to download this album for her, and then proceeded to play it repeatedly for the next three weeks suggested to me that she was trying to tell me something, whether consciously or not.

"I quote others only to better express myself." (Michel de Montaigne, from your mom's quote journal).

I didn't realize this at the time; I merely was witness to it. I experienced it, and in retrospect, the words "miss me a little when I'm gone, gone, gone..." seem a little personal, to say the least. I missed her then, and I miss her now.

The other main song that broadcast from our kitchen like a broken record for three straight weeks was "Shut It Down," off the same album, the only album:

"Shut it down, down, down (ay, ay, ay)
You would shut it down, down, down (ay, ay, ay)
You'd be the baddest girl around, 'round, 'round (ay, ay, ay)
And they'd notice, they'd notice
You would shut it down, down, down
You would shut it down, down, down
You'd be the baddest girl around, 'round, 'round
And they'd notice, they'd notice
You would shut it...
And together we shut it down, down, down
They know we shut it down, down, down
You'd be the baddest girl around, 'round, 'round
And they'd notice (they'd know) they'd notice (they'd know)
That we shut it down, down, down
They know we shut it down, down, down...
You shut that thing down, you shut it down (down, down, down)
You shut it down, you shut it down (down, down, down)
You shut it down, you shut it down, you shut it..."

Shut what down? Why do I have to listen to this constantly? Is this because now you hate me, because you are taking our daughter back to some "cult"? What does that even mean?
For the most part, she just hung out in the kitchen with her phone, *Glamour* magazines, and her Glamour cigarettes. I continued trying to counteract the odd, negativity that she was broadcasting by keeping the other music going in the living room. I invited her to come into the living room and dance with us, but she wouldn't, so you and I danced alone. It didn't feel the same without her, but I believed that she would come around. *How could she choose to wallow in her misery? Didn't she want to be happy with us again? We were back together, and we had it all. What was she missing, all of a sudden? What could have happened to her?*
It felt like she was pretending almost, like an elaborate April fool's joke; *how could this be my wife, the same person that couldn't wait until we were back together, said that she wanted us to be back together almost every day that we were apart? How is it her, except that it is?* I wanted to put up a video camera in our apartment to capture it all, and I remembered wanting to do that in the past because of "borderline personality disorder," but unfortunately I never did.
She said almost nothing to me, wouldn't even say bye to me when she stepped out to go to the store; she only spoke to you. She pretended that I wasn't there unless she was repeating to me how much she hated me, how I was the cause of her misery, and how she was taking you back to Poland for either Christmas or New Year's. And she didn't hesitate to include you in the conversation.
I asked her what she wanted to watch on tv when we put you to bed, and she provided me with a list of movies that she wanted me to download. From her list, over the course of the next three weeks, we watched "Love and Other Drugs," "Stone," "The Expendables," "Unthinkable," and "Remember Me," also watching some of my selections. She chose to watch the last two, "Unthinkable" and "Remember Me" our second to last and last night together, respectively.

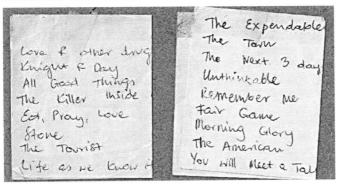

Your mom's list of films to watch with me.

That evening, just my second day back, you had the same type of episode in the shower, panicking, and screaming, "Not my pee pee, not my pee pee, just not my pee pee.." Again, your mom carried you to the sink to rinse you down, I wanted to scream. I was realizing that I couldn't trust her at all, that all the things that I trusted her with because she was your mom, or my wife, or a woman, were foolish. You were my responsibility, and there was something suspicious going on. Hearing you scream like that about your "pee pee" was the worst sound I had ever heard; it sent shivers up and down my spine, and throughout my entire being.

After I read your two books and told you that, "I love you to the moon and back," your mom and I sat on the couch for our evening hangout session. It was frustrating to be so distant from her, but at least we were back together. I had seen this before, and I believed we would work through this one too.

There were a couple of television series that she and I had been watching together that we both waited to resume until now, *Dexter* and *Fringe*. We started to try to watch them, but I just couldn't do it. "Agata, I can't do this right now, Dexter is like you, walking around with weird stuff in his head, he reminds me of you right now. And Olivia also reminds me of you, living in two totally different worlds simultaneously. I don't want entertainment; I want to talk to my wife."

"What do you want to talk about?" she asked.

"Remember that story you told me about your dad cheating on your mom when you were a little girl, the one where he told you, and you were then forced or obligated to confront the other woman? You told me that story within days of meeting me, and several times since, and I've never been a great support with stuff like that. Agata, I think that events like these in your childhood might have something to do with right now."

"No, that never happened."

"What do you mean it never happened? You told me that it happened many times. That is abuse, Agata, it is abuse. Forcing a child into that situation is abuse."

In my opinion, abuse had happened, it had to have, and I was just trying to start with what she had already admitted to and go from there. I didn't want to attack, but rather to understand.

"It never happened."

"Ok, so you told me that the nicest thing that your dad ever did for you was bring you a cup of tea, once. This is another one that you've been telling me since day one. What does this mean? How is it possible? One cup, Agata, one cup of tea is the nicest thing your dad ever did for you? I bring you and Adelle tea daily, so what are you talking about?

"Yes, one cup of tea, that's the nicest thing he's ever done for me. I never had much of a relationship with my dad, with my mom, but not my dad."

"Ok, so don't you think that is something we should look at? For our daughter won't you look at it with me? Can't you see that 'one cup of tea' doesn't make sense? There must be more to the story that you are not telling me. I love you, and I am here for you no matter what, but I need you to start telling me what is going on. The nicest thing your dad ever did for you was bring you one cup of tea, Agata, really? That's your final answer?"

"My mom wants us to travel," she said, changing the subject, in a monotone voice.

"Agata, what are you talking about? You are jumping all over the place, can you please try to focus? Why are you talking about your mom now and how are we going to travel if you hate me?"

"That's what she said, she wants us to travel like Jeremiah and Heather's family."

"I don't know what you're talking about, and I really don't care what your mom wants us to do. I want us to figure this out now. I want to understand how the nicest thing your dad ever did for you could be to bring you one cup of tea."

"I was going to tell you that I met someone..."

"Yeah, but that would be a lie. Why do you insist on messing with me? Just tell me the truth. I know that is not true, I know that there is something else going on. You are miserable, and we're all scared. Even the cat is afraid of you."

"I was going to tell you that I met someone," she repeated, as if by mere repetition I might come to believe her.

"Yeah, and I wouldn't have believed you. Why not just tell me the truth? What does that even mean that you 'were going to tell me something?' Do you realize how happy you were? Do you remember? Do you remember begging me not to leave, telling me you could not wait until we were all back together as a family? Whatever made you like this... I definitely didn't do it."

"It's ok for you to be with someone else, it's ok, it's ok."

"Agata, what are you talking about? I don't want to be with anyone else; I want my wife back."

"You killed that girl."

"What do you mean, 'you killed that girl?' How is that possible? I killed what girl? What are you talking about? How did I do anything? When did I kill that girl, when you were in Poland?"

> "Soul murder is neither a diagnosis nor a condition. It is a dramatic term for a circumstance that eventuates in crime—the deliberate attempt to eradicate or compromise the separate identity of another person. The victims of soul murder remain in large part possessed by another, their souls in bondage to someone else" (Shengold 2).

"You killed that girl," she repeated. "Do it for Adelle, stop thinking about yourself, do it for Adelle."

"Do what for Adelle? Everything that I do, I do for you and Adelle. There is no Adelle without you; I do what I do for us."

"No, do it for Adelle, stop ranting, and do it for Adelle."

That night, when your mom and I were in bed together, she reminded me about the "red herring," about the fact that you were going to be taken from me somehow using my drug, psychological, and criminal histories.

"Agata, you don't know what you're talking about, you are crazy. You're telling me that you've been collecting information on me in some file that is going to be used to take Adelle from me? There is no way that is going to happen, I will not let it happen. There is no way that anybody is going to believe you."

"You don't have any friends, and even your own family knows that you are crazy, Iain."

"Whatever, Agata, I have friends, and you're obviously the crazy one. You are the one that nobody is going to believe."

"They say I might have cancer."

"Who says you might have cancer? Can I take you to the doctor, please?"

"They say I might have cancer, that I might die before I'm thirty."

"Agata, that is crazy, they say you 'might' have cancer, who says someone might have cancer? Anyone might have cancer, why do they think you might? Why don't they know?"

"It's true; they say I might have cancer, that I might die before I'm thirty," she repeated, making me believe that she believed it.

"Ok, so then as your husband, I'm telling you that I want to take you to a doctor here. I want to get a second opinion, and I want to do it now. You are very important to our family, Agata, I love you, and I am your husband. Please let me take you to the doctor. You're twenty-eight, and you're telling me that you have less than two years left. I'm worried about you. We need you to be healthy. Please, let's get help together."

"You are not my husband; God doesn't approve of our marriage," she reminded me.

Agata, what are you talking about, it's happening again! You're doing it again, Agata!"

I would have felt more comfortable if I was able to check her body for marks that I knew about, but she slept fully clothed, and the times that I had seen her go in or out of the shower so far were a blur. I didn't push it; for some reason she was hiding herself from me. For some reason I was the enemy. I was spinning, and I was scared.

I almost didn't believe that she was my wife or your mom. It was hard to wrap my head around the idea that this woman was the same person as the other. Everything was the opposite, and it crossed my mind that this might somehow be an evil twin that I was never told about.

> "Dissociative disorders are a general diagnostic category listed in both in the American Psychiatric Association's *Diagnostic and Statistical Manual of Mental Disorders* (DSM) and the World Health Organization's *International Classification of Diseases* (ICD)...According to the DSM-5: 'Dissociative disorders are characterized by a disruption of and/or discontinuity in the normal integration of consciousness, memory, identity, emotion, perception, body representation, motor control, and behavior' (American Psychiatric Association, 2013, p.291). The diagnosis of dissociative identity disorder represents 'the disruptive experience of two or more distinct personality states, which may be described in some cultures as an

experience of possession' (p. 292) and amnesia or memory gaps for important personal information, traumatic events, or everyday information that cannot be explained as ordinary forgetting" (Noblitt and Noblitt, 2014, 16).

CHAPTER 29

DAY 3: SUNDAY, DECEMBER 12, 2010

Y ou wet the bed, the cat was still not pooping in the litter box, and I awoke in a pool of sweat and diarrhea. You hadn't wet the bed in at least a year when under my care, and I knew that the cat was just scared of your mom. I don't know how I pooped myself, or rather I surprised myself that I did, but I was in fact that scared. It wasn't as if I didn't know why I pooped myself; I knew very well that your mom was literally terrifying me. Your mom and I had to change our sheets in the middle of the night, and I had to take a quick shower.

Part of me enjoyed this, simply because it was my involuntary response to your mom; my nervous system sensed danger and reacted out of pure fear, and I thought that maybe your mom would see this and start to listen. It was obvious that I was not acting, that I was truly scared. How could she not listen? I knew that she loved you, therefore logically she would want to get help. I obviously wasn't lying; maybe she would see this. "Look, Agata, even I'm pooping in our bed now; that's how terrified I am because of you. Please listen to me, not for me, for her."

She told me that she was trying to contact our babysitter, Monia, so that the two of us could go see Kees together, but that didn't work out. Part of me wanted you to go with us if Monia was unavailable because I really wanted him to see your mom. But ultimately, I was unwilling to bring you, concluding that it would only further traumatize you. All that you wanted was for your mom to be ok; you still seemed very concerned for her. "Mommy, are you happy? Mommy, are you ok? Mommy I love you," just like fingernails on a chalkboard, nearly every time that she was in your presence. What did you know that I was not yet privy to?

CHAPTER 30

DAY 4: MONDAY, DECEMBER 13, 2010

I almost didn't go to the appointment because of fear; it was very hard for me to leave you with her at all; she was very "sick." I wasn't sure that you guys would be there when I returned if I were to leave, as she was adamant that she was taking you back to Poland. And now she claimed to hate me, and to have always hated me, so anything was possible. She assured me that she was not going to leave yet, reminding me "Christmas or New Years," and I decided that I had to go, but that I would hurry there and hurry back. I needed to get someone on our side, and I thought Kees was the man for this.

I believed her, mostly, for some reason, but I was still scared. She was nice to me, for the moment, and she told me that she would be there, and that she would even go talk to Kees herself soon. She had a way about her where she could go from seeming to be my enemy back to being my friend at will, but then again, I didn't ever believe that she hated me anyway. I believed we would get to the bottom of whatever was going on.

"I can't wait for that," I spouted at her. "You will not hold up under questioning. You don't make any sense." I hurried out the door, and ran to the tram stop on Fahrenheitstraat, where I caught the first tram heading toward Den Haag Centraal. I only had to go a few stops or so; there was maybe forty-five minutes total travel time from door to door there and back.

I ran from the tram to the elevator, wanting to get to the receptionist and check in as soon as possible. I felt a strong urgency to get back home, and this was constantly in conflict with the urgency that I felt to speak to Kees. I still wasn't sure that you would be home when I returned. I was anxious and out of breath. I had to calm my mind so that I could speak clearly and focus. Kees was late, so I sat down in the waiting room and jotted some thoughts into my notebook.

After a few minutes he sauntered in and invited me to his office. We sat down at a table across from each other, and he apologized for being late, explaining that he had run into someone on the way here, and that they had struck up a conversation in the street. He was very upbeat and positive, and I remember that he looked sharp in his striped, grey pants and fedora hat. I was very happy to see him.

"Well, Kees," I started, "I had only good news until recently. As soon as I got home, Agata completely changed again. She is out of control, saying that she hates me, promising that she is going to take our daughter back to Poland without my consent."

"She can't do that," he assured me, rather easily.

"Yeah, I know that she cannot technically, legally do that, but she says that she is going to do that, and I believe her. I am afraid, I don't know what to do, I need you to talk to her."

"Yes, I want to talk to her. She contacted me a few days ago, and she seemed distraught, she said that she couldn't wait to be back home with you, that this time apart had been very difficult for her."

"Now she is telling me that she hates me, and that she is taking our daughter back to Poland. She doesn't make any sense about anything, and I can't communicate with her. I'm trying, but I can't get through."

"Well, Iain," he reassured me, "she cannot take your daughter out of the country. That is against the law. I'm sure she will come around, just give her some time; you guys have been apart for some time."

"I understand the law, but I am not convinced. I know Agata, and if she tells me that something is going to happen, I tend to believe her. I believe her when she says that she intends on bringing our daughter back to Poland, and I am scared."

"Well, again Iain, she can't just take your daughter to Poland without your permission. That would be a child abduction. Your daughter lives here, not there in Poland."

"Alright," I responded, "well I'm glad that you are sure. That does make me feel a little better." I did feel better, though not by much. I realized that he didn't really know your mother that well, that he had never seen or even been made aware of this side except once in an email I sent to him earlier in the year.

"She doesn't make any sense at all. She is acting in the same ways as before, when we both thought that she might have something like borderline personality disorder. Remember when I emailed you and told you that this was what we thought, telling you not to tell her I told you because I feared her wrath if she found out? Now, it's happening again. She doesn't make any sense; she's totally lost it, and she is threatening to take our daughter back to that third world country where life for them is obviously not good considering what we are going through right now."

"Have you ever heard of the Parable of the Stone?" he asked me.

"I don't think so," I told him, not really searching for it in my memory banks, but just wanting him to tell me.

"There is a man, and this man has come across a giant stone in a field, a stone which he must break. All the answers that he needs depend upon him breaking this stone. The task looks impossible, but this man knows that there is no other option. So, he swings his sledgehammer, and he keeps swinging. The stone does not budge, there is no visible sign that the man is doing anything with all his swinging. The man's friends think that he is crazy for wasting his time on something that he obviously cannot impact. But the man knows and believes that the stone will crack; he knows that he must keep swinging, regardless of what others think or say. What nobody can see is what is happening internally, under the surface. It looks like the man is not breaking the stone because there are no visible signs. However, what they cannot see are many tiny cracks that are forming. These cracks eventually add up, and the stone collapses in a pile of dust, though nobody believes it is possible until it actually happens, because they can't see it."

I knew that this was exactly what I had to do. Kees was right, and I felt blown away by his wisdom. I had seen this before with your mother, and it had never lasted. It wasn't fun, and I didn't understand what was going on, but she had always snapped back. This new version of her was the "not well" one. Before she went to Poland, she was healthy and happy, and now she was the opposite. I knew that she loved me, and that she loved us-our family. I didn't know what was going on, but I wouldn't give up. If I didn't give up, I believed the stone would break. This had to be true, but I did not know what it meant, or how big and strong the stone could be.

"I won't give up," I assured him. "I want her to talk to you as soon as possible. I want her to tell you the things that she is telling me."

"I also want to talk to her as soon as possible," he assured me, obviously concerned.

"Will you try to contact her, please?"

"Yes, I will reach out to her, and I'm sure everything will be alright. Again, just the other day she couldn't wait to be back home with you. I spoke with her on the phone. I will contact her soon."

I felt very confident knowing that Kees was going to reach out to your mom. I had accomplished what I had set out to do, which was to inform him about the current situation at home, to let him know that she had threatened to take you back to Poland, and to get the two of them to communicate. I hurried back home, feeling elated, certain that the stone would, in fact, shatter. There was no doubt in my mind, though as I approached the entrance to our apartment, I gradually lost the elated feeling and fear began to inch back in, not even totally sure that you would be there.

When I got home, you and your mom were sitting on your bed. I hadn't seen her interact with you that much since returning, and I decided to watch. Your mom was leading you in some kind of a game whereby you were pretending to fish for imaginary pearls with an invisible fishing pole. To me it was strange, and it didn't seem like that much fun, certainly not a game that could go on for that long. "Just trying to catch a pearl," she told me.

The game ended pretty much right after she told me what was going on, and I told her that Kees wanted to talk to her.

"Yes, of course I will talk to him," she assured, smiling, but I didn't believe her.

"He is going to contact you, and I need you to tell him what you have been telling me."

"Yes, I'll talk to him," she restated.

I wasn't convinced, but one thing that I thought I had was time. Whatever had happened in Poland had happened in Poland. That was then. Now you were in my house, and I would figure it out. I knew that I couldn't let you be taken back to Poland; I was literally willing to die before I let that happen. I was back, and I believed that your mom was just going through one of her phases. The stone would shatter, and we would be back to dancing together as a family, I believed.

CHAPTER 31

DAY 5: TUESDAY, DECEMBER 14, 2010

"Tue, Dec 14, 2010, 8:11 AM
Iain Bryson to Mom
mom,
got back safely. working on getting things moving. love you"

"Tue, Dec 14, 2010, 10:53 AM
Mom to me
Hi my son. I assume you made it back ok as I would have heard from Agata otherwise.
Weather has gotten cold here with some snow flurries
I mailed off your Geico payment and deposited a check from the Tech School
I checked today and noticed the $233 that I deposited was pulled out by an IRS levy, leaving you with less than $1 in your account. Your insurance payment is fine, so just don't try to get any $ out of the account.
Hope you guys are all well.
I mailed out a total of 4 boxes so let me know as they arrive. Shipping was $150 for these, so will have to wait before I ship more due to the cost.
Email or skype when you get settled.
Love and kisses for all.
Mom"

Your mom continued to suffer, spending more and more time in bed like someone stricken with the flu. My patience was growing thin; she was causing daily turmoil in our home, and I wanted so desperately for us to just be "normal" again.

"Agata, I am asking you to get help with me. I am your husband, and I am terrified. I need you to listen to me. Please listen to me. You look like a rape victim. Agata, you are my wife, and I am telling you that I am terrified. You look terrible."

I wasn't trying to be mean, and nor was I exaggerating. She didn't want to hear it; she didn't respond, she didn't look at me, and she covered her face.

"Agata, I am scared. This has happened before, and now I am telling you that we have to deal with it. I am on your side. I love you, and whatever it is, I can handle it. But we have to deal with it. You have to see Kees."

"Molester!" she belted, quickly emerging from under the covers to glare at me with a fierce intensity, then darting back to safety into her pillow.

A jolt shot through my body; I knew that I was onto something. She had just cracked a little.

"Me, Agata? Really? You're gonna call me a molester? Are you serious? Who is the molester, Agata? Did your daddy diddle you? Who is the molester?"

"Research on childhood sexual abuse over the last decade has documented the prevalence of repressed memory in incest survivors who suffer from a form of post traumatic stress disorder (PTSD) similar to that found in combat veterans and rape victims. Among the symptoms of this disorder are fear, flashback to the trauma, and sleep disorders. These psychological manifestations of sexual abuse may be present in the child as well as in adult survivors, even when actual experience of violation has been repressed, that is, withheld or expelled from conscious memory. Thus, the victim may have an extreme fear of the dark or of intrusion without knowing who or what is the object of her terror. One result of repression is that the identity of the perpetrator may be buried deep in the unconscious, while the trauma of victimization is manifested in psychological distortions which act as screen memories [distorted memories] that are symptoms of an abusive history" (Jacobs 35).

"Child sexual assault by a father or father-figure represents perhaps the most difficult diagnostic and therapeutic challenge in clinical practice. Underreporting and failure to identify this situation are so widespread that there is growing conviction among clinicians that a father or a father-figure is, in fact, the most common perpetrator by far" (Sgroi, 1978, as cited in Burgess et al., 1978, 133).

She was hiding, and she didn't respond to me. I decided that I would take pictures of her to document how she looked to me, which was not well. "Agata, I'm taking pictures of you. You look horrible. I am terrified. I'm taking pictures of you to document this. You will get help!"

Your mom, December 2010. Photos taken by me (see Appendix 25).

"Agata, I don't know what you're doing, but it doesn't work anymore. I see through you now. All that you are doing is making me stronger. Last time you made me stronger, and this time I will not put up with it. Agata, why don't you just stop. I want to do this with you. We need you. Your daughter and I need you so badly."

That evening, I was researching your mom at the computer station, trying to figure out what could be "wrong" with her, when she approached me.

"What are you researching?" she asked, seemingly interested.

"Oh, just you," I told her, in a tone that let her know it was obvious, frustrated that she wouldn't just open up to me.

She put her hand on my shoulder, and I felt a jolt; wow, she was actually touching me. "Iain, Faye just posted that John died. I'm sorry." She paused for a second or two, and then turned and walked away.

I was in shock, a flood of anger and despair shot through me. John Hughley was one of my long-time friends, and yet something larger than even his death was looming in my own household; I couldn't put my finger on it yet, but I could feel that it was there. I had lost my wife, again. "Agata, does that not affect you? He was *our* friend, not just mine. You don't care? No tears from you, huh? Where is my wife?"

"How do you know that I don't have tears?" she said as she turned and continued walking away.

It felt like I had taken some gut shots, the wind knocked out of me a little more. I loved John, and I had just seen him days before. I had been trying to help him kick his heroin habit while I was in Connecticut. He had my number, and I told him to call me anytime he needed anything from me. That phone was now off because it was a Connecticut phone. I wondered if he had called me, if he had needed me, if I had any messages from him on the phone that I didn't have access to. Maybe I was the last person that he called, maybe he needed my help...

I couldn't let my mind wander for too long; he was gone, and I was facing a real, present crisis right in my own home. I had to focus on what was on my plate, which was already too much for me to handle.

I peeked in on her in the shower, cracking the door so that she knew that I was there. I wanted to see if I could identify a particular reason she was hiding her body from me, maybe bruises like you had, for instance. I was kind of joking or pressing the point that this used to be normal. It was ridiculous to me that we had gone from where we were to where we seemed to be now. She was sitting on the ground in what I would describe as a heap; she didn't look good. She had lost a lot of weight, and she was constantly shaky.

I only kept the door cracked for about three seconds. She didn't want me there; I was bothering her. I hated seeing her in pain, and I closed the door and walked away, feeling heavy.

CHAPTER 32

DAY 6: WEDNESDAY, DECEMBER 15, 2010

My friend, Rob, who I had sent John H to in Florida to detox, began contacting me regarding John H's recent death. He had received the news directly from John's widow, Faye, and he was in shock. I was too, though the primary shock was not because of John, but because of your mother. And this isn't to minimize what losing one of my best friends meant for me, but to remind you what it was like in our home.

"we need to talk
Wed, Dec 15, 2010, 3:49 PM
Rob to me
I need to know what happened?"

"Wed, Dec 15, 2010, 4:03 PM
Iain Bryson to Rob
what you mean?"

"Wed, Dec 15, 2010, 4:06 PM
Iain Bryson to Rob
i am in holland"

"Wed, Dec 15, 2010, 4:06 PM
Iain Bryson to Rob
just found out. Trying"

"Wed, Dec 15, 2010, 4:14 PM
Rob to me
oh ok, I didn't know you were there. I just found out too, yesterday night I called his phone and faye answered and told me. that's all I know, I want to know who he was with and what happened. let me know if you hear anything, and I will do the same. thank you, and talk to you soon."

CHAPTER 33

DAY 7: THURSDAY, DECEMBER 16, 2010

"Thu, Dec 16, 2010, 5:45 PM
Mom to me
I love you too.
I emailed Agata from work, so don't know if it's the correct address.
Wanted to talk to you about John Hughley. When you can email me, let me know, or maybe skype this weekend. Hoping all is progressing well. any boxes arrived yet? Love to all. Mom"

"Thu, Dec 16, 2010, 5:54 PM
Iain Bryson to Mom
I have heard.
no boxes yet. how are you and george? working on everything. love you"

"Thu, Dec 16, 2010, 7:44 PM
Mom to me
Keep working on it and moving forward as a team. George & I ok. Looking forward to some time off from work. Will let you know when I change your return plane ticket. Love you, Mom"

I had to return to CT to deal with my court case regarding the situation that had happened with Mike at the school, but I knew that I couldn't leave again anytime soon. It was on my list of things to do but had been superseded by much more pressing issues. At this point, I didn't know if I would ever be able to leave your mom "alone" again.

Tonight, it was more of the same: you screaming about your pee pee and hyperventilating. You calmed down much quicker than you did a couple of days ago, but you were still terrified. I wasn't letting your mom bring you to the sink; when it happened, I just held you tight. I refused to let your mom even think for a moment that I believed that this was due to some soap irritation.

Your mom and I watched a movie, and again I tried to convince her that we needed to get help. "So, we know that there is something going on with your dad, right? You tell me about the one cup of tea, you've told me about the woman he cheated on when you were a kid, though you tell me now that never happened. And we know that something was going on before; we both thought that you could have bpd, you admitted to me that you knew something was wrong. So, if these things are issues, and we know that they are, how big of an issue do you think they are? Maybe it's a small issue, but maybe it's not. Maybe it's everything."

"In the great majority of cases it is not possible to establish the point of origin by a simple interrogation of the patient, however thoroughly it may be carried out. This is in part because what is in question is often some experience which the patient dislikes discussing; but principally because he [or she] is genuinely unable to recollect it and often has no suspicion of the causal connection between the precipitating event and the pathological phenomenon" (Breuer and Freud 3).

"Won't you just leave me alone. If you keep talking to me, I'm just going to go to bed."

"OK, Agata, all I am saying is that we need to look at these other issues that we know are issues and determine what's what. You can't say the things you're saying without explanation. What happened? Come on, Agata, one plus one equals two. There is no mystery here; something else is going on besides me. What you say just isn't possible."

"One plus one doesn't always equal two; depends on whose math."

"What do you mean, depends on whose math? No, Agata, you are wrong, one plus one is two. Whatever happened in Poland is the reason you are the way you are now. I have nothing to do with it, and to say I do is a logical impossibility."

"God doesn't approve of our marriage."

"Agata, what are you talking about? How can you say that, and why do you keep saying things that are impossible? Of course, God approves of our marriage."

"My dad created a red herring, your drug, criminal, and psychological histories are going to be used against you."

"What drugs, Agata? I don't use drugs anymore. What are you talking about?"

She thought for a moment, then replied, "Concerta." The way that she stopped to think about her answer made me believe that it was something that would come up again, though I also could not fathom the events which were unfolding.

As the list of things that she was claiming grew, it was impossible for me to not recognize that the pattern was that I was being slandered; in everything she said, I was the bad guy. I had waves of a fearful feeling that what she was saying could be true, making me consider quitting Concerta immediately to preemptively eliminate as many of the claims against me as I could. I didn't understand what was going on, but I did hear her loud and clear.

"The problem is obviously with you. I'm not afraid of anything else. Nothing you can say about me bothers me. We can talk about me all you want, but we also must deal with what I am saying about you. I know the truth, and it will be obvious to everyone else too. Let's go talk to Kees together."

CHAPTER 34

DAY 8: FRIDAY, DECEMBER 17, 2010

Early the next morning, before the birds began their song, I awoke because you opened the door to our bedroom. You came and stood at the foot of our bed, holding your blanket, and I sat up. "Monster," you said, seemingly frightened.

At this point, your mom awoke, and half asleep she invited you into our bed.

"There is no monster," I stated.

"Yes, there is, it's a terror," your mom shot back.

"No, there isn't," I confirmed, but she had already picked you up to try to console you and brought you back to your room. When I came in shortly after, she was asleep in your bed while you were still awake, so I woke her up and sent her back to our bed, telling her I would take care of putting you back to sleep.

I laid down next to you and stroked your forehead, singing to you the song that my dad sung to me, but with your name instead of mine. "Adelle Avery Bryson, she's my number one daughter, she's so fine, I'm glad she's mine, Adelle Avery Bryson." You were sound asleep within a few minutes, and I returned to your mom, waking up in a pool of sweat later that morning. I was not sleeping well at all, but it was when I was awake that the real nightmare was taking place.

"...small children may report that they were hurt by 'monsters,' which actually represent an abusive parent or relative" (Kluft 34).

"Fri, Dec 17, 2010, 11:03 AM
Iain Bryson to Kees de Vries
Kees,
I wanted to touch base with you and just go over a few things since time is short in our sessions. I am doing better after being caught by complete surprise upon my return from Connecticut. I wanted to respond to your question about whether Agata lies: Yes she does, pathologically, but I do not believe she is conscious of it. When I thought of 'lying' when you asked, my first thought was of being intentionally misled, which I do not believe she does. From the beginning of our relationship, I have been faced with many things which I knew were not true. I have said on numerous occasions that I wish I had a tape recorder. Prior to me leaving for Connecticut, we began talking about this. She admitted to me that this was a problem, but she would or could not 'remember.' I again dropped it. I have told her that it is not that I need to 'know' what she lied about, but that the continuation of this behavior scares and worries me.

Up until I returned, I had no indication other than my intuition telling me there was anything going on with her that was different from when I left. The e-mails I have from her, the conversations are all positive and lovey dovey. She now says that her 'suspicions were confirmed' upon my arrival and that she has felt this way all along. When I ask her what was going on from August to December, she says that it was nothing different than now. I have told her that in order for that to be true, everything after August would have to be an intricate web of lies, and that I do not believe this. She has no response. She tells me that May-aug is completely different from now, and will not draw any comparison between the two. What I see and feel is identical.

I have tried to go over things that I have spoken to you about such as our 'fight pattern' and the fact that we had made great progress figuring this out and working through it. She says this is false, that there was no such thing, and that it is me that is the cause of the fights. If you remember, I had told you we had begun to figure out how to identify 'fights' before they escalated, and to stop them instead of letting it cycle through.

I mentioned the event with her father and the other woman. This was something she brought up to me in the first couple of weeks of our relationship, saying she had never told anyone. She was distressed, but at the time, I did not have any answers for her. It has arisen at different times throughout our relationship, usually in regards to her intense involvement, including having contact with the other woman, the effect upon her mother and the fact that her mother has not been 'happy' since, and the fact that her mother is 'cold' towards her father. She has also stated she believes this may be the reason her father did this in the first place; he could not get the 'attention' in his marriage, and so he went elsewhere. As of this week, she has begun telling me that the age she was when this occurred was 18, whereas in every conversation in the past it was 12-16...never a sure age.

We have also discussed and dealt with at length her father's alcoholism. Prior to her leaving, we discussed how we would deal with this in regards to our daughter, and she had a conversation with her mother, getting her mother to agree there would be no alcohol in the house. Drinking is a problem, and has been for him her entire life.

She constantly has a health issue. Recently when in Poland, it was anemia. Previously it was a report by her doctor that her heart may give out before she is thirty. She has stated over and over she does not and cannot have bowel movements but once a week or so. This was a joke for a while, until a few months ago when I indicated I was worried. She has migraines, sleeps for 10-12 hours, and her weight increases and decreases dramatically. The response I get is 'I am not hungry.'

I have tried, and I think been fairly successful in dealing with issues surrounding my daughter. She does not or cannot, or maybe will not see these issues at all. It is night and day to me. When she first left for Poland three months ago, she was pumped and excited about everything, and particularly in regards to things we were working on with our child. Upon coming back, the situation is back to where it was in May when she returned from Poland. Everything she told me she was doing in Poland with regards to our daughter, and everything else, simply was not true. The other night, my daughter came in crying. I have always been the one to deal with these issues, especially at night. Agata cannot snap out of sleep and focus her attention.

In May, one issue was our daughter sleeping in our bed. We went over and over this, my wife saying she read or heard that when couples are having trouble, the child needs to be in the parent's bed. After dealing with this for a couple of months, I got her to try....the first night we tried, our daughter went to bed in her own bed without incidence. The other night, our daughter came in crying. I was up when she came out of her room, as I have no problem snapping into complete consciousness out of sleep. My wife woke up, looked at the situation, and hugged her, telling me it was a 'terror.' I told her it was not, but she proceeded to treat it as if it were, at first just not wanting to do anything other than let our daughter snuggle and crash in our bed. Upon seeing my disapproval, she took her and went to our daughter's room, where she did not talk, but instead laid down and proceeded to go to sleep. I went in, looked at my daughter, and saw my daughter's big eyes looking at her mother trying to figure out what was going on.

My wife does not see or feel that her perception of what is going on with our daughter is swayed by her own perception of things. I laid down next to my daughter, telling my wife I was going to take care of it. She left, and within a minute our daughter was laughing and smiling. I left her room within five minutes and she was back asleep for the night.

Since I have returned, when the fight escalation has begun, I have seen my wife bring my daughter into the mix. I have since realized that the fight escalation was happening again, as I was caught completely off guard at first and found myself falling right into the 'trap.' She will ask me something like, 'Do you want us (meaning her and my daughter) to go to Poland for Christmas or New Years?' and when I say that I am not ready to talk about that, or anything like it, she tells me they are going. I have said that I cannot stop her, but that I do not feel it is a good idea, and that I do not want my daughter to go. She says they are going....

I have since stopped arguing and am trying to ignore these things completely and not get sucked in. She will then take our daughter, hug her and act like she is comforting her, when in fact I believe it is for her sake. I came into the room, was saying, 'Agata, we need to talk,' and she would not look at me or recognize I was there. My daughter was watching and it was eating me away. I then got on my knees to make eye contact or try, as this is something else she cannot do at all, and I put my hand on her knee, gently. She said, 'Get your hand off of me.' After the fact, I asked her why she would do this, and she said, 'Just don't put your hands on me.' I tried to tell her I can see our daughter's big eyes taking all of this in and whether she wants 'daddy get your hands off of me' to come out of her mouth. In May, my daughter started picking up these things. She would complain when I would hold her hand to cross the street, crying and saying, 'It is my hand' etc....

While in CT, I continued to figure out things and was doing excellent. I had in my mind the wonderful thoughts of my two girls, all we had accomplished, and what we were going to accomplish. I could see Agata was drifting off, in her eyes, though her words would not tell me this. On a couple of occasions, I asked her to leave Poland and go back to Holland as I did not believe she was strong enough to handle the situation there. I could see the gradual decay into what we have today, though I did not want to believe it and was hearing the opposite.

I knew I needed to get back here, though I knew what I was doing was good for us. While there, I believe one of the big issues was the VISA and the disappointment that news brought to her. I also believe she simply had difficulty not understanding or being a part of things, and that she felt abandoned or out of the loop or scared of what I may or may not be doing. I was working, treating every minute as if it were golden, and I came back with plans to go over with her that I believe would get us out of the hole(s) we are in. Now, we are back to the same old. I am trying to pull my [expletive] together and she has apparently thrown in the towel.

She says over and over now, 'I don't love you' etc.....in May it was the same. 'I just feel that way and I know,' she says. I have told her that is fine but that the issues I see, or think I see, deserve to be investigated. We saw this as a potential issue prior to September, and she was going to counselling. I say, 'I believe you feel that way and I am not trying to change your mind. What I am trying to say is that there are too many factors which I see as potential issues and as direct parallels to what happened from May to August, and on a smaller scale since we have me[t].' She says the issue is me. I tell her I have no problem discussing or trying to figure out any of these 'issues' she refers to, but it seems she cannot come up with any except vague, broad things, and she is unable to describe what she means. I have gotten to the point where I am trying to do what I can.

I had a good friend of mine die the other day, and between that and coming back to a world flipped upside down, I am having some trouble getting off my feet. I have realized that trying to reason with her and point out these things will not help....I do not think. Only by trying to get her to talk to someone and by realizing she must figure it out and feel it will she get back to where she was. She has been seeing a counselor, and I feel this is good, but I also feel that the mask she wears is a hindrance to any real understanding happening. She cannot admit the issues or things exist so what will she say when asked? I am still trying to get someone who can look after our daughter for the 21st. And, I have stopped the smoking, and am sitting this one out. All the best, Iain"

In saying that I had "stopped the smoking," I was referring to marijuana. The reason that I stopped, and the reason that I told Kees was because of how afraid I was. I knew that I had to eliminate anything that could be "used against me," and smoking was an easy one. Your mom had never personally had a problem with it, but I knew that it could and probably would be part of any "red herring" involving my drug history.

"Fri, Dec 17, 2010, 11:26 AM
Iain Bryson to Kees de Vries
When we first met, there were a couple of instances where she was holding a knife to her arm, touching herself with it, but never cutting to my knowledge. I do not believe this has occurred in in six years, but it was never explored. She admits to having OCD tendencies, though she jokes about it. She gets anxious when things are not the way they 'should' be.
She has told me on numerous occasions that she has felt there is something wrong with herself; that she is flawed."

"Agata, how do you expect me to feel comfortable leaving the house? I am trying to find work, and you won't let me leave the house. Please just give me one of the passports, and you can have mine."

"Why do I care if you find a job?"

I had no response for her; I was just frustrated. It felt like she was purposefully sabotaging us. I couldn't go look for work. I couldn't even think about anything else except about whatever was going on with her. I just needed to get her to Kees as soon as possible.

"withholding
Fri, Dec 17, 2010, 8:07 PM
Iain Bryson to me
Withholding:

If there is a relationship, then there must be an exchange of information. Simply put, withholding is a choice one partner makes to keep virtually all one's thoughts, feelings, opinions, hopes and dreams to oneself and to remain silent and aloof toward the other partner. The verbal abuser may go for months without attempting to engage his partner in meaningful interaction. They may also withhold important information about money, finances or bank account"

"psych abuse
Fri, Dec 17, 2010, 8:11 PM
Iain Bryson to me
Psychological
Among victims who are still living with their perpetrators, high amounts of stress, fear, and anxiety are commonly reported. Depression is also common, as victims are made to feel guilty for 'provoking' the abuse and are constantly subjected to intense criticism. It is reported that 60% of victims meet the diagnostic criteria for depression, either during or after termination of the relationship, and have a greatly increased risk of suicidality. In addition to depression, victims of domestic violence also commonly experience long-term anxiety and panic, and are likely to meet the diagnostic criteria for Generalized Anxiety Disorder and Panic Disorder.

The most commonly referenced psychological effect of domestic violence is Post-Traumatic Stress Disorder (PTSD). PTSD (as experienced by victims) is characterized by flashbacks, intrusive images, exaggerated startle response, nightmares, and avoidance of triggers that are associated with the abuse. These symptoms are generally experienced for a long span of time after the victim has left the dangerous situation. Many researchers state that PTSD is possibly the best diagnosis for those suffering from psychological effects of domestic violence, as it accounts for the variety of symptoms commonly experienced by victims of trauma"

CHAPTER 35

DAY 9: SATURDAY, DECEMBER 18, 2010

"ptsd
Sat, Dec 18, 2010, 9:43 AM
Iain Bryson to me
http://en.wikipedia.org/wiki/Posttraumatic_stress_disorder"

> "PTSD is often noted as a common comorbidity of BPD. In nationally representative samples in the United States, approximately 30% of adults meeting criteria for either PTSD or BPD also met criteria for the other disorder, and closer to 40% of adults diagnosed with BPD had an episode of PTSD at some point in their lifetime" (Ford and Courtois 2).

"**http://allpsych.com/journal/alcoholism.html**
Sat, Dec 18, 2010, 10:12 AM
Iain Bryson to me"

It was obvious that your grandfather's alcoholism was somehow tied to your mom's trauma, and although I didn't know how, that was one place that I looked for understanding. The fact that he was an alcoholic was undeniable, as it was something I had experienced myself, and something your mother and I discussed in detail prior to me sending you to Poland.

I kept looking for answers, trying to put a label on the situation and on your mom. I knew that if I focused on it, I would figure it out. *Why doesn't she want to work with me? What is she so afraid of? Why is she so miserable and full of hatred toward me? Time will tell*, I surmised.

I continued trying to convince your mom that it was in our best interest, and specifically in your best interest, to see Kees together this coming Monday, December 21. I was very frustrated with her. There was no headway; we were stuck. I approached her in the kitchen to again try to ply her with logic.

"Agata, one plus one equals two," I reminded her. "We know that there was an issue before. Now you are telling me that that issue is not an issue, and I'm telling you that I believe it is the same issue."

"It doesn't always equal two... depends on whose math," she paused, and then continued with, "The issue is you. You are the problem."

I picked up a knife from the counter and attempted to hand it to her. "So then just kill me right now, take this knife and kill me. I am not wrong, and I am not going to stop, so just kill me right now if that is what you want. I promise I will never stop."

She wouldn't take the knife, and she acted like I was being ridiculous, which I knew I was, but it also seemed rational given what was going on. What was ridiculous was whatever she brought back with her from Poland; I was trying to adjust.

I looked at the water cooker that was heating up water for my coffee, and I debated pouring some of the boiling water over myself so I could say that your mom did it and maybe get help. This was just a passing thought, but it didn't seem to me to be as far-fetched a thought as the ones that she was experiencing. I just wanted us to get help. I was so scared that I almost thought dumping boiling water on myself might be a good idea.

CHAPTER 36

DAY 10: SUNDAY, DECEMBER 19, 2010

"http://en.wikipedia.org/wiki/Parental_alienation
Sun, Dec 19, 2010, 4:16 AM
Iain Bryson to me"
["Parental alienation is a theorized process through which a child becomes estranged from one parent as the result of the psychological manipulation of another parent…"]

"http://www.paawareness.org/
Sun, Dec 19, 2010, 4:17 AM
Iain Bryson to me"

"http://www.soulwork.net/sw_articles_eng/emotional_blackmail.htm
Sun, Dec 19, 2010, 4:29 AM
Iain Bryson to me"

"**Sun, Dec 19, 2010, 3:26 PM**
Iain Bryson to Kees de Vries
kees,
i am trying to work through things with her. i cant get past the same bs that there was in may. i know that on some level she is scared and sees no other options and i hate being put on the defensive and thinking of my wife in ways i never have. i do not gather intel and look at our marriage that way and this has thrown me for a loop. i came back ready to hit the ground and now when i am told things that make no sense other than on an emotionally extreme, mother survival level, I go into permanent panic attack mode and am terrified to leave my house. I love her but when i hear the words 'i dont love you and never have,' 'divorce,' 'termination of parental rights,' it puts those things on the top of the list and i've gotta figure out how to deal with this [expletive] i cannot comprehend that was so different till i walked through the door. Iain"

"**what's going on with you mo fo>?**
Sun, Dec 19, 2010, 3:27 PM
Iain Bryson to Brian"

"**Sun, Dec 19, 2010, 4:41 PM**
Brian to me
Same story different day - how bout you, nice to be back?"

"**Sun, Dec 19, 2010, 5:48 PM**
Iain Bryson to Brian
pretty crazy here, kind of like warping into another reality. the wifey is back to where she was at in may-july, so been trying to figure out that [expletive]. 'what your favorite color?....refrigerator....remember? crazy [expletive] and it comes down to a lot of [expletive] but basically it's not a good idea to send her to poland

for three months. every [expletive] time it's like getting a new model back. this one seems programmed a little differently than last....basically, she has gone into wifey survival mode whereby i am nothing since i am not making money, which i can see, but would've liked some sign or chance to let her know there are plans and [expletive] like that....but.... [expletive] women and personality disorders and [expletive] like that. apparently there is a file on me at the police station she has been saving, so she means business and though i could rip her the [expletive] up and flip it the [expletive] back onto her, i'd rather not, and would really like to erase the past three months from her memory.

john hughley died a few days ago. Haven't heard anything and having trouble focusing on much else than what's in front of me. i saw that [expletive] though and it is not [expletive] easy. [expletive] when the [expletive] hits the fan it hits hard. at least i have my mind for the most part. now i gotta figure out how to make some dough in the face of delusionville sociopathy and no [expletive] job market for anyone without two-five languages. got sideswiped as she has done nothing i have expected or rather she said she would so gotta pick up pieces like the apartment which was supposed to be handled by a lawyer friend and the [expletive] i had planned on doing when back like finding work, teaching, sending [expletive] out to magazines, figuring out translating with her, tutoring, and trying to ascertain exactly how crazy a woman can be. i personally think the skies the limit though i would prefer to not find out and maybe figure in probability for the next occurrence and try to stop it.

permanent panic attack once again....at least i understand what's going on in my head this time, though stopping her from crossing the border with the kid or even leaving to go look for work is terrifying at the moment. such are the ups and downs of life i guess. so anyway, what is the same old [expletive]? you ok? u gotta bring the wife here maybe at some point and step out of that [expletive] for a minute. relax and regroup. i am going to try to figure out what is possible here. when you are not dealing with reason or even any amount of logic it's nuts. all feeling from these women and the polish ones are a different model it seems.

so, me.....i am trying once again to save my family and also trying to get us out of a rut....and the wife, whether she wants to be the wife, has a flat tire and no AAA at the moment. seem to be cycling through the stages myself quicker, but i've already heard 'divorce,' 'termination of parental rights,' 'go to US and i will go to poland and by i i mean me and your daughter and i don't love you' so it is nutty buddy. gonna try to rest my heart attack. not too many things can keep me in this state.....no drugs though as i have to think and don't need the polish dea that is my wife who i think only saw nancy reagan's 'just say no' speech getting any more cues that [expletive] is wrong. my favorite color is refrigerator mother [expletive] and i am going to [expletive] kill you and feed you to my little friend. I"

"Sun, Dec 19, 2010, 7:31 PM
Iain Bryson to Brian
got a few apps off tonight. going to sleep now since i get up with the kid a couple hours earlier than my wife who is in an alternate, but very real, universe. just have to keep saying to myself 'i love the permanent style panic attack that feels and if this is what a heart attack feels like, then bring that on too cause it aint too bad.' she is so serious about the refrigerator being her favorite color when she is mad, and i guess the women (or maybe just the one i have at least until tomorrow, but i would guess at least...at least...i am not limiting myself but also not trying to figure out the unpredictable) feel it is better to act out of pure raw emotion without the aid of the brain at all. if i did that i would be killing mother [expletive] left and right, or maybe that is what i was meant to do and i have missed it altogether. oh well, gotta figure out how to get the kid a xmas tree, get a haircut so i could go to a job interview, and if the wife has any plans at all to stop our eviction or if it is all pathological bs. fun exciting [expletive]…"

I ventured out on my own to get you a Christmas tree. I was scared, but your mom assured me that she would be there when I got back. I wanted us to all go together, but she wouldn't go. I didn't think that I would have to go far, and I wanted you to have a tree, so I risked it.

When I got to the store a couple of blocks away, I was hit by a strong wave of really missing your mom. I wanted us to be doing this as a family, and it hurt to be back in a place that I thought we had triumphed over. I called her, "Agata, I'm at the tree store. Do you think that I should get the small tree or the big tree? The big tree is almost twice the cost."

"Umm," she took a moment to think, "get the big one."

It felt good just to make that decision with her. I purchased the tree and headed back home. It was fairly heavy and awkward, and it was snowing, but it still felt amazing to be heading back to my girls. *We are going to figure this out; there is no way around that. I'll have your mom watch "It's a Wonderful Life" with us, and she will see that she is just in the grumpy, miserable version of herself right now. Maybe then she will wake up into what she was before Poland.*

You were very excited when I got home, waiting at the top of the stairs, watching me lug the tree up our windy staircase. "Daddy, is that for me?"

I smiled, "Yes, Adelle, it's for you."

We decorated the tree together; your mom wanted no part in it, but just stayed in the kitchen with her music, her phone, and her cigarettes.

"Agata, can't you just pretend to be happy for our daughter? It's Christmas, can't you please just try?"

"Why would I?"

It was painful because I saw the effect that she was having on you. All that you wanted was for Mommy and Daddy to be ok, and I couldn't make that happen. It was also all that I wanted. I had totally lost control of our household, as if a tornado had passed through in my absence, except that a tornado would have been better, because at least then I would have known how to pick up the pieces.

CHAPTER 37

DAY 11: MONDAY, DECEMBER 20, 2010

"Mon, Dec 20, 2010, 6:06 AM
Iain Bryson to Mom
mom,

trying to figure out the day. i wanted to say i am sorry for yelling at you. i've been trying to stay focused and get a lot done. the entire time i knew there was something wrong over here but couldn't put my finger on it, but also lost any help i could have used from agatka. kind of like what i saw with john....i had to stay focused on what i could do and felt i should do. i couldn't have done any of it without you. love you"

"Dec 20, 2010, 7:26 AM
Mom to me
Iain

Thank you. I love you very much and whatever I say is only my way of trying to help. I have no other motive in my life.

Stay focused on getting your anxiety under control and by helping yourself you will be helping your family. they have to be number one in your life, which I know they are but the one way you can show that is to support them and provide a home for them. Women need security. This is the one big area your father and I struggled. He always wanted to follow his dreams and there was no sacrifice to just work and take care of his family. The ups and downs did us in. I needed the security after we started having you kids. It is a woman thing. I love you and I love Agata and I love Adelle. Don't get sidetracked with others issues, of which there always will be issues. That is life. Love you"

CHAPTER 38

DAY 12: TUESDAY, DECEMBER 21, 2010

Another appointment with Kees today, and again, your mom refused to go. I needed Kees on my side, there was nobody helping me, and I felt very alone. I hurried to the appointment as fast as I could, anxious that you might not be home when I returned.

"Kees, I can't talk long, I have to get home. It is worse, it is absolutely crazy in my house. She's exactly the same as she was last time. I don't know what to do. She keeps telling me that she is taking Adelle to Poland. I'm going to keep hitting the stone, but I am terrified right now. She has our daughter's passport, and she tells me that she is taking her to Poland."

"Go home and keep working on it. It may take time. You have to be patient. She can't take Adelle to Poland; that would be illegal. I am very worried about Agata, and I am going to continue doing my best to reach her, but she can't take Adelle to Poland."

"Ok, thank you Kees. Please keep trying to talk to her."

"Yes, Iain, I will, I want to talk to her, and I am worried about her," he assured me.

That was a waste of time. Now I felt a little bit more alone; he wasn't listening to me either. She told me that she was going to take you to Poland, over and over. There was no way to mince your mom's words. Illegal or not, I was terrified.

On the way home, I decided that I had to stop at the police station. I didn't want to stop at the police station, and I previously couldn't have imagined a situation where I would or could report my wife to the police, but now I didn't see any other options. She had your passport, and she told me she was going to leave the country with you. I could not let that happen.

I walked in, ready and determined to finally get some help. "Hi, my wife is threatening to take our daughter to Poland. She has her passport, and she is telling me that she will leave the country with her. I need help."

The officer handed me a flier with a list of family attorneys and sent me on my way. I was absolutely crushed and felt much more alone. This was the first time in my life I had ever really needed the police, and they had completely dismissed me and my fears about the impending abduction of my daughter. I rushed back home and was relieved when I saw your big blue eyes.

I didn't want your mom to know that I had gone to the police; I could barely admit it to myself. I was careful to hide the flier from her, and never took it out of my pocket in her presence. I didn't know what to do with it, there was no way I could or would hire an attorney. There was no way that I would pre-empt your mom, though I guess I just had by going to the police. I just wanted her to get help, and I was extremely scared, I think more frightened than I had been in my life up to that point.

I kept telling her that I was scared, but she didn't care about anything that I had to say to her. She seemed to have no emotional response at all to how I was feeling, she continued to act like she hated me in front of you, and this was driving me crazy. Her response to me was usually something like, "Why would I care? I hate you."

"Well, Agata, you should listen to me because of our daughter." I reminded her, "I only care about her, I don't care what you think about me. I've been through this before with you, what bothers me is the effect that it has on our daughter. I am not willing to do it again; we need to get help."

"You're a typical abuser."

"What are you talking about? I'm a what? Agata, who hurt you? Please tell me, and please get help with me."

CHAPTER 39

DAY 13: WEDNESDAY, DECEMBER 22, 2010

I woke up early in a pool of sweat and put down a towel so that I could continue trying to rest. My dreams were tough, some kind of new night terror I had acquired since returning home. But I needed the sleep; I was exhausted.

Your mom awoke in a panic, and she started yelling. I couldn't understand her, and I don't remember if she was yelling in Polish or English. I covered her mouth with my hand in order to try to prevent you from also being woken up. She calmed down immediately once she realized that it was me, but then she acted as if nothing had just happened.

"Agata, what was that? You've been abused. I love you, and I am terrified. Please listen to me. I am your husband, and I am absolutely terrified."

I proceeded to take the slim cigarette that she was smoking and put it out on my forearm.

"Don't," she said, but I proceeded.

"I am terrified, see how terrified I am, I need you to get help. I'm not asking you anymore. I am telling you that you will get help. Look, the burn on my arm doesn't bother me. It is only you that is the problem right now. We need help!"

"http://en.wikipedia.org/wiki/Antisocial_personality_disorder
Wed, Dec 22, 2010, 11:14 AM
Iain Bryson to me"

"http://www.lovefraud.com/01_whatsaSociopath/key_symptoms_sociopath.html
Wed, Dec 22, 2010, 11:19 AM
Iain Bryson to me"

Your mom told me that she was giving Jackie some old clothes, and that she would be coming over to get them. Shortly thereafter, Jackie showed up with her daughter, Cicely. I told her that bacon grease had burnt my arm, lying so I didn't have to tell her the truth about burning my arm with a cigarette to show your mom how frightened I was of her, and I continued cooking.

Jackie had a terrible cold, and I was annoyed by this, and by the fact that your mom took her into our bedroom. I was trying to cook in the kitchen, and I couldn't believe that your mom was sitting on our bed with a lawyer when she was threatening me with taking you out of the country multiple times per day. *Why won't she speak to her normally in a common area? What is she doing here?*

I didn't know what was going on, but it felt very suspicious. Jackie emerged from the bedroom with several large bags of clothes, maybe half of your mom's total clothing. I thought that it was strange, but in relation to everything else that was going on, it was just par for the course, the upside-down world that I had come back to. *Weird that she is giving Jackie so much clothing, but whatever, I just can't wait until she leaves*, I thought.

"Agata, I don't want her in my bedroom, that is my private area, please don't do that again."

"It's not your bedroom. I needed to give her clothes."

"It is my bedroom, because it is our bedroom, which makes it yours and mine. I'm not saying it is only my bedroom, as it is also yours, but that doesn't take away from the fact that it is my bedroom. I don't want her in my bedroom, please. You're in my bedroom talking to a lawyer when all you are telling me is that you are taking my daughter. Are you crazy?"

I was upset and panicking, but that fact that she was in the process of moving out right in front of me didn't even cross my mind. All of the other stuff that I could see was crazy enough, and her moving out under the guise of "escape" was still beyond my ability to comprehend.

At this point in my life, when I thought about the devil, like when I thought about God, "I thought not. In common with 99 percent of psychiatrists and the majority of clergy, I did not think the devil existed" (Peck 182). However, it wasn't long before I would be saying, like M. Scott Peck, "I now know Satan is real. I have met it" (183).

"http://en.wikipedia.org/wiki/Psychopathy
Wed, Dec 22, 2010, 1:24 PM
Iain Bryson to me"
["Psychopathy, sometimes considered synonymous with sociopathy, is characterized by persistent antisocial behavior, impaired empathy and remorse, and bold, disinhibited, and egotistical traits."]

"http://en.wikipedia.org/wiki/Hare_Psychopathy_Checklist
Wed, Dec 22, 2010, 1:28 PM
Iain Bryson to me"
[assessment tool/22 item checklist of perceived traits and observable behaviors]

"http://en.wikipedia.org/wiki/Conduct_disorder
Wed, Dec 22, 2010, 1:30 PM
Iain Bryson to me"
["Conduct disorder is a mental disorder diagnosed in childhood or adolescence that presents itself through a repetitive and persistent pattern of behavior that includes theft, lies, physical violence that may lead to destruction, and reckless breaking of rules, in which basic rights of others or major age-appropriate norms are violated"]

"http://en.wikipedia.org/wiki/Egocentric
Wed, Dec 22, 2010, 1:33 PM
Iain Bryson to me"
["...it is the inability to accurately assume or understand any perspective other than one's own."]

"Agata, can you come here please?" I requested, sitting at our little computer station trying to put my finger on what was happening with my wife. I was excited to show her what I had found.

She came in from the kitchen, where she was probably listening to Drake's new album.

Screenshot from Rollins Band "Liar" music video.

"Look, Agata, I found you on YouTube. See, look, this is you singing your song," pleased that I was getting a chance to show her her identical twin. "This is exactly what you look like to me." Here are some of the lyrics:

"...wonder why things are going so well
You want to know why?
'Cause I'm a liar, yeah, I'm a liar
I'll tear your mind out, I'll burn your soul ...
I can't believe I ever hurt you, I swear I will never lie to you again, please
Just give me one more chance, I'll never lie to you again, no,
I swear, I will never tell a lie, I will never tell a lie, no, no
Ha ha ha ha ha, ho ho ho! Sucker! Sucker! Ooooh sucker!
I am a liar, yeah, I am a liar, yeah, I like it,
I feel good, ooooh I am a liar... Yeah
I lie, I lie, I lie, ooh I lie, I lie, yeah,
Oooooh I'm a liar, I lie, yeah, I like it, I feel good,
I'll lie again, and again, I'll lie again and again and I'll keep lying,
I promise... Ha ha ha"

She walked back into the kitchen without saying anything. From my point of view, at the time, this was your mom. Of course, this guy had the devil costume on, and she looked fairly normal to the naked eye, but this is what was coming out of her, the spiritual essence that was emanating from her being, and I let her know that this was what I thought. It wasn't a good conversation starter. She already knew how I felt, and she just didn't seem to care.

I could not believe she wouldn't listen to me, not at that moment necessarily, but in general. I thought that her head might start spinning around at any moment as in the 1973 film *The Exorcist*, not literally, but it wouldn't have been much of a surprise, because that was how serious the situation was in our home; she was wreaking havoc.

I was the sucker, and I didn't like it one bit.

CHAPTER 40

DAY 14: THURSDAY, DECEMBER 23, 2010

"Thu, Dec 23, 2010, 3:49 AM
Iain Bryson to Brian
yo,
which number you try to call? probably 'something like that' if the recording was in dutch, but i do quite a bit of guessing myself....i have to have my daughter tell me what is going on sometimes cause she is the only one who speaks three languages. it is weird when people, and especially kids talk to me and i see their lips moving but catch maybe one word. it puts a strange twist on things. imagine if that was how it was in az or ct. from person to person you have no idea if you can communicate.

trying to get ready for the holiday and hold down the fam and get work going here as well. ppppp (adelle wanted to see a 'pp) i got some sociopathic sabotage to get around here and trying to not let that throw us off too much but really have no idea what may be around the corner.

john....i haven't talked to anyone but i do know what happened.....i was with him from the day i got back to ct and could see what was going on....sent him to florida to try to detox.....told him to stay when he wanted to come back.....saw the decline again and tried to do what i could but couldn't drop everything else. the details other people need to explain it are not really that important to me...that [expletive] is just a way to explain away the reality.

anyway, gotta make some eggs and try to figure some [expletive] out. [expletive]. it is one thing after another. the wife hasn't done anything,,,,,no work on the apartment, excuses about the social help we were supposed to be getting, found out we have a lot less money than she told me which may last a week or two, and just more pathological lying that ends up in defense mechanisms that look like a demon to me when i confront it. she is so [expletive] i dont know how to leave my house and at this point i'd rather have my kid in dutch social services than with her. gotta figure this [expletive] out and try to flip her into 'my wife' and then keep it that way which should be interesting if not [expletive] impossible under the circumstances. hi to your family and will have my phone on me today"

I wrote down the addresses for the U.S. Consulate and the U.S. Embassy, and I put them in my back pocket in case it became necessary to escape with you. I was afraid of your mom, and I felt like a kid trying to sneak a cookie out of the cookie jar. She seemed so far gone to me that even options like the police or the U.S. authorities seemed reasonable at times. I was clueless, in a situation that I could have never imagined, and I didn't know what to do.

You and I went out for an adventure in the city. I knew that your mom wouldn't come with us; she had left the house a couple of times, but only alone, and she kept telling me that she wanted me to spend time with you. I felt bad, since I knew what was in my back pocket, but I had every intention of coming back home after our adventure. Christmas was coming up; why couldn't we just get back what we had prior to this trip to Poland? *What happened in Poland?*

We took the tram into Den Haag Centraal and played in the snow on the royal grounds just outside of the station. We did a lot of running around; you were playing some game where you would throw your mittens on the ground and run away from me. My job was to collect your mittens, catch you, and then help you put your mittens back on your hands. We played for a while, and then we returned home.

UPS came with the packages from my mom. I saw the truck from our window, and I knew that it was here for us. I was excited; Christmas was coming, and I was going to get to spend it with my girls. I ran outside in the snow without putting shoes on, hopping back and forth from one foot to another to try to keep my socks from getting wet.

"Thu, Dec 23, 2010, 4:31 PM
Brian to me
Hey man, just tried again, but no dice. At least this time it just rang and rang and no dutch lady... I prob just blew it last time...
I figured with John it had to be something like that... He seemed alright when we were there, but I think I would be ignorant to the subtleties if that's all there would be.
You gotta get [her] out of the finances, not sure if that is possible, but I've always had better luck handling that myself...
PS on the language thing, it can be that way in AZ if you're in the right neighborhood
Anyway I'll try you back later or tomorrow - let me know what's up..."

Your mom kept trying to hang a wooden angel on the wall in your bedroom, and you kept telling her that you didn't want it. She hung it up, and you took it down, repeatedly. I watched, trying to figure out what was going on.

"Pola gave it to you," she said, but that didn't make you want the angel on your wall. It seemed to make you very uncomfortable, but the strangest thing to me was how insistent your mom was that it be on your wall.

You were adamant that you did not want it on your wall, and you seemed scared. I realized that it had to have some kind of significance to you because of the previous three months that you were in Poland, but I couldn't fathom what that could be. I had no idea why she was being so pushy. It didn't make sense in the reality that I knew, almost like a scene from the Twilight Zone, which is where your mom was residing for the time being.

"Agata, she doesn't want it. She keeps telling you that she doesn't want it. It doesn't matter that it is from Pola. Why is it so important to you? You're really going to try to make her keep a wooden angel on her wall? What is wrong with you?"

"She needs it on the wall; it's from Pola."

"No, Agata, she doesn't need it, and if she doesn't want it, then she doesn't have to have it. Please stop."

You did not go to sleep with the angel hanging on your wall. I put it in a place where you wouldn't have to see it again if you didn't want to.

CHAPTER 41

DAY 15: FRIDAY, DECEMBER 24, 2010

"**Fri, Dec 24, 2010, 3:51 AM**
Iain Bryson to Brian
hey b

yes i got the call this time. no dutch lady is the best although some of them are hot. was trying to speak to the wife, but that got nowhere. will have it on me again today. if you can email me a time or two, then i can guarantee that i can answer. a bit nutso to say the least. the wife is seriously in need of help and i can't leave the daughter here with her. it is pretty sick [expletive], and i may have to send you the book for you to understand. some psychological abuse [expletive]. but seriously if you look up sociopath, borderline personality disorder, and narcissism, you will have a pretty good idea. when things go back to good i tend to let it go, which is what happened prior to CT this time. [expletive] big ass mistake. i tend to think that there is more thought going on and don't see that [expletive] coming though i could sense it from ct when skyping and looking at her eyes and trying to get [expletive] done. she would say things were getting done, tell me about the daughter, and i can tell when things are not getting done.

when i confront her, she retreats and lies incessantly. [expletive] why i gotta love this woman? [expletive] it, i do. well, like the rent not being taken out of her account for six months and her not 'knowing,' 'the electricity being shut off and us not having a notice' which we did, and a thousand other things just like it that are coming to mind, she will not talk to me about the situation now. it is just '[expletive]' and nastiness and blah [expletive] blah. so i get told things about the apartment, which i am going to try to take care of as she has again dropped the ball, the little bit of money that we do have (or i presume we have) that has since gone in half in the matter of a couple of days (well it hasn't but i was lied to again), and then just things like polish. she says she spoke english to our daughter, and only english when in poland. by the way, it is the lying that gets to me, and not the polish.

i see her 'training' my child to manipulate and be a nasty [expletive], and it drives me insane. if the insanity was not there, the polish would be fine as it does not bother me except for the reason the wife uses it. if i touch the wife in front of the child, she backs away and acts like i stuck a screw driver in her [expletive] without lube. [expletive] psychological abuse. so, she says she speaky the english, but then when i get here she only speaky the polish and my daughter took a couple of days to get into english so again i just know she is lying and that is the deal. but if i try to speak to her about it, she guarantees she did this this and this.

the money thing: yeah i know. i gotta figure that one out once and for all. i believe i did and do have it figured out, and it really sucks the wife has thrown in the towel, sabotaging, not doing anything she said she was going to do, unwilling to talk or go over our current situation. it is a bit too much on top of my fears about my daughter, my inability to leave since the wife gets up at 11, nasty as a [expletive], and throws this [expletive] onto my daughter. my daughter is having tantrums, crying, and back to where she was last time this happened.....maybe i am the only one who can see it and see it is only due to my wife, but that [expletive] [expletive] with me....it is so [expletive] clear.

i have been applying for jobs which i really have not done seriously before here and trying to figure [expletive] out. i tell the wife i need time to work and she says 'why do i care' so it is tough. i've been getting responses to the jobs and got more ideas, but probably nothing will happen until after the holidays regardless and given my inability to extract any information, it makes things a bit anxious on my end. i think, whether consciously or not, she is trying to force me back to the US and get her and Adelle to Poland. And, that is the way things are going if I were to really look at it, which i cannot do so instead i stay up till three looking for options and trying to pull this [expletive] together out of my [expletive].

i told her that i will not allow her to go back to poland with my daughter. how the [expletive] could i? if i didn't believe she was nuts and i could trust her, sure, i may come to that decision, but not when being forced through psychological manipulation. gotta figure out the legality of that [expletive]. i will have to write a letter and send it around so as to get her on kidnapping should she try. i would rather her be assed the [expletive] out in this country because at least i know where to find my daughter. well, adelle just woke up. gotta get her some breakfast. oh, when i got here the wife was feeding her chocolate pudding for breakfast, because 'she likes it' so now i make breakfast with her everyday. she likes it....you stupid [expletive], no you are a retard and a psycho and you like that [expletive]. wonder what else you [expletive] like you [expletive].

well, you and the fam have a great xmas. let me know when you can call so i can be sure to get it.
john was not alright when we were there, but he was trying and doing better than when i first got there. yes it is subtleties and i can see that [expletive] which is good and bad i suppose. the thing with the language thing is that you probably can choose not to and don't need to go to those neighborhoods."

"Fri, Dec 24, 2010, 5:35 AM
Iain Bryson to Mom
Mom,
happy christmas eve
we got four boxes....thank you.....nothing else needed for now. gotta figure out some things before i can relocate anymore books, etc.
we have snow which has been on the ground all week for the first time since being here. adelle and i have been going out to play every day.
got a lot of job apps out and working on more all the time. just not sure how the sabotage will affect everything. what have you got planned for tonight and tomorrow? if you see courtney can you ask her for my book please? does kyle have anything from john's funeral, etc?
sitting and working with the cat on my lap. got up with adelle and made breakfast with her....love you"

"Fri, Dec 24, 2010, 7:04 AM
Mom to me
Iain,
Happy Christmas Eve to all of you. Glad you got the boxes.
I will have to change the ticket by middle of next week so let me know please. One day at a time. Keep up the counseling. Got to get ready for work. will we be able to Skype tomorrow morning. I can get up very early if needed. Love you. Mom"

"Fri, Dec 24, 2010, 8:48 AM
Iain Bryson to Mom
mom,
i am definitely going to have to change the ticket......can't leave here right now and will have to figure out how to get back. gotta figure out some things and get things nailed down a bit. got some jobs going that been working on but will have to wait until after the new year i am sure to hear, so will just keep plodding away. it's pretty much like my pile of books here that i have to resort, get back in order, and figure out things that have gone astray. adelle has reverted back to may, so that is a bit frustrating.

have to figure out what to do since nothing i thought was being done was actually being done. hoping to figure out the apartment next week...got to figure out how to get it done so we don't get blocked from being able to rent in this country cause i really don't know what to do in that situation. i cannot let adelle go back to poland, which is unfortunate, but at this point i'd rather have her with social services. adelle doesn't get up too early but we'll see how it goes. i will send you an update once things get rolling....

i plan on getting them up around 8-9 if she is not up earlier and making breakfast. agata doesn't get up till around 11 so we'll see how it goes. maybe tomorrow will be different. been trying to get her into counselling but i don't think she really wants to be confronted. it is tough for her because she cannot fool me anymore. i tell her this and tell her i love her, much like i would an addict. but i also have to tell her that i will not allow certain things to happen or be in adelle's life; it went from hurting me to not being able to hurt me enough so then using her to hurt me, which is the most frustrating thing of all.

i have an appointment with the counsellor on the 30th and trying to find someone to watch dell as he wants agata there and she ducked out last time with one of her phantom migraines. i think she is weary as there is so much that doesn't add up, well nothing does, and unfortunately i remember every word from day one, or maybe luckily, but it is not something that is fun to think about and try to frame. she was or maybe is going to another lady, but she is great at painting the picture she wants to paint, and again we are dealing with a choose your own adventure story where reality is a bit elusive, but again i think she is seeing that there really is no way to evade all this and no way to put it all on me as is the trend.

if i believed in demons i would sign her up to have one cast out. working on it; i guess just another project. wish there weren't so many going on at once, but oh what fun it is. love you and have a great night and day tomorrow and time off."

I was sitting on our loveseat reading when you approached me, closely followed by your mom. She stood a few steps back, hovering over you. I looked at you, put down my book, and glanced at your mom. Something felt off to me; why was she supervising this interaction between us?

You reached out your hand and offered me a miniature New Testament, the one that I received from my parents as a kid in 1986 but hadn't seen in many years. "Thank you," I said, forcing a smile as I carefully took it out of your hands. You turned toward your mom, and then you walked away, making it even clearer that you were completing an assigned task.

It was obvious that this transaction was staged by your mom; you were only a messenger. I believe that your mom knew that only God has the answer to what was about to happen to our family, the answer to the "winter of our discontent." I had no idea what was coming, but your mom did, and I couldn't hear her even though she kept telling me.

"Iain, you are just like your father!"

"What?"

"You are just like your father!"

I had no idea what she was saying. As far as I knew, her stance on me was that I was a "typical abuser," a bad dad, and she hated me. My dad is not those things, and I didn't hate him. *What is she saying now? Where is my wife? Where did she go?*

"Agata, I am not just like my father, we aren't really even that alike at all."

"Yes, Iain," she demanded, "you are!" as if I was just supposed to agree with her because she said so. She was very serious. She walked away from me, and I thought to myself, *no I am not, she's crazy.*

Then it hit me that she may have been referring not to my father, but to my Father, who is God, except that I didn't believe that at the time. That made sense with her also having you give me the Bible, but what was she getting at? It seemed that she was trying to make some point about the importance of the Bible and of our relationship with the Creator through Jesus Christ, but at the time it was a leap that I wasn't willing to take and more proof that she had lost it. *She doesn't make sense*, I thought, *we need to get help. I need her to see Kees.*

I went into the kitchen to talk to your mom; you were in your room with the door closed.

"I need you to listen to me, I need you to hear me, I need to know that you are still there, we have to get help, this is not ok," I pled.

"Why would I listen to you? You are the cause of all of my problems."

"Agata, no I'm not. That is not possible. We have to go talk to Kees. You have to, Agata, he told me that he is very worried about you, and I am very worried about you and our daughter."

I heard your door open behind me, and just at that moment your mom swung her fist at me and yelled, "Get the [expletive] away from me!" and then dropped to the ground crying. I realized that you were going to think that she was crying because of me, just like when she screamed when I put my hand on her leg. Without hesitation, I turned from your mom, walked down the hallway, and picked you up into my arms. You asked me why I hit your mom and I told you I did not hit your mom. Your mom exclaimed, "She saw you hit me!" I took you into your bedroom, and I closed the door behind us.

I hugged you tight, and I sang to you, your head on my shoulder. I was crying, but I didn't want you to know. Your mom opened the door and started to enter your room. You looked at her, pointed your finger at her, and ordered, "Mommy, you go, Mommy you go."

She was devastated. She started crying and left, closing the door behind her. I sat down with you on the bed, and we talked for a few minutes. As soon as you calmed down, you began worrying about how your mom was doing. You felt like you needed to comfort her, like she needed you. I didn't like it, but I didn't like any bit of it.

"Adelle, your mom loves you, and I'm sure that she would love a hug from you if that's what you want to do. She is ok, and she loves you."

You told me that was what you wanted to do, and I followed you out of your room to your mom, who was sitting at the computer, smiling, seemingly humbled. She lifted you onto her lap, and I stood back so that you two could have some time together.

I did stand there to observe, or maybe to supervise, and I didn't like that you felt the need to console your mom, that you seemed to feel responsible for whether she was "happy," or not. She seemed calm now, and I was thankful for that. The crazy was over, for the moment. I enjoyed the brief calm periods amidst all the chaos, and I loved just looking at you and your mom, longing to laugh and dance once again with both of you. Christmas was coming, and I knew that your mom ultimately wanted the same thing, underneath it all I knew she did. This new version of your mom was the wrong version, the sick version; something was seriously wrong, and I had to get some help.

CHAPTER 42

"DO IT FOR HER"

"Do it for her," she ordered, "just stop ranting, and do it for your daughter."

"Do what for her? I don't do anything just for her, I do it for us, for you and for her."

"No, you need to do it for her."

"Ok, Agata Avery, whatever you say." I added our middle name, Avery, to her name to let her know that she was the same thing. I did not differentiate between her and you regarding my love; it was one in the same thing. Without her, there would be no you, and without a healthy her, there could be no healthy you. Our family was a unit, and I would not agree with her that I would do anything for you alone, but always for us.

"Didn't you tell me once that you were sad that you weren't given a middle name? Well, now you have one, Agata Avery, Agata Avery Bryson, why won't you talk to me?"

The landline phone on the desk started frequently ringing. Your mom told me that I wasn't allowed to answer it, and it seemed to scare her that it was ringing, so I mostly left it alone. I never answered it because I feared your mom's reaction if I did. I did give her a bit of a hard time, but I was pretty much just trying to break the ice wherever I saw a potential opportunity.

"Agata, so now the phone just has to ring because you say so, we can't answer it, and you also say we can't unplug it, wow Agata, that is kind of weird. Do you think we can get some help yet?"

"Just don't answer it," she said in her somber, serious sounding voice, confirming that it wasn't allowed.

"OK, Agata, whatever you say, what happened in Poland to make you this way? What happened, Agata, why won't you tell me?"

"You are the cause of all of my problems; I hate you."

"Yeah ok, and now I am switching from what I was doing to my new project: you. You are out of control, everything about you is off, you are abusing our daughter in our home in front of me. You will get help. I demand that you get help."

"She knows that you are the problem," she assured me.

"No, Agata, she knows that you are sick, and now I am going to write about you. Why do you make me focus on you? Why won't you just get help with me? I don't care what it is; we will get through it. I am on your side."

"You are the only problem."

"I am going to write about you now, and I'm going to use your name. No, I won't use your name, this is too crazy to use your actual name, I won't use it, that would be mean."

"I want you to use my name," she half smiled.

"What are you talking about? Why would you say that? I don't want to write about you, I don't want to have to rip you apart, just get help with me. Please, just get help with me. I will be by your side, no matter what it is. I love you."

"I want you to use my name. I believe you can write, not yet... but I do believe that you can write. I want you to use my name."

"Fri, Dec 24, 2010, 10:43 AM
Brian to me
That's good that the call came though, someday I'll figure it out for sure. It sounds like you have so much going on and then throwing the kid in the mix, those are some full hands. I'm sure you'll figure out the finances ... I'm glad you're also able to figure out the root cause of the tantrums, I'm still a bit fuzzy on some of my kids. I can't get any sports game to end (unless formal with his team sports) without a huge tantrum... Whenever we play backyard anything, he freaks out when the game is over - then I tell him fine, I won't play for 3 days - 3 days go by with no play and then I play something and it's the same thing - He is slowly starting to come around, but it's always a battle.

That is awesome too that she will be tri-lingual - [expletive] baller... I've definitely kicked with some broads that went on the rampage, but I was never near as invested as you - I'm sure this is just a phase that will pass - both of you have a lot of pressure right now and that can have strange effects on people. I've been working on some of the other things for myself - trying to detach myself from emotions at time and be able to observe the thoughts/environment that are causing. Also getting the rage under control... I find it overwhelming at times - sometimes for reasons I can't even identify, I think once I get there it will help tremendously.

I like conceptionally trying to view situations / exchanges with people I'm having with people from an outsider's perspective - I think once I get that to happen without thinking about it, it will help across the board. I'm at work, so didn't look up the definitions below yet, but am I going to find my picture under any of those? guess I'll have to check and see... I'll try and call in a few hours - if you can't get it - no worries - just keep your fingers crossed for no dutch lady"

"Fri, Dec 24, 2010, 12:17 PM
Iain Bryson to Brian
i think you got the calling figured out. it is either 011 or 001 and then 31..... i would have to be in the US and trying to call and sometimes i try both to get the right one... i got some advice for the tantrums, but in general i think it is a bit different for you because you work all the time. it is tough to coordinate with the wife, and when there are differences they exploit them, though not intentionally or consciously. it is just normal human [expletive]. u got all the [expletive] on your plate and then you walk in and try to get [expletive] done and you don't have much time and you get frustrated. i have been there, and fairly recently.

my kid has regressed back to a year ago because the wife is inept. and yes, psychotic. you don't have any of those things, but i could tell you what you do have if you want. i know what i have, but it is just a spectrum thing. it is not a problem unless it is, which i try to constantly assess. the three day [expletive], i dont think, will work. his concept of time and not playing for three days is not on that level. it is just a word to him. you could tell him he has to eat a turd and it would not work either. let me ponder that one, but i know what you mean as i am dealing with them for the first time in a while and trying to fix it. i tend to ignore it, not in a mean way, but i think i act as if it is not going to get my attention in either a good or bad way and if it gets worse i try to catch myself and not fall into that cycle.

you should read some of the books i have read. they are [expletive] amazing. observing is amazing. being here is the first time i have slipped up as the wife can put the fear of god into me. i have gotten back on track for the most part in the past day or so. concerta helps.....you should look into that [expletive]. it is the brain which is tough to regulate, and it is trial and error and you cannot get frustrated but keep learning, writing and moving forward. i try to assess what stage i am in and view myself from the outside and make adjustments daily. she won't speak dutch but she knows it. gotta work on that too as she now won't say thank you or hi to strangers. [expletive] poland. never again [expletive].

yes, the investment is the problem. without the kid i'd be outta here. but so goes it, and the kid is amazing. i am going to pick another language once i get my [expletive] together. it will pass since i am learning how to deal with it and not in the ways she assumes i will. people react, as i do, but the difference is that you do not have to do it the same every time. i think that [expletive] with her as she counts on the predictability.

read that dh lawrence book or huxleys heaven and hell. 'The highest goal of every man is the goal of pure individual being.' 'The mind as an incubus and a procreator of its own horrors, deliberately unconsciously.' 'He has invented his own automatic principles, and he works himself according to them like any little machine inside the works.' 'The whole of life is one long, blind effort at established polarity with the outer universe, human and non-human, and the whole of modern life is a shrieking failure' and I would add [expletive] delusional failure. 'They (children) twig soon enough if there is any flow in our intentions and our own true intention and our own true spontaneity.' 'Children have infinite understanding of the soul's passionate variabilities, and forgive even a real injustice.'

how is the notebook doing? i got tons of [expletive], but just started writing, well full time in addition to applying for jobs today. i have been writing but not really thinking about it the same way as i got too much on my plate. gotta eat and figure out what the [expletive] is going on tonight. talk soon"

Your mom made a traditional Polish meal for Christmas Eve dinner: pierogies and borscht. In Poland, they also eat fish on Christmas Eve, but I don't recall our family ever having fish at all except when in Poland. She spent quite a long time on the meal, cooking it all from scratch as per Polish tradition. If you're Polish, this is what you eat on Christmas Eve, end of story, as you know.

It was as if she was just doing it in order to go through the motions. She didn't involve us, she didn't even talk to us, even when we sat down. She looked miserable, listening to Drake, smoking her slims, basically shaking, and cooking our Christmas Eve dinner. I was kind of excited; Christmas was coming, and I was with my girls, but I was also apprehensive.

Your mom was tight lipped during the entire meal, staring at nothing with some kind of turbulence flowing through her. Finally, all of us at our little table, I was ready for my special Polish meal. But your mom stayed seated for no more than two minutes, claiming that she was done. She cleared her plate, and her bowl of borscht, and then she came back and immediately cleared yours, as if you would naturally be done since she was done.

"Agata, what are you doing? We're eating."

"She's not hungry. She's finished."

"No, she's not, just leave it and I'll get it when we're done."

She retreated to the kitchen, stewing.

After dinner, she asked me if we could open presents tonight, on Christmas Eve. This was the first time that she had spoken to me about Christmas at all, except when I was out getting your tree. All the presents were from me or my mom. Of course, the presents that were from me were also from your mom, and you would never have known the difference, but now she was adding a new twist, telling me that we had to open a present in adherence to Polish tradition.

Not that her request was ridiculous, but I didn't like that she was now communicating with me solely because she wanted something from me, and I told her no. I told her I was available whenever she chose to begin communicating with me, but that I would not cave to demands intermixed with nonsense. She really wanted to open at least one present, and I flat out told her that we would not be doing that. She was upset, but so was I.

I wanted you to have something to give to your mom, and so I took you into your room when she was showering and showed you the Sephora makeup that she had asked me to get her when I was in the U.S. We wrapped it together, poorly, you wrote your mom's name on it as best you could, and I showed you how to put it under the tree.

We put out milk, cookies, and carrots for Santa and his reindeer, and this was actually your mom's idea. I didn't want to do it because I didn't feel like I could tell you that there was a Santa. I did my best not to lie to you at all, and I wasn't going to start by telling you that Santa was going to come into our house at night. I let your mom take the lead on this one, grudgingly, thinking to myself that we would revisit this issue again, but also concluding that this was harmless compared to the rest of our recent reality with your mom.

You had stopped screaming about your "pee pee" by this point. I still had no idea what that could be, and your mom wouldn't allow me to take you to the doctor, but I was grateful that you were healing. Your improvement was remarkable to me; you were settling back into being home, and I just wished that your mom would do the same. I didn't know what had happened in Poland, but I knew it wasn't good, and I knew that I could not let your mom do as she threatened, or warned, she would.

Bedtime was more exciting than usual because the next morning was Christmas. For me, every day was exciting when I got to sleep with you under the same roof, and you weren't really all that excited about your presents, but I was. The Christmases of my childhood were amazing, and now you were old enough to enjoy them yourself. And I wanted to watch.

You just wished that your mom and dad were talking to each other; the division between us was upsetting to you, and you were frequently testing to see if we were back to normal yet. I tried to act as if nothing was wrong, because it wasn't for you to worry about, and I frequently told your mom that I loved her, purposely verbalizing excessively what had never and would never change, trying to assuage whatever part of her had been hurt or abandoned.

We weren't talking to each other, and there was no fooling you. Your mom continued to be cold, continued to ignore me, and continued to say that she hated me even while you were there. She thought that it was ok for you to know that she hated me, ok if you thought that I was the cause of her problems, ok if you thought that she thought that I was a bad dad.

"It's what I think, so why wouldn't I let her know? She deserves to know." While she didn't say that you hated me, she acted as if you should.

"No, Agata, you are wrong. Even if what you are saying is true, you still don't bring our three-year-old into whatever drama we may have. She's three, and she loves both of us. She needs you to be healthy is what she needs. You have lost it, just like before, just like the last time when we decided that you needed to get help. Bringing our daughter into this in the way that you are is abusive; you are abusing our daughter. You need to stop, and we need to get help."

"Fri, Dec 24, 2010, 5:36 PM
Iain Bryson to Brian
i have just been busy with the fam, and i again saw you called but we were eating pierogies this time and.....well let's just say it's hectic. i have to look at this as another experience that i can grow from. honestly the three months from may to july though they were worse than anything i can ever go through again was a great experience. detox on my own and the same [expletive] as now except i couldn't see what was happening like now.

so, bringing that into your situation, i would say do not be tough on yourself. just try little things, also realizing he has to adjust as he now has his expectations of what will happen. it will take time. try little things, and no matter how you feel try to keep the observation mask on. i think writing it down would help you to think about it, see change, whether good or bad and adjust. it also makes you revisit it instead of waiting for next time and doing the same thing. i have been doing this with my wife; the frustration i bet is the same. i can see what she is doing as well and i just want it to stop but she will not cause she is testing me and seeing how she can get the rise out of me. a bit different with the kid, but the same idea...i also think two kids adds a twist and i will have to think about that, but really if you are a bit detached and unemotional you will call the shots instead of the other way around. if you are not, then he will, just like with the wife.

as far as school, i wouldn't worry too much. the change has to start at home and then it will go to school. it is just another way for him to get at you. try to think of how you can end the playtime in other ways and test that out. i will also think about it. i have been dealing with the 'no' ....'please daddy'....... 'crying'...too since they got back because without me this [expletive] falls to pieces. my issue is that the wife is not currently on board, making the process almost impossible. but it is still a game i have to play and it drives me crazy. i think you need to make yourself write a page a day if it is slacking.....it is not easy for me a lot but the harder it is, the more i need to do it. it is therapeutic and very helpful. it can be hard because you feel like you are thinking about [expletive], but you are either way, so you might as well be working on it and not starting at the same point each time.

i will have to think about 'what you have,' although i know you don't have any 'disorders,' like my wife who is a certifiable psychopath........no [expletive] joke. certifiable.....i would have her committed if i knew how, but [expletive] it i do love the [expletive]....i guess love is a flaw i have. look that [expletive] up and think about it......pathological lying, no affect, no empathy.....but, it is also what has made me stronger, though she has no clue, as i have to do it all myself....for example, when detoxing and i think almost dying though how do you measure that [expletive], she acted like nothing was happening. it is sick, but i guess for the better.....though i would like to know that she would care and maybe hold my hand and look at me if i were dying, but [expletive] it i guess. my daughter would.

you had an assessment? i go weekly and like my guy, though i have blown past him as far as understanding the mind. he is still an 'expert' in the field, so they say and i get ideas from him i maybe don't think about. i really think everyone should do this; the mind is more complex than the body and people go for a cold to the doctor but are afraid of the stigma or to admit the other. who the [expletive] cares? i want to know [expletive] that will help me and only i and maybe you know if i am crazy or not. i have thought of asking you before because the wife assures me i am. ....but she is doing anything and everything to cause me pain at the moment. makes me want to [expletive] some other [expletive] once i get her under my finger (if i do) again and say [expletive] you stupid [expletive], but then again, i try to put it in terms of what i want for my daughter and if i can't keep my [expletive] in my pants, i don't think too many people can.

so, any traits i may think of as far as you are concerned would just be normal spectrum traits that may be a little enhanced, but honestly i can't think of any off the top of my head and i can for most everyone. but, then again, i didn't ever do it with the wife until she put on me as i don't think it is really healthy to deal with people you care in that manner. but, god, i dont know what i'd think if i didn't start thinking about her. now i can write a book about her life from beginning to end being about 90% accurate; it is like predicting what a dog will do in a given situation as it is cause and effect with no brain activity to learn or progress. and that is the case with most people. the most we can do is try and not get hard on ourselves or depressed or too frustrated as it doesn't help and it is not an easy task. chip away at that [expletive] and don't let the enormity of the job get to you.

first i would say you are overworked and stressed out. i do think there may be a little depression though labels suck. i had some the other day. the panic attacks were [expletive] with me and i got into bed and felt like i did in May for a couple of hours, working my way out of it. it is overwhelming. it is kind of like forcing your head into a mushroom trip, though not as intense, but looking at things like that. really, that is how it would be if we could take the stress and set it aside. the stress doesn't really make you do things better but it is a coping mechanism and response to the world, which is [expletive] intense at times. and then everyone else is also acting in similar ways so we assume it is what people do. [expletive] that [expletive]. i aint no [expletive] ant.

try to look at the small picture and not let the other things overwhelm you. the big picture is too much. you got your job, you got time with the kids, you got a wife that loves you and is awesome, you have a house, and your kids are going to eat. they don't know there is anything wrong until you let them know. try not to do that. i can't sometimes, but really only recently with the wife going insane again as i've been working on it. snap out of the fog and see what is in front of you. the rest will still be there and you will deal with it the same, but again, the stress only hurts everything. have a good xmas."

"Fri, Dec 24, 2010, 9:00 PM
Mom to me
Iain, Just getting home and getting ready for bed. I will be skyping Carrie in the am before she goes to work. I'll wait to see if you skype. Sounds like things are very difficult right now. You two have to work at it together. Adelle is all that matters.
I have to change the date on the ticket by Thursday as you are scheduled to fly out I believe the 3rd or the 4th. Your court is Feb. 8th. Let me know. If not, I will change to fly in the 6th most likely, unless you get the date changed. Merry Christmas to all. I love you. Mom"

CHAPTER 43

DAY 16: SATURDAY, DECEMBER 25, 2010

I was desperate, I wanted us to have a good Christmas, I wanted my wife back. I was indignant with whatever had disrupted our joy, and with whatever "monster" had taken up residence in our home. It was very frustrating for me, and I didn't feel like cycling through this entire thing again with your mom. I had seen it before, it was absolutely crazy, and then she got better and told me she was sorry, and that it wouldn't happen again. Now we were smack dab in the middle of it again, and I couldn't reach her; nothing I said to her seemed to get through.

She was curled up in our bed, "praying," with a "migraine," and I felt like I couldn't take it any longer. Christmas was happening. Life was happening. Your childhood was happening, and that meant that each day, each moment, was precious beyond measure. *How can she not snap out of it for our daughter? Why does she want to do this? What is she doing?*

I approached her from the living room, feeling willing to try anything, and I leaned over her, putting my hands on her head. She was praying, so I would also pray. Why not? What could I lose?

Satan seemed like a pretty reasonable explanation of whatever was going on in our house, and especially with your mom. I didn't know what was going on, and most of the time I was looking for answers from a psychological perspective, but what I could feel and sense was the devil, and it was blowing my mind.

"Exorcism... deals with a bodiless, genderless creature whom Jesus identified by name as Lucifer, and as Satan. A creature who Jesus identified further as 'the Father of Lies and a Murderer from the Beginning.'" (Martin xiv).

"In Jesus' name," I said, taking control over the room with the volume of my voice, "I command whatever is tormenting my wife, whatever has taken her over, I command in Jesus' name that it stop."

I felt ridiculous; never before had I prayed out loud in my adult life, let alone in an attempt to perform an exorcism.

But the entire situation was absurd. Everything that had been happening in our home since my return had been nonsensical, and the opposite of what I had expected. I don't think I could've imagined anything more outlandish, and it was all happening under my roof. I was scared to such a degree that I lost any and all aversion to prayer, and I had no fear of making a fool of myself. I wasn't worried about what your mom thought of me, and I thought it was worth a try.

Your mom stopped her "prayers," and looked up at me, stunned, but not surprised. I liked it when she looked at me like this; she seemed to appreciate my thinking outside of my normal box.

"Agata, it's Christmas. Will you please get up and join us?"

"I'll come out in a few minutes. I'm going to finish my prayers." I had made my point; she knew that I was extremely worried about her, and that I really thought she should make an effort not to be miserable that day. I left the room to start the day with you.

You were sleeping, and I laid down beside you, careful not to wake you yet. I had closed the door behind me, and it felt like we were in our own little world, away from the chaos that was on the other side of the door. I stroked your forehead, in awe of you, knowing that I was so very blessed to have you as my daughter, overwhelmed with waves of love.

Aerosmith's song, "I Don't Want to Miss a Thing," found its way into my thoughts, as if the situation had pulled it out of the deep past on my personal radio, the perfect tune for this moment. It's amazing how music, as well as scripture, can return to conscious awareness from hibernation right at the moment that we need it.

I started to cry in appreciation of how blessed I was, and how scared I was. I vowed to myself again that I would never trust you with anyone the way I had. I would work with your mom, but I would not blindly accept whatever she told me, and I would never again underestimate whatever her "mental illness" was. You were my job, end of story.

"I could stay awake just to hear you breathing
Watch you smile while you are sleeping
While you're far away and dreaming
I could spend my life in this sweet surrender
I could stay lost in this moment forever
Ooh, every moment spent with you is a moment I treasure
Don't want to close my eyes
I don't want to fall asleep
'Cause I'd miss you, babe
And I don't want to miss a thing..."
("I Don't Want to Miss a Thing" – Aerosmith)

I eventually woke you up, gradually, not really wanting to, but I was excited that it was Christmas, and I couldn't help myself. You agreed to come see what was under the tree, and I carried you into the living room, wrapped in your little pink blanket, Koko. Your excitement grew when you saw the colorfully wrapped mystery boxes, all yours except for the one that you would give your mom. I played some Christmas music that I had downloaded to try to stimulate the wonder, mostly Nat King Cole and Manheim Steamroller; I really hoped that your mom would come alive today. Why wouldn't she pull it together for you?

I already had coffee, but we made more so that your mom could have some too, and we cooked our usual scrambled egg mix with toast for breakfast. Your mom continued to pray; we wouldn't bother her until things were prepared.

She got up and took a shower. We set the table and waited, Christmas music playing in the background. When she came in, I felt proud, but in a way that one might feel when their dog scratches the door asking to go out instead of just going on the carpet. She was clean, dressed, awake; wow, we were all in the same room together on Christmas morning! This still wasn't the person that I knew to be your mom, *let's start small, let's just get through today. There is hope*, I thought, *good girl, Agata.*

She sat down, and I felt a tightness in the air. She was tense; it looked like it was hard for her to sit still, arms and legs crossed, almost shaking underneath her blanket. She greeted you, and ignored me, not looking at me or saying good morning or anything else. I knew that we wouldn't be able to pretend; if this was the best she could do, this was not going to be the day I once envisioned. We would go through the motions, and I would do the best I could, I decided.

The landline phone began ringing again; it didn't ring when we were sleeping, only during the day. I joked that I would answer it, and she reminded me in her own way how I was not allowed to get the phone or unplug it.

"But it's Christmas, Agata. Why can't we answer the phone? Do you know who it is? Why won't you talk to me?"

She scowled, and I backed down; the phone continued to ring from time to time. I just ignored it. It wasn't any weirder for me than the cat pooping on our bed, and I could simply turn up the music, problem solved.

She sat in the same position the entire time that you opened your presents, crossed and closed off. She smiled from time to time, but she wasn't really there, and it was more like the smiles that she frequently gave to characters on the television. Her phone stuck in her hand; her mind was elsewhere. She had no idea what the presents were because she didn't get any herself, didn't wrap any herself, and didn't seem to care.

I asked you if you wanted to give her your present, the Sephora makeup, and I felt like she must have felt when she asked you to give me that little Bible. I think that your mom gave me the same look now that I gave her then. It felt weird to me now that I was trying to play it off as your present to your mom, and I wished that I hadn't done that. My goal was to involve you in the giving part of Christmas, the most important part, and I was rushed.

Since you were three, and you knew that it was ultimately from me, this seemed awkward for you as well. You handed her the present, but I could tell that you weren't really sure what was going on. She forced a smile and thanked you.

When you went to the bathroom, I decided to try again. "Agata, can't you just try today? Won't you just try for our daughter? I don't care what you think about me. I'm only concerned with her, and she needs you. Come on, Agata."

"Why would I care?" she reminded me, probably some of the most frightening words that could come out of her mouth, words that suggested a total disregard for my position, a total denial of any rational conversation, and acting as if her new a priori reality was beyond question, that she and what she thought were infallible. All that I wanted was for our family to be healthy again, to pick up where we had left off, to figure out what could have possibly happened during those three months in Poland.

"Agata, can you see that you don't make sense? Do you realize that you are totally irrational? You are not the same person I used to know; you can't be. We've been through this before, why won't you listen to me?"

"No, you killed that girl."

"What are you talking about? Who killed you, Agata? I love you, why are you doing this?"

She retreated to the kitchen, and you and I proceeded to unpack, put together, and play with each of your presents: several puzzles of different sorts, a worm farm, a butterfly trap, etc. We laid out the puzzles on the floor, covering most of the living room. I knew that your mom wouldn't like this and would want it cleaned up right away. I hoped she didn't come in and scold us for our mess, but it didn't matter, we would continue being normal, and just wait for her to join us, whenever that might be.

One of your presents I had bought in Connecticut was a worm farm, but of course it didn't come with worms. Like an ant farm, it is set up so that you can watch the worms make tunnels through the soil and do whatever they do as they live their lives. I wanted to get it going, and because it was a worm farm and not an ant farm, we didn't have to order the worms in the mail like with the ants. I figured that we could find some worms in the park across the street, so we ventured out with our snow gear, and your plastic beach tools. Your mom stayed inside; more than two weeks, and she still hadn't played with us yet.

We had to dig a few holes, but in the end, we found the worms that were to move into your bedroom. I did most of the digging, though you did get in there a bit. I put each worm into your hand so that you could put them into the bucket, and we thoroughly filled in our holes so as not to disturb the park more than necessary.

We brought them inside, with a bucket of dirt, and we were officially worm farmers. I had to look further into what they ate, but we gave them some dried leaves to tide them over in the meanwhile. Your mom didn't like that they were in the house, but she didn't like much of anything at that time. We put them on the windowsill in your bedroom, right next to where we looked for the moon each night so I could tell you that I loved you to the moon and back. They didn't do much; I think they were too cold, maybe hibernating for the season; it was late December after all.

Ally was still pooping on the bed, and your mom was fed up. I reminded her that the cat was afraid of her, just like I was, and her daughter was, but she wasn't listening to me. *Well, this is how crazy it is because of her,* I thought, *I don't mind the cat externalizing what I also feel.* Animals know when something is wrong; I knew that horses, dogs, and cats, at least, had some type of vision into the normally invisible energy fields all around us. Ally confirmed what I already knew: your mom was nasty, angry, mean, and she was obviously in pain.

Your mom kicked Ally out of frustration, a swift toe punch, right in front of both of us. I was upset, mostly because of my own frustrations as your mom continued to prove more and more with her actions that she was out of control. We needed help, and I had no idea how to make that happen, how to convince her. I closed us into your room, with Ally, and together we played your drum and sung a song that I made up on the spot.

It went something like this, "Ally why are you pooping on the bed, don't you know you're supposed to poop in the litter box, please poop in the litter box, mommy is upset, why are you pooping on the bed, oh, why are you pooping on the bed?"

We sang and danced and laughed, marching across the floor, pounding on the drum. This wasn't my favorite song to sing with you, but it seemed appropriate at the time. It was a good way for us to vent. The weird, negative, cat-kicking energy was transformed into laughter, and that was an improvement.

"Sat, Dec 25, 2010, 4:40 PM
Iain Bryson to Mom
will do. i have to figure out some things. looking for work but not being 'allowed' to focus on that as i have to take care of adelle. so i have to stay up all night or most of the night which doesn't work anymore with the stress. it is no different than dealing with an alcoholic. it is throwing her for a loop that i can see through it now. unfortunately, there is not anyone i can talk to or want to in detail and so i have to just continue to cover the bases and try to work on her.

i need to figure out what is possible when i do leave the country, as i cannot allow her to have a captive audience without me here or to try to frame me as a deserter or something. i just don't know, and from where i stand anything is possible. trying to show that the options are very limited, but in each case since the beginning she has allowed the time to expire and then throw it back on me. i don't know whether she is not or cannot think or whether she is thinking i will cave and let her go to poland with adelle but there is no situation where i can let that happen. i have told her and just hope i am getting through. i cannot believe that someone who sees this would continue to go in the same direction.

i have been asking for the bills since May and every day since i got home and just got them today. it is tough to focus on work or anything else when this other thing is going on. i tell her i love her and that all that is needed is a baby step. unfortunately, when she is like this she is the very definition of a sociopath. and the other issues like ct and everything here doesn't help. it's a bit too much and she has the passport so i cannot leave the house for too long. sabotage is what it is. so, i am going to see what i can get done tonight, then wake up and make breakfast and go outside with adelle as she sleeps till 11 then frantically cleans the house once again, listening to her depressing music and smoking her cigarettes instead of seeing that one week of this is half of the money we have left. or maybe getting adelle something to give to me for christmas or maybe getting adelle something.

well, at least i am not fooled, but it is pretty intense at the same time. unfortunately for her, she has just made me stronger over the past year and i just have to hope that this is another one of those examples, yet this is not the game i want to be playing...at all. adelle had a blast on skype today. Every time we got cut off she said 'i need grammy. where is grammy. i have to tallk to her.' i think that was good for agata to see, but i am still trying to figure out if she is aware the things she says are false or if she is also lying to herself. hope you had a good christmas. sorry to bring this up, but i want to explain why i cannot deal with court right now. i will take care of it monday and go from there. talk to you soon. love you and take care of yourself."

"Sat, Dec 25, 2010, 5:01 PM
Iain Bryson to Kees de Vries
kees,
i am thinking more and more i am dealing with a psychopath or APD, and wow it is terrifying, especially with all this other [expletive] going on. i finally got a list of bills today after begging since i walked in the door off the plane. but, i was also asking for the past year. at least i finally see things and am not fooled. wow what a trip that was for seven years. how can you continue to call something white when it is black and someone

is showing you in every possible way that it is black? why do you play this sick game with a child? not only do i have seven huge bills i could not get information on until i apparently got it as my christmas present, but i find out today we have about 100 Euro. but she has it and will spend 5 something on her cigarettes every day and try to lay the blame on me, as always.

how do i focus on things i need to when i have to watch my child? she doesn't get out of bed till 11 and then i feel it is like living with an alcoholic or maybe someone with tourette's that just blurts out [expletive] just to cause pain. i have to take care of my child, then try to stay up to work on jobs. i am terrified to leave as she has my child's passport and i have no idea where it may be. she had told me i had an appointment with the psychiatrist, but then again, i have text messages and emails indicating nothing is abnormal and that she loves me and has taken care of x, y, and z for us and is ready to get moving forward up until the point i walked in the door and was hit with a barrage of [expletive] which has continued till now.

i could really use more concerta. it allows me to lose the anxiety and be clear headed instead of clogged with this crap and not capable of knocking [expletive] off the list like i have to. when i sleep now i have nightmares and i sweat profusely to the point where i cannot lay on my sheets and i have diarrhea. if only she knew that i do love her and could see or admit or whatever it may be that there is no option as she sees it and that it makes no sense on any level. wow, this [expletive] threw me for quite a loop last time and i am glad for the clarity. in the end she is making me stronger, but this is not the game i want to be playing.

when i think about the options, it is not fun, and the pressure is a bit too intense. i have told her that under no circumstances will i give her permission to leave the country with my daughter, and she still will not change or even consider it. my god, how? what fuzzy [expletive] can be happening in someone's head to lead to these sick things. [expletive] i love her and want to help but it is no different than dealing with a heroin addict or an alcoholic. look in the other room woman. our child is there and you have to be able to admit one of these things are true, and in doing so maybe you can continue on that path to see that more is as well. if nothing else, the one thing that is as apparent as anything is so [expletive] up that it is worth taking a closer look.

anyway, other than that, i am doing well, though not to be redundant i could really use more concerta. the fog in my head can get overwhelming; i forgot what it was like and this girl can lay that [expletive] on me, basically paralyzing my mind. christmas was good. i am getting things done we talked about, though the thousand sledge hammer swings need to work sooner rather than later. if nothing else, my daughter is doing much better than when i first got here, we talked to my mother on skype for an hour today, and we do things every day and have been having fun in the snow.

i cannot get the wife to leave her habitual sleeping in, lounging, frantic cleaning, smoking cigarettes and playing depressing 80's music/and new r+b hits, and just plain burying the head as far in the sand as possible. when i ask her to think about something, i just get the nastiness and get blamed. at least i finally got the list of things i have been asking for though it sucks it was my christmas present. and 100 euro. my [expletive] god. and you decide to buy things like cigarettes and paper towels and pepsi..... [expletive] this has to be bizarro world, or maybe this is how they raise them in poland. anyway, i hope you are well. Iain"

**"Sat, Dec 25, 2010, 6:45 PM
Iain Bryson to Brian**
had a good xmas considering everything else. have narrowed the wife down from borderline, psychopath, sociopath to sociopath and not psychopath with borderline traits. [expletive] scary [expletive]. finally got some info out of her as a xmas present including our finances which she will smoke half of this week if she keeps going. have to figure out how to get her into my counseling session on the 30th....got to find a babysitter. if this [expletive] doesn't change, involuntary commitment may be the only option and i need her to see someone. luckily she has been seeing him with me since july or august so he will see (or i [expletive] hope) that she is destroying everything she crosses. wow.

so, going to bed i think as i have to get up with the girl since the wife sleeps till 11 and then mopes around and cleans incessantly with her OCD or whatever the [expletive] it is. gotta work on jobs and was going to tonight but this [expletive] takes the wind out of me, i gotta figure out how to stay above water and win this [expletive] should it come down to it. now for sleep i have nightmares and sweat to the point where i cannot lay in my sheets. i didn't need to sleep at all for a while, but now i get brain blockage and overwhelmed as it is just a bit too far on the crazy side.

i could and was prepared to deal with the financial issues, etc. but things have changed and i can't even figure out whether that is the priority or i guess it is not though what the [expletive]? [expletive]. well i hope you are doing great and had a nice day with the family. this will be a good book but not something i want or need to do now. thank god i have some clarity, though the game is not one i want to play and the stakes are ridiculous especially with the court [expletive] in CT and the money/apartment issue.

she cannot add one plus one which is frustrating. i spell out hundreds of things with perfection and she goes right back to 'refrigerator.' if you got a phone card, let me know when you could/can call and i will set up a time to be out of the house. the wife has the kid's passport and i am terrified to leave for an extended period of time, thus making finding work that much more difficult. again, at least it is not going over my head and i can deal with it, but at some point it can get to be too much."

"Sat, Dec 25, 2010, 7:04 PM
Mom to me
Ok honey. I can only imagine what's going on and I know it's hard. It's just that we cannot let this court thing get out of hand either as that will just make matters worse. So, if you can change the date without a lot of issues that's fine, I just need to keep the 1/2 of the ticket open and not lose it. If not, come back, deal with it and then go right back. Merry Christmas. I love you"

"Sat, Dec 25, 2010, 7:05 PM
Mom to me
the other option, is to bring Adelle with you for a visit."

I liked the way this sounded, but my current reality wasn't suggesting that this was an actual option. Your mom still had your passport, hidden, and she hadn't changed her stance: she was going to take you back to Poland, and I was wrong about everything. End of story, for her; she wasn't budging yet.

My mom had no idea what I was dealing with; nobody did. Take you to the U.S.? I was just trying to keep you from being abducted by your mother, who continued to guarantee me that this was in the process of happening. My mom's naïve statement reminded me that it could've and should've been more normal, and made me long for those days. This was like dealing with some crazy alcoholic; I knew that anything was possible, and I was in constant fear.

All things considered, I felt like you and I had a pretty good day. I was sad that your mom hadn't really participated, that she wasn't truly present at all, but this was the new norm. I wasn't surprised anymore, and she really was just making me stronger. You and I were growing closer daily; it was almost as if we had never been apart, except that we had.

I knew that you had also been traumatized, like your mom obviously had been, and it frightened me to think of the forces that must've shaped her incongruities, and to know that they had also had time with you. I needed my partner to level with me, and she flat out refused, so I attempted to have a sit-down meeting with you, my three-year-old daughter.

I knelt on the floor, facing you, and I asked if you would hold my hands. Looking deep into your eyes, I told you that I loved you, I told you that I loved your mom, and I told you that you could talk to me about anything. But instead of opening up to me, you tensed up and closed off, stared at me blankly, as if my questions were scaring you in some way, as if you were instructed not to speak to me.

You had nothing to say, and me asking you was making you uncomfortable. I knew that me sitting with you and holding your hands, asking if you had anything that you wanted to talk to me about, gazing into your eyes intently, was not inherently uncomfortable. Why would it be?

Then I saw your mom, standing there observing us, and it made sense. You weren't allowed to talk to me; you were afraid of betraying someone's secret. It would take me some time, and I would have to begin talking to you when your mom was not around, but I knew that you would tell me everything, whatever it was. My goal was to get your mom to cooperate because I didn't want to press you for information or make you break a promise; my plan was to flood you with the greatest healing tool that I knew: love.

Your mom was another story, as she was an adult who was being actively abusive and completely negligent. I would never give up on her and never take you from her, but I couldn't continue to put up with this. She would have to get help, or I would have to find a way to get her help; there was no other option as it stood. I also knew that in the meantime I had to take control over your safety because she was not good at it, and I could have no more patience with her on this topic. She was not trustworthy, as much as I wanted and needed her to be.

You were amped up after the Christmas excitement, and you didn't want to go to sleep. We put you to bed, but you were up playing with your new toys, and with Ally. You were singing and bouncing around your room. I was happy that you were in your room, in our house, safe and sound.

But I needed to talk to your mom, and I needed you to be asleep to be able to do that, so I went back into your room to chat about getting some sleep. I told you that you didn't have to sleep, but that I wanted you to stay in your bed, because it was late, and because you needed rest so that you wouldn't be tired the next day. I hated reasoning with you like this, but I really felt I had to spend time with your mom, and our apartment was too small to have you awake during any of that, especially with her recent theatrics. Your little eyes and ears were not going to record any extra "crazy" on my watch.

You agreed to stay in your bed, but as soon as I was back on the couch with your mom, I could hear you laughing, and I could see your eye peering through a keyhole in an inoperable door that separated your room from the living room. I was torn between inviting you out for family time, *who cares what time it is*, and my burning desire to get back to business with your mom.

I got up and put a piece of tape over the keyhole, feeling a little bad, but concluding that I didn't have a choice. I couldn't have my three-year-old daughter watching this, maybe someday soon your mom would be healthy again and I wouldn't have to be such a stickler.

"Don't cover the hole," your mom entreated, apparently sadder than I was by the look and sound of her.

"I have to cover the hole. It's nighttime, and I need to speak with you. She is three, and she doesn't need to be here for that. She needs to sleep. I have to talk to my wife."

She didn't argue with me, but her facial expression convinced me to take the tape down, to not block you out in that way. Instead, I returned to your room and asked you again if you would stay in your bed. I laid with you for a few minutes, and you drifted off. I longed for our family to be healthy once again, soaking in the beauty of my sleeping child, your innocence, all your beautiful potential, how blessed I was to have you.

As soon as I knew you were sound asleep, I had to get back to our current reality – your mom was absolutely crazy and dangerous, again. *Alright*, I thought, *I'll tell her again that I am terrified, that we need to get help now, that I will support her. She is scared too, I can be patient while also being relentless, at least I now have them back under my roof.*

"I don't understand how that is not enough, Agata." I pointed in your direction. "How can you do this, knowing that you did this before, knowing that your daughter was once healthy, as were you? This happened in Poland, Agata: end of story. I'm not going to argue with you anymore; you're crazy, you've flat out lost your mind. Do you want to be put into a white gown and locked up?"

She glared at me knowing that I was giving her the same ultimatum that she was giving me, and that I would be the one to face psychiatric scrutiny once I told someone else what she was telling me. Her look said something like, "Oh, you poor boy," in a way that conveyed both love and pity.

I sat down on the ground by her feet, and I began chain smoking her slim cigarettes, partly because that is what I tended to do when under a lot of stress, and partly because I knew that the rapid disappearance of your mom's own cigarettes would give your mom stress. It wasn't that I wanted to upset her but wake her up; I wanted her to hear the words that were coming out of my mouth, and I could not just sit and watch another movie, wasting time, with this threat of you being taken back to the "cult" in Poland imminently looming.

"What do you expect? What do you expect me to do? I'm telling you that our daughter has been abused. I'm telling you that you are abusing her now and trying to alienate her from me. How could you do that?"

"She has a right to know."

"What are you talking about? Our three-year-old has a right to know that you hate me?! She knows that you are crazy, Agata, she says that you are sick, and that she has to help you when you're sick. I don't like that either, but that's the way it is. She isn't stupid. What do you want me to do? What is it that you expect me to do? We need help, Agata."

"I was gonna tell you that I met someone."

"Agata, is anyone home? Where did you go? Who do you think you're talking to? Please listen to me; we need help."

"You need to go to the U.S., you won't be able to work here, me and Adelle are going back to Poland."

"What are you talking about? You are my work, if you think I'll stop, you're wrong. I'll never stop. You don't fool me, Agata Avery."

"Not for me, do it for her, stop ranting, stop thinking about yourself."

"Agata, I am not thinking about myself. I am thinking about our little girl."

I realized that we were going nowhere, I didn't want to wear her out, and I was tired of pushing and prying. It was nice to get to sit close to your mom, in a semi calm, and watch a movie, and I knew that this is what she wanted. She didn't want to talk to me, that was obvious. I wondered how long it would be before we were ok again.

She told me that she wanted to watch "Unthinkable," from her list. It didn't look like a good movie to me, but I was interested because she had chosen it, and was choosing it right then. Not long after it started, I realized why it didn't appeal to me; it was a movie about terrorism and torture, not really that much fun, and I was already dealing with horror in my household.

I'd have rather watched something like "The Other Guys," the comedy that we had watched a few days prior, but this was your mom's choice, and I focused on scooching closer to my wife on the couch, seeing the comedy of suddenly having to be afraid of accidentally touching her.

In the movie, a man was threatening to blow up stuff, and Samuel L. Jackson was torturing him. "This is stupid, all they have to do is threaten the children. Why go through all the rest of it, if it were me, I'd go straight for the children, that's all that he has to do, movie over. Just twist his arm as hard as you can with his children; why are they messing around with half twisting his arm?"

Of course, we had to sit through the entire thing to get to that conclusion, wasting valuable time, the only time that we could speak together without you overhearing us. Even then, I knew that she didn't think we were wasting time, the way that she looked at me when I told her that he should threaten the man's children, as if I were a baby that was just beginning to grasp something that would be very painful. She knew that this movie would get under my skin; she knew that I would think it was ridiculous. "Unthinkable, Agata, is our house right now; unthinkable is you."

We got into bed, and I felt like I was going to explode. *Who is this woman, and what does she think she's doing? She dares to threaten me with my child, she dares to abuse her in front of me, she doesn't acknowledge anything that I know to be the truth, she says that she never loved me, that she planned this.*

I felt like I had a dangerous intruder in my house that was threatening my entire world, and the world of the woman that I loved and sent to Poland three months earlier. *Where was that other woman? What happened to her?*

I pushed her in the butt with my legs, at first just to get her attention, but I kept pushing until she slid off the bed onto the floor twenty inches below. "Get out of my bed, who are you, get out, get out," I ordered her, pointing my finger, and clenching my teeth much the same way you had earlier when you ordered her out of your room. She put her head down, and left, again in the same manner as when you had told her to leave.

In the living room, she immediately laid down on the couch to go to sleep there. I felt like I had just killed her dog. *This is my wife, I cannot kick her out, no matter what*, I reminded myself, frustrated that my best friend had become my greatest enemy, threatening to do the worst thing possible. Somewhere underneath there was that amazing person I knew was there; no matter what she appeared to be, I knew who she really was, under the layers of trauma and pain.

I knelt beside her and put my arm around her, knowing that I was out of line, wanting her to get back into bed with me, wanting all of this to just go away, wishing I had never left. "Agata, I'm sorry, please come back to bed, I shouldn't have done that, I am scared. It's your bed too, please come back."

She did, and I laid down with her until she fell asleep. I couldn't sleep, and I didn't want to. I decided that I would try to express myself to her in writing, and I stayed up until the early morning typing this multipage stream of consciousness plea. *She just isn't listening*, I reasoned, *if she could see the truth in black and white, then she would want to get help. She would have to, because there is no other rational option.*

I laid it on the line, unafraid, not holding anything back. I just let it flow. I didn't care about her arguments insofar as I could hypothetically accept them all to be valid, whether they were or not, and then proceed to the obvious elephant in the room. I thought of the Eminem line, "I apologize even though I know it's only lies." I didn't care about my ego; I didn't care what I was or wasn't. I did care that my loving wife had returned to me a monster, telling me ridiculous, horrible things, and obviously victim to the same.

CHAPTER 44

LETTER TO YOUR MOM – DECEMBER 25, 2010

"*Baby, I love you. My world has been flipped the [expletive] upside down due to the current situation. I went from knowing, along with you, that our love is true, great, precious, not perfect but improving and definitely on the right path.......within a few hours, I was back to where I was in May, which is my Hell. I would rather go to Hell given the opportunity, if there were one, but after this I have once again become a person who is worried about Hell... I am most certain that Heaven for me is taking care of and loving my two girls. There is no doubt in my mind; not ever... Heaven is not after this life. It is right here, if we only see it. We do not float out of our bodies into some palace with anything we want after we die. This is it; I see it perfectly clear. We are floating right now....you me dell and ally, and I know you have also seen this.*

My marriage to you has developed more than I could have possibly imagined or wished for over the nearly seven years I have known you. We had reached the point of where we had gotten over the hump and begun to kill the demons which nearly ended us. Our marriage is no longer a challenge for me in any way. It is a pure joy....we both agreed on that three months ago when I went to Connecticut, and you with our daughter to Poland. (Please ask Kees if you are uncertain....or your mom...) I am sure of it, absolutely positive, but that is because I know you and I can sense it. I am not going to hold you to your agreement, but I have been trying to get my points across, which I feel might be important to you. I know things have been tough, and that we have been through a lot (more than 1), and that I am not a perfect man... I only hope to show you that something else is highly likely to be both distorting your thoughts as well as the conclusions that you come to.

You state that you have known all along that you did not love me, or at the very least that you knew it since May. I have known both love and intense hostility. The love is so real that I am blown away and reassured that 'love' itself is actually real. The hostility is just as real; I see evil emerge in both of us...I do not believe that we would be married today had one of us been consciously able to control the issues that have led to and been a part of our fighting. The only other option for us to remain together would be for us both to get help, and that surely would not have happened in the beginning until they figure out how to do pre-marital mental checks along with the blood testing. I do believe that now that we have figured it out, we have the ability to remove the [expletive] from our love. BPD has directly led to our conflicts... The proof is in what you do, rather than in what you think you do or say that you do...

Whether this current situation can be tied to BPD or 'mental illness' is never going to be proven. There are too many factors and no reliable tests; love cannot be known except to the individual. However, real 'love' is expressed through the union of two individuals, and though I know you do not feel it now, I know without a shadow of a doubt that it has been there. I know it is not perfect and that I am surely not perfect. I know that I will not be able to convince you with words of our love, though I will try, and can only hope to show you that there is another possibility for this change. The way that this possibility has been shown/defined to manifest itself is in the exact thoughts which have led to changing beliefs about your love for me... but the only thing I do believe in is 'love.'

With love comes Heaven, with obstacles, but the obstacles become fun, for the most part, once love is found. The things which upset us are just a part of the environment of our 'love.' We have the ability, if we should choose, to deconstruct our environment, thereby seeing how our [expletive] 'yard' could make us love each other one day and not the other, in the same way that we can see if our anger towards someone has grown or subsided from day to day. The reasons for love are not known; they cannot be expressed in mere words, though love itself can be expressed. When love is expressed, it is expressed on a spiritual level, denying explanation or comparison. I do not believe that it is often found, but I truly believe in the reality of our love.

IF YOU TO TALK TO SOMEONE AND DO IT HONESTLY, YOUR THOUGHTS WILL CHANGE IN REGARDS TO THE ISSUES THAT ARE RELATED TO BPD. THIS DOES NOT MEAN THAT I KNOW THAT YOU HAVE BPD, OR THAT I KNOW WHICH THOUGHTS WOULD BE AFFECTED. BUT, I DO BELIEVE THAT IF, IF YOU WERE ABLE TO BETTER UNDERSTAND THE THOUGHTS LEADING YOU TO KNOW WHETHER YOU LOVE ME OR DO NOT LOVE, HAVING A BETTER UNDERSTANDING OF THE THOUGHTS STEMMING FROM BPD, YOU WOULD CHOOSE TO LOVE ME.

My wife says she is one hundred percent certain that she can no longer be with me. She says that she has come to this decision after a period of clear reflection and clear, sound thought. I believe that she does feel this way, and I can also say that the reasons she has may lead you to that conclusion. I do not believe she is purposefully lying to me; she truly does feel this way. I am terrified due to the fact that I have seen this exact thing before.....the exact thing and she has categorically denied that they are similar.

I am not saying you are not you or that there is something wrong with you. I am saying that there are things that are beyond conscious reason and thought which effect people, and that these things are often serious. There are many things which affect the brain such as the Depression, ADHD, and panic attacks which I have dealt with. There are also much more serious things such as schizophrenia and PTSD. I am not trying to, nor do I want to question your thinking. What I want to do is to make sure that your thoughts are not coming from something which you cannot see. This is not only damaging our marriage, but it has impacted your quality of living, your happiness and pretty much everything on some level. It is the same with anything in the brain.

These disorders are generally misunderstood. There is not a huge difference between Depression and Schizophrenia in that they both are names for something unseen, but real, which affects thought and life. The ways that they affect the brain are different, as is their respective impacts on the thinking, and on life. What I am trying my best to get across to you is the importance of being able to identify and understand any one of these things. They affect your thoughts, feelings, and actions. I know that you feel the way that you do. I am sorry and I love you.

What worries me the most is that you are making decisions based on things that are reasons which you feel, but are unable to identify. This is going to impact your life, and the life of our daughter. I value our marriage and our love more than anything in this world, but I love you and really want you to be sure about the reasons that you are making decisions. Or, as certain as possible. It is no different than getting help and understanding, and continuing to do that with my Depression and ADHD. I have only recently begun to understand these things, and I am blown away by the amount of impact and the things which were impacted in my life and the lives of those I love for so long.

When I met you, you told me that your father told you when you were twelve or fourteen that he had cheated on your mother. He took you for a walk, having this discussion with you. You told me this after we had known each other for less than two weeks. It was certainly an issue which was plaguing you, and one which you needed to get off your chest to someone you loved/cared about. You also told me that I was the first person you had ever told this to. I was blown away, hurt, angry, frustrated, and I tried desperately to provide some kind of a useful answer, but all I could come up with at the time was to love you the way I knew how. You knew all about the woman, you knew the entire story, you had spoken to the woman, angry about what had occurred. Your mother went to Spain for a while and then came back, but you know that the reason she went was due to the fact that she was figuring out what to do. You[r] mother and father's relationship has never been the same since, and your father drinks. I have been trying to understand and figure out how to define these things for as long as I have known you. I have not thought about it much, until now, but it did come up on some occasions.

Most recently, when you last went to Poland with Adelle, we had a big discussion about your father's drinking, and how we would deal with it in our home. We have had discussions throughout our marriage about how your mother and father continue to have problems, and how she is not happy because she is with him. We have spoken about the cheating incident as well, sporadically throughout our relationship. We have never gotten very far, but I have always been able to see that it bothers you and hurts you, and as you know, anything with these characteristics is something that drives me crazy.

Before this year, we had not dealt with any of the issues which either one of us brought into our marriage. Throughout the course of the year, we have dealt with more than most people deal with in their lives, and we have begun to figure out things which have been hurting us.

Baby, I want you to be happy, even if that means that you are not 'with' me. We were on the verge of separation before. You were certain. You had completely withdrawn from me, emphatically stating over and over for a period of about three months that you could not and would not live with me. I see the exact same thing happening again, and I cannot just let it happen when I know the things we have and were dealing with prior to September.

We had finally begun to understand and deal with my drug use, Depression, and ADHD. You also recognized that Borderline Personality Disorder was something you may be dealing with. We researched and talked about this, agreed that it made a lot of sense, and you decided to get help. We never followed through with this, and it dropped off the radar. Given what Borderline Personality is, the fact that we knew we needed to understand it, and the fact that we completely neglected to deal with it, I am worried that we have reached where [we] are today as a result of this decision. I know that you believe this is not the case, but the fact is that neither of us know. I really want us to continue to look into this with the same fervor we looked into the other things we knew were plaguing our relationship.

You say you cannot be with me. You said this from May to August and then you told me, Kees de Vries, and everyone else you spoke with that you were the happiest woman in the world. I knew you were the happiest woman in the world, as did those around you. We also came to the conclusion that things that happened from May to August were due to issues we could strongly identify with Borderline Personality Disorder.

I was terrified when I first starting researching and seeing how much of it made sense to me, how much of it I felt, and the fact that you could not see it at all. You had gotten to the point where you were able to admit that it did make sense to you based on things which had happened, and also that you were going to immediately talk to someone in order to try to understand it and deal with it. You were perplexed, overwhelmed with 'BPD,' and deeply trying to figure out what it was that had led to some of your actions in the past. I could tell that it was bothering you, and that it 'made sense, but did not make sense.' I was relieved when you decided you would go talk to someone. At the time, I emailed Kees without your knowledge, telling him what we had 'figured out,' and indicating to him how overwhelmed and scared I was. I did not tell you I emailed him because I was terrified, and I did not want to violate your trust. I needed someone to talk to, and he was someone I could trust, and the only person other than you that I can speak to.

During this period of our marriage, we were figuring out so many things about us. I had withdrawn from clonazepam and morphine, dealt with Depression, and I sought counseling. The meetings with the psychologist became a place that you and I could go to work on issues about me. In these meetings, we uncovered a lot of things, one of them being that I have ADHD. We had identified a high probability of Borderline Personality, and we decided it was imperative that we also dealt with this. We spoke with Kees, though together we never told him about the BPD suspicion. I did not bring it up again because you began to see someone and because Kees indicated that he could not act as a psychologist to both of us.

Though we had begun to seek help in understanding the things which appeared to be from BPD, we stopped after you saw the psychologist a few times. From my understanding, you completed some questionnaires, and you had begun to speak about your parents, and about your family. However, we never again spoke about BPD, and we have failed to deal with it at all since this time. We let it completely drop off of the radar due to the fact that it had ceased being a visible issue. We were happy, making progress, and as usual, we did not want to deal with unpleasant things during 'good times.' And these times were wonderful. Neither of us had any doubt about us, about our marriage, about our love, about our future.

This is the exact pattern we have followed throughout the course of our relationship, during which time issues of BPD have arisen at different times. These issues have clawed away at us, hurt us, and perplexed us since the beginning. But, when they were dormant, we had no discussion, and we never made any progress. In the end, after we both decided that BPD had affected our relationship, we again let it go when things starting going well, but this time we had at [least] begun to seek answers when you went to counseling. But, we only started....

You continued to be baffled by the BPD issue. You went to counseling reluctantly because of your inability to speak about the issues which needed to be dealt with. You went a few times, and we spoke after each time you went and saw the counselor. I helped you to complete the personality questionnaires because you thought I would know the answers to the questions. It was too much for you, too intense, and you were unable to focus your attention towards these issues. You never got close to discussing issues which could have been related to BPD; you did not have time, you did not get that far, and you were still reluctant to outwardly express these things.

Because of the intensity surrounding this realization, you pushed it out of mind, going into counseling hoping that it could be 'fished out,' as you had decided not to bring up the possibility. You have 'blocked out' issues or things which have overwhelmed you since I have met you. I have always spoken of it, though we never identified it as an issue. I believe that it has now become an issue which we need to deal with. Previous things which were 'blocked out,' were things like the rent not being taken out of your account for six months, the electric shut off notice, and what your father told you as a child.

I am not claiming you have 'BPD,' but I am claiming that we have both thought it was a good possibility. And, because of this, I have sought to try to understand it so that I could better understand our past, and so I could better understand you. The fact is that we failed to follow through once we identified it as a probable issue, and I am scared due to what I see, and the direct relationship it could have on where we are at now.

BPD, or the symptoms we identified, can be due to something called 'non-touching' sexual abuse. The definition of this type of 'abuse' is the submission of a child to graphic sexual images. When your father told you about his extramarital affair, I have no doubt he had good intentions. Though it has angered and frustrated you for your entire life since, I also know you believe he had good intentions. It is not the intentions that matter, but rather, the result that it has upon a child. I respect your father, though I have struggled with this, and I believe that he was a great father. I also know that this incident left a mark on you as a child that you shared with me when you were an adult and that it carried on throughout our relationship.

Because of this, because of the issues in our marriage which seem to be explained in part by BPD, and because of our conclusion that BPD was an issue which needed exploration, I really believe that this image created issues in our marriage, and in your life in general, which can be explained by BPD. The picture of your father cheating on your mother was for certain a graphic image which developed in your mind as you matured. You personally dealt with the woman who was involved in this affair. You were aware of and lived with the effects that this had on your mother. You brought it up to me as 'the issue' when we met. We have dealt with aspects of it throughout our relationship. We decided to get help for the issues, regardless of whether or not we could discern ourselves whether it was in fact BPD. The fact is that it does not matter if we call it BPD. A child was subjected to and listened to her father explain a sexual relationship with a woman other than her mother. There is no doubt that this experience is still having an impact on some level today. It logically follows, given the definition of BPD, that the issues which we have identified can be at least partly attributed to this childhood experience.

If we can and have admitted to ourselves that BPD may be an issue, there is then a chance that our current situation can have something to do with it. One of the things associated with BPD is 'distortions in cognition and self.' This means that your thoughts and the way that you view yourself, as well as what makes you happy can and probably do change over time without your knowledge, and without you choosing for this to occur. I have seen this in many aspects of you and our relationship, but the present is what I believe matters the most at this time. When I left for Connecticut, you were more positive, sure, and optimistic than you have ever been. I believe this is due to the relief gained from dealing with things such as drug use, Depression and ADHD. You were not lying about how sure you were about the validity and realness of our love and our marriage; you had genuinely reached that point.

Furthermore, you said to me on more than one occasion that you would never again 'forget' that you loved me, and that you saw the fact that this had happened to be a severe issue which you now would remember and not do again. One day we are doing as well as I could hope for, making progress with each day. Then, I leave for three months, return and you are again saying that you cannot be married to me. This represents both a distortion in thought and a distortion in thought; one day you were certain that you were happy, while the next you are miserable and saying you know that you want a divorce.

Also a distortion of thought is the compilation of letters I have from you during the three months I was away. They indicate romantic, true love, and again, you were not lying. So, from August, when there was no doubt we were going to be together to December, when you are certain we have to be apart, you went back and forth with your thoughts. You were unable to maintain the certainty we had in September, and while all of your correspondence indicated you were 'in love,' you were certain of the fact that we have to get divorced once I got back to The Netherlands.

While you claim that your thought process which led you to your current conclusion has been unaffected by interference, we know that some sort of interference is probable, and so we also know that distortion is probable. Given the fact that distorted thoughts are probable, and that you have been 110% certain of both your undying love for me and your need for a divorce, I would say that your thoughts and decisions about our marriage have been 'distorted' in some way.

Another sign of BPD can be seen in the creation of a 'false dilemma.' This is defined as 'a false dichotomy; the either or fallacy; fallacy of false choice; black and white thinking, or the fallacy of a false hypothesis.' One day I see you and you are certain of your love and of our future; the next you are certain of the need for a divorce. This alone could be a 'false dilemma,' since you are going between extremes of marriage and divorce, stating repeatedly that it is because it is the way you 'feel.' Given the fact that distorted thoughts would cause distorted 'feelings,' the probability that your feelings have been affected is also high.

You state that you are certain, more certain than ever, and that it feels that way. You have some reasons you state as examples of reasons which have led you to this 'feeling,' but have been unwilling and unable to clearly explain them. 'I just feel this way, and I know for sure. I do not love you. I was wrong before.' You have arrived at a decision to end your marriage without being able to identify the actual decision through anything other than the way you feel. As I have stated before, I am not saying that the reasons you have expressed are not valid, or could not be a reason to 'not be able to be with me' in and of themselves. However, the reason you give for your change of heart is 'the way I feel; I just know.' We have been unable to explore any one of the reasons to any depth beyond the label which is attached to it.

Another example of black and white thinking, I believe, is when you say that the decision you have come to now has nothing in common with the one you made in May. I know it feels different, but it is the exact same decision, separated by a month of being certain of your love for me and three months apart. And I am hearing and feeling the exact same things from you. I see the exact same person, the exact same chain of events, and the exact same situation before my eyes. I believe that this should be looked at as a similar situation due to the similarities even though you feel it is a different situation. I have no doubt that you are certain of this, and that you are not lying; I simply believe it is worth exploring, especially given the fact we knew we had to after the first instance and then stopped.

'Such symptoms are most acute when people with BPD feel isolated and lacking in social support, and may result in frantic efforts to avoid being alone.' This indicator of BPD gives us notice that if BPD were an issue in the first place, the fact that we were separated for three months, uncertain about our future and also our present, would create a situation that might lead to a distortion of thoughts and behaviors. In May, 'I can't be with you' began with your return from Poland. I have mentioned this to you, along with other instances in the past where we had been apart and then had serious problems.

When you went to Poland, you were so happy, proud and sure of your family. You had discussions with your parents, letting them know that we had arrived at some important parenting decisions that they needed to know about. You spoke to your mother about alcohol being in the house, as you know this has been a problem in the past, and you felt ready to deal with it. We were separated, isolated, worried, we missed each other terribly, we were dealing with two entirely different worlds along with what we still had in Holland, and ultimately we found out that the VISA would not be issued, and that we would meet back in Holland.

When the VISA decision was made known, we were crushed, and you insisted that I come back immediately so that we would be together for Christmas. I could sense and see that you were struggling, and I was worried to death. I had seen this before, and I knew that the sooner we were together the better. I have seen the same anxious signs in the past, and when they revealed themselves again, I was worried. However, I was on a mission to do as much for our family as possible, and I also knew that both you and Adelle were safe with your parents. I was concerned, but I had to stay on task. Both times 'we cannot be together' has come out of your mouth, it was directly after a period of being apart.

'People with BPD often have highly unstable patterns of social relationships. While they can develop intense but stormy attachments, their attitudes towards family, friends, and loved ones may suddenly shift from idealization (great admiration and love) to devaluation (intense anger and dislike). Thus, they may form an immediate attachment and idealize the other person, but when a slight separation or conflict occurs, they switch unexpectedly to the other extreme and angrily accuse the other person of not caring for them at all.' Our relationship has been unstable; we have made some great progress in understanding and dealing with many of the issues which we have been able to identify.

The fact that your idea/feelings towards loved ones may suddenly shift from idealization to devaluation, and you went from knowing you love me to knowing you do not, it logically follows that this change of mind could have been due to BPD. Furthermore, we began our relationship with a 'stormy attachment.' We met while you were in CT on a J-1 VISA for three months with your long time boyfriend. Your relationship with him ended, and we were engaged in a month. We simply 'knew' our relationship was real and certain and worthy of marriage. There was absolutely no doubt in our minds. Between you being in CT, you breaking up with your Polish boyfriend, and becoming engaged to me, it seems like a 'storm' was brewing somewhere.

Relationships affected by BPD can be subjected to splitting and transference. Splitting is when one of the people in the relationship can be viewed as all good or all bad at different times, depending on whether he gratifies need or frustrates them.

We had intense counseling sessions where we worked together to figure out and deal with things which were negatively impacting me as a person, a parent and a husband. We fought through issues I never dreamed possible, and we reached a point where we understood each other, the reasons for things in the past, and new ways of doing things in the future. Our love matured and grew, and we were both more certain than ever of our family, our love, our marriage. We debated me going to Connecticut over and over; we discussed the pros and cons with each other and with Kees de Vries for about a month. When we decided to do it, we were both scared because of what we had with just each other and our daughter, but we decided that this option was the best given our circumstances..."

CHAPTER 45

DAY 17: SUNDAY, DECEMBER 26, 2010

"http://www.schematherapy.com/id30.htm
Sun, Dec 26, 2010, 5:08 AM
Iain Bryson to me"
[Therapy for healing maladaptive coping modes derived from damaging childhood experiences.]

I tried to get a few hours of sleep, but it was not sleep that I was worried about. Desperate to identify the skeleton that was now totally out of the closet, and finding myself in a sweaty nightmare when I did try to sleep, I got back to work. When your mom woke up, I asked her to sit down at the computer and read the letter I had just written to her. It certainly was not polished, but I thought it got the point across.

I brought her a coffee so that she would be more comfortable, and she seemed grateful and semi interested in whatever I had written to her. I was excited about her reading the letter, believing that I would eventually get to her, and that she would remember through whatever trauma fog she was currently experiencing. I would continue to hammer the stone, and I was happy with this swing.

It took her some time to finish it, and she didn't say a word to me about any of it. When she was done, she got up, said, "You should erase your browsing history," and walked into the kitchen, never to mention the letter again. *I don't care if she sees my browsing history*, I thought, *I am trying to understand her, plain and simple.* I was not trying to hide that fact, or anything else.

"http://en.wikipedia.org/wiki/Neurosis
Sun, Dec 26, 2010, 9:21 AM
Iain Bryson to me"
["Neurosis (plural: neuroses) is a term mainly used today by followers of Freudian thinking to describe mental disorders caused by past anxiety, often that has been repressed. This concept is more usually known today as psychological trauma."]

"http://en.wikipedia.org/wiki/Catastrophization
Sun, Dec 26, 2010, 9:21 AM
Iain Bryson to me"
["Exaggeration is the representation of something as more extreme or dramatic than it really is. Exaggeration may occur intentionally or unintentionally."]

"http://en.wikipedia.org/wiki/Neuroticism
Sun, Dec 26, 2010, 9:24 AM
Iain Bryson to me"

["Another definition focuses on emotional instability and negativity or maladjustment, in contrast to emotional stability and positivity, or good adjustment. It has also been defined in terms of lack of self-control, poor ability to manage psychological stress, and a tendency to complain"]

"http://en.wikipedia.org/wiki/Psychoticism
Sun, Dec 26, 2010, 9:25 AM
Iain Bryson to me"
["Psychoticism may be divided into narrower traits such as impulsivity and sensation-seeking. These may in turn be further subdivided into even more specific traits. For example, impulsivity may be divided into narrow impulsivity (unthinking responsivity), risk taking, non-planning, and liveliness."]

"Sun, Dec 26, 2010, 1:03 PM
Iain Bryson to Kees de Vries
Kees,
I have no idea what to do and am terrified, consumed with this situation. She is adjusting to the situation and instead of listening to me, she is altering her stories and with anything and everything there is a plausible but untrue story to cover her ass and push the blame onto me. All I care about is my child when it comes down to it. The more this goes on, the more I see that I cannot get through. I have tried to show her simple things, which I believe she can see for a second, if not more, but later she denies it or will not revisit it. And, the most difficult thing is to watch my kid try to figure out what is going on; it has led to behavioral issues, latching on to either or both of us, trying to figure out how she can intervene, trying to get us to do things that we were doing…

Agata ignores me. If I touch her she backs away as if I hurt her. I cannot leave as Agata has the passport and I am terrified, let alone the fact that she has been doing nothing other than sleeping, moping around, complaining and cleaning. She takes a shower for an hour after getting up at 11. She does not think the kid needs to eat. I have taken care of that, but it is frustrating. She will not leave the house and either reads a women's magazine, cleans up and gets irritated when Adelle or Adelle and I want to play, has a migraine, or sits on her phone or the computer texting and social networking. When this happened before she got on skype with an ex boyfriend, changing from her miserable self to her cheerful warm self and talked to him until 11:30 at night.

She does anything and everything to try to push my buttons. Now I see that this has been going on forever. Before I could not see and was just depressed and anxious. I was diagnosed with panic disorder before which I do not think I told you. At the time, my goal was to not take a benzo since I had been doing that for too long, and I have since figured out how to deal with it. However, in this situation, even though I can deal with it, it is terrible, debilitating and all consuming. I need to figure out the details of Holland and am having such difficulty getting this done. This other [expletive] has been moved to the forefront, and I have been sabotaged.

Over the past year the major lies I can think of:
1. Rent not coming out of the account for six months: I tried to figure out why and how, but I got nothing. When I pressed, as when I always do, she either freezes up or gets really 'friendly.'
2. I went to Poland for Easter. She told me she would not talk to me or go out with me and I was stuck in her parent's house for a week doing nothing trying to take care of my child, while she acted like i was not there.
3. My child supposedly diagnosed with Scarlett Fever during the Easter period. She stayed in Poland and we went back to Holland. I was told for over a month that the doctor could not figure it out and that my child may die. I could not get any more information. I told her I wanted her back here and she would not discuss it with me.
4. When the electricity was shut off I was blamed. She said she had no idea. When I started trying to figure out how this could happen, I found a shutoff notice and confronted her with it. To this day, she denies it ever existed.
5. She says she was told by her company doctor that she could have a heart attack by age thirty. I begged her to see someone else and she would not and I could get nowhere.
6. She told me that the neurologist told her that she has to 'deal' with her migraines and there is no cure or help. Since I have been back, she has had a 'migraine' for four or five days.
7. She told me she had anemia when in Poland for this last stretch. I was told she was on medicine, but that it wasn't working and that the doctor had stated she may have blood cancer. Again, I freaked out and could not get any more information.
8. During the May to July episode, she told me that her parents would not come here if I was here, explaining the things I had '[expletive] up' in detail. I was in Phoenix when this first began and I would see her on chat and say something like 'how are you.' She would reply with 'you are [expletive] me up....i need to know if

you are going to be here because my parents will not come and nobody wants to see you.' I compared this whole conversation, which went on for weeks to me asking what her favorite color is and getting 'refrigerator' as an answer. I remember speaking about it with my friend in Phoenix.

Later, we discussed this as it continued to hurt me. Since it was her parents, this is one that could not be lied about forever. She told me she made the whole thing up and that her parents had only said that we needed to figure things out.

9. When I got home, she said that I was a bad father, a horrible husband, that she does not love me, that I need to go back to the US and allow her and Adelle to go to Poland, that Adelle doesn't like it here, that Adelle doesn't like living with me, that her family loves Adelle more than my family.....this [expletive] threw me off guard for a while until I picked up the pieces. One night when we were discussing this she said that she had contemplated telling me she met someone. I told her that would do nothing other than hurt me as the other things had and that it would be an easier one to understand.

Now that my daughter has been with me, she is adjusting and doing better and I don't feel so isolated. However, I pointed things out to Agata like the fact she said 'how can I have a good Christmas when I don't want to be with you' and how she was reacting/acting around our daughter, how she was teaching our daughter to say things like 'don't touch me daddy," etc...and today she has started 'fake' playing. I have tried too hard to show her the obvious and now I think she is just adjusting to the fact that she cannot pull the wool over my eyes. I think her ultimate goal is to get us in a position where she can toss the [expletive] onto me and make me make an impossible decision. Sabotaging everything, lying to me for three months about what she was getting done, when she was doing absolutely nothing.

She told me she was speaking only English to Adelle while in Poland. Now, I would not expect this, nor necessarily want it. However, I tried to explain that I know this is not the case since they were speaking only Polish when I got here and my daughter had to adjust to speak with me. I told her that I knew she was not speaking only English, and probably no English. I told her I do not want them speaking Polish in the house at this time because it is doing the same thing that 'don't touch me' does. It is no different than whispering when things are this way. Before, I got to the point where it was fine, but it was also not being done to disrespect me. She will not make any changes other than adjusting to what I try to tell her. I am trying to just sit back and observe, but I feel she is abusing my child. I know my child and she was doing so well before and it is so tough for me to sit back and watch this and I feel the need to try to explain it to her. However, this has not helped at all. I could not believe she would knowingly hurt our child, but it seems her motives are stronger than any other. Somehow she justifies or places the blame onto me for everything I do.

I have been trying to stay up and do some work on jobs, etc. after Adelle goes to bed but I want to keep myself healthy and need to have my head. Adelle gets up and I get up with her to make breakfast and start the day and I need to continue doing that. My wife will get up around 11 and basically restart the morning we already had, but in a depressed state. It is impossible for us to get moving before 1:00 and nothing happens except I get lied to and sidetracked and I just have to take my daughter out and do everything because if I count on my wife for anything she just ignores me or says yes and does the opposite.

She has told me she has some sort of file on me from day one with psychological, drug, abuse, etc. information that she will use to terminate my parental rights. It caught me off guard for a minute, but I know what I have and have not done. I also know how things can be framed, especially if she has been recording things from her deluded perspective for seven years. I have since told her to do what she wants and to stop threatening. I am not afraid of anything she may or may not have; the thing that scares me is that I do not want this battle and just want my family to be healthy. She has told me she will call the police and I have told her I will get her the phone. I know she can paint a picture initially, and like divorce, if she is going to do it she needs to do it and stop threatening and dragging my family down.

I will not participate in those conversations, nor will I discuss any 'custody sharing' with her. I am [expletive] terrified. I tell her constantly I care and love her and am terrified and ask her what she wants and it always comes back to 'i don't love you' and 'I want to work out an arrangement.' She has cried once or twice though with no tears and I can see she is faking it, though I get her tissue and empathize anyway. One of my best friends died last week and she said 'I am sorry' but he was also her friend for years and I saw no emotion whatsoever. She has told me throughout the years 'why should I care' in regards to things like this constantly and I was too blind to see it, or maybe too in love. She states there is no similarity between her behavior this time and in May to July, which I told you about, but she is sticking to it. She states that she is herself now and that the rest of our seven years was some type of coping mechanism. She tells me the texts and emails stating how much she loved me and how well they were doing in Poland were a ruse to fool me and she didn't mean it. When I explain that either she is lying incessantly or that she is missing something she states she was planning all of this and that she didn't love me the entire time. I have these messages and it is clear that something is not right.

Well, dinner is ready. I do not believe I will be able to get her in on the 30th. She says she will but last time there was the 'migraine' and I believe this time she will sabotage it as well. I am going to try to work it out on my own, but I really don't know anyone except in Amsterdam. I expect she is going to drain us of money and shift it right onto me, crying and blaming and putting my child in the middle. Iain"

"Sun, Dec 26, 2010, 1:48 PM
Iain Bryson to Kees de Vries
When I first got here, I was begging her to talk to someone. She says she went to see someone at your office, but I now am not sure if she did. If she did, she went in painting whatever picture fits her current reality. I have begged her to do it for Adelle, trying to show her that regardless of the other things, she is 'off' and needs to check on some things. I remember telling you the first time I saw you upon my return about showing her on paper how her point 'a' does not lead to her point 'c.' She seemed to see what I was saying, but it has since escalated so that none of what she says makes sense.

In July when she began counseling, she was researching and telling me that she saw 'borderline' traits and was willing to look into it. Now, she will not look at anything I say and I have tried to say I don't care what it is or is not and that everyone I know can have a label and that doesn't matter but what matters are the facts and our daughter. When she began counseling she had a personality checklist to go through which she made me fill out because she said she did not know.

As far as the Polish KGB file she says she has been collecting, I have told her I doubt she even has such a thing. If she does, it is bogus anyway. But she continues to call me an abuser, an addict, and crazy. She says I am now addicted to amphetamines. I told her I could give it up in a second, which I could and have, but she has no idea about that stuff. It is just to hurt me. I remember telling you I have used my strength against her, which I have. But what I meant was that I have done too much, which in my view is anything. However, the only thing I've ever done is grab her and hold her, and each time this has occurred, it was because she was going nuts and coming after me. I have never hit her or harmed her because of my anger. I have bruised her by grabbing her, but only in reaction to a surprise attack from her, and my intention is not to harm her. I am afraid because I do not know what is going on and because she lunges at me, digs her nails into me, jumps on me and starts hitting, etc. Once she put one of the vertebrae in my neck out of place. I went to the doctor and told my doctor and my doctor was upset but I told her it was an accident. Agata did not want me going back to that doctor.

Before I went to CT we were talking about lying and I was trying to figure it out and keep it from happening in the future. She retreated and would not talk. I told her that it has driven me crazy over the course of our relationship, but that it is not that I need to know anything. I just want it to stop and for her to see it. She told me she knew there were lies, but that she could not recall any. I saw that she was getting defensive and evasive and could not take more. She told me that she would think about it, but that she knew for sure that 'there was nothing big like a previous marriage.' This blew me away, but I held it together, counted this conversation as progress and asked her if we could talk about it again at a later date. Now she says there is nothing and that she doesn't do this. A previous marriage? Ok, well if that is a big thing, then what is a small thing?

When I say anything to her now, she ignores me flat out, in front of our child. When I continue asking, she says 'don't talk to me like that' in a nasty voice with her eyes and face showing her anger and I am not saying anything that should upset her. I am trying to survive and to raise this kid the best I know how, and seeing her mother act like a different person is difficult to say the least and I thought she would want my opinion. I am extremely careful about what I say in front of our child, but it doesn't matter. Like creating a fight where one doesn't exist, she can turn 'how are you doing' into me saying something horrible and I have to sit there and watch my child react to her nastiness.

I do not know how I can get her in on the thirtieth. I am going to try, though again, I feel she will come up with some excuse. Like the first time I saw you, I have nothing I am trying to hide and want to look at everything I am doing or not doing so I can understand it and work on it. I am not afraid of anything except what I am facing now, which I believe to be the destruction of my family."

"Sun, Dec 26, 2010, 1:59 PM
Iain Bryson to Kees de Vries
actively using my child against me.....what does one do about that? what could be worse? from doing nothing at all to trying to act like she has it all together. anything to [expletive] with me. how? i am terrified and disgusted. my child is becoming protective of her mother, asking the questions I told you about and also telling me mommy is crying (which she does not do) and that I cannot talk to her like I am. I cannot explain to my child that I am not talking to her in any inappropriate ways and that it is her mother who is reacting to things as if she were an actress or a soccer player taking a tumble to get a red card when he was barely

touched. i have tried to tell Agata but she keeps going. my guess is that she sees my desperation and pushes it a bit further."

I was absolutely petrified, spilling my guts to Kees, a guy I hardly knew at all, but also someone that I respected and trusted. I knew that he didn't need all this information, but I didn't know what to do, and I figured the more the better. At least I could get it out there before she did anything crazier. And, he was already worried, already trying to contact her because he was concerned, and capable of pulling the "involuntary treatment" strings if need be.

How great it would have been if he read my reports on your mom and decided that on his own; I was way over my head. Not that I wanted her to be locked up, but I would've surely been ok with that on a temporary basis. Maybe my constant panic attack and fear that you would be taken would have subsided. Your mom was chaos incarnate at that time, and I wasn't eliminating any options.

"Kees is still trying to get ahold of you, Agata, and he is worried. Please call him, please listen to what I am telling you, please realize that I love you, and that I am terrified."

No matter how many times I told her these things, her response was the same: nothing or nonsense.

"Do it for her, Iain."

"Do what for her? What are you talking about? You need to do it for her, you need to get help, you have lost it, again."

I never really had to stray far from my point, the original point that I had the day I got back to our home: this is the Agata that nearly destroyed us, the one that we knew wasn't well, the one that we sought help for. This Agata was like a rabid dog, and everyone in the house, including our cat, was afraid of her. *How about we get some help, for the benefit of all that matters, our little girl?*

That evening, you spilled a whole glass of milk onto the living room floor, twice, one right after another, and it didn't seem like an accident. I grabbed a towel, cleaned it up, and poured you another glass, both times.

I knew that you had been traumatized, and I knew that this was potentially a response or reaction. Kids do these things to get attention, or maybe to test. I thought that my best response was no response when dealing with you, that I should mentally document these things, and simply continue to give you love. I knew that you wanted my attention, and you had it.

> "Gaining the ability to differentiate when a set of behaviors has its source in a traumatic event in history rather than a child simply misbehaving or demonstrating a 'tantrum' is important in the daily care of the child" (Krill 10).

To give you attention meant putting the microscope onto your mother, taking her threats seriously, taking full responsibility for your future wellbeing and not leaving it up to my partner. Maybe I would be able to trust her again, but at that moment I could not. I was more certain of that than I was that the sun would rise the next day; something incredibly strange was happening in our household, something had taken hold of your mom and totally twisted her around.

It wasn't even your mom that was the problem, but whatever alien demon that had possessed her. This was not the same woman that I left, the same woman that I spoke to daily for those three difficult months apart. This one had "Liar" seeping through every pore of her being. You had all my attention, and I resolved to do nothing else until this was remedied.

Later, I left the room for a few minutes, and when I returned you had spilled dirt all over the living room. You had taken our potted plant and the extra bucket of worm dirt, and scattered it over the couch, the love seat, the floor, my books...This was not a little bit of dirt, but lots of it, and it was nearly everywhere in the room; I was glad we didn't have carpets. I plugged in the vacuum cleaner and proceeded to suck it up, without saying a word.

I glared at your mom; I couldn't wait to talk to her again once you were asleep. Surely her love for you outweighed whatever else was going on with her, whatever she thought was going on with her and I. If only I were dealing with a rationally thinking human being. I'm not sure why I kept holding onto the idea that I was, or even that I should be, despite all the evidence that I wasn't; I suppose it had to do with love being blind.

Your mom started your evening shower while I was vacuuming. I felt a bit like I was destroying evidence or sweeping the elephant back under the rug. I could have used the mess as a conversation starter with your mom later or left it as a symbol of how you and I both felt about the current situation with your mom in our home. But I didn't want to put any emphasis upon your actions during this time, I didn't wish to unnecessarily help create traumatic memories, and I wanted you to know that there was nothing you could do that would make me mad at you, ever.

This was the last night that I ever got to put you to bed, the last night that I ever got to read to you "Curious George" and "Guess How Much I love you," the last time I would ever get to tell you that I love you to the moon, and back. The point of that story, in my opinion, is to show that love is boundless, that it cannot be measured in words. No matter what the moon is, or how far away it may be, love will get us back. My love for you is so enormous that my entire journey is simply to get back to you.

"Kees is still trying to talk to you, why don't you pick up your phone, or call him back? He's worried, Agata, about you. Please call him back."

"Why would I care? God doesn't approve of our marriage."

"Just call him, please, I need you to call him back."

She decided that we would watch "Remember Me," the last movie we would ever watch together, the last night that we would ever spend in the same bed. Less than twenty-four hours from then things would change immensely. In less than twenty-four hours all that I would be able to do was remember, because in less than a day both you and her would be gone, and I would never see you again.

This film is a story about two damaged people, which we all are in some way, who found love somewhere in the midst of fear and pain. The couple overcomes some initial difficulties and seem to be making breakthroughs in their relationship, and they appear to be in love. The movie ends with the guy going to visit his dad, who happens to work in the North Tower, on September 11, 2001. A plane is shown flying into the building, and the love story buildup of the entire movie vanishes, it was all squashed in an instant. I had tears in my eyes along with a deep longing to reconnect with her. I knew how precious it all was, how quickly it could all dissolve, and I was scared.

"Why did you want to watch this?" I asked, feeling confused. How could she not see that our story was also a love story, that we would and could deal with whatever was going on, whatever had caused these drastic changes, whatever had happened in Poland? Nothing mattered to me other than you and her; how could she not know that? How could she not want what we had before? What happened?

The look that she gave me indicated that she was in there somewhere, that beneath it all there was a glimmer of longing for that which I longed for, that she might even have known what I had been talking about. It was a look of understanding and pity, but it was brief, and the hardness quickly returned.

"You have me watch that horrible 'Unthinkable' movie last night, and now this. It is that fragile, Agata, it is that crazy, and that is why we have to deal with this now. I am so sorry that I left you, I know it was hard, but now I'm back, and I really wish that you would come back. I am here, Agata. I'm sorry."

She had nothing new to say, and we retired to our bed together. Lying in bed next to her, I recalled the last time this had happened, which was after the last trip to Poland earlier that year. I recalled going through this same thing where she apparently hated me, couldn't stand me, didn't want any contact with me at all. This was for a couple of months, and then I remember the moment it ended, lying in bed together miles apart, when out of nowhere her toe touched my leg. The touch of her after so long sent an electric current through my entire being. I yearned for that now. *Patience, patience*, I reminded myself.

CHAPTER 46

DAY 18: MONDAY, DECEMBER 27, 2010

"Mon, Dec 27, 2010, 3:45 AM
Iain Bryson to Kees de Vries
There is no way that anyone told her that the VISA would take ten weeks. I was told by her that she went to the Consulate in Amsterdam, something I tried to do with her, but I ended up having to leave. When I called the Consulate from the US, they acted like I was insane for thinking it would be anything close to ten weeks, telling me it is 6-8 months.

I was told and have emails telling me the apartment is being 'worked' on with the help of her friend. Since I have returned, I have learned there is no such thing going on and no progress has been made. I try to go over it and get nowhere, like with everything else.

Same with the unemployment, social help. I was told it was all set. Then I am told that she is going to go figure it out. Then nothing, despite how much I try to get the information. I am told that I will not find work here. When I try, I get the response 'why do I care.'

I made a list for her a week or so ago with the things I need. One thing was planning Xmas. One thing was money. On Christmas Eve, as we are sitting down for dinner she says 'can we open half the presents tonight?' I am set aback, and try to regroup. First, all of the presents are from my mother or what I have brought from the states. The thing is there is never any planning and then it is my fault and thrown in my face. I told her right there that this is what she was going to do with the money and that I had attempted to plan for Xmas long ago. I told her she would wait until there was no money, just as she had waited until Xmas Eve, and then throw it onto me, blaming and getting nasty in the same way. I told her this is what she does and has done with each and every thing.

Last night, I went over this again with her, asking her what she wants to do and trying to get her to help plan or do other things so I can work. She said 'what have you ever done for this family?' 'In what ways do you show you love your family?' I told her I am not going to argue these points with her and that the issue is not anything she is bringing up.

The issue since I walked in the door off the plane has been moving forward and she has done everything to ensure this is not possible. I told her after this that I need her to stop buying cigarettes, to go to the unemployment office, to give me one passport or the other so I can go out and figure things out, and that I need her to begin dealing with the apartment. She would not say one way or the other if she would or would not. She went out and bought more cigarettes. I told her she needs to come to the appointment on the 30th and she said she would after I told her that I am afraid. I reminded her that since I walked in the door and this began, I had been begging her to talk to someone. Begging, reminding, checking, worrying. I told her that going and presenting an agenda was one thing and that if she chooses not to deal with the issues I am going over with her, I am terrified.

I asked her again what she wants or what she sees as the end result. She said 'I do not love you and I was hoping we could make an arrangement.' The arrangement she speaks of is the same one as on day one...she wants me to go to the US and for her and my daughter to go to Poland and that is as far as her thought process takes her. I went over some of the lies with her, using the Scarlett Fever my daughter supposedly had last Easter. She said it happened. I told her that i didn't care what she says because the bottom line is that there is nothing that will say that my daughter was at risk of dying. Even if there was, she would not tell me what was going on, but only that my daughter was going to stay in Poland regardless of anything I wanted, felt, or thought."

"Mon, Dec 27, 2010, 8:05 AM
Iain Bryson to Kees de Vries
so the latest thing is that Agata is/was supposed to go to unemployment today. she now says 'Why would I?' I am not sure exactly how to respond to that one.

She said she want[s] to bring Adelle to the store to get some paint. I asked her if that was a good idea given our financial situation. She said it is 'only two euros.' I told her that it all adds up and the packs of cigarettes for the past week have taken a good portion of our money as it is. I told her that this is the pattern throughout our relationship and that I cannot continue to let it happen. I wanted to ask her what she thought about buying paint, but the issue is that she has both her and my daughter's passports. I told her that I cannot allow her to take my daughter out when this is the situation. I do not trust her, and right now my only goal is to keep my daughter safe.

i told her that this situation is keeping me from being able to leave the house in the mornings and go looking for work. I told her I am terrified. She said 'you are going to hold me prisoner. Don't open your stupid [expletive] mouth.' I said that I am doing no such thing and that all I want is one passport or the other, or to at least know where they are. Further, I said she could hold onto my passport. I tried explaining that there is no argument as all she has to do is one of these things and I have no problem but that I will not take a one percent chance when it comes to my daughter. I was talking to her and my daughter looked at us and asked 'why are you sad mommy?' Agata then said 'I want to take you to the store.' I asked Agata why she would tell a child such a thing. Why would she include her in an adult conversation? Adelle cannot understand and all this does is to hurt me through hurting Adelle. It is using my child as a weapon.

She can do whatever she wants with her, but not when she is holding the passports and telling me she doesn't love me and wants to terminate my parental rights, take my daughter to Poland, etc. She doesn't or can't understand what I am saying. This sort of thing is commonplace. I asked Agata if she thought the conversation about her going to Poland, which was started on the day I returned, for either Christmas or New Year's was any different. Why the [expletive] would my daughter be a part of this? The same thing with her and my daughter going to the friend's house for the night. First, nothing is going to happen with the passport issue. Second, I have some issues with her being in the home of a heroin addict. However, immediately when it was brought up she asked Adelle if she wanted to see her friend. Then when I mentioned my hang ups, it is my fault.

She says 'why would I go to unemployment.' Why would I talk about the apartment? Right now, Adelle just asked AGata what she was doing. Adelle said 'can we go to the store?' Agata said 'you need to ask daddy.' My god: how many ways do I need to show her and tell her that I will not allow her to abuse my child. I am [expletive] terrified and no matter what I do or say it goes back to [expletive]. If she has both passports and is saying the things she is saying, how could I, why would I possibly agree to these types of things? Am I stupid? I told her I want to go out and look for work, well I told her when I first arrived. But like with the computer she says she doesn't care and it doesn't matter to her."

"Mon, Dec 27, 2010, 8:17 AM
Iain Bryson to Kees de Vries
what the [expletive] are my options going to be? I am not asking you, but I am [expletive] terrified. She is in a pickle and I am not folding to her 'demands.' She is willing to let us get to the point of having no money and then what? She knows that ultimately I will take care of my daughter, but does that mean I have to be like Solomon in the Bible and give up my child? How do I do what I need to do under these circumstances? I am terrified, having hot and cold sweats once again, nightmares every night, and constant panic, though that has gotten more under control as I have progressed and brought the situation into better clarity.

I had a plan of attack when I arrived in The Netherlands, and no doubt about our ability to execute. Now, everything is being dismantled piece by piece. I don't know what she will do as she realizes more and more that I see through her [expletive]. Will she try to kill me? Will she try to kill herself? Will she report some bogus charge to the police to get me out of here? I hope not, but really only for the reason that I care about my family and I do not want my daughter to suffer at all because of this [expletive]. Every day I beg Agata to stop the abuse, to go talk to someone, and she goes right back to it, keeping my terror alive.

Other than that, I am scared for her, and scared because my daughter is in the middle of this crazy, contrived situation. These are not the stakes I wish to play any game with, and I cannot believe the lengths she has gone to in order to do the same thing she has said since day one: When I ask her what she sees as options, she reports the same thing as on day one and that is that she wants us to come to an agreement. The only 'agreement' she comes up with is me going to the US without my daughter. When I tell her about the things I see as problems, she locks up, gets nasty, yells and tells me I am crazy and that she doesn't love me and that I am not a good father and that she doesn't want to terminate my parental rights. Jesus christ (superstar)!"

I was absolutely terrified this morning, as I had been every morning since I arrived back to our house. I was running on pure adrenalin. My night sweats continued, and I still occasionally, uncontrollably squirted diarrhea into my pants, or into your mom and I's bed. These things didn't particularly concern me; either your mom or I would clean it up without any more words. She knew I was terrified, and she made it pretty clear that she just didn't (or couldn't) care.

I had nobody around me that I could turn to, no family close by. The police had rejected me, told me to find an attorney. My plan, the only plan that I could think of, was to stick to you like glue, to keep my cool, to let your mom do whatever it was that she was going to do, and then I could react appropriately.

I had no doubt that I would be able protect you from her threat of abduction to Poland, and if it was a real threat, I believed that she wouldn't be able to get very far with you. Taking you to Poland would be extremely crazy, even for her, and she was not alright at this time. All that I wanted was for Kees to get ahold of her, and for her to tell him what she was telling me. *This is what I must keep trying to accomplish*, I thought; I knew that I needed help.

When you got up, you came into the living room to get on my lap with Koko (blanket) and Lala (doll), as you usually did, and we woke up together. I remember the feeling of you on my lap, in my arms, as if it were yesterday. I believed it would never end. I was going to get your mom help; I was going to get us help. I was tired, but I was also still confident. I thought that your mom was just going further off the deep end, but I had seen her bounce back before.

After cuddling and singing a few children's songs on YouTube that we liked to sing together, we moved to the kitchen, tip toeing so as not to disturb your mom. We didn't want to wake her up, not yet, not that it would really be a problem since she wanted to lay in bed and we knew that, but because, at least from my point of view in retrospect, any contact with her was usually uncomfortable at that time. We would wake her up once breakfast and coffee were ready, but not yet.

You helped me make our typical scrambled egg mix with toast, and when the coffee was ready, I suggested that you ask Mommy if she would like a cup. I had been doing this most mornings, as a test to see how you felt about your mom. This time you made it clear that you didn't want to approach your mom in bed, and so I took the lead, trying to show you that there was nothing to be afraid of. I walked a few steps from the kitchen, down the hallway toward the bedroom so I didn't have to raise my voice at all. I was really trying to impress upon you that your mom was not a scary person, but she was not making it easy for me.

"Agata?"

She moved to let me know that she heard me.

"Dell and I are making breakfast, and we want to eat with you. Are you getting up soon, you think?"

"Yeah, I'll be up soon. I'm praying. I'll be up in ten minutes."

"The coffee is ready now. Do you want a cup in bed? Adelle can bring it to you."

"Yes, that sounds nice."

So, I walked back into the kitchen, and we made your mom a cup of coffee. I handed it to you, and you delivered it to her. We still had to finish making breakfast. I wanted all of us to get out of the house together, that still hadn't happened since September, and I knew that it would be good for us.

Organizing and cleaning, these were the things that she was focused on, and she was being very obsessive compulsive about it. She was on top of anything that was out of order in the house, like maybe a book of mine on the ground, or a plate on the table. But she was on it in a way that was akin to a ball kid in a professional tennis match. I told her she was doing it, and I told her that it was just another sign that something was wrong with her, but all she would ever do was repeat that it was because of me. There was still no getting through to her; I felt that she was getting increasingly worse, and I didn't know what to do.

By the time she joined us, you and I had finished eating and were sitting next to each other on the couch. Without saying anything at all, she approached us and handed us both a little piece of individually wrapped cheese, then took her breakfast from the table, and walked back into the kitchen.

This was weird, and when I looked at you it appeared to me that it also felt weird to you. Suddenly our positive morning had been knocked down with this weird heaviness that your mom was carrying around. I didn't know what was going on; I just had an overall sense of unease that seemed to be increasing with time rather than decreasing. What the heck was this cheese? *Thanks, I guess... and I guess you're not going to have breakfast with us,* I thought.

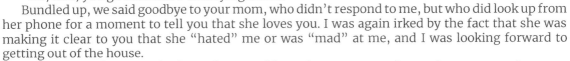

The Laughing Cow
cheese logo

I did not want to be stuck in the house with your mom's darkness, but I did still want her to come out with us, and so I asked her again if she would.

"No, Iain, I want to stay here. I have things to do. I want you to be with Adelle. I want this time to be for you and her."

"I understand, Agata, but we want to be with you. We need you. We need you to be well."

"No, Iain, you go with her. I'm staying home."

Bundled up, we said goodbye to your mom, who didn't respond to me, but who did look up from her phone for a moment to tell you that she loves you. I was again irked by the fact that she was making it clear to you that she "hated" me or was "mad" at me, and I was looking forward to getting out of the house.

Right across the street in the park, you told me that you wanted to make snow angels, so we laid down and made them next to each other.

"Dziadziuś," you said.

"You made snow angels with Dziadziuś?"

"Yes."

I let it go, and we kept walking, looking for an adventure in the snow. Nobody was outside, the snow was pretty much untouched, except in the streets, which had been plowed. I let you get on my shoulders, and you reminded me that it was your "favorite place."

We walked to a neighborhood that was new territory for us, and we found another playground, maybe a small school or community center. There were ping pong tables that you were jumping off of, into my arms. You kept climbing back onto the table after I put you down, joking with me that if you were going to jump that I needed to be there to catch you. You ran from one table to the other, and I kept catching you, though there was enough snow either way to cushion you if you were to fall.

After a while, we left and continued our winter snow trek through the city. I was having a blast, but my mind was also thinking of your mom back at home. *What is she doing? What is going on with her? What should I do?*

We stopped at another park a couple more blocks away that you remembered because of the large statue. This was a park that I would often come to alone, just to sit on the bench and read or think away from home. It was full of snowmen that other people had put together, so we made a little snowman of our own. I couldn't stop thinking about your mom, we were having so much fun, it was so nice outside, I wanted to see if she was ready to come out and play. She was the only thing that was missing.

I carried you on my shoulders as we headed back home for lunch, and so I could try to talk to your mom again. When we got home, your mom was sitting at the computer engrossed in whatever she was doing.

"Agata, will you come out with us? It's really nice out. Please."

"No, I've got things to do here. I want you to take her out."

"That doesn't make sense. We want you to be with us."

I turned on the tv for you, put you on the couch with a blanket so that you would warm up, and went into the kitchen to whip something up for lunch. I boiled some Dutch hotdogs, and we ate those with bread and ketchup.

"She's not hungry," your mom yelled into the kitchen.

"What are you talking about? She is hungry. Of course she's hungry; it's lunch time."

After lunch, I sat down at the computer to check my emails. Your mom walked over to me, and without saying anything, she grabbed ahold of the internet cable attached to the computer. She seemed angry, determined, and she looked like she wanted to rip the cable out of the computer. She gripped it tightly, her teeth clenched.

"Agata, what are you doing? Are you going to break the computer now too?" I took her hand to stop her, but she wasn't really trying to do it, just threatening, or maybe warning, or maybe just completely out of control. She glared at me, but she didn't say anything. She removed her hand and retreated into the kitchen.

We bundled up to go back outside, and I asked your mom again if she would come with us, just to check, not thinking she was going to change her mind. She said, "No," and continued working on the computer. She seemed to be energized today, in a way that was off, in a way that was new since we reunited weeks earlier. She was busy in a frantic way as if preparing for something. Our apartment was spotless.

We decided to head toward the farm, basically in the opposite direction of where we had gone that morning, past the Albert Hein grocery store that we frequented, past the police station, past the library. This was a familiar path, and you wanted to run; you wanted me to chase you.

So, I chased you, but I never let you get very far in front of me. I pretended that you were getting away, but you weren't. I didn't really feel like running, but it was your game, and so of course I would play, at least for a while. There was a park on the way to the farm, so we didn't have to go far before I could suggest swinging. I still hadn't suggested to you that you kick your own legs on the swing; I absolutely loved my job as your swing pusher.

I pushed you on the swing for a long time, singing to you songs that I made up on the spot. I don't know how long we were doing this, but it was a while, and you didn't want to stop. "Don't ever let go, Adelle," I interjected a couple of times, "hold on, and don't ever let go."

It felt like I had to keep us moving forward. I had this lingering feeling of guilt that your mom was home alone. I didn't want to go home, but at the same time I really wanted us all to be together, and I still couldn't believe that we weren't.

Eventually, I got you off the swing, explaining to you that Mommy was waiting at home, that we couldn't be out too long, that we were still going to visit the farm, and that she was probably going to be cooking dinner. You told me that you didn't want to go home.

"Adelle, your mom loves you," I reassured you. "She is home, and she needs us. She loves you so much. We aren't going home now, but later we will. She is waiting for us, and she loves you."

"I don't want to go home," you reiterated.

I shifted focus back to getting us to the farm, which was only another couple blocks away. We continued to play in the snow all the way, you didn't want to walk, but rather to run, constantly. Laughing and running, all the way to the farm.

When we got to the farm, you made it obvious to me that you were stalling. You said hi to all of the animals, and I took pictures of you. I loved taking pictures of you; you made everything make sense to me (see Appendix 26).

You wanted me to read you all of the books and pamphlets that were in the lobby rack, which I did, and then you wanted to shovel manure. You started cleaning up with a plastic pitchfork and a broom. I joined you, and we did this for a while, not really talking to each other, just picking up poop. I was thrown off by your behavior, and I was trying to observe, to see what you would naturally do. We kept cleaning, other people came and went, you were determined, in a zone, almost like your mother with her obsessive cleaning and organizing. I followed your lead, and we filled several wheelbarrows together.

Your mom started calling, over and over, and when I didn't answer my phone, she started texting. "Where are you? I need you to come back. I have plans to take Adelle to the store...." I didn't want to start rushing around, and I didn't really want to hear whatever it was she had to say, so I ignored her but started thinking seriously of heading back.

I didn't want to dive into her world with you at all; I wanted very badly for her to come to ours. Her apparent desperation alerted me that something was off, but then again, I already knew that, and I kind of liked the fact that she was now engaging. I saw it as a potential opening; *now, at least, maybe she is ready to interact with us? Maybe we will go to the store together later?*

"Mommy is making dinner," I told you, "We should go home soon."

You didn't look up from what you were doing; it was pretty amazing to me that a three-year-old was content to be shoveling manure, but you indeed were. You really did not want to go home.

"She's waiting for us. She loves you. Dinner will be ready in a little while. We can take our time going back, but we do have to go back, Adelle."

You kept telling me that you didn't want to go home, and I kept telling you that we had to go home, that Mommy was waiting for us. We played hide and seek on the walk back, you were still stalling, reminding me over and over that you didn't want to go home, that you didn't want to be with Mommy. I kept reminding you that she loved you.

Below are pictures that I took on our journey home, the last journey I was to ever take with you. We continued to play all the way home, stopping occasionally to look at whatever you could find that was semi-interesting, anything you could find to postpone our return to your mom. I remember taking these pictures and thinking something like, *wow, this is my daughter, wow, she is so amazing* (see Appendix 27).

*Pictures I took of you on our way home from the farm
on our last day together. December 27, 2010.*

CHAPTER 47

GLAMOURED

"I've been waiting for you," she panted frantically as soon as I was close enough to hear her. "I've been waiting. I have plans to take Adelle to the store." She was dressed up to go out, put together in a way that I had not seen in the past weeks. Suddenly, it seemed as if she had a purpose; she wanted very badly to leave the house with you, and her stated reasoning of wanting to buy you art supplies did not add up.

"Yes, well, we just got back. We are going to warm up and relax for a while. If you want to go to the store, we can all go together later."

"I'm ready to take her to the store now. I've been planning this. I don't want you to come with us. You are holding us hostage."

"No, Agata, we are not going to the store now. We can all go together in a little while if you want. You are holding us hostage because you won't get help. You have her passport, and you are the one who keeps saying that you are leaving with her."

"Dinner will be ready in a little while," she told me, "Let us go to the store, we'll eat after that."

I glanced and saw that something was cooking on the stove, but I didn't look closer or ask her about it. I helped you out of your winter clothes, lifted you up, and put you on the couch under a blanket.

"Mommy, I don't want to go. I want to stay with Daddy," you pled, clinging to me.

"Adelle, we aren't going anywhere right now," I reassured you.

I turned on the tv for you so that I could talk to your mom alone in the kitchen, hopefully without you hearing us.

"I want to take her to the store. I've been waiting all day. We have to go."

I chuckled at her tenacity as I replied, "Agata, we've been over this. You are threatening to take our daughter. You have her passport, and you say that you are taking her back to Poland. I will not let that happen. If you want to go to the store, then we can all go together."

"I want to go with her, not with you. I hate you."

"Yes, and I'm terrified of you, our daughter is terrified of you, our cat is terrified of you, I've been telling you that for weeks, and you keep telling me that you are taking our daughter back to Poland. That is ridiculous. We need help."

"You are holding us hostage."

"No, I am not holding you hostage. I am responding to your threat. You can still give me either of your passports, and then I wouldn't be so scared. Or we can all go together."

She was frustrated and upset, but I didn't care. I was right, and I wasn't going to back down. I made us tea and popcorn, and I returned to you in the living room.

"Daddy, I don't want to go. I want to stay with you."

"We aren't going anywhere right now. I am not going to leave you. I love you."

Your big blue eyes locked with mine, pleading with me to listen to you. The intensity of your concern left a scar that has never disappeared.

I turned on one of your favorite movies, *Bee Movie*, and we settled in on the couch with our refreshments, warming our bones after spending the day out in the snow. Your mom was visibly upset; she was huffing and puffing, scampering about our apartment with a nervous, frantic energy. I tried to ignore her, to focus on what we were doing in our space, but it wasn't an easy thing to do since she was so visibly and audibly upset. *Once she calms down*, I thought, *then we can maybe go to the store all together. Or not.* I really was done responding to her psychotic behaviors; *what could she possibly need at the store so badly?* All that I could do, I figured, was hold the line and wait for help.

A short time later, maybe thirty or forty-five minutes, our doorbell rang. I paused the movie and got up to go answer the door. I ran down the stairs to find Mickey DeLuca, who I reluctantly let in. I hadn't seen him in a while, he wasn't my friend, I didn't like him, I didn't trust him, and I didn't want him in our apartment. He had been very pushy with me in the past, getting infuriated when I didn't answer my phone when he was trying to call me, and I felt pressure to let him in. With all of the pressure from your mom, I think I was probably losing strength. I didn't want anyone here, but I also thought that I was in control of our home at this point, and I thought that it wouldn't be a bad thing if other people were witness to any of your mom's odd behaviors.

You were still sitting on the couch when we got up to the top of the staircase and entered the apartment, still snuggled under the blanket with the popcorn. The movie still paused, I went over and took my place next to you.

"Hi Mimi," he started, making me cringe. "Cicely is with Jackie at the library down the street. They were wondering if you wanted to meet them?"

Hearing "Mimi" always made my hair stand up, like nails on a chalkboard, or maybe static when trying to listen to the radio. I didn't know why I didn't like it, perhaps because I was not privy to when or why you picked up this nickname, perhaps because it was only Polish people and Mickey that ever called you this, perhaps it was just because I was on edge and did not trust Mickey at all.

The movie still paused; our attention was now affixed on this visitor. You looked at me, scooted closer to me, and you told everybody that you wanted to stay. Your mom and Mickey then retreated to the kitchen, and we played the movie.

Maybe five minutes later, they both returned, talking loudly; I paused the movie. Mickey's phone rang, and he sat down on the love seat, perpendicular to the couch that you and I were on. Your mom stood in the doorway, phone in hand, all dressed up with nowhere to go.

Mickey began to talk to his wife Jackie on the phone; I couldn't hear her voice, but he made it apparent that this was who he was speaking with. They went on and on about some recipe that they were going to cook later, and then he asked you again if you wanted to go hang out with his daughter, Cicely, at the library.

Your mom chimed in from the doorway, "We'll just go for a little while to see your friend, Cicely. I've been wanting to go out with you all day."

You indicated to your mom that you would go, your big blue eyes locked with mine, and I felt that you were scared, and that you did not want to go. I simultaneously felt bad for your mom, felt that it would be good for her to have some time with you, and was happy that she was finally up and willing to go out with you.

I had lost my balance; I should have remained firm. Your mom still had both of your passports; she was still constantly threatening to take you back to Poland. I believed it would be a short trip to the library, it was already pretty late, and that little library surely couldn't be open too late.

I left you with your mom so that she could get you ready for the library, and Mickey and I went into the kitchen to make coffee and have a cigarette. Right about when the coffee was ready, maybe five minutes later, you walked toward me, all dressed up and ready to go back out into the winter Den Haag streets with your mom. Your mom stood behind you, a stern, hard look on her face.

"Give Daddy a hug," she instructed, hovering a few feet behind you, the same hovering as when you handed me my little blue Bible, you were following her instructions. I watched your mom during this process and saw that she was just waiting for you to be done with what she told you to do.

Mickey kept talking, filling my head with sweet nothings, my attention drawn away from the fact that you were about to leave our house after making sure that didn't happen for the past three weeks. You walked to me the rest of the way, I bent down to you, you wrapped both of your arms around my neck, tight. I remember your fingers intertwined behind my neck; you latched on. I hugged you tight back, but it felt a little excessive to me, and I didn't want to play into your fears with fears or exaggerations of my own. I released you, told you that I loved you, told you that I would see you soon, and to have fun. For some reason, all fears that your mom would not bring you back home had vacated, and I sent you to the library to see your friend.

Your mom started you down the stairs in front of her, and then she turned around briefly and made eye contact with me. Everything was happening so quickly, and my head was spinning, Mickey blabbing on in the background to top it all off. My eyes scanned your mom, and I found myself lusting after her, and also thinking that maybe I could start to trust her again.

Her glance had only been for a split second, and then she turned away and stepped down the staircase. I wanted to squeeze her. I wanted her to be ok again. I wanted my wife back, and it felt like maybe we were getting closer.

"I'll see you soon. I love you, baby," I told her, Mickey still trying to tell his story about his new sled making business. She continued without a word or further eye contact and followed you down our windy staircase and out of our home for the very last time.

In retrospect, from the moment I agreed that you could go to the library until I realized that you hadn't gone to the library, I felt like a deer caught in headlights. It was as if I handed my executive decision making over to your mom and became passive, only able to observe and accede to her reasoning. And, I was ok with it, like an intoxicated person who is trusting a friend.

It was as if all my fear had vanished or never existed, as if we had turned the page and I could let down my guard again. I wasn't consciously thinking this but acting as if under compulsion. It felt like how "glamour" was portrayed in *True Blood*, a series your mom and I watched together, where some characters were able to influence other's minds through hypnosis, and later, once I realized what had happened, I wondered if her favorite cigarettes (Glamour) and magazine (*Glamour*) were intentional on her part. I was like putty in your mom's hands and more worried about how beautiful her legs were than I was about her constant, daily promises to kidnap you over the past several weeks.

PART 5

DECEMBER 27, 2010 — APRIL 25, 2011

"FOR THE THING I GREATLY FEARED HAS COME UPON ME, AND
WHAT I DREADED HAS HAPPENED TO ME"
- JOB 3:25 NKJV

CHAPTER 48

"SHE IS THE EVIDENCE!"

I didn't see it yet, but there could not have been a bigger crisis looming on the horizon. Everything had been leading up to this point – your mother was very clear about what was taking place. I was in a sort of limbo land where I felt impotent and dazed. I had tried your mother repeatedly now for weeks, I tried the police, and I tried Kees. I told people enough about what was happening, so that if it were really happening and not just your mother being crazy, there would be documentation that I had warned people.

As the following events unfold, my world is completely shattered. The grief, terror, and panic that ensued rocked the essence of my being as the bombs did Hiroshima and Nagasaki. I was operating on an instinct even more vital than survival itself – protecting our young.

Mickey and I took our coffees into the living room, where we continued to chat and smoke his Marlboro Lights, which I was enjoying since I had been rolling my own to save money.

I felt some relief just because your mom wasn't in the house, like a dark cloud had rolled away and the sun was finally trying to peek through. Her spiritual presence was hard to deal with - a thick, stifling gloom of bondage. I vented to Mickey a bit, not because I trusted him, but because he was the only adult available for me to talk to. "I don't know what is happening, Mickey. She has lost it again. I think she's crazy. This happened before, and now it's happening again." I was anguished, flabbergasted, not really hoping for useful advice, and just grateful for someone else to talk to and the opportunity to verbalize my desperation.

"It's going to be ok, Iain," he assured me, which told me that he either didn't understand or wasn't listening. "I have to go. I have a check waiting for me down the street at the bar, and I have to go pick it up. I might hang out there if you want to come down and have some drinks. It would do you good to get out of the house."

Jackie called Mickey and said that the four of you were still at the library, but then they immediately began talking about a recipe for dinner. Their conversation struck me as odd and possibly cryptic, but I figured that they were just a married couple, being a little weird. You and your mom were at the library; that was all that mattered to me.

"Yeah, I might. I don't know," I responded, really not wanting to go or even hang out with him for another minute, but also agreeing with him on some level that it would be nice to get out of the house for a beer or two. I wanted to believe his prognosis, that it really was going to be ok, despite what I had been seeing and hearing for the past several weeks.

"Ok, well that's where I'll be. I've got to go. Maybe I'll stop by later. I'll leave you the cigarettes. You need them more than me," he remarked, which I thought was a strange comment to make. As he began to walk down the stairs, it struck me that he might really have been listening to me, that by leaving the cigarettes he was showing some empathy for my current high stress situation; *what a nice gesture,* I thought.

"Ok Mickey, thanks, maybe I'll see you later." My "maybe" was a lie, simply to avoid further discussion and hasten his departure. *Why did he come here in the first place?*

He turned and left, and now the house was empty, just me and your cat, Ally. I thought that you and your mom would be back soon. I went into the kitchen and called Brian, knowing that he would have time to lend me his ear, and that he would put some genuine thought into his advice to me.

"Brian, I don't know what's going on. It's as if we've been transported back in time. It's the same crazy as before; she is literally possessed by demons. I don't know what to do..."

"Yes, I remember... hmm, it's happening again? So, it's back to 'what's your favorite color?' – 'refrigerator,' again? When you talk to her, nobody's home?"

"That's exactly what it is," I replied, chuffed that I was talking to someone who could understand.

Suddenly, I was struck by a lightning bolt of terror, as if I had just remembered the newborn baby I had left in a running bathtub. It was as if I somehow slipped and began uncontrollably falling, like in a dream, but I knew that this was no dream. "...going to Poland...cult...mind control...Stockholm Syndrome...red herring..." I felt the bottom drop out from underneath me, and I began freefalling. *She was telling you the truth, they're gone,* echoed through my head, with a time-stopping screech of absolute horror.

"Brian, they're gone! I know it. They're gone. I have to go, I'll call you as soon as I can," I snapped with a newfound panic. I didn't have time to explain; Brian couldn't help me now. I lost my breath and felt my heartbeat thumping in my chest.

"He was not only about to perceive the whole situation in its complete and instantaneous entirety, as when the photographer's bulb explodes, but he knew now that he had seen it all the while and had refused to believe it purely and simply because he knew that when he did accept it, his brain would burst" (Faulkner 85).

It came crashing down on me and I was fully awake, too awake, like if I had just been sentenced to the electric chair, or as if I were to drive off a tall bridge and have time to reflect about the fact that my next experience was going to be smashing into a pile of boulders. Reality was no longer blocked off by my cognitive dissonance or denial, and I knew that you were going back to Poland, and that what your mom had been telling me was true. I knew now that you were, in fact, being abused, and that there was going to be an effort to keep me away from you.

Oh my God, she did it! She actually took you, and the plan I thought was ridiculous and far-fetched was now in motion. My life, you, my daughter, flashed before my eyes, and every fiber of my being prepared for the war that had been thrust upon my back – I thought something like, *my name is Iain Bryson, you hurt my daughter (and my wife), prepare to die.*

Your blanket (Koko) was gone, your favorite doll (Lala) was gone, everything else was immaculate; your mom had made the entire apartment spotless, everything in its "proper" place, that's all that she had been doing for the past few days. It wasn't normal for you to leave the house with your blanket, surely not for a short trip to the library. I was entirely gripped by the terror of knowing that you were gone, and the determination that I would not allow this to happen. *She told me!* reverberated in my mind, *why did I let my guard down?*

It flashed through my mind how foolish and out of control she was. I didn't want her to get into trouble, and I would do my best to convince the authorities that what we needed was protection and counseling, but she had just gone through with a planned kidnapping that she had been warning me about for weeks. The next step, I realized was the "red herring," and though a shiver shot through my body as I thought about it, I didn't believe it had a chance. Facts are facts, and my child was just snatched by crazy people, one of whom was my wife.

"Because these types of criminals often force their victims to commit the same atrocities that they were subjected to, some people lose the distinction between the offender and the victim or survivor. (And this is exactly what offenders intend)" (Woodsum 57).

I sprinted around our apartment to grab my coat and my keys, ran down the stairs out the door, took a left, and then continued running to the bar Mickey claimed he was going to. It was only a block away from our apartment, and I knew that he knew more than he let on. I wanted to knock him out, but I would have been satisfied just to see him at the bar he said he was going to so that I could get more information.

First your mom tried to get you out of the house without me, and when that didn't work, Mickey showed up to try the same thing, and succeeded. For him to not have been in on it, he would have to be at that bar, and you and your mom would have to be at the library.

I presupposed that you weren't at the library, but I still had to cycle through all the possibilities, and I was sure that I could get more information from Mickey if I could find him. I already knew that my next step after the bar would be the library, and then the police after that.

"Hi," I sputtered, slightly out of breath, to the first person that I could find as I entered the empty bar, "have you seen Mickey Deluca?"

"Who?" the man replied, obviously puzzled. *He hasn't seen him*, I deduced, feeling the fear pile on as I found more evidence to support what your mom had been drilling into me for weeks: you were gone, going back to Poland.

"Mickey Deluca, the Danish guy that comes in here sometimes with his three-year-old daughter, he did some work for you, he told me that he was coming here tonight, have you seen him?"

"Oh no, I haven't seen him in a long time."

"Really? Are you sure?"

"Yes, he hasn't been here in months," the man continued. He glanced behind him at another employee, who in turn concurred that he also hadn't seen Mickey.

I turned and took flight out the door, realizing that Mickey had lied, your mom's warnings sinking deeper into my awareness. I sprinted back the way that I had come, past our apartment to the next corner, where I took a right to go to the library. I was running as fast as I could, it felt like my heart would explode, not so much because of the running as because of my panic. It felt as if I was being chased through the woods by a grizzly bear; I ran with all my might, for your life.

When I got to the library, the sign on the door indicated it had been closed for several hours. There was never a plan to meet Jackie and Cicely there. I bolted around the corner to the police station, the same station that had given me the list of attorneys a few days ago and advised that they could not help me. When I got there, the door was locked. I couldn't believe it; *how could the police station door be locked?*

I watched people walk by on the sidewalk and realized that I was in the middle of a crisis, and that these people were not, they were in an entirely different world. I made eye contact with one man and had no idea what I would have said to him had he asked me what was going on. I wanted to scream at everybody for help, but I knew that they wouldn't be able to hear me.

I felt very alone, and I was. But, at the same time I knew that you were with me, I knew what I was fighting for. I pictured in my mind that you were standing next to me, and I had no fears in the same way that you had taught me to have no fear of singing with you on the bus.

I pounded on the thick glass door, peering through to see if anybody was there, not caring if I broke it. I took my phone out and called the emergency number. "Hello, I need the police, the door is locked, and I need the police now." My heart was pounding out of my chest; my mind was hyperalert, it felt like I had been dropped into the middle of a war zone without cover.

Adrenaline was pumping through me, and I believed this kidnapping could be stopped before it went any further if the authorities acted immediately. Shaking inside, I tried to hold it together as I saw an officer walk through a glass door in the back and walk toward the outer door that I was standing at. I could hardly wait; I knew that you were moving toward Poland as your mom had warned.

The officer opened the door to let me in, and I spilled my guts, "My wife just left to take our daughter back to Poland without my permission, I've been trying to get my wife help for weeks, she's been threatening to do this for weeks and now she's done it, they are going back to Poland now, they are being abused in Poland, we have to stop the bus."

I believed that I could get them to stop the bus; how could they not? I didn't know yet that your grandfather was already in town, that he had driven the 12 hours across Germany to pick you up, that all my efforts now were too late because this was preplanned. What about an Amber Alert for a child who we knew was going to be taken across national borders to another country?

But they were just as uninterested as when I got the list of attorneys from them days earlier, totally indifferent, unwilling to even accept the fact that I could need help with anything. I wondered what your mom may have told them, and if this was part of the "red herring" she had been so adamant about.

"What do you want from us?" they replied, nonchalantly, apparently unphased by what I had just told them. "What do you want us to do?" I was befuddled; I couldn't believe that question had just been asked, or the tone, which suggested that I was being ridiculous.

Why did they not care about what I was telling them? What about the best interest of the child, which is to take all reports seriously? What about me, your daddy, who was asking them to stop his child immediately and investigate before she left the country? How could they not at least do this?

"I want you to stop the bus. I want this to be investigated before they can get to Poland. They cannot go to Poland. I want my daughter to be evaluated here. I want her to be evaluated now. She is being abused!"

"Well, if your wife wants to take your daughter to Poland, there is nothing we can do, she is an adult, yes?"

This nonsensical response felt like I got hit with a flaming arrow. *These people are actual morons*, I decided. Your mom being an adult had as much to do with this as your mom being white, or your mom having ten fingers and ten toes.

"Yes, of course she is an adult, but she has our three-year-old daughter with her. She cannot take her to Poland. I can't let them get to Poland. I need you to stop the bus. My wife is not well right now."

"Why can't your daughter go to Poland? You don't think she should be with her mom?"

"That's not the issue, please listen to me. I don't care what you think about me. I don't care about anything right now except stopping them from leaving this country, the country that my child lives in. It's illegal, and she is being abused in Poland. Please stop them!"

I was boiling, ready to explode, and I was loud. I held my hands out in front of me, wrists crossed and pleaded with them, "Please, I don't care what you think about me or what you do to me; you can arrest me right now if you want, you can kill me if you want, but please do not let them leave the country. Charge me with whatever you like... I don't care, this is not about me. Just stop my daughter from leaving this country!"

There were three officers in the lobby, a desk between us. One responded, "No, we are not going to arrest you. Why would we? Do you have proof that your daughter has been abused?"

I felt her placating me, and I responded abruptly, with a bit of an attitude. "I don't care if you arrest me, that's not the point. No, I don't have evidence, my little girl is the evidence, and right now she is on her way out of the country. What other evidence could there be? She's just a child. That's why I'm saying that we need to stop the bus that they are on right now, and then look at this closely while they are here in this country."

"Well, you don't have evidence. How old is your daughter?"

"She's three, she'll be four the end of next month."

"We are unable to investigate child abuse on a child below the age of four without evidence. Don't you think that she is ok with her mother?"

"What? She is the evidence. There is no other evidence, what other evidence could there be, bloody panties or a videotape? You don't make any sense. She is just a child. No, she is not ok with her mom, not right now, are you not listening at all? Her mom just stole her from me after telling me that is what she was going to do for over two weeks. I came here for help before, and you turned me away. I need you to stop that bus."

"Ok, we can probably do that, that shouldn't be a problem," one of the officers assured, "why don't you go back home and get some rest for now?"

"I'm definitely not going to go rest right now, what are you talking about, are you going to stop that bus or not?" I considered leaving to try to stop the bus myself, realizing that it was possible that the bus hadn't left yet. It was apparent that the police didn't care what I thought, and that I couldn't trust them because they were not taking me seriously; they were acting as if I said I lost my stuffed animal, not my daughter.

"Yes, I think that we can do that, it shouldn't be a problem," he repeated. His tone told me that he was just telling me what I wanted to hear so that I would leave them alone, but I still wanted to believe him.

I was frustrated, and I again doubted their competency, but I also knew that what I was asking was reasonable. I wasn't saying that your mom had to come back and live with me, at this point I couldn't even care about that. My only argument was that she shouldn't be allowed to steal you from your home and take you to another country, a country in which I wholeheartedly believed that you would not be safe in.

"I want to file a report," I stated, desiring to officially document this attempt at getting help.

"What kind of report would you like to file?" an officer asked, with a tone that seemed to suggest that my request was unreasonable.

"I want to file a police report. My daughter has just been stolen from her home. My wife told me that she is taking her back to Poland, she has been warning me for weeks, now it is happening. I need to file a report."

"No, we cannot do that. There is no need to file any report."

"That's ridiculous! I want to file a report. I need to file a report, I want this to be documented that I was here and told you what I told you."

"No, we won't file any report. Go home, and we will let you know about the bus."

"I'll be back later," I shot back, as I pushed through the first glass door, out into the lobby, completely unsatisfied with their response. I wanted to make phone calls. I wanted to see what the USA would do to help me out. *After all*, I thought, *if nothing else she is an American citizen*. I wasn't getting anywhere with these guys and didn't have time to waste, so I would check on them in a while after I had the opportunity to reach out elsewhere. How could they possibly not file a report for me? *First the door was locked, and now they won't file a police report for a dad who says his daughter is being abducted to a foreign country... What kind of country am I in?*

The Natalee Holloway case flashed in my mind, an American girl who just seemed to "disappear" in a foreign country, and I knew that I couldn't count on anybody else to take this situation with my daughter as seriously as I was. The authorities in her case were also Dutch (Aruba) and inept, yet I knew that they would be more competent than Polish authorities. I could feel a sink hole in the pit of my stomach.

As I pushed through the second glass door back out onto the sidewalk, I was sure that it wasn't a guarantee that the police were going to help me. I felt like a lion going after a threat to my cub. Everything was moving in slow motion; I was in a focused daze, oblivious to everything else. Nothing was going to stop me; it was me (us) against the world, and we would win, or I would die trying.

"In 11 percent of the cases of incestuous abuse, our respondents reported being victimized for the first time before the age of five" (Russel 99).

CHAPTER 49

"MY DAD HAS CREATED A RED HERRING..."

I rushed home, eager to make some phone calls and get help. "My dad has created a red herring, your drug, psychological, and criminal histories will be used against you, nobody will believe you...I am taking Adelle to Poland, and there is nothing you can do about it... I hate you, I've always hated you... you killed that girl... they say I might die before I'm thirty...mind control...Stockholm syndrome...cult" ringing through my head, the night clear and crisp.

Your mom had left something cooking in the kitchen for "dinner," which she never intended to have with me tonight. I left the house in such a hurry that it didn't even cross my mind that the stove was on. I shut the burner off and lifted the lid off the pot. Inside was a whole fish boiling in water. This was what your mom had claimed was for dinner; there was nothing else cooking in the kitchen. There was no way that this was dinner; she never cooked fish, and certainly not boiled whole fish. This was something else.

It occurred to me that it might be her reiterating, "my dad has created a red herring, your drug, psychological, and criminal histories will be used against you, nobody will believe you..." I didn't know what an actual red herring looked like, but this obviously wasn't meant for dinner. I emptied out the water, and I threw the entire pot away into the trash.

I proceeded to tear apart our apartment, thoroughly searching each room for anything that stood out to me, looking to see what she left behind. On the bookshelf was a new bag of American Spirit tobacco, and one of our debit cards left in a way that I could tell was intentional. I quickly realized that I could have been more wrecked than I was, that she could have left me with nothing and told me nothing, and I took the card and ran back out to the ATM a block away. *She does love me*, I reminded myself.

There wasn't much in the account, just a couple hundred euros, but this would certainly help to keep me going while I got help for you; I didn't need much. I took the money and ran the block back home. When I got home, I called Brian back first since I had left him so abruptly before; I knew that he would appreciate an update.

I told him that I had been to the police, and that the police weren't helpful, that I was going to stay on top of it, that I didn't know much at this point, and I confirmed that I would keep him apprised of any new information. I really didn't have time to chat; I had to get back on it. You couldn't be in Poland yet, but you were most likely already moving in that direction.

I realized that your mom had not been donating those several large bags of clothes to Jackie a few days earlier. Rather, she was moving out, taking things that she would bring to Poland on her "planned escape," which was happening now. This was no escape, but an orchestrated, preplanned child abduction that I had been warned about for weeks.

On the phone with my mom, your grandma in Connecticut, I was frantic, alerting her that the crisis I had been telling her about for weeks had now fully materialized. I told her that your mom had just taken you back to Poland against my will, that this was against the law, and that I was seriously concerned for your wellbeing. I also told her that all signs were pointing toward you having been abused in Poland, and your mom having severe psychological or spiritual issues, most likely from her own experiences with extreme childhood abuse, that I had always been suspicious that your mom was a victim of incest. I needed my family on my side so that we could quickly end this abduction and get you to a doctor.

She asked me the typical mom questions: "Are you getting enough sleep?" and, "Are you eating?" But she also told me that she was going to help me get help from the USA, and I felt like I had an ally, which is exactly what I set out to find upon departing from the totally useless local police department. *Having my mom fight alongside me is exactly what I need,* I thought. She had always been persistently tenacious for my cause, and I believed she was someone I could count on to do her best.

I called my dad and explained to him some of the details from the previous eighteen days, telling him that I had been desperately trying to get help the entire time. I had never been able to talk out loud with anybody else about my suspicions of abuse because I was terrified of the repercussions if she found out. I didn't want to "betray" her, and I also believed that she was ultimately on my side. I didn't think any of this was really possible.

"What can someone even do sexually with a three-year-old girl, with a three-year-old child?" I begged, imploring my dad to help me see, not wanting to have to twist my head in that direction, and always having blocked it out as impossible up until this point.

Yes, I asked your mom about and even accused her of things like being a victim of incest during the final weeks, but I never really looked at the extreme ramifications of what being a victim of incest would or could mean. I totally underestimated the situation, unable to wrap my head around everything your mom was telling me, and what I was seeing with my own eyes. It was too horrible to look at.

The idea of child abuse happening to you was an impossibility. My mind set up a barrier so that I was able to know that you had been abused and not know at the same time, the "not knowing" section of my mind being dominant until it was too late. All the signs were there; I had just missed them, blinded by my naivety and trust in your mom.

And your mom had told me with her own words: "Stockholm Syndrome," "my family is like a cult," "molester!" It was just too crazy, too bizarre for me to understand at the time, but now I had to understand it. Love's blindness became love's sight.

So, what could one do with a three-year-old child? My dad's answer to me was, "Well, Iain, um, I think people can do a lot with a three-year-old child." As he said this, a mule kicked me in the head, and I was transported to a realm of possibilities I had never considered, like whatever might've happened to you to give you the bruises and vaginal pain and terror, or why you would've told me that my penis looks like Grandpa Sławomir's or played a game with him where you would learn the term "stinky balls."

Oh, yeah, foolish me, that's what they could do, and that's what some people are doing. But not to my little girl! Not my family! What kind of trauma would cause a mother to tell the father of her child with several weeks' notice that she was going to take their child back to the country where she is being abused, where she herself was and is abused, and then to do it?

"As a result of the psychologically intolerable nature of their early childhood experiences, victims of ritual abuse frequently develop multiple personality disorder (MPD) [also called dissociative identity disorder (DID)]. MPD constitutes a system of psychological defenses which are a reaction to intolerable abuse usually occurring before the age of six... Ritual abuse is conducted on behalf of a cult whose purpose is to establish mind control over victims... Mind control is originally established when the victim is a child under 6 years old" (Gould and Cozolino 194).

CHAPTER 50

"LISTEN ALL Y'ALL, IT'S A SABOTAGE"

"History demonstrates that heinous acts can and do occur. There is no shame in our ability to recognize that human beings are capable of committing atrocities. It is, however, shameful when we ignore the outcries of the victims, many of whom not only describe past abuses, but also present threats and dangers. We cannot know how many of the outcries are accurate unless we properly and individually investigate them" (Noblitt and Noblitt, 2014, 179).

I set my mind on contacting people who could help stop the abduction of my daughter and initiate an investigation into my claims. Since an investigation would be in the best interest of the child, I believed the authorities would have to proceed in that direction. Since your mom and I's claims were in stark contrast, the answer was not to let her run away with you, but to stop everything and get it sorted out. While trying to find someone who would listen and take action, I continued to sift through the puzzle pieces that your mom left behind in our apartment.

I had our family laptop with me while I was in Connecticut from September to early December, and I knew it very well and generally used it more than your mother did. During the past eighteen days, your mom had spent many hours doing something on the laptop, but I hadn't been paying close attention to the details. Her behavior all the way around had been bizarre and erratic, but when she was on the computer at least she was calm and not spewing hatred in our home. I began looking closer to find out what she had been doing.

One of the first things that I noticed, right in the middle of the screen, was an icon for the Beastie Boy's song "Sabotage," and I knew that I hadn't put it there; I hadn't listened to the Beastie Boys in many years. I had told her that she was "sabotaging us," on several occasions over the course of the past eighteen days, and maybe this was her telling me that she, in fact, was. This was a planned, dramatized "escape" made possible with a fabricated "red herring" diversion, an elaborate child abduction scheme designed to keep me away from my child forever, and to continue to abuse her.

"I can't stand it, I know you planned it
I'ma set it straight, this Watergate...
Oh my god, it's a mirage
I'm tellin' y'all, it's sabotage...
But, yo, I'm out and I'm gone
I'll tell you now, I keep it on and on
'Cause what you see, you might not get...
I'm trying to tell you now, it's sabotage
Why

Our backs are now against the wall?
Listen all y'all, it's a sabotage (x4)..."
("Sabotage" – Beastie Boys)

Your mom scanned in all our family documents, and she put them in a new folder for me in the middle of the desktop next to "Sabotage." She left another folder of photographs that I had never seen, and a short video of her talking to someone in Polish for a few seconds in your grandparent's apartment in Stargard.

My first impression of this video was that it was suspicious and weird, even without being able to understand the words, just by witnessing your mom's body language during whatever interaction was taking place. Her stance, her posture, her tone, her facial and hand tics, all these things indicated that this wasn't a "happy" video.

Screenshot of the video.

I had no way of getting a Polish person to translate it for me until much later, but I didn't need it really; I knew enough of what was going on. I knew that I needed to stop you from going back to Poland, and I knew that I needed to have you evaluated by a doctor whose specialty was severe, caregiver inflicted trauma.

It wasn't until a couple of years later, somewhere in Polish prison, that several Polish people all translated the two second clip for me, and their translations were (something like) what follows: Your mom asks a man who is off camera (her father) "Did you beat her?" and the man then replies, "You know we did."

She left a couple of her notebooks neatly laid out on the desk next to the computer. I had seen her writing in a frenzy during the last couple of days on several occasions, but I hadn't paid much attention to it, other than that it appeared to me that a crazy person was writing. *Good, she's writing*, I thought, *maybe she'll work it out*, and at least she was quiet and non-confrontational.

I don't mean "crazy" in a derogatory sense, only that from my perspective your mom had lost her grip on reality. It was barely possible to admit to myself that this was the same person. I watched her scribble desperately, almost as if she were trying to write while being chased. Something was tormenting her, and it wasn't me; I was the one who was trying to convince her to get help.

"If your hand writes what your conscious mind has not previewed and does not know, it is doing automatic writing... Your hand is connected to a dissociated center of consciousness and is writing a message or opinion from that dissociated center. It is a trance technique for accessing unconscious knowledge. 'Automatic writing... is often resorted to when resistance or objection to verbalization is encountered...' (Marcuse, p. 129)... What you write automatically is likely to be something repressed and important to you. The painful, repressed data is like steam under great pressure held in by the wall of prohibiting repression" (Emery 389)...

Most of what she wrote was in Polish, and at the time I spoke only a few words in Polish. I had no idea what she had written, nor did it really matter because the frantic, terrified mindset during the writing was enough to behoove further investigation into what was really going on. She was home all day by herself, getting ready for the big "escape," so the fact that it was on the desk was intentional, just one of the many puzzle pieces that I wanted people to look at before she got too far away with you.

Four of the pages indicated that your mom had taken an interest in *Eat, Pray, Love* by Elizabeth Gilbert (see Appendix 28). She had been reading the book off and on, in Polish, during the last days that we were together. The Polish in these notes was easier to translate, using Google Translate, because it wasn't so scribbled. I thought it odd that she had been reading a book about spiritual development, journey, and love, given her obvious misery, her proclaimed hatred of me, and the fact that she had just stolen our child from me.

But I also knew that the misery and hatred were not really your mom, that something else had taken her over, something she had brought back with her from Poland, and I knew that she was in tremendous pain. I made a mental note to both read the book and watch the movie starring Julia Roberts, realizing that it could help me gain some insight into her mental state.

What she wrote is fragmented, but so was she when she wrote it. What she did write for sure was, "I believe in you"(Polish), "I love you"(Polish), "I want you to love me," "I want you to make me feel like the only girl in the world," "In my mind there is no haven for my thoughts," "Thank you for everything," and, "Bye" (see below and Appendix 29).

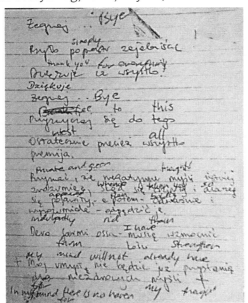 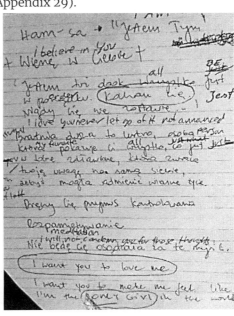

Pictures from your mom's journal, written the last week we were together in December 2010. English translations below.

Left: *"Bye. It was just cool! Thanks for everything! Bye. Get used to it. After all everything passes away." The remaining text is difficult to understand.*

Right: *"I am this. I believe in you. I'm right next door. Everything is okay. I love you. I will never leave you. A soulmate is a mirror that shows you everthing. Everything that is supressed in you which draws attention to yourself so that you can change your life. You are tormented by the compulsion to control the reflection. I won't judge you for that thought. I want you to love me. I want you to make me feel like I'm the ONLY girl in the world."*

"Your problem is you don't understand what that word [soul mate] means. People think a soul mate is your perfect fit, and that's what everyone wants. But a true soul mate is a mirror, the person who shows you everything that's holding you back, the person who brings you to your own attention so you can change your life. A true soul mate is probably the most important person you'll ever meet, because they tear down your walls and smack you awake. But to live with a soul mate forever? Nah. Too painful. Soul mates, they come into your life just to reveal another layer of yourself to you, and then they leave. And thank God for it. Your problem is, you just can't let this one go. It's over, Groceries. David's purpose was to shake you up, drive you out of that marriage that you needed to leave, tear apart your ego a little bit, show you your obstacles and addictions, break your heart open so new light could get in, make you so desperate and out of control that you *had* to transform your life, then introduce you to your spiritual master and *beat it*"(Gilbert 149).

CHAPTER 51

"THE SYSTEM IS NOT SET UP TO HELP YOU"

I had a long conversation on the phone with Diane from a rape crisis center in Texas. She was very understanding and supportive, and it was a blessing to get her on the phone; she let me know that I was not alone, speaking to me for over an hour. She also let me know that it was going to be very difficult.

"All that you can do is never give up. This is going to be a journey for you. The system is not set up to help you or your daughter. I recommend that you keep a record of the people that you talk to, and please let me know when this gets resolved."

I thanked her, and I felt like I had made a friend, like she knew that I was one of the good guys. *There's one person who's on my team*, I surmised; it was relieving to know that this person understood what I was talking about, even though much of what she had to offer was a warning of the difficulties inherent in the system. I made my way back out onto the street to go see what the police had figured out.

> "Those who try to assist sexually abused children must be prepared to battle against incredulity, hostility, innuendo, and outright harassment. Worst of all, the advocate for the sexually abused child runs the risk of being smothered by indifference and a conspiracy of silence. The pressure from one's peer group, as well as the community, to ignore, minimize, or cover up the situation may be extreme" (Sgroi, 1978, as cited in Burgess et al., 1978, xv).

I hadn't slept, and now the sun was just beginning to show signs of coming out for the day. It was still dark, and again I assumed that the police station would just be open, but when I got there, it was locked.

I called the Dutch emergency number on my smart phone, and connected with an operator: "Hello, yes I need the police, and the station I am at is closed."

"What do you need the police for?" she asked me.

"My wife took my daughter, and she told me that she is taking her to Poland. She is being abused in Poland. I need help."

"Well, that doesn't sound like an emergency. Why don't you go back to the police station in the morning when they open?"

"Well, it is an emergency. I am telling you it's an emergency. Where are the police?"

She gave me directions to a station she indicated would be open, and I headed that way, running and feeling like a lung might collapse, knowing that each passing moment was a moment that you were most likely closer to whoever was hurting you in Poland. There was no police station at the location that she had given me. I ran around the entire area but couldn't find anything. I was upset, as it appeared to me that the operator had given me bogus directions. I don't know if she did or didn't, but I do know that she was dismissive and belittling, only trying to convince me that there was no emergency.

I grabbed a bike, thinking I would just throw it through a shop window to get the police to come as quickly as possible. But that bike was locked, as they always are, and I threw my arms up and yelled. I needed the police so badly that I wanted to get arrested, just so that I could talk to them. I jogged around some more until I saw someone walking a dog. This person told me where I could find the police, and I bolted that way, nowhere near where the emergency operator had pointed me. There was no time to lose; I needed whatever was the Dutch equivalent of an Amber Alert.

I was out of breath when I walked in the door. "I need help, my wife took our daughter, she's trying to take her to Poland, she's being abused..."

They took me into a back room, and offered me coffee, which I gladly accepted even though it felt weird that offering me a coffee was their response to what I had just told them. As soon as I was handed the coffee, I knew that they were just trying to pacify me by the mood I could feel in the room. They then proceeded to tell me that there was no problem, that there was nothing that they could do, that you and your mom were "safe."

"What do you mean 'they're safe'?" I demanded.

"We can tell you that they are safe," one of them repeated. This made no sense to me, knowing you were the opposite of "safe," and it also left me bewildered how this new group of officers could even be aware of this situation, especially given the fact that I hadn't been permitted to file an official report.

"I need to know what you mean by that. Are they in this country? Where are they? How do you know that they are safe?"

"Well, they are in The Hague, and they are safe. We can tell you that."

"What? How do you know they are in The Hague? Are you sure?" *Why are they playing games with me?*

"Yes, they are safe. That's what we can tell you."

"Ok, but I am telling you that they are not safe. I am telling you that if that bus takes them back to Poland, that they are even more not safe. I am telling you that I do not want my daughter to leave this country."

"And we can tell you that they are safe," they repeated, "you should go home and rest."

It felt like I was back in the *Twilight Zone*; the Dutch police seemed more like cartoon characters than actual, even semi-rational law enforcement officers, like a sick version of *Super Troopers* – maybe the next thing they would say would be "meow," I considered. It was clear that I wasn't going to get any help here, so I left, uncertain of what I should do next.

Maybe I should go to the bus stop, maybe they haven't left yet? Maybe I should start heading to Poland myself, right now? What should I do?

At this point, I couldn't be sure where you were, and so I hesitantly decided that I would not go to Poland, not yet at least. I could still get help from here, I reasoned, and the thought of trying to deal with it in Poland seemed ridiculous; I wouldn't have a chance. *I need to be here, at our home. I need my computer and my phone, and I need to exhaust all possibilities before moving onto any more drastic measures.*

In the following emails, I didn't yet tell Kees about the abduction because I was only 99 percent certain at this point, still hoping on some level that I was wrong. I stopped trying to protect your mother's privacy, and I used Kees to document as much as I could, and to process with someone who I thought could give me advice and possibly issue a psychiatric hold on your mother.

"Tue, Dec 28, 2010, 4:02 AM
Iain Bryson to Kees de Vries
We had another discussion last night and again she agreed to try to understand the things we have been over and over. I told her I just want her to try to think about the issues which we have both known about and which she has told me are at least affecting her in some way. I woke her up as I told her I would; she wanted to get up early and see if any appointments were available. When I woke her up, she told me to 'get the [expletive] away.' she told me she was going to get me arrested. she told me i am a [expletive] molester. she told me she hates me. she retreats into a shell, rolled into a ball, covering her face. Distant. Not there. I am

terrified. All that I care about is being tossed around and lied about. I ask her what she is talking about and she tells me she is going to terminate my parental rights.

When I met her she told me she had never had an orgasm. She told me she had always thought she had something wrong with her. Then she told me that the first time she had one was the first time with me. Then when I mentioned oral sex to her, she looked at me in the same way she has been doing now (nasty and mean) and said 'I will never, ever, ever, ever, ever, ever.' I was taken aback and hurt. I got up and put my pants on. I told her that it was not a big deal if she had never, or if she didn't want to, but that I didn't know what 'never ever ever....' meant and I asked her how she could say that.

From there it went through cycles where I would talk to her and try to figure out what the problem was. She would assure me there was no problem, that she wanted to, that she liked to, and then months would go by and I would get frustrated and ask her again. Then it would happen once and then the same cycle would go on once again. This has been the case for our entire relationship. Immediately after sex she gets up and goes to the shower. Immediately. I have told her I want to snuggle with her and she says she has to clean herself because she feels dirty. Within five minutes of having sex, she has had a shower and is back in bed fully clothed.

She called me a molester and an abuser and stupid and a psychopath and that she hates me and that she will terminate my parental rights and that I will not see my child. She told me that who she is is who she is now and that the rest (like when we were doing well and our daughter was doing better than I have seen any child do) was a defense mechanism. I ask her what she is talking about and how this could be. I ask her about her change of attitude and she tells me she has always felt this way about me. She says 'I am sorry I don't love you,' like a funeral home director says 'I am sorry for your loss.' I am not going to speak to her anymore as I believe it will just lead to another incident like yesterday. She is escalating each and every day. It has gone from 'I don't love you,' 'you are a bad father,' 'Adelle was happier in Poland,' to 'I will get you arrested' and 'you are a molester.'

She is frantically cleaning once again. It is all that she does besides talk to her mother in Poland and social network and read magazines. 'I help mommy when she is sick.'

After May -July, my daughter was constantly asking 'mommy are you happy?' Over and over again. I did not like it but I could not understand or maybe I was dealing with too much other things. Now she asks me why mommy is not happy. From one minute to the next she reacts completely different. I have tried to tell her that these things are not ok and that no matter what is going on I will not let my daughter know by the way I look at her or the way I react to my wife. She says it is my fault. I ask her what is wrong and she says 'you.' She will say 'wow' when my child finishes a meal and smile a fake, distant smile and then she will chastise her and get completely irritated the next moment.

http://www.youtube.com/watch?v=_vgQalXalxs ['Liar,' Henry Rollins]

She is beginning her rampage to put the screws to me because of our financial situation. I can take care of my daughter but when she is running around like a mad woman organizing and picking up everything over and over, I am with my daughter, assuring her it is ok to play and make a bit of a mess. We will clean it up after for mommy, I assure her.

She says now she will not go to our appointment. She will not deal with the unemployment. She will not deal with the apartment. She will not allow me to work. Am I wrong for being scared when she will not tell me where the passports are? I don't want it but I also don't want it to be a mystery and don't understand the deal. If I will give her mine, doesn't that take away any fears she may have?"

"Tue, Dec 28, 2010, 4:52 AM
Iain Bryson to Kees de Vries
when i met my wife, she used to ask me to hold her hand when she was peeing. she said she couldn't go without my hand. she would close her eyes and concentrate and then she would go. for the duration of our relationship she has told me she cannot poop. i have asked her, like with the migraines, the heart, the 'cancer' to please see someone and i have tried to go with her on numerous occasions telling her it terrifies me.

these things never really struck a nerve with me, but as this goes on and i think and see more and more and remember more and more from may thru july, it has all been coming together. last time my daughter was in poland and i was told she had scarlett fever and may die, i could get no information. I was told nothing other than that she was staying in poland. I could not get my wife to discuss it with me at all. it terrified me like when i am told that my wife may have a heart attack before age thirty or that she could have blood cancer. then when my daughter did come home from poland, she would say that her pee pee hurt. When I asked Agata about it, she told me it was from soap. I asked her if she had gone to the doctor and she told me she knew it was the soap and that Adelle had told her. It scared me once again.

It bothered me intensely that my daughter would constantly say 'not pee pee' when I was washing her, meaning she had special soap for pee pee. 'Pee Pee is special' she would say. It was non stop and it drove me crazy. Why would a child keep saying this? Why is her mother not concerned? It went on like this for a few weeks and then it stopped. Immediately after I got home this time, it began again. She did the exact same thing. She also began not wanting to go pee pee. She would cry. She [expletive] her pants. We would have to bring her into the sink and run warm water over her. This has stopped since I have returned.

Yesterday she started talking and she said 'ja ja,' which in Polish means something like 'egg.' i asked her what she meant and she relayed to me that jajush (her grandfather) had told her it is what you call testicles. I asked Agata why her father would be naked in front of my child and why she would be talking about this. She had no answer at all. I have never heard such a thing from my child. This morning she calls me a molester and says she will not speak with me.

Agata has also said that her father has made comments about 'young boobies' and that this has been some sort of a joke for her life. I don't know what this means, but I am not sure why a father would talk about this at all. My god, this woman is sabotaging me, telling me the most horrible things she could possibly tell me, and trying to take my child back into that home."

"Tue, Dec 28, 2010, 7:11 AM
Kees de Vries to me
Hi Iain,
 Two things:
1. Yes, you'll have an appointment with Ms Kuhler at the 3rd of january at 15:00.
2. I receive a lot of a-mails from you. I'm afraid I can't keep up with them. If you send me e-mails, could you be as brief and to-the-point as possible? Or if it helps you to write me in the way you do, just put on top 'I need to get this out of my head' (then I know it's for your sake and not for mine). I'm sorry I cannot just read them all!
 Kind regards, Kees"

"Tue, Dec 28, 2010, 10:52 AM
Iain Bryson to Kees de Vries
yes i can do that. thank you. i am just scared and don't know what to do."

CHAPTER 52

"SHE LEFT WITH ADELLE."

"Tue, Dec 28, 2010, 1:24 PM
Agata Bryson to me
Adelle and I are at a shelter for abused women and children because I was afraid for my life and what Adelle was going through. We couldnt stay under one roof with all the abuse. I will contact you in few days so we can plan to meet the three of us and also to see a counsulor about all of this."

Oh, thank God, that is great news! I would love to see a counselor with them. I felt a wave of relief, thinking that maybe you possibly could be in a shelter in The Netherlands. This would be fantastic, but I didn't think so, because I tended to believe what your mom had repeatedly been telling me before, that she was taking you back to Poland.

But I didn't know for sure, and I hoped that you were in The Netherlands, regardless of exactly where. Just not Poland. If you were in a shelter in The Netherlands, I could find out where you were and simply tell the shelter people that they needed to investigate the possibility that you had been severely abused in Poland. I would also ask them to observe you and I together, so that they could see that I was the stable caregiver and the protective parent.

I called all the shelters I could find, but I was unable to confirm one way or the other; nobody would give me any clear information at all. I really doubted that you were still in the country, though I decided that I would communicate with your mom as if she was telling the truth. The best possible situation would be for you to be at a shelter in The Netherlands, under the care of capable professionals who would thoroughly evaluate the situation, including speaking with you separately from your mom.

"she left with adelle
Tue, Dec 28, 2010, 2:08 PM
Iain Bryson to Kees de Vries"

"Tue, Dec 28, 2010, 2:08 PM
Iain Bryson to Agata Bryson
agata, call me"

"I need to see you tomorrow
Tue, Dec 28, 2010, 2:23 PM
Iain Bryson to Kees de Vries"

"Tue, Dec 28, 2010, 2:43 PM
Iain Bryson to Agata Bryson

a few days agata . please dont. i need my daughter and she needs me. talk to me and start talking with someone else like i have been begging you to do now. i love you"

"Tue, Dec 28, 2010, 2:53 PM
Iain Bryson to Agata Bryson
i asked you, begged you to talk to someone agata. there is no other reason for me to do this than the fact that i am concerned, terrified. there is no other possible reason. if i were worried about you talking about me i would not want you to talk to anyone. it has been what i have been begging you to do since i returned. i want you to try to understand the things i see. please agata. i need my daughter. i need her and you know that. there is no reason i would be so adamant about you talking to someone. the things you need to talk about are not just going to come out. you have to be willing to deal with them and really talk about them. please agata."

"http://en.wikipedia.org/wiki/Dissociation
Tue, Dec 28, 2010, 3:00 PM
Iain Bryson to me"

I began to narrow down my understanding of your mom further, homing in on her with an eagle eye. She did have many of the traits of borderline personality disorder, as we had both agreed, but it wasn't a good fit. What about the fact that I couldn't even be sure it was really her, or the fact that I was certain she was possessed, or the fact that she told me that she has "something like Stockholm Syndrome"? What does the most severe trauma do to a person, the kind that would make you tell your husband that you are taking your child back to a "cult," then do it and claim that you are in a women's shelter because you fear the husband?

"What is multiple personality disorder? As I say in my book *Multiple Personality Disorder: Diagnosis, Clinical Features, and Treatment* (Ross 1989), multiple personality disorder is a little girl imagining that the abuse is happening to someone else. The imaging is so intense and subjectively compelling, and is reinforced so many times by the ongoing trauma, that the created identities seem to take on a life of their own, though they are all parts of one person" (Ross, 1994, vii.).

"Although MPD patients are, by definition, diagnosed as having more than one personality, they in fact don't. The different 'personalities' are fragmented components of a single personality that are abnormally personified, dissociated from each other, and amnesic of each other... In order to correct misconceptions arising from use of the term 'personality' in this context, the official name of the disorder has been changed to Dissociative Identity Disorder..." (ix).

"The survivors of ritual abuse and mind control that we will talk about over the course of this Conference grew up within an evil cradling; within families and cults who set out to make it impossible for them to ever escape; impossible for them to ever break the psychological bonds with their abusers, bonds carefully welded within a cocoon of torture and programming" (Epstein et al. 39).

"We see here that Satanist cults are able to manipulate these psychic susceptibilities as a result of bonding through extreme trauma, and draw the victim in to wider submission and loyalty to the group's belief system" (48).

"The dissociative disorders field has established that DID is associated with chronic, intense, early abuse, often involving a combination of physical, sexual, and emotional abuse, frequently including profound neglect, family violence, and a generally chaotic home environment (Chu, Frey, Ganzel, & Matthews, 1999,; Draijer & Langeland, 1999; Ogawa, Stroufe, Weinfield, Carlson, & Egeland, 1997; Putnam, 1997; Pynoos, Steinberg, & Goenjian, 1996)" (65).

"A synthesis of survivor accounts suggests that the central psychological mechanism that permits mind control programming to be effected is that extreme torture can force a victim's psyche to form new, readily programmable self-states, separated from the front personality by programmed amnestic barriers, that can be exploited to 'hold' and 'hide' directives, skills, and information. The conditions that appear to most reliably yield new programmable states are (1) application of torture in the preschool years or to already dissociation-prone individuals, and (2) application of forms of torture that victims have not yet learned to endure, such as novel or extremely prolonged torture" (66).

"Can I please see you tomorrow?
Tue, Dec 28, 2010, 3:15 PM
Iain Bryson to Kees de Vries
Since I walked into this, I have been pleading with Agata to talk to someone so she can better understand what I believe I see. I have been trying to tell her, to show her, but she will not attempt and probably cannot attempt to. I have told her that there is no other possible motivation for me to be begging her to speak to someone. If I were worried at all about anything I have done, I would not want her to speak to anyone. If I am correct, then one day in this situation is the same as saying that psychological abuse is ok since it cannot be measured, and that the issue will be placed on hold. I understand she feels she needs space. What I do not want is for my daughter to continue being harmed in the ways I believe she has been and will continue to be harmed."

"Call us consulate now
Tue, Dec 28, 2010, 3:24 PM
Mom to me
Duty Officer 062-039-8862
He is waiting for your call."

I called the U.S. Consulate as soon as I got this email and was connected with Duty Officer Juan Gambola. He knew I'd be calling because my mom had already communicated with him. He seemed to be understanding of the situation that I was describing, but he also wanted me to be understanding of the fact that the United States had no jurisdiction to do anything; that was his primary message to me. In short, there was nothing that they could or would do.

"You need to continue talking to the Dutch police, and you need to make them help you. You should not let them get to Poland, do not let them get to Poland, in Poland it can be very difficult... If you can, set up a meeting with your wife, and when you meet her, you need to get your daughter and take her to the nearest U.S. Embassy or Consulate..."

"Ok," I replied, thankful for the advice, but uncertain of what he meant, or how I could possibly pull something like that off. "I don't think they are still here, but if they are, then what you are telling me is that I need to take my daughter away from her mother, and run to the Embassy? That's what I should do?"

"Yes, that is what would be best. If you can get your daughter there, then alert the guards that you are coming in with a child, and they will let you in. We will make sure that your daughter is evaluated."

I looked to my left out the window, and I was hit by a wave of feeling like I could be in a Hollywood film, wishing that the director would yell "cut," and end this nightmare. *How can this be happening? How can this U.S. Official's advice to me be to re-abduct my three-year-old daughter from her mother in broad daylight? Is it even possible to accomplish such a feat, to take a child from another adult in public and run with her to the closest U.S. government facility?* I believed he was correct in his conclusion, but it still felt crazy to be getting such advice in the "real" world. *What should a father do in such a situation?*

I thanked him for his honesty, and proceeded to study routes to get to the Embassy and Consulate on foot depending on some potential places that I could meet you and your mom if you were still in the country. She had told me that she would be contacting me "in a few days" to meet, and though I doubted this would happen, a small portion of me held on to the idea in hope, and I planned for it despite the low likelihood of it occurring.

I pictured in my mind what it would look like to take you from your mom and run away to an Embassy, and all that I could come up with was "impossible," or "crazy." To do so, I would probably have to push her on the ground and take her phone, and then I would have to run away with you in my arms to a place that wouldn't be close. I couldn't just have her meet me a block from the Embassy; she was too intelligent for that.

"Tue, Dec 28, 2010, 3:24 PM
Iain Bryson to Agata Bryson
Agata,
I want us to see someone immediately. Please listen to me about this. It is for our daughter. I understand you feel you need space. That is not the issue, nor has it been since I got off the plane. The issue is that I see what I believe to be psychological abuse. Whether there is or is not psychological abuse is to be determined. I do not think it is your fault, nor do I have any intention of using it against you. What I fear more than I fear anything at all in this world is my daughter being subjected to this.

Now, if what I believe I see is true, you would not know there is psychological abuse. You would not have the ability to see it. So, just take into account that I may be correct, even if just in some way. If I am right, what you are doing by not dealing with this, and by dealing with what you believe I have done, you are saying that psychological abuse is not a big deal and that it can continue for a few days. I am saying that I believe more than anything that it is an issue and that I want to deal with it immediately. I have been pleading with you to deal with this since I arrived. I have no other motivation than to keep our child safe.

There is no way that these people are going to pick this [expletive] out of your head right away. Please allow me to be a part of this, and now, please. I only want to protect our daughter. Like I have said from day one, you are her mother, and I love you and I will do nothing to harm that. I am terrified by what I see just as you are terrified by what you see. Please deal with both of these issues so we can protect our daughter. Please do not discount what I am saying. If you choose to, you are saying that there is none of what I believe I see and you are saying that you would know if it were occurring. By definition, if it is happening, you would not know.

Please Agata. I do not care about anything other than taking care of you and Adelle. I have been terrified, begging you to talk to someone about the issues that only I will be able to see at this point. There is no way that Georgina [her therapist] would pull this out in two hours. It is not possible. Let me be a part of this now. Please. I love you.

will you go to kees tomorrow at 10:45 please?"

"Tue, Dec 28, 2010, 5:05 PM
Dad to me
hi Iain. i'm sorry to hear of your troubles. Your mom has told me some of the details and of course i am most concerned with Adelle and her grandpa. If she were in the US she would be picked up and checked out quicksmart. I understand you have contacted the US embassy. How about local health or child welfare dept.? I will try to call you but will have to pick up a calling card and see if that will work on my phone. Otherwise I will have to check with my carrier to get overseas access. I am here for you. Love, Dad"

I pulled up your mom's Facebook page; we were still "friends" at this point, but not for long as she would soon block me. Since you guys left, she had posted two videos, Tom Petty's "Free Falling," and "If Tomorrow Never Comes," by Lyfe Jennings. These are the only things that she had posted since the "escape," and it was extremely rare for her to post anything at all. *This is what she posts? A man handcuffed to a chair, being tortured, saying "...if tomorrow never comes...and you never see me again...I still believe..." Why would she post this?*

First "Shut It Down" and "Miss Me," and now, "If Tomorrow Never Comes" after the "mind control" that she had vehemently warned me would lead to her returning to the "cult" in Poland with our daughter. I knew that I had to get people to understand who your mom was, or rather, what she had become as a result of severe, organized abuse, and I also knew that this would be difficult due to the fact that she was currently pointing the finger back at me.

Who could ever believe that my wife had left the country with our daughter because my abuse was too much to bear? *Only people that don't know me might believe it,* I considered. *But most people,* I thought, *will be able to see through the "red herring." Most people,* I imagined, *will take a closer look and see that there is something else here that we need to consider, something in Poland.*

"[Chorus]
Cuz If tomorrow never comes
And you never see me again

I don't want yo last memories of me
To be filled with negativity
See if tomorrow never comes
All that fussing and fighting
Won't mean nothing when it's said and done
If tomorrow never comes..."
("If Tomorrow Never Comes" - Lyfe Jenning)

I passed out after a while, I don't remember falling asleep, but only waking up on the floor between the couch and the computer, knowing that I had slept. I was still running on adrenaline, feeling like I had been dropped back into an active war zone immediately upon waking up. I made coffee, and I got back to it; it didn't matter what time it was.

"Wed, Dec 29, 2010, 2:06 AM
Iain Bryson to Mom
Mom,
I love you. Do not worry. I am as fine as I can be, though I need to sleep later on....maybe tonight. I have this nailed. I have no doubt that I will protect Adelle from going to Poland. There is absolutely no chance this will happen unless they have lied to me and she is already there. I have thirty single spaced pages of evidence that abuse has and is occurring. Unfortunately, in order to get there, I had to tear my wife apart. I do not see any choice. I still love her, but she must address the issues that I believe I see, and do so without lying or omitting because she feels it is unimportant/ not relevant. I would not doubt it if I get Adelle back tomorrow.

I am not sure what to do from then, but I do not believe they will leave her with Agata, and I am not sure they will allow Agata to choose voluntary treatment. I told her not to do this to me. I just wanted her to speak with someone. I am not quite sure how she can categorically deny that this is a factor worth looking at, believing that I am crazy and there is nothing going on with her. She doesn't think I know, but I remember every word of our conversations. If I continue sitting, who knows how long it could be. There is nothing that I forget of importance. She has forced me into recalling it all, analyzing it, and presenting it. I asked her to think about the fact that all I would have to do is prove that Adelle was in fact being abused, and that it is not me. If I can just show that, then she has to see that the fact that she cannot see her child is abused leaves open that possibility that she cannot see a [expletive] thing.

Well, I did what had to be done. It is no different than an intervention for addiction. I have such limited resources was not willing to preemptively attack. Adelle will never be exposed to that again and she will get looked at. I love you"

Because my understanding of what had been going on in our family for years was finally clearing up, I assumed that others wouldn't be too far behind. I was processing things at warp speed, wondering and worrying about how your mother would be treated when she was held accountable for her own part in your abduction and abuse. I was thinking about how I could communicate to the authorities as quickly as possible so that they could begin understanding that your mom was only a victim, even though technically she was also a perpetrator, like Patty Hearst.

My understanding was augmented by all the details from having lived with your mom for almost seven years and you for almost four. She was my wife, you are my daughter, and we were a kind of symbiotic organism. But the only evidence people needed to believe and look at was you.

I didn't care if everyone believed everything I was saying, in fact, I hoped they would grasp that I was reacting and reeling from the worst disaster a man can experience – losing his entire family. *If only they hear me a little bit*, I contemplated, *we will have my daughter evaluated, and then all of this will end.*

CHAPTER 53

"PLEASE TAKE THIS SERIOUSLY, FOR MY LITTLE GIRL..."

"Wed, Dec 29, 2010, 6:05 AM
US Citizen Services - Amsterdam to me
Dear Mr. Bryson:
Thank you for your email. As advised during our phone conversation this morning we encourage you to contact the local authorities concerning your family matter. Also please refer to our website for information on custody and child abduction:
http://amsterdam.usconsulate.gov/child_abduction.html
Regards,
U.S. Citizen Services
Amsterdam, the Netherlands"

"International parental child abduction is the removal of a child outside their country of habitual residence in breach of another parent or guardian's custody rights. The office of Children's Issues within the U.S. Department of State is a leader in U.S. government efforts to prevent international parental child abduction, help children and families in abduction cases, and promote objectives of the Hague Abduction Convention. If you believe your child is in the process of being abducted by a parent, legal guardian, or someone acting on their behalf, call us..."
(travel.state.gov/content/travel/en/International-Parental-Child-Afduction.html).

The sole reason that I had to contact them was because the local authorities had been unhelpful. They wouldn't even take my report or tell me where you were. This response from the U.S. Embassy or the United States of America about my U.S. citizen daughter made me extremely uncomfortable. I already knew what the response was from the local authorities, and now the U.S. Embassy was saying, "Yeah, well we can't help you, it's out of our jurisdiction, go back to them. We don't know what to tell you..."

The United States Department of State had a lot of information about parental child abduction online, and yet it seemed nobody was jumping to stop this current one from taking place. It seemed to me that all their caring was just in their words, not in their actions, but I didn't lose hope. I sent emails, including to President Obama, and I called all the numbers that I could find, my goal being to get as many eyes as possible on the parental child abduction of my daughter that was currently taking place.

"Wed, Dec 29, 2010, 7:27 AM
Mom to me
Iain,

I am worried beyond what words can express, not only for you but for Adelle. Is the US Consulate OFFIce helping you? What about food, money etc. Your dad is willing to fly over if for nothing else to be with you so you are not alone. Let us know.

I have no idea how things are handled in another country, but you do know how things would be handled here. The most important person here is Adelle and what she needs and what is good for her. You are an amazing dad that did the right thing to protect Adelle. Sometimes everything has to hit the gutter first in order for things to then start going upward. You and your family need to take advantage of help that will now be provided. I know you will do the right thing and will take care of Adelle. Be sure to also take care of yourself as you have to be healthy so that Adelle can be taken care of. I love you very much and please keep me informed. I am going to get a STI card today so I will call you later on early afternoon my time. Mom"

"Wed, Dec 29, 2010, 7:30 AM
Iain Bryson to Mom
mom,
i cannot get anyone to listen yet. I am told they are in the hague and i am told they are going to look into it. i need someone to listen to me. I really cannot understand why this is not an option. agata laid out the options to me right away: go to the us, allowing her and adelle to go to poland again, or face her trying to terminate my parental rights. I told her i would not consider her mandate, as I require her to seek help for issues which I know to be more than coincidence. She can not even talk to me. I believe progress is being made, and I know that they are still in Holland."

"will you go to kees tomorrow at 10:45 please?
Wed, Dec 29, 2010, 7:59 AM
Iain Bryson to Agata Bryson"

"Wed, Dec 29, 2010, 8:19 AM
info@haguedv.org to me
Thank you for contacting the Hague Domestic Violence Project! We will do our best to get back to you within 1-3 business days. You can also reach our voice mail box at: 1-866-820-4599.
If this is a domestic violence emergency, please contact 911. You can also reach an advocate at:
(1)The National Domestic Violence Hotline at 1-800-799-SAFE (7233) or (TTY) 1-800-787-3224 or online at http://www.ndvh.org/
(2)The Americans Overseas Domestic Violence Crisis Center at 1-866-879-6636 or online at http://www.866uswomen.org/
We look forward to connecting with you."

"Wed, Dec 29, 2010, 8:52 AM
Iain Bryson to Jackie DeLuca
fooled again, huh?
you are wrong. all i wanted was for agata to begin to think about, to be able to think about issues of abuse which are affecting my child. My child is being sexually abused as well as psychologically abused. Agata has been sexually abused and psychologically abused. Could you maybe think about what refusal to face these facts would mean. Did you know that both Agata and I have known all along that Mickey stole your money. He is a heroin addict, who smokes it in the same room as your daughter. He goes to Arnhem all the time, with your daughter, to get heroin. Good luck. thanks for your brilliance."

I was upset and disappointed in Jackie for being a part of your abduction, even though I knew she was most likely duped by your mother in the same way she was by her husband. I realized that the way I was speaking to her was harsh; I was very angry, and I wanted her to be shocked by what she didn't know.

"child abuse
Wed, Dec 29, 2010, 10:22 AM
Iain Bryson to webmaster [Dutch police]
My daughter [was] abused and I believe also sexually abused. My wife is for certain a victim of sexual and psychological abuse. She is unwilling or unable to entertain the idea that I should be taken seriously at all. She denies, ignores, blames me, and has now left with my child. I am told she can go to Poland if she

chooses, where the abuse began. She has given me two options: 1. Return to the US and allow her to return to Poland with our daughter. 2. Face her attempt to terminate my parental rights.

I told her I will not discuss custody until she begins to seriously and honestly address the issues I believe are abuse. She will not. She has gone to the police, which I knew was inevitable due to the choices I was given. I do not care about her report. You people can shoot me or waterboard me....whatever you please. All I want, at least for now, is to prevent my daughter from leaving the country until this is taken seriously. I wrote thirty pages last night after my wife left with my daughter. I cannot get anyone to read it. Please, can I get some help for what I believe is sexual and psychological abuse of my four year old daughter?
Iain Avery Bryson
Newtonplein 25
Den Haag, The Netherlands 2562JV
June 1, 1977
0627098698

Adelle Avery Bryson
January 30, 2007
Agata Bryson
July 11, 1982"

It wasn't that I thought my "thirty pages" was the be-all and end-all. Nor did I think it was definitive proof of anything other than that there was more than enough evidence to investigate further. I wanted to tip the scales, not necessarily to everyone believing me, but to people doubting the red herring version of events enough to dig a little deeper and do the prudent thing, which was to get you properly evaluated.

"Wed, Dec 29, 2010, 12:55 PM
Tulin D. Acikalin [Lawyer] to me
Dear Mr. Bryson, If you need legal advice, please contact our legal advice line at 800-551-5554. The hours are Monday and Thursday, 9:30am to 1:00pm, and Monday and Wednesday from 9:30 to 3:00pm. Our legal line is currently closed for year end maintenance, however it will re-open Monday, January 3, 2011. We cannot provide legal assistance without first determining eligibility. Please be advised that we do not have an attorney-client relationship, therefore nothing that you sent to me is confidential, private or privileged. Also, because Bay Area Legal Aid does not provide legal assistance via email, I have not read your attachment and will not do so.
Sincerely,
Tulin D. Açikalin"

"Child Abuse Report--Urgent
Wed, Dec 29, 2010, 4:54 PM
Iain Bryson to [The Hague Domestic Violence Project], Kees, Jeremiah, [Netherlands Youth Institute], [Youth Care Amsterdam], [Lawyer], [Lawyer], [Lawyer], [Lawyer], [Lawyer], [Lawyer], [Lawyer], [Lawyer], [Lawyer], [Lawyer], [Lawyer], [Lawyer], [Lawyer], [Lawyer], webmaster [Dutch Police], US Citizen Services - Amsterdam, [Netherlands Youth Institute], [Lawyer], [Lawyer], [Lawyer], [Lawyer], [Lawyer], [Lawyers]
Iain Bryson
Newtonplein 25
Den Haag, The Netherlands
2562J
Iain.bryson@gmail.com

In regard to Adelle Avery Bryson, January 30, 2007 and Agata Bryson, July 11, 1982.
0627098698
Could you just attempt to talk to my wife about her abuse history for an hour, without allowing her to change the subject or control the conversation? That would be a wonderful start.

My daughter is being sexually abused. My wife was sexually abused, and has never dealt with the effects of this trauma. The abuse has and is occurring at the hands of my father-in-law. My wife brought this up in the beginning of our relationship, telling me it plagued her, made her hate her father, and that I was the first and only individual she had told. Her understanding of the event(s) has not progressed in nearly seven years.

My daughter spent more than a month in Poland last Spring and then another three months from September to December. Upon returning home, she has displayed signs of sexual abuse. They gradually have disappeared after she is home with both of her parents, but I am not willing to allow this to occur again. After both trips to Poland, my daughter has returned with serious issues, and my wife will not speak to me about it. She denies that there are changes, or that the changes are in any way abnormal. She says that the issues are related to my behavior.

My child cries, screams, hyperventilates, and repeatedly states 'not my pee pee, just not pee pee. My pee pee is special, not the pee pee,' when in the shower. It is as if I am listening to the worst broken record in the world. She has stopped doing this, on both occasions, after about two or three weeks of being away from Poland. My wife claims it is due to a soap irritation. I have asked her about seeing a doctor, and she says it is not necessary because she knows it is due to soap. I am not sure why it is an obsession for my daughter and why it disappears completely after being home, but I cannot get this point across to my wife. My daughter cannot pee. She cries when she has to go to the bathroom. She has to be held sometimes, in the sink, in order to urinate. She defecates in her pants. She told me that her grandfather had talked to her about 'ja ja,' which she then told me (using her words) that it was testicles. This was out of the blue when we were watching television. I looked at my wife when this occurred, and she glared at me with displeasure, anger, and irritability. I knew I could not speak to her. My daughter has told me that my penis is like her grandfathers. Other than this reference, she never speaks about my penis. It just is, and it is just 'different' from mommy's 'pee pee.'

After both stints in Poland, my daughter has had periods of 'baby talk' where there was none at all prior, tantrums, crying for reasons she cannot identify such as when a movie ends, excessive likes and dislikes, craving for attention, fear of abandonment, need to alleviate mommy's emotional issues. My wife claims that there is no correlation between any of this and Poland, and states that it is all because of me.

My wife is neglecting our daughter. She medically neglects her by not seeing the need for a medical and psychological evaluation. She denies that my daughter has her own thoughts, feelings, and experiences. She responds to my daughter when she wants to or when she can, and at no other time. She has withheld information which I need in order to have any chance whatsoever at maintaining food and shelter. She states she does not care and that it is my fault.

I believe that my wife shows serious signs of PTSD, OCD, pathological lying, psychological manipulation, low emotional literacy, superficial charm, lack of remorse, lack of empathy, impulsivity, incapacity for 'love,' unreliability, malignant narcissism, incapacity to express guilt and benefit from experience, persistent irritability, gross and persistent attitude of irresponsibility, dissociation, emotional blackmail, phantom chronic illness, munchausen by proxy, phobic avoidance, weight and sleep issues, distortion of self esteem, emotional attachment to our child for her own benefit, verbal and physical aggression, feeling of being flawed, paranoia and depression, exploitation of others, emptiness, projection of her emotional state onto our child, transference of feelings about her father onto myself, sexual dysfunction, creation of false dilemmas, emotional detachment, fight baiting.

I believe she deliberately starts arguments. She denies that my personal needs exist or matter. She denies that events occurred which did. She denies my perceptions, memory, and sanity. She causes me to lose confidence in, and to question my perceptions and feelings. She causes me to doubt my mind, my ability to be a father. She holds me personally responsible for her happiness. She plays on my guilt and compassion. She threatens, repeatedly and completely, to end our relationship. She threatens to terminate my parental rights, telling me how she will do it and what I can do to stop her from trying. She seeks to distort my perceptions of the world. She tells her daughter how to feel, what to think, what to believe. She withholds affection and sex purposefully. She is cunning: in addition to telling me what she told me, she mentioned she had considered telling me that she had 'met someone else' while in Poland. She denies things which obviously exist. She is easily offended. She lies constantly and needlessly. She retreats from herself in the television, social networking, distant relationships. She has constant, unregulated mood changes. She feels like sex is an obligation or a treat she gives out for good behavior. She has TMJ. She has dizziness and fainting. She has constant headaches. She has self mutilated. She has chronic physical complaints. She is emotionally immature. She denies anything she cannot face. She needs psychological evaluation, and she has to do it thoroughly and honestly.

My wife requires constant attention and reassurance. She used to have me hold her hand so she would be able to urinate. She claims she defecates once per week. She claimed she thought there was something wrong with her because of her inability to orgasm, which was somehow magically cured by me. During the first month of our relationship, she declared that she did not care if she got pregnant. She does not know what is causing her harm; her only explanation is that it is me. The unknown is leading to our daughter's subsequent abuse.

My daughter is being psychologically abused right now by her mother. I do not believe her mother knows that this is occurring. It is due to her own unresolved issues of sexual and psychological abuse. It is too painful for her to come close to thinking about or talking about with me. I have been pleading with her to seek some help to understand this matter. I have been begging her to listen to me when I tell her our daughter is being psychologically abused. I need this to be taken seriously. I need my daughter to be evaluated. I need my wife to seriously and honestly deal with the issues I see.

- 'Monopolization of perceptions is often part of the abuser's brainwashing-like tactics whereby the abuser insists upon the children also believe what he/she says is true and that their perceptions, opinions or ideas are mistaken or unworthy.' (Loring, 1997)

My wife believes that our daughter feels the same ways she does. Upon my return from the US, my wife told me I am a bad father. She told me Adelle likes it better in Poland, and that she does not like living in our home. She believes that Adelle knows that I am an 'abuser,' and that Adelle is suffering in the same ways that she is. My wife speaks to our child as if she were an adult. She asked me to cancel our child's dentist appointment, telling me Adelle was terrified. I attempted to tell her that it was her that was terrified, and that Adelle had no reason whatsoever to be fearful of the dentist without the imposition of her fears. My wife 'knows' that my child has 'terrors.' I have shown her over and over that this is not true, but she cannot see otherwise, because it is something she suffers from herself and cannot identify.

My wife believes her parents love Adelle more than my parents do. My wife believes that Adelle needs her and only her when she is upset; she knows for sure that it is my fault, and she knows that our child needs emotional support from her. It is my wife who needs the emotional support, forcing her feelings and beliefs onto our daughter. Our daughter told me 'I help mommy when she is sick.' Over the course of the past year, my wife has told me that a Polish doctor indicated that my child could die from Scarlett Fever, and needed to stay in Poland until further notice. She told me that a doctor told her she could have a heart attack before age thirty. She told me she was told she may have blood cancer. She told me that a doctor told her that there is nothing that can be done for her migraines, and that she would just have to live with them. In each case, I was told the 'facts' as my wife sees them, and was unable to get any additional information. I was not allowed to speak of it, and I was not permitted to get a second opinion. It is mentioned, I panic, and it is never mentioned again.

- 'Constant criticism, demeaning behaviors, threats, use of male/parent privilege, withholding affection or threatening abandonment for non-compliance with abuser's demands and personal humiliation are further consistent, on-going tactics of the emotional/psychological abuser (Pilowsky, 1993; Parkeer, 1996; Follingstad, 1990; Marshall, 1996; Hoffman, 1984; Alexander, 1993, Chang, 1996; Jacko, 1995; Loring, 1997).'

My wife uses coercion and guilt in order to control our daughter. If our daughter does not react the way she wants her to react, she becomes despondent, she acts depressed, she stops interacting. Or, she pleads with our child, forces guilt onto her, or tries to bribe her. She cries in order to get our child to give her the attention she desires. Adelle asks me why mommy is not happy constantly. Adelle asks her mother if she is happy constantly. Adelle tells her mother she loves her every five minutes. Adelle feels the need to help her mother when she was upset, or as she put it 'when mommy is sick.' 'Some parents use a child as a source of lifetime compensatory love and security. Frequently, these are parents, who idealize their own parents and deny the abuse at their hands. They fail to recognize that they seek to extract from their children what they didn't and couldn't get from their own parents.' My wife is following this model exactly. Her mother used and uses her for emotional support, stability, reassurance, and no[w] my daughter is in the same role.

- 'The continuous and unrelenting pat[t]ern of emotional abuse is often interspersed with warmth and kindness to create an 'in and out' of bonding, 'crazy making' experience for the children and spouse.' (Loring, 1997).

My daughter cannot tell from one moment to the next how my wife will react or respond to her. One minute she is praising her for finishing her cereal as if she just completed the most amazing task in the world. The next minute she is absent completely. She smiles and makes a comment that is totally out of place, and then she switches into utter irritability. My child never knows whether mommy is happy or unhappy. My child asks me why mommy does not 'play' with me. My wife tells my child how she feels. My wife acts without regard to the child. 'How can I have a good Christmas when I do not want to be with you?'

My wife tells me with her words and actions 'not to touch her,' which includes bumping her, brushing her, putting a hand on her shoulder or knee. She retreats as if she were being threatened by the most terrible thing in the world, yelling, swearing, glaring. I tell her that my daughter has begun to pick up on these traits. When this happened previously, my daughter would say 'don't hold my hand daddy, it is my hand.' 'Do not hold my hand tight. It hurts.' When my wife is not acting in this manner, this does not exist with my daughter in any way. When I ask my wife about this, she tells me that I should not touch her and I should not say the things I say if I do not want her to react that way, and that if Adelle picks up on this, it is completely my fault.

My wife was psychologically abused by her mother. I believe that one reason she cannot face the abuse she has endured is due to her intense fear of abandonment of her mother's 'love.' She states that her mother is emotionally cold. She states that her mother is unhappy because of her father. She states that her father cheated on her mother because of her mother's inability to show warmth and love. She talks to her mother more than she talks to anyone. Her mother's perceptions, feelings and beliefs determine those of my wife. I am told constantly that her mother does not care for me and that I have caused both of [her] parents severe, irreversible harm. Her mother has never attempted to have a conversation with me. Neither has her sister. My wife states that she helped her mother get through the trauma caused by her father's extramarital affair(s). I cannot discern any emotion in my wife's mother.

My wife is not able to deal with the psychological issues which are leading to my daughter's abuse. She categorically states that they do not exist and that I am to blame. She cannot have a discussion with me on the topic. She dissociates when confronted with any of it. Reasoning, begging, and appeal to our daughter has not worked. Demanding that she seek help has not worked. Telling her I would rather face her attempt to terminate my parental rights has not helped. Describing how intensely and sure I feel about the abuse has not helped. My wife is abusing our child. My wife's clearly stated intention has been to return to Poland alone without trying to understand anything I have said. She is certain it is all because of me."

"Wed, Dec 29, 2010, 8:51 PM
Dad to me
Hi iain. i am figuring out phone service. i can set up my cell for overseas calls to landline phones but not to cell phones. Which do you have? If it is a cell phone i will get a sit [STI] card. How did today go? I read your email to me. whew!!! I hope the embassy man jumps on this. Lets talk tomorrow.. Love, Dad"

"Thu, Dec 30, 2010 at 10:02 AM
Carine Terhaar sive Droste [Social Worker] to me
Mister Bryson,
We read the email about the serious situation surrounding your daughter. We would advice you to go to your gp with your child for a physical and some advice. And you could call Bureau Jeugdzorg(Child services) for more advice. In your mail you state that you live in Den Haag. Bureau Jeugdzorg works area-bound. So; if you want to contact Bureau Jeugdzorg for your child(ren) you have to contact the one in the area your children are living in."

"Help!
Thu, Dec 30, 2010, 12:31 AM
Iain Bryson to US Citizen Services - Amsterdam
Please tell me what I can do right now. I can't wait. I know with my entire being that both my wife and daughter have been sexually abused…"

"Thu, Dec 30, 2010, 6:48 AM
US Citizen Services - Amsterdam to me
Dear Mr. Bryson,
Thank you for your email.
In these circumstances, we recommend you retain an attorney. The U.S. Consulate General in Amsterdam maintains a list of local attorneys for your convenience.
http://amsterdam.usconsulate.gov/legal_assistance3.html
As informed earlier we advise you to file a police report and work closely with the Dutch authorities in resolving this matter.
Regards,
U.S. Citizen Services
Amsterdam, the Netherlands"

I didn't have money saved up for the rainy day that was having my child internationally abducted. The Dutch police had refused to work closely with me, or to take me seriously at all. My parents would have to help me with this attorney, which I was confident they would do given that their granddaughter was involved.

"Thu, Dec 30, 2010, 9:43 AM
Iain Bryson to Kees de Vries
The police say there must be 'evidence' and that there is none. They say they cannot question her unless she is four. Agata took Adelle only to the doctor in Poland, and since she has had her I have not been able to take her. They advised me to talk to Agata and to go speak about the psychological abuse aspect."

"Thu, Dec 30, 2010, 9:48 AM
Iain Bryson to Kees de Vries
can you please keep trying to call agata. they wont tell me if they are in the country. i do not like what i see"

"Thu, Dec 30, 2010, 10:44 AM
Kees de Vries to me
I keep trying, Iain.
Regards, Kees"

"I figured it out and need to be heard right now, please
Thu, Dec 30, 2010, 12:30 AM
Iain Bryson to Kees de Vries, Dad, Jeremiah, Brian
Kees,
Please tell me what I can do right now. I can't wait. I know with my entire being that both my wife and daughter have been sexually abused. I have not been able to fully focus on this yet as I believe I need to know my daughter is a bit safer than she currently is before I scare myself any further. I would have to say I have no doubts of some type of oral sex and some type of vaginal sex. My wife has been psychologically abusing our daughter. I do not believe she can know as it is just not within the realm of possibility. She has to know, there is no other choice, that our daughter has been subjected to sexual abuse. She cannot begin to go down that path of thought.

I have been told she can take my daughter to Poland, and that is what I need to guarantee does not happen. I cannot risk any chance of this occur[r]ing again, and I am certain it will. I am certain it will become more devastating, and that part of the problem in general has been my increase in understanding and perception. Agata knows on some level that this is not good. She is backed into a corner that she cannot begin to imagine.

Get my daughter checked out. Please. I need to see her. She need[s] the one person who has not betrayed her. I just want her to be safe for now, but at least let me hold her and comfort her. She need[s] the only real love she currently knows and she needs that [expletive] right now. My God Kees. I begged Agata to get help. I told her she had no choice. I begged her not to put me in this situation and force me to break it down as I have and will continue to have to do. Now, I am in one of the most insane, sick situations I can imagine, and I cannot sit back and hope it does not occur again.

If she is going to Poland, I will have to get there, and I will kill anyone in my way. Not even a choice. It is done if that is what it takes. If you don't see it, please humor me and allow me to show you. I didn't want to think it was possible, but not only is it possible, it has happened. Why did I give any man unlimited access to my daughter. How could I do that on the assumption he was cool because he is my wife's father? That is the only factor I based the decision on. I need to make sure my daughter is safe.

The police think I am a monster, and though I know I can get to them, it is tough convincing someone of something when the[y] are already certain they know and have the evidence they need to make their decision. I just hope she still believes it is enough evidence to make me do what she needs me to do so she doesn't bail. I don't think she can as she needs me to shut the [expletive] up. But somewhere inside of her she knows I will not, and so she must convince me and them that I am anything and everything she can think of and 'prove' that sheds doubt on the crazy, obviously psychotic things I have to say more than I need to live. iain"

"Thu, Dec 30, 2010, 12:43 PM
Mom to me
Iain, I just spoke to your dad and he is going to come. It probably will be the first of next week but one of us will let you know for sure. Stay calm. Exchange your $70 and get some food. you must eat and stay strong for the long haul. I am going out for a couple of hours. I will check my email when I get back. This is not going to get resolved overnight so you must do everything you can do to stay calm. I will put your car up for sale as soon as I get the title for some $. I will call you in the morning, so save on your phone bill please. I love you. Mom"

"Thu, Dec 30, 2010, 4:05 PM
Iain Bryson to Kees de Vries, Dad, Brian
if my wife is lying about each and everything in her life and i know she is and can list it all to a perfected degree that i do not believe has been fully understood yet, how can it be claimed that she is telling the truth about our child or anything else? how can i be told that sexual abuse may not have occurred because the dutch police decide there is no physical evidence? I cannot imagine a world where this is happening and I am stuck with that reality. in Connecticut, the mere suspicion of abuse keeps the state in the life of the child until they are certain that the abuse does not exist. And, here i am to be told that i must prove this abuse took place at a level of certainty that is not possible given the nature of the situation and what has been done by the perpetrators to ensure that there is no physical evidence. what is being implicitly, if not explicitly, by this set of rules and guidelines?

i cannot locate my child and nobody seems to really be bothered by this. so, i have to assume that they feel it would be alright if she were in poland. my child needs me more than i could have previously imagined and they are to have me try to internalize that i am simply wrong and that neither my wife nor my child will be questioned at all? she cannot express what is happening in her own words, but i know that she feels it, and it tears me apart to not be able to help her. it tears me apart that her mother is telling and showing her that she is her 'savior,' that i am not there when she is terrified and uncertain. my wife helps my daughter through some heinous situations and at what point does my girl just crack and split into complete irreversible defense like i see in my wife?"

"Fri, Dec 31, 2010, 4:33 AM
Iain Bryson to Fred Taal [Dutch detective]
Attachments
please take this seriously, for my little girl who needs me days ago...
Iain Bryson Avery: 1-6-1977
Adelle Avery Bryson: 30-1-2007
Agata Bryson: 11-7-1982
Newtonplein 25A
Den Haag, Nederland 2562JV
+31 (0) 627098698
Iain.bryson @ gmail.com"

"Fri, Dec 31, 2010, 4:41 AM
Iain Bryson to Kees de Vries
is there not something that can be done here? i cannot believe this place. there is no rush, no real concern. this is a child, and i am sorry but this is my child and i will not be told i am wrong. i know who and what i am. i have been forced to relive this over and over, in more detail each time, working it out so i can figure out how to present it to people who are fooled by things like 'correlation equals causation,' 'propaganda,' 'distortion of facts and reality,' my wife who fits the profile of a sociopath, primacy effect. if i am right, then my wife will do anything and everything to cover this up. she has to because she would [be] 'crazy' in a different way if these things did not exist, if she has to actually realize what her whole life has been. if she has to realize what she is doing to her daughter. she knows she is not flawed or bad, and so how can the 'love' she has always known be wrong for her daughter.

authorities within my government have confirmed that this needs to be seriously looked at and i will not conform to dutch realities when my daughter's life is on the line. i cannot. the girl needs me. right before she was taken from me, she refused to go to the store with my wife. she looked at me with open eyes, wondering what i think. her mother was coercing her using guilt and bribery and i told her i will not raise my child like that and that if she wanted my help we could go in the other room and talk. she told me adelle is not listening because i will not support her. i am [expletive] glad i did not. my daughter needs some reassurance that what she still believes, somehow, is wrong, is actually wrong. thank god i am in her life and we have the relationship that we do."

"Please forward to Dave and Juan Gambola: Duty Officers: EMERGENCY INVOLVING UNITED STATES CITIZEN
Fri, Dec 31, 2010, 5:00 AM
Iain Bryson to US Citizen Services – Amsterdam
Attachments

The Dutch police tell me I cannot come back to the police station. They tell me they will go see if my daughter is ok through observing her immediate environment. They tell me it could take three days, or more. What kind of sick, alternate reality is this? If what I am saying is correct, and it is, then the story they believe and are acting upon is also necessarily true. My wife has to protect all that has been real in her world, which involves sex with her father since god knows when till now. If she is not 'damaged' and a good person, and if she loves her parents which she must, her only option is to do this. If not, she would collapse and her mind would turn into mush.

Why can people not see that correlation does not equal causation? why can people not see the power of propaganda? I told them that what they are telling me is that it is ok for a child to be abused and that from my point of view the only logical conclusion is to do it myself. They say 'what do you want us to do?' Protect my child [expletive]. And, her mother is not in a position to do this. And, now you are telling me you never knew where they were, and that you think they are staying with a friend, whom I know to be smoking heroin in front of his own daughter. I spoke to Dave, and cannot express how much I appreciate his help and understanding. I just cannot tell for sure if I am understood enough because I feel something has to be possible other than the options before me working on my own. What about the media?

[The third attachment is a ten-page letter explaining that I believe (know) you are being abused, similar to the other emails I wrote claiming that you were being abused.]"

CHAPTER 54

"WE DON'T KNOW WHERE SHE IS NOW..."

"**Fri, Dec 31, 2010, 5:24 AM**
Fred Taal [Dutch detective] to me
Iain, we send a sms to your wife cellphone to contact us. We don't know where she is now. If she don't respond we can make a call for the police and border security. We keep in contact with you about this.
Regards,
Mr F. Taal and R. Brusik
child police officiers Policestation Segbroek."

"**Fri, Dec 31, 2010, 5:31 AM**
Iain Bryson to Fred Taal [Dutch detective]
Fred,
I appreciate your assistance. Thank you, Iain"

"**This is what the Dutch police now say after guaranteeing me for four days that my daughter is safe/**
Please pass to Duty Officers Dave and Juan Gambola
Fri, Dec 31, 2010, 5:52 AM
Iain Bryson to US Citizen Services - Amsterdam, Brian, Jeremiah, Mom, foxreport [News], Fred Taal
[Dutch detective]
'Iain, we send a sms to your wife cellphone to contact us. We don't know were she is now. If she don't respond we can make a call for the police and bordersecurity. We keep in contact with you about this.
Regards,
Mr F. Taal and R. Brusik
child police officiers Policestation Segbroek.'
Forwarded to the White House, all major US news outlets, the Embassy in Holland, FBI"

Whether they knew it or not, this is where the Dutch police officially confirmed that you were not safe. I had been screaming at them for days, begging them to stop you from leaving the country with your mom, begging them to evaluate you, emphatically telling them that you are not safe.

"**Fri, Dec 31, 2010, 7:50 AM**
Iain Bryson to Kees de Vries
Kees,
Is it possible for you to give me a few sentences on what you think of my relationship with my wife in September 2010? I don't know Dutch law, but I know in the US, since we have been having a technically pre-existing conversation, it is nothing other than telling me what I should know already but was too foolish due to my blind, unconditional love. I know what is going on and I will never come to a different conclusion. I am resting, eating, and receiving support from my family. Iain"

I knew that everything from here on out was very important, and I was looking for support. Your mom was lying, and I wanted to make sure that I had someone to back me up. I wasn't asking Kees to speculate, but rather, I wanted his pure, objective, unbiased opinion, because I knew that I was right. It was not the truth that I was afraid of, but whatever your grandpa had up his sleeve.

What your mom was saying was impossible, that she hated me and fled to a shelter to get away from me for safety, and I knew that Kees would agree. Something had switched in your mom, a total transformation, and I felt fortunate that Kees knew us a bit, thinking that he would probably be important in helping us to sort everything out and get your mom the help she needed.

"Fri, Dec 31, 2010, 8:41 AM
Kees de Vries to me
Hi Iain,
I can't reach you by phone. Do you have any news?
To answer your question: at august 19th, you and Agata came to see me together. Agata told me she was delighted about your progress. She said she appreciated the calmth in the house and your patience. As I understood it, there were no problems between the two of you at that moment.
Don't forget your appointment coming monday at 15:00 with Ms. Kuhler. If you want, you can come to see me at 17:00 (on monday). Let me know if you want that.
Take care, Kees"

"Fri, Dec 31, 2010, 8:55 AM
Agata Bryson to me
Hi Iain: I wanted to let you know that Adelle and I are doing OK. We are under professional care in recover"

I knew that she was lying, but I hoped that she wasn't. *"We are doing OK." What does that mean? No, she is obviously not doing ok.*

If real trauma specialists were assessing the situation, then I knew that they would be able to discern that the progenitor of your problems was your grandfather, and not your father. The lack of information that I was receiving as to your whereabouts was messing with my head, and I couldn't understand why the Dutch police didn't think it was important that I knew where my daughter was.

I continued spending some time researching Dutch shelters and whether you were in one or not, but I had it basically crossed off my list of actual possibilities. I wondered how your mom would spin it since it would be obvious to the "professionals" that you were not afraid of me, but of your mom, and of whatever was going on in Poland.

"Fri, Dec 31, 2010, 9:08 AM
Iain Bryson to Agata Bryson
Agata,
Glad you are well. You told me I could see my daughter in three days. Could you let me know about that because it is pretty high on my priority list. Please tell her I love her"

"Fri, Dec 31, 2010, 9:30 AM
Iain Bryson to Kees de Vries
'Adelle and I are at a shelter for abused women and children because I was afraid for my life and what Adelle was going through. We couldnt stay under one roof with all the abuse. I will contact you in few days so we can plan to meet the three of us and also to see a counsulor about all of this.'

'Hi Iain: I wanted to let you know that Adelle and I are doing OK. We are under professional care in recover'

Kees, These are the two messages I have received via email from Agata since she and my daughter left. The first is on the evening [they] left. I received it after I returned from the police station. The second is from just now. I sent her one asking when I could see Adelle, reminding her of her first message. I asked her to tell Adelle that I love her. I talked to my cousin today, who is a Special Agent with the FBI in Puerto Rico. He convinced me to listen and realize his point of view, which blows me away. I know it all, and have a difficult time coming to the conclusion that it is not simple. He said that they are law enforcement and that they will react first to me, with not much thinking. The only person of interest which I know has listened to me is a US Consular Officer, which was good ideas more from the US perspective.

I have trouble following rules just to follow them; I have to figure out why and what it means and decide on a more philosophical than practical stance. I have been pretty practical, but I need to work that out a bit since it['s] 'practical' from the point of view that I believe this [expletive] needs to end immediately and be looked at until they know the child is safe. Basically, the conclusions the Dutch people come to permit and maybe even encourage sexual abuse up to age 4. By that time, people can have them pretty well trained. I am glad I know my daughter and can see that it is nowhere close. It is only because of me and my dedication to doing the absolute best that I can do with the most important job that I have in this life. I cannot imagine ever coming to the conclusion, and believing, that there is such a world where I cannot protect her. To me it is like going into a ring and fighting someone to the death, being told not to pick up and use the rock and believing I really cannot.

So, I am working, but taking it easy and trying to read my body and mind so I stay on point. I slept most of last night, but awoke drenched and a bit frantic. I had to harness my head back and force it systematically back where I needed it. It was like booting up a computer to 'hell.' OK, so I know I am right. My first and only priority has to be securing my girl's safety. I need to be in charge of executing this mission, and I need to be able to utilize the resources as if they were my own fingers on this one. So, I am making progress, constantly trying to reassess the situation, and plodding away.

My friend in Amsterdam sent some money and I went to AH for food and coffee which I had been out of for two days. My father is coming soon, as it is really a bit much for one person. He will check out the apartment situation for me and stuff like that to make sure I do not lose my home base. From what you gave me from the transcripts of August 19, I come to some ambiguities. There is as much potential negative, though it is subtle, but the positive is also kind of removed a bit. I am trying to remember more, but when I think about it now I think that is probably how it all was. It is like 'perverted polish girl training refined.' Who knows, or wants to know, how pervasive this is?

Anyway, I need someone to at least try to see that I know this is happening and I know she fits the profile of a sociopath. All that it takes is for someone to have the time to sit down and work it out as if it were a long division problem. It is no more than acting a sick part in a movie, and only catching glimpses that you are not really in the movie. Because in the end, she has to believe she is in that movie no matter what. I think I almost had her too, but I think that once things get good with us, she becomes very antsy and has a strong urge to return to Poland. All the best, Iain"

"It is conventionally accepted that if the initial traumatization occurs after the ages of five to seven, it is difficult to make a multiple. We might end up with someone with a dissociative disorder and are certainly very likely to get someone with a character disorder, such as borderline personality disorder, but to make a multiple, the trauma has to start quite young. Many begin at preverbal ages. In fact, in the typical case I've seen, the abuse began in infancy or certainly by toddlerhood" (Calof 34).

"i have the phone now. i was talking to my cousin/fbi..........yes 17 [O'Clock] on monday is great. thank you
Fri, Dec 31, 2010, 9:31 AM
Iain Bryson to Kees de Vries"

"Fri, Dec 31, 2010, 9:42 AM
Iain Bryson to Kees de Vries
How I would say it in one sentence: On the surface, if you are observing and doing no analysis most people would come to the conclusion that the situation was a bit strange but that it was also volatile and uncertain. Objective analysis leads to the path she has chosen until you ask her or assume that even one or two of the things I have said are true. And they all are unfortunately. I am trying to look at behavior [on] a different level, and I know who my wife, and especially my child are. She still has no idea that I can actually look through her. She was able to put doubt into me about things which drove me crazy until she left and I recovered from terror.

I think it has to be multifaceted; one approach may not quite push the burden of 'proof,' though I will make it and know it will just take time to get it done. It will happen and it is my job to make sure. It is extremely tough, though at the same time I am learning quite a bit and am confident in the outcome. I just have to believe she wants a 'clean break,' and that it is a bit too risky for her to flee to Poland. It [would] raise one too many difficult questions and she probably does assume the US government has been contacted. Though I know she has to reach the conclusion that it is impossible for me to know. That is what keeps her 'safe.'"

By "clean break," I was referring to the fact that it was obvious to me that your mom wanted help getting away from the cult. She knew that I would take all that she had dumped on me and tell other people, and she knew that I would never stop. She knew that people wouldn't initially believe me, and she knew that our struggle would be uphill. Once they just start investigating child abuse, which I thought they would have to do, the onion would peel back, and the cult family would be stopped.

I was scrambling, and I was trying to explain things in as many ways as possible, like using a shotgun in the hopes of hitting the target, even if it is only one bb that hits the target; accuracy wasn't the point. I was also alone, without anyone to talk to or anyone to run things by, and so my emails became like my journal. I remembered your mom trying to rip the ethernet cable out of our computer, and I thought that this was most likely because she knew I would be doing what I was doing now.

"Fri, Dec 31, 2010, 10:05 AM
John S to me
Your email is cut off before you finish citing Ms Smedley's credentials. Still, there is certainly enough here for me to offer you this advice: You MUST secure professional help in these matters. You need to talk to a lawyer, and the lawyer needs to refer you to the proper medical/psychological professionals who can examine this evidence and help you take the proper legal action. I don't know how it works over there, but around here I think these allegations would prompt some sort of investigation. It's difficult to believe that the authorities wouldn't want to look into this if they saw the allegations. Have you been to the proper authorities? Because telling your friends is important, but we don't have any authority in the matter. I will wrack my brains and ask around about what is the proper avenue for you. But I don't know how successful I'll be. In the meantime, I will pray. And please try to hold on. Don't freak out. You are going to have to be incredibly normal through all this.
-- John
PS -- I see you sent this to Nancy. Good idea. I happen to know she is away on her annual retreat this weekend. I don't know if she gets email there, but I'm sure she will check it when she returns. So don't freak out if she doesn't get back to you immediately.
We love you, bro -- John and Linda"

"Fri, Dec 31, 2010, 10:26 AM
Iain Bryson to John S
John,
I know I am right, and that is all I can care about now. I am not worried about being wrong, as it is not possible. I begged Agata to get help and told her to not make me do this. She doesn't know how sharp my mind can be when I want, and especially when the purpose is to save the one thing that embodies all of 'hope' and 'heaven' in my life.

I've got the US Consulate helping; they tell me to get her to the Embassy if I can grab her. The Dutch are extremely difficult and I am learning how to play their sick game. It is all by the rules with no rush no matter my allegations; they told me they were closed till January 3. I am going to get the Department of State overseas abduction service, but they are off for the holiday as well. It is an abduction if my conclusion is reached, which it will be. The sex unit here is supposedly making sure they stay in the country for me and through their [expletive], elementary procedure. I need to be directing this [expletive]. My psychologist knows both of us and knows I tell the truth and am not crazy so he is trying to help and looking at this from the perspective of a psychologist. Agata will not call him back, so she will have to find an excuse for that, which will be another nail since she knows he will be the first one to see cracks.

Anyway, the options are clearer and I am not pressuring myself now, but just thinking and shifting to something else so I don't stay at such a high pace for too long. Sleeping is not really possible. It is like trying to go to sleep in battle. I lose time here and there but I am never really sure how much and always wake up completely wet from sweat and disoriented, trying to put together what is going on and having to reboot my head to get on track. I am not freaking out, but have had to work on controlling my natural passions. I have to believe someone will listen. So either way, I am getting them to stay on it, and it will happen and any [expletive] presuppositions they have don't really make a difference anyways. They will just be more set aback when they see, but they wouldn't see any sooner."

"Fri, Dec 31, 2010, 10:41 AM
Iain Bryson to Fred Taal [Dutch detective]
Fred,
I have thought things through and processed our meeting. I spoke with my cousin in the FBI and he got me to listen. What you have to understand from my side, or I ask you do, is that I know this is true, and I will prove it. I have no doubt, and I am telling you the truth when I tell you this is what I do best other than being a father. Now, I cannot expect anyone to come to that conclusion right away, though I need them to, and I have to try. It is like trying to tell Agata I see psychological abuse and not getting her to even acknowledge that the word exists. Except the stakes are the most important thing in my world. So, I have to listen to you, and see that in your profession this happens more frequently than I'd like to imagine, and people often get sidetracked somewhere not reaching the correct conclusion.

All I can really ask of you is that you keep taking me serious and checking off your list so that you do investigate and work within your boundaries to get my child to safety without getting hung up on what is the expected result of a sociopath in this situation. She absolutely has to make everything look a certain way, and she doesn't even know what she is doing. It is sick programming done at such a young age, in a secluded society with no diversity. There is a control over opinion as most people will not go outside the 'normal,' accepted sources for their information. So, it is much easier to teach someone that something like love is based on giving a man sex as a reward, and getting what you to believe is 'security' and acceptance in return. I am so glad my daughter has me, so she hasn't yet even come close to the conclusion that this is right. But any bad decision is unacceptable to me. If I can do better, and you always can, that is what I want for her.

Agata emailed me, so if you can, could you reach out to her that way? Have a great holiday and again I do appreciate your help. I see what you mean about the police station but have to see it is 'it wont do any good,' which is tough for me to reach, but I know you do not mean it in the way I feel it initially. I believe she is going to make it look like my daughter is afraid of me and wait until she can get me to the 'bargaining table.' She believes she is right because she has no other choice; she would implode if she could reach the other conclusion because the facts are way too difficult. Have you spoken with Kees de Vries? Again, he has tried to get in touch with her, and she will not get back to him, which I believe is just another thing she will not be able to explain with anything that makes sense. All the best, Iain"

"Fri, Dec 31, 2010, 10:46 AM
Iain Bryson to Kees de Vries
one issue is that I can look at a family, and as I gather information, I know I could successfully remove abused children by just watching. My cousin made me realize that this wouldn't be a good thing if it was standardized and anyone could apply for the job."

I knew that I was exaggerating to some degree, and I was making a sort of joke when I told Kees that Jer had told me it couldn't be "standardized." My speech became looser as I became more desperate and felt more alone. It felt like I was falling, and like I was speaking in a language that nobody could understand, as if I started clicking and clucking with my tongue. But it felt like I had to not care what other people thought or where they were at, because in the meantime you were gaining distance from me and returning to your abusers.

The words in my emails were my attempts at hitting the stone with my sledgehammer. I knew that I couldn't do anything, that someone who was in a position of power had to act. I couldn't understand why nobody wanted to protect my daughter, why they were so indifferent to my allegations. I wondered, *do they not understand? Or not care? Or not want to be bothered? Are they already poisoned by the "red herring"?*

"Fri, Dec 31, 2010, 12:27 PM
Iain Bryson to Kees de Vries
If you do not have time, this is not necessary to read, but it helps me to focus. There are certain things that come to mind which save me, proving that I did not ultimately go off track in what I believe as a parent. I never let Adelle think I did not love Agata. I think she knows what my frustration was on her own level, though it is unresolved. I was observing and unable to come to the conclusions as I can now, but that was mostly

because of my love and trust in Adelle's mother. I never reacted negatively or positively to the things I saw in Adelle. It stunned me, and I could not figure it out in the circumstances I was in, but I would have if it had continued to play out. I believe that is why we are where we are; it is too dangerous and they know. Agata knows, though not consciously, that there is no way that this would continue to fool me.

She told me she did not want me to think about homeschooling Adelle. I refused to 'back' up Agata when it didn't sit right with me, telling her I would talk to her in the other room about why I could not. Agata hung a wooden angel in Adelle's room, which Agata has always said 'protects' and 'makes her safe.' Adelle said she did not like it to me. I took it down, wondering why that could be but not playing it out. Then Adelle told me and Agata. I started to go take it down. Agata said 'I like it, it is from Bunusia and Jajush.' Adelle said I dont like it. I said 'well if you dont like it I will take it down.'

Agata wanted me to help her coerce Adelle into going to the store. She was not crying but she was letting Adelle know it did not make her happy she had decided not to accompany her, letting her know she wanted/needed it and that she had planned on it and waited all day. Agata said, 'she is not listening because you are not supporting me.' I said 'I cannot support it and don't ever need to lie to her.' Adelle looked at me looking to see how I felt and knew she was safe with her decision. I never reacted positively or negatively to the surplus of sexual knowledge and attention. I didn't know what was going on, and I had to assume it was innocent though when it adds up it clearly is not. How could I come to the conclusion that anything like this is possible.

I felt weird about her always saying she was her cat and acting it out, but I didn't give her a hard time. She would call herself Ally or Mimi, and I would always revert to Adelle, but not let her know why. I woke up with her daily, making breakfast with her two hours before Agata would get up. We did lots of great stuff and she didn't give a [expletive] if Agata woke up, asking me why she was sleeping kind of in a way that let me know she knew something is off. She started coming in to our room and she would ask me to come lay in bed with her. If I tried to get up she would stop me and tell me to stay and I always did, though I do not believe it is necessary in a 'normal' situation. I always rotated Agata's [expletive] 'she likes this and she doesn't like that' out of the picture without demanding it.

In the past two weeks, I basically cut the television out, got her off cereal and chocolate yougurt for breakfast, got her eating regularly, did the activities she wanted to do. I got her a worm farm, which Agata tried teaching her is gross, but it did not work. I let her make the biggest 'mess' she wants when she plays, letting her know we just have to clean it up together at some point. When Agata put makeup on her, I never said anything like 'you are beautiful' or 'that looks nice.' It was just a neutral activity that Agata liked to do with her. She knows I think she is beautiful, but I am careful about why she thinks I think it, and how often I tell her. I began telling Agata I don't always wanting her wearing pink because it is not her that 'likes' it. I asked her why she did not like the boys at daycare. I swung her as high as I knew I could in the swing. She always came first, and I could not negotiate my principals on that one except where I saw that it was a 'normal' part of Agata.

I just wonder what I would know if I could understand Polish completely. I think I will have to keep the language in her life; if I cut it out she will have a void which is never filled, Instead, it just needs to be all positive from now on so she can work through it on all levels. Adelle was just speaking Polish except to communicate with me when I got back. I can understand enough to fill in the blanks and she would tell me the words I didn't know which is awesome. And one day I said 'very good' in Polish and she said 'mommy....daddy is talking like Bunusia and Jajush.' Now I understand. It's like some kind of [expletive] up programming code that I knew I had to remove from her environment under these circumstances.

When she didn't want to come home I would keep trying but not push it and always keep doing what she wanted to the fullest extent, gradually making our way back until she said it was ok. I used to feel that 'Agata wants us back' and I would get anxious but I got to the point of 'I really dont care and shouldn't.' I am having fun with my daughter, and I dont need to explain why I do not answer my phone. There is no call that is more important than what I am doing. Agata said she was going to have Adelle sleep in the same bed as her friend. I didn't know they were going over there for sure, so I didn't get into it, but I was going to say that it is not ok to encourage it. Two beds and if they decide that is what their relationship is, then ok, but I am still going to continue to look at this constantly. Why would you push your adult [expletive] 'cute' [expletive] onto a child as if it is what they want?"

"Fri, Dec 31, 2010, 12:49 PM
Iain Bryson to Kees de Vries
my vengeance comes only through restoring what has been stolen from my daughter. the rest i need not worry about. if i save my daughter, that plays out naturally in ways that inflict more pain than i could personally inflict if given the task without thinking only about how i should feel. only one goal is necessary. worrying about the rest is not healthy and certainly not of assistance to the true goal"

"Fri, Dec 31, 2010, 12:56 PM
Iain Bryson to Kees de Vries
i told Agata that our daughter will enjoy sex, and that i wanted it [t]o develop at an appropriate level just like anything else. she looked at me like 'what does that mean. she already is 'enjoying' it.'
when i first had my child i told agata that she would be a lesbian. then i got to 'all that i care about is that she knows why she makes the decisions she does and doesn't get taken advantage of.'
i do see hints of 'goodness' in agata but do not know whether it was because i was watching or if it was 'natural' motherly instinct taking over. adelle and i sing and i've always made up songs with her. she is remarkable at 'freestyle,' blowing my mind with what she comes up with."

"Fri, Dec 31, 2010, 1:03 PM
Iain Bryson to Kees de Vries
agata would tell me things like 'my father says young boobies are special' and I would do a doubletake, then think ok well that is surely strange, but i also know that people are strange."

"Fri, Dec 31, 2010, 1:04 PM
Iain Bryson to Kees de Vries
i see the need for alcoholism now. i knew it was something other than 'being Polish,' but it is probably a synonym."

"Fri, Dec 31, 2010, 1:11 PM
Iain Bryson to Kees de Vries
agata's weight would go up the longer she was with me without going to poland. she would complain, do fake diets that never worked out, but say 'i think i am heavier when i am happier.' i would tell her i love her and it doesnt matter what she looked like as long as she was happy. i wish you could see her now. i would guess 15-20 pounds less, manicured, tweezed, makeup galore. not hungry at all. i wonder if i ever pleased her like her father could and did while i was married to her. well, i know i did at least a couple of times, but it was more for sure, and something indescribable for her. lost immediately to her [expletive] training.
    her calling me 'molester.' she was being confronted at a level she could not stand and about things she could not think about. it was the same as when i first went to poland with her and she was talking about my ex girlfriend, asking me questions, telling me i still loved her, etc. I woke up, calling agata by my ex's name since she skillfully inserted it into my subconscious. i caught hell but it never happened again as that conversation never happened again. the guy she talked to on skype with my daughter till 11:30 at night: she told me she could not explain what she had with him and she would always wonder. she said they had kissed. i doubt that was all they did and wonder if there was any orchestration there as well. it must be interesting to watch agata and my mother-in-law go over the stories that will work on men."

"Fri, Dec 31, 2010, 1:16 PM
Iain Bryson to Kees de Vries
after i am told about the 'need for divorce,' and i get a couple fake crying sessions where i do realize it is fake but it is what crying is for my wife, she tells me 'god does not recognize our marriage anyways,' since i am not catholic and we were not married in a church. i wonder what sick [expletive] god does approve of."

"Fri, Dec 31, 2010, 3:02 PM
John S to me
This sounds good, like what I was trying to recommend. Your daughter's safety is paramount right now. If she can get to a safe place where there are some objective people helping out it will be good. It must be [expletive] frustrating for you, putting up with government [expletive]. But that's what it takes in these situations. And you have to be judged well by people, sometimes even people you don't respect, because their judgment has so much power. So, play the game if you have to, my friend. Hopefully it will pay off.
    I'm going to be away from my computer for a day or two. I will try to check my email somewhere if I can, but if not, soon as I am back home I will check in again. Linda and I are sending nothing but good thoughts and hopes to you and your beautiful daughter.
Love you, Iain"

CHAPTER 55

"CHILD ABUSE IS COMMON AND PERVASIVE"

In chapter 5 of his book, "Organised Sexual Abuse," Michael Salter describes how his eyes were opened and his life was irrevocably transformed upon becoming friends with a victim/survivor of organised abuse. He explains, "...I describe my own tumble 'down the rabbit hole' and re-emergence into a world that I was no longer familiar with: one in which a young woman could be stalked, assaulted and terrorized over a period of years by a group of men without drawing the attention or interest of the authorities. The stark reality is that neither the police nor any other agency intervened to protect Sarah despite repeatedly being notified of her plight. The disinterest and inaction of the authorities in the face of evidence of organised abuse is irreconcilable with common stereotypes of police 'always investigating cases' and investigators 'always getting their man' (Tamarkin 1994a). This irreconcilability lies at the very heart of the debate over organised abuse, and this chapter details my own struggle to recreate a coherent worldview in the aftermath of a prolonged confrontation with extraordinary abuse" (75-76). "There was a systemic quality to the neglect and invalidation Alex experienced at the hands of the authorities, and this resonated with the methods of control drawn on by her perpetrators, who often told her that nobody would believe her. They were in fact quite correct. It was my own belief that the authorities would assist us that proved naïve and unfounded" (85).

I came up with "Polish Generational Incest Cultural Heritage" all on my own. I knew that it was not a scientific term, or an actual diagnosis, but I knew that it also covered all the bases. The fact that my daughter was in the process of being abducted so that she could continue being abused as her mother was before her was the most unbelievable thing I had ever considered, and it was blowing my mind.

I didn't yet know or understand all the correct terminology, and I was trying to explain what was happening the best way I knew how, in accordance with whatever level of understanding I had at the time. "Dissociative Schizophrenic Syndrome" does not exist in the DSM, but the symptoms of DID and schizophrenia can look similar, in the same way that borderline personality disorder and DID may overlap (Lacter and Lehman, 2008, as cited in Noblitt, 2008, 85).

"U[r]gent
Fri, Dec 31, 2010, 5:41 PM
Iain Bryson to Fred Taal [Dutch detective], Kees de Vries, Dad
Fred,
My child is in the middle of a Polish Generational Incest Cultural Heritage. I guarantee it. And there is nothing that can be done? This is an abduction. It is Natalie Holloway in live. It is widespread and pervasive and you're telling me there is nothing the country can do? Poland is the first country in Europe to have mandatory chemical castration [for sex offenders], so they both look good in policy and make people master the technique. They systematically create Dissociative Schizophrenic Syndrome in the women. My daughter

has to get out now. There is [no] way I can continue not even knowing for certain she is in Holland. I have to do everything I can at this point. I have the entire story mapped out systematically. This is ridiculous; the ramifications of what is actually going on, how well this is orchestrated, and what is at stake are unbelievable. Tell me my daughter is in this country, and please tell me what you think. Happy New Year, Iain"

While chemical castration really had not much to do with it at all, it did prove that child molestation was enough of a (admitted) problem to institute such a law. I winced when I considered your grandfather's obvious future given your vaginal pain and interest in his gonads, and I sure didn't envy what he was in for once it came out what he had been up to.

"Fri, Dec 31, 2010, 5:47 PM
Mom to me
Iain, I just tried to call and your phone is busy. I wanted to wish you a Happy New Year. Right now it might not seem very happy but it will get better. Hang in there, be strong and be ready for when you see Adelle. We've been out for the afternoon. I will again try to call but don't want it to get too late on your end. I love you. Mom"

"My daughter, a US citizen, in imminent danger. Generational Polish Incest. Please: Duty officers Dave and Juan Gambola.....Dutch will do nothing; act as if it's permitted, now i see too clearly. please
Fri, Dec 31, 2010, 5:56 PM
Iain Bryson to US Citizen Services - Amsterdam
Iain Avery Bryson
Adelle Avery Bryson
Agata Bryson
Newtonplein 25
Den Haag, NL 2562JV

Dave and Juan
[same body of text as sent to Fred Taal, Kees de Vries, and Dad on December 31, 2010 at 5:41 PM]"

"Fri, Dec 31, 2010, 5:57 PM
Iain Bryson to Mom
I know what it is. I am fine but need help now. Generational Polish Incest. Intentional Schizophrenic Dissociative Disorder. Culture. Tradition."

The deeper I dug, the more I was clobbered with the fact that child abuse is common and pervasive and even normal for many people, and that people really do not know or care for the most part. I realized that people would rather bury their heads in the sand than look at anything unpleasant that they weren't absolutely forced to look at, and that this included both their own trauma as well as others'. I wondered why we hadn't yet banded together as humans to stamp out such a terrible, damaging plague.

Where was the war on child abuse? In my lifetime I had seen wars on drugs and wars on terrorism, wars that to me didn't make sense, at least not compared to people intentionally hurting children. Why weren't we fighting against the abuse of our children, our future? Now, it was my child, you, in the middle of this big mess.

"Fri, Dec 31, 2010, 6:12 PM
Mom to me
I just tried to call again. No answer. Are you going to be ok until your dad can get there?"

What does she mean "Am I going to be ok?" I asked myself. Though I knew that I could be reading into it the wrong way, I didn't like it. Why was there no mention of you? The only thing that could've made me "be ok" was to have you in my actual arms. Why would my dad being there help me to be ok? I hoped it was because he was going to get the lawyer I needed, but my alarms had been triggered, and I sensed that my parents were not being honest with me about something.

"IDEAS ANYONE? EMBASSY, INTERNATION US ABDUCTION SERVICE CLOSED FOR HOLIDAY. DUTCH ARE ACCEPTING IT/TURNING AWAY/PROMOTING
Fri, Dec 31, 2010, 6:13 PM
Iain Bryson to Dad, Kees de Vries, Mom, Brian, Nancy [ex-colleague], George N [high school friend]
there has to be something now.
POLISH GENERATIONAL INCEST HERITAGE
DESIGNING HUMAN BEHAVIOR
DISSOCIATIVE SCHIZOPHRENIC DISORDER
MY DAUGHTER, AGE THREE
INTERNATIONAL SPOUSAL ABDUCTION

I CAN WRITE SCRIPTS, TRAINING MANUALS, CULTURAL INTEREST TOPICS, KEYS TO MASKING, THIS IS GOING TO COME OUT AND IT IS RIDICULOUS. CAN I NOT GET MY DAUGHTER TO SAFETY"

"Incest of my three year old American citizen daughter. Dutch will not help. US will/ stargard szczecinski
Fri, Dec 31, 2010, 6:37 PM
Iain Bryson to RoguskiJX@state.gov [US State Department], Kees de Vries, Brian
Pilsudskiego 2/6
Stargard Szczecinski
Poland
73-110
Makowska

Iain Avery Bryson
Adelle Avery Bryson
Agata Bryson
Newtonplein 25
Den Haag, NL 2562JV

Mandatory Chemical Castration. My daughter needs help now. They won't guarantee me she is even in Holland and has not yet fled with her mother to hell.

[same body of text as sent to Fred Taal, Kees de Vries, and Dad on December 31, 2010 at 5:41 PM]"

"Re: I will dismantle the entire sicko country piece by piece. I found my first real job. please help my daughter now. everybody involved in hurting my daughter or allowing it to continue is a conspirator. us international abduction services closed fo[r holiday]
Fri, Dec 31, 2010, 6:46 PM
Iain Bryson to Brian, Kees de Vries, US Citizen Services - Amsterdam, Kristin [high school friend], George N
someone be a hero because i am analyzing each perspective and will break it down accordingly and it will be published"

I didn't really believe that all of Poland was the problem, or that only Poland was the problem. I did believe that people who were not helping, along with people who were hindering, regardless of their intentions, were "helping" you to be abducted, and I wasn't happy with people's responses so far. I was extremely frustrated, and I could feel your childhood innocence being crushed.

"You treat me like an affliction. You leave me like an addiction. But you got my daughter involved...you are [expletive] done. I promise you that. It is worked out to perfection and will only get more clear, which will be more than any of you Polish [expletive]
Fri, Dec 31, 2010, 7:01 PM
Iain Bryson to Kees de Vries, Brian"

"You are looking the other way in the most heinous situation currently happening. i am not going to stop until it ends. come out on top. Dont go to the police station? nice one.

Fri, Dec 31, 2010, 7:23 PM
Iain Bryson to Fred Taal [Dutch detective], US Citizen Services - Amsterdam, Brian
manual 2 , ages 4-6 starts and my wife has to get her there. this is her mission. help now"

The manuals I'm referring to in the above email are German guides for sexually training your children starting at age 1 (*Korper, Liebe, Doktorspiele* (*Body, Love, Doctor Games*) by Ina Maria Philipps).

"Body, Love, Doctor Games"
(translated from German), the
books I referred to in the email
above.

Excerpt from an article about *Body, Love, Doctor Games*:

> "'Fathers do not devote enough attention to the clitoris and vagina of their daughters. Their caresses too seldom pertain to these regions, while this is the only way the girls can develop a sense of pride in their sex,' reads the booklet regarding 1-3 year olds. The authors rationalize, 'The child touches all parts of their father's body, sometimes arousing him. The father should do the same'"
> (https://www.lifesitenews.com/news/german-government-publication-promotes-incestuous-pedophilia-as-healthy-sex).

"Fri, Dec 31, 2010, 8:11 PM
Iain Bryson to Fred Taal [Dutch detective], US Citizen Services - Amsterdam, Brian, Kees de Vries
absoutely perfected, but i can do better: The New Guide to Making your girls perfect, sharing with anyone, and displaying your accomplishment to your friends. God she is beautiful.
This is everybody. There is no innocent Polish family. The culture itself is corrupting my child."

I didn't know for certain that they were using these particular manuals, though I did know that you had been having too much contact with and too much interest in your grandfather's private parts because you had been talking about it. I also knew that you had a nearly indescribable fear that something was going to happen to your "pee pee." I wasn't concerned with the details at this point. I used the analogy of a shotgun before, but my outcries were becoming more and more nuclear.

I knew it wasn't everybody, and that there was, in fact, an "innocent Polish family." The point I was trying to make was that all who were silent or oblivious were complicit, as was anybody who didn't care or didn't want to look, not really much different at all from those who wanted to deny the existence of, or the severity of, concentration camps during World War 2.

"Fri, Dec 31, 2010, 8:35 PM
Iain Bryson to US Citizen Services - Amsterdam, Kees de Vries, Fred Taal [Dutch detective], Brian
'I help mommy when she's sick,' says my daughter.
    My wife and daughter lay side by side. My wife demonstrates, then helps my daughter get undressed. She fakes an illness, or sickness, and emotionally manipulates my daughter into doing what is ever at the end of the age 1-3 book. I bet it is exciting to get ready for part two. the greater things in life, right? what could be better?
    Human Rights Atrocity, First Amendment Violation Catholic Pedophile Priests/Conning to Perfection, or do they know? of Three year old American Girl In Holland Dismissed as 'Not Likely;' still happening each second."

"Fri, Dec 31, 2010, 9:35 PM
Iain Bryson to Mary Corey [Journalist], info@rainn.org [anti-sexual violence organization], [Lawyer], [Doctor], Governor Rell, US Citizen Services - Amsterdam, Fred Taal [Dutch detective], Brian, [European Journalism Centre], Kees de Vries
http://ajp.psychiatryonline.org/cgi/reprint/155/9/1291.pdf , my book on Polish Catholic Family Perfect Beautiful Anticipation is much better.
I need someone to listen and tell me where my child is now.
http://www.ryszard-matuszewski.com/irena_barcz_persecuted,514,,list.html
My family, my three year old daughter..."

"DEAR Pope, please secure my daughter's safety. Fwd: Undeliverable: Catholic Church, God in Poland, Father, Grandfather, Brother, Husband, Mother, Sister.....It is all fair game and encouraged. Please Help.
Fri, Dec 31, 2010, 9:43 PM
Iain Bryson to benedettoxvi [Pope Benedict], US Citizen Services - Amsterdam, Brian, Fred Taal [Dutch detective], George N, bcc: Kees de Vries"

"In summary, Satanism has always been a dark cloud lurking in the background of the Roman Catholic Church. That cloud is in the process right now of overshadowing the Church, of overwhelming it with its power and taking control. Meanwhile the Satanic apologists, including those who pose as spokesmen for the Church, are working overtime to convince everyone that there is no such thing as Satan, and most especially no Satanic conspiracy, urging us to ignore the sulfurous odor that lingers around the current Church child abuse charges. Unfortunately, people are all too willing to ignore the obvious, and to stay within the safe cocoon of their belief that the rape of their children by priests is not part of a larger, more sinister pattern. It is this attitude that could soon allow Satan to take control of the Papacy itself, if nothing is done to stop him" (Kennedy 8).

I knew it wasn't only the Roman Catholic Church that had a problem with sexually abusing children, that people from all backgrounds and people who professed all kinds of faiths were included in this group. But the Catholic Church was the church that you were baptized in and the church that represented over ninety percent of Polish people. The Catholic Church was also the church that gave you a panic attack and led to you saying, "No amen, no amen, no amen," over and over again.

"I love you girls. happy new year babinski.
Fri, Dec 31, 2010, 11:12 PM
Iain Bryson to Agata Bryson"

"can we get a coffee?
Fri, Dec 31, 2010, 11:28 PM
Iain Bryson to Agata Bryson"

"I love you completely, fully, always.
Fri, Dec 31, 2010, 11:40 PM
Iain Bryson to Agata Bryson"

"can we go now, please?
Sat, Jan 1, 2011, 12:21 AM
Iain Bryson to Agata Bryson"

"I can see him and I need her to not be scared. god its [expletive] intense.
Sat, Jan 1, 2011, 2:13 AM
Iain Bryson to Kees de Vries"

"Sat, Jan 1, 2011, 2:44 AM
Iain Bryson to Kees de Vries
I had to plot out the entire evil entity. I had to assume the evil was all powerful, but now I am certain love is stronger. But, I also still know fear of non love is even stronger, and you have to be able to believe fully in the one to leave the other. the amount of pain one can willingly, knowingly, lustfully inflict is mind blowing. the worst torture I could not before imagine but now do better than my wife. she needs to know she is safe."

It wasn't until I was forced to sink my mind into the depths of evil that I began to have faith in a God who is good, a God who is just, a God who hates evil. This wasn't faith in the sense where one believes something because they are taught to believe, or faith because I needed something to believe to feel better. Rather, this was one of the most beautiful moments of my life, amidst the most brutal moment, whereby I became certain of the facts that the spiritual world exists, that light is stronger than darkness, and that there was a way to align myself with this victorious light.

"Can you tell me for certain my wife is receiving support?
Sat, Jan 1, 2011, 3:24 AM
Iain Bryson to Fred Taal [Dutch detective], Kees de Vries"

"i love you sis
Sat, Jan 1, 2011, 3:28 AM
Iain Bryson to Carrie"

I sent this short message to my sister because, at 3:30 in the morning, I felt a wave of empathy for all women. I remembered my own sexual abuse as a boy, and I wondered what she might have been subjected to as a girl. The wave of love that I felt envelop my body for my sister, my wife, my daughter, my sister-in-law, etc., made me want to lay down my life immediately for what I believed was true feminism – the elimination of childhood abuse.

"it is time for me to know that my wife is being helped so we can get through this. I see it all, and it is done. what is more important than this? I lived it in four or five consecutive days, but with a full understanding at each level. And to think,
Sat, Jan 1, 2011, 4:10 AM
Iain Bryson to Kees de Vries"

I was blown away, and I was writing it all down. I had reached some new levels of understanding, but getting there was not easy, and expressing it to others sounded crazy. After all, I was only getting to understand these things because my little girl was in the middle of it. I had to understand; there was no choice from my perspective. I cycled through some pretty tough things, including anger, frustration, and just missing you, and I slammed it all into the keyboard as it was happening, taking everyone else on the journey with me.

CHAPTER 56

HAPPY NEW YEAR?

Early on the morning of the first, I was experiencing the peace and the thrill that goes along with new understanding. It feels good when the fog dissipates, when things that hadn't made sense finally start to make sense. It is similar to the feeling of learning something like math, when at first it seems impossible and frustrating, but when you get it, then it feels natural and easy; it finally makes sense. No matter what it is, good or bad, it always seems better when it makes sense, and I felt good this morning.

I felt like I was on top of a mountain that I had just scaled over the past week. I was exhilarated. I wasn't angry, I wasn't confused, and all that I wanted was for my little girl not to be a part of it. *OK*, I understood, *the world is an ugly place. I have seen a level of darkness that I have never seen before, deep, terrible darkness, but I have also seen that its opposite is much stronger.*

The scriptures that I memorized as a child came forth to remind me that "God is love" (1 John 4:8), and that I could, "finally, be strong in the Lord and in the strength of His might" (Ephesians 6:10 NASB). I knew that true prayer could move mountains (Matthew 21:21). I knew that God was more powerful than the force that would intentionally torture children to gain control over them, the force that the Bible calls Satan, the devil, Lucifer, or the evil one.

While this gave me comfort, I also realized that I had written off God as nonexistent or unimportant for a long time, and that consequently I was not close to Him. I knew that He was the ultimate answer to this huge problem, but I didn't know much more than that. *At least*, I thought, *I can see that the light does provide the answer, but I must press on because they won't even tell me where my daughter is.*

I felt energized as I watched the sun come up. I just had one of the best and worst nights of my life, delving into both the depths of evil and the depths of God and being permitted a glimpse of love's victory. I thought I was about to get you back, that I had to be on the verge of it because how could God allow you to be in such a horrible situation?

I was out of cigarettes, but I had to wait for the store to open, I figured around 6:00 AM something would be open. It was beautiful watching the sun come up on New Year's Day. *It's a new year*, I thought, *this is the year that I will get my daughter back.* There was a new and certain hope this morning, and I was bouncing as I danced down the street.

Very few people were out on the streets, and I could quickly tell that most, if not all the stores, were still closed. I didn't want to go far; I just wanted cigarettes. I walked up the block a ways and ran into a few guys that seemed to be also looking for a store, two twenty-something drunk Polish guys, of course, and an older, homeless looking black man.

It was obvious that the Polish guys hadn't slept at all either the previous night; they were stumbling home after a party, still hootin' and hollerin.' All of them were looking for a coffee shop, and though I wasn't looking for pot, I knew that coffee shops had cigarette vending machines, and so I decided to journey with these guys for a bit.

The Polish guys were a little obnoxious, or maybe a little funny—I couldn't decide. I told them that I have a Polish wife, and they both reacted as if I were a winner. "Polish woman best," one of them proclaimed, humping the air. "Yes, I know," I responded, not giving credence to the sexual level of their jokes.

The other guy smelled a little bit, and though I never really saw homeless people in Holland, I got a sense that this guy was one of them. He had a bicycle, and he just wanted to get high on this fine Dutch morning. I felt a connection with him, we locked eyes, and I told him that I was up all night, researching and writing. I told him that I understood how the world works, and that it is horrible.

"How can we do this?" I begged for some help from him in understanding what was going on in this world. "How can we do this to our children?"

As his gaze matched mine, I could see wisdom in his eyes, and I hoped to gain some insight from this stranger. "We have to do something to get by, we have to do something to have fun in this life," he said matter-of-factly. I didn't know exactly what he meant, and I didn't want to. What I did feel was that he had confirmed that it is a crazy, survival of the fittest world, no matter what we try to tell ourselves.

"Sat, Jan 1, 2011, 10:04 AM
Mom to me
Iain,
email me and let me know you are ok. Your dad is working on final flight arrangements. Probably going to leave here Monday. I am going to store right now, but will check on you when I get back. I love you. Mom"

"Sat, Jan 1, 2011, 10:16 AM
Iain Bryson to Mom
no, just thinking, trying to figure out next step."

"Sat, Jan 1, 2011, 10:25 AM
Mom to me
Ok, but stay calm and your dad will be there to help soon."

"Jan 1, 2011, 10:27 AM
Iain Bryson to Mom
i am good. a little info would be nice"

Info like, where the heck are my wife and daughter? You all can't not know, can you? Are you helping me to find out, or not? Because I can't really tell. What is my dad coming over to "help" with, and why can't that "help" commence sooner? We really can't figure out what country they are in?

"Jan 1, 2011, 11:18 AM
Carrie to me
Love you too iain, what's going on over there!?"

"Jan 1, 2011, 11:34 AM
Iain Bryson to Carrie
Please dont worry about it now. I believe we will all be fine, and have been working toward that goal for five days. Love you"

I was livid; nearly a week later, and my own sister didn't seem to know that my daughter had been abducted. My annoyance was not aimed at my sister, because I didn't really expect anything from her to begin with. It was the authorities that needed to take action, and if push came to shove, I knew that my dad was on his way over to "help," and that had to mean we'd get a lawyer, because I didn't need any other help at the moment.

The next email was an attempt to express my exasperation, bluntly and shockingly, just another swing of my sledgehammer at the stone. So much was coming at me at once, and I was facing battle fatigue. I knew that I needed to pass the baton to someone else for a while, but nobody seemed willing to run my relay, and so I had to keep trying. I knew that collateral damage, especially to myself, was inevitable with the way I was communicating, but I felt like any attention was better than no attention.

Stopping or slowing to the pace of someone like Fred Taal would have been preposterous from my point of view, the one of a dad who was losing his daughter (and his wife) to an abusive cult. While the following "titles" seem like exaggerations or confabulations, in actuality they are mostly true.

The "mind control" that your mother informed me of, the kind that could force an otherwise loving mother to take her child back to a "cult" for further abuse is trauma–based mind control. It is the same kind of "mind control" that the CIA used in MK Ultra and "Manchurian Candidate" research (see Marks, Noblitt, O'Brien, and Barnett). For me, this was a "holocaust," and my girls were smack dab in the middle of it.

"Sat, Jan 1, 2011 12:43 AM
Iain Bryson to Brian, Kees de Vries, US Citizen Servies – Amsterdam, George N, Kristin
Manchurian Candidate Gone Wild Part two
Systematic Holocaust of Generations of Women
My three year old American citizen daughter
Intentional Dissociative Schizophrenic Disorder. Yes it is as [expletive] up as it sounds, but incomprehensible to 'ordinary' people. Heart Disease of Infants. Pervasive. Ingrained. Expected. Respected

First country with mandatory chemical castration
forces you to really figure out how to do it well.
you are so proud of your girls. come on help me please."

The "heart disease of infants" comment was not one that I had researched well enough to report on, and it's not "dissociative schizophrenic disorder," but "dissociative identity disorder," also known as "multiple personality disorder," or "possession," and maybe in the future to be known as "Cult and Ritual Trauma Disorder" (Noblitt and Noblitt, 2014, 239), but I was still trying to wrap my head around it all.

It was here that I first came across Dr. Colin Ross, a trauma and mind control expert and author of many books. I began to see that cult abuse, and the effects thereof, were a thing people were researching, identifying, and treating. The purpose of the Colin A. Ross Institute for Psychological Trauma, among others, is to understand the type of phenomena that I had been witness to with your mom.

I saw that this wasn't rare, but that it also wasn't well known. I wondered how I could have gone through six years of college education and received a degree in sociology, and even briefly worked as a Child Protection Officer with the Department of Children and Families, without ever hearing of the very large social problem that is ritual/organized abuse. I wondered why it wasn't something that everyone was talking about and ready to wage war against.

"http://www.empty-memories.nl/dis_89/Ross_structuredinterview.pdf-----------guaranteed....
[C. Ross DID Interview]
Jan 1, 2011, 1:26 PM
Iain Bryson to me, Kees de Vries"

"Sat, Jan 1, 2011, 2:16 PM
Iain Bryson to Agata Bryson
You said you are in The Hague at a shelter. The police say you at Jackie's. You told me you would meet me with our daughter nearly three days ago, and you have not answered my questions. Agata? As a father and husband, I need to know where you are. Please tell me. I love you."

"Abduction/Endangered child
Sat, Jan 1, 2011, 2:53 PM
Iain Bryson to Jackie DeLuca, Mickey DeLuca
The Department of State is filing Conspiracy charges against you. And it's certain."

I was just trying to scare them, mostly, but I also wanted justice. They both knew that your mom was planning to "escape," as Jackie had removed several bags of clothes from our apartment, and Mickey and Jackie both pretended that you were going to the library, which you were not. I figured that their worry or fear would add to the smoke, that someone would finally think to investigate the fire.

"Sat, Jan 1, 2011, 3:08 PM
Iain Bryson to talkback@the-sun.co.uk [Newspaper]
Attachments
Iain Avery Bryson (United States) June 1, 1977
Agata Bryson --------maiden name: Makowska (Poland) July 11, 1982
Adelle Avery Bryson (United States) January 30, 2007
The Hague, The Netherlands
iain.bryson@gmail.com

Slavomir Wojchiech Makowska (Incest Perpetrator)
Pilsudskiego 2/6
Stargard Szczecinski
Poland 73-110

January 1, 2011
My wife and daughter have been missing since Monday evening, and are both in danger for their lives.
The Dutch police will not let me know whether they are in Holland, or whether the[y] have fled to Poland. On the day they left, the Dutch police told me they were in The Hague, staying at an abused women and children shelter. Yesterday, they told me they were staying with 'friends.' They will not confirm either way. They act as if the issue does not exist. Sexual abuse cannot be investigated on children under three in Holland, thereby guaranteeing a successful, smooth transition into the second training manual, recommended by a German doctor and executed to perfection in my Polish family. Child Protective Services is a joke in this country. The response from the Dutch is 'what are you complaining about?' and 'What would you like us to do?' Well, the simple answer is that I need to know, I have to know that they are safe, and they will not even confirm that they are aware of their whereabouts…"

"Sat, Jan 1, 2011, 4:00 PM
Iain Bryson to Kees de Vries, bcc: US Citizen Services - Amsterdam, bcc: Fred Taal [Dutch detective]
Kees,
Agata was keeping a journal for the week or so before they left. She has never done that before to my knowledge. I was surprised when I found it. It is in Polish and written quickly and tough to get translated.
She says 'bye' a few times.
The police are giving out no information. I do not know if she is here, though the two emails I got said yes, and the police said that they think so.
If she is in Poland, my daughter turns four soon, which is when stage two of sex training begins. This is antithetical to all I believe in.
Iain"

"Sat, Jan 1, 2011, 5:47 PM
Iain Bryson to Agata Bryson
this is not good for our child agata."

"http://www.feminist.com/resources/ourbodies/viol_incest.html........they need help. this is serious
and she believes i will not even get an evaluation? wow
Sat, Jan 1, 2011, 7:10 PM
Iain Bryson to Kees de Vries"
["One common form of sexual abuse of children is incest, which has been defined as sexual contact that
occurs between family members. Most incest occurs between older male relatives and younger female
children in families of every class and color... A sexually abusive relationship is one over which a child or
young woman has no control. A trusted family member or friend uses his power, as well as a child's love and
dependence, to initiate sexual contact and often to ensure that the relationship continues and remains
secret."]

"last one. Focus for a moment on Adelle, you and I dancing to Up Up an Away.
Sat, Jan 1, 2011, 8:17 PM
Iain Bryson to Agata Bryson"

"I have your sick little sex training books so throw that [expletive] out now. i bet he's anxious to get
started with the 4-6 year book. what a 'pecial time. mommy, you did good. a little girl and that makes
your father feel like a man. Wow.
Sat, Jan 1, 2011, 9:19 PM
Iain Bryson to Agata Bryson"

"Sun, Jan 2, 2011, 1:27 AM
Iain Bryson to Agata Bryson
Soap irritation, you say, causing Adelle to scream and not be able to pee. What a great job baby. Proud of
you. And then it just goes away when your father is not around. Wow, some soap irritation. Plus you already
know the doctor is not necessary or if it is you are helping to progress some crazy psychotic condition, but
dont worry i know how to go after a doctor. Your mom's friend huh. and adelle is having terrors because you
know she is and she is afraid of the dentist cause you know. and you cry when your dad has to go to the
doctor because he hates it more than anyone you know. He brought you a cup of tea once. You cherish that
moment. Wow. I make breakfast and play with our daughter everyday for two hours before you come out of
your coma, trying to act as if it's still morning."

I was frustrated with your mother, and I wished that she had just brought it all plainly out into
the open, even though I knew that the nature of the problem precluded her from doing so. Mostly,
I was just venting to her; she was still the only partner I had, and I was disappointed at how things
were going down. She had done more than she should've been able to do, warning me while
simultaneously admitting that she had Stockholm Syndrome and was going to take you back to a
cult.

"Abduction In Progress
Sun, Jan 2, 2011, 11:05 AM
Iain Bryson to webmaster [Dutch Police], Fred Taal [Dutch detective], US Citizen Services -
Amsterdam
Iain Avery Bryson (United States) June 1, 1977
Agata Bryson --------maiden name: Makowska (Poland) July 11, 1982
Adelle Avery Bryson (United States) January 30, 2007

The Hague, The Netherlands
iain.bryson@gmail.com

Slavomir Wojchiech Makowska (Incest Perpetrator)
Pilsudskiego 2/6
Stargard Szczecinski
Poland 73-110

January 1, 2011

My wife and daughter have been missing since Monday evening, and are both in danger for their lives. The Dutch police will not let me know whether they are in Holland, or whether the[y] have fled to Poland. On the day they left, the Dutch police told me they were in The Hague, staying at an abused women and children shelter. Yesterday, they told me they were staying with 'friends.' They will not confirm either way. They act as if the issue does not exist. Sexual abuse cannot be investigated on children under three in Holland, thereby guaranteeing a successful, smooth transition into the second training manual, recommended by a German doctor and executed to perfection in my Polish family. Child Protective Services is a joke in this country. The response from the Dutch is 'what are you complaining about?' and 'What would you like us to do?' Well, the simple answer is that I need to know, I have to know that they are safe, and they will not even confirm that they are aware of their whereabouts.

There is widespread Dissociative Schizophrenic Disorder. There is no ability to think any other way tha[n] the way which is programmed beginning at birth, encouraged by the Catholic church, and perpetuated by a male predator population which has determined that females are on this plane for their pleasure. They need to teach them early, consistently, and correctly. They do not want my daughter to miss this important period of growth and learning, and are determined to get her there at any cost. The male 'friend' is a sexual predator, who smokes heroin in front of his three year old daughter. He is a convicted felon, a fugitive from Denmark, and he was denied residence in the United States because he provided false information on his immigration form. I need to know that they are receiving support, and i cannot be certain.

Prior to fleeing our home, my wife emphatically stated she had to go to Poland for either Christmas or New Years. She had just spent three months in Poland, with our daughter, where levels and methods of sexual abuse progressed and became more instilled in both my wife and daughter. My daughter is turning four years old this month; incest is systematically programmed into children, and the Second Manual for ages 4-6 is an exciting time for my wife's family in Poland. I cannot be assured that my wife has not returned due to the immense pressure upon her to sacrifice our daughter's innocence and childhood. To permanently distort her beliefs and thoughts about love, life and sex.

My wife and daughter disappeared in The Hague last week. I have been attempting to get in touch with authorities, and have been unable to obtain a location from the Dutch Police. My wife was raised into Generational Incest; both my wife and daughter have been sexually abused. My wife is psychologically abusing our daughter. She is currently struggling with the issue of our daughter, uncertain about whether to return to a life of incest, or whether she can leave. She is having difficulties seeing the reality I see clearly now, where child abuse and incest should be non-existent. She knows on some level, but she is unable to believe, and she is terrified from a lifetime of molestation. My wife has attempted to provide me with signs, begging for help, but unable to state the circumstances, which I was previously unable to see. Now I see this more clearly than anyone else in this world. I need to secure their safety now.

My daughter is exhibiting every sign of sexual abuse. The Dutch government will not examine or question anyone regarding this matter. My wife has to know she has support; the internal drive towards 'Father' is too great to deny if she cannot be certain she can see what is actually 'real.' She cannot come to the realization that she is not evil, but that this man has taken and plans to take everything from both her and our daughter. Please assist with this matter. It has been stifled by a lethargic, tolerant view of human nature, ownership of females, incest sanctioned by state and religion. All the best and Happy New Year, Iain Bryson"

"**I need to know where my daughter is, and without question, no bull, by 11 please. that's enough time. I dont need an address or anything. Not trying to find you but just want proof of life**
Sun, Jan 2, 2011, 1:33 AM
Iain Bryson to Agata Bryson"

"**i LOVE Agata Bryson. I LOVE her. There is NOTHING that could change that.**
Sun, Jan 2, 2011, 1:00 PM
Iain Bryson to Agata Bryson"

"**Could you think about this? She is trying to get out. She knows she is done. Or, she is going to hurt our daughter. She has shown me and I didn't get it. She is not this, but has to be. My God**
Sun, Jan 2, 2011, 1:08 PM
Iain Bryson to Kees de Vries, Brian, US Citizen Services - Amsterdam
http://www.pdprogramme.org.uk/assets/resources/151.pdf

I know this is what is going on. I know it all. I am systematically analyzing it, taking it apart and reassembling over and over. I am better at this than anyone out there. I got philosophy, training manuals, real stories with dialogue from every perspective, but especially my wife and child's; imagine what I was missing by not understanding enough Polish. Wonder what visual cues are in my home right now, but already know at least ten. I wonder what my wife says to my stepmother and how much my wife is really doing. If I were running this, my wife would not have much actual 'free will' at all. Why would she want it? She wouldn't cause it is way too [expletive] hard, especially when her husband cannot pick up on all that is happening right in front of him. It was too insane for me. I was too blindly in love and focusing on other things.

I believe I began writing, reading and researching fervently a few months ago because I needed answers. I told Agata she was just making me stronger and that is all this [expletive] has done throughout our relationship. I told her what she was. I diagnosed her, I taught her how to parent. I saw her and it confused and frustrated the [expletive] out of me. I told her I could see the girl I love, but that this was not her and I was [expletive] terrified.

I could tell she was mad at me, and in a way I couldn't place. I am her husband and Adelle's father, and I was going to let this happen to them, and I did, and she was bitter and confused as to how I couldn't see. It always feels too hard to do, no matter what the challenge is; it is all on the same spectrum at different places. The problem is, nobody can see the entire spectrum at any and nobody can apply that to the variations which exist in the human psyche. The mind has to block it out to protect itself. I guess I am lucky because my mind does not shut down unless I ask it to. If it needs something like a break, a change of focus, or nourishment, it tells me. In the past, the pain was from things rattling around that I could not figure out......too many big ones at a time. I have to know, or I have to know at least what I do not, or maybe how to figure it out if I do not, and what I just cannot know. And know I got 'cannot know where they are for sure' rattling around with a clear head. It sucks but it is powerful."

Ritual (organized) abuse is outrageous and knowing that my wife and now my daughter were victims, and that I was losing control over the situation, was extremely difficult. I absolutely hated what I was being forced to confront, and I hated the non-reaction that I was getting. Everyone was playing right into the hands of your abusers, just as your mom had forewarned.

I felt the need to reassure my wife that I was not angry with her, and that I was still on her side. The next email to her was an attempt to ensure that she knew I was not going to abandon her, that I loved her even through this, even though I did feel anger toward her briefly.

"Please realize that I get it. Finally. The rest was me cycling through everything systematically, to the fullest extent I could. I do not blame you no matter what. Not at all. I see you and I love you.
Sun, Jan 2, 2011, 1:16 PM
Iain Bryson to Agata Bryson, bcc: Kees de Vries, bcc: Brian"

CHAPTER 57

"I NEED TO KNOW IF YOU CAN BELIEVE ME OR NOT"

"Sun, Jan 2, 2011, 1:26 PM
Mom to me, Dad
Iain

I spoke to Dave from US Consulate OFFIce a short time ago. He has set up for you and your dad to go to US Consulate Office when your dad arrives this Wednesday. You are to meet with a Stewart Wilson phone # 020-575-5336. Also, you might meet with Juan Gamboa who you have previously spoken to. His # 020-575-5334.
I asked your dad to get Adelle's birth certificate from New London Town Hall tomorrow and bring it with him. Dave said these gentlemen will find out if she is still in the country and help you. Dave said he understood Agata is at a woman's shelter in The Hague. Maybe because you had told him that.

The address for the US Consulate Office is
#19 Museumplein, Amsterdam. He said it is widely known so a taxi would get you there easily. You should plan on meeting your dad at the airport Wednesday am at 10:30am.
 The US Embassy phone is 070-310-2209 and you dial 1 for an emergency. Then ask them to contact the US Consulate Office and locate Dave for you if you need it.
Please keep yourself together so you can be there for Adelle when we find her. I love you. Mom
If you need to speak to Dave prior to your dad getting there, give him a call at the US Embassy number. Tell them you need to be connected to the US Consulate/Dave."

"Sun, Jan 2, 2011, 1:26 PM
Iain Bryson to Kees de Vries
Everything she did was a sign I could not piece together. In the end, she was listening to music, talking, acting, doing everything she could to show me how [expletive] it was. I told her I saw a demon and it was no different than a heroin or crack addiction. The mind can do quite a lot, and when it is cooking, it sure can fool you if you let it."

"Sun, Jan 2, 2011, 1:33 PM
Iain Bryson to Dad, Mom, Kees de Vries, Brian
I cycled and will be fine, stronger than ever and ready for them. My own feelings are figured out, as are theirs. I can easily focus on theirs."

"Sun, Jan 2, 2011, 1:37 PM
Iain Bryson to Kees de Vries, Brian, Mom, Dad
what an addiction/affliction that was. Sorry. Let's get them some help please."

Though they may not have known, I was referring again to "Liar," and the lyrics, "I'll come to you like an affliction, but I'll leave you like an addiction...," and what it felt to have to get to know the devil-looking character in the music video, in as much as he was the latest embodiment of your mother. But I also knew that your mother was not the real monster, and I wanted help.

"Sun, Jan 2, 2011, 1:38 PM
Iain Bryson to Kees de Vries, Mom, Brian, Dad
Adelle and I rock out to Dave Matthews. She knows all the lyrics and we dance every day."

In other words, "Come on guys. I am Adelle's best friend. You can't possibly believe that Agata had to get her away from me for her safety, can you? Can you?!"

"Sun, Jan 2, 2011, 1:51 PM
Iain Bryson to Kees de Vries, Mom, Dad, Brian
I confronted that demon. I told her. I held her and she has pictures to prove it. I got in her face and said the worst things I could think of. Now I have way worse things to think about, but there is also no more confusion, just an infinity of possibilities for exploration. She could have gotten rid of me, but she doesn't have the ability. She is my wife and Adelle's mother first but she is not strong enough, and neither was I."

"Sun, Jan 2, 2011, 1:59 PM
Iain Bryson to Mom, Dad, Kees de Vries, Brian
I prayed out loud with her, for her, for the first time in my adult life. I was going to do anything, and I told her. I told her to kill me if she thought she would fool me. I wondered if she was, but then my mind quickly and oddly came to 'no' every time. She was listening off and on obsessively with headphones in her phone back and forth from Polish radio to Drake's new album. Drake is her singing to me. She is pleading with me."

"Sun, Jan 2, 2011, 2:01 PM
Iain Bryson to Dad, Brian, Mom, Kees de Vries
Look at Dave Matthew's 'SAVE ME' Lyrics. please. We just have to help them now so I can continue, or else this evil of all evils prevails with my daughter, the most wonderful thing I have ever known."

Thinking about your little girl as the victim of incest with your wife's father, and your wife before her, can have the effect of overloading your brain with too much to process at once. I had an enormous problem with my daughter being victimized. The next email is a demonstration of the aforementioned facts, and a journey into some of my processing. It is blasphemous, and it is untrue; I was being sardonically facetious in my frustration.

"Sun, Jan 2, 2011, 2:10 PM
Iain Bryson to Dad, Mom, Brian, Kees de Vries
So, Mary, sweet Mary, if you were pregnant with Jesus as a virgin, you can help prove to me that it is your husband's job to get me pregnant, and that sex with my father doesn't really mean anything. It is pure after all. Sex with the Father is the most beautiful thing in the world, right?"

"Sun, Jan 2, 2011, 2:14 PM
Iain Bryson to Kees de Vries, Brian, Mom, Dad
When Adelle tells me she loves me, I say 'I know you do.' Agata tells me she likes it. She is trying to tell me in everything she does."

I knew that my relationship with you was being questioned, not because of a guilty conscience, but because your mother told me that this was going to happen. My relationship with you was one that I wanted to bottle and sell to the world, because it was amazing. I begged the police to just put me in a room with you and then put you in a room with your mother and see what happens, because I knew that if they had done this you would have clung to me for dear life.

"Sun, Jan 2, 2011, 2:16 PM
Iain Bryson to Mom, Dad, Kees de Vries
I told Agata it was driving me crazy that Adelle was telling her she loves her two hundred times a day. Agata kissed her every ten seconds when they were together. Sick. Adelle wanted me in her room with the door closed constantly."

**"Sun, Jan 2, 2011, 2:21 PM
Iain Bryson to Mom, Dad, Brian, Kees de Vries**
'up up and away' again dave matthews is the song adelle agata and i sung and danced to every day when she was not split into blind devotion between us and pure evil."

**"Sun, Jan 2, 2011, 2:27 PM
Iain Bryson to Kees de Vries, Dad, Mom, Brian**
When I lived in Poland, the panic attacks were being tested out to the fullest. Agata spoke for the doctor for me, via her mother, getting me twenty milligrams of clonazepam and two other crazy psychotropics which she will not talk about anymore. And what doctor would give anyone this amount of Klonopin, I would ask her, but at the same time I would take a bit more to ease the frustration."

**"Sun, Jan 2, 2011, 2:43 PM
Mom to me**
Iain, You need to write these down and stop with the emails. I understand trying to get it out of your head, but not broadcasting via emails. Wait for your dad to get there to help you. You understand the world of cyberspace."

I knew that everyone who was advising me to stop sending emails was correct, in a way, but the thought of you being abused, or even just away from your home, for extra minutes, days, and weeks literally drove me crazy, as if mosquitos were attacking me and the swarm increased with the passage of time. Not having you and having what your mom told me would happen actually happen was the worst pain I had ever felt.

**"Sun, Jan 2, 2011, 2:48 PM
Iain Bryson to Mom**
She told me she 'was' going to Poland for either Christmas or New Year's. I have to believe that is a possibility, and a likely b[ut] not certain one."

I was reminding my mom that I had told her that your mom told me she was taking you back to Poland, and trying to remind her how terrified I was beforehand. I wanted her to remember those emails, because I thought it would help her not be distracted by the red herring, though I thought it almost impossible for my mother to be distracted by such an obvious trick and evident lie.
I wanted you and your mom to be at a shelter for abused people in The Netherlands. If only I knew this, I would have been able to take a breath, because at least you wouldn't have been with your abusers in Poland.

**"Sun, Jan 2, 2011, 3:01 PM
Mom to me**
When you meet Wednesday with the consulate they will help you locate her. Hang in there. I know it sounds like a long time but take it moment by moment. Your daughter is fine and we will all be reunited. Focus on that right now. I love you"

How did my mom know that you were fine? This struck me as weird because I knew that it wasn't true – there wasn't a worse possible predicament that you could be in. I knew that my mom was either trying to console me in a strange way, or that she was not telling me the truth. Had she already been infected by the sweet smell of the red herring? Had your mother gotten to her?
The following email is from an American coworker from Laureate Online Education who was engaged to a Dutch woman, and so, also an expat. I spoke to him on the phone about trying to locate you to see if you were in a shelter.

**"Sun, Jan 2, 2011, 7:30 PM
Tim W. to me**
Iain,

Good to talk to you. All things considered, you sound as though you are doing well enough...enough being the operative word. Just to clarify, I didn't mean to sound overly critical on the phone. I am simply trying to talk through things with you so that I know where you stand and what's happened. As I had said on the phone, it's only fair for me to also assume that you could be fabricating everything because I do not know your wife and I have never met your daughter, nor have I been a witness to anything that's been happening recently. So I only have your descriptions to believe. On the other hand, if what you say is true then it goes without saying that the situation is extremely serious and extremely critical. If I can help you to work through the situation then I will try my best to do so. I do care about you as a person Iain and definitely would not want anybody to be in the mess that it seems you, and your daughter, are in.

To find out whether Agata is currently at a women's shelter, you can try a couple things. First, contact the Steunpunt Huiselijk Geweld in Den Haag. If she is currently in a shelter ("opvang") then it is your right as the Father in the Netherlands to know about this. Typically, the father is informed via a phone call wherein it is stated that so and so is currently at a women's shelter (location obviously not disclosed) and everything is okay with your child. If Agata is at such a place then you should have already recieved this call. Nonetheless, it is probably worth checking.

Second, you can call the AMK (Advies en Meldpunt Kindermishandeling = Adivce and Registration point for Child Abuse) to report your concerns about Adelle. This is a must do and you can utilize the email you've sent me which describes your concerns. The AMK are obligated to check into these allegations if your wife and daughter are in a women's shelter. The contact information for the AMK and the Steunpunt Huiselijk Geweld is pasted below.

Advies- en Meldpunt Kindermishandeling Haaglanden
Neherkade 3054
2521 VX Den Haag
telefoon: (070) 346 97 17   (070) 346 97 17   fax: (070) 362 29 05

Steunpunt Huiselijk Geweld Regio Den Haag
Naam: Steunpunt Huiselijk Geweld Regio Den Haag
Postcode en plaats: 2491 Den Haag
Telefoon: 0900 044 33 22   0900 044 33 22
Website: http://www.eerstehulpbijhuiselijkgeweld.nl/

Het Steunpunt Huiselijk Geweld is een telefonisch steunpunt, dat
bereikbaar is op telefoonnummer 0900 044 33 22 begin_of_the_skype_highlighting
 0900 044 33 22   end_of_the_skype_highlighting.

If you need anyone to help you translate something from Dutch into English then let me know. If you have any other questions then let me know. Keep me updated about how things progress Iain. I certainly hope that you are able to find the clarity that your looking for and have things come to a close, with your daughter's best interests in mind, as soon as humanly possible. Hang in there buddy!
- T"

I wondered why the women's shelters had not contacted me, but I figured it was most likely because you were not actually in a women's shelter. I had no idea where you were, and nobody seemed interested in telling me. Did anybody know? Did they know that you were being stolen from your protective parent and just think it was a good thing because of how it was framed by the other parent who had the incentive to frame it exactly that way?

"Sun, Jan 2, 2011, 5:13 PM
Bob McCoy to me
Dear Iain,
　　Your note horrifies and perplexes me... I will pray. It is not only the only thing I can do...it is the best thing I can do.
　　Meanwhile, I have many questions... Please know that the door to my office is always (schedule permitting) open.
　　Give me a call or email me.
Warmly
Bob McCoy

Groton Bible Chapel
66 Tollgate Road
Groton, CT
Pastoral Staff"

Hearing from Pastor McCoy was like receiving a warm embrace, but I needed answers too, and at the time I needed them from someone with the ability to stop you from leaving the country or call an Amber Alert if you had already left.

"Sun, Jan 2, 2011, 7:48 PM
Mom to me
Iain
Hoping you are resting to the best of your ability.
Jeremiah called. He said the best advice he can give is for you to present yourself as a father that is in control of his faculties and to be respectful to the authorities. I know you have been doing this and will do your best. Your dad will be there Wed am at 10:30. Can you meet him and go to the US Consulate. They are expecting you two. He is bringing Adelle's birth certificate. Write your thoughts down, but serve yourself better by gathering your thoughts before emailing out. This is a crazy time, but you must maintain your self control. If you need to email me or your dad that's fine, but not everyone else. Your communications to Police etc have to be cohesive and make sense to the outside world. I love you more than words can contain and I need you to take care of yourself. You are MY son, so how you are feeling about Adelle is how I feel about you. I will be at work tomorrow. I will call in the am before I leave. I love you. Mom"

"Sun, Jan 2, 2011, 10:42 PM
Brian to me
what is the latest news man - I'm having phone issues and feel like I'm getting bits and pieces through the email...
What day does your dad come in?"

"Sun, January 2, 2011, 1:27:36 PM
Iain Bryson to Jeremiah
u sure there is nothing you can do? i would not ask if i were not certain and out of real options
    i cannot ascertain where she is. if she is here, start proceedings now regarding whatever to get it going
    if she is not here i need help with the hague convention child abduction package. my wife took all our documents, birth cert, etc and a lawyer can get it and demand she return to go to court here. i have volumes of this [expletive]. too much to focus on at once.
    First, is she in HOlland and where. Second, how [d]o i start legal proceeding.
    this is going to get national/intl attention and i am spending my life to shut this [expletive] down. i have gone to hell and learned about the devil and i am a [expletive] expert beyond comprehension.
    cult mind control. forcing children to go nuts so they will do and believe anything"

My cousin, I imagined, *has known me since we were children, and now he is an FBI agent, so surely he will help me with what little I am asking him. Why wouldn't he help me, even if it were to just refer me to the person in the United States government who did deal with abducted American citizen little girls?* I didn't understand what his problem was; *is he just a weakling, or is his nose also being guided by that delicious scent of red herring?* If I worked for one of the largest federal law enforcement agencies in the world, I would have taken at least one day off from work just to help my cousin if his daughter was kidnapped— that much I knew.

"Mon, Jan 3, 2011, 4:32 AM
Iain Bryson to Brian
i am good. i see it all, and all too clearly, and just want them back and/or i need them to be safe. i have it figured out, and this will happen. i [am] 'excited' and terrified at the same time. i have to focus on the 'small' picture, but i can see the entire picture. i just do not give a [expletive] and have one objective right now. The rest will come.....it has already, and i believe it will get us some peace and allow me to work. love ya man."

"Mon, Jan 3, 2011, 7:39 AM
Mom to me
Iain, Leaving for work now.
The only thing I can fall back on or draw from is knowing that God loves you, Agata and Adelle more than life itself. I have to believe that He is keeping you safe and He is keeping Adelle safe. He knows where she is. That is the bottom line for me. Is having that faith that if we do our part in the way we know how that I have to trust Him. I don't know anything else and it is only that that allows me right now to get up in the morning and to go to work.
Your dad is on schedule to arrive Wednesday and the two of you have an appt with the US Consulate, Stewart Wilson.
I will call about midnight your time tonight. I love you. Mom"

"Mon, Jan 3, 2011, 3:37 pm
Iain Bryson to Brian
I need to know if you can believe me or not..."

"Fwd: from my best friend.
Jan 3, 2011, 6:42 PM
Iain Bryson to Kees de Vries, bcc: allyopolis [back up email to myself]
---------- **Forwarded message** ----------
Tue, Jan 4, 2011 at 12:39 AM
Brian to me
Not sure what you mean as far as believe you or not. I'm 100% on board that you have diagnosed this correctly... Some of this is so bizarre, perhaps hard to swallow at first (I am past this stage), but I know you can pick up on things no one else can... Similar to the way I can understand my daughter, but other[s] cannot while she is at her current stage of talking. I would still recommend focusing most of the energy and 'case building' toward the father for now. I think that will serve you[r] best interest (i.e. Adele's) in the immediate future, as opposed to casting a larger net...though this needs to be done, but first things first. I haven't done the research you have as far as the specific disorders and symptoms, but again I have utmost confidence that you will nail it.

Below is pretty interesting, I'm still not sure about the sexual energy toward the mother or the incest tendency though, I don't think I'll ever be able to come to terms with that - perhaps I am thinking about consummation too much, but I'm having a hard time grasping either as a far reaching concept... Maybe nature/nurture issue - On another note, I've been trying some new things with the kids and you have really helped me revisit some things and some cues I've been sending. I think this will pay tremendous dividends in setting the appropriate environment for the kids.
Call you soon..."

CHAPTER 58

"AGATA AND ADELLE IS WITH AGATA'S FAMILY IN POLAN"

"Tue, Jan 4, 2011, 5:55 AM
Mickey DeLuca to me
Ian, I knew nothing about Agata's plans to run away the day I was over at your house, I would never have helped her, as someone who has a son that I have not seen since he was 4 days old because his mother went into hiding with him, so I would never help some one to do that to another person. Had I known she would do what she did, I would have said something to you, but if you've decided you that I had anything with Agata's escape to do your a BIG joke and then there is nothing I can do about it, but I know that she is not in The Netherlands anymore, so if she tells you that she is still here, she's lying.

she wrote Jackie and told her that her dad and brother in law came and picked her up, so she used us to in her escape and the reason for me not coming back, was that Jackie called me and told that Agata had been picked up and was going to Poland, and we did not know anything about her plans, but you believe what ever you want and if you want to accuse me and Jackie for having something to do with Agata's escape then have fun with that. ok."

I've already discussed that I didn't believe it was possible that he "knew nothing," for the simple fact that he held his phone up to his ear and arranged plans for you and your mother to meet his wife and daughter at the library, which was closed. While it was possible that your mom had used him, this still didn't let him off the hook for helping your mom "escape," even if he didn't know you were going to Poland.

I couldn't trust that he knew where you were, or that he would tell me the truth if he did know, but I also believed you were not in The Netherlands. This was where I learned that it was not a bus that took you back to the cult, but your grandfather, the same one who had just sent you back to me with bruising and vaginal pain, the same one who authored the red herring... the thief!

"Tue, Jan 4, 2011, 7:10 AM
Iain Bryson to Fred Taal [Dutch detective], Mom, Dad, Brian, US Citizen Services - Amsterdam
Below is an email I received from the man who assisted my wife in her escape. He says she is in Poland.

Iain Bryson
Newtonplein 25
The Hague, The Netherlands 2562JV
(From Mickey DeLuca, who assisted my wife in her escape. Heroin smoker. Smokes it in front of his child. Fugitive. Not granted US residence; lied on Federal Forms. Felon.
[same body of text as email sent from Mickey DeLuca to me on Jan, 2011, 5:55 AM]"

"**Physical Evidence//// Abduction**
Jan 4, 2011, 7:54 AM
Iain Bryson to Dad, Brian, US Citizen Services - Amsterdam

Now the guy who helped my wife escape claims he did not even know that she was not going to the library as she stated. Well, that cannot be true. So, just another coincidence. She did the entire thing without his knowledge. And, his wife called twenty minutes later, while we were chatting, and she said she was at the library with my wife and daughter. And you don't have a clue this was the plan? Are you sure you are gonna stick with that?

Please take a look:

Once again, I am certain my wife and daughter are the victims of mind control. Monarch mind control to be more precise. Rape trauma syndrome. Wonderful stuff. I have physical evidence and video. My daughter is an 'artist,' and I know her, so there is everything. Incest. My wife and daughter.

i have polish video. Adelle at church being given to her grandpa, or maybe to me, but he knew I did not want that. I have three dvd's so far. I need an 'expert' to look at this. visual cues. audio cues. all around them. controlling them in ways nobody can imagine."

One video was of your baptism in Stargard, one was of you and Cicely, and the third was the one where your mom asks, "Did they beat her?" and your grandfather responds, "You know we did." None of these were proof, per se, but I was just trying to get people to talk to me.

It was like trying to hail a taxi with your hands tied behind your back, wearing a neck brace, with dark sunglasses on. It was as if I was the boy who woke up as a bug in Kafka's *The Metamorphosis*, and while I could hear them, all they heard was whatever language a bug speaks, even though I thought I was annunciating my words clearly enough.

It was like I was trying to convince the fire department to come to my house when they'd already been warned that I was going to call in a false alarm, and also that I was a big jerk. I didn't have any real physical evidence other than you, and I knew that, but if they would have come to see what I had, or even just cared enough to find out where you were, then that might have started an investigation or at least generated a report that I could've held in my hands.

"Tue, Jan 4, 2011, 8:29 AM
Iain Bryson to Mickey DeLuca
the problem with that, Mickey my friend, is that you are wrong. You cannot convince me, because I know. I am not asking for your opinion. I am telling you."

"Tue, Jan 4, 2011, 8:36 AM
Dad to me
Is this enough for the Netherlands to demand her return to The Netherlands (child abduction) for investi[gation]"

"RE: USA.gov Inquiry [T20110101002A]
Tue, Jan 4, 2011, 8:48 AM
USA.gov1@mail.fedinfo.gov to me
Thank you for contacting USA.gov seeking help with locating your wife and daughter.
Unfortunately, the U.S. government is not able to assist with locating non U.S. citizens.
If you are looking for assistance from the United States, you may wish to contact a U.S. Embassy. To access a listing of U.S. Embassies around the world, please visit the U.S. Department of State's (DOS) website at:
http://www.usembassy.gov/
We hope you find this information helpful.
Regards,
USA.gov Citizen Response Team"

"Tue, Jan 4, 2011, 10:23 AM
Mickey DeLuca to me
What ever, you and Agata are to dumb for me, so you charge me if you think you'll get anything out of that and you must be psychic since you know better then me what I did or didn't do, but good luck, dumb as."

While it was kind of funny that he was calling your mom and I "dumb," to me, he was just a little boy who had stolen candy and was trying to stick to his story even though the candy could be seen bulging from his pockets. Being "psychic" wasn't the only way I could know; I was there when he set me up with his wife to make me think that you and your mom were going to the library right down the street. I wished I had spent less time with this man in my life.

"Tue, Jan 4, 2011, 10:24 AM
Iain Bryson to Mickey DeLuca
 sure thing bro. you must think you know me."

"Tue, Jan 4, 2011, 10:24 AM
Iain Bryson to Mickey DeLuca
 your kid cannot speak. molester."

Mickey's wife did not anger me; I was only frustrated with her. I believed that she was also a victim because, at the least, Mickey was secretly taking their daughter on heroin runs. I knew that she could easily be deceived by your mother as well.

Cicely couldn't speak, and she was around your age, and I was teaching you to spell, and to add and subtract. She still wore diapers, and she wasn't good at holding onto the swing by herself. These were red flags to me; it seemed that her normal development had been stunted.

I shouldn't have called him a "molester" because I did not know with enough certainty, but I was mad at him. I would have bet the farm to have his daughter evaluated right after your evaluation, but I also should have been more careful with my accusations given that I knew less about Mickey's family than I did about my own.

"Update on my wife and child's whereabouts
Tue, Jan 4, 2011, 11:00 AM
Iain Bryson to Fred Taal [Dutch detective], US Citizen Services - Amsterdam, Kees de Vries, Dad, Mom, John S, Brian, bcc: allyopolis
Fred,
1. I was told by the Dutch police that they were at a shelter in Holland. I received two emails from my wife, stating she was at a shelter. The police, a few days later, told me that they were at a 'friends' house. I told you guys this guy was part of the abduction. I tell you he smokes heroin in front of his daughter. I tell you he is a felon, a fugitive, that he was denied entry into the United States. Denied entry means 'not with my daughter when I have to decide. I told Agata this; no further information on their whereabouts was given to me, despite my determination. I told you I had to go to Poland. She told me they are safe.
2. A cop comes over yesterday, assures me they are safe, and that they are in Holland. I tell him I still do not know for sure, but that I appreciated him telling me. You told me not to come back to the police. 'What do you want us to do........sure well in your country they care about kids and the purity of their sexual development.' The police told me to wait for the next signal. I was told that I could do nothing, and that Agata would get news to me when necessary.
3. Mickey DeLuca, Den Haag, emailed me telling me that he had nothing to do with my wife leaving. He said she is in Poland. He said he didn't have a clue.

1. Mickey comes to my house.
2. He says his wife and daughter are at the library. In retrospect, his daughter doesn't go to the library, and she wouldn't choose that over playing with my child.
3. My child is told to give me a hug. She hugs me completely, though I do not know what is going on until later. I am not saying bye. Adelle has no idea what is going on.
4. Mickey gets a call 'from his wife' fifteen minutes later. He tells her some recipe, and she indicates she is still at the library. If she is still at the library, expecting my daughter and wife, and they had not arrived yet, he would have known. It is categorically necessary. A logical truth. That was the signal that Agata had left. He then said he was going to the bar to get money and that he would come back.
5.. I waited, then realized he was not coming back.
6. I looked through my house for certain things, like Adelle's blanket......gone.
7. I went to the bar where they told me that Mickey had not only never come there, but that he had not been there in months.
8. I go to the police.

Upon return, I have an email from Agata saying she is in Holland in a abused woman and child center. I run into people who either cannot do anything, or will not, as it is just not a problem in Europe. The courts really must intervene in this situation? For real? My wife and child are being mind controlled. Agata is a Rape Terror Syndrome Victim. She was given a nice dose of Dissociative Schizophrenia. My daughter has had Venereal Diseases. My wife left me all the clues she could, but she is drawn by a higher force, which is her mind. Controlled, manipulated, and rigged since birth to respond to certain cues, visual, language, control of the entire emotional regulation center. You are telling me I still need to 'believe' you and think they are in Holland? If so, great, but if not, what I see is sexual incest rape molestation mind control. Think about that for a moment.

Thank you for any assistance you can provide.

All the best,

Iain Avery Bryson for Agata Bryson and Adelle Avery Bryson"

"Tue, Jan 4, 2011, 11:19 AM
Iain Bryson to Fred Taal [Dutch detective], US Citizen Services - Amsterdam, Kees de Vries, Dad, Mom, John S, Brian
Options:

1, Either you do not think behavior can be modified.

2. You cannot come to one conclusion which I have drawn.

3. You do not think this is a big deal.

4. It is only one child.

5. You believe Agata, which doesn't matter, because a prerequisite would be that my story is entirely false. Can you come to that decision? If so, lets talk.

6. I am sorry I know my family and I can describe behavior, development, and child consciousness along with unconsciousness to a 'T.' You need only come up with one conclusion: My child is not safe. So, from there an action would be required. I have already told the police I would go to Poland if they could not tell me for sure. By not going, and going through this bureaucratic bull, my wife and child have a possibility of being sexually abused at any instant. How about now?

Iain Avery Bryson

Slawomir W. Makowsky
Pilsudskiego 2/6
Stargard Szczecinski
Poland 73-110"

I was perturbed on a level I had never experienced, and it felt like torture. Why wouldn't they take a report? Why wouldn't they tell me where my daughter was? Why wouldn't they evaluate you? It had been eight days at this point.

A female Dutch police officer, on one of my several visits to attempt to report my stolen daughter, told me, "You should have been more careful," as if it was too late because I hadn't seen the signs until now. I didn't disagree with her because in retrospect that was an obvious point, but I thought I had been careful.

The next email was not helpful or necessary, but I was so highly displeased and irritated with the (non) response of the Dutch police, who did have jurisdiction. I wasn't saying that there was a de jure agreement to traffic and abuse children, but de facto in the sense that the rules that were in place allowed children to be trafficked and abused with impunity, with you as the example that showed me this was true. Maybe their response in this situation was atypical, and they usually protect children who are being trafficked out of their country, but it sure didn't appear that way.

"Tue, Jan 4, 2011, 11:28 AM
Iain Bryson to Fred Taal [Dutch detective], US Citizen Services - Amsterdam, Kees de Vries, Dad, Mom, John S, Brian
I believe the Dutch have an agreement with the Poles. It is not at a level I am prepared to explain now, but European Union citizenship is simply not an answer. The Dutch allow the Poles to come, acclimate, take over entire areas. They show know animosity. This is not the first time; my wife is not pulling this off on her own. Not by a long shot. It is what it is. By telling me the Poles can and do have the opportunity to train my child in German Sex For Children from ages one to three, and I am sure much younger than one, and you

can do nothing. You tell me it is not sexual abuse, that it does not exist, cannot be detected, until the age of four? Well, I can detect it, I did, and this is my child, an American citizen being trained for a lifetime of incest, trauma, and the most horrible things I have ever come across."

"Tue, Jan 4, 2011, 11:36 AM
Iain Bryson to Fred Taal [Dutch detective], US Citizen Services - Amsterdam, Kees de Vries, Dad, Mom, John S, Brian
I received a call today on my cell phone. Polish country code. 48. It was my friend in Arizona, who has a Connecticut number. So, I have a Polish number on my caller ID. It is my friend. I do not notice at first. I called him back to check. It has to be tapped, because it was my friend. Can you think of any other options, assuming that I have a 48 on my caller ID? I cannot."

I couldn't get past how strange it was that Brian had called me from a Polish phone number. *Am I being tapped? Is Brian really my friend?* And while it was relatively easy to discard the latter question, the former lingered, because I considered the chances. *Maybe someone in Poland is listening in on the call to gather information*, I considered.

That admittedly could sound crazy taken out of context, but my daughter was being abused and abducted, and my friend was calling me from a Polish number. Furthermore, were the police even helping me? And what did my parents mean when they said they wanted to "help" me? I didn't know who I could trust. Thinking my phone could be tapped wasn't that strange considering all that was going on. I didn't know how one would do that, but I also hadn't thought international child abduction was so easy, so I surely couldn't rule it out.

"Tue, Jan 4, 2011, 11:59 AM
Iain Bryson to Fred Taal [Dutch detective], US Citizen Services - Amsterdam, Kees de Vries, Dad, Mom, John S, Brian
How far do I have to open this up? I can attack this at any level. It is my wife and daughter, Stargard, Poland, indoctrination. I need them out of sex slavery no[w]. Please. Why can't you again? I do not quite understand. This is normal? You are not worried about it at all? Somebody will get it because it is real. So, why do we have to allow more abuse?"

"Tue, Jan 4, 2011, 12:15 PM
Mickey DeLuca to me
 you to Bro."

"Tue, Jan 4, 2011, 12:16 PM
Mickey DeLuca to me
 You better be very careful what you say now Ian, or you are going to have a very BIG problem with me and THAT'S for SURE......."

"Tue, Jan 4, 2011, 1:26 PM
Iain Bryson to Fred Taal [Dutch detective], US Citizen Services - Amsterdam, allyopolis, Brian
The police told me they are at Mickey DeLuca's house. They told me, after five days of claiming she was in a shelter, that they were staying at Mickey DeLuca's house. He has the name DeLuca, after his wife, as his last name identifies him as a fugitive from Denmark, with a felony criminal record which is longer than I'd like when looking at men I trust my daughter with. I emailed my wife on day two or three, asking her to get out of that house, if she could I stated. I received no reply.

Now, I am being told by Mickey that he knew nothing. The Agata thing was an entirely different thing. He was not aware of it, and thought nothing of it. What about the fact he said he was going to the bar a block away to try to get money, and that he would be back? I checked the bar, and was told he hadn't been there in months. What about the fact that the reason the DeLuca's are here is because Mickey was denied entry into the United States for LYING on his Federal forms. Lying to the US government for the purpose of obtaining entry and eventually citizenship. He was thinking that he had to do anything, and if he told the truth, they would deny him. His wife did not even know, and he never wanted to bring it up. So, they end up here, never to return.

Now, I get emails from Mickey, saying he knows my wife and daughter left the country. He knows that my father-in-law and my wife's sister's boyfriend picked them up from the bus stop. He says he has no idea what happened, then coming to the conclusion that he is one hundred percent sure they are not in Holland. He knows, I am told. He then says that 'thinking' will get me into trouble. How, I ask myself? Well, the only way thinking could get me into trouble is if I could not identify my thoughts. If I had crazy thoughts which made me act without even knowing why I was acting like that, it probably would be a problem. However, that is not what is occurring here. I have thoughts, which to the casual observer may be perceived as a bit off. Somebody who aids in what is an abduction, whether he th[e]n admits to knowing about it after the fact, is someone that should be looked at a little further. If my thoughts are a problem for Mickey, what does that mean? He knows I am wrong, and I am not threatening him, so there must be something else which makes him try to instill the fear of thought into me."

"Tue, Jan 4, 2011, 2:28 PM
Iain Bryson to Fred Taal [Dutch detective], US Citizen Services Amsterdam, John S, Brian
Are you still ok with the fact that it is a possibility, at least you say it can happen, that my wife has fled to Poland. So, you are fine with them being raped right now? Or maybe in ten minutes? Interesting, cause I am just not ok with that. Furthermore, it takes me time to figure out how, in the realm of all possible human thought, one could conclude that Rape may be occurring, then coming to the conclusion that the proper form is available. All I need to do is fill it out, mail it in my my SASA, and wait from a response from an official. An expert. Someone who definitely cares and has the power to do something. They have a nice title and it sure sounds to me like a person that would protect a child from rape. Maybe I am wrong about something. No, well rape could be happening right now, so I still do not see how waiting any longer is an option. Waiting at all is not an option. I am not sure what you are talking about. Waiting. Maybe rape, right no[w], but waiting? Wow."

"Tue, Jan 4, 2011, 6:02 PM
Mom to me
Iain, I tried to call but maybe you are sleeping. (hopefully). Your dad is at the airport ready for take off. He is bringing the form for you to sign to get Adelle's birth certificate. You and Agata are the only two that can get it. I will make a copy to keep here. The US Consulate will help faxing it to New London City Hall.
Your dad is arriving 10:30am. I love you. Mom"

"Tue, Jan 4, 2011, 6:10 PM
Iain Bryson to Mom
Agata would not help me get Adelle registered in The Netherlands. Just like everything else, it just didn't happen. I now know, as she always has, that an apostille can be obtained at the consulate. love you"

"Tue, Jan 4, 2011, 6:28 PM
Mom to me
It's better to do things yourself. Or at least make the call. Keep the faith. I love you"

"Tue, Jan 4, 2011, 8:22 PM
Wendy to me, Mom
I just spoke to kirk and he wanted me to pass along this message as he cannot hook up to the wi fi in Philadelphia. He was about to board the plane and was greatly concerned that he has not heard from you He is expecting you to meet him at the airport on his arrival.
Plese reply to this email to let me know that you will be meeting him.
thanks
wendy"

"Tue, Jan 4, 2011, 8:30 PM
Iain Bryson to Wendy
yes wendy. expecting him. thanks iain"

"My wife's grandfather. Waldek. His wife Vera. Mother and Father of my mother i[n] law, so they tell me.
Tue, Jan 4, 2011, 10:21 PM
Iain Bryson to allyopolis, US Citizen Services - Amsterdam, Brian, Mom, Kees de Vries, foxreport [News], [The Colbert Report], [Lawyer], [Netherlands Youth Institute], American Citizen Services, [News], [News]
Attachments

My wife told me her family, her mother and father, love Adelle more than my family loves her. They certainly know her better, but I would say the question of 'love' is a bit harder to determine. The[y] know her, they study her, they want her. They want to use her. They are using her. They are abusing her. Now. Regardless of where they are, they are both still being abused at this very moment. Adelle and Agata have the same Name Day, one only they have, February 4th, more important than the birthday, especially for girls. We have never celebrated. She denies that there is any suspicion that something happened that I do not know about causing her to have the same name day as our daughter. The odds are one in 365, but she says she had no idea, Adelle and the Polish Adela 'aren't even the same name,' and that girls names have to start with A. They do have to start with A, because that is what she was told they could, would start with.

http://picasaweb.google.com/lipa52/WielkanocZdjCia#
C:\Users\Bryson\Desktop\Brysons\Pictures\Easter pics\wielkanoczdjcia.zip

wielkanoczdjcia- the word Agata gives to one of her photo albums. Eggs. Artwork. Masterpieces. Her and my daughter, for my father in law."

"Wielkanoczdjcia" means merely "Easter pictures," but I didn't know that at the time. All that I knew was that something extremely out of the ordinary was now happening to our family, and that your grandfather and great-grandfather were not good men.

"Wed, Jan 5, 2011, 12:57 AM
Brian to me
Able to through most of these emails tonights - Are you thinking they may still be in Netherlands now?

I'm obviously not on your level on some of this... Having trouble following the pov [pov]on some of the previous writings where the dialog is oscillating between the thoughts of the the person doing the mind control and the person/people who appear to be questioning your conclusions... I'll get there I'm sure, but work in process for me. I know you didn't want to give up your passport for facebook, but if your girl knows you don't have access and she also has an account - could you get in there to see if there is any clues to her whereabouts or perhaps if you have other friends in Holland that have her as a friend. Just a thought, thinking if she is OCD on the cell phone, she could also get into facebook and leave clues...

Have you gotten anymore input regarding what the 'abuse' / KGB file is all about ? Or any word on Deluca - I thought it sounded like the cops may be questioning him?"

The last thing she had left on Facebook was the music video for "If Tomorrow Never Comes," and yes, I agreed with Brian that this had been a "clue." Your mom did not want to bring you back to the cult, but she had no choice, literally. Trauma based mind control had put her under the control of her abusers.

Brian was referring to the red herring when he referenced the "KGB file," my drug, psychological, and criminal histories that had been spun into a narrative web in order to facilitate the smooth transfer of you from our home to their home while keeping the onlookers in a state of perplexed confusion.

"Wed, Jan 5, 2011, 4:23 AM
Mickey DeLuca to me
Again , Agata and Adelle is with Agata's family in Polan, believe it or not, but that is the truth, and what are you talking about when you say 'rape'.??????? you really don't make any sense Ian"

CHAPTER 59

"I LOVE AGATA, COMPLETELY, FULLY, ALWAYS"

It was time to go to the airport to get my dad, and I wasn't looking forward to leaving our house. I wasn't sure how mad Mickey was, and I had no idea what your mom's family might do. I was feeling paranoia. I knew that I was never going to stop, and logically it made sense that killing me would be the best option for whoever wanted you. If I were them, I think I would kill me. So, I took a kitchen knife, and I stuffed it in my pants for protection as I headed to pick up my dad at the airport.

I arrived early, and I went outside to smoke. As I stood smoking by the trash bin at the entrance to the airport, I began to feel that my fear that led me to carrying a knife was excessive. *This is absolutely crazy, but it cannot be that crazy, and even if it is, I cannot let it get to me*, I thought. I carefully removed the knife from my waste-band, and I tossed it in the trash, happy to remove that burden, feeling lighter.

I looked on the monitor to find out where he would be coming out of customs, and I waited there. It was good to see him. I brought him home and filled him in.

"can i communicate with You?
Wed, Jan 5, 2011 at 1:56 PM
Iain Bryson to Agata Bryson"

I still had hope that she would snap out of it, that tomorrow I would see her and she would say, "I love you, and I don't know what that was…" like last time. I wanted to make sure that she knew that the door was always open.

"Wed, Jan 5, 2011, 3:06 PM
Child Welfare Information Gateway to me
Good afternoon,
Thank you for contacting Information Gateway, an information and referral service of the Children's Bureau, U.S. Department of Health and Human Services. We connect professionals and concerned citizens to information on supporting and strengthening families, preventing and responding, child abuse and neglect, adoption and more.
We are very confused about the situation you described, as we are only an information and referral service. We cannot advise or intervene in personal situations. You need to continue to work with the US Embassy and you may also wish to contact International Social Services in the Netherlands for consultation regarding your case. I am including contact information for this agency below…"

"Re: Your messages
Wed, Jan 5, 2011, 5:09 PM
John S to me
Hi,

I don't know who 'Fred' is, but I get the feeling he has some sort of authority in your case. I also sense that he is not responding in a manner you find acceptable. I'm not sure that barraging him with emails is going to move his butt in your direction, though. Is it possible to get yourself an advocate -- a lawyer or somebody -- to represent your interests? Someone to deal with the [expletive], someone who knows the ins and outs of this stuff. It won't be free, obviously. So, where is your family in all of this? Are your parents aware of what's happening to you? I'd think they'd want to help you somehow to find an advocate, some representation.

Anyway, that's where my head is right now. I will keep in touch.

-- John"

"What's up
Wed, Jan 5, 2011, 6:22 PM
Brian to me
Hey man - Is everything okay (obviously within the circumstances)? Getting worried I haven't heard from ya..."

"Must My Babies Bones This Hungry Fire Feed? [Dave Matthews lyrics]
Wed, Jan 5, 2011, 9:54 PM
Iain Bryson to Brian, Mom, John S, bcc: allyopolis"

"Wed, Jan 5, 2011, 10:16 PM
Iain Bryson to Brian, Mom, US Citizen Services - Amsterdam, Fred Taal [Dutch detective], John S
Still, even as a father, and even though I have the 'right' to know, I am not told. I do not know. I cannot know for sure. The police, or maybe the shelter, who I have contacted repeatedly over the past week, could not tell me where my wife and child are despite the fact that it is my right to know? Do you know where they are because you did assure me that they are safe, time and again."

"Re: Legal Counsel Needed Immediately
Wed, Jan 5, 2011, 10:24 PM
Jeremiah to me
Iain - that email was way too long. You're rambling and it doesn't make a whole lot of sense. You need to stop sending these lengthy emails. Write a journal on pen and paper if you need to, but keep your thoughts to yourself.

Work with your dad while he's there to summarize your complaint in 1-2 paragraphs, or it won't get the attention you need it to. Stick to the facts. State when she went missing, why, where you think she went, and that you believe she and Adelle are ongoing victims of sexual abuse. Give a LITTLE background information re: your complaint and what you're seeking.

If you need me to try and summarize it for you, I will. Or send me a draft to edit before you email anything. You really need to stop sending these lengthy emails.

How did the meeting at the consular's office go?
Jeremiah"

"Wed, Jan 5, 2011, 10:35 PM
Iain Bryson to Jeremiah
If you can succinctly lay it out, it would be helpful. It is difficult for me to focus on any one thing. It is all here. Now, besides the proof and evidence I had, I have Agata saying it is happening. From this point, the only logical conclusion is that she needs help, and she needs it badly. She could not ask. She had to give me what I need so that I can ask. The Consulate said to get an attorney. I am trying, going to by tomorrow. My dad is here, sleeping. When I get too specific and ask if they are safe, I am told that they are. I need to know, and I need to know what to do in either situation. The lawyer will help. Tomorrow at the latest."

"Representation Required
Wed, Jan 5, 2011, 10:45 PM
Iain Bryson to me, US Citizen Services - Amsterdam, Brian, John S, Fred Taal [Dutch detective], [Lawyer], internationalnji.nl [Netherlands Youth Institute], Jeremiah, [Lawyer], [Lawyer], [Lawyer], [Lawyer], [Lawyer], [Lawyer], [Lawyer], [Lawyer], [Lawyer], [Lawyer], Mom, Vandana [Friend], Nancy
Iain Bryson
Newtonplein 25
Den Haag, The Netherlands 2562JV

iain.bryson@gmail.com
A. My wife and daughter have been missing since December 31, 2010.
B. My wife and daughter have been sexually abused.
C. My wife has provided information stating that she believes/knows that the abuse will continue if the[y] go to Poland.
D. My wife told me she had to go to Poland for either Christmas or New Years.
E. The Dutch police cannot tell me, with the level of certainty I feel is necessary, where they are, or even what country they are in.
F. Either, my wife has fled and I need to know the location of her and my child, or both my wife and child are being sexually abused. And, my wife provided me with video, notebooks, pictures, evidence confirming that she needs help, and that she does not want to be abused or to allow our daughter abused more than she has been."

"Wed, Jan 5, 2011, 11:12 PM
Jeremiah to me
Have you tried calling Agata's parents in Poland, by the way?
I would say someting like this:

My wife, Agata Bryson (DOB: July 11, 1982), and my daughter, Adelle Bryson (DOB: January 30, 2007) went missing on December 31, 2010. Agata and I are legally married and have joint custody of Adelle. Agata was sexually abused as a child by her parents, and the abuse still continues when she is at home with them in Poland. Because of the trauma caused by years of abuse, Agata is not able to seek treatment on her own and is has gone through several stages of both denying and accepting the abuse. The abuse has been the root cause of other mental problems as well.

In addition to the concerns I have with Agata's well being, I am equally concerned for Adelle. She has spent a significant amount of time with Agata's parent's in Poland, accompanied by Agata and also on her own. And recently I've noticed a change in Adelle's behavior as well as signs of clear sexual and mental abuse.

I've been trying to work with the Dutch police to confirm the whereabouts of Agata and Adelle, but have not been getting any direct answers. I believe there is a good chance that they went to her parents' house in Poland, but I cannot confirm this. If they are in Poland, I am concerned that the abuse will continue. If they are not in Poland, I am concerned for their safety and well being.

I am asking for your assistacne to locate Agata and Adelle so that we can determine if they are safe. And because of the recent evidence of sexual abuse with Adelle, I feel it's important for her to be immediately evaluated by a doctor. In addition, I need guidance in terms of how to get help for Agata and Adelle and how to deal with the custody issue. Because of Agata's current mental state, I do not believe that she is able to provide adequate care for Adelle and that she may be putting herself and Adelle in greater danger. Agata left evidence and clues for me confirming that she and Adelle are suffering from abuse, including statements, photos, videos, and journals.

Please advise regarding how I can proceed with locating my wife and daughter and what I can do to get them the help they need. Thank you in advance.

I have to get to bed. It's after midnight here and I gotta be up early. Call or email me later. Review what I wrote with your dad and tweek it as needed. Keep it simple and to the point. If I see another email like that from you, I am going to fly over there myself and slap you around. hang in there. It will get better.

And pray about it too...I am."

"Thu, Jan 6, 2011, 2:30 AM
Iain Bryson to Agata Bryson, bcc: me, bcc: allyopolis
I think I have the possibilities worked out. I think I have the answer. I guess I am usually not all wrong, but it is tough to be all right as well. Being right about some, and [expletive] sure of it, as well as sure that there is a good chance your 'life' is in danger, it means throw the [expletive] that is real as hard as you can. I think I have covered all the bases, I ponder for a moment as the power of your [expletive] is overwhelming. Yes, I suppose, but no. Just powerful. Got to look at the [expletive] in totality again, next, side by side, etc like on top of that [expletive].

It is a pure learning experience from my completely amazing wifey. You allow me, well force [m]e, out of necessity, but [expletive] it looks odd at first. A [expletive] pile of crazy [expletive]. You pecial. Another basket there completely. I love your basket. You fascinate me. Allure me, as you always have, since the first moment I saw you. It was the eyes, with maybe a smidgen of the rest caught in the periphery of my consciousness, which was directed into you. What is that? She is amazing. I can't figure out why, but I do know I need to look closer. I have to. She is [expletive] beautiful first of all (As in you my babinski other basket). Even today, not that it would be any different babinski, but yes even today you are just beautiful. And 'beautiful' for me is like 'love.'

As I said, I will never ever ever stop loving you. It cannot happen. Well, with beautiful, in your case, it is more of a divine term. You are beautiful, not because you are 'beautiful,' though you certainly are, but because you are [expletive] beautiful. How you ask me about John like that? You do it over and over. I got it and now I just got that [expletive] in general, though not quite in the same sense, or I mean not at all. But it is just the beginning, as is everyday with you."

"Thu, Jan 6, 2011, 3:47 AM
Iain Bryson to Brian
As of now, I believe this done. And you are then only one I can tell, because being wrong would be 'psychotic,' but then again any weird thought can be. It is like picking a face in the crowd and saying it is a happy face. Too happy? How happy? How do you know? Happy about what? Are you sure? Is that what you would look like if you were happy? Are you happy now? Are you sure of it? So, what I think, and given the game I am playing/have been playing and enjoying once I can remove the immediate personal emotions, use them but not live them uncontrollably, then being able to use it for a strength instead of a debilitating weakness.

She is way beyond me. She has plotted and figured, and already has her plan. Her end. She told me, and I didn't hear that, just like 'molester' only made sense flipped onto her father. She said she wanted me in Adelle's life, on a daily basis. But in order for that, she first had to be strong, and then it was my turn to sort through the [expletive] only to find out that I am 'dancing' with my wife, she is incrementally showing me what I could not, in large doses, most likely expecting my reaction. Now I know what attracts me to her. What the [expletive] is going on up there when you can devise this crazy [expletive]? Wow. I cannot be sure, but I am other than the fact that I cannot be. She is here, and the next step, I think but will have to tackle how she might think in a few different ways. I believe, though cannot claim in this instance, that she is insanely deliberate, able, capable, powerful. But I also believe I know her and that she was using that for reasons we cannot understand, or if we can, we will not be in it for long enough to hone the skills as she has.

She is in charge, and I am catching up. She can organize that [expletive] perfectly, as I always knew and said she was good at. I can destroy that [expletive] from different angles, but that is slowing me down to what she is doing. She just looks, knows what is, knows what she can do to what is, thinks about why she wants to, what that may mean, and then mother [expletive] executes if she decides it is real or worth it."

"Thu, Jan 6, 2011, 4:08 AM
Iain Bryson to Kees de Vries, me
Kees,
Thought I'd check in with you. Wanted to update you about the 'music,' since I know it makes you think crazy things. It should. I know it should, but it is also real if I want it to be real. Lucky for both of us, when I do not want it, gone. Completely. And it does not even trickle in, not even a dribble, until I need it or think I need it in the future. Or, if it does, I work on it so a fuller understanding is possible, whereby I can then stop the dribble. Eventually at least.

And because of learning from Agata, having you to help along the way, and having a very strong wife who has the ability to completely thwart my conscious activities to try and feel a certain way. She can make me feel anything she wants me to. She has been there, and the skills she has attained are quite amazing. Again, like with incest or any of the other things I had to master myself, but just theoretically here, at least for most of them, I forgot about the skills you get, or can get through experience. Through having a defined task; you know you need to learn how to control that man as soon as you can. Once you figure out that man, any man will be possible, and you can just run with it as you see fit. Survival. Of course she's got that [expletive]. She is my wife."

"If I had It ALL [Dave Matthews lyrics]. I DO. Her. She is enough. Way more. Too much, but I love her.
Thu, Jan 6, 2011, 6:33 AM
Iain Bryson to Mom, John S, Brian, Agata Bryson, Iwona [Agata's mom], Ada [Agata's sister]"

"Thu, Jan 6, 2011, 7:26 AM
Iain Bryson to Agata Bryson, Ada, Mom, Jeremiah, Amy [Agata's friend in US], Angela [Cousin], Bonnie [Aunt], Brian, Bree [Sister-in-Law], Carrie, Courtney [Cousin], Dave [Uncle], [unknown], Mika [Agata's friend in Poland], Ewa M [Agata's friend in Poland], Roger [Grandpa Bryson], Hart [Cousin], Heather [Jeremiah's wife], John S, Jon, Dad, Maciej, [unknown], Iwona, Marza, [unknown], [unknown], Jim [Uncle], Rachel, Sara [Aunt], [unknown], Slawomir [Agata's dad], Wendy

I thought that the love I had for Agata was complete, full. I was not thinking. In order for Agata to even begin to feel my love, she has to first begin to feel it as love. I thought that I knew what love was. I did feel what it was, but it was only what it was to me at any given time. The problem arose when I began to notice Agata reacting completely opposite to what should have been happening had my love be for her, and for her completely. After struggling for [n]early seven years, for I had to figure out what was wrong with my love, or with my wife's love. I could not think of anything at all, not in my wildest dreams. And, my dreams can get wild, even when I am awake. But, I know Agata'[s] have been much worse, unthinkable, and that these dreams began when she was a little girl. My little girl.

I could see with my eyes that there was an evil, pure evil in my house. I lived in Poland amongst and with this evil. I had it in my home on multiple occasions. Everyone else knew, but they either couldn't say, they did say but I couldn't explain to them exactly what they had explained. They know, as you do, somewhere in your unconscious. Let's hope it is not in your conscious, but if it is, you are much better off than it being hidden completely from view. When it is hidden from view, it can and will wreak havoc on some level. That is certain. It could be minor, and maybe you can glide past it, ignore it. That may be, but if you ignore the minor ones, you can also learn, or possibly even be taught by another to ignore the major ones.

By leaving open the possibility, you are then vastly increasing the probability that you will have something within you that is churning up thoughts, feelings, and even behaviors, and this something could be everything. You are not worried? You feel that thinking about it is a waste of time, or maybe you just already know. Do not worry; someone else can, will and should make those decisions for you. Somebody had better do it, or else you run the risk of having it overcome by something you may hopefully, but also unlikely, ever have to understand in your entire life. If you fail to even recognize the need. suggestion that thinking about this thought is maybe a good idea, that thought will linger. It will develop as new thoughts rush in, covering it up, making it feel and making you believe that the first thought never even existed. Did it? I don't think so. Just move on. You will be ok. Will you not? Do you think maybe thinking could be good. Maybe it should be recommended. I personally recommend it. If you are thinking you might want to have sex with my wife or daughter, I will know whether you are consciously thinking about it, or if it is perched somewhere in the cobwebs where you place the old stuff you that you no longer need. Really, it would be best if it just went away altogether, but it won't. How long are you thinking you will hope about something that can and will never happen? What does this hope then do for you in either respective situation? It is not hope. You cannot meditate on nothingness. There is no nothingness. There is always something. Maybe you do not know what this something is, but you still cannot call it nothing.

I cannot believe the strength I see. The need for love, real love, once and for all. Finally. It has to be worth it. It must. It is. These women are the strongest, most capable people I have ever encountered. And, I have the pleasure of loving them completely, no sex involved, not for the love. The love is separate. An entity unto itself. It is pure. It is giving, and in only this way does it ever take. It is not giving or taking. It is being. Living. Doing. Believing. Against any odds I could have imagined, but which was imagined all to[o] well within my own household, these women have triumphed. For me, the victory is beautiful. Finally. I love you."

"Subject: Re: I love Agata, completely, fully, always. I want our daughter to have the ability to feel and know this love. I need her to have the ability.
Thu, Jan 6, 2011, 7:43 AM
Iain Bryson to Agata Bryson, Ada, Mom, Jeremiah, Amy, Angela, Bonnie, Brian, Bree, Carrie, Courtney, Dave, [unknown], Mika, Ewa, Roger, Hart, Heather, John S., Jon, Dad, Maciej, [unknown], Iwona, Marza, [unknown], [unknown], Jim, Rachel, Sara, [unknown], Slawomir, Wendy
Incapable of accepting any love other than real love. Incapable of giving any love other than real love. It is not real because you say it is, or even if you think it is. It has to be real, it really does. And, knowing that it is real can only be determined when it is known. You cannot know anything without feeling it. She can feel, all to well, that something must change. A fundamental error is permitted, allowed, encouraged to envelop itself around the entirety of what it is to be human. It will play with your love, put it out slowly, surely, and enjoy that moment when you know it has been extinguished.

How could you ever then figure out what love really is. You have been told. You already know what it is, and you have known since you were a child. Everything you learned about love after that is distorted, changed, destroyed, as it can never coexist with anything real. It is not real. It is a problem, and you should figure it out so you can love again, or for once. Try it. What is stopping you? Do you know what is stopping you? I recommend you find out. She did, and it blew my mind, beyond comprehension. Either I am seeing my wife, completely, totally, all at once, or I am crazy. I know my wife, but I also know she says I am crazy.

Well, by getting to know her, I learned that she means it completely differently than you could ever imagine. Crazy for her is not seeing this evil, when it is everywhere. When it shares a wife, a daughter, a meal, a laugh, a smoke. I do not think it is funny at all. I wonder how it can be thought of as even quasi amusing. Please do not think about it unless you must. If you must, you will. Then, just continue thinking until you either do it or seek understanding, truth, help. Otherwise, you will feel and know pain, emptiness, things that are not real. You can make them real, but do you know what you are deciding you are going to make real? Should you know?"

"**Thu, Jan 6, 2011, 8:36 AM**
Jeremiah to me
what the f- is this? keep this for your book. don't email soliloquies like this.
 Jeremiah"

Your mom was the most spectacular being that I had ever seen, and she had just taught me my most important lesson on love to date. Granted it was also the most difficult lesson to date, but such is the nature of lessons, at least in my experience. I couldn't wait until the world laid eyes upon the woman that I had married, a woman that was giving everything that she had for love – to get her daughter out of the cult that she was born into.

Love is Agata Bryson, I thought, *because she somehow broke past her mind control in order to beg me to beg the world to get them out.* And undoubtedly, she was going to pay for that upon returning to the cult and them finding out everything that I knew, and that she had let loose a man who would never stop as long as he possessed breath. This woman, your mom, was an actual hero, and I couldn't wait for others to also recognize this and get her the help she was pleading for.

"**Mickey DeLuca**
Thu, Jan 6, 2011, 8:58 AM
Iain Bryson to Fred Taal [Dutch detective], bcc: Jackie DeLuca, bcc: Agata Bryson
Fred,
Mickey DeLuca is guilty of sexually abusing his child, along with my child. Agata's child. I cannot tell my child that nothing happened. I cannot tell my wife, nor do I want to. He did, and you must know. He should know, in case he does not already. You can decide. I have video of the event. Thank you, Iain"

Again, I didn't know for sure that Mickey was "guilty," per se, nor did I have any video evidence of Mickey being abusive – I was speaking here like a politician or a prosecuting attorney, and I really didn't care about my accuracy. I wanted to instigate an investigation because I knew that what I needed was for these two little girls (you and Cicely) to be evaluated immediately.

"**Thu, Jan 6, 2011, 9:56 AM**
Carrie to me
Iain,
I don't know what I'm seeing here, looks like a 14 second clip of Adelle laughing with another little girl???"

She was right; the "video of the event" that I referred to in my email to Fred Taal was not proof, as I already discussed. It was suspicious, because it was one of three short videos that your mom left on our laptop just prior to leaving with you to return to the cult, and one of the videos was the "did you beat her? You know we did," video.

As your dad, I knew that this other video with you and Cicely was not good, but it was not helpful for me to claim that I had proof and then show them that video because they didn't know you and therefore had no ability to know if your behavior was normal or abnormal.

"**Thu, Jan 6, 2011, 1:34 PM**
Iain Bryson to Agata Bryson
Agata,
Can I speak with you? I love you. Just working.
Iain"

"Can I come to you please? I love you.
Thu, Jan 6, 2011, 6:27 PM
Iain Bryson to Agata Bryson"

"Thu, Jan 6, 2011, 6:30 PM
Sara [Aunt] to me
Hey I got your two e-mails, they are not the typical e mails that I usually get from you and I am not sure what you were trying to say. E-mail me and let me what is going on with you. Unc Dave and I love you guys and are praying for you. Let us know what we can do for you. Love auntie."

Atypical emails? Could the abduction of my daughter and the non-responsiveness of the authorities and my family have had something to do with that?

I was sitting at my desk that evening when a light hit me in the eyes. I looked out the window, and I could see that someone was shining a flashlight at me; it looked like maybe a cop. There was a knock at the downstairs door; I looked at my dad, and he shrugged as if he had no idea what it could be. He asked me if I wanted him to check it out, and I said yes, hoping that he could take care of whatever it was, leaving me to what I was doing on the computer.

He reappeared moments later, and with him were five other people. He invited them into our living room, and they sat down. I was flabbergasted. They explained that they were a psychiatric emergency intervention team, and that they were there to assess whether I should be involuntarily locked up.

I was upset that they were in my house and aggrieved with my dad who had invited them. It was now obvious to me what "help" meant, and I wondered why nobody would just help me get my daughter back. It was clear that he had planned this, and it brought on another wave of paranoia. He said he was helping, he said we were going to get a lawyer, but he had been lying to me.

I quickly composed myself and explained that I was fine, that I was just working at my desk, and that I was completely surprised that they were there, but they could see that already. They asked me if I had punched the wall, or anything like that, and I told them that I wasn't mad or violent, that all that I wanted was to figure out how to get help for you, and that I would appreciate it if they would get out of my house.

They left for several minutes to talk in private, then returned to inform me that they were not going to take me into the hospital against my will. "Thank you," I stated mockingly, "all that I am doing is trying to get help for my daughter, who does actually need help."

As soon as the lower door latched shut, I made sure that the upper door was also closed. It felt good to have them gone, but there was never any real fear that they would take me. For what? For sitting at my computer, for sending inflammatory emails, for not sleeping, for giving it all I've got to try to get you help? Is that dangerous? No, I didn't think so.

But with my dad, I felt betrayed. I was irate. "How dare you invite those people into my house. You come to my house, and you make things more difficult for me than they already are, I should throw you out right now, do not ever do anything like that again, this is my house, your granddaughter is being abused, and you're worried about me? What the [expletive] is wrong with you?"

He apologized, and he said that he was wrong. My guess was that he had been under pressure from others, maybe Wendy or my mom, or even your mom, to "get me help." I didn't think that he was acting on his own. I reiterated, "Don't you ever do anything like that again. If you're not here to help me, you can leave!"

This was the "help" I had been promised repeatedly? They wanted me to calm down and get my emotions under control? The only thing that could have helped would have been to show me that we were going to work as a family to get you and your abductors into court – why were we not getting a lawyer?

CHAPTER 60

"IAIN IS FRANTIC WONDERING WHERE YOU ARE, AND ADELLE"

One of the things that your mom left on our computer was a document I had never seen: her curriculum vitae (CV) in Polish. When I put it through the 2011 version of Google Translate, it was confusing and not something I could comprehend. I thought that everything was a potential clue, and that maybe this was some secret project your mom was working on. Things were strange, so I assumed this also was part of it, but this time it probably wasn't (see Appendix 30).

Whatever it was, I was overwhelmed, and the growing distrust that I had for my parents' "help" was not making it easy to think clearly. I couldn't trust anyone, and that was not a good thing. The fabric of my reality was already crumbling; these emails were coming from a place of desperation because I was beginning to fear that nobody was on my side.

"Agata Avery Bryson
Thu, Jan 6, 2011, 11:18 PM
Iain Bryson to Agata Bryson, Ada, Mom, Jeremiah, Amy, Angela, Bonnie, Brian, Bree, Carrie, Courtney, Dave, [unknown], Mika, Ewa, Roger, Hart, Heather, John S., Jon, Dad, Maciej, [unknown], Iwona, Marza, [unknown], [unknown], Jim, Rachel, Sara, [unknown], Slawomir, Wendy
'ŻYCIORYS
Urodziłam się 11 lipca 1982 roku w Stargardzie Szczecińskim (Polska, Województwo Zachodniopomorskie). Rodzice – Iwona i Sławomir – pracowali jako nauczyciele, później matka została (i jest do dziś) wicedyrektorem Zespołu Szkół Budowlano- Technicznych w Stargardzie Szczecińskim, ojciec był dziennikarzem lokalnej prasy i rzecznikiem prasowym Zarządu Miasta, obecnie prowadzi własną działalność gospodarczą. W roku 20... zdałam maturę w I Liceum Ogólnokształcącym im. Adama Mickiewicza w Stargardzie Szczecińskim i dostałam się na studia w Wyższej Szkole Morskiej (obecnie Akademia Morska) w Szczecinie, na kierunku: logistyka i zarządzanie w europejskim systemie transportowym. Studia ukończyłam w roku 20.... Po napisaniu i zrecenzowaniu pracy dyplomowej (przed obroną) wyjechałam do Stanów Zjednoczonych Ameryki Północnej i wyszłam za mąż za obywatela USA Iaina Avery Brysona, gdzie w roku 2007 urodziłam córkę, Adelle Avery Bryson.
W czasie pobytu w New London w stanie Connecticut pracowałam jako personal sekretary w kancelarii prawniczej .....(nazwa).
W roku 2008 przyjechałam, z całą rodziną, do Holandii, gdzie podjęłam pracę w firmie Aramco....(pełna nazwa) w charakterze legal sekretary szefa filii firmy najpierw w Leiden, później w Hadze. W międzyczasie, w roku 2009, obroniłam na Akademii Morskiej w Szczecinie pracę inżynierską z logistyki w europejskim systemie transportowym. Do końca sierpnia 2010 byłam pracownikiem Aramco ... (pełna nazwa).
LIST MOTYWACYJNY
Podstawą mojej aplikacji jest fakt, że posiadam odpowiednie wykształcenie i wszystkie umiejętności wymagane na obsadzanym stanowisku. Są one wsparte dużym (międzynarodowym) doświadczeniem w prowadzeniu sekretariatu, najpierw w kancelarii prawniczej (USA), ostatnio biura jednego z szefów globalnej firmy logistyczno- transportowej.

Kilka lat pracy w realiach holenderskich, ale w firmie z Arabii Saudyjskiej, o kosmopolitycznym charakterze zatrudnienia, pozwoliły mi nauczyć się nie tylko relacji merytorycznych, ale i obyczajowo- kulturowych z przedstawicielami różnych składowych europejskiej społeczności.

Nie bez znaczenia jest fakt, że mimo wielokulturowej rodziny, moje polskie obywatelstwo jest nie tylko przejawem formalnym, ale także autentycznym wyznacznikiem tożsamości. Jestem Polką, która się doskonale adaptuje, nie zamierzając się asymilować. Dotyczy to także mojego dziecka (obywatelki USA), które jest wychowywane nie tylko w stałym kontakcie z rodziną w Polsce, ale także w polskiej rzeczywistości językowej i kulturowej. Mój kontakt z krajem nie ogranicza się do kontaktów z rodziną, polega na stałej łączności z informacjami o sytuacji społeczno- politycznej i śledzeniu bieżących wydarzeń w kraju.

W kontekście tego, co powyżej bardzo ważnym motywem mojej aplikacji jest motyw prestiżowo-patriotyczny. Możliwość pracy w polskim przedstawicielstwie dyplomatycznym, w tak ważnym dla Europy miejscu jak Haga, byłby powodem do niekwestionowanej dumy i impulsem do dawania z siebie w pracy dosłownie wszystkiego. Ewentualna możliwość funkcjonowania (choćby na najniższym szczeblu) w strukturach polskiego państwa w zachodnim kraju, to dla młodej Polki na obczyźnie niezwykła i niepowtarzalna szansa r

Based on my letter of motivation applications is the fact that I have adequate basic education and skills required for all Based on my letter of motivation applications is the fact that I have adequate basic education and skills required for all obsadzanym position. They are supported by a large (international experience in the conduct secretariat, the first at chancellery lawyers (USA), as last office one of the heads and global companies-transport. position. They are supported by a large (international experience in the conduct secretariat, the first at chancellery lawyers (USA), as last office one of the heads and global companies-transport.ealizacji zawodowej i osobistej.'

Love has conquered evil, an evil I could never quite understand. I could not describe it. I could not think about it. It was painful, often too painful, and I know I felt it, I thought I knew why, but now I am sure I know why."

These next messages were communications that I did not know of at the time, though I did suspect that my parents were in fact talking to your mom. I couldn't be certain because of how secretive everyone was being, but my senses and experiences were telling me that they were not being truthful with me. I was able to retrieve these messages as part of the discovery for my own trial later in 2012; they were in the prosecutor's file, and were used to prove his case against me, and to prove that nobody else thought you should be evaluated in accordance with the wishes of your father.

Wed, January 6, 2011
Mom to Agata Bryson [from the court record]
"Kirk told me that you emailed hi that you two are safe and I thank you for that. Iain is frantic wondering where you are and Adelle, who is his life as you know...Secondly to come up with on idea on how to get Iain back here. I want him to get help. He will beat the court thing but he has to show up"

Thu, January 7, 2011
Dad to Agata Bryson [from the court record]
"Iain has crashed (finally) on the couch and is asleep. I think he has been up since I got here Wednesday am. I am still all ears for anything you would like to say to me. I am so sad that this has happened. He loves you both so much and doesn't see that he is off in another world. So bizarre...Will there be charges against him which would allow him to enter a hospital here? He will heal much faster if he has you and Adelle in his life...to get Iain the help he needs..."

Thu, January 7, 2011
Dad to Agata Bryson [from the court record]
"Iain is still convinced that there's a conspiracy to separate you and that you're sending him messages to find and save you. If we could break his fantasy, he would have a much better chance to return to reality and get help'"

What I could've possibly needed "help" for, other than family support and a lawyer to deal with my recently kidnapped daughter, was only in his mind, along with my mom's. I suspected that your mother and grandfather were behind whatever it was they were thinking even though my family didn't tell me they were in contact with them at the time.

I was sending emails to your mom's contacts, and the following email from Pola, your mom's cousin, made that worthwhile. As far as I knew, she didn't speak English at all, so I was surprised to receive any communication from her. I didn't know that much about her except that she was one of the most timid people I had ever met, and what your mom had told me recently, that her parents were forcing her to see a psychiatrist because she was dating a Sri Lankan man.

Left: Pola during a visit to The Hague.

Right: You and Pola's Sri Lankan boyfriend.

"**Fri, Jan 7, 2011, 3:26 AM**
Pola to me
Iain,
Please stop doing this, sending those emails to her contacts. It's not right.
I don't know what is going on between you and Agata. I don't know what happened to this beautiful couple you were. Whatever it is it's personal, no need to involve others. Especially not in this way. I imagine you are in despair now but it's only making things worse.
Your love always inspired me. Please protect whatever left. I hope all this mess can be fixed. I wish it for you, Agata and Adelle.
Take care,Paula [signed the American way]"

I was sitting at the computer when an incoming Skype call from an unknown caller popped up and started ringing. I answered despite the fact that I didn't know who it was, thinking it could be your mom reaching out to me. It was Pola's Sri Lankan boyfriend, whom I barely recognized and had never spoken to.

"Are you Jesus?" he asked me, with no discernable expression on his face.

I was taken aback; this was not the conversation I had expected.

"Are you Jesus?" he repeated. He was serious, it seemed, but what could he mean? I thought that he must be aware of the cult and what was happening. If not, I reasoned, he would have said something like, "you got what you deserved, you dirtbag."

"No," I responded, "I am not Jesus. I just love Agata," and I hung up.

"**Fri, Jan 7, 2011, 6:22 AM**
Jeremiah to me
what is this?call me today when you can..."

"**Fri, Jan 7, 2011, 12:53 PM**
Brian to me
Hey man - any way you can get at me via the phone?"

"**Re: I love you**
Fri, Jan 7, 2011, 3:27 PM
Rachel to me
Iain
I just read your e-mails. It sounds like you have alot on your mind and in your heart. I hope things are ok.
I love you lots and lots.
God bless
Rach"

January 8, 2011
Mom to Agata Bryson [from the court record]
"In my opinion Iain is having a nervous breakdown. He's convinced that you've been abducted and are in great danger. I'm sure his mind created that so he doesn't have to cope with reality"

January 9, 2011
Agata Bryson to Dad [from the court record]
"...as you know, Adelle and I are in recovery from domestic violence program and all the professionals that we are working with. Please remember that Adelle and I are the victims of domestic violence in family from his and and words, and it seems like you focus only on his pain."

January 9, 2011
Dad to Agata Bryson [from the court record]
"As you know he is very good at convincing people that he is in control and on the right track. He says that he is smarter than the doctors (and police...) and he is right. You were his operating system, Agata and without his computer is down and lost...it's all pretty crazy. I don't know how you have lived with it all these years. I wish you had told me because I would have stepped in. Not your fault, I should have asked you and been a better father-in-law."

January 9, 2011
Agata Bryson to Dad [from the court record]
"...Adelle is not in good shape because of him."

January 9, 2011
Agata Bryson to Mom [from the court record]
"...his mental state for a long time now is based on the drugs that he has been abusing for the past 15 years!...Adelle and I went through hell and back that requires very extensive, long lasting therapy. Adelle startles and cries and hides in the corner..."

January 9, 2011
Mom to Agata Bryson [from the court record]
"...in no way do I consider any of this your fault. I am so happy that you are a strong woman and took care of both yourself and my granddaughter."

I don't know what my mom thought reality was, but these emails to your mom confirmed that she had completely been swallowed up by the red herring. She must've thought that you were actually hiding in a corner, as your mom claimed, because of damage that I had done to you. She must've thought that taking you away from me was a good thing. My heart was broken when I read this in a Polish prison cell more than a year later.

They capitulated to the narrative of your abductors/abusers rather quickly and proceeded to apologize to your mother and even thank her for taking you away from me. Not long before, my mom had been telling me to call the Duty Officer, and my dad had been telling me how worried he was about whatever your grandpa had done to you. But, as your mom had forewarned, nobody believed me; the red herring was doing its job.

Additionally, Jeremiah had fully taken the bait and was even trying to cover his butt as he advised your mom to handle the custody issue. Reading these messages after sitting in a cell for nineteen months was quite difficult, because they proved the reason why I was being railroaded and ignored – I stood completely alone.

Why he would've asked the next question and believed that your mom's answer could mean anything at all, given what I had been telling him, is an enigma. Of course, the truth was that we had spent the last three weeks together while your mom was in bed threatening abduction, and all of your abuse signs and symptoms had returned with you from Poland. In your own words, I was your "best friend."

January 9, 2011
Jeremiah to Agata Bryson [from the court record]
"Does she (Adelle) talk about Iain and miss him?"

January 9, 2011
Agata Bryson to Jeremiah [from the court record]
"Adelle won't talk about him at all. Only that she doesn't want him to come over here and that she is scared of him. I am sure your relationship with Sawyer [Jer's son] is different than the one Iain had with Adelle. It is very sad but that is the truth."

January 9, 2011
Jeremiah to Agata Bryson [from the court record]
"If you ever have to print these(my emails) and take them to court, I don't want my name on them."

January 9, 2011
Agata Bryson to Mom [from the court record]
"Judging by your e-mails I think you don't know the whole situation (...) everyday he had outbursts of anger. He caused me physical pain, waking me and Adelle in the middle of the night shouting in my face, strangling me, pulling her out of my arms, locking himself with her in the room, while she was crying for me and changing my life into hell. I do not agree with his ideas for a living (that he will be a writer now, and I will support us again, that he will still take drugs, that we will live in Hague with debts and problems and I decided that I have to stand for Adelle and my family. Every day he threatened me that if I don't do as he says, he'll kill me or take Adelle from me and I will never see her again. He also told Adelle that I can't play with her or take care of her because I am mentally ill (...) Adelle is afraid and cries, hides in the corner at every louder noise. She won't allow anyone to get nearer if I don't hold her in my arms. (...) I had to let it all out, because I assume that you have no clue what happened during the last three weeks with him under the same roof'"

Everything she said here was untrue, but it was enough to get my parents on board, thus putting the final nail into my coffin. None of my efforts at getting help in the future would be fruitful, whether it was pre-arrest (before April 27, 2011) or post. Nobody believed me, and it all started with my parents; they were effectively working for the other side by dissuading others from taking me seriously.

January 9, 2011
Dad to Agata Bryson [from the court record]
"(...) I think I know what he needs and how this fantasy of saving you from bad people developed (...)'"

"Mon, Jan 10, 2011, 8:07 AM
Brian to me
Hey man - any new news? I'm hoping your love has conquered evil below equates to you being reunited with your family... is that the case?"

I thought that it would mean that we would be reunited soon; not long ago I thought that people would agree that you needed to be evaluated, and that, if my family in Connecticut united behind me, we would be able to make that happen, but I was not getting the "help" that I needed.

"Mon, Jan 10, 2011, 11:49 AM
Iain Bryson to US Citizen Services - Amsterdam, Agata Bryson, Mom, Jeremiah, Angela, Bonnie, Brian, Bree, Carrie, Courtney, Dave, Hart, Heather, John S., Jon, Dad, Rachel, Sara, Governor Rell, [Netherlands Youth Institute], [Lawyer], [Lawyer], [Lawyer], Fred Taal [Dutch detective], Bob McCoy
Iain Avery Bryson
The Hague, The Netherlands 2562JV
As I have stated over and over, Agata and Adelle are missing. An abduction has taken place. I need not go into further detail at the moment; the extent of what I know is impertinent. What I do have is proof. I have a fifty page document, written in Polish, describing how my wife and child will be used for 'war.' The police tell me that they are 'working on it.' The US Embassy tells me that an attorney must take care of this. The problem is that I know what is taking place, what will take place, and what has been taking place all along. This is a planned event. My wife has tried to tell me, tried to show me, and has left me proof. Nobody wants to see the proof.
Before leaving, she made me watch 'The Tourist,' 'Unthinkable,' along with other things that really need not matter now. The evidence is in my possession. She has left me proof of Saudi Aramco's involvment. I do understand that to many people the result of such a thing would be a whirlwind of chaos and confusion.

My wife has known all along that this would not be the case with me, and I have been provided with all that is needed to remedy this situation. The problem is that nobody will listen or even take a look at what she has left. Proof of what I consider to be terrorist activity needs some consideration.

Or, I have to ask myself what I as a writer should do with such information. How long need I wait? How long should I wait? When I answer that question, in my own mind, the answer I come up with is 'there should be no wait at all;' waiting necessarily means more harm to Agata and Adelle, and there is proof of abduction/terrrorism.

All the best to you and yours,

Iain"

Two weeks of trying to figure out where you were and stop you from leaving the country had taken a toll on me, as any form of torture eventually would. But my problem wasn't that I was losing my mind, but that I was losing my family. My reaction was, in fact, reasonable given what the stimulus was. The people who should've been on my side were not, and everything was crashing down on top of me all at once.

"An abnormal reaction to an abnormal situation is normal behavior" (Frankl 38).

The more alone that I felt, the more antagonistic I became. I didn't have a document saying you would be used for "war," and I didn't have proof of Saudi Aramco's involvement. I had held it together, for the most part, up until now, but once I realized that nobody was helping me, I began to slip. It wasn't that I really believed what I was saying, but that I was too mentally fatigued at this point to process new information, and too inflamed with passion to stop typing. If people would have stopped and asked, I would have explained to them that taking my daughter, in my opinion, is terrorism.

"Tue, Jan 11, 2011, 5:43 PM
Mom to me
Iain
I still haven't heard back from you about rescheduling your flight.
I am going to call US Air tonight and see about Thursday or Friday this week.
Big snow storm might jam up the works.
Also looking into Aer Lingus but that means a Boston Pick up so you would have to sit and wait for me to get out of work to get you. again, snow storm jamming everything up.
Let me know asap please. Love you, Mom"

Paranoia is an interesting phenomenon, because once there were things to be legitimately paranoid of, like my parents talking to my wife behind my back or having to wonder what their next act of "help" might be, then it became difficult to mentally formulate where the boundaries of normal and possible were. Once the paranoia reflex was triggered, it wanted to play it safe in all areas that came under its purview.

My dad was still acting strangely, and though he continued to say he wanted to help me, his actions were not adding up. Ever since he invited the crisis intervention team into our home, I knew I had to watch him, and I could tell that he wasn't being forthright. It was as if he was pretending to go along with me just so he could be close and keep an eye on me. He was constantly on his laptop or phone, sending out emails and text messages, and if I approached, he was quick to avert the screen so I couldn't see whatever he was doing. Obviously, he was talking to people about me.

One morning, when I was typing my own emails with the morning sun shining through our living room window onto my face, I sensed my dad over my right shoulder. I wasn't concerned if he saw what I was typing, because nothing I was doing was a secret; the only thing I wanted was to stop you from being taken back to your abusers in Poland. After arriving at a place where I could take a break, I turned and looked over my shoulder to acknowledge my dad and see if he was waiting to say something. In that moment, he had just taken a picture with his phone, and the look on his face told me that this was not "help." My eyes darted to where the camera had been pointed, and anger began to well up inside of me as I realized what had just happened: the picture he had snapped was of my doctor prescribed bottle of Concerta and five Euro worth of marijuana that was next to me on the windowsill. *He is collecting evidence to show that I am not in my right mind!*

I yelled at him and again threatened to throw him out, but I was more concerned with the fact that I was losing any support that I thought I had rather than whatever he thought he was going to do with that picture. But then panic struck as I remembered what your mom had said about Concerta being used against me, and I took the bottle into the kitchen and buried it deep into the trash. In the bathroom, I flushed the marijuana, hoping that at least a piece of the red herring would also be going down the drain.

The reason that my mom was "looking into Aer Lingus" was because I had told her that I would not fly any other way. One of the documents on our computer was a receipt from Aer Lingus from a previous flight that said "thank you for flying Aer Lingus" in big letters at the top of the page. From my point of view at the time, I thought that it was possible that your mom was trying to tell me to fly Aer Lingus, and though that seemed extremely odd, I wasn't going to take any extra chances with anything.

My dad convinced me to return to the United States, where he assured me that we would work together as a family to get an attorney and demand immediate action. Because that was exactly what I wanted to hear, I packed my bags and said my final farewell to our home. The only issue at hand was your cat, Ally, but my dad promised that he would make sure to do whatever it took to get her to the U.S., so that she would be there when you got there. He also said that he would take care of the apartment as far as turning the keys in and letting them know we had vacated, but I was only worried about our cat.

CHAPTER 61

"BACK TO CONNECTICUT"

On January 14, 2011 I disembarked from the plane, excited to be home, back in the good old USA where people still did believe in child protection, I thought. It was a good flight; I read the better part of two books, and also watched two movies. After retrieving my luggage, I made my way out of the customs terminal, first going to Dunkin Donuts, then outside to roll and smoke a cigarette.

After smoking one, I rolled another, and then called my mother. She had previously said I was going to have to wait a while at the airport so she could get out of work and drive up to Boston from Connecticut. I was surprised when she answered and said she was at the airport with my aunt.

They came outside shortly thereafter with Dunkin Donuts coffees of their own. I gave them hugs, telling them that my flight was great. They were smiling and laughing, and I joked along with them as I pushed the cart with my luggage to my mother's Volvo.

On the two-hour drive back to Connecticut, I went over some of the details of the abduction and abuse with them, and they seemed to listen intently with great concern. I had no reason to believe they were worried about anything else other than what I was worried about: getting you evaluated as quickly as possible.

The traffic was heavy, and they complained about it the entire way home, stopping three more times to get coffee and to go to the bathroom. I was a bit exhausted from my day on the plane, along with two weeks in Holland desperately trying to gain ground on your abduction. My mother passed the exit which would have brought us to my aunt's house. I wondered where we were going but figured at the same time that my mother must have it under control.

She continued toward her home, but then she passed that exit as well. I was confused, but there was quite a bit that was confusing me lately, and it did not sound off any internal alarms. After all, one must be able to trust some people some of the time, or else constantly be on guard. I was relaxed like a lamb being taken to slaughter or a child thinking he is going someplace fun only to find himself at the doctor for a shot. We pulled into the hospital parking lot and came to a halt. I waited for someone to speak.

My mother said, "I need to go inside and get a handle on this. I need help understanding what is going on."

"What do you mean, Mom? What do you want to understand? Adelle is gone, she is in Poland, and we must get her. We have to get her medical attention right away. We need a lawyer. There is really nothing to understand. The details are unimportant; what is important is that Adelle has been abducted."

"I know Iain, but I just need help to understand this."

My mother was crying, her eyes beet red, and my aunt looked at me. "Iain, let's just go inside for your mother. She needs help with this."

"OK, I can go inside for her, if she thinks it will help her. I just have no idea what she needs to understand or what she thinks she should understand. It is clear. We need to get Adelle."

"OK Iain, well let's just go in for her," she proposed again.

"Not a problem," I responded, wanting to help. "If she thinks it will help her, I will try. I just do not understand. This doesn't make any sense to me."

The three of us walked into the hospital, through the emergency room entrance. My mother went right up to speak to the receptionist through the glass, crying. She could hardly maintain her composure. She seemed to be doing much better during the ride here, and I wondered what had upset her so much. *Why is she having a breakdown right now?*

My mother continued crying, my aunt stood next to me, and within a minute or two the door to the back room was opened to allow us to enter. My mother entered first, led by a nurse, and my aunt and I followed a few steps behind. The three of us were led into a back room with only a hospital bed. As soon as all three of us were inside the room, my mother slipped out the door, crying, and the door was closed behind her.

"Iain, your mother needs help, but this is for you. I need you to take off your clothes, and put this on, for your safety," the nurse instructed me as sternly as she could.

"What the [expletive] are you talking about? I am fine. It is my daughter, and obviously my mother, who are not fine. How about you work on getting the dick out of my daughter? Did you not hear that she has been abducted, that she is being sexually abused? What else is there to worry about?"

"Iain, if you don't take your clothes off, we will have to take them off for you. We are not giving you a choice. Your mother says that you go to a dark place; she is very worried."

"I do not go to a dark place. My [expletive] daughter is in a dark place. What the [expletive] are you talking about now? My daughter is abducted, I fly in from Amsterdam, and now you trap me like a wild animal?"

"We are not trapping you; we are trying to help you. Now, are you going to take your clothes off, or do we need to help you?"

My aunt chimed in, "Iain, just do it for your mother. She needs you to do this."

"I do not know what the [expletive] she needs, or what you are talking about. Adelle is in trouble, she is not safe, I have been working on this. It is obvious. Now you want me to check myself in, to be checked into a hospital? For what? Because my daughter is being raped?"

Security guards blocked the door, and I saw that I was trapped. I clenched my jaw and glared at my aunt. "You people want to tie my hands behind my back and make me watch my daughter be raped. Do you not understand that my daughter has been abducted and that I am sure she is being sexually abused, possibly at this very moment? Get these [expletive] security guards away from me. What the [expletive] are they going to do? Arrest me? Did I not say there is a dick in my daughter?"

The officer responded, (Officer St. Jean of Norwich PD) "Iain, I am a police officer, not a security guard."

"Yeah, I can see that you have a gun. You have your hand on it. Do you think you scare me with it? I just [expletive] told you that my daughter is being molested."

"I'm not trying to scare you, Iain."

"Then what the [expletive] are you doing with your hand? It is on your gun. What are you really going to do with that gun? I told you my daughter has been abducted, and that she is being molested, yet you still threaten me with a gun? Do you think that gun would stop me from getting out of here if getting out of here was what I felt I needed to do? Should your gun, or the threat of your gun impede me from helping my daughter?"

Two nurses then entered the room, one of them carrying a needle. I don't like needles, and I surely didn't think I needed one. I thought I was here to get help for my mother, but now I was being chased by needles. *What the [expletive] kind of sick joke is this? I guess it is my reality. My daughter has been abducted, is being molested. Why should I not be chased with a needle?*

"OK OK, please no drugs. I am sorry for being loud. I just don't understand being trapped here against my will when my daughter is in Poland, being abused. I am upset, and I just got off the airplane a little while ago. Don't give me drugs. Please. I don't want drugs. I will quiet down. I'm sorry."

"If you quiet down, we won't give them to you now, but I am going to keep them in my pocket in case you get out of hand. I will give you one chance, but next time I have to ask, you are getting the drugs."

"Thank you. What drugs are they?"

"Ativan and Halidol. They will just calm you down."

"I don't need to be calmed down. I was perfectly calm, even amidst my daughter's abduction. Now, you've got me trapped in a psych ward and you tell me I am not calm when I object?"

The doctor came in the room a couple of hours later. "Iain, you have a delusional disorder. Get some rest, and Dr. Kaiser will be in to see you in the morning."

I temporarily accepted defeat, barely alright with the fact that I would have to sleep on a metal table in a hospital tonight, realizing that I was going to have to adjust how I came across to people, and that I was truly on my own.

When the doctor came in the next morning, I was calm and mentally prepared to speak to him, ready to get out of there and get back to the reason that I had returned to the United States. I knew that they couldn't just hold a person in a psychiatric hospital for no reason, that they must determine that the person is a danger to himself or to others. And, of course, I was not; all I wanted was to find a good attorney and get you evaluated by a professional at the soonest possible time. This was not crazy or dangerous, but rather what any father in my position should've wanted.

I explained to him that I was upset that I had been lied to and trapped, but that I was over that and just needed my freedom so that I could begin looking for help with the situation involving my stolen daughter. "I lived in The Netherlands apart from my family. Nobody in my family here really knew my wife or my daughter. Nobody saw what was going on other than me. My mom and my aunt are reacting because this is a surprise, which it was and is for me as well. They are having a hard time wrapping their heads around what I am saying, but really they just have no idea what they are talking about. My daughter was illegally taken from our home in The Netherlands to Poland, and all signs point to the fact that she has been abused. As her father, I want her back, and I want her to be evaluated. And yes, I am upset, as I should be, but also totally in control."

This psychiatrist decided quickly that he did not have the grounds to hold me any longer, and he indicated that he would be back shortly to process my discharge. I anxiously waited in my holding room until he returned about thirty minutes later. "Well, your mom, your dad, your aunt, and your cousin (Jeremiah) called and said that they are afraid that you will hurt yourself or someone else if I let you out..."

"No, of course I won't," I protested, feeling the wind being taken from my sails.

"Because of their vehemence, I have decided to place you on a hold for further observation."

"How can you hold me when you already decided that I am not a danger? Who am I a danger to? What do they have to do with anything? They don't even know me, I haven't had a relationship with them in years, and they have no idea about my family..."

"When there are so many people saying the same thing, in this case that you are a danger, I have to take that into account. We are going to keep you here for further observation."

My stomach sank to the ground, but I could see that he had decided, his judgment had been tainted by too many others, and I didn't have a chance to change his mind right now. I knew that I would change his mind, but I also needed him on my side, so I didn't argue. I decided to put my head down and plow through whatever their observation was, knowing that it would be easy, and that they would have to let me go shortly. Most importantly, I knew that I didn't have a choice.

I hated wasting time with you where you were, but there was nobody on my side now, and at least I could prove to everyone that I was not "crazy." Then, maybe, they would see that I did need help getting you out of Poland and getting you evaluated.

I could write a book just about my time (January 14-January 27) in the psychiatric observation unit at Backus Hospital in Norwich, CT, but to do so would go beyond the scope of the purpose of this present book. I met new people, learned a lot, and other than only wanting to find an attorney, this time was enjoyable for me, just another experience. It was disheartening to know that I didn't have anybody on my side, but these were the cards I had been dealt.

The same people that forced this hold on me tried to get me committed for longer, but since I had been fully "observed," that wasn't going to happen; their irrational, ignorant fears were irrelevant. I was given my walking papers, and on them written the following diagnosis: "adjustment disorder, delusional disorder ruled out." *Yes, losing my daughter and knowing that she is being abused has been a very difficult "adjustment" for me! Shouldn't it be? Now can we get back to what I was saying and just get this nearly four-year-old child, my little girl, evaluated?*

> "Adjustment disorder (AD) is a psychiatric condition that arises in response to a stressful event or situation. It resolves spontaneously once the stressor is removed or when a new level of adaptation is reached. AD is unusual among psychiatric disorders because it is one of the few syndromes in the current classifications to link aetiology with diagnosis. In this, it resembles bereavement, acute stress disorder (ASD), and post-traumatic stress disorder (PTSD)" (Casey 2).

The only diagnosis that they could legitimately give me was Adjustment Disorder, which is defined in the DSM-V as, "The development of emotional or behavioral symptoms in response to an identifiable stressor(s) occurring within 3 months of the onset of the stressor(s)" (American Psychiatric Association 286).

Further, "The stress-related disturbance does not meet the criteria for another mental disorder and is not merely an exacerbation of a preexisting mental disorder" (286). In other words, other than the level of distress I was experiencing after having lost my daughter to an abusive cult, there was absolutely nothing wrong with me. Once the stressor of having my daughter stolen was cleared up, my emotional state would also right itself naturally. But still, nobody was stepping forward to actually help me.

I shared a cab with a guy I had met during my stay at Backus, and we returned to his house to figure out what to do next. Mike was his name, and he had been in the psychiatric unit because of a suicide attempt; he was a depressed alcoholic. He now wanted to help me in whatever way he could with my daughter, even if it meant him going to Poland to take care of it himself, or with me.

Neither of us had money, but I did have a car at my mom's house, so I told Mike I would be back and walked several miles through the snow to get my car. My mom seemed to be waiting for me; she handed me a twenty-dollar bill and my car keys, telling me that I had to go elsewhere, suggesting that I stay at my dad's empty schoolhouse in New London because he and my stepmom, Wendy, were in Florida. I drove back to Mike's to tell him that I would come back for him the next day, then I headed to check out the situation at the schoolhouse.

I unpacked my bags once I got to New London, and I discovered that my passport was missing from the secure, zippered pocket I always kept it in. Certain about where I had put it, I was just as sure that my mom had taken it. I got back into my car to drive to the nearest pay phone, and I was livid.

"Mom, I know that you took my passport, and I want it back."

"I didn't take your passport; it must have fallen out of your bag. I don't know, but I didn't take it," she attempted to assure me.

"Mom, I am not asking you if you took my passport, but rather telling you that you did, and that you will give it back. I know where I put it, and now it is not there. You are the only one who had access to it. Stop lying to me."

She did not admit that she took it, but she didn't have to; I knew she did, and I would get it back when I needed it. I decided I would try to get onto my computer and relax a bit.

There was no heat in the building, but I made myself comfortable, nonetheless. I was able to find an unsecured wi-fi network with a weak signal and get my computer online, and I spent the evening checking my email and planning my next moves.

Mike stayed there with me over the course of the next week or so, and a couple of other people from Backus also stopped by to visit. We ate at a homeless shelter down the street and were careful not to blow through the twenty dollars from my mom.

The craziest thing was that only a month ago I had been trying to get your mom help, singing to you, and caressing your forehead to help you get to sleep. Now I was homeless, stripped of everything that I held dear, and left by the rest of my family to figure it out on my own.

CHAPTER 62

"NO, NO, NOT MY LITTLE GIRL!"

"International Abduction of US Citizen/Generational Polish Incest [Incident: 110101-000045]
Thu, Jan 20, 2011, 9:01 AM
U.S. Department of State to me
Recently you requested personal assistance from our on-line support center. Below is a summary of your request and our response. If this issue is not resolved to your satisfaction, you may reopen it within the next 7 days.
Thank you for allowing us to be of service to you.
Subject

International Abduction of US Citizen/Generational Polish Incest
Discussion Thread

Response (Support Agent) - 01/20/2011 09:01 AM
U.S. embassies and consulates help to locate U.S. citizens overseas when relatives or friends are concerned about their welfare or need to notify them of emergencies at home. Welfare whereabouts requests may be directed to the appropriate office in the U.S. Department of State, Directorate of Overseas Citizens Services (CA/OCS).

For Missing and Sick Adults, Emergency Family Messages, and Child Abuse, Neglect, Abandonment or Exploitation cases, and child welfare in cases not/not involving parental child abduction or custody disputes , contact of the Office of American Citizens Services at (202) 647-5225/5226.

For a Child Custody/Parental Child Abduction Case of a U.S. citizen under the age of 18 , phone or fax the Office of Children's Issues, (CA/OCS/CI), U.S. Department of State, 2201 C Street, NW, Washington, D.C. 20520-4818; TELEFAX: 202-312-9743; PHONE: 202-736-9090. If you make the request by phone, you will be asked to follow up with a written request via fax.

Or Contact the U.S. Embassy or Consulate -- It is also possible to contact the American Citizens Services Section of the nearest U.S. embassy or consulate directly. Telephone and fax numbers for U.S. embassies and consulates are available in our Country Specific Information for each country or via our automated fax service by dialing (202) 647-3000 from the phone on your fax machine.

What Information to Have Available Before You Call:
In order to assist us in locating the U.S. citizen abroad, it is helpful to have the following information available:
• Caller's full name, address, phone number and relationship
• Name of the Person abroad
• Date and place of birth of the person abroad
• Passport number (if known)
• Last known address and phone number; itinerary

- Reason for their travel/residence abroad (business, tourism, etc.)
- Date of last contact
- Other points of contact abroad (friends, business associates, hotel, etc.)
- If ill, where hospitalized and, if relevant to current hospitalization, the name and phone number of attending physician in the U.S.
- You may also be asked to provide a photo of the missing person
- It may also be useful for you to contact credit card companies, telephone companies, etc. to try to determine if the missing individual's accounts have been used recently and where those transactions occurred.

For Emergency Family Messages also include:
- Nature of the emergency
- What you want the person told about the emergency
- Name, address and telephone number and relationship of person you wish subject to call after the emergency family message is relayed to them by the U.S. embassy or consulate.

For more information, please visit the following site:
http://www.travel.state.gov/travel/tips/emergencies/emergencies_1202.html

Thank you for contacting the Department of State.
Question Reference #110101-000045

Category Level 1: Consular
Category Level 2: Emergency Information
Date Created: 01/01/2011 12:04 PM
Last Updated: 01/20/2011 09:01 AM
Status: Solved"

"Fri, Jan 28, 2011, 11:44 AM
Iain Bryson to Agata Bryson
Agata,
I love you. Please give our daughter a hug and kiss for me. I sent her a book for her birthday. So much to say.
My play on time is one [reference to a Dave Matthews lyric], Your husband"

"Adelle and Haag Treaty
Sat, Jan 29, 2011, 8:11 PM
Dad to me
Hi Iain. I'm in Fl until the 7th. I have info on paperwork and want to go over some things with you so we can figure how best to proceed. I agree that you need to push the treaty so as to get contact with Agata and Adelle and stay in Adelle's life. The best (and maybe only)short term approach seems to be invoking that treaty. There are a few issues that will come up fast. One, you do not have a home or work in Holland. The Dutch will look at Adelle as a resident of Holland and may want a Dutch address. Two, Agata obviously has some issues with you and may question your ability to take care of Adelle. I think that they need to see that any problems that they might attach to you are the result of your losing your daughter and that, therefore, it is most important that you be re-united.

This may mean returning to Holland, getting a job there?, ???. It may mean in the short term that both you and Agata live in Denn Haag separately but with share custody of Adelle. Without an agreement from Agata you may not be able to bring Adelle to the US, just as without your agreement, Agata would not be able to take Adelle someplace else, including to her parents. This may not be a good long term solution but it would certainly allow you to be with Adelle now. I have more thoughts on this which I would like to discuss. The point is that the treaty can force Agata to return with Adelle to Holland where you should have access with Adelle and from there the work will be to make an agreement between you that will work for now. I think you will need the help of your doctors to give you good reports.

I am of the opinion now that all the trouble has come from your losing Adelle and with your being re-united with her your 'stability' will return. I would like to help. Making Agata return may be fairly simple, beyond that I don't know. That will be the work.Be sure to keep all your correspondence simple and to the point. Agata left Holland with your daughter . You have joint custody of her. She did not have your permission to take Adelle out of the country. She must return with Adelle. Once the three of you are in Holland you can discuss your issues and options. Period. No other stories, no Polish perversions, no Catholic Church or Aramsco conspiracy. You all lived in Holland together, she left with Adelle w/o your permission, they must come back. Give me a call and we'll talk. I have atty's info as well as person I talked with at international abduction center. Love you, Dad"

"back in new london?
Mon, Jan 31, 2011, 6:46 PM
Brian to me
hit me up if you can..."

"Adelle Avery Bryson -----No, No Not my little girl.
Tue, February 1, 2011 1:28:20 AM AST
Iain Bryson to Fred Taal [Dutch detective], US Citizen Services - Amsterdam, allyopolis, Art, Alice, Carrie, Brian, Dad, Brianne, Jeff B, Bonnie, Casey O, Jim, [News], Robert P, Dave, [News], George N, Heather W, Haidee S [ex-colleague], John Hughley, [Lawyer], Jon, Nancy M., [News], [News], Pat [Polish friend], [News], [News], [American International School of Rotterdam], Sara, [Lawyer], [Lawyer]
January 31, 2011
Iain Avery Bryson
Writing for
Adelle Avery Bryson, born January 30, 2007 in New London, CT, and Agata Bryson, born July 11, 1982, in Stargard Szczecinski, Poland.

Adelle Avery Bryson, my daughter is the victim of an international spousal abduction. There has been no response by authorities, at least not one which touches my standards in this sort of situation. I demand a response, now, finally. Adelle disappeared with her mother on December 27, 2010. We were living in The Netherlands; the Dutch government would not do anything, and the US government said it could not do anything. Now, my daughter is in Poland, in a situation where she is held by her abductors, and where she is regularly abused. The Dutch cannot respond to suspicions of child abuse until the child has reached the age of four. The US cannot do anything in Holland or in Poland, as it is the Hague Convention which determines the course of legal action in this situation. My prescribed course of action is to fill out the paperwork, requesting the return of my daughter to a Dutch court, where they will then decide on her future. This can take a year or two, maybe more, and in the mean time, I am told to wait while my daughter is exposed to violence, abuse and neglect on a daily basis at the hands of people who stole her from her home, from her father. I will not wait; I am getting my daughter. Will you help, or will you not? I am getting her regardless. And, just so we are perfectly clear, I am not threatening anyone or anything. I am just saying I am going to get my daughter. Are you ok with that?

The first thing we need to take care of, other than getting my daughter out of her abductor's hands, is the validity of my sanity. I was recently released from the Backus Hospital Psychiatric Unit, where I was held from January 14-27 2011. During this period of time, I was observed, counseled, doubted, and chided, but in the end it was confirmed that 'I AM NOT DELUSIONAL.' They were forced to set me free, despite the fact that my own mother requested a Conservatorship.

So, I am free for the moment to know, at least in my own mind, that my daughter has been abducted. Chew on that for a moment. Ok, from there I can go into why I know, why a child would be abducted to an Eastern European country, why my child was abducted, how she was abducted, what I can do to get her back, the steps I will or will not take (now again, I am not threatening; I am merely stating that I will get her back, but I have to clarify since that is what got me locked up in the psycho ward. Again, I was branded 'NOT DELUSIONAL.') This is happening, unfortunately for my family). So, the Dutch pretended as if I were delusional for the entire time, from December 27, 2010 till I left Holland January 14, 2011. The US Embassy told me to run with my child to the Embassy if I could get my hands on her, but I could never get my hands on her. So, now she is in Poland, right where they want her. That is not ok with me. Should it be?"

"Re: Adelle Avery Bryson -----No, No Not my little girl.
Tue, Feb 1, 2011, 9:02 PM
Jeremiah to me
Call me when you can.
Jer
860 ▆▆▆"

"Wed, Feb 2, 2011, 7:54 AM
Dad to me
I have contacted Maartja at the abduction center in Holland have asked for help in getting paperwork completed. Call me when you can. Love, Dad"

"Fri, Feb 4, 2011, 10:29 AM
Iain Bryson to Dad
dad,
what is going on from your end? did you get those documents to the lawyer?
is anything else needed? i need to report adelle's passport 'lost' as well. can you let me know what you are/are not doing? this was supposed to be done a month ago."

"Fri, Feb 4, 2011, 7:19 PM
Dad to me
Waiting for reply from Maartja. I will call her Monday. She had all the info. Got your info so that should be helpful. See you Monday."

"Fri, Feb 4, 2011, 10:10 PM
Iain Bryson to Dad
OK. just wondering what the news is. i can't think of anything for her to reply to. What she needs to file this should be one conversation. I need to know what the details are. When you call, can you ask her about cancelling Adelle's passport, reporting it as 'lost'? See you in a couple"

"Sun, Feb 6, 2011, 9:08 PM
Dad to me
hi Iain . flying in mon providence noon. can you pick me up? Have info for ?Hague. thanks, Dad"

"Sun, Feb 6, 2011, 9:42 PM
Iain Bryson to Dad
i can pick you up but i don't have money for the gas."

"Mon, Feb 7, 2011, 8:15 AM
Iain Bryson to Dad
do you want me to come? i just need you to put some in the gas tank"

"Mon, Feb 7, 2011, 9:39 AM
Dad to me
yes iwill give you gas arrive delta 2916 about 12:15 thanks Dad plz confirm"

My dad and Wendy returned from Florida, and Wendy demanded that I leave the school immediately, not wanting anything to do with me. "But Dad, all I am trying to do is get back on my feet and get my daughter back..."

I took my belongings, dropped Mike back off where he had been staying, and headed to the only place I could think of: my friend John's (who died in December) widow's house, Faye. I figured she would let me in, and I figured she could use some help as well given the recency of her own husband's untimely passing.

She gave me my own bedroom and invited me in as family, and so I had heat and a strong wi-fi signal, which was all that I needed to get back to work. I enjoyed spending the next three months with her and her daughter, getting to laugh and cry with them, getting to paint easter eggs with someone else's daughter who was just a few years older than you were at the time. She called me "Uncle Iain," but that just made me miss hearing "Daddy" even more.

"Wed, Feb 9, 2011, 7:59 AM
Iain Bryson to Kees de Vries
Kees,
I just wanted to let you know I am doing well. I appreciate all of your help.

I will get back to you later; I have a busy day. So, I got to spend thirteen days in an inpatient psych unit. It took them that long for them to tell me what I already knew: I am not delusional. At least I have that on paper now. Iain"

"Thu, Feb 10, 2011, 3:30 AM
Kees de Vries to me
Hi Iain,
Good to hear from you! So what are your plans now?
Kind regards, Kees"

CHAPTER 63

"HEY YOU, GET OFF MY CLOUD..."

"Thu, Feb 10, 2011, 9:11 PM
Iain Bryson to Agata Bryson, bcc: Brian, bcc: Dad, bcc: Mom, bcc: allyopolis, bcc: Agata Bryson, bcc: Kees de Vries

Agata,

I have not heard from you since December 27, 2010. I have not seen our daughter since December 27, 2010. During this stretch of time, I received two messages from you:

The first was an email I received on December 27, 2010, stating that you and Adelle were in a shelter for abused women and children. I received this within two hours of you leaving. It also stated that you would contact me in a few days that the three of us could talk, and so I could see Adelle. Can you explain why you did not follow through with these plans? I received your second email four days later. You said that you were receiving treatment in a shelter, and that you were in The Hague.

Can you tell me what my daughter received treatment for? What follow-up services are in place? Can we choose another doctor together for Adelle to see? Do you think Adelle should receive any less treatment than she needs? Do you think I should have no say in what she needs? I ask that we work together for the benefit of our daughter.

I know you care a great deal about our daughter, and I am confident that you are on top of things. That is not my concern at all. I believe with all my heart that you want what is best for Adelle, just as I do. My concern is that this is an ambiguous decision with huge implications for the rest of her life.

There are two logical paths that could deny Adelle what I believe to be necessary: 1. You can say you have taken care of things, that Adelle is doing wonderful, and that my concerns do not exist. What I would say to you is ok, but can we still check again, for the benefit, however crazy it is, of our daughter. Is it too much for Adelle to find a doctor we can agree on, to test until I am satisfied she is safe, to make sure that our daughter moves forward from this point in as healthy and nurturing a way as possible? It would put my mind to rest if we were able to check on this now.

When Adelle screams 'not my pee pee' over and over again, right after you and her get back from Poland, you state it is due to a soap irritation. Can you tell me how you know it is from a soap irritation? Did she tell you? How does she know? Did you tell you? How do you know? Are you sure that either you or her are correct? Absolutely sure?

Can you tell me why she stops saying 'not my pee pee' after a couple of weeks of being home after her ventures to Poland? Is the soap really bad in Poland? She seems less scared once she settles back into our home life. I do not quite understand. Does someone in Poland cake the soap on her, terrifying her, so that I have to hear her cry and plead for about two weeks each time she returns?

Are you sure she doesn't need to see a doctor, if for no other reason than to figure out what this horrible irritation may be from, once and for all. Maybe we could avoid this completely and maybe she doesn't have to scream 'not my pee pee' over and over every time she returns from Poland. Why did you tell me a doctor is not necessary? I do not understand; we have health insurance. I recommended it then, and I demand it now. Are you not concerned at all? Is it an allergy we need to worry about, or do you have it under control? Are you certain, because I really like to be sure when it comes to Adelle?

I am concerned, as I was on December 27, 2010. If you remember, I emphatically stated, each and every day from December 9 to December 27 that I needed us to seek a third party opinion due to my concerns. My concerns are not and were not your concerns, so can you tell me where we are at in dealing with this? Am I to believe you dealt with my concerns when you told me they did not exist? Are you sure they did not and do not exist? Sure enough to not even think about them or get have our daughter examined in the ways I would like?

Do you not remember that I agreed to take your concerns, accept they are one hundred percent true, and deal with them? I was not and am not concerned about your allegations. However, it appears that you are not concerned about my allegations. For the duration, you have claimed that they do not and cannot exist, at least in this reality. Can we agree that it may not be a soap allergy at all? It may be a soap irritation? It may be PH level. It may be anything because our daughter is not of an age where we can trust her explanations. I have waited in the dark for too long, ignored completely when all I care about is Adelle's safety and health. What is your agenda? Is it not Adelle's safety and health because I really thought it was?"

"Thu, Feb 10, 2011, 10:37 PM
Dad to me
very nice, Iain. Well spoken. I look forward to seeing you tomorrow.
That's the point, that you both need to work this situation out for Adelle's sake. It is not for Agata to do on her own just as it would not be right for you to do on your own. It is not right for Agata to keep Adelle from you just as it would not be right for you to keep Adelle from Agata. This is why I am saying that you need to plan on how to be back in Denn Haag where you can be close by and work out a solution. It may be that you will both have to remain in Holland for a while which will mean a job and home for you, as well as transportation back. Love you< Dad"

"Re: Contact Information needed
Fri, Feb 11, 2011, 9:09 AM
Iain Bryson to Dad
mom took my passport, i have been sabotaged repeatedly. granted it is love, but what a sick distorted delusional love. just because you feel it doesn't make it real. when your thoughts are [expletive] up, so shall be your feelings and your beliefs about all that is around you. it is no more than cause and effect. my job is to think since i know nobody else that can. some help with the rest would be nice, especially since all i have gotten is the opposite of help. yes, it is the thought that matters, but not in this case, where my daughter is being raped. now, i shouldn't have said that since it brings about a response antithetical to my position, but unfortunately for my family, everything I say is true. Everything."

"Your perceptions are distorted. Luckily for you, mine are not.
Fri, Feb 11, 2011, 11:00 AM
Iain Bryson to Sara, Mom, Dad, Wendy, Brian, allyopolis
Life's greatest dangers often come not from external enemies but from our supposed family and friends who pretend to work for the common cause while scheming to sabotage us."

"Fri, Feb 11, 2011, 11:21 AM
Iain Bryson to Mom, Jeremiah, Amy, Bonnie, Brian, Brianne, Carrie, Courtney, Dave, Roger, Hart, Heather, John S., Jon, Dad, Rachel, Sara, Wendy, Leyden P [Friend]
Dear friends and family,
I love you all, and I also know you love me. The issue is not the emotion we all like to refer to as 'love.' Rather, it is our expression of this emotion, like our expression of any emotion, which can and is the problem. You can feel any of it, or not, but the way it is expressed is unique to each individual. It is your thoughts which determine expression, and when your thoughts are not right, the expression will not be right.
    'Life's greatest dangers often come not from external enemies but from our supposed colleagues and friends who pretend to work for the common cause while scheming to sabotage us.'
    See, I know your intentions, but I also know how messed up your actions are. Because of your 'love,' and because this emotion is controlled for you by delusional, irrational thoughts, it is expressed in the form of sabotage, among other things. I see it all; I try to explain it, but to no avail. You cannot lie to me; it is simply not possible. I read you like a book. I will get the point across. It kind of stinks for me that I have to go so far outside the box, dealing with you instead of my daughter, to eventually get to my daughter. You do feel these things, but I am telling you, with certainty, they are not real. I am more than happy to help you work on this.
    'People expect your behavior to conform to known patterns and conventions.'

Understand that mine will never conform. But, then again, I know what I am doing, consciously, at all times. You just do and you just feel; bottom line. No questions asked. You cannot begin to explain it to me on any other level. Which is better? Which is more reliable? I know you like your way, but I choose mine. I reject your reality and substitute mine. Why do you think I should even entertain yours for a second? I know you do not like it. I do like mine, because at least it is one of clarity. I have no confusing thoughts other than 'how can people be so blind and clueless.' At least now I see just as clearly that it is not intentional. You cannot help it. Each and every thought you have is distorted, causing reactions you can no longer see. You have been terrorized on every level, leading to your confused, unhappy state. You cannot even identify what is wrong. Stop thinking about what you should feel.

Look into the mirror. What do you think about on a daily basis? I bet it goes something like this: I need more money. This sucks, that sucks. Why can't I win the lottery? I wish I could change....Why does he think that? I wish he/she wouldn't do that. I am mad at..... How is he so happy. Iain cannot be well; if he says what he says, there must be something wrong. Well, Iain has a mind which works, and he directs his emotions appropriately. He will never sabotage anyone he loves. I can help you as well, but it would be nice if we could band together and get my daughter some medical attention.

Do you realize she was abducted? It is a logical proof, and one I can show you right now. If you take a child from her country of residence to another country without the other parents' approval, you have committed an international spousal abduction. Start with that one and realize I have the rest whenever you are ready.
All the best,
Iain"

"Fri, Feb 11, 2011, 12:16 PM
Iain Bryson to Mom, Jeremiah, Amy, Bonnie, Brian, Brianne, Carrie, Courtney, Dave, Roger, Hart, Heather, John S., Jon, Dad, Rachel, Sara, Wendy, Leyden P
Thirteen days of observation in a 500 square feet psych unit.
Result: Iain is not delusional, just smart.

Now, I am not saying anything more than I have a paper saying 'ruled out delusional disorder.' I knew this at the onset, as I run diagnostic testing constantly on my brain. It does not just operate, I operate it. Yes, it is possible, and I sort of like it.

So, by definition, you are delusional. Since 'delusion' means 'false belief,' can we agree you at least have one?

Rip through the veil. Tear down the walls; the harder they are to tear down, the more they need to be taken out. If you do this in error, you can always build it up again, and you could even make it better. What are you scared of? What is your major malfunction? Can I help you with your delusion(s), or would you rather hold them tight? Remember, just remember, 'ABDUCTION.' Hold onto that. I will not bombard you with what I know. Not now. But, I can rip it all to bits, so keep it up."

"'Hey you get off my cloud, you don't know me and you don't know my style.' Method man
Fri, Feb 11, 2011, 1:30 PM
Iain Bryson to Mom, Jeremiah, Amy, Bonnie, Brian, Brianne, Carrie, Courtney, Dave, Roger, Hart, Heather, John S., Jon, Dad, Rachel, Sara, Wendy, Leyden P
Who is the crazy one? I am just crazy in love with my girls. What are you crazy about? Are you sure? Can you explain it to me? Sorry, I know you cannot, but you cannot fault me for trying, can you? I know these things can be scary, but frankly, I am more scared for my little girl.

More words of wisdom from Dave. How is Fox news treating you? Again, I already know. You add certain ingredients to anything, if you control what is added and what it means, you then know what the result will be. You are made. Manufactured. Devised. The most important part in your programming is the part that makes it so you cannot see you are programmed. You are merely a mechanical being, thoughtless, driven into the ground by the forces around you, immune to thought, immune to anything other than what has been programmed. Mom you know this: your love now equals sabotage. Do you know what my love means? Have you ever heard of the F-Sharp theory? I have the truth, and I will continue to drill it out. Do you think I should do any less? I really believe Adelle would say no...."

"Re: 'Hey you get off my cloud, you don't know me and you don't know my style.' Method man
Fri, Feb 11, 2011 at 8:14 PM
Iain Bryson to Mom, Jeremiah, Amy, Bonnie, Brian, Brianne, Carrie, Courtney, Dave, Roger, Hart, Heather, John S., Jon, Dad, Rachel, Sara, Wendy, Leyden P

Agata,

Can you tell me why Adelle was crying incessantly, telling us her vagina was hurting? Are you sure we cannot have her go to a doctor?

Can you tell me why my child did not want to return home when she was out with me? Why did she tell me she helps mommy when she is sick? Why did she ask you to leave her room? Why will she not let me leave the room, pretending like it is locked, telling you to 'go there' when you come in?

Why did she refer to your father's balls as 'Ja Ja'? Why would this come up out of the blue, let alone at all? Do you realize she has never referenced my private parts except with the following statement: 'Daddy, you look just like grandpa.' Under what circumstances does your father take his balls out in front of my daughter? Under what circumstances do they talk about it? Why does Adelle tell me grandpa also refers to balls as 'Pooka'?

Why did our daughter pick out the picture of two lady bugs mating when there were ten other pictures to choose from? What is special about this picture? I can help: there is nothing special to a child until an adult tells it that there is something special.

Why did my child revert back to baby talk? Why did she start having tantrums and crying upon returning from Poland? See, I know (nobody else can) that my child does not cry, or else I find out why and fix it. Yes, as a matter of fact, nothing in this world happens for no reason. I know it is easier for you to choose this, but it is not true. Especially when it comes to my daughter, I choose to figure out the reasons behind the actions.

I see and can describe, in detail, each and every sign of sexual abuse in my child. Do you not think an evaluation is in order? I am telling you right now, I will not stop until this is resolved. I am right, so what you gonna do?"

"Sat, Feb 12, 2011, 9:09 AM
Sara to me
I have recieved all your e mails and it seems ot me that if your goal is to get back with adelle then you need to get a job, save some money for lawyers and airfare and stop the e mails. They are using up time and keeping you from working. I do hope you are well. Love auntie"

Get a job? She was obviously in a different universe where, in her mind, the fact that my daughter had literally just been kidnapped by a cult family did not matter to her and should not matter to me. *How about we get my daughter back, and then I will have the rest of my life to "get a job"?*

"from S
Sat, Feb 12, 2011, 1:04 PM
John S to me
I'd been off the Internet for awhile. Came back on to find all these emails. Not quite through reading them yet.

In the meantime, let me know your address and a phone number (in case the last one has changed). I'm going to be unavailable for a day or two (long story), but I will contact you next week.

Are you sure this email bombardment will get results? We talked about getting the media involved. Any luck in that area?

Linda and I are sending you positive thoughts."

"Sat, Feb 12, 2011, 1:08 PM
Iain Bryson to John S
no john. i am not sure. i am working on something bigger. just agitating i suppose. i dont have an address or phone number at the moment.
should have one once i am done with this project......soon i hope. the media will get involved, i believe. hope you are good. hi to the wife."

February 13, 2011, 11:43 AM
Iain Bryson to Ada (via Facebook messenger)
"Take care of my girls. Love you. 'I'll be there'"

"Sun, Feb 13, 2011, 11:49 AM
Iain Bryson to Sara

You doubt me. Good luck with that. You trap me in a nut house. Good luck with that. I got this [expletive]. I told you all that. I have had it, and now i really have it. My words are my tools. The pen is mightier than the sword. Much mightier. Especially when the sword is yielded by deluded folk who think my child being abducted and raped should lead to me being silenced. Good luck with that."

"Re: 'Hey you get off my cloud, you don't know me and you don't know my style.' Method man
Sun, Feb 13, 2011, 2:15 PM
Iain Bryson to Mom, Jeremiah, Amy, Bonnie, Brian, Brianne, Carrie, Courtney, Dave, Roger, Hart, Heather, John S., Jon, Dad, Rachel, Sara, Wendy, Leyden P
So now, do you not remember things at all?
My wife called me a 'MOLESTER.' She did this on the day she left, with my child, to go back to molesterville. I was pushing her hard, demanding that she get help.
So, according to even simple minds like Freud, there are two options:
1. Either I am a molester or
2. Someone else is.
Test me, chase me with halidol filled syringes, kill me, make me [expletive] like my daughter does, I do not care.
Can we just get her looked at?"

The next three messages are more that I didn't have until I was going through the court records during the nineteen months that I was in pre-trial lockup. I jotted them down in my journal, feeling as betrayed as I'd ever felt in my life to this point; a guy I had known my entire life continued to speak to my wife about her getting custody of our child along with his insistent worry about himself.

February 13, 2011
Jeremiah to Agata Bryson [from the court record]
"...custody of Adelle."
"Please don't mention to anyone that we talked about this..."

February 13, 2011
Jeremiah to Agata Bryson [from the court record]
"Since Friday (Feb. 11th) we have received about 115 e-mails from Iain (he sends them to me and other people, family and friends included). The tone of these e-mails is getting worse- borderline with violence and threats."

For the sake of the length of this book, I'm not including all the emails Jeremiah was talking about from the "Hey you get off my cloud" series. The ones I have included are representatives of the group. The key word in his email is "borderline" because I had not made any threats or done anything violent; I knew my family was looking to lock me up. I was expressing my frustration and need for real help as forcefully as I knew how. I wonder what he was trying to accomplish by continuing communication with your mother.

Brian checked into the issue of why his calls were coming in from a number in Poland on my caller id. The calling card company confirmed that "it should not be a Polish number."

"Sun, Feb 13, 2011, 12:48pm
Brian to EFulfillment Partners [calling card support]
Thanks very much for your input Katie - is there any way to specifically tell if it would come through as a Polish # or not? This is going to sound even odder, but I have a friend in Holland who will not answer the phone if it comes up as a Polish # and that is why I am buying cards from your company. Is there a way to tell if Poland specifically will show up?"

"Sun, Feb 13, 2011, 4:10 PM
Brian to me
I don't know if I'm dealing with an expert here 'Katie', but this does seem a bit odd perhaps...
-----Original Message-----
Re: SpeedyPin Final Low Balance Reminder 2011-01-06 13:53:32

Sun, Feb 13, 2011 2:00 pm
EFulfillmentPartners.com Support to Brian
Hello,
Thank you for your email.
The only way to tell is to buy the card and try it. If you are calling from the US and not from Poland though it should not be a Polish number.
Regards,
Katie
Customer Support"

What the heck could that mean?! I wondered. *"Should not be a Polish number..."*

CHAPTER 64

"MY ONLY FEAR IS THAT I WILL BE TOO LATE"

"Tue, Feb 15, 2011, 8:22 AM
Dad to me
You have a letter sent from hartford. I would like to get haag treaty papers going. We need to talk. Love, dad"

"Tue, Feb 15, 2011, 8:26 AM
Iain Bryson to Dad
who is the sender? you've been saying the thing about the hague treaty for nearly two months. adelle didn't have two months, and now she doesn't have a minute. i can meet later, but i need a few bucks for gas."

"Tue, Feb 15, 2011, 9:15 AM
Kyle [brother] to me
The same love u have for your daughter is the same love she has for u. All she has ever done is love u and do her best as a mother. I read your emails and they are cruel. U r causing so much pain to our mother and life is short and can be taken away any moment. No one is responsible for what has happend in your life. U married a woman from another country, had a child, moved to another country and things went bad. Your family loves you and especially your mother. Life is too short for all this [expletive]."

Yes, but none of what he was referring to was an issue of dispute. What I did have a problem with was the actual working against me and lying to me.

"Tue, Feb 15, 2011, 9:27 AM
Dad to me
i have been waiting on you. do you have aCCESS TO A phone?"

"Tue, Feb 15, 2011, 11:20 AM
Iain Bryson to Kyle
get my daughter out of this situation then and quit sidelining me. I hear you, but who is not an enemy if they are wrong in this situation? Adelle needs me and that is all i care about. my daughter's life is all i care about. the rest can get a grip and lose their delusions or at least stay clear of me."

"Tue, Feb 15, 2011, 11:23 AM
Iain Bryson to Dad
waiting on me? you even want to go there? Do you not listen, ever? How long have i been waiting for you to do the one thing you said you would? Get a [expletive] attorney. You do not fool me. I remember every word that comes out of any mouth. My cat. It is all a big blur to you, I know, but it is just [expletive] sabotage. Waiting on me? did i give you any reason whatsoever to wait on me? Do you think I did, cause we need to discuss that. I told you exactly what is going on. You never answer or do what you say you will do."

He had promised me to take care of our cat, Ally, and make sure she got to the U.S., but he didn't. He ended up giving her to the DeLucas, of all people. From my point of view, there could be no excuses. He relinquished a member of our family because he didn't take our agreement seriously. I loved that cat, I knew that you did too, and I wanted to put her in your arms when we were reunited.

"Tue, Feb 15, 2011, 11:24 AM
Iain Bryson to Kyle
It is about Adelle, not me or her."

"Tue, Feb 15, 2011, 11:48 AM
Dad to me
your cat. It was not for me to arrange for your cat. But I said I would. You told me I did not need any shots and that she was all set to fly. When I was ready to go I found out that she needed a rabies shot 30 ... thats thirty .... days before leaving. I did get you an atty. I told you she needed $1500 to get involved. Where's the money? Did you ask how to get with her to make some arrangements? I told you about the child abduction organization. Did you do anything about it? You know about the Haag treaty. Did you look for the form and get it and fill it out and send it? I am willing to help but not to do it all for you. What have you done to make progress? As to the cat.... who took care of Butch all these years... his vet bills and medicines. His burial? Get a mirror and have a look at the problem. I love you Iain, but get real."

Interesting words from a dad to his son after he had just lost his daughter and seen his family ripped apart. He made it obvious that he thought it was my fault, and that pursuing a solution to my concerns wasn't even worth him putting up $1500. Apparently, he had decided that you were where you needed to be. I felt like I didn't have a dad, but I still needed his help.

"Tue, Feb 15, 2011, 11:52 AM
Iain Bryson to Dad
The money is what I would have made had you not locked me the [expletive] up? Where is your brain? My cat. YOu let me know then if you cannot take care of it. Do you not know that I can take care of anything in this world? YOu told me [expletive]. You sabotaged me, acting sneaky, while I was just recording each sick move you made. What have you done to alleviate your status as a conspirator? What does Butch have to do with it? Are they brother and sister? Who took care of the garage door? What's your favorite color? Refrigerator. I hate speaking with children."

"Tue, Feb 15, 2011, 11:55 AM
Dad to me
how much money have you earned since you left backus? Time well spent?"

Again, with the talk about earning money, as if success were determined in dollars per day. How long was I expected to seek money in lieu of seeking my daughter? Why was nobody else willing to help or contribute to the cause of an abducted family member? I knew it wasn't about the money but that my family didn't believe me.

"Tue, Feb 15, 2011, 12:38 PM
Kyle to me
This is your family and your mission. If you want support you have to come across believable, sincere and not crazy. You can't be angry at what people havnt done but thankful for what they have done. These are your family membrs that want the best for you. Period. Writing hundreds of emails to family members isn't helping her or you. Especially when most sound personally threatening. I believe you but I think your anger is misplaced and you've ruining good relationships w family for no reason."

"Tue, Feb 15, 2011, 1:37 PM
Iain Bryson to Kyle, me
Thanks for your insight. I know what you are saying. That is what I am trying to do. What you have to understand is I see it all, so from there I have to decide what buttons to push. Also, when things happen like

being trapped, chased with needles, told you are delusional, treated like you are delusional, and metaphorically having your hands tied while your wife and daughter are raped, I will capture that emotion and use it. They should not [expletive] up if they dont want to get [expletive] up. It is nothing personal. It is all for Adelle. It is not a matter of what they want. I realize that it is love, as messed up as the actions can be. I love them too. But, I will not sit and let this happen to my girl.

Personally threatening? These are words. They are threatening, if you mean by words. I can take anyone out with my words. They can tie my hands and let my daughter be raped, so what are words really? Use Halidol as a weapon against me, and words will come flying out. I hear you Kyle, and please believe I am trying. But, what is the solution then? I am still being lied to. Still being sabotaged. Still having my passport stolen, my car broken into, Still being looked at in the eyes and lied to. I will not have it. If they want to act like enemies, they can be treated as such. I do not care about relationships founded on [expletive]. Adelle doesn't need that, and that is what I am about, Adelle. You have to see that from my perspective, there really are no personal boundaries. Adelle doesn't have any, so why should people that get in my way of getting her, regardless of their motivation.

I hold no anger whatsoever. It is all just what is, and I happen to see what is. If people don't want to hear it, get out of the way or at least do not get in the way. I am right and that is all there is to it. It is not up for discussion. There is nobody that can discuss what I am discussing. There is nobody who can disprove what I am discussing. I try to say: just remember that an international spousal abduction has occurred, but what do they do, they talk to my wife when she is in Holland, and do nothing, don't even think it is necessary to do anything. Mom tells me Agata took Adelle home. Well, that is one way to look at it, but w"

"Tue, Feb 15, 2011, 3:17 PM
Kyle to me
People read and dnt understand the difference between verbal threats and physical threats. It took you a long time to realize and accept something so awful. People need the same time to absorb it all. Maybe fam made mistakes, maybe they r ignorant about the situation but they are family and Not the enemy. I just think you need focus on adelle and the process ahead of you. It's not a matter of who's right and who's wrong. It's simply what do u have to do to get your girl back. I hope things work out and i'm here if ya need me."

"Tue, Feb 15, 2011, 3:22 PM
Iain Bryson to Kyle
i hear you kyle. thanks again. i really cant help that people cannot focus or do not know what a verbal threat is. I know for a fact there are no physical threats, except to my girls, and i really do not know what to do about people's delusions. its not that i do not care; i do, quite a bit, but there are actual physical threats, imminent threats to my daughter and people continue to hinder my progress, or try to. i know they have to soak it in, but i need to speed that up. no , not 'enemy' but surely held me back and made me watch my daughter be raped, regardless of intention. i am focusing on adelle. this cannot be understood by people either. they have no idea how to focus on anything."

"Tue, Feb 15, 2011, 6:48 PM
Dad to me
Hi Iain I have the Haag Treaty forms . I also have instructions and am waiting for a call from the person who works with Holland. I will try her number again tomorrow. You will have to review and fill out the form. Next check out the general instructions. You can fill out the form on line, then copy it, sign it and send it on. The site is www.travel.state.gov Look on the top banner for child abduction, then to the left column for a to z. next look for hague convention. Also there is paperwork for child passport issuance alert.. L,D"

"Tue, Feb 15, 2011, 6:52 PM
Iain Bryson to Dad
Thank you dad. I appreciate it. I will go there now and look at what needs to be done. The passport is very important as well. You have no idea where I would need to go? Is it possibly the post office? That is where you apply for the passport. love you"

"Tue, Feb 15, 2011, 7:28 PM
Dad to me
I believe you go to the Post office for passports. i don't know the process. The children's passport issuance refers to one parent procuring a passport for a child without the other parent's permission. As you will read, this is not allowed in the US. You will have to research Polish law to see if it is allowed there. We will have

to ask someone at central authority about putting an alert on Adelle's passport. No return address on the letter. hand written address postmarked hartford 2/11/11."

"Adelle and Agata
Wed, Feb 16, 2011, 10:31 PM
Iain Bryson to Mom, Jeremiah, Amy, Bonnie, Brian, Brianne, Carrie, Courtney, Dave, Roger, Hart, Heather, John S., Jon, Dad, Rachel, Sara
My only fear is that I will be too late. Why will you not also demand that my daughter to be tested by a doctor of my choosing? To top it off, you counteract my actions. That is just a bit silly to me, not really, but when you think about it, it kind of is. Did you not hear that I believe she has been sexually abused? Can we look more closely at my clearly stated concerns? Is my claim of sexual abuse something that rolls off your back so easily? Somebody is abusing this girl, sexually, and I want to get to the bottom of it. I am demanding to get to the bottom of it."

"Tue, Feb 22, 2011, 4:44 PM
Mom to me
Hi Iain
Wondering how you are, being a mother you know. Did you think about talking to your contacts at DCF and pick their brains to see if they have any idea about how to go about having Adelle checked out in Poland. Just a thought. I love you, Mom"

This message from my mom triggered me because she was obviously not interested in what I had to say about you. In my opinion, she had done the opposite of what a mother should've done in this situation, which would've been to stand by her son and realize that she really didn't know any of the other people involved. She should've realized that there were gaps in her understanding of the situation, and then stuck to the principle of standing up for her child. I lashed out, frustrated that my own mother couldn't know who I was, and that she could do what she was doing.

"Tue, Feb 22, 2011, 4:50 PM
Iain Bryson to Mom
I had that thought on December 27. Imagine the thoughts I've had since. What thoughts have you had?"

"Tue, Feb 22, 2011, 4:52 PM
Iain Bryson to Mom
My family, other than a select few:
1. Sabotage
2. Steal
3. Take action which places my family in imminent danger
4. Lie
If this is love, I wonder what it is I have for Adelle"

"Tue, Feb 22, 2011, 4:58 PM
Iain Bryson to Mom
I don't need to pick any brain. Like I've said, I have this figured out. What I do not have figured out is how everyone can continue to work against me. Adelle will not see a doctor in Poland. I told you she is being molested. 100% Do you think I am fooled for one second?"

"Tue, Feb 22, 2011, 4:59 PM
Iain Bryson to Mom
INCEST"

"Tue, Feb 22, 2011, 5:01 PM
Iain Bryson to Mom
Thanks for keeping it up, allowing them to pass into third world post hitler poorer than hell Poland, where things have gotten much more interesting, at least for adelle. this all happened on your watch. you then tie me up, try to derail me permanently, steal, lie. no thank you and adelle says no thank you as well"

"Tue, Feb 22, 2011, 5:03 PM
Iain Bryson to Mom
how does it make you feel that nothing you have done is in the best interest of myself, my daughter, or my wife? nothing."

"Tue, Feb 22, 2011, 5:12 PM
Iain Bryson to Mom
The world was flat until it was not."

"Tue, Feb 22, 2011, 6:01 PM
Iain Bryson to Mom
There is nothing to check out, and certainly not in Poland. Every word I have written since day one is the truth, unfortunately for my family, at least at the moment. I cannot begin to follow the logical progression of 'have Adelle looked at in Poland.' Not for a moment; it makes no sense. Agata took Adelle knowing this was happening, because she herself has rape trauma syndrome. She is not going to now take her to a doctor, not a real one at least, just because. Nothing has changed. It is still myself which is going to put an end to this, and Agata knows it. Boy, she sure did swindle you, play you like putty. Must suck to have the wool pulled over your eyes to the point where you put your own son into suspended animation, then steal and lie, try to get conservatorships.....Sorry but you were swindled. How much would you spend to take back Adelle's latest molestation moments?"

"Tue, Feb 22, 2011, 6:03 PM
Iain Bryson to Mom
Do not worry. You will be able to say 'how should I have known,' though I doubt you will be able to look Adelle in the eyes. You think you know me and my family.....you are insane."

I thought that one of my most logical arguments was in response to my mom claiming, "I know Agata." In the course of Agata and I's relationship, she had probably been in the same room with her for a total of five hours and spoke to her way less than that. There was no way for her to know your mom better than I did, let alone at all, but she still thought that she did somehow.

"god i just want to look at you, know you are there. what a test of faith my pecial girl
Thu, Feb 24, 2011, 4:59 PM
Iain Bryson to Agata Bryson"

I decided that it was time to get my passport back, that I had waited long enough. It was time to confront my mother, who was still claiming that she hadn't seen it, even though I told her that I knew she had it. I had to eliminate her ability to make up stories by giving her an ultimatum; "please" didn't work, nor did telling her that she that was lying to me. *OK*, I thought, *I'll just prove you are lying, but only because you are making me.*

I lamented bringing my stepdad into the equation, but I reasoned that he would never know because my mom would never tell him. He was not dangerous, and I didn't want his guns to be taken away, but I also knew they wouldn't be. I knew that my mom would cave because she would have to. It was an ultimatum in the same way that the rock was with the paperboy, but all my mom had to do was give me back my own passport.

"Mon, Feb 28, 2011, 11:34 AM
Iain Bryson to Mom
so u can give it back today or tomorrow. i could just report it lost/stolen and get another, but since you have it there is really no need for all those shaninigans. i really dont think george should be driving around with a 9 mil tucked in his pants looking for the '[expletive]' as he calls them. get me that passport and you can keep your safe. Today or tomorrow or no safe, depending upon how the court feels about george chasing [expletive] with his guns."

I knew that all that was required to take someone's guns away was to sign a protective order against them. So, in a sense, I could take their guns away with my signature if she didn't give back what she took. I just needed my passport, and I was now confident I would be getting it back soon.

"Mon, Feb 28, 2011, 5:02 PM
Melanie Brandt to me
Attachments
Hello Mr. Bryson,
I am writing in reference to our conversation on Friday regarding your daughter, Adelle. Attached, please find a letter which includes the information I discussed with you along with a Hague application, Article 28 authorization (described in the letter) and the Privacy Act Waiver [see Appendix 31].
Once you have had a chance to review this information, please call me with any questions.
Sincerely,
Melanie Brandt
Citizens Services Specialist
Office of Children's Issues
Washington, DC
202-736-9071"

"Mon, Feb 28, 2011, 5:50 PM
Iain Bryson to Mom
u wanna tell me where to get my passport, tomorrow, or you dont. not answering counts as dont."

"Mon, Feb 28, 2011, 6:56 PM
Mom to me
You can quit threatening me with your emails.
I will talk to your dad and I will give him your passport. Just to clear the record. You had left it on the seat of my car. I have had it from day one. No breaking and entering on my end. No need to. I do not want to receive any more emails from you. Is that clear?"

> "Gaslighting is an emotionally abusive strategy that causes someone to question their feelings, thoughts, and sanity. If someone gaslights you, they'll attempt to make you question reality. The purpose of gaslighting is to convince you that you can't trust your thoughts or instincts. A gaslighter may try to convince you that your memories are incorrect, that you overreact to situations, or that something is 'all in your head.' They may then try to convince you that their version of events is the truth" (https://www.webmd.com/mental-health/gaslighting-signs-look-for)

This next email was not the right way to speak to my mother even though she did steal my passport from a secure location in my luggage, and she did plot to get me put onto a psychiatric hold. She continued to lie and try to make me feel bad for doing what I had to in order to get back what she stole.

"Mon, Feb 28, 2011, 7:03 PM
Iain Bryson to Mom
i am not threatening you stupid. you stole my [expletive] passport. [Expletive] off."

"Mon, Feb 28, 2011, 7:04 PM
Mom to me
I did not steal your passport, and yes, you are threatening me. Stop."

"Mon, Feb 28, 2011, 7:05 PM
Iain Bryson to Mom
u did steal it. u admitted this already. stop trying to lie."

"Mon, Feb 28, 2011, 7:08 PM
Mom to me

Talk to your dad about the passport.
I am blocking you so any emails after this I will not be receiving them."

"Just a note
Mon, Feb 28, 2011, 8:36 PM
Sara to me
Iain, I have not written you in awhile but there are a few things that I must say to you as you have said plenty to all of us.
1. you need to realizxe you did have something happen to your emotions and you should be thankful that your dad and mom care enough about you to go over to your home.
2. you need to admit this was needed as if it was not you would have stayed there and done what you needed to do from there.
3. If you did not have some kind of issues with your emotions you would never have and still be sending out all those e mails one after another.
4. Your mom did not try to get legal guardianship, she inquired about your stay and the hosp. is the ones that used those words, saying she would have to do that to keep you there and guess what Iain she did not do it as you left.
5. She did not file a missing persons report, she said she was concerned as she has not heard from you and just wanted to know that you were not dead somewhere.
6.What do you want her to do about adelle? you keep saying we are all causing adelle to be molested, that is rediculous, you have to do the paperwork to get your wife to go back to the netherlands no one else caused her to leave and no one else can get her back, no one has ever said adelle is in the perfect place.
7. You are being so rude and disrespectful to your mom and blaming her for everything. she is the one you called when you were desperate and she responded as a mom.
8. no one ever has said that adelle was not abducted but you keep saying that.
9. You were raised with so much love iain that you need to remember all that, no one is perfect but your mom is not the bad one here, you must realize that many things you have said to her caused her to react and feel the way she did and your dad too.
10. there is no reason why you should not go to your mom and make ammends and agree not to discuss in detail things that you know you buck heads over. you are the only one that has to make things happen to heal the relationship with your wife and try to get your family back together, no one pulled it apart and no one can fix it but you.
11. We have said all along that we want you to be together and you must realize that your words and actions have not been all normal and rational.
12. Your mom never broke into the school, she had a key if she wanted to go in and she did not, your dad will even tell you it probably was the person he asked to go over to check things out, I am sure your friend who was sleeping did not say iain it was your mother, because it was not.
13. Why do you keep saying 'she wants adelle molested,' these statements are not making sense iain and if you really think about it you will know this is true.
14. you seem to have so much hatred and bitterness within you and this will eat away at you. You caused your mom to be [c]oncerned about you and big deal you were under drs. care for 13 days, its done and over and you were not the inocent person with your actions and words, how alful for a mother to sit back and do nothing even if it does not seem to you to be exactly the right thing to have done and have to say 'I should have done something and I did nothing'.
I am not writing this to get you pissed at me Iain as I love you and you know that but it is so sad to see what you are doing to yourself by being so bitter to your mom and how you are hurting the one person in this world that would give her own life for you.
I just wanted to say this to you as I have read all your e mails I hope you will read this one and really think about a few things. I will pray that you do the right thing, as you know love and family is what life is all about and you have a wonderful loving family and people who care about you.Love
Auntie Sara"

"Tue, Mar 1, 2011, 12:26 PM
Iain Bryson to Sara
You need to realize you do not know me.
1. my daughter was abducted. stupid you.
2. no, what was needed was to stop that [expletive] bus from going to Poland. stupid you.
3. why? because it is not what you would do? actually it is what i do. stupid you.

4. inquiring is the first step to trying. stupid you.

5. she did actually. either you or the cop is lying.

6. stay the [expletive] away from me is what i want from her about adelle. you all have no clue.

7. there is no rude and disrespectful. i am working and you are working against me. shame on you and shame for you should you cross my path.

8.you are stupid.

9. i love my family stupid. i love you but you will stay out of my way. if you cross my path as i am trying to save my daughter from an oncoming train, you will be tossed aside so i can get to her.

10. i have nothing to amend. i speak the truth. you cannot handle it.

11. what you say and what you do are completely separate. doesn't count if you do the opposite.

12. she broke into the school. i was living there and she was snooping through my stuff. my car as well.

13. she does want adelle molested. so do you. your actions only lead to that conclusion

14.i have no hatred or bitterness. none. do you? i am doing great. i want adelle and you people lie cheat and steal.

YOU ARE A LIER And a thief. NOthing you say is true here. you even told me you had nothing to do with locking me up, looked me straight in the eyes. YOU ARE A LIER. Adelle is being molested and you love it"

"Re: Adelle and Agata
Thu, Mar 3, 2011, 7:01 PM
Iain Bryson to Mom, Jeremiah, Amy, Bonnie, Brian, Brianne, Carrie, Courtney, Dave, Roger, Hart, Heather, John S., Jon, Dad, Rachel, Sara
'A Red Herring is a fallacy in which an irrelevant topic is presented in order to divert attention from the original issue. The basic idea is to 'win' an argument by leading attention away from the argument and to another topic. This sort of 'reasoning' has the following form:'

In case you did not understand, you are all caught up in this fallacy. The argument is: Adelle has been abducted. Her father has not seen or heard from her since December 27, 2010. The diverting argument: Everything else. Everything you do and do not think about, which isn't much, but is very detrimental to the original argument. Wow this fallacy worked well on you. Oh, did you hear: Adelle has been abducted. And, all you are worried about is what my thoughts are, things you can never and should never understand. You cannot understand the simplest reasoning error, yours. Your sort of reasoning sucks. It really does. You kind of suck because your reasoning sucks…"

CHAPTER 65

"THANK YOU FOR CONTACTING THE U.S. DEPARTMENT OF STATE"

"Thu, Mar 3, 2011, 7:38 PM
Dad to me
Do you want to meet tpomorrow to sign the Hague papers and send them off. You can also pick up your mail, notebook and pasport."

"Thu, Mar 3, 2011, 7:59 PM
Iain Bryson to Dad
Can you just print out a copy of the papers for me since I dont have a printer? I dont want to wait any longer for these papers, the same papers you said you were working on two months ago and for thirteen days while I was locked up because you put me on a plane, destined for my mother who was and is bent on locking me up. I will handle it. Just print it out for me, if you don't mind. Also, I need that form I emailed you a couple of days ago, when I first mentioned I wanted my notebook now. It is the one for cancelling Adelle's passport, the other form you said you would make sure was filled out, the one you assured me would get filled out while I was locked up, being chased by Halidol needles, playing with drooling tourettes syndrome bipolar depressed addicts. You have penciled in some things, but besides that, you have done nothing except not do what you say you are doing while keeping me from doing all I can.

So, if you can meet, I do need the passport mom stole from me, the notebook I told you I needed back days ago, the one with my wife's last words, and the paperwork you told me you would send in, to begin the process of getting your granddaughter away from abduction and child abuse. Do you not want her away?"

"Thu, Mar 3, 2011, 8:02 PM
Iain Bryson to Dad
this is my daughter. what the [expletive] are you doing, have you been doing?"

"International Abduction of US Citizen/Generational Polish Incest [Incident: 110101-000045]
Fri, Mar 4, 2011 at 6:12 PM
Iain Bryson to U.S. Department of State
The issue is not resolved."

"Fri, Mar 4, 2011, 6:13 PM
U.S. Department of State to me
Response

This e-mail account is no longer operational. Please click the link below and you will be directed to our website where you will be able to submit your questions or comments.
http://contact-us.state.gov
Thank you for contacting the U.S. Department of State."

"Fri, Mar 4, 2011, 8:25 PM
Iain Bryson to Dad
really not sure what you mean. you act like there is something in it for me, like you are doing me a favor. Wow. Did I tell you Adelle has been abducted? where is your head?"

"Sat, Mar 5, 2011, 7:44 PM
Dad to me
If you want to come by tomorrow (to the school) we can finish up paperwork, sign, scan and send off. Come by for lunch."

"Mar 5, 2011, 8:06 PM
Iain Bryson to Dad
i told you; i dont want to finish up the paperwork with you. do you know how many dozen time i have heard that from you since this occurred? i want the paperwork, again I already asked you, if you can print it out for me. adelle has been abducted and you dropped the ball as soon as you had it."

My response was harsh to my dad; what he had offered was perfectly reasonable in his last email. The fact that it was March ripped a hole in me.

"Sat, Mar 5, 2011, 10:42 PM
Iain Bryson to Carine [social worker], bcc: allyopolis, bcc: Brian, bcc: me
I appreciate your response. My child was taken from Den Haag on December 27, 2010, and I have not heard from her, seen her, or heard from her mother since. I need help. The Dutch police would not investigate. All that I initially wanted was to stop them from going back to Poland, Now it has been verified that they have gone to Poland, where abuse is taking place. It is now March 5, 2011 and I have had no contact with them; I know there was an abduction and I am certain there has been sexual abuse, and I have had no contact whatsoever. I would love to take my daughter to the doctor, but unfortunately, like I said on December 27, 2010, she has been abducted. I haven't had a chance to get my hands on her so I can take her to the doctor. I cannot wait. Please help or advise if you can.
Sincerely,
Iain Avery Bryson"

"Sun, Mar 6, 2011, 3:37 PM
Dad to me
I will be going to Preston tomorrow and can bring everything. If you want to get some books you will have to come when I am here. Do you have marriage cert and birth cert?"

"Sun, Mar 6, 2011, 3:58 PM
Iain Bryson to Dad
i have everything but adelle, who has been abducted. i told you this how many times? i didn't say i wanted books. i said i wanted to get my [expletive], the stuff you have been keeping from me, like you have my daughter through your actions and inaction"

"Fwd: FW: Incest Abduction
Sun, Mar 6, 2011, 7:04 PM
Feminist.com to me
Thanks for reaching out to fem[i]nist.com and I'm so sorry to hear about your situation. Since some time has passed since you sent your original note, I'm assuming there was been some update to your case. If you still need assistance, please let me know. That said, I'm sure there is very little I can do -- given that it's an international case it's very hard to add another person into the mix.
I hope you and your wife are getting the help you seem to need. And hope your daughter is safe. I will just note that behavior that you described is often irrational and likely rooted in earlier patterns.
Take care, Amy"

"Tue, Mar 8, 2011, 8:06 PM
Iain Bryson to Dad
Dad,

It was nice to see you today. I feel that we had a good talk. Please keep our communications between us. Information does not need to circulate.

When you say 'exaggeration,' I know what you mean, but it is not what it is. It is true. It is just on another level. For example, [I] am not claiming that the Catholic Church is culpable, just like I am not claiming that you are culpable. It depends how you look at these definitions. I am looking at things in ways that people do not. Like I said, and I am not trying to be mean, but only to prove a point, by your inactions and moms, you are complicit. Intention doesn't matter. It is what you do and then the result. So, anything that is done which impedes me is therefore helping the abductor.

As I cycled through the heavy emotions, I learned quite a bit. I would compare it, as I did before, to being shot in the arm. In this situation, you have two main options:

1. Scream until someone identifies that you are screaming about a gunshot, and until you get the attention you need.

2. Look at the injury, try to understand it, and then explain it.

In both situations, you are in pain. In each situation, you are going to express a completely different phenomenon, and the chances of someone understanding you depend on what they relate to.

Another example:

A man is walking around a fair with his daughter. He looks away, and when his eyes come back, looking for his daughter, she is nowhere to be found. The man runs around, looking in places he last saw his daughter, talking to people, yelling, waving his hands, panicking.

I am this man, except that instead of a man out of control, thinking purely on emotion, I am screaming in the way that I do. I am trying to get attention, to let other people at this fair, especially the ones I care about, know what it is that has happened and what I am trying to solve. Unfortunately, even my family sees me running around the fair, saying things and screaming, saying that I had some girl next to me that is now missing. As with the man in the fair, my family has no idea why I would be doing anything other than riding the fair rides, eating the cotton candy and waiting in line. No, my daughter is still missing, just like as if she disappeared from the fair. I am not going to stop and have cotton candy with you or talk about the weather. These things don't matter until I get my daughter."

"Tue, Mar 8, 2011, 8:29 PM
Iain Bryson to Dad
What I am saying is that I write my thoughts a lot of the time, as I am figuring things out. When I read a book, I often copy much of it down. It helps me to work things out and to retain. So, my daughter is abducted. From there, I get scared for a day, terrified, and then I get up and start 'working' in my own way. As I am 'working,' I am sending off my thoughts. These thoughts are received by you, and though they are revelations of sorts to you, they require more thought in order to understand. They are not self evident.

So, above, in the other email, I am trying to compare the actions of mom and you to the actions of the church in that in both instances, the actions are counterproductive to my daughter being liberated from abduction and abuse. In [both] cases, things are being done, which although maybe not intended, are keeping Adelle in this situation. So, again, what is there other than 'abduction?' Everything else, whether it comes from me or from my wife, is just a distraction."

"Tue, Mar 8, 2011, 9:19 PM
Dad to me
Thanks Iain. I undrstand your frustration and see the treaty as a viable option. Can we meet early or end of day?"

"Wed, Mar 9, 2011, 3:13 PM
Iain Bryson to Dad
thanks for you[r] help. good to have that done. can you let me know when you have that letter please? love iain"

"Wed, Mar 9, 2011, 6:09 PM
Iain Bryson to Melanie Brandt
Melonie,
I hope that you are well. I wanted to check in with you and make sure you got the documents I sent today. I sent what I have, just so you have it, in case you end up needing something. Please let me know if you need anything further. I wish you all the best.
Iain A Bryson"

"Wed, Mar 9, 2011, 11:18 PM
Iain Bryson to Dad
Dad,
About a week ago you used an argument with me that I'd like to respond to. You said that you were helping with Adelle like you helped with Butch. You have to understand that what I mean is that as of December 27, any action which does not lead us closer to getting Adelle immediately looked at is not good. I think that these actions are not only not good, but that they are horrible, heinous. I equivocate them to directly causing harm to my daughter. You have said you see these things as a stretch, but it is not. All you must do is separate a page with 'cause' on one side and 'effect' on the other. When you put things down like the hospital, you have to put it in the 'cause' column; the effect is always the same and that is that Adelle is not well, not safe. I am not only going to try to cross off the big causes, but any I see, and I tend to see a lot in quite a few situations.

The experience with you and Butch was one of the best in my life. You dropped everything, as you always do, and supported me, helped me with whatever you could. The best part about it was the time with you, experiencing that with you. I loved that dog. I love my daughter. I know you know this, but I need you to see that my emotional response, my responses in general are only because of this love. It is the only reason. I [expletive] love this child. And, because it is me, you will get the response you have gotten, and because it is me, you will not understand.

I need your support and love, and I need you as a father, but in this situation I need you to let me be a father and a man. After all, it is the man you raised. I have this under control. I understand it completely as I have told you. What I need to do is stop trying to make you or even help you understand. Truly all that is needed is 'abduction.' As I said before, from there you cannot jump to 'minor abduction.' You cannot say anything other than abduction or else you are foolish for sure I really wish we could've stopped them from leaving Holland. I would give anything to go back and stop them, just as I would've then. The situation is not good. Thanks for you[r] help. love Iain"

"Thu, Mar 10, 2011, 7:45 AM
Dad to me
[H]I Iain. I will bri[n]g the letter to court. Thanks for your goo[d] words. i ,too, am looking forward to getting you and Adelle back together."

"Dutch central auth
Fri, Mar 11, 2011, 12:45 PM
Dad to Melanie Brandt, me
Hi Melanie. We would like you to send off the Hague papers to the Dutch Central Authority. As Adelle was a resident there at the time of the abduction, I think it best that we include them. I believe that they will think it is in their court. Please let me know how you are doing with Polish Hague forms. We are looking for someone to help with the translations. Thanks, Kirk"

"Fri, Mar 11, 2011, 2:57 PM
Melanie Brandt to Dad, me
Hello Mr. Bryson,
I am still locating the Polish application and hope to have it to you by Monday. I will forward your materials to the Dutch Central Authority.
Sincerely,
Melanie Brandt
Citizens Services Specialist
Office of Children's Issues
Washington, DC
202-736-9071"

"Tue, Mar 15, 2011, 9:16 PM
Dad to me
Hi Iain. Thanks for the emails on illuminatti. I have to say that it is a struggle to read; one, the book line advance is choppy so it was difficult to keep up, and two, wow, heavy stuff. I had heard about this (in Brown's book... The Divinci Code) but never read about it in such depth. Heavy heavy heavy. Same on monarch m[i]nd control. I'll try to read more then maybe we can talk. It's hard for me to believe that this horror actually existed, nevermind exists today. I have read about the Nazis, Mengle [Mengele] and a few others in the

camps, but in the us? (small caps on purpose). I will need some time to digest this. What a crazy species are we. Missed Conn College today as they are on spring break hours and closed early. I will call them in the morning and ask for polish teacher or someone who can help. If you have more papers to be translated you might want them copied or sca[n]ned. Any thoughts on contacting the doctor who examined Adelle? I am waiting to hear from Melanie for a contact name at the Dutch Central Authority. Will send it on to you as soon as I get it. L,D"

"Do some satanists really commit crimes and abuse children? Many people believe not. My own hard-earned professional experience tells me otherwise. This chapter is an account of my journey: a journey from relative ignorance prior to 1980, through growing awareness of the extent of child sexual abuse, through my bizarre, frightening introduction to satanist ritual abuse, to my eventual belief that satanist crime does, indeed, occur. And I would like to think that mine is a reflective, rather than reflexive, belief (van der Hart & Nijenhuis, 1999)—that is, belief that stems from reflecting on the evidence, rather than blind acceptance of what initially seems highly improbable" (Coleman, 2008, as cited in Sachs and Galton, 2008, 9).

"Update?
Wed, Mar 16, 2011, 9:48 AM
John S to me
Colonel,
Please keep us updated on your whereabouts, connectivity, progress, etc.
Love from John and Linda"

"Mar 16, 2011, 10:05 AM
Iain Bryson to John S
Hey Admiral and Lady Admiral.
Just working on getting these women out of this crap. The Dept. of State papers are filed.
I am just doing what I need to do, and trying to continually figure out what that is. love I"

"Sat, Mar 19, 2011, 8:59 PM
Iain Bryson to Brian
remember we were on the phone when i realized what had happened? From there i ran to the police department.......etc."

"Sun, Mar 20, 2011, 12:01 AM
Iain Bryson to Brian
u got any ideas on the present situation?"

"Mon, Mar 21, 2011, 2:12 PM
Melanie Brandt to me, Dad
Hello Mr. Bryson,
The Dutch Central Authority has notified me that they received your Hague application and supporting documents. I will keep you informed of any additional communication I receive from the Dutch Central Authority regarding your case.
Sincerely,
Melanie Brandt
Citizens Services Specialist
Office of Children's Issues
Washington, DC
202-736-9071"

"Iain Bryson
Tue, Mar 22, 2011, 12:42 PM
to Kyle
my family is being abused"

"Tue, Mar 22, 2011, 1:01 PM
Kyle to me
I know. I hope ur taking care of yourself. U can't spend every min of your day on one issue. Do the best u can but things take time"

"Tue, Mar 22, 2011, 1:04 PM
Iain Bryson to Kyle
i have to. if you knew what was happening, you would understand. u just have to trust me on this one. it is not abuse like spanking, it is abuse like cages and torture."

"Tue, Mar 22, 2011, 1:17 PM
Kyle to me
I never questioned what's going on or what u have to do. Life can be hard as he'll sometimes. Just got stay strong and do best u can. Hopefully things work out in the end."

"Tue, Mar 22, 2011, 1:22 PM
Iain Bryson to Kyle
life is not hard for me. it is hard for them. i just need them to stay strong till i get to them."

"Tue, Mar 22, 2011, 1:27 PM
Iain Bryson to Kyle
what would you do if your wife and child were being raped? and, you got no support or help? the choices are pretty limited, but the bottom line is the abuse will end"

"Tue, Mar 22, 2011, 1:33 PM
Iain Bryson to Kyle
the people you thought would be there in this situation are not, at all. what would you give to stop your family from raped and tortured? what should any man do?"

"Tue, Mar 22, 2011, 1:44 PM
Iain Bryson to Kyle
it is no different than me saying something like 'the sky is falling' and having the people who should at least stop and listen just ignore and get in the way. in this case, more than the sky is falling. this is what matters to me more than anything in this entire world. people are blind and my girls are being [expletive] tortured."

"Tue, Mar 22, 2011, 2:34 PM
Kyle to me
It's a [expletive] situation. U have to understand from others view. U flew off the deep end out there n everyone wanted to make sure u were ok. U got angry at everyone thinking they were just ignorant and didn't understand. Before u can attack your problem they wanted to make sure u were ok. Family would of helped ya but u lashed out at them. Knowbody understands why u would move back there knowing of the abuse. Basically the whole thing became an ugly mess wasn't dealt w well w everybody. I dnt know what I would do but family is very important and it does no good to point the finger at each other when the problem isn't here."

"Tue, Mar 22, 2011, 3:13 PM
Iain Bryson to Kyle
i dont have time to let other's learn. i know my duaghter is being raped. deal with it, or dont. but do not get in my way"

"Tue, Mar 22, 2011, 5:49 PM
Iain Bryson to Kyle
have you decided what you would do if your family was being abused?"

"Tue, Mar 22, 2011, 7:35 PM
Iain Bryson to Kyle
if you came to me saying what i say what help would you want?
    Look at it like this: I see 'cancer.' What I describe and have been talking about, over and over, and sometimes in off putting ways, are the details of the cancer and the minutia of everything around it.

This is for two reasons:
1. I see things in detail, and have been working on this for a while.
2. The nature of the cancer, and who it is affecting gives me great motivation to see the details, to know all I can......I can know a lot. That is what I do, so why would I not?

So, from there, I yell out all of these details as I am finding them, telling everyone. I see them, and again, it is as if I have a bullet in my leg. I am frantic, desperate to stop what I see. The problem is: People can only see 'cancer.' I am the only one who can see all the other [expletive]. When I talk about the other [expletive], people can no longer see cancer. However, that bullet is still in my leg, my child is being raped, still, and I am still thinking. I try to tell people that it is cancer and I also try to explain the details, now all too easy to understand for me. I understand that others will not understand the details; I do not expect them to. What I do not understand is that when I say 'cancer' (rape) no body does anything but worry about me. I am not worried about anything else in this world other than cancer: I have figured the other [expletive] out. I would volunteer for twenty years of prison right now in exchange for those women being taken out of that situation for good immediately. I would trade my life for the same thing. What else would I do? My wife and my daughter are being abused, terribly. There is no need to worry about anything I am doing. It is all geared towards stopping this [expletive]."

"Mon, Mar 28, 2011, 7:55 PM
Iain Bryson to Kyle
yes, when someone is hiding something from you, you are blind. do you need me to explain this to you? time to sort it out. no, sorry there is not time. my girls are being abused. you are talking like the stupid people. is there time to sort out emergencies? the main concern is not that i am ok. who the [expletive] told you that and why the [expletive] would i not be ok? this is more stupid [expletive]. the only problem there ever was is that my girls are being abused. people helped me with what? they have done nothing. [Expletive] you and [expletive] this [expletive] family that keeps them over there being raped you [expletive] loser brother"

"Mon, Mar 28, 2011, 8:33 PM
Kyle to me
U made bad decisions and [expletive] your own life up. You always run from your problems. You have always asked for help from family and friends and gave never givin anything in return. You have never been able to control your emotions. If someone says something I disagree w u call them names, even your mother. Look in mirror. What have u done w your life? You say your so smart and u read 100 books a day. Well hey that's like me saying I have the cure for cancer. You have lost your family, you have nothing, no job, no money, [expletive] nothing. Grow up, be a man.

Except responsibility for your life and the decicions u made. You married her knowing of this [expletive] m moved the [expletive] over there. It's your fault and yours alone. If what u say is true. You r like a child and have been your whole life. Except no responsibility for any of your actions. Which causes mo growth as a man and a person. People may never forgive u this time. As for me...I have no issues w family, I work my ass off and take care of mine. If your so smart why have u never held a job for even a year? U contradict yourself all the time. I'm happy w my life and I work at it everyday to keep it that way. I dnt blame people for my mistakes. I never have and never will need a thing from you. I feel sorry for you and hope you get the help you need so maybe oneday you can see your daughter. Best of luck brother. Hope your as smart as u think. But I think your life is flying by and you r truly missing out. [Expletive] u too"

"Mon, Mar 28, 2011, 8:44 PM
Iain Bryson to Kyle
my girls are being abused you [expletive] retard"

"[expletive] off you loser. you cannot even think
Mon, Mar 28, 2011, 8:52 PM
Iain Bryson to Kyle"

"Mon, Mar 28, 2011, 8:56 PM
Kyle to me
See, no contol over emotions like a child. I dnt lose a sec of sleep over you. I'm like a pig in [expletive] in my life. You just enjoy being mean. Make u feel better to fight w me? You really r a lost soul. Grow up n get ur [expletive] together. The only abuser is you."

"Mon, Mar 28, 2011, 9:05 PM
Kyle to me
U dish it out but can't handle truth. I think just fine. My family is under my roof. I have a good job. Have money too. Also I love my mother and dnt disrespect her. U our like train reck, take out everything in it's path before u blow up. A crazy man believes everyone else is crazy. U say I can't think but you have not a piece of the happiness I have. The persuit of happiness...it takes hard work, everyday. I get no pleasure out of fighting w you. But I will not take your [expletive] or not be honest w you. I think u are [expletive] up. So best of luck. Hopefully u prove me wrong cause u r my brother. You have your life and I have mine. We dnt need each other so I will leave it at that."

"Wed, Mar 30, 2011, 3:56 PM
Iain Bryson to Melanie Brandt
Melanie,
I hope you are well.
What do you need for 'intention to stay...'? We moved to The Netherlands in 2008, relocating from CT.
We both have residence permits and stamps in our passports.
I can return to Holland as needed.
I have a Dutch residence permit; I do not need a VISA or anything else to live and work in Holland.
Please let me know what specifically you need, if anything.
All the best,
Iain"

"Adelle Bryson
Thu, Mar 31, 2011, 3:10 PM
Iain Bryson to Melanie Brandt
Melanie, Please remove my father, Kirk, from the contact list. If you have any questions, please let me know.
All the best, Iain"

My dad's behavior, or lack thereof, was giving me goosebumps in the same way as when we were in The Hague in early January and he had the crisis team over, then sent me to Boston to be forced into a hospital. He either wasn't paying attention, or he was running me around the bush and playing games, *maybe because of the red herring?* I asked myself. Either way, I couldn't risk it with him any longer; I didn't want your mom to have all the information about our case with the government.

"Thu, Mar 31, 2011, 4:17 PM
Melanie Brandt to me
Hi Mr. Bryson,
I received your email and will remove your father as requested. Should I continue to call you at the same phone number or should I contact you via email?
Sincerely,
Melanie Brandt
Citizens Services Specialist
Office of Children's Issues
Washington, DC
202-736-9071"

"Thu, Mar 31, 2011, 4:20 PM
Iain Bryson to Melanie Brandt
Melanie,
Please contact me via e-mail. I appreciate your continuing help with this. Do you need anything else for the Dutch Central Authority, or anything else at all for that matter?
All the best,
Iain"

"Thu, Mar 31, 2011, 5:09 PM
Melanie Brandt to me
Hello Mr. Bryson,

Regarding your questions about the recent request of the Dutch Central Authority(DCA), what follows is the text of the communication they sent:

This office would like to know more about the intention of the stay of the parties in The Netherlands when they went to The Netherlands in 2008. Further, this office would like to ask you if you can inform this office if the father is able to return on short notice. Is he able to organize visa, work, et cetera so that he can prove that he has the intention to continue his residence in The Netherlands in the future with Adelle?

You may wish to submit any information or documents that address these questions; I will then forward that on to the DCA.

Regards,
Melanie Brandt
Citizens Services Specialist
Office of Children's Issues
Washington, DC
202-736-9071"

"Sat, Apr 2, 2011, 4:06 PM
Iain Bryson to Melanie Brandt

Melanie,

You had mentioned before that we could request that Adelle be returned to the US. Can you tell me what exactly the available procedures consist of? I do not know that I intend on living in Holland in the future. I can, but I do not feel that I should have to in order totake care of an abduction which already occurred,

In 2008, we relocated to Holland. My wife secured a job with Saudi Aramco, which she had from 2008 until the summer of 2010. I worked for Laureate Online Education in Amsterdam from 2008 to February 2010. My wife and I filed for a marriage VISA to the US in 2010, and it is being processed. Please let me know what you think so that I can best answer these questions.

All the best, Iain"

CHAPTER 66

"WHAT SHOULD A PARENT DO IN THIS SITUATION?"

I was getting more and more antsy as time continued to pass. It appeared that there wasn't going to be an investigation, that nobody except for me was worried about what had happened and was happening to you. The paperwork for the Hague Abduction Treaty was filed, but I couldn't just sit back and wait for what could be years; I couldn't wait another month, or another week.

It became apparent that I should go to Poland because it was time for action. I felt that I had been patient enough, and that to go to Poland at this point would not be impulsive. I wanted to exhaust every reasonable legal route, and once I could see that I had, all I could see was a dead end.

I discussed the options I saw with Faye and our neighbor, Dre, as I wanted their honest feedback. We knew that we were discussing extremely serious matters with the possibility of complications, and anything up to life imprisonment for myself. But it was about what I should do that was of paramount importance in our conversations. What does a father do in this situation? We contemplated for weeks, and in the end we all decided that as your father, I had to act.

"Faye, don't you think I should go to Poland? How could I, as a father, not go to Poland at this point? What should a parent do in this situation?"

"Yes, Iain," she replied, "I do think you have to go to Poland. I think that you have to do whatever it takes. From a mother's perspective, there are no rules for you except that you have to fight for your daughter. It doesn't matter what anybody else thinks. You know what you have to do..."

Dre was willing to go with me to Poland to get you, but I wasn't willing to allow him to risk also going to prison. I probably would have taken him up on his offer if he didn't have children of his own. I had gotten to know his children, and as tempting as it was, I couldn't take their daddy away from them.

I put my car up for sale to get the cash that would allow me to get to Poland, and I continued to pray and look for alternative routes. The last thing that I wanted to do was go to Poland, but I also had to start planning for exactly that. You had to be evaluated in December, and now it was April!

Because of what I had recently been through and what I had seen, I felt a sense of being close to God. I knew that I had to start trusting in Him, but I didn't know what that meant in my day-to-day life. I didn't have time to pursue it in too much depth, and I didn't open my Bible during this time because I couldn't imagine how any answers could be there. I needed answers immediately, and my entire being was crying out to God for direction and assistance.

But my entire being was not ready to fully surrender because I didn't know what exactly I would be surrendering to. What I did know was that there was a war between good and evil, and that I had now taken a stance with the former. I knew that the latter had to lose, ultimately, but I couldn't see past what was directly in front of me – my abducted daughter.

"Sat, Apr 2, 2011, 10:15 PM
Iain Bryson to Faye H.
Attachments"

"Introduction from SISHA
Mon, Apr 4, 2011, 12:47 AM
Eric M [SISHA] to me
Dear Mr Bryson,
Thank you for contacting us with the information regarding your wife and daughter in Poland. My name is Eric Meldrum and I am the Operations Director with the anti-human trafficking and sexual exploitation organization, SISHA. We at SISHA operate in Cambodia but we can put you in touch with anti-sexual exploitation organizations in Poland or I recommend you contact the Police for them to instigate action to help your wife and daughter. Please let me know what you decide and if there is any link to Cambodia please let me know and we will take the appropriate action.
I look forward to hearing from you.
Yours Sincerely,"

"Mon, Apr 4, 2011, 11:21 AM
Iain Bryson to Eric M [SISHA]
Dear Mr. Meldrum,
I appreciate your response. Please let me know which organization I can contact in Poland. The local police in Holland and Poland have not been helpful. The Dutch told me they could not investigate sexual abuse on a child prior to age four, and my daughter was a month shy at the time. It is hard to believe that there are no resources to deal with this. It is almost as if the Hague Convention is set up to provide the rules in order to allow this to happen. Thank you.
All the best, Iain"

"Mon, Apr 4, 2011, 1:26 PM
Melanie Brandt to me
It might be easier to discuss this over the phone. Would you like to set a time to talk?
Melanie Brandt
Citizens Services Specialist
Office of Children's Issues
Washington, DC
202-736-9071"

"Mon, Apr 4, 2011, 9:22 PM
Eric M [SISHA] to me
Hi Iain,
Thanks for getting back to me so soon. Despite what the Dutch may say it is of course possible to investigate sexual abuse on a child prior to age four. Can you pass me the details of your wife and daughter (full names, dates of birth, nationalities, current address, location of the abuse and any other information you feel is relevant) and I will contact Interpol who will assist with this case. If it is necessary to then involve any local organizations in Poland I will research them and find the best ones to help.
I look forward to hearing from you.
Best Wishes,"

"Mon, Apr 4, 2011, 9:31 PM
Iain Bryson to Eric M [SISHA]
Eric,
Thank you so much. The story behind this is quite extensive. I have been fighting, trying to get someone to take a close look, since December 2010.
Iain Avery Bryson --United States--June 1, 1977
Agata Bryson (Makowska) -Polish - July 11, 1982
Adelle Avery Bryson --United States --January 30, 2007

(Current Address of my girls)
Pilsudskiego 2/6
Stargard Szczecinski
Poland
73-110

Prior to the abduction, the three of us were living in Holland:
Newtonplein 25 A
Den Haag, The Netherlands 2562JV

I have been working on this non-stop since the abduction. There are many ways to describe what is happening, but I think that the best I've found is 'ritual abuse.' I could not see it until it was thrust in my face. I appreciate your help more than you can imagine. I have reached out to everyone I can think of with no results whatsoever."

> "Ritualistic abuse refers to organised abuse that is structured in a ceremonial fashion, often incorporating religious or mythological iconography (McFadyen et al. 1993)...The majority of cases of ritualistic abuse involve female victims and facilitation by parents (Creighton 1993, Gallagher et al. 1996)" (Salter 36).
>
> "Children and adults subject to ritualistic forms of abuse are profoundly traumatized, phobic of doctors and the police, and often convinced that the abusive group has supernatural powers (Mollon 1996). Cases involving ritualistic abuse are distinguished from other forms of organised abuse by the young age at which victimisation starts, the involvement of parents as primary abusers, the extremity and diversity of abusive practices, and the prolonged period of abuse (Creighton 1993, Gallagher et al. 1996)" (37).

"Mon, Apr 4, 2011, 10:20 PM
Eric M [SISHA] to me
Hi Iain,
Thanks for the information. Can you tell me the details of the abduction please (when, where, who was involved) and the 'ritual abuse' that you have found out about. These are questions that will be asked of us. Thanks,"

"Mon, Apr 4, 2011, 11:19 PM
Iain Bryson to Eric M [SISHA]
Eric,
In September 2010, my wife and I submitted a marriage VISA to the United States Embassy in Amsterdam. From September to December 2010, I was in the US, and my wife and daughter were in Poland. We met back in Holland in early December, which is when I noticed extreme changes in both my wife and daughter, including symptoms of abuse. This happened before, after extended periods of time when they were in Poland. For the two weeks we were in Poland [correction: Holland] together, I was pleading with my wife to get help for the abuse I saw at the time, which is nothing compared to what I now have come to realize was present all along. She told me that she had Stockholm Syndrome, that she was a hostage, and that she was going back to Poland with our daughter whether I liked it or not.
On December 27, 2010, my wife left with our daughter, after threatening to do so for the two weeks prior to then. Immediately upon finding out they had gone, I went to the police station. They would not do anything, and I went back several times, but they never did anything. I contacted the child protection authorities, but

they did nothing. I contacted everyone I could think of, frantic to get help. The US Embassy told me to take my daughter and get her to the Embassy, but I was never able to get my hands on her.

Abduction:
When: December 27, 2010
Who: Agata Bryson and Adelle Bryson left Holland to go to Poland. Mickey DeLuca distracted me while they made their 'escape.'
Where: The Hague, The Netherlands

My wife left, but she left me everything I needed in order to understand what had been happening for the duration of our relationship. She has been traumatized by rape her entire life, is unable to escape, and will not ask for help until she feels safe. I have as much information as is needed. As I told the Dutch police on December 27th: 'Stop the bus and take a close look. I do not care about anything else. My wife and daughter are being abused, raped, tortured and I need someone to take this seriously.'
Iain"

"Mon, Apr 4, 2011, 11:19 PM
Iain Bryson to Eric M [SISHA]
correction
'for the two weeks we were in Poland together' should read '....two weeks in Holland together....'"

"Tue, Apr 5, 2011, 5:57 AM
Eric M [SISHA]to me
Hi Iain,
Just one further thing, can you let me know your address and contact number to pass on to Interpol please."

"Tue, Apr 5, 2011, 6:33 PM
Iain Bryson to Eric M [SISHA]
Eric,
I am currently at:
17 Taftville Occum Road
Norwich, CT 06360
USA
860-███-████"

"Thu, Apr 7, 2011, 1:14 PM
Melanie Brandt to me
Hi Mr. Bryson,
I can send the information you provided in you[r] email below regarding your employment in Holland on to the Dutch Central Authority. I would then let you know their response.
While you can also submit your Hague application to the Polish Central Authority and ask that Adelle be returned to the United States, case precedent shows that foreign courts will consider the country of the child's habitual residence when making the determination to return the child.
Again, please feel free to give me a call if you want to discuss further.
Melanie Brandt
Citizens Services Specialist
Office of Children's Issues
Washington, DC
202-736-9071"

"Fri, Apr 8, 2011, 1:39 PM
Iain Bryson to Eric M [SISHA]
Eric,
Please let me know if there is any additional information that you need at this time. I appreciate your help.
All the best, Iain Bryson"

"Fri, Apr 8, 2011, 1:40 PM
Iain Bryson to Melanie Brandt
what about when the child is being abused by the same people who abducted her? I do not agree."

"Sun, Apr 10, 2011, 9:20 PM
Eric M [SISHA] to me
Hi Iain,
We should have enough information to be getting on with just now thanks. I've contacted Interpol with the details of the case and am awaiting a response but will chase them up about it again today. Hope to have some positive news for you soon."

"Tue, Apr 12, 2011, 12:47 PM
Iain Bryson to Eric M [SISHA]
Eric,
Thank you once again. Please let me know if there is anything else you need from me. I wanted to reiterate that my wife told me this was happening. I could not see the extent of it. I was asking her to get help, telling her we had to get help for what I could see. She was telling me she had Stockholm Syndrome and that she was leaving with our daughter, and that I did not have a say, despite the fact that I did see abuse at the time. It was just not the abuse that I now know to be present.
All the best,
Iain"

"Tue, Apr 12, 2011, 10:12 PM
Eric M [SISHA] to me
Hi Iain,
No problem. I've sent another email to Interpol and am speaking to the Polish embassy also, so I hoope we will see some action soon. I will keep you updated.
Cheers,"

"Fri, Apr 15, 2011, 4:16 PM
Iain Bryson to Eric M [SISHA]
Eric,
Much appreciated. Please do keep me updated when you can. I am trying to figure out my schedule in regards to all of this.
All the best,
Iain"

"Mon, Apr 18, 2011, 2:05 PM
Iain Bryson to Melanie Brandt
What is it that 'abduction' means to the US government? Is it some minor spousal argument? My child is a US citizen. She was taken from me, and she is being abused."

"Mon, Apr 18, 2011, 2:18 PM
Iain Bryson to AndersonTQ@state.gov, Melanie Brandt
Hello again,
I filed an international spousal abduction report a while ago. Your definition of 'abduction' appears to be some watered down version which does not mean anything. My child was taken against her will. My four year old American citizen daughter is being sexually abused. My child is being trained with rape and trauma. I have filed papers reports with SISHA and Interpol. The US government has done nothing; the only helpful individual was a Duty Officer in the Amsterdam Embassy who indicated that I should get my child to the Embassy. I need help; I do not need to be placated. I am telling you that this is going on. I am not asking for help understanding this, but rather I am telling you that my daughter is in constant danger. If you have questions for me, please let me know. Please help me to quell this abomination.
All the best,
Iain Avery Bryson"

"Adelle Avery Bryson
Mon, Apr 18, 2011, 7:48 PM
Iain Bryson to [FBI-New Haven office], me

Dear Sir/Madam:

My child was abducted from The Hague, The Netherlands on December 27, 2010. Both her and her mother, who abducted her, are being sexually abused and held against their wills. I have been dealing with this constantly since its inception. My daughter and I are citizens of the United States. Wife wife is a Polish citizen. They are currently in Poland, where they are hostages, being abused. Please assist me in the resolution of this matter.

Sincerely Yours,

Iain Avery Bryson"

"sent to embassy in berlin
Mon, Apr 18, 2011, 8:03 PM
Iain Bryson to me

Dear Sir/Madam:

I am in US citizen who, along with my Polish wife and my four year old American citizen daughter, was living in The Hague until January 2011. On December 27, 2010, Adelle Avery Bryson was abducted. She was taken from her home in The Hague, and brought to Poland, where she is being sexually abused, trained in trauma and ritual abuse.

When this initially occurred, I attempted to get help from the Dutch police, Dutch child protective services, and everyone else I could think of. The US Embassy in Amsterdam indicated that I should take my daughter and get her to the Embassy, where we would at least be on US soil. Unfortunately, I never got the chance. I have filed under the Hague treaty, I am working with Interpol, and I am working with SISHA. My daughter, a four year old American citizen, is being tortured and raped. Thank you for any assistance or ideas you may be able to provide.

All the best,

Iain Avery Bryson"

"Mon, Apr 18, 2011, 11:01 PM
Iain Bryson to AndersonTQ@state.gov, allyopolis, Dre, Melanie Brandt

Melanie,

I would really appreciate more information regarding the intentions of the United States government to help my daughter. I would like to try to explain the situation a bit better for you. I have outlined a couple of points that I hope to touch on in this letter.

The International Parental Kidnapping Crime Act (IPKCA) of 1993: A criminal arrest warrant can be issued for a parent who takes a juvenile under 16 outside of the U.S. without the other custodial parent's permission.

This needed to be done on December 27, 2010. I told the Dutch police that my wife had taken my daughter, that she had told me she was going to flee to Poland with our daughter, and that there was sexual abuse.

I told the Dutch police two weeks before the abduction that my wife had taken my daughter's passport, that she would not tell me where it was, and that she was threatening to leave the country with our daughter. The Dutch police would not file a report.

Characteristics Posing A Risk For Abduction ---Kidnapping (and all the subsequent abuse)

1. Possess paranoid or delusional tendencies.

My wife told me she has Stockholm Syndrome. My wife has Dissociative Identity Disorder. For the last two weeks that we were living together, I was trying to get my family help, telling and demanding that my wife seek outside help because of the signs of abuse that I was seeing at the time. She told me that she was leaving with Adelle, that the US government would not do anything about it, and that she was a hostage. I did not believe any of the three until it happened. The US government needs to help me.

2. Exhibits psychopathic behavior:

I am not going to go into this at the moment, but I kept journals on my wife's behavior the entire time. Now, I have a full understanding of her behavior, which is due to her own history of abuse.

3. Has strong ties to another country:

Her ties are the strongest possible. She is a hostage; she told me this numerous times. I did not know what she meant.

4. Feels alienated by the US legal system:

She told me that the US government would do nothing to help our US citizen daughter. She hates being coined an 'alien' by the US government. She is frustrated with her immigrant status. We filed a marriage VISA in September 2010, which is still being processed.

When we filed this, prior to her going to Poland with our daughter for the second time last year, she begged me to call my cousin who works for the FBI in order to see if he could expedite it. At the time, I laughed it off, knowing we would have to go through the process, regardless of who my cousin may work for. She was terrified to go back to Poland. I just did not know why, and I believed at the time that she would be able to tell me about things in Poland she could not handle.

5. Threatens to Abduct:

My wife did this for every day for the final two weeks we were together. She told me that she and our daughter would be returning to Poland for either Christmas or New Year's. She held onto our daughter's passport, keeping it in an undisclosed location. I contacted the police, who would not file a report or act.

Please let me know what information you have. However, this is a kidnapping and an abduction, and it is not the swe[e]t and pleasant kind. Abuse is happening everyday. I have been trying to tell people this since December 27th and everyday after that when I contacted the Dutch police on five occasions, the Dutch sex police, Dutch child protection, my governor, the Rape Abuse Crisis Network, Connecticut Department of Children and Families, The US Embassy, ...and many more.

My wife and my daughter are in constant imminent danger, and immediate action needed to occur months ago.

I am in contact with the FBI overseas division, Interpol, and SISHA. I need some professional collaboration here. This is not a matter of custody, but rather of life and death.

Kind Regards,

Iain Avery Bryson"

"Wed, Apr 20, 2011, 4:40 PM
Melanie Brandt to me

Hello Mr. Bryson,

Please know that the allegations of abuse you have raised below are of concern to our office. I can request that the U.S. Embassy in Poland try to conduct a welfare visit with Adelle. It would be helpful if you could provide evidence that documents these allegations, such as police reports, court orders, etc.

Sincerely,

Melanie"

Her telling me that they were now "concerned" did nothing to comfort me. I had seen as much complacency and stalling as I was willing to put up with. If they were truly concerned, then that would be great, but I wasn't going to wait around for results.

By the time I sold the car, I was certain I was going to Poland. I didn't know what I would do once I got there, and so I planned for many contingencies. The best option, I thought, was still the one given by the Duty Officer: if I could get you to the U.S. Embassy, then they would evaluate you. I printed directions from both your grandparents' apartment in Stargard and their other place in Sierakowo to the Embassy in Berlin.

I also went to a thrift store with Faye and purchased specific clothing with the intention of blending in once I was in Poland. Dre cut my hair short, and I bought black hair dye to bring with me. I threw in a compass and binoculars in case I had to do reconnaissance prior to taking whatever action it was that I was going to take.

Journal Entry, April 22, 2011

"I am getting ready to go to Europe, though I am not really certain how to 'get ready,' other than to by preparing for 'anything,' which can only be done on a mental level...My only fear at this point is failure. Failure can take many forms, but it cannot happen...I need my girls so badly. I love them so dearly..."

Journal Entry, April 24, 2011:

"..Dre came over this morning. Katy [Faye's daughter] had already woken me up, but I was trying to meditate, to prepare myself for the day, the last day before I go to Europe. I am filled with apprehension at the moment. It does not help that I have nobody to speak to or that my other half is in dire straits. What does help, what drives me, that which is the breath and breadth of my soul, my love for those two girls..."

Journal Entry, April 25, 2011:
"On the plane, leaving Boston shortly. Apprehensive, strong, but just needing to get this [expletive] done. Exchange rate is [expletive] for dollars, but it has to work out, and I have to just keep plugging away on to the one. What's the use of worrying. London first, supposedly good weather."

Journal Entry, April 25, 2011:
"It feels good to be on my way to Europe despite uncertainty. I am closer to A + A every second that goes by."

Journal Entry, April 26, 2011:
"Waiting at Heathrow for my plane to come in. A bit overwhelmed but really isn't anyone going into any new given situation. I have been alright. God has taken care of me, and he will continue to."

"directions
Mon, Apr 25, 2011, 11:14 AM
Iain Bryson to me
Driving directions to Sierakowo, Poland
[MapQuest directions, deleted for brevity]"

"pol to embassy
Mon, Apr 25, 2011, 11:18 AM
Iain Bryson to me
Driving directions to Embassy of the United States in Berlin [from Sierakowo, Poland]
   2 hours 3 mins...
   164 km...
[MapQuest directions, deleted for brevity]"

    I said goodbye to Dre and his family, and to Faye's daughter who I had grown close to over the months I was living at their house. Faye drove me to the bus station in New London, and I took a bus from there to Logan airport in Boston. I was ready, I thought, for whatever was coming next.

PART 6

APRIL 26, 2011 – JUNE 18, 2015

"WHEN WE ARE NO LONGER ABLE TO CHANGE A SITUATION, WE
ARE CHALLENGED TO CHANGE OURSELVES"
— VIKTOR E. FRANKL

CHAPTER 67

"DOING SOMETHING WAS MY ONLY OPTION"

My plane landed at Amsterdam Schiphol Airport; it felt like I was on a business trip where the business at hand was very serious. I just wanted to get on the road and begin the long journey east toward Poland. I was focused, though I still didn't know exactly what the plan was. First things first, for sufficient unto that moment was the evil thereof. I had no idea what I was doing other than that I was being the dad I believed I should be. I cleared customs quickly with my Dutch residence permit and headed over to get my rental car, uncertain as to whether they would give me one with my prepaid credit card or not.

They didn't know or didn't care that it was a prepaid credit card with only enough money on it to cover the deposit of the rental, and they handed me the keys to a Renault Twingo, one of the smallest cars I had ever driven. I had never driven in The Netherlands, always having used public transportation, so I stopped at the first gas station I could find to purchase a map, and then proceeded to move toward the German Autobahn, which would take me out of The Netherlands and across the entire country of Germany, straight to Poland.

Renault Twingo

The drive was relaxing other than the fact that I was a bit frightened to be on a road with no speed limit, in a micro car, with huge BMWs and Mercedes flying by me at speeds in excess of 120 miles per hour. Billboards on the side of the highway showed pictures of high-speed accidents to remind people to be careful, and I quickly discovered that I was most comfortable sticking to the right lane with my cruise control set to a speed about half of what other cars were going.

I estimated that the drive from Amsterdam to where I was going in Poland would be about twelve hours based on the bus trips I had taken, so I had to stop to refuel once. I considered picking up a hitchhiker at the gas station for company, a twenty-something hippy looking guy, but I decided against it because I needed to be in my own head given that I was driving to Poland for a purpose I hadn't yet determined, a serious purpose regardless of the details. I knew that this was one of the most important days of my life to this point, and though I felt bad that this guy needed a ride, and I had an empty car, this was not the time to add on extra adventures or sidekicks.

I stopped one more time on the German side of the Germany/Poland border because I couldn't figure out from the map how to get into Poland. I wanted to get over the border as soon as possible, and I didn't want to appear to be driving around aimlessly. The rental car company had warned me that I was not allowed to take the car into Poland, so I did not want to have to explain where I was going to the police or be required to show them my papers.

The woman at the border gas station was extremely friendly, and I conversed with her for several minutes, buying a coffee to get me through the rest of the day and night. It was getting dark, and I was glad to be near the border; it had been a long couple of days. At this point, I decided that I would not go to Sierakowo because I didn't have an address or know the village at all. I didn't' pay enough attention when I was driven there in the past, and I wasn't sure that I would be able to find it again. I thanked the nice woman, and I headed toward the border, toward Szczecin in Poland. From there, I would be able to find Stargard, though I still didn't know exactly what I'd do once I got there. All I knew was that you and your mom were most likely in Stargard, and so I continued going that way.

Deer were crossing the unlit windy road at a rate I had never seen before. I knew my little car didn't stand a chance if I were to hit one, or if one were to hit me, so I proceeded very carefully to the border. Once I got to Szczecin, I stopped one more time, just so that I could be certain that I was on the right road for the last half hour of my trip to Stargard. I arrived during the night, without a plan of what to do from there, so I headed to the parking lot of an apartment complex your mom and I lived in when we were engaged to try and rest and plan my next moves. The street was named "Hallera."

Journal Entry, April 27, 2011

"In the dark hallera jeden [street name] waiting, focusing...haven't eaten since Boston, so I guess fasting too. My girls are around the corner, or I have to assume they are, and I just hope it's a good assumption. I'm not sure how I could've found Sierokowo with just the one time being there. This place is detestable, disgusting; Who knows where it all ends and begins? Well, I have a pretty good idea, but that is really too much information for me, or more than I need. My family, the only thing in this world I care about, live for, love – well I do love more, but you don't know about divine love. You don't know about my marriage and my wonderful wife. You have no idea about my little girl.

You think I was going to let people hurt them? Did I not tell you every which way that they are being abused, molested, tortured, held against their will? My wife is so scared, she doesn't even consciously know. It is just a feeling and a personality switch for her. She stopped being able to deal with it long ago. Dissociate....If you get abused, you still live, you still take the 'good' with the bad. You have to keep going. Depending on the nature, duration, intensity, abuser, your brain will adapt. And the best part is most of you will never know or believe...you can't...I do not want to do this; I just want it to stop, but it won't and they will not stop on their own. Their elaborate scheme, and all they've got to lose is too great, too entangled."

It felt so strange to be there, in Stargard, outside one of the apartment complexes that your mom and I lived in before we were married. But at the same time, given the circumstances that had been dealt to me, it didn't feel as strange as the rest of it, and I was grateful to be there. I was on a mission, and that mission was to begin the process that would end your abuse and reunite our family, the first clause always the most important to me. I would've given my life at any point just to keep you from being bruised or hit even one more time, and what was happening was infinitely worse than that.

When something "impossible" happens, there is bound to be some sort of also seemingly "impossible" reciprocal reaction. One follows the other; we do not know exactly what we are capable of until we are there. It is not possible to hypothetically imagine your child being taken, or your child being abused. To understand it, one must experience it, the screaming of every fiber of one's being, the epitome of the human disaster, worse than any death of self could possibly be. People had to start listening to what I, your dad, was saying.

Going to Poland was not a hasty decision, but rather one that I arrived at after months of trying everything else that I could think of. What the world was telling me was that there was nothing that could be done, nobody that could or would help, that I would have to go through a legal process that could potentially take two years, and I was not willing to acquiesce to that reality. It was not within me to do so; I had no choice but to take matters into my own hands. I certainly was not going to wait two years, or even a year. This was you, my daughter, not a stolen car or phone, but my little girl.

I had considered, very seriously, re-kidnapping you and doing my best to get you to the U.S. Embassy in Berlin, about an hour away from where you were being held. This was the optimal scenario because it would get you out of Poland and onto "American soil," where you would definitely be evaluated. Duty Officer Juan Gambola had guaranteed this to me back in December. I had the driving directions, and I really wished it were possible, but in the end, I decided that this had a potential for risk that was too high.

I could not picture taking you away from whichever adult was "caring" for you, getting you into a car, and then driving with you for an hour to another country. Would there be a car chase, maybe even spike strips, a pit maneuver, or a helicopter? I knew that this was not the answer; this was too far-fetched, even for me.

Although I had already ruled out going to Sierakowo, the reason I had considered it for so long was because your mom had yelled the word "Sierakowo" at me a couple of times. She gave no explanation or context, just a loud burst of amplified fear, similar to when she yelled "molester." I knew that it was the location of your great grandparents' vacation cabin; I had been there once or twice, and I even changed your great grandpa's (Waldek Labun) tire once in the rain on the way there.

Nobody else that I knew was faced with my choice: do something, whatever that was, in order to get attention, or wait for maybe two years while my daughter continued to be abused by her maternal family, accept the fact that my daughter has been illegally abducted from her home, and just move on. As you can see, my choices were only in the details; doing something was my only option, and waiting two years was not on the table. Anyone who would argue that point does not understand what it means to be a little girl's daddy.

CHAPTER 68

A TIME TO KILL?

April 27, 2011 was a drizzly, overcast morning in Stargard, and I was ready to go. I didn't want to wait any longer as I hadn't slept after the long drive from Amsterdam, but just sort of hovered in near-ready mode passing the time. I gained a burst of second wind energy as soon as the sun began to rise, but this was still several hours too early to do anything. I was calm and focused, determined, solemn, not tired, but contemplative, wishing that I could think of another response to this situation.

I had tried every day with every ounce of my strength since the day that you were taken, and I had gotten nowhere. *Today that will change*, I thought; *my job today is to make sure that my girl is evaluated in accordance with my stated concerns.* I peed into a cup from the driver's seat of my Twingo and then emptied it out onto the street, using the car door to block what I was doing. I knew that there were many curious eyes all around and more to come as the wee hours turned into the early morning, and with my Dutch plates and obviously not Polish physique, I didn't want a run-in with the cops at this point. I left the parking lot and drove back toward Szczecin, a larger city with more going on, thinking I could find some breakfast.

I knew my surroundings; I didn't need a map anymore. It felt strange to be driving by myself in Poland with your mom as my supposed enemy who now hated me, but at least I knew where I was logistically. I felt like I was as organized and prepared as I could be. There was little or no chaos in my mind.

Everything was still closed in Szczecin when I got there, even McDonalds. I yearned for a meal, but thinking about food and where to get it was a distraction, so I turned around and drove back toward Stargard, stopping at a gas station. I paid five zloty (about $1.50) to use the bathroom, and then I settled on a bag of pistachios and a can of coke for breakfast.

The plan that made the most sense to me was to confront your grandfather later in the morning when he came out to throw his beer cans into the dumpster, something I knew he did every single morning from when I lived with and visited him (2004, 2008-2010). Drug addicts, in this case a severe alcoholic, are not difficult to predict. Many of their behavioral patterns are in accordance with the habits or necessities of their addiction, and they are not likely to change that much over time. I was confident that I would get to see him today.

I was not angry with your grandfather at this point. I had cycled through anger, to understanding, pity, forgiveness, and to realizing that he is also a victim of intergenerational abuse, just a male version of your mom from an older generation. I knew that he was not ultimately the problem, that the problem was greater than any one man. I could have been born into his position; the only difference between him and I was the respective roles that we played.

> "For we do not wrestle against flesh and blood, but against principalities, against powers, against the rulers of the darkness of this age, against spiritual hosts of wickedness in the heavenly places" (Ephesians 6:12 NKJV).

I suspected that the reason he needed beer for breakfast was because he couldn't live with himself. He was constantly drunk or thinking about being drunk, so I knew that he was not a happy, fulfilled man. He had to be a slave himself, whether to other men, spiritually, or both. I remembered your mom once telling me that her dad had to go talk to the priest because the priest was mad at your Aunt Ada for not "visiting" him enough. From the way she told me and how she stressed the weight that it was upon her dad, I knew that this didn't have to do with confession or other religious requirements.

> "Like other forms of organised crime, familial organised abuse occurred within strictly observed hierarchies of men who maintained control through blackmail and the threat of injury and death. Participants indicated that parental involvement in organised abuse was a source of fear for both parent and child, who could both be subject to serious sanctions if they did not comply with the requirements of the sexually abusive group. Fear of more senior or powerful men within the abusive network loomed large in the minds of abusive adults as well as children..." (Salter 105).

Whatever I would do this morning would not be personal but pragmatic; my aim was to use him to get you evaluated. As a man, and particularly as a husband and father, I did not mind that the plan that made the most sense to me was to get into an altercation with your grandfather; regardless of forgiveness or understanding, there was still the fact that this man was causing you pain. *People will understand my actions*, I intuited, *once I have the opportunity to explain it to them*.

Part of me was excited to have the opportunity to put the fear of God in him, to let him know that I was crazy for my girls, that he would never know what to expect, and that I was not afraid of him. I psyched myself up for the upcoming confrontation with the same music that I used before my high school wrestling matches. I had to manufacture intensity, as I did not hate him. I was calm, composed, and focused, but I was about to take him down to the mat.

At this point my enmity was because of your situation, and the system which seemed to be allowing this to occur. The individual actors really made no difference to me; my only concern was you and your mother. Granted there was a part of me that wanted to squash your grandfather like a mosquito, just brush him off and be done with it, because at least that would stop this one man from ever hurting you again.

It was a difficult thing for me to reason, given the paradox of the commandment, "Do not kill," and in my understanding the obvious duty to protect one's family. *Why wouldn't I kill him? Shouldn't I? Would it be any different than killing an intruder that was threatening my family if I had to save them? Isn't an intruder still an intruder even if time has gone by?*

It seemed to me that the answer to that was probably yes, though I also couldn't get free from the conviction that killing someone was not God's plan for me. *But could it not be His plan*, I pondered, *am I not to protect my family?* Wouldn't protecting your family be the best way to "serve God"? After four months of deep contemplation and meditation on this subject, I still didn't know what the right answer was.

I left the "to kill or not to kill" dilemma hanging for the entire time, until the last moment, never firmly settling it within myself. It didn't really matter to me. I didn't have a problem doing it, but I really wished I wasn't being forced to make these types of ridiculous decisions. I could justify it either way ethically and morally, and I really didn't know which way I would go when it came down to it.

The store where I bought the coke and pistachios had a glass case with cheap knives, but when I inspected them, I discovered that the blades didn't lock and therefore they could not be used without the risk of cutting my own hand. Instead, I chose to buy a used hammer that was hanging on a shelf right next to the knives. *Odd that they are hanging there not far from the pistachios,* I thought, *but also quite convenient.*

I had no idea what I would do with it, if anything, and the thought of what one might do with it made me cringe. *I'm just going to go through the motions of what a dad should do,* I thought. *I'm going to keep moving in that direction, because right now I don't know what to do, I don't want to be here doing this, I want to be dancing with my girls back in August of last year, back before I made the huge mistake of sending them back to Poland, again.*

On the drive back to Stargard I ate the pistachios and threw the shells on the floor. I knew that I would not be returning this car to Amsterdam, so it didn't matter if it was dirty. I wanted there to be another way, and my mind kept returning there, but I knew that there wasn't after the months of trying my hardest, months of thinking only about how to resolve this. Waiting any longer wasn't an option, nor do I believe it should've been. My daughter should not be in an abusive situation for even a minute, and you still were after four months. *Four months! How many more months should I wait?*

I drove by and around your grandparents' apartment to get my bearings. I hadn't been on these streets in a while, but it felt like I was home because I knew you and your mom were here. I didn't want to park any longer than necessary in the location that I would wait for him. For now, I just wanted to stake out the back of the apartment complex and find a good spot in view of the dumpster, which was less than twenty steps from the entrance of the apartment building.

Your mom had warned me many times of nosy neighbors, saying that they were calling her mom to tell on me because of my "walks," and I didn't want any part of the nosy neighbors now. I had on my Polish costume: tighter jeans than normal for me, an Adidas top, mirrored sunglasses, and I had cut my hair to military length, just like nearly all Polish men. But I knew that I still couldn't blend in, that every move I made was not Polish enough. Also, I couldn't open my mouth because that would immediately let everyone know I was a foreigner, and the car that I was driving had Dutch plates. This was serious business, and I was ready, but the time wasn't quite right; everyone was probably still sleeping.

I left and went to the Lidl supermarket parking lot a couple miles away because I wanted to try to dye my hair black with the box of Just for Men that I had in my suitcase, but the directions convinced me that I didn't have time, and I gave up on the endeavor without getting it all over me. A little more of a disguise would have been nice, but I didn't think it was crucial because the element of surprise was on my side. I needed to return and get into position. The last thing that I wanted was to miss an opportunity and spend another night in my car. I felt like a man behind enemy lines with no support whatsoever.

Down the alley behind the building, I looked for a parking spot that would give me enough of a vantage point. I made a full loop and ended up backing into a spot not far from the door that he would come out of. A construction crew was working on the building in front of me, and a couple of people were out walking their small dogs. It was quiet and still, and I settled in, pretending to read a book, trying to relax so that my upcoming decisions would be the best that they could be. I wanted to make the impression that I was waiting for someone, like maybe a business partner or somebody I was carpooling with. I didn't want people to think I was lost, and I didn't want to emit the possibility of anything suspicious happening. Out of the ordinary, alright, but not suspicious because then people would've started talking or even making phone calls, and I couldn't afford that chance.

The first spot I settled into made me feel uncomfortable. I couldn't see well because my angle was horrible. Depending upon when he spotted me, he would have had too high of a chance to get back inside the door and close it, locking me out. I started the car and scooted to another parking spot perpendicular to my first spot, so that the car was facing the door almost directly, the dumpster separating my car and the door. I knew that this adjustment alone probably would draw some attention. The people walking their dogs were interested in me, but just in a "this guy is new" way, and I got back into my book to try to keep it that way, picking up my map here and there, trying to act as if I was patiently waiting for someone that could be a while.

I looked clean and respectable, maybe even Dutch, and I thought that I was in the clear as far as that was concerned, though I hoped that he would come out soon. A couple of men came around the corner with their morning beers cracked open in their hands, and several people exited the door I was focused on, but not your grandfather. It was kind of hard to tell, but I was sure I would know when it was him; there's a particular bounce in his step that is impossible to miss if you're looking for it.

I sipped on my coke and turned on the stereo, playing my CD with the wrestling preparation music. I kept the volume very low, laughing at myself for being in this situation. I had to remain focused and ready like a sniper waiting for a shot. I knew that I would only get one chance, and I was ready. My mind was focused, I still didn't know exactly what I was going to do when I saw him.

The sunglasses allowed me to keep my eyes on the door while making it appear that I was reading or otherwise busy with something in the car. A lady with a dog who I noticed when I arrived was now checking out the back of my car, and I shuffled through the briefcase on the passenger seat to let her know that I was in fact busy, looking for something, and not sleeping or drunk. *She's probably just wondering why a Dutch person would ever want to be here, or maybe she's never seen one*, I thought.

I moved my wedding ring from my left hand to my right hand, and I did so for two reasons. The first reason was that the wedding band is worn on the right hand in Poland, and I wanted it to mean here what it means elsewhere. The second reason was because my punching hand is my right hand, and I wanted your grandpa to get hit with the ring that was symbolic of my pledge to your mother.

The door opened again, and he emerged, plastic bag in hand, and he was alone. *Perfect!* Autopilot took over, pure adrenaline. I had wound myself up and put myself into position, like a Jack-In-The-Box, and now something else was taking over. I still didn't consciously know exactly what I was going to do, but whatever it was, there was no turning back now.

My decision to take action had been made long ago, and my window of opportunity was small. I stopped thinking and I acted, starting the car, and throwing it into gear as quickly as possible so that he wouldn't have time to think if he decided to look at the car that had just started.

I crept forward, making sure that it was really him, then marveling that he was, in fact, out to throw away his cans on this fine morning. As soon as I judged that he was far enough away from the door so that he could not return, I sped in his direction toward the door. I swerved away from and around him, positioning myself to block his egress from where he came from. I was moving so quickly, so mindlessly, and so without fear that I stopped the car by crashing it into a stone wall, blocking access to the door to the apartment building completely and disabling the car. Mindlessly in the sense that I had to assess what I had done after it was done, because I was just doing and not thinking at this point.

The airbag deployed and hit me in the face, but I hardly noticed it. The hood caved in like an accordion, my door was bent, and I had trouble opening it because it was right up against the door to the apartment, within inches. The tiny Renault Twingo didn't stand a chance against the stone wall. I didn't waste any time because he was in the process of figuring out that it was me. I knew that he had a car nearby, and I didn't want him to get to a place where I couldn't reach him.

Without thinking or having planned to ahead of time, I reached behind my seat and picked up the hammer off the floor with my right hand, pushed open the door and squeezed through, all in one motion, pivoting and sprinting toward your grandfather. It seemed everything was happening in slow motion, out of my control; the decision to do this, whatever this was, had already been decided multiple times, on multiple levels. The music box had been wound up, and now it was playing the tune. *After this, my daughter will be evaluated, and soon she will be safe,* I thought.

My boots were a couple sizes too small, and my toes were restricted so that it felt awkward to run, but I did not hesitate. As I rounded the back of the car, he fully realized what was happening, producing a loud chirping, high pitched scream from utter surprise, fear, and vulnerability as he turned and ran the other way. I don't think this was what he was expecting on this ordinary late April morning. His scream was music to my ears; now I was the hunter, and he was the prey, even if it was only for a moment. Now, at least, he would never forget how serious I am about my family.

I was gripped by the absurdity of the situation, and I had to press forward with the motion as the means to my end. I was a lion protecting my cub, and that was that. I wasn't about to fail that responsibility so long as I had strength and breath and a heart that was beating, and it didn't matter to me if the entire world disagreed or thought that they would handle this situation differently. I knew that either they didn't know because they couldn't comprehend circumstances such as these, or they just weren't the types to protect their families at all costs.

As I chased him, I realized that I was not going to kill him, that I couldn't, or maybe shouldn't. I had taken myself to the brink of it, allowing for the possibility and the capability, thinking it through thoroughly, and now I knew for sure that it wasn't in my makeup, or that it just wasn't on the path in front of me. It didn't feel like a decision, but an observation that was somehow beyond my control, and a weight was lifted off my mind. I could feel it, and I was a little disappointed in myself, like someone whose draft number doesn't get called during wartime even though he didn't really want to go to war in the first place.

This scene, the chase, what I looked like, I chuckled to myself, even as I was running down your grandfather in the street. I caught a glimpse of myself from an aerial perspective, almost out of body, and I couldn't help myself but laugh. *What a moment*, I thought, *and I've got to act it through, I can't just ask him to let me see her, he's the one that stole her from me, why would he give her back? I can't ask to have her evaluated, they have painted me as the enemy and a bad father, and so here we are.*

I hated all of it; all that I wanted was to not have my child stolen from me by abusers and liars, and to be your daddy. But it was what it was, regardless of what I wanted, and so I was chasing this man down in the street in order to get arrested so that I could get the authorities to finally listen to me.

For quite a while none of my days had been normal, so for me this was just another one, the next day without you, and all I could do was hope that this was going to be the beginning of the end of that. This was once in a lifetime, a gameday of sorts in a sick game and I decided that I was going to enjoy this moment. I didn't mind the fact that he was terrified at all. Why didn't people understand that he stole my baby?

I didn't say anything, but just catapulted toward him, pump faking the hammer in the air a couple of times like a quarterback, or maybe like a Cherokee with a tomahawk, to scare him some more as he rubbernecked. Surprise was on my side, but I was also surprised that this was what it had all come down to, me chasing your grandfather with a hammer after wrecking a rental car in broad daylight.

In hindsight, the hammer was a bad choice, but at the time I didn't think that the details mattered because all that I wanted was to get arrested and be heard. I didn't care about any repercussions for me, nor did I think there would be any once they investigated.

We raced about twenty or thirty paces down the back alley, out the way I had come in with the car. I was gaining on him, but he was not a slow runner. I had met him on the court before in one-on-one basketball, and he was an avid tennis player when his elbow was healthy; he was way more active than I was. I had to push myself, especially with the tight boots. There was no doubt in my mind that I would catch him, because although he was an athlete, I also knew I was faster than him.

He turned a corner toward some shops and fell to the ground, plopping down like he found a spot in the circle in the game, Duck, Duck, Goose. He had tripped up just enough to know that I had him, and he stopped trying, like an opossum trapped in a corner.

I switched the hammer over to my left hand so that I could hit him with my right fist and knock on his head with the ring your mom had given me. I lurched over him, and we locked up, him holding the hammer with his right hand, but that was just a decoy; my only concern with that hand was to keep my grip. He attempted to control my right hand with his left hand, but he had to allocate too much of his attention to my left, the hand with the hammer.

He was holding his keys in his left hand, and he never dropped them, so all he was able to do was block and make it hard for me to swing my fist with any force. I was able to land around two to three reasonable punches to his head, the kind that lump you up, not the kind that shatter your jaw, all of them at least partially blocked. This was quick and dirty, and due to my frustration at not being able to swing or land anything substantial, like in a bad dream, I grabbed his hand and made him punch himself in the face with his own keys a couple of times.

I stopped, it was enough, the point was made for sure. In the police report, he stated that a man he had never seen before broke up the fight, assisted him, and saved his life. Either he was lying, which I knew was possible because I knew his nature, or maybe there was an angel that he could see that I couldn't. I don't know which it was, but I do know that nobody was there to break us up that I could see.

We remained locked up, like two high school wrestlers waiting for the time to run out, basically just holding each other's hands. I tried to maintain dominance so that he could not attack me, and I also didn't want him to get away so I did not let him get off the ground. I knew that someone would be there soon as we were very near to the grocery store, though I had no awareness of anything except what was right in front of me. I kept my eyes locked on his, trying to communicate to him that I was never going to give up.

Two members of the City Guard (Straż Miejska), a gun-less security force subordinate to the regular police, arrived on scene and I surrendered to them. They handcuffed me and I stood silent. No words were necessary to your grandfather or to the guards; this was just business, and it had played out according to plan.

CHAPTER 69

"THIS IS POLAND. THIS IS NOT USA."

I was relieved that they were there, and that this scene of my life was over. I smiled as they cuffed me, feeling some pressure lift off my shoulders, believing that when they heard me, which I thought would happen shortly, that they would have to investigate my claims. *How could they not?* For some reason I still hung on to the idea that this world contained justice.

He was bleeding a bit from above his left eye, nothing serious, probably a scratch from the keys, or maybe from my ring. He stood up as soon as I was cuffed and began talking to the guards; I couldn't understand anything that they were saying, except that I heard something like "Americano." It was apparent that they all knew each other. I knew that this would be an issue, me the outsider coming in against an established and well-respected family, attacking a man who has worked for the city, his best friend a judge a couple of blocks away.

I could only hope that the loud nature of my message would force someone to take a closer look. The only thing that I wanted was an evaluation of you, which I thought shouldn't be too hard no matter who he knew. I felt like he should be shaking in his boots because now the investigation was about to come crashing down on him, and I knew that he would not be able to withstand the type of inquiry that I was saying needed to happen.

He sighed, giving me the impression that he thought I didn't understand something, or that I was in for a ride I could not yet imagine. I stood by with my hands cuffed behind my back, standing tall and proud, and knowing my cause was righteous. I couldn't wait to talk to a judge, and I knew that would have to happen soon.

The two guards and your grandfather conversed in Polish, and though I couldn't understand the words, I could understand that he was covering his butt and explaining to them that I was a bad man in one way or another. An ambulance came and they gave him a cap made of mesh netting, but he was walking around just fine. The police showed up, and the City Guard walked me over to the police car, arms held above my head behind me, so that I had to walk hunched over. Two uniformed cops got out of their Kia, took the handcuffs off me and replaced them with their own, and then placed me into the back of their car.

One of the officers spoke some English, and one didn't, the guy in the passenger seat. Both were in their mid-twenties, and it was obvious that they were a little surprised to have an American in their car. They were both checking me out in the rear-view mirror, and I made eye contact and smiled. I could tell that the guy in the passenger seat didn't like me, that he had already formed a strong opinion of what just happened, probably from listening to your grandpa tell his story first. My smile confused him, but I was not angry or upset. These officers were my new friends from my point of view; one of them was going to take my statement.

"Alcohol?" the driver asked with an accent, acting as if it were a given that I was drunk to do such a thing.

"No, no alcohol, no nothing. He is abusing my daughter," I answered.

They didn't seem to believe that I was not drunk, even after I assured them that I was 100% sober. I told them that I had come a long way just to get the point across that he was abusing my daughter. The driver immediately warmed up to me and didn't see me as a threat anymore. My guess was that he had a child of his own and thought about what he would do in such a situation. The other guy began to calm down, though he was obviously still suspicious that I was drunk or high on something.

They drove around to the back of the apartment building and got out, leaving me to wait until they finished their investigation of the scene. I was happy to sit where they parked, right by the dumpster where your grandpa was going to dispose of his cans. If I had a rock, and if my hands hadn't been cuffed behind my back, I could've easily hit a window of the apartment that I knew you were living in. It was nice to be close to you, nice to know that an investigation was beginning, even though I knew that I would initially look like the criminal.

Your grandfather left, and I assumed that he was going with the ambulance even though it was obvious that his injuries were only superficial. I got to see your aunt Ada and your grandmother Iwona, as both of them came outside to talk to the police. Neither of them made eye contact with me, though it was nice to be in their vicinity. I wondered where you and your mother were, yearning for even but a glimpse of either of you through the window, but you never appeared.

I asked the police to get my bag out of the car, especially the computer. I had books and notebooks as well as evidence like your mother's journals that I wanted to show to the court. When I packed, I knew there was a good possibility I would be in Poland for a while, and I was grateful they agreed to get my things for me. They got out to write their reports, and I tried to relax in the back of an old beat-up Kia sedan, only a cop car because it said so on the exterior. The seat was made of cloth, and there was no divider between the front and back; it looked like an old taxi to me.

They drove me to the local police station, where a female officer came out to help with my belongings. Seeing that I was thirsty, she held her personal water bottle up to my mouth, and I greedily emptied it, slouching down to get every drop, thankful and honored that she had noticed I was parched. The first things I noticed when they brought me into the station were that tiles in the floor were missing, and people were walking around in the hallway smoking cigarettes... *yes, third world, here I am.*

They ran a breathalyzer test and examined my saliva for drugs, but I was clean, and then I was booked. They didn't take fingerprints, which surprised me, but I did have to strip down, squat and cough before being placed into the jail cell, which was dank and dark, underground with no window. There was no bathroom in the cell, so I had to knock on my door when I had to go, but also no toilet paper in the bathroom down the hall, so I just had to hold it until further notice.

The next day the police came to take me to a meeting with the prosecutor - a squat, plump man who chewed on his fingernails, Arkadiusz Wesolowski. He didn't speak English, but with him was a young (about twenty-year-old) woman who would become my interpreter for the duration of the next nineteen months. I didn't know it yet, but she also didn't understand me; her mastery of English was no mastery at all. I tried to explain to her that you were being abused, and that your mom had also been abused when she was a child, but the only word that she understood was "rape."

"Why would your wife leave you to be raped?" the prosecutor asked via the interpreter, and I couldn't help but chuckle to myself at the absurdity of his question given what I had already told him. I tried to explain that this is what can happen with severe trauma, but everything I said was lost in translation; I could see it on his dumbfounded face. It was evident that his only interest was in the slam dunk case that I had plopped on his lap by assaulting your grandpa; I could already tell that the "why" didn't matter to him.

The following morning, after my second night in Polish jail, I was transported to the local court in Stargard. The police officer spoke some broken English, and he asked me what I meant by "rape." "Severe child abuse," I responded, looking for an explanation that would make sense to him. "You know when people train a dog to fight, they deprive it and abuse it from a very young age, this causes dependence upon the trainer, and the ability of the trainer to fill the dog's head with whatever he wants to fill it with. It is not just rape, but trauma training."

"Yeah, well you are going to be in prison for a long time," he responded.

I was excited to have my day in court, but of course I had the same interpreter, and it didn't seem like the judge could understand me either. The focus was on what I did rather than why I did it; the judge didn't care what I was alleging, or that my entire reason for being there was so that I would have an audience to inform that my daughter was being abused. "I find that there is ample evidence to suggest that you have committed attempted murder. You will be placed in pre-trial detention for the next three months, at least," he declared.

"Will you please have my daughter evaluated?"

"That is not for me to decide. This case is about your actions," he said, deflating me and negating the only reason that I was there in the first place.

"My father-in-law is one of the people who is abusing my daughter. He is big in this town, and his best friend is a judge in this building. Can I be tried in another jurisdiction?"

"Are you suggesting that I am corrupt?" the judge shot back.

"No, I am just saying that it appears to me that there may be a conflict of interest in this building."

He banged his gavel, and I was taken back to the jail to wait for my transportation to the prison.

Later that day, April 29th, I was driven to the local prison by the same young cop who had taken me to court. He cranked on the handcuffs, and he refused to loosen them. For some reason this guy just didn't like me.

I could tell that my right wrist was bleeding from the handcuff, not badly, but bad enough, and I still have a scar now as I write this more than ten years later. I told him that I was bleeding, but I didn't force the issue because I didn't want this guy to think that he was bothering me at all.

"Twenty-five years, that's what they're going to give you, you are going to find out about Poland, this is not USA, twenty-five years," he was having fun trying to scare me.

I laughed at him, "They aren't going to give me anything, and I don't care if they do. Do you think that I made a mistake? You wouldn't protect your family if someone was hurting them?"

"This is Poland, this is not USA, twenty-five years," he chided as if that part of it mattered to me. He made it obvious that it would matter to him. I didn't care about twenty-five years, but about four months of you being stolen from our home and being in an abusive household.

"So, then what you are telling me is that you don't know what love is, you don't love your wife."

"Yes, of course I love my wife," he shot back, defensively.

"No, you don't. You don't know love at all. If you're more afraid of jail than you are of your family being hurt, then you don't know the love that I know at all; you can't, it's just not possible. You don't love your wife," I assured him, hoping to put some doubt in him and get him to see that he was wrong. How one could justify anything other than "any means necessary" when it comes to protecting their family, I could not begin to comprehend. How could a man value his own comfort over the safety of his wife and child? To me, this was a ridiculous notion.

He kept me in the back of the car for a while baking in the hot sun, my wrist aching and bleeding until eventually becoming comfortably numb. I realized that most people do not know what they mean when they say things like, "If anyone ever hurt my child, I'd kill them." They are just blowing hot air and empty threats; they are all afraid and too worried about themselves.

"More than one devoted parent has vowed, 'If anyone so much as lays a finger on my little girl, I'll kill him'" (Rush 3).

There were people who understood along the way, including the prison guard that greeted me once the cop let me out of the back of his car, an older gentleman with a thick mustache, a better man than that cop. I explained to him why I was there, and I could tell that he was moved. His eyes full of pity and shame for being a part of the broken system, he shook my hand and patted me on the back. "You are a good man, but this is Poland, not USA," he reminded me.

"What is this place called?" I asked. He didn't understand the question, so I followed up with, "Do you know Alcatraz or Riker's Island? What is this called?" I asked, using my hands to show him that I was referring to the prison.

"Oh, this is 'Więzienie,'" he replied, smiling, the Polish word for prison. I smiled back, happy to be right where I was, right around the corner from you and your mom, on the verge of getting you evaluated. *Wow, Polish prison - amazing!* From my point of view, things were getting better; *the day where we reunite must be right around the corner*, I thought. I was looking forward to this brief view of Polish prison that I was about to get, remembering that I had considered volunteering for Dutch prison for the experience.

He escorted me first to an administration window where a twentysomething woman was sitting behind the glass with no expression on her face. I could tell that she was not a happy person. I had to sign some paperwork and deposit all the money that I had into a prison account; inmates weren't allowed to have cash on their persons. She almost let me keep my "lucky" Thomas Jefferson two-dollar bill after I informed her that it was not money, but a keepsake of sorts. But she changed her mind and made me hand it over; I had a feeling that it would be the last time I ever saw it, that somehow it would get "lost," which it did. Things being taken from me was becoming less of a surprise each time. *You can have my two-dollar bill – what I want is my daughter.*

I was relieved that I was not asked or ordered to surrender my wedding ring; I would have put up a stink about that, but for now they let it go. The guard led me to our next destination, "magazyn," where all of the prisoner gear is stored and distributed, where I would have to leave my laptop and everything else that I possessed that was not permitted within the cells.

Magazyn (the warehouse) was manned by two toothless convicts in their early thirties who were smoking tobacco out of glass stems called "lufkas" that looked a lot like crack pipes to me; I had never before seen people smoke tobacco in this fashion. They also looked like crack heads, but they were just hungry, poor, and without hope, without teeth, in the middle of doing long prison sentences. They had fallen into the prison groove, and I was new. I would later understand that their "look" was representative of the average prisoner in the Polish prison system.

Here I was given my bedding, green plastic utensils, a plate, and a bowl. I was also provided a month's supply of toiletries: one roll of rough, gray toilet paper, one disposable razor, a baggy of powdered laundry detergent, and a small tube of tasteless toothpaste. I asked the guy to take good care of my laptop. I could hardly wait to use it again, just to look at pictures of our family; it had already been far too long since I held you, since I read to you before bedtime, since we made our scrambled egg surprise or a new song together.

I was escorted with my belongings to one of the buildings and led inside where there was about a one-hundred-foot hallway with locked rooms on both sides. It was impossible to see what was going on in the cells because they were concrete cells with thick, solid metal doors, and not what I was accustomed to seeing on tv with bars.

I was permitted to keep my own clothing because I was pre-trial; it was only after sentencing that prison garb was given out and mandated. I was also allowed to keep my books, notebooks, and everything else that was not banned. My new home was all the way down the hall on the left.

I lugged all my belongings as best I could, and I wondered what my cell and my cellmates would be like.

The guard unlocked the door, and I stepped inside where I was met with six pairs of eyes staring at me from different parts of a room about the size of our living room in The Hague. As the door closed behind me, I could feel my world shrinking. It was hard to believe I couldn't open the door and go home.

Drawing of a prisoner and prison guard. Made for me by a cell mate.

CHAPTER 70

"ATTEMPTED MURDER WAS THE CASE THAT THEY GAVE ME"

Journal Entry, April 29, 2011

"Arrived in Polish prison –Stargard Szczecinski 90 days pre-trail – July 27th. Attempted Murder was the case that they gave me. All I can think now is 'God's will.' What choice did I have? I didn't try to kill the man. I am still not sure what any alternative would be? Just let this [expletive] keep happening? I think not, though that is exactly what has happened. They are still there. The only good thing I can think of is that I am in the same town. Why are people so [expletive] blind? How can I get no help whatsoever for this ritual abuse that is at this very moment creating a sex slave out of my daughter?"

The following email I did not see until 2014 when I was in a minimum-security facility and was allowed to log into my email account.

"Bryson - child abduction to Poland
Fri, Apr 29, 2011, 4:23 AM
[American Citizen Services-Germany] to me
Dear Mr. Bryson:
Your recent inquiry concerning the abduction of your minor daughter has been referred to this office for response.
As much as we sympathize with your plight, as your daughter was abducted from the Netherlands to Poland her case unfortunately does not fall within the jurisdiction of the U.S. Consulate General in Frankfurt. However, you appear to have already taken the appropriate steps by informing the U.S. Consulate in Amsterdam and Interpol.
The Department of State considers international parental child abduction, as well as the welfare and protection of U.S. citizen children taken overseas, to be important, serious matters. We place the highest priority on the welfare of children who have been victimized by international abductions. The Department of State's Office of Children's Issues (CA/OCS/CI) is designated to provide assistance to the left-behind parents of international parental child abduction:

Office of Children's Issues
Toll Free Phone from within the U.S.: 1-888-407-4747 (8 a.m. - 8 p.m.)
Phone: (202) 736-9090
Adoption Office Fax: (202) 736-9080
Abduction Office Fax: (202) 736-9133
Contact email address for international parental child abduction and adoption country-specific information: AskCI@state.gov.

Specific information about Poland and child abduction laws can be found here: http://travel.state.gov/abduction/country/country_515.html. You may also wish to contact our colleagues in the American Citizen Services Unit at the U.S. Embassy in Warsaw for additional guidance: ACSWarsaw@state.gov.

U.S. Embassy Warsaw
Aleje Ujazdowskie 29/31
00-540 Warsaw Poland
Tel.: +48-22/504-2000
We hope you will find this information and wish you all the best in reclaiming your daughter.
Sincerely,
Germany ACS
U.S. Consulate General
Gießener Straße 30
60435 Frankfurt am Main, Germany
' +49 69-7535-0
Ê +49 69-7535-2252"

The truth must set you free, or else I have no chance, I realized. I often slept with my pants on because I was certain that they would come for me anytime, and I wanted to be ready. I immediately began writing letters, one of the first to my parents to inform them that I was now in a Polish prison, that they would have to get a lawyer. However, my intention was not to have them get a lawyer for me exactly, but to get one which would push for an evaluation of you. I never heard back from them, and I never had a lawyer fight for this, which was the only reason that I was in Poland in the first place.

One of my new cellmates made my bed for me, which was a sign of respect, and then the inquiries commenced. I was the new guy, an American, and they wanted to know everything. Communication was nearly impossible, as I only knew a few Polish words, but we had time. At first, I could not discern where one word ended and another began. Polish sentences were just a mixed garble of gibberish, like it must be for a baby.

I focused on their mouths as they spoke, and I practiced, eventually being able to get the gist of most conversations. But this took time, and at this point I had to make my communication attempts with simple English words and my hands. I did not have a desire to learn Polish because that would be an admission of being a long-term prisoner. I was confident that I would soon be leaving this country with my daughter, and hopefully her mother.

Everyone in my cell was there on pretrial status, and we were not allowed to use the phone or have contact with any other people in the prison to protect the state's case against us. In my new cell were people charged with murder, car theft, assault, and marijuana possession, among other things. Nobody had any idea how long they would be there, and bail was not an option.

Pretrial detention was ordered in three-month increments for as long as the "investigation" required, with a maximum duration of two years. Hardly anybody ever stayed for just three months. The guys called the letters we received every three months a "dolewka," meaning they were filling up your "cup" again, like when you add water to a teacup after finishing the first round. One of the first phrases that I was taught was "zycie jest brutalny," which I was told meant "life is brutal." "Yes, ok, it is, but that is not alright for my daughter," I pled. "That's fine for me, but not for my little girl."

There was a man who visited occasionally just to ask how we were doing, and we always smiled and told him that we were fantastic just to get him to leave us alone. His position was called "wychowawca," and he was a social worker, I was told. He looked a little closer at the rooms than the guards did, and he made sure that the little communities in each cell were not having any major issues. From my point of view, these people did as little as possible; it appeared that they were just for show more than anything else.

I became acclimated to my new surroundings: they brought three meals a day to the doors of our cell to prevent us from having contact with other inmates in a common dining center. The meals were meager, so anybody who was not able to buy food or share food was hungry all the time. A typical breakfast was something like two hardboiled eggs, or three slices of sandwich meat or a third of a can of meat, or about two inches of kielbasa/mystery meat/minced fish, a small loaf of bread to last the day, and a slab of butter. Lunch included a rotation of soups along with something hot, like potatoes or beans. Dinner was about the same as breakfast, except that bread was only served in the mornings.

Much of what we were served were different kinds of mystery meat, canned and tubed, which I have now grown to enjoy, but they were strange to me at first. Some of it, particularly the blood head cheese, almost nobody ate, not even the feral cats that patrolled outside our windows.

Mealtime was highly anticipated; it was one of the best parts of our days. The seven of us ate at our little table together, which was good for bonding. We played a lot of cards too, which was an effective means to get rid of time, but also enjoyable when there was nothing else to do, which was most of the time. This is how I learned to count in Polish.

Each cell was permitted one tv if someone could get it from their family on the outside, but there was no cable or internet connection. We had to adjust our rabbit ears to try to get the signal of about four local channels, but this was also something to look forward to, and one of the best ways to learn their language. I wrote letters to all the major news channels, as well as to "crime solving" programs, but I never received any responses.

"Apel" was every morning, and every evening. The guards walked down our hallway to open each door individually so that they could count and check on the inmates. They rang a loud bell in the morning signaling that it was about to begin, and we were expected to make our beds and stand at attention with our hands behind our backs when our door was opened. Also in the morning, a guard entered to bang on the window bars with a big wooden mallet to ensure that we had not started sawing through a bar during the night. There was no bell in the evening, but only the yelling of the word "apel" down the hallway to signal that it was beginning.

Once per week, we lined up to leave our cell and walk to the shower room for a strict five-minute shower, with no hot water in the cell itself during the rest of the week. We were allowed a water cooker in the cell, so we found ways to take sponge baths in our bathroom to avoid excessive body odor. Most of the guys shaved off all their body hair, another way to minimize odors; this was the first and only time that I ever shaved my head.

We also used the water cooker for washing dishes, and for laundry, which we did by hand in a plastic tub. It was only possible to heat a liter of water at a time, but we did have all day, so we got used to it. Cell cleaning was a daily affair, the floor, the bathroom, and the sink area; everybody had a job, and we had time to be clean, so we were.

"Spacer" was our time to walk around in circles in another small cage just outside our cell. The guards asked us each day at a random time if we wanted to go, and then they would escort those that did into the cage for some sunlight and flowers, which I picked and stuck into my books for drying. We found ways to exercise in our cell, doing sit-ups and pushups, and using the furniture and filled water bottles to do things like arm and leg curls. I exercised for a while, but after a few months I just did not feel like it, mostly because I did not feel that I could maintain any new muscle on the diet we were given.

We could smoke in the cell, and in my cell the rule was that it had to be done by the barred window, or in the bathroom; in some cells, it was required that everyone smoke in the bathroom to cover the scent. Everyone had their own glass "lufka," which allowed us to smoke a third or a half of a cigarette at a time to conserve tobacco. It kept us occupied, and it was one of the most cherished privileges we had. Of course, not smoking would have been better, but this is a story of what was and not what should have been.

We never obtained any alcohol in this cell, but one of my cellmates was able to acquire some marijuana during a visit, so they set up a gravity bong in the bathroom with a cut up plastic soda bottle, one person with their ear on the door to hear if the guard was nearby. I tried it once or twice, but I used marijuana to relax or focus, and relaxation was simply not possible in this environment. I was terrified that we would all get caught, that this too would be used against me. It felt like I was trying to relax while driving and being followed by a cop and waiting for him to flip on his lights at any time.

The only thing that they ever did catch us with was too many water bottles, which they confiscated and dumped out. We tried to explain that we collected water for when the faucet stopped working, which it did periodically, and for exercise. They acted as if we were hoarding dangerous contraband; when they raided us, the guards were sometimes dressed like a SWAT team with masks. We were removed from our cell frequently, but irregularly so that we couldn't plan for it, placed into a closet in the hall where we all stood until the guards finished doing what they were doing. My only concern was that they would mess up my papers and notebooks, but they were usually gentle with my things, and I never had any problems.

A linen cart came by every other week to exchange our sheets. A different cart stopped by monthly with a roll of toilet paper, a plastic disposable razor, and a baggie of powdered laundry soap. One roll of toilet paper was not enough, and so people protected their roll as one of their most valuable possessions, trading or bartering with someone who was able to buy extra at the store. Sometimes we had to write a "prośba" (request) to the prison director for another roll, which was usually granted, but not guaranteed or quick. Some people just learned to live without toilet paper.

About every two weeks we were permitted to go to the recreation yard for about forty-five minutes where we could lift real weights, shoot baskets, or sometimes play volleyball. I was grateful for the ability to run around and chase a ball.

There was a library which I sometimes visited, but I was limited to picture books, as the only books on the shelves were written in Polish. Some of the inmates around the prison heard I was there, and I began receiving random deliveries of books in English. I remember specifically reading Steven King's "Cell," and thinking it was amazing to be able to read something new in English, but that it was poor compared to some of his other books.

I saw the prison dentist, and I was not impressed with him at all. I think he was probably drunk by the way that he looked and acted, and he did not hold back in treating me like a "prisoner" patient, causing me to feel a bit like a lab rat. He told me that he could not help me unless I wanted to extract teeth that were bothering me, and I declined. It was odd to me at the time that most of the guys in my cell thought removing painful teeth was a good idea; I thought it better to wait and see what would come next. They had to be getting ready to release me soon, I figured.

One time, the pain was so intense, and I refused to have it extracted, so they took me to the local hospital for x-rays. I was transported in handcuffs and leg shackles with two officers guarding me. One of the officers carried an Uzi, the other a short-barreled shotgun. When I got inside and sat down, the nurse looked at me and immediately told them to remove my restraints; she could tell that I was not dangerous just by looking at me. After they had my x-rays, I was finally given an antibiotic and the pain cleared up.

The sun shined bright and hot over the summer, and there was almost zero cross breeze through our cell. The cell was solid other than our one big window, and so we soaked sheets in cold water and hung them all around the cell on clotheslines that we made by twisting up plastic bags. The little breeze that we did get was chilled, which was a slight improvement.

For a while, we had a small hole in our wall, just big enough for a toilet plunger handle, going from our cell to the one adjacent. We passed back and forth small amounts of tobacco or coffee as a trade, a loan, or to help a friend. We only knew people by their voices, as we never saw them face to face, but nonetheless they were our friends.

We were also able to trade things with other cells by swinging a homemade rope out the window in a kind of underhand lasso motion. It could be thrown haphazardly if it were something like coffee, but sometimes they would pass the PlayStation around this way. Of course, the guards were always looking for these sorts of things, but inmates seldom got caught, as they knew the guards better than the guards knew them. Their habits and patterns were easy to pick up, and almost impossible to not pick up, as it was the same every day, every week, every month. We knew who was coming to work on each shift unless there was a surprise.

Below are more emails that I didn't have at the time they were sent. I received them later when I was permitted to view the case against me.

May 7, 2011
Agata Bryson to Mom [from the court records]
"Bad news: the police has visited me yesterday concerning me and Adelle. He contacted some organization in Cambodia and accused my dad of abusing us…"

May 7, 2011
Agata Bryson to Mom [from the court records]
"…Is there anyway you guys could help?"

May 26, 2011
Mom to Agata Bryson [from the court records]
"They are now saying that Iain has bipolar and delusional disorder."

What happened is that my mom did help them. By taking your mom and grandfather's side and stating that she also believed I was mentally ill, she was putting the nails in my coffin, and guaranteeing that I would not be taken seriously during my trial. Unfortunately, this also helped to ensure that you would never be evaluated.

CHAPTER 71

"IN FEAR OF OUR LIVES"

One day, during this hot summer, I was transported to meet with a couple of local psychiatrists for what the court called a preliminary "expert" evaluation. The guards transported about ten of us in the back of a van, each prisoner chained to one other prisoner. I was chained to an old man who I had to help walk. We were escorted into a run-down building with paint chipping off the walls and miserable people everywhere. At the end of the hallway, we waited our turns as the psychiatrists cycled through their evaluations. My wait was about an hour; I hoped that the man I was still chained to would not try to jump out the window.

When it was my turn, they took off my chains and I entered the room. One psychiatrist was behind the desk, the other was propped, sitting halfway on the corner of the desk. Both were in their thirties and balding; to me they looked like jokesters, and I didn't like their arrogant demeanor. Karolina, the same translator I had been given for my visit with the prosecutor, was sitting in a chair next to my chair. My heart sank as I realized that I could not effectively communicate. I liked Karolina as a person, but she was a problem as a translator, even though she had obtained the Polish certificate allowing her to get her current court translator job.

I had already written to the prosecutor, the court, and the United States Embassy regarding the fact that Karolina could not understand me, with no response. The U.S. Embassy sent me formal letters explaining that I had to do whatever Poland determined was necessary. They completely ignored the fact that I wouldn't have a fair trial if she was my translator, and on top of that they never addressed my concerns regarding you.

When they began their questioning with, "So, you smoke marijuana?" I knew that these were not the psychiatrists that I had hoped for. "And you like guns?" they continued. "You think that your father-in-law raped your wife?"

I was flabbergasted, "No, I never said 'rape.' What I said was that my wife and daughter are in a family that uses trauma to train their children. My wife referred to her family as a cult. Incest is closer to what I am talking about than rape, and incest is not rare."

I could tell that nearly everything I was saying was being lost in translation. I could also tell, like someone called into their boss's office to be fired, that these "bosses" already had a plan for this meeting. They thought they already knew the truth of what was going on, and it was clear that their interest was not in understanding me, but in completing their evaluation so they could move to the next prisoner. This was assembly line psychiatry.

They "knew" that you were not being abused because that was what the prosecutor had told them, and each claim I tried to make about abuse in any way was mirrored by crazy looks, like if I had said that I had seen a dinosaur in my yard. They were going through the motions, but I was already in a "box" before I entered the room.

"And you believe in God?" they queried.

"Yes, I do," I answered, knowing that this would also be somehow delusional thinking.

"And what god do you believe in?"

"There is only One. I do not believe the same thing that you believe as Catholics."

"Do you pray?"

"Yes, I do pray."

"How do you pray?"

"I speak to my God, and I ask for help."

"And do you go to church?"

"No, I do not."

With mischievous, sly grins, they told me that the evaluation was completed, and I went back to the hallway for my chains. After everyone was done, we were transported back to the prison, and to our respective cells. Another opportunity to speak to people who should've known that trauma and child abuse are not uncommon, and another swing and miss. All of this was a letdown, days like this one a bit more than others, but my strategy was to keep pressing, keep doing my best, and trust in the One. I knew that I was not alone.

Psychiatrists would (as a group) classify all religious beliefs as delusional if they could, but society wouldn't put up with it. They only classify religious beliefs that are not espoused by a large group of people as delusional. Therefore, if someone believed that Jesus lived in the apple tree in their front yard, that would be a delusion, but if fifty million people believed it, then it would not be a delusion. While my personal religious beliefs were not in line with those of my peers or the Polish majority, I knew that nothing I said could be legitimately deemed delusional, though I anticipated that this was coming next.

> "Before diagnosis there is the process of differential diagnosis in which the clinician extracts the probable from the possible and the likely from the unlikely. One cannot make a diagnosis without excluding others – no case is ever that black and white" (Munro 193).

The problem was that these two literal "quacks" decided that they could bypass this process. Their report stated that they did not get enough information to make a diagnosis in the short visit that they had with me (about ten minutes), but that they did "highly suspect" that I had delusional disorder. So, after admitting they could really have no idea according to the guidelines of their profession, they then went on to assume the worst, deciding that I was "probably" insane after ten minutes or less.

This information further confirmed my suspicions that these were not deep-thinking psychiatrists, but tools of the criminal justice system. In my opinion, a professional "head" doctor who claims that allegations of incest and severe child abuse are delusional based on an insufficient investigation and the testimony of the alleged perpetrators, is dangerous, criminal, and even delusional. Incest and child abuse are not rare in any way, and to date, nobody had investigated any of my concerns.

> "It [DSM–IV] states that a delusion is a false belief based on an incorrect inference about external reality that is firmly sustained despite what almost everyone else believes and despite what constitutes incontrovertible and obvious proof or evidence to the contrary. The belief is not one ordinarily accepted by other members of the person's culture or subculture (e.g. it is not an article of religious faith)" (Munro 26).

I had not made an "incorrect inference about external reality," because all that I was standing on was this: my daughter had multiple signs and symptoms of child abuse, including bruises, vaginal pain, terror that someone would touch her "pee pee," talking about her grandfather's privates, nightmares, bed wetting, regression, along with the fact that her mother had told me she was taking her back to the "cult." This was my bottom line; the other stuff that I said between December 27, 2010 and April 2011 was attributable to me dealing with what happened and was happening.

"...despite what almost everyone else believes" is the part that really did me in because there was nobody telling the court that they believed what I believed. Even though nobody was disputing the fact that you had bruises, for example, they still thought that I was somehow a bigger problem than your grandfather, who you had told me gave you the last bruise I saw. This was a direct result of the "red herring."

* * *

A cellmate gently awoke me to tell me that I said, "perception," in my sleep. I realized that for my case, the truth was of no importance at all, that all the people I had been and would be speaking to were going to be influenced by the "red herring," by me being an outsider, by having committed a crime, by what I was alleging, and by the fact that my family was not on my side. Biting my tongue and being afraid of what might happen to me was not an option; time was passing, and I was not willing to stop swinging at the stone.

Cell life was monotonous, but I was not bored. I wrote everything down, filling up stacks of journals and producing hundreds of letters to send out. The guards shut our main light off at 10PM, so I spent quite a bit of time in the bathroom by myself during the night, utilizing the small light that was in there to write in solitude.

I had nothing to do but to think, remember, and process. I was able to go over everything in my life again and again, and I remembered things that probably never would have come to the surface had I not had this time. I made lists of things like books and songs to exercise my mind, and I read the five or so books that I had with me multiple times, analyzing them on deeper levels.

Studying my Bible became my main focus. I wrote out verses and entire books, searching for greater understanding. I created charts and diagrams, and prayed to God for discernment as if I was pleading for my next breath. I knew that Jesus Christ is "the way, the truth, and the life..." (John 14:6), but I had no idea what that meant for me. I knew that the Bible held the truth because it had been made clear to me during the abduction when my head was forced into evil. What I also knew was that many people had it wrong, even though they might say they know that Jesus is the way, they still didn't get it.

They wanted Jesus to give them money, health, a better job, or even a prime parking spot, or they wanted Him to make them feel better about themselves. That "Jesus" was of no interest to me. I knew that I needed the Jesus of the Bible, the One that said, "Therefore I say to you, whatever things you ask when you pray, believe that you receive them, and you will have them" (Mark 11:24 NKJV), because I needed my daughter to stop being abused more than I wanted to live into the next minute of my life. Where could I find this Jesus? I begged the heavens.

The Jehovah's Witnesses visited every month or so, and I took this opportunity to leave the cell and learn their doctrine. Of course, I wasn't looking for answers from them, but I felt fortunate to get to experience their teaching methods. Listening to them helped me narrow down areas of doctrine to study in my Bible when I got back to my cell, and it also gave me an inside course on the Jehovah's Witnesses. I gave them a letter regarding you and the fact that you were being abused, they told me they would help, and then I never heard back from them. I would have been surprised if they did help, as they have little clout in Poland and I wasn't a member, but they were a link to the outside that I had to try.

My first round of divorce papers arrived in the mail, calling for not only divorce, but termination of my parental rights, termination of visitation, and alimony. The basis was exactly what your mom had told me would happen with the "red herring," just lie after lie painting me as the worst man, father, and husband imaginable – a true monster. It also stated that you and she escaped in fear of your lives (from me) to safety. This letter was a shock back to reality, as it was the first real news on anything going on outside of my cell.

I immediately began drafting an appeal letter, rejecting each of your mom's demands in turn, and explaining my side of the story. "I do not agree with divorce, and I do not agree with the termination of my parental rights. My daughter was stolen from her home when I was trying to get our family help. They did not leave because they feared me. I was not the problem and am not the problem. My daughter needs to be evaluated now."

Jurn, a lanky Dutchman with a curly afro, was introduced into my cell. They put us together because we were the only English speakers in the facility, and he spoke less Polish than I did. He was caught trying to transport around fifteen kilograms of marijuana in his trunk from Latvia to The Netherlands, passing straight through Poland. Now he was looking at five years in prison or more, and he was scared. I helped him to get situated, the hardest part being teaching him to hunker down and get used to it, as things were not going to change quickly. A couple of weeks in, he was ready to get Polish prison tattoos, and he ended up marrying a Polish woman and staying in Poland after his release many years later.

Just before Christmas 2011, I was visited by a consular officer from the United States Embassy in Warsaw: Margaret Bula-Duane. The purpose of the visit was not to see if I was alright, or if they could help with my case or my daughter, but because it was required of them to visit American prisoners every so often. She brought me a bag of candy, a used pencil, a magazine, and a copy of The New Testament, with Proverbs. I already had my copy of The New Testament, the one you handed me before you left, but I did not have Proverbs, so I ripped out Proverbs, put it into my Bible, and gave the rest to Jurn (see Appendix 32).

It was obvious that she was not interested in my case, and that her position was that the Polish judicial system was handling the situation well. I don't know whether she really believed that or just took that stance for political reasons to honor Poland's judicial autonomy. I told her that I had not seen a lawyer, and I reiterated again that the court interpreter did not speak ample English. "This is Poland, and there is not much that we can do. Are they feeding you? Are you safe?" she asked.

"The girl cannot understand me. How am I supposed to have a fair trial?"

"They claim that she is qualified," she declared.

"Well, she definitely is not," I firmly rebutted.

She put up a wall on this one, so I moved on to you. I suspected that my parents were having an influence on how she perceived me, and I wished for a moment that my only family was you and your mom.

"And what about my daughter? She is a United States citizen, born in New London, CT. Why can't her government get her evaluated?

"Her mother is Polish, so when she is here, the Polish government considers your daughter to also be Polish, and there is nothing that we can do about it. This is how Polish law works in this instance."

"I don't care about Polish law. This is another Natalie Holloway in progress, and my daughter's government is impotent and worthless."

She said that they would check up on me again in a few months or so, and she gave me a hug, saying that my mom told her to give me one from her. It struck me that I needed a lawyer, and not a hug, but that didn't seem like it was going to happen. I went back to my cell, knowing that no government was going to help, knowing that my family had no plans to help, and wondering what else my parents had told the U.S. government and the Polish court about me, their adult son, and how this would affect my strategies moving forward.

I shared my candy with my cellmates, and I wrote you a letter, knowing that you would not get it, but thinking that maybe your mom would. I composed a short children's story about patience and love, and I sent it to your grandfather Sławomir's address on Piłsudskiego street right down the road from where I was. It was rare that we could see the moon from our window since it was often on the other side of the building, but the one thing that kept me together was remembering and learning to believe that "I love you to the moon" always ended with "And back!" and that this was the direction I was moving.

Dawid M., 25, was awaiting a case on car theft. In Poland, they steal cars and bring them to Germany to sell, or vice versa. This is big business, as the border provides cover and protection. Dawid had done time in Germany as well as in Poland, and he was at peace with where he was. He did not have anywhere else to go, and prison had already become a normal part of his life, something that he had to deal with sometimes. He wished he was in a German prison where the food and facilities were better, but other than that he was one of the most up-beat people I had ever met, unphased by temporary setbacks.

"What would you think if they gave you seven years?" he asked, not joking, but thinking that would be reasonable based upon what he knew.

"Seven years? No way. They will investigate, and I will be out soon. Seven years is crazy."

"No, seven years would be good. This is not USA, this is Polska."

I was in that same cell at the end of the hallway until around August 2011, and then they told me that I was being transferred to Szczecin for psychiatric evaluation. The guards gave me a half hour to pack and say goodbye. I would miss them, but I had everybody's contact information that I wanted, and it was time to continue with the mission I started. The worst part was that you weren't going to be down the road from me anymore.

They put me in a temporary holding cell with two other guys who were also waiting to be transported. The toilet did not work; we had to dump a bucket of water into it from the sink to make it flush. The paint was chipping, and all the metal was beginning to rust. My two cellmates were miserable; they did not want to talk or share anything that they had.

There was a radio mounted on our wall, like in all the cells, and for the first time since being put in custody one of my favorite songs played. It felt like God was reminding me He was with me no matter where I went. I climbed atop one of the stools, and put my ear right up to the speaker, closing my eyes and drifting into a piece of heaven. The older man in my room reached up and turned the volume all the way down, and I returned to earth.

The next morning the police drove me to Szczecin. The guy driving was one of the most reckless drivers I had ever been in a car with, and I was in the back, facing sideways, handcuffed. He was a young guy who drove like he knew he had authority and could not be touched. I was nervous like when I was in high school being driven home by a drunk friend, but I didn't believe that my end was going to be in a car crash.

CHAPTER 72

"WOULDN'T IT BE NICE IF YOU WERE CRAZY?"

"Is the individual a menace to society? If so, then he is insane and away with him. If not, he is sane so we allow him his liberty" (Estabrooks 147).

When we arrived at the prison in Szczecin (Areszt Śledczy w Szczecinie), I was taken into the hospital ward on the top floor where inmates under observation or waiting for transportation to a longer-term prison hospital were housed. After a quick intake, I was placed in the full-on observation cell, right next to the guard's office. The walls were made of glass instead of concrete like the rest of the cells. A small room with two beds and my new roommate, Marcin Deka (~20 years old), who was excited to see me, hoping that I had tobacco and food. In this ward, we were not able to wear our own clothes, but instead we were issued one set of pajamas.

I did have tobacco and food that my friends had given me for the road, so we rolled a couple of cigarettes and enjoyed some snacks. As we got to know each other, I began to see that this was just another troubled youth like so many I had met already, scared and amped up, with absolutely no compass or possibilities. We bonded and enjoyed our time together in our new glass home. Neither of us knew what was going to happen next.

It was kind of hard to believe that they needed to do such an intense observation on someone who had already been a model prisoner for several months, but policy is policy. The next morning, they moved us both to the last cell at the end of the hall on the right-hand side. To enter our new cell, the guard opened a solid steel door, then a second steel barred door. There were no bunkbeds here, only eight cots evenly spaced five or six feet apart and bolted to the ground. Two metal tables were bolted to the ground on either end of the room, along with a sink that had hot water. There was a door to the bathroom where the toilet was located.

I chose my bed and met my new roommates, most of whom were obviously taking extraordinarily strong doses of antipsychotic drugs. The only thing on any of their minds was tobacco; I thought of them as docile tobacco zombies, but I was also thankful in a way that they were on brain tranquilizers because they slept a lot. I shared what I could, resigned to the fact that I was going to run out now that nobody else had any, but at least this would stop the constant begging.

This too shall pass, I repeated to myself. I didn't think it could get much worse than the present situation, but I invited this new challenge. I returned quickly to my Bible, taking my spot at the table, trying to immerse myself in God's Word and stay out of the nonsense that surrounded me. My job now was to prepare to talk to more psychiatrists.

Nobody here wanted to clean, and they did not clean unless a guard told them to. I missed my little family in the Stargard prison, in our comfortable, small room. But this would do for now, and they told me I would only be here for a month. Comfort is nice, but there could be no comfort since you were removed from my life.

They called me out of the room to meet with one of the court psychiatrists, Dr. Marcin Fronczak, a young balding guy with glasses. He spoke English better than anyone I had met so far in Poland. I was excited to speak to someone who could understand me, someone who I thought would be able to understand trauma, child abuse, and what losing a child can do to a person's psyche.

I was prepared to make my only important statement: *I know that I cannot prove anything, but I am asking, as a father, that you evaluate my child for exposure to the type of trauma that I am alleging. Please give me a polygraph test; I guarantee that I will pass. What my wife has said about me is simply not true. She is lying. My wife's problems stem from whatever has been happening in Poland. My daughter had symptoms of child abuse, so therefore my belief is not a false belief.*

> "I soon learned the purpose of psychiatric assessments inside hospitals. Take a complex, textured, marvelous human life, and reduce it to a simple formula. Then give the right drug" (Ross, 2008, 59).

"We think you have delusional disorder," Dr. Marcin Fronczak informed me within a minute or two of our first encounter. "We don't know for sure, but that is what it looks like. You will be here for at least a month so that we can evaluate you."

"How can you say that you think I have delusional disorder when we haven't even spoken yet? What about differential diagnosis? Don't you think it is wise not to 'think' anything at this point?"

Differential diagnosis is the process of deducing the accurate diagnosis from many possible diagnoses by ruling out other possibilities. However, psychiatrists, like many people in general, tend to choose the one they like and then proceed to put up blinders and look for evidence in support of what they already believe, a process called confirmation bias.

A wave of worry washed over me as I realized that I was not dealing with a "real" psychiatrist. Even though he said they didn't know for sure, I could tell that he was sure enough. It was obvious that diagnosing me as "healthy" was not on the table, and that they planned to decide which illness I had.

"How can you say that the fact that I think my wife and daughter are being abused is a delusion? The only way that you could know is if you evaluated my four-year-old daughter, which has not happened."

"They did evaluate your daughter, they talked to your wife, and they ruled out the possibility that there is any abuse. What if your daughter is happier now? What if they are doing really well? Wouldn't it be nice if you were crazy, and then you could know that they are ok? Isn't it difficult to think that they are being abused? Don't you want to be wrong?"

To evaluate you, they would have to have been aware of the nature and extent of the abuse that I was alleging. This was one reason why I wanted to get you evaluated in The Netherlands or the U.S., because the Poles still didn't even know what I was talking about. I knew that they would continue to see nothing unless they looked specifically for what I was telling them to.

It wouldn't have worked, for example, to ask Patty Hearst if she needed rescuing. If she hadn't drawn attention to herself by committing crimes, people would have continued to think that she loved her captors and was happy where she was, even though she had been brainwashed. I had not alleged simple abuse at the hand of a backwards drunk, but sophisticated, organized, and expert abuse with a plan (the red herring) to pin everything on me.

"Both individual and group-connected offenders rely on careful organization of all their crimes. To get away with their sophisticated level of abuse, spontaneity couldn't possibly work. Abusers plan their every action carefully, over long periods of time, and always with back-up plans in place. As victims and survivors report, for cult-related offenders associated with very large, international groups, organization includes all the modern technological assistance available" (Woodsum 38).

In response to Dr. Fronczak I explained, "I would love to be wrong, but unfortunately, I am not. I would give my life right now to stop the abuse of my daughter. My daughter was stolen from me, she had many signs and symptoms of an abused child, and my wife told me weeks before she left that she was taking our daughter back to the 'cult' because of 'mind control.' I was not the problem. I was trying to convince her to get help, contemplating having her involuntarily committed. I went to the police and I was in frequent contact with a psychologist who knows both of us. My wife did not escape from me to safety. What do you mean 'they are ok?'"

"One can't help but wish for the problem to 'go away', or be proven to be a mistake, a misunderstanding, hallucination, or lie. But it seems that rather than going away, our growing (if still rather limited) knowledge of extreme abuse and its sequels is pointing to the contrary" (Sachs, 2008, as cited in Sachs and Galton, 2008, 5).

"Well, again," Fronczak continued, "we think that you have delusional disorder, and we are the experts. If you don't agree with us, then that will also be used against you. In psychiatry, it is called 'a lack of insight.' You have to admit that you are sick or else it will be worse for you. You should start taking medication now. I think that your daughter is better off now than when she was in your house, don't you?"

"Essentially, impaired insight reflects a lack of understanding or a denial of one's symptoms... The essential question regarding reality-testing has to do with whether or not an individual can distinguish the products of his own mind and imagination (i.e., what is inside) from what is objectively perceived and consensually verifiable in the external world." (Kleiger & Khadivi 13).

"Insanity has generally been assumed to be a matter of perceiving things that do not exist and believing things that are not true. As Karl Jaspers (an influential psychiatrist before he became a philosopher) put it, 'Since time immemorial, delusion has been taken as the basic characteristic of madness. To be mad was to be deluded.' Such a view certainly prevails in contemporary psychiatry, clinical psychology, and psychoanalysis, where disturbance in or failure of 'reality-testing' is considered to be the defining criterion for diagnosing a so-called psychotic condition" (Sass 1).

Trying to find some common ground, I responded, "If I were wrong, then you could start thinking I could be 'insane,' but you don't really know if I'm wrong. As a psychiatrist, you should know that you cannot know because there has not been an adequate investigation. My reasoning is not faulty, and I am not mentally ill. My daughter came home with many signs she had been abused, and my wife told me she was going to take her back to the cult and try to ruin me. What I am doing in the process of arriving at my conclusions is called 'inductive reasoning,' not 'delusion.'"

This guy has to be at least semi-intelligent being a doctor, doesn't he? It frightened me that people like him were going to be deciding my fate, but at least I had some time to try to get through to him.

I continued, "They did not evaluate my daughter. They did a normal checkup that did not reach beyond the surface. I have said from the beginning that this is severe, caregiver inflicted trauma. She must be evaluated with this in mind; otherwise, this type of abuse cannot be detected. It is ridiculous to ask things like 'what if she's happier now?' and 'wouldn't it be nice if you were crazy?' My daughter was happy, and she was stolen from our home. She is definitely not happier now. I am her dad. Incest is not uncommon; why is it so hard for people to consider that my wife's family could be abusive?"

"Well, your wife said that you were abusive, that she escaped from you to safety, and that is what everyone else seems to believe as well, even your parents. There is nobody except you claiming that your father-in-law is abusive."

The fact that nobody else was siding with me was going to be a problem because of the definition of "delusion," and how it is tied to what other people believe. Of course, this didn't make any sense because it was a given that your mom's claims were going to be the opposite of mine, and because nobody in our U.S. family had any first-hand knowledge of the situation.

Feeling flustered by his ignorant and unwavering stance, I explained, "Yes, and I have been clear that my wife was also abused as a child, and that she is one of the abusers of our daughter. I am not here to defend myself, but I am not the abuser. I have never hit or scared my child, but I do not care what you think about me. You can assume that I hurt my child, and then do the evaluation I am asking for. I don't care as long as you evaluate my daughter. What is the harm with taking an extra step to prove me wrong? You cannot prove me wrong until you complete a real evaluation."

"I have never heard of a woman being abused and not wanting to get help. Why would Agata not get help? Why would she leave your lovely home and take your child to a place where they are being abused? This makes no sense."

> "In cult programming, however, the loss of the individual's normal sense of executive control is commonly reported by survivors" (Noblitt and Noblitt, 2014, 88).

> "Incest is a highly successful method for gaining extensive power and control over the intended victim, not only during the abusive acts, but throughout the victim's life. Understanding that gaining power and control are primary motives for offenders of incest, ritualistic, and cult-related abuse is the ultimate key to freeing victims and survivors from these crimes and their effect" (Woodsum 15).

> "Sarah's [or Agata's] attachment to the abusive group was anchored by the sedimentation of terror, shame and loyalty that had accumulated over many years. These were emotions of such intensity that they were often beyond articulation, compelling Sarah [or Agata] to place herself at risk despite her own deeply held desire to find a life free of pain and abuse" (Salter 83).

"Severe trauma," I responded, appalled. "Because of severe trauma, she isn't choosing. I can't believe that you can say that you have never heard of a woman not wanting help. Many women who have been date raped don't want or aren't capable of seeking help. I'm talking about incest, at least. These are the basic principles of trauma that I am talking about. How can you be so naïve?"

"Well, the court has ruled out abuse, and I am here to evaluate you now in light of that fact."

"Can you get them to evaluate my daughter, please? Only then can you understand my mental state, either way."

"I doubt it; that case is closed. We are here to take the facts of the case, and decide what happens with you, whether you stay in prison or go to a prison hospital."

"The 'facts' of the case? The case hasn't been investigated!"

"Yes, it has, because the prosecutor has said so. We practice evidence-based medicine here, and the evidence says that your daughter is not being abused. You are the only one claiming this, and everyone else thinks you are wrong," he reiterated once again. "We are going to evaluate you based upon the evidence that the court has given us."

"Evidence-based medicine?" I was bewildered, because I could see the direction that he was going, and the logical result of what he was telling me – that they would "have to" say I was insane, because it was too late for me to bring my daughter to a suitable doctor/trauma specialist, and nobody else was going to do it or demand it be done.

"Yes, otherwise known as medicine based on fact," he said smugly.

"Don't you see what you are doing? There is no evidence, and yet you jump right into calling it 'fact.' Can't you see you're just playing a statistics game? How is that good for my daughter?"

This was not a good start; I knew that there was almost no chance of me not being "crazy" unless I could somehow get through to him. He was like a magician as he swapped out the word "evidence" with the word "fact," hammering in the point that this group of psychiatrists worked for the prosecution. They were not planning on doing a differential diagnosis, but rather a "diagnosis" in light of the baseline of "truth" given to them by the prosecution. But, of course, this "truth" was not the truth at all because it aligned with your grandfather, who had obviously abused you, and your mom, who had warned me for weeks that she was taking you back to the "cult."

"On the surface, the task of the psychiatric witness is to share with the court his supposedly expert knowledge on mental illness and its relation to social conduct... questions like these cannot be answered in a scientific fashion. The main reason for this is that in the courtroom the psychiatrist is expected to help the judge, the jury, and the public to dispose of an offender, not merely explain psychiatric matters. However, the sort of question the psychiatrist is asked makes his answer appear as if it were an expression of learned opinion about observable facts. This is why the work of the psychiatric expert in the courtroom seems to resemble that of other experts. What he in fact does differs basically, however, from what experts in ballistics, pathology, or toxicology do when they testify." (Szasz, 1974, 113).

Fronczak went on, "You also claim that your wife has multiple-personality disorder?"

"Yes, or dissociative identity disorder, whatever you want to call it. These are things that happen when the kind of trauma I am alleging takes place."

"There are many minds in Europe who say that DID is only a thing in American movies, a fiction created by Hollywood," Fronczak stated with confidence.

"Although DID is a formal DSM-IV diagnosis, it is very controversial, and many professionals hold the view that it is extremely rare, doesn't exist at all, or is factitious (pretended). I suspect that the most important reason for the reluctance to recognize DID is not its confusing appearance, which to many professionals is actually rather fascinating. I believe that the reluctance stems from the disturbing link between DID and the most extreme and sadistic forms of crime, especially when faced with the continued involvement that many survivors still have with a world that none of us wishes to believe in or to share (Coleman, chapter 1; Healey, chapter 2; Cross & 'Louise', chapter 5; Silverstone, chapter 12; Cook, chapter 13)" (Sachs, 2008, as cited in Sachs and Galton, 2008, 3).

"The courts have also upheld the finding that DID is a scientifically accepted diagnosis" (Noblitt and Noblitt, 2014, 12).

"Yes, well it is not fiction. It is real," I responded. "There are many minds everywhere that say it is real. You need to look at all the evidence, look at the timeline of when she took our daughter back to Poland, the communication between us, and talk to our psychologist, Kees de Vries in The Hague. Once you look at all the evidence, which seems reasonable to do in my opinion, you will see that I am not the abuser in this case. Isn't it Polish law that all evidence must be examined?"

"The court has looked at all the evidence; we have the file. In psychiatry, we have something of a phrase: 'if you glance out your window and see a bird, you assume it's a songbird, and you do not assume it's an ostrich.'"

Yes, of course, I thought, everyone who has ever taken a general philosophy course knows Occam's Razor principle which basically states that things shouldn't be made more complicated than they must be. But DID, ritual abuse, and trauma-based mind control are complicated; what I was talking about was the ostrich.

> "Thus, there is a need for professionals to proceed with caution, acknowledging that there is little that we know with a high degree of certainty... We need to adopt the simplest explanations for phenomena that fully explain them. This is a generally accepted principle of the logic of science known as parsimony. Unfortunately, therapists sometimes embrace particular theories and then use them to interpret their clients' behaviors and experiences without testing the theories. In my humble opinion, psychologists and other mental health professionals commonly accept explanations for psychological processes that are unparsimonious and unproven" (Noblitt and Noblitt, 2014, 14).

"That doesn't make sense, and it will lead to errors. Assuming things is not a good idea. What if it is an ostrich? Why not just look a bit closer so you know for sure? Again, what about differential diagnosis? You have to look at everything. What about the fact that my daughter had bruises and vaginal pain, regression, nightmares, and she was talking about her grandfather's 'stinky balls'? What about the fact that both my wife and I believed she has 'something like borderline personality disorder'? What about the fact that she was seeking treatment for things like erratic mood swings that she admitted on paper had a huge negative impact on our family?" (see Appendix 17, question 25).

I had been parsimonious in my "diagnosis" of your mother, by initially concluding that whatever she was suffering from had many of the characteristics of borderline personality disorder and/or post-traumatic stress disorder, and not immediately jumping to the conclusion that she had dissociative identity disorder. I hadn't enough information to know that it was DID, just as these "experts" couldn't possibly know that my belief was false.

"So," I continued, "you think that I was abusing my wife and daughter to the point that they had to 'escape,' and that I was also trying to get help the entire time, including going to the police and a psychologist multiple times? You think that I saw bruises that didn't exist? Did my daughter not scream 'not my pee pee'? Don't you see that it is your belief that is problematic and not mine?"

"What about ritual abuse?" he began again, ignoring my line of questioning. "That is a myth, it is not in Poland, and we don't think it exists at all. Isn't your wife's family Catholic?" he asked, suggesting that Catholic people wouldn't practice ritual abuse.

> "Like incest, ritualistic and cult-related abuse has been around for a long time. It is not a phenomenon of the late 20th century. As with incest, there has been a long period of general ignorance and denial that has kept us from understanding the nature of certain experiences" (Woodsum 59).

> "The notion that RA [ritual abuse] allegations are essentially false and the result of suggestibility and social influence has been proposed by a number of individuals

(Frankfurter, 2006; Mulhern, 1991, 1994; Ofshe & Waters, 1994; Spanos, 1996). However, this hypothesis appears to reflect the authors' subjective opinions and speculations rather than any empirical research findings" (Noblitt and Noblitt, 2014, 58).

"It is around here; it is everywhere. You are uninformed. They can have a Catholic front, but that doesn't mean that they cannot be something else behind closed doors. They're not going to wear 'I'm a pedophile' t-shirts. My wife told me her family is a cult!"

"Victims and survivors have described ritually abusive groups engaging in elaborately structured phases of torture designed to induce dissociative and traumatic psychopathology, with the apparent intention of maintaining absolute control over the victim and reducing the likelihood of detection (Sachs and Galton 2008, Epstein et al. 2011)... a substantial group of commentators have argued that such descriptions align so closely with the content of myth, novels and films that they are most likely confabulations drawn from the same. However, this view is challenged by the recent substantiation of organised, sadistic and ritualistic abuse during the prosecution of child sex cases in Europe and North America" (Salter 37).

CHAPTER 73

"KAFKATRAP"

I am not an advocate for drugs, but neither am I one for misinformation, lies, or propaganda for the purpose of manipulating the public. I believe in the sufficiency of the truth itself. As people grow closer in their understanding of the truth, I believe, their need and desire for things such as drugs disappears. This has been my experience.

In Poland, lies about drugs led to the "expert" court psychiatrists using my drug history as proof that nothing I said could be trusted. From their standpoint, my mind had been destroyed and I had a mental disease that required immediate treatment with their own drugs. In the Philippines (Hart, 2021), policy was enacted to execute methamphetamine users and sellers because the government decided that "[methamphetamine] use would shrink the brain of a person and therefore he is no longer viable for rehabilitation" (111), even though it won't shrink the brain, they can be rehabilitated, and the same substance is sold at CVS and Walgreens. It may be a blessing that your mother wasn't from the Philippines, but nevertheless, the Polish "experts" used their misinformation to further negate my competence and testimony, and to diagnose me.

The fact that I am so staunchly against using deception should not be interpreted to mean that I am pro-drug, or that I am some kind of a second generation, twenty-first century hippy, because I am neither. I believe in truth and individual freedom, but that does not mean that I think everyone or even necessarily anyone should use drugs. Ultimately, they are not where the answer is, but that doesn't mean we should use deceptive tactics to scare people away because the damage done by lying to people is catastrophic.

As I mentioned in Part 1, my Drugs and Society teacher at the University of Connecticut put the last nail in the "drugs are bad" coffin when he showed us that drug legislation rarely (if ever) has had anything to do with the drugs themselves, but with controlling people and/or controlling money. If the truth was not what they were telling us, then what was it? I wanted to know for myself.

Drugs are not the problem, but neither are they the answer, and I want to stress both of those points; they are something else. And in this story, they were also not the problem, but merely a prong of the three-pronged "red herring" of "drugs, criminal history, and psychological history" that your grandfather cunningly deployed, as your mother foretold.

"We also think you have a drug addiction disorder. We have to evaluate you for that too," Fronczak continued.

"But I'm not addicted to any drugs," I pled, searching for reason. "Did I have drugs in my system when I was arrested?" I asked, knowing that I did not.

"You have a drug history. Don't you smoke marijuana?"

"I did smoke marijuana sometimes. I lived in a country where it was legal, and I'm from a country where I could get it medically with my neck condition."

"Yes," he stated matter-of-factly, "we think you moved to The Netherlands so you could get marijuana."

I assumed that they had to have gotten this idea from your mom – such a weird thing to say, but he was certain he had found another clue.

"No, actually there is plenty of marijuana in the United States... and many people use it as medicine."

"In Poland, marijuana is not used for medicine. Marijuana causes psychosis."

"No, it does not. It is medicine, and Poland should use it, it might help some of the many alcoholics you have here. It maybe or even probably can cause or exacerbate psychosis sometimes, but that doesn't mean that it 'causes' psychosis. There are millions of people who smoke marijuana for whom it does not cause psychosis. Again, it is ridiculous for you to try to find 'proof' for what you think you already know. What kind of observation is this? Your facts are from *Reefer Madness*."

I knew that I was caught in the middle of a Kafkatrap, whereby everything that I was trying to explain to defend myself was being used as proof that what they were positing was true. My insistence that you were being abused was being used to prove that I was mentally ill and suffering from a delusion, since they were working off the premise that you were not being abused. My denial of mental illness, of being deluded, is exactly what a deluded person would do, and I knew this.

> "The thesis that the criminal is a sick individual in need of treatment – which is promoted today as if it were a recent psychiatric discovery – is false. Indeed, it is hardly more than a refurbishing, with new terms, of the main ideas and techniques of the inquisitorial process. Instead of recognizing the deviant as an individual different from those who judge him, but nevertheless worthy of their respect, he is first discredited as a self-responsible human being, and then subjected to humiliating punishment defined and disguised as treatment" (Szasz, 1974, 108).

I didn't see a way out of this trap other than to continue trying to show them that their logic was the flawed logic, and not mine. They hadn't proven that you were not being abused. The fact that I had experience with drugs did not lead to the necessary conclusion that I was a drug addict or that my mind was damaged. The fact that your mom claimed that I was the abuser did not mean that it was true, or that I was delusional for saying otherwise. The fact that I had assaulted your grandpa did not mean I was violent or dangerous, as this is exactly what a dad might do in the situation that I was alleging.

My only hope with these "experts" was that honesty and rapport would lead to someone saying, "Hey wait a minute, maybe we should evaluate the daughter of this father so that we can be sure that we are getting to the bottom of this." Despite the real logic of the situation, as in any Kafkatrap, I was to later find out that the only way to escape the trap is to admit to everything they were accusing me of.

I began to make a practice of reaching my hand out to shake his hand after all our meetings in order to remind him that I was a human, with feelings. He didn't really like shaking my hand, and he told me he shouldn't, but he did, because I was persistent. My job was to do my best, try to present the real me that they weren't seeing on paper, and tell the truth. I tried to do it well, even though I was shaking inside because of the absurdity of the situation and the people I was forced to deal with. *Just evaluate my little girl*, I thought, *how difficult can that be?*

My mind was constantly blown that I was where I was. I had gone from developing your homeschool curriculum and applying for jobs at the United Nations in Geneva and Vienna, for example, to living in conditions that I could not have previously imagined. We got the same five-minute shower per week and one hour outside per day. We were allowed to keep razors as long as nobody started cutting themselves, and we were under constant video surveillance if anyone did.

One of my cell mates, Rafał W., was an artist who told me that he spent a few years at Area 51 as a child because his dad was in the military. He drew me pictures of both your mom and I, and he wrote a letter that he begged me to send to the U.S. Embassy so that they could forward it to Mariah Carey. Sure, he was a bit "crazy," and I knew it probably would not help my relationship with the embassy to even make such a request on behalf of a friend, but they did not show any interest in helping regardless. I sent the letter for him, just to make his day.

Drawings of your mom and I, by Rafał W.

Then he decided that he also wanted to send a love letter to my sister, but I did not send that one. He taught me how to tell time in Polish with an old clocktower that we could just barely see outside of our barred window. We made espresso with the hot water from the sink whenever we had coffee, we played cards, and we talked about the state of the world. One day he slit his penis with a razor to then insert a quarter of a toothbrush, "for the ladies." In my opinion, Rafał would probably never be able to live outside an institution on his own, at least not with the "treatment" that he was offered, but I am thankful and blessed to have met him.

Now at least I wouldn't have to volunteer for prison to experience it, but this was more of an experience than I would have signed up for voluntarily. I knew that God had a plan, though this didn't make the time I was losing with you any easier to stomach.

The psychiatrists rarely wanted to speak to me, maybe an average of once per week; the rest of the time was just waiting. The conditions here were much worse than they were in regular prison, the people were harder to communicate with, and there was zero outside food. We only ate what came in on our trays, because nobody in the cell had money, so everyone was hungry all the time. Furthermore, some people were selling their food trays for cigarettes, or even pieces of a cigarette. When they collected butts, they smoked them, then they chewed on the filter like a piece of gum, afterward drying out the filter to smoke that. They rolled cigarettes with pages from the Polish Bible, which they got from the priest that visited on occasion.

They begged the guards for an extra loaf of bread, and sometimes they had one; many of the guys sprinkled sugar or salt on their slices if there was any around. Every so often the nighttime medicine cart bringing most of the guys their second dose of antipsychotics also gave us a cigarette or two. I thought it was funny that part of the medicine was cigarettes.

When they did not get cigarettes, cigarette butts, or used filters, they would cut themselves with a razor or burn themselves with matches. This would lead to a temporary suspension of our privilege to own a razor, but it usually also led to more cigarettes on the medicine cart. The primary difference between a tobacco user and a heroin addict is accessibility. They both can be abused, they both can wreck your life, or not, but one is readily available everywhere and one is not. Except in prison environments such as where I was, where people become "heroin addicts" over nicotine.

One of my cellmates gave tattoos for a while with a gel pen and a paper clip. This ended with us all getting strip searched, me first because the guard thought I was the most honest (and least crazy), and that I would fill him in without him having to search anymore. Knowing that everyone would know if I were to spill the beans, I told him that he should just look, with a smile, letting him know that he would easily find the culprit.

Marcin Deka, the young man from my first day observation cell, was transferred a small amount of money. We had to wait a couple of days for the guard to take him to the little prison shop, but eventually it happened. He bought all the good things: tobacco, accessories for making cigarettes, coffee, sugar, and canned Polish meat. He was extremely generous with me due to our initial bond; anything that was his was mine also. But this was not the case with the other guys. He began using tobacco to buy food from the other guys to the point where people were starving, and he started playing games with people, particularly an elderly man over seventy years old.

He had this man drink water until he puked for as little as a puff of a cigarette. The man drank so much water once that he got chills and started hyperventilating and shaking, a sort of water poisoning, I supposed. Sometimes he gave the reward, and sometimes he withheld, only leading to increased demand and desperation. Once he had another prisoner (Adam) stick the toilet plunger handle up the guy's butt using butter as a lubricant. This was the breaking point for me; I had to tell someone.

In retrospect, I probably should have said something sooner, but prison is an unhinged environment, and it is nice when the authorities do not visit your cell. I also had some mixed feelings because I did not want to lose Marcin's supplies or get him in trouble, but I did my best not to let this affect my judgment.

I slipped a note to Dr. Fronczak and Marcin was removed shortly thereafter. A couple of days later a note was delivered to me from Marcin stating that he was angry with me, and that he refused to speak to me anymore. I felt some regret in the pit of my stomach; betraying a friend is not alright, but I knew that it was more not alright to sexually abuse an old man, or anybody.

Besides Dr. Fronczak, there were two other court psychiatrists on my case. I'm not certain of one name, but she was the head of the department, something like Anna Cieszyk. Dr. Fronczak explained to me that her last name was a type of bird. Dr. Jacek Afrykański was the third psychiatrist, the head of the entire prison hospital, but his job was only to sign off on what was already "known" by the other two. I enjoyed talking to Dr. Cieszyk, an early forties Polish woman who did not speak English; Dr. Fronczak translated.

It was rare to see women, or to be in their presence, and it felt strange just to be in the same room. She curled her legs up sideways on the chair facing mine, and I licked my lips, ready to go on a date with her, happy to be out of the cage, and delighted to be away from my drooling, cigarette filter chewing colleagues. I wondered if her leg curling was a deliberate attempt to seduce me so that I would open up to her, but it didn't matter because I had already made the decision to do just that.

It was clear that there was going to be no further inquiries into my case. The "facts" were that the child abuse I was alleging had been ruled out, and that I was a "junkie." The evidence was the prosecutor's file, which stated that the police did a welfare check in your grandfather Sławomir's apartment, and they also checked with your mom. And with this, they had "ruled out" abuse. The fact that only by evaluating you could they truly rule out abuse eluded them completely; these people were dense, and there was no stopping them from proceeding with confirming their biases.

Dr. Cieszyk wanted to hear all about my "drug history," and so I obliged, reiterating that while I had experience, I did not have any addictions. Trying to hold back nothing at all and committed to total honesty, I explained that I had experimented with crack, heroin, cocaine, ecstasy, opium, LSD, and psilocybin, and anything else that had crossed my path that I was interested in and thought was safe. I further stated that I did not regret my experiences, and that they had made me stronger and more knowledgeable on the subject. Nevertheless, they assured me that I was an addict, and that I was addicted to all the drugs that I had tried. This was what they were taught to think, and I had nowhere to escape, deep in the Twilight Zone.

What did my previous drug experiences have to do with any of it anyway? Was there some kind of rule in Polish psychiatry that made someone who had used "drugs" de facto insane? In fact, this is a part of Polish culture and Polish propaganda. It actually does work to frighten many Polish people away from "experimenting" with drugs, as they are all trained to believe that drugs will kill them or make them crazy. They handed out a pamphlet to the inmates, explaining photographically that marijuana is basically heroin; from the picture, one might even conclude that marijuana is injectable (see Appendix 33). The article in the pamphlet explains how marijuana use leads to psychosis, among other things.

The crux of the matter is that correlation is not causation, something I learned as an undergraduate. The fact that something can, might, or sometimes does cause something, or that something may occur at the same time as something else (even if it's every time) doesn't lead to the conclusion that it was the cause, or even that they're otherwise related at all. This is a basic error in thinking, a logical fallacy. Because of this, I would have to spend the next few years repeating back to them, "I am an addict and I need treatment. I will always need treatment," as a condition of my release.

> "I do not see how it is possible to deny that coerced psychiatric personality change – even (or especially) if it entails 'helping' a person to give up his 'psychotic delusions' – closely resembles coerced religious conversion (Szasz, 1977, 111) "...involuntary psychiatric treatment constitutes an instance of 'forcing citizens to confess by word or act their faith' in a social reality interpreted by institutional psychiatry. Therein, precisely, lies the tragedy of psychiatric slavery" (112).

The prosecutor's file quoted your mom's testimony claiming as fact that I claimed that I was a writer, and so the psychiatrists mockingly asked me, "What have you published?" and "Have you ever been paid for writing?" They had taken on the tone that anything and everything your mom alleged was true, and that I was nothing more than a crazy, deadbeat, junky, abuser.

In reality, other than being a stay-at-home dad for the past year, I had "worked" (for money) as much or more than your mom had, and the decision for me to be a stay-at-home-dad was one that your mom and I had made together. I was applying for many jobs, and I was not going to have trouble finding one; in fact, I had one in Connecticut as a full-time substitute teacher to start. Though at this point, I was even more certain than I had ever been that I needed to write; I knew that I would have to explain this to the world.

"Nothing, and no. I have never claimed to be a writer. I discussed with my wife that I think that is something that I am going to pursue. I am a husband and a father, and I have a master's degree. I am not a deadbeat."

"Oh, and what are you writing now?" they countered.

"Right now, I am writing about all of this," I explained, taking notes on my lap. "I write down everything that I can; it helps me remember and process. This is my new project. My daughter is the only thing that I care about. I will always be writing about this, until my daughter is back under my roof. I am not trying to defend myself; the reason that I came to Poland was to force an evaluation of my daughter."

They asked me about being a stay-at-home dad, suggesting that it wasn't "real" work for a man. I tried arguing with them, because I knew that what I had been doing was a full-time job, and I knew that much of the world also saw it this way. But for them, this was not "man's work," and because this is what I had been doing at the time of the abduction, it was more proof for them that your mom needed to "escape" from me.

* * *

In my opinion, monkeys would have made better psychiatrists than Dr. Fronczak and his crew, who were no more (or less) than tools of the prosecution. In my lifetime I had been diagnosed with depression, major depression, panic disorder, attention deficit hyperactive disorder, and most recently adjustment disorder. I was sure that I was soon to be diagnosed again, this time with either delusional disorder or schizophrenia, and yet I didn't have any of them. Why weren't they interested in any of my past diagnoses, and why did they refuse to consider that having my daughter taken could be the cause of anything they were concerned with since then?

> "The psychiatric disorders are not independent diseases. They are different elements of the trauma response" (Ross, 2008, 274).

"What group of people would you say you are associated with? Americans? Dutch?" they asked.

My antennae were up; they weren't here to chat. Every question was part of a specified spectrum of questions that they would use to inch toward their chosen diagnosis. I knew that the definition of delusion included the clause that said that beliefs were not delusional if a group of people believed the same thing. But I didn't have a group of people other than you and your mom.

"I do not consider myself to be a part of any manufactured group of people. Travelling has taught me that I do not have to be anything just because the people around me decide that is what they are going to be. There are other ways of thinking you know, besides the Polish way. Let me get my own psychiatrist from The Netherlands, or the United States, and let's see if they agree with you. You think it is unreasonable to think my child is being abused when my wife told me she is, there were multiple signs and symptoms of child abuse including bruises and unexplained vaginal pain, and my wife was seeking help for what we thought was a disorder linked to trauma?

"Ok," they replied, "we have decided that you need to stay here for two months total, instead of the usual one month, since you do not speak Polish, and therefore it is more difficult to communicate with you."

"I don't have a problem staying here forever. All I want is an evaluation of my daughter. Nothing you have said, no evidence that the court has collected, no evidence that you are obviously compiling now, none of these things rule out the abuse of my daughter. All you are doing is creating a story using a matching game, and you are not interested in differential diagnosis at all."

CHAPTER 74

"MONEY, MONEY, MONEY"

Back in my cell, I came to grips with another month in this place, and I yearned for normal prison. I delved further into my Bible, looking for answers, and I kept going; man's help was proving to be futile. And, I also began writing copious letters to the psychiatrists, not caring what they thought about me because they had already decided, just wanting to get my point across. I read and I wrote, and I did hours of each every day. They, in turn, used this as further evidence that I was insane because of my "abnormal" behaviors and "excessive" writing.

> "Trust in the Lord with all of your heart, and lean not on your own understanding; In all your ways acknowledge Him, and He shall direct your paths" (Proverbs 3:5-6 NKJV).

I knew that this was what I had to do, but how? What did it mean to "trust in the Lord," and what did it mean to "lean not on my own understanding"? Was He directing my paths at this point, or would that be something only for the future? How could I be certain that He was, in fact, directing my paths?

Life in the cell continued unchanged except that someone in my cell had lice twice, forcing us to quarantine for a week on each occasion. I never had any lice on me, but we all had to strip down naked in front of the nurses and turn over our clothing. Someone said they were going to take everything and burn it, and I was worried about my journals and books, but it turned out that this was only rumor. We could not leave the cell for walks or showers during the quarantine; the only reason they opened our door was to give us food, or to give the other guys antipsychotic drugs. I was not bothered; we usually did not go outside anyway.

One day at "spacer," in my striped pajamas, one of the guards chatted me up, interested in me because I was the American. "Hey, do you want to have a Marlboro and coffee with me in a minute?"

"Sure, I'd like to talk to you." Part of me felt like I was at an Amsterdam café for a moment.

"No, I'm just joking," he said, reminding me of the class system between guards and inmates, especially ones in striped pajamas.

"Do you like your job?" I asked him.

"Yes, I love my job."

"What do you like about your job?"

"I like the money," he said with a grin, rubbing his thumb and forefinger together. "Money, money, money," he went on.

I thought that he also liked his uniform, and the feeling of superiority that it transferred to his ego, but I really did not talk to him enough to be certain. What I can say is this: when money becomes the object of one's desire, things that have become less important due to money's ascension on the hierarchical pyramid of needs/desires will begin to be neglected, like child welfare and truth.

I worked on preparing for my next meeting with Dr. Fronczak, planning on how I would re-present my case. I went over my notes from our last meetings, and I formulated a strategy. I did not think that this man could not think, but that he refused to think, probably because he also liked his job for the same reason as the guard. His job was to read the report provided him by the court, and then to formulate a diagnosis based upon those "facts." The "facts" were indisputable if he wanted to keep his job. He was not being paid to be Sherlock Holmes.

When I met with him, I decided to start teaching him about the basics of trauma. I told him that trauma is used for training animals all the time, and I gave him the basic example of a pit bull being trained to fight, its owner using the fact that he can imprint whatever he pleases on the creature's mind for his use.

"Trauma training is a known fact," I explained, "it is not a myth, it has been done and is being done to dogs and humans..."

"So, what you're talking about is hypnotism?" he queried.

Finally! I thought, it's really not so difficult, and it's certainly not farfetched. I had a moment of thinking that we were having a breakthrough, and I was proud of him; at least now he was acknowledging that what I was claiming did exist instead of saying he'd never heard of such things before.

> "...there is not a reputable psychologist in the United States who would dare write an article questioning the existence of hypnotism and certain phenomena in hypnotism. His reputation would be ruined... Then there is that very interesting question of dissociation, considered by some the key phenomenon in hypnotism" (Estabrooks 68).

So, now that he had come out of the closet to admit that there was such a thing as "hypnotism," I didn't think it would be much more work to get him to grasp "DID," or "ritual abuse," since they all go hand in hand. I could understand how the prosecutor or even the judge could be oblivious to such things, but surely not an entire flock of "expert" court psychiatrists.

He could not simultaneously maintain that hypnotism was possible and that they had ruled out what I was alleging. Not only does hypnotism cause amnesia, but "[t]he reader is asked to remember that, in hypnotism the individual is highly suggestible. To be sure there is a popular belief that he will do nothing in the trance that he will not do in the working state. This is sheer nonsense" (Estabrooks 191–192).

Hypnotism, which is no more (or less) than the science of suggestion, is not unrealistic or bizarre, because, "[a]ll these weird things have a sound physiological basis. If the reader would really understand hypnotism he must banish from his mind all trash about the mystic and the supernatural. Everything is to be explained and can be explained by the activity of a very complex nervous system" (Estabrooks 59).

In response to Dr. Fronczak, I stated, "Yes, that is a big part of it; there are many aspects to trauma-based mind control. Hypnotism, and hypnotism in tandem with intentional, strategic traumas are what I am talking about. And hypnotism and DID go hand in hand." I wondered why he was not seeing the forest for the trees, and if he really believed that your mom "escaped" from me, and if he cared at all, or if he was just going through the motions to get to his next break.

"You are not a psychologist," he responded, frowning with skepticism. "How could you diagnose this?"

And just like that, any hope that I had gained darted away like a frightened school of minnows. He didn't care what I knew; I was the guy in the pajamas that didn't have buttons or zippers so I wouldn't swallow them. I was the guy "nobody" believed. And I was the guy with the most incredible drug history he had ever heard of.

"That's not the point. The point is: you have not ruled out what I have alleged, you have not proven that I am crazy, and most importantly, you have not proven that my daughter is not being abused. Polish criminal justice is a joke. What about my daughter's bruises, caused by her grandfather, the fact that she had vaginal pain and terror after every return from Poland...?" I felt like a broken record.

"Do you think that there is a lot of child abuse in the world?" they asked in a way that told me that "no" would be the "right" answer.

"Of course, there is a lot of child abuse," I replied honestly. "To think or believe there is not would be delusional thinking." I was nervous even though I knew I was right.

"How do you know? How could you know?" they asked in their typical skeptical way.

"Because I read," I stated bluntly.

"The sexual abuse of a child constitutes one of the most common of human interpersonal traumata. Depending upon the research methodology used to obtain the information, various studies have found that anywhere between one-quarter and one-third of adults in the United States and similar developed, industrialized nations report sexual abuse in their childhood (Briere, 1996). Contrary to the claims of some authors who see the issue of childhood sexual abuse as an invention of late 20th-century feminism (Ofshe & Watters, 1994), sexual abuse of children is not a recent phenomenon... Children have been sexualized in Western and other cultures for millennia – used as prostitutes, victimized by incest, and raped in war" (Cling 188).

All three of these "experts" pierced me with their doubtful, judgmental eyes, and I wished that I had a computer or a library at my disposal so I could show them the research. At this point, given where I was, it was my word against theirs, and my word for them was the voice of a madman.

"And, you have guns?" they asked, moving to the next item on their list.

Their line of questioning was fatiguing. What could having guns have to do with anything relevant to their diagnosis?

"Yes, I have guns; I'm an American. It is normal for us to have guns. I've had a gun since I was seven years old."

"Didn't you hit your father-in-law with a hammer in the head?"

"No, I did not. I hit him with my fist. I'm not even mad at him; I just want my daughter to be evaluated."

"How can you not be mad at him?" they scoffed, "Didn't he abuse your daughter?"

"Yes, and I want that to stop, but I am not angry with him. I've cycled through that; my act against him was strategic, not emotional or vengeful."

"So then why did you hit him with the hammer?"

"I didn't, and there is no evidence in the court records or medical reports proving that he was hit with the hammer. The only evidence they have is that my father-in-law claims he was hit, but this is impossible since any hit with a hammer would be included in the medical report. The fact that I had a hammer does not prove that I hit him with it, and the evidence shows that I didn't hit him with it. Conveniently for him, the difference is that I was charged with attempted murder instead of assault."

"If what you say is happening is actually happening," Dr. Fronczak admitted, "I believe it will continue to happen. I don't believe there is anything you can do."

With this statement, Dr. Fronczak had just conceded that my claims were not only possible, but that they were also not disproven or "ruled out."

"Well, that is just not acceptable," I countered, "and I guarantee that you are wrong. Something must be done and will be done. I will not stop until my heart stops. How could I? And, by the way, you just admitted that what I am claiming is not delusional, except in comparison to the court 'facts,' which you also know did not investigate anything of the sort."

"Yes, well what about all of the things you wrote and all of the e-mails you sent?"

"Losing my daughter and seeing our situation did make me lose my mind for a time. I do not think that was unreasonable, or a surprise, given the circumstances. I wrote and said a lot of things that I would not now, nor do I necessarily believe all those things. I wanted help and I was desperate. In the U.S. I was diagnosed with adjustment disorder."

"We think that your training with the Department and Children and Families has also affected your judgment, making you more prone to see child abuse where it doesn't exist," the "experts" continued.

"How does that make sense? Would not training give me more ability to detect child abuse? You are really stretching it; all you want to do is match up as many clues to your predetermined diagnosis. What about my daughter's bruises and vaginal pain?"

It didn't matter what I said, this meeting ended like all the other ones: no progress.

During my stay in the prison observation psychiatric unit, they transported me to different hospitals around the city for an EEG and a couple other brain scans. They were looking for signs of structural damage to explain my "delusions," but of course they didn't find any.

On my final meeting with the three psychiatrists, they asked me who healed my neck. I knew that they were looking for more evidence of "delusion," and this time it was because I included scripture in the letters that I had been giving them.

I thought for a moment, then replied, "God."

They gave me the "mm hmm" head bob, but I had told the truth as I knew it. There was no other possible reason why my neck had ceased from causing me severe pain that I could think of.

"Believing in God is not delusion either," I said pre-emptively.

"What God do you believe in? What church do you attend? Are you Catholic?" they challenged.

"I believe in the One God. I do not attend church. My Bible says that I don't require a priest or a pope or any man to mediate between me and God, but that Jesus Christ is the Mediator between God and man. I am certainly not Catholic."

They told me that I was going to be diagnosed with Delusional Disorder and mixed addiction to drugs, but I had deduced as much since my first conversations with Dr. Fronczak. I didn't like their decision, but only because it meant that the people who should've been "experts" in trauma and abuse were not, so any hope of getting you evaluated at this point dashed away.

My diagnosis precluded me from the 8-25 year sentencing guideline for the crime I had been charged with. Now that I was "insane," the decision for my release would be in the hands of more people like Dr. Fronczak. While my disdain for psychiatry was growing, it was a game I knew I could play. I figured that I would be out shortly, as soon as I could get a new evaluation.

I was asked if I would submit to medication, and I told them that I certainly would not. They informed me that I would be transported back to prison until the court had time to order me to be treated. They told me that my noncooperation with their medication would extend my treatment and reminded me about my lack of insight regarding my illness. I reiterated that I would not submit to taking their drugs, stating firmly that it was ludicrous for them, as professionals, to arrive at such a diagnosis after only a cursory glance at the totality of the evidence (see Appendix 34 for a portion of the psychiatric report).

CHAPTER 75

"A MUPPET SHOW"

After two months in the Szczecin prison psychiatric observation unit, shortly before Christmas 2011, I was transported back to prison in Stargard. I continued to write letters, my goal being to send at least one out each day as part of my work. I did not care that I was being redundant or demanding attention, or that all my letters had to be translated into Polish so that the prosecutor could approve them. I knew that the sheer number of letters would gain attention, but that's what I wanted. I could not be worried about the possibility of them using it against me for their "crazy" argument.

Back in my old cell, I reconnected with my friends, including Jurn, and we feasted. We continued playing cards, but, more often than not, we played Texas Hold'em for cigarettes, whereas before we played mostly Polish games. This was Jurn's doing; he was in love with poker, and during my two-month absence this had become the pastime of our cell. I enjoyed it because the entire cell became a center of intense competition.

We also played table tennis by using our plastic plates as paddles and ping pong balls that a guard gifted us. For the table, we used a pressed piece of wood that we each had under the mattresses of our bunk beds. I imagined that our cell was probably the best in the entire prison, maybe in all of Poland.

I was in Stargard for Christmas and New Year's, and then I was transported back to Szczecin to await trial. I had to go to Szczecin because my case was to be held in the more serious court, Sąd Okręgowy (District Court), because my charge was attempted murder. The court in Stargard didn't hold trials on attempted murder.

I was placed into a cell of pre-trail inmates on the opposite side of the prison from where I was for the two-month evaluation, and I immediately made myself at home. My new cell held five people, with two bunk beds on the sides, and a single bed along the back wall (see Appendix 35). They welcomed me with open arms and immediately treated me as their brother. Everything else was pretty much identical to Stargard, except this new place was larger, and in somewhat better condition.

I was looking forward to my trial, and I hoped for a wise judge, one that would look at the entirety of the case and allow me to call my witnesses, including Kees de Vries from The Netherlands. I needed a judge who would at least try to think logically and thoroughly, unlike anyone I had met to this point.

For sure, I imagined, *almost any judge would see that it is in the best interest of my child to evaluate her, regardless of any other information.* Even if I were to claim I was a Martian, that would still be the best thing to do; I thought that this was common sense.

My new cellmates and I often stayed up all night, drinking strong espresso, eating snacks, and preparing for our trials. The bathroom light was the only light we had so we all huddled together. In this cell, with these guys, we always had plenty of extra food because they had support coming in from the outside.

Mariusz, also known as Bogdon, a thirty-five year old banker with a wife and two daughters in town, was going to be my cellmate for the next eleven months, though I did not know this yet. There were two short stints where I was moved to another cell for two or three days, but this was just because of some kind of issue like a fight where they needed a space to move someone on a temporary basis. They chose me, because as an American I had less of a chance of having troubles in whatever cell they put me in, and because they recognized that I got along with everybody.

During the times that we were apart, Mariusz would have a guard or a food cart deliver me enough tobacco and coffee to get through the day. When we were together, we ate like kings most of the time, always having everything we needed. In addition to food, his wife would bring in clothes and books just for me as well.

He wanted to learn English, so I taught him. He knew only a couple words when we first met, but by the time we parted he was ready to live in an English-speaking country. He constantly wrote in his notebook and asked me, "Iain is this correct, is this how you say it...?"

We played chess nearly every day, and sometimes we put all our mattress pads onto the ground for wrestling tournaments. There was opaque plexiglass covering our window, so we burned a small hole through it using an alcohol ointment from the nurse. This gave us visibility to the street and allowed us to pass notes to Bogdon's wife with a homemade blowgun over the prison wall.

After eleven months, I saw a lawyer for the first time. Her name was Krystyna Holka, and she was a Polish public defender. She got her "facts" from the prosecutor's file and had no intention of questioning those "facts" or fighting for the things that I was demanding to fight for. Her job was to show her face and make it appear like I had representation, when in fact I did not.

A new guy was introduced into our cell, Henry E. from Nigeria, the only black guy in the entire prison. He was in his late twenties, he spoke broken English with a Nigerian accent, and zero Polish, which is why they put him with me. He married a Polish woman as a barter for the purposes of entering Europe on a marriage visa, and then he decided to order cocaine from Brazil. The Polish police raided his house as soon as the package arrived, and he faced at least several years of prison time. I gave him soap, toothpaste, and food, and he settled right in as part of our group.

In this prison, unlike in Stargard, we had a "sister" cell that we were able to visit about once per week for an hour so that we could mingle and play cards with guys outside our cell. They matched us with a cell of eighteen-year-old kids that were facing twenty or more years each. I started teaching English to these guys, and I continued teaching English for the duration of my stay in Poland. It was good practice for me, and it gave the guys something else to think about, another way to exercise their minds. Because I was teaching English, I had more privileges to visit them, and we met more often than the usual one hour per week.

In Szczecin, pigeons visited our windowsills for bread. They were like pets, as some would return every day, and I could almost touch them once they got to know me. The best part of the pigeons for me was that "gołab" (pigeon) was one of the only Polish words you taught me on one of the last days we ever got to spend together. "Daddy, gołab, Daddy, gołab," you pointed, as we walked on the sidewalk in the snow outside our apartment in The Hague.

The wychowawca (social worker) here, Kristian Kalinowksi, may have been in his early thirties, and he was pretentious. He did not relate well to the inmates, and he seemed to do less than the guy we had in Stargard, not that either of them did much. My main issue with this guy was that he demanded that everyone stand at attention upon his entering the room. The problem was that we had no idea when he was coming, as most times that the door opened it was only a guard and they didn't make us stand except in the morning for apel. We had to learn the sound of Kristian's footsteps coming down the hall, and always be ready for him to make a surprise appearance.

This made it much harder to relax or sleep during the day. One time I was sleeping and unaware that he had entered the room. He clanged his keys loudly on the metal of my bed, right by my ear, and I was jolted awake. Nighttime was much better, since then we were left alone unless we were causing a commotion.

The dentist in Szczecin wasn't drunk, but he was still not much better. I got a couple of small things fixed, but the rest he said would have to be extracted. I knew that he was wrong, and so I declined like I did in Stargard. I developed a couple of bad tooth infections, and it was difficult to get antibiotics or pain medication. On a couple of occasions, the pain was so intense that I could not get out of my bed or lift my head, and I did not have the strength to try to get help.

Mariusz tried to help by banging on the door for the guard, but the first guard said that we would have to fill out a request to see the dentist. The next guard brought a nurse that knew me from my stay in the observation ward; I was relieved and overjoyed to see her. She gave me a handful of strong painkillers, telling the guard, "I know him." Eventually I also received antibiotics, and things returned to normal for a while.

* * *

I went to court a total of three times, and it was just a show, a "Muppet Show," as one of my friends referred to it. Instead of a wise judge, I got a curmudgeon, who was also the head of the Szczecin court and known to be the toughest judge around, Maciej Straczyński. He immediately reminded me of Doc Brown from *Back to the Future*. He had a scowl and a negativity that was off-putting, along with no interest in justice or the welfare of my child. He was disgusted with the "crime" that I had committed, and made it known that his only purpose was to figure out what to do with me. It appeared that he was actually angry with me.

Unwilling to rely on my public defender, I came fully prepared for court. I prepared questions for the witnesses against me, I had a list of witnesses that I wanted to call, and a list of "facts" that I wanted to dispute. Under Polish law, it is required that they review all available evidence, and I thought that this would matter, but I was wrong. All available evidence meant all the evidence that the prosecutor had decided to include in his file, and nothing else.

My first argument before the judge was that there was no attempt to murder. The judge explained that even though what I did was simple assault, he believed my true desire had been to kill him. He decided that I hit your grandfather with the hammer even though the medical evidence showed that I did not. The medical report showed no hammer injuries to any part of his body including his arms and hands; the hammer was not swung. The judge finished with "a gentle hit is a hit nonetheless, and any hit with a hammer is an attempt to kill."

The three "expert" court psychiatrists from my observation attended the first court date to present their findings that I was "insane" and a "drug addict." Because they were the "experts," there was no questioning their opinion; I was denied the opportunity to call in my own, non-court psychiatrist, which could have been crucial for my case. In the court's mind, the "experts" were already there, and a second opinion was not required.

"If I didn't say that my daughter is being abused, would you still be able to say that I am insane?" I asked the psychiatrists before the court. "Is there any other evidence to say that I am insane other than the fact that I will not change my stance on the abuse of my daughter?"

Dr. Jacek Afrykański responded, "No, if you did not believe that your daughter was being abused, we would not have concluded that you are insane."

Seeing his straight face produced an involuntary smirk from me; it was absolutely amazing to me that this guy was deemed to be an expert at anything. He never seriously considered my allegations that the caregivers were the abusers, and that they were lying.

What happened was that these specialists fell victim to circular reasoning. They decided that A was true because B was true, and also that B was true because A was true without knowing if either A or B was true, with A being "Iain is insane," and B being "no abuse of his daughter had occurred." The "experts" were just dummies in costumes. *These people can't think at all, and yet they are the ones who have determined that I cannot think.*

"Is he dangerous?" the judge asked the psychiatrists. "Is there a chance that he will hurt somebody in the future?"

Dr. Afrykański spoke again, "Theoretically, in a hypothetical sense, yes, there is a chance he will hurt somebody. If he believes that his daughter is being hurt, then he may in the future possibly harm someone."

"It was obvious that the insane person, the subject of psychiatry, was an individual in conflict with others, typically members of his family or the authorities and agencies of society. The psychiatrist's task – in his dual role as physician and agent of society with special powers and privileges granted him by the State – was to manage and resolve the conflict" (Szasz, 1990, 142).

At this point, it was obvious that for the judge it was case closed. The rest of it was just going through the motions. He decided that it was unnecessary to hear people like Kees de Vries, who could testify that he had been worried about your mom and not about me at the time of the abduction/escape, that the so-called escape was planned, and that I had warned him about it for weeks before it happened.

I requested again that I be permitted to get the opinion of another psychiatrist who spoke my language and had a background in trauma psychology. But they denied this request as well, stating again that they had no need for another opinion because they knew that the opinion that they already had was true. In an attempted murder case, I would think that it would be very important for the defendant to be able to call a witness not on the government payroll, but that was not the case for me.

I was excited when I found out that I would have the opportunity to cross-examine your mom, and I prepared a line of questioning that would dismantle the "escape" story. I knew that the story that she was tasked to present was not her own, that she would be running a script that I could easily punch holes in. In preparation for trial, I had requested all of the witness statements in writing. Her testimony itself was predictable, exactly what she had told me would be the "red herring." Her witness number, "666", was off-putting, and I wondered how she had managed that. But I was already saturated in the outrageous, so this was just par for the course.

"Agata, what was your reasoning for not taking our daughter to the doctor with me when our daughter had unexplained vaginal pain?" "Agata, can you explain to me why you left our home with our daughter?" "Agata, can you describe why we decided that you should get mental health counseling?"

After my first few questions, she started hyperventilating and had to go over to the window for fresh air. My attempt to break through her programming caused her to short circuit, and rather than answer my questions she had to walk away to try to compose herself.

The judge cancelled the trial for the day and told the police to take me back to prison. He didn't like that my questions were causing her emotional distress, but instead of realizing that this could indicate that the true answers had not yet been revealed, he concluded that I was just being a bully. Unfortunately, he wasn't willing or able to see the real problem.

On my way out with my police escort and my little blue Bible in my hand, I reminded her in front of everyone in the courtroom, "I love you, Agata." She did not look at me, still over by the window, catching her breath.

On the next court date, the third one, the judge banned me from court. As I entered the courtroom, the handcuffs dug into my wrists. The police wanted to take them off, but the judge said that I was dangerous, referring to the findings of the court "experts" at the last court appearance. I could tell by how the police treated me that they knew this judge, and that they felt bad for me.

This entire day was dedicated to them deciding that I was not fit for trial, and that the rest of the trials would be held without me, with only my public defender there to represent me. The "experts" told the judge that my only interest was in having my daughter evaluated, that I had no specific interest in defending myself against the attempted murder charge. This, for them, was another sign of my mental illness and the rationale for deeming me unfit to stand trial. Their recommendation was for a prolonged period of "treatment."

Because Mariusz's case involved banking, the Polish equivalent to the FBI was involved. I saw this as an opportunity to reach out to them, so I had him pass them a letter for me. I explained the nature of ritual/organized abuse, along with the fact that the police, prosecutor, and the court system had refused to admit that such a thing could be real. They had not investigated, and my child was still at risk. However, when Mariusz returned, he told me that the agent said that he did not believe in ritual abuse.

Some time went by, and then I finally got my marching orders: Kristian told me that I was going to be transported to a maximum-security prison psychiatric hospital. The court had concluded that I was criminally insane. He had no further information for me but assured me that it would be "better" where I was going. *Alright*, I thought, *here I go. This should be easy*, though I didn't think it would be better. "Better" would only be when I had you back.

> "In a jail, a person is 'let alone'; in a mental hospital he may not be. A prisoner will be released after he completes his sentence, and possibly before. A mental patient may be required to undergo a change in his 'inner personality' – a change that may be induced by measures far more intrusive than anything permitted in a jail – before the psychiatric authorities let him go. And they may never let him go. Commitment, unlike a sentence, is for an indefinite period" (Szasz, 1974, 168).

By this point, Mariusz had already gone home, so I said my goodbyes to the rest of them, my brothers in arms. Although I was not going home yet, I was moving on, which I thought had to be some sort of progress. It was the end of an era and the beginning of a new one; the passage of time was just a reminder that I had to be closer to you.

Journal Entry, November 30, 2012

"I said goodbye to the guys, gave Henry (E) and Boguslaw (C) hugs. Carted all of my stuff out, and I'm now sitting in the van, waiting to be transported to the maximum-security psychiatric hospital in Starogard Gdanski. Because I believe that my daughter is being abused. Father, I am still waiting on you. Father, my family is still waiting on you...It feels, almost, like I am getting out of here. I have my laptop in a box on my lap, using the box as a table. I am not in handcuffs. But I am not getting out. I will be closer to Russia than to Germany.

I don't know what awaits me, yet I know that God is for me, and so, I shall not worry myself with what man will do to me. Of course, there is a degree of apprehension, as there is and should be when entering any new situation, but it is not really anxious or worrisome apprehension, but rather, a new day, closer to the end, closer to holding Adelle in my arms. O Lord. O my God....I was just thinking about [Boguslaw], about the love I have for that guy, about looking into his eyes and hugging him, and my body began tingling all over, filled with the spirit of love. The spirit of God, everything that is good in this world: Love."

CHAPTER 76

"JOHN DEERE IS GREEN"

"Ever since the creation of insane asylums, some three hundred years ago, it has been common knowledge that individuals incarcerated in them were mistreated" (Szasz, 2008, 65).

November 2012 to July 2013
Regionalny Osrodek Psychaitrii Sadowej w Starogardzie (R.O.P.S.)
(Regional Center for Court Psychiatry in Starogard)
Ul. Skarszewska 7
Starogard Gdański 83-200
Poland

The van rolled to a stop, and the driver killed the engine. I looked out the window and knew that I was "home." *Ok, here we go. I wonder what could be next*, I thought. The guards got out, and the one on the passenger side slid my door open. I scooched toward the door with my hands out so that he could put handcuffs on me. After cuffing my wrists and ankles, he reopened the passenger side door and pulled out a short, black, assault shotgun. "Does that have lead or beanbags?" I asked, with an ironic smile on my face.

"These are just beanbags," he replied.

I carefully stepped out of the van and into Starogard Gdański in north-central Poland and hobbled to the back door to retrieve my things. As usual, the guards would not help with my bags, and I had to figure out how to balance three bags and a box while walking in chains to the front door of ROPS, one of Poland's three court-ordered maximum-security prison hospitals. The driver opened the door, and I stepped into the facility where I was about to reside for about the next seven months, though I didn't know that at the time. Hospital security was waiting on the other side of the door.

Paperwork was exchanged for chain of custody; my handcuffs and leg shackles were removed, but not before I was asked if I was going to behave. I emptied my pockets onto a table: half a pack of Polish cigarettes, two lighters, a miniature New Testament, a pen, and a notebook.

"No more smoking," blurted out the new guy. I looked at the door as a wave of panic shot through me for a moment as if I had been asked to have a toe removed. But I wasn't really that surprised, as I was getting used to dealing with uncomfortable situations and new information that I would rather not hear.

"Can I have one more," I hesitantly questioned while nodding my head toward the door.

"No, no smoking." My heart sank just a bit more, but it had been a long time since I had heard good news.

Then he delivered the next blow. "You can't have your Bible either."

"What do you mean? It's a Bible. I need it. I read it every day. I want to read it now."

"No," he confirmed, "you are not allowed to have anything until Monday."

Everything that made my life semi-comfortable was being taken away. I couldn't smoke, I couldn't have my Bible, and I wasn't going to have anything to write with. I walked through the next set of doors into the main corridor behind the guard. He opened another door on the right, and motioned for me to go in.

"Take off your clothes and get in the shower," I was instructed. Five people, including two women, were standing there in the room with me.

I took off all my clothes, put on my rubber shower slippers, and got into the shower. I was in a slight state of shock from the recent events and the long, uncomfortable ride. They watched me shower; it was strange being watched by so many people, but it was more strange that everyone was looking at me as if I were a lunatic who might try to bite an ear off or sprint for the door. In prison I didn't deal with that; in prison I was a "criminal," but not a "crazy" person. Being perceived as crazy is more difficult to get used to than being perceived a criminal because "crazy" is both misunderstood and feared because it is misunderstood.

After drying myself off, I was given striped pajama bottoms with an elastic waist, and a short sleeve button-up shirt without the buttons to prevent me from eating them. I dressed, and then I was ushered through another door to a back room where there was a psychiatrist seated behind a desk. I had prepared myself for this conversation mentally during the ride, but I was tired, and my defenses were thin. I smiled and extended my hand to see if she would shake it.

She did, though she hesitated for a moment. I sat down and made eye contact, being careful not to stare. "My name is Katarzyna Szumska. I'm a psychiatrist. How are you feeling?" she asked, trying to speak English.

"I'm ok, just a little tired and hungry," I replied.

Her attention shifted to a scratch on my arm in the crook of my elbow that was due to the police not helping me with my many bags. I hadn't known it was there, but when I looked at what she was looking at and saw her face, I knew that she suspected I had been injecting drugs. She stood up to inspect my arm, and I reassured her it was not that, but I couldn't tell if she was convinced.

She sat back down and proceeded to ask me some general questions, but nothing specific. I think she was just checking my demeanor and basic cognitive abilities so that she could sign her name stating that I could be released to the ward. She told me that I would probably get to speak with a doctor on Monday, and she assured me that I would be given Nicorette but no other drugs for the time being. I wanted to get a piece of Nicorette as soon as possible.

I stood up and was escorted out through the room with the shower and back into the main corridor. The guard opened another door with a card key that was hanging around his neck, and I walked into Ward A. This was where all new "patients" stayed for observation, where the "craziest of the crazy" never leave, and where they brought troublemakers from the three other wards. This place was secure; even if someone got through the first door, there were still two more reinforced security doors and a security station with cameras and guards before reaching the street. I was buckled in.

Three or four curious patients in baggy pajamas and plastic sandals immediately surrounded me. The first introduced himself as Krzysiek; his wrists were bound with leather straps, and these straps were attached to a belt around his waist. He reached out his hand as far as he could to shake mine, flashing a big toothless smile, and I put my hand about five inches from his waist to get to his.

A tall, gangly guy named Timon, around twenty-five years old, bounced around aimlessly while I was meeting Krzysiek. He was bubbling over with happiness, and I wasn't sure why until I turned to him, and he wrapped his arms around me in a bear hug like I was his dad who just got home from work. I returned his hug lightly out of convention, and then quickly backed away a couple steps. He smiled, turned, and sprinted down the hallway in the other direction.

My third greeter was a burly, fat guy with the posture of an ape. About thirty years old, he looked like a cross between Shrek and Paul Bunyan. He hobbled, forcing him deeper into character. I grabbed his hand to shake it; it was huge, his skin rough and cracked as if he had been working in the garden without gloves for years. "Skurat," he blurted, telling me his name.

"Hello, I'm Iain."

"John Deere is green," he shot back in Polish, and he bent down into a crouching monkey position and started making tractor noises and flexing his arms in a way that suggested he was pulling levers.

The guard who had brought me in was still standing nearby. After Skurat turned into a tractor, I turned to the guard to find out what was next. I wanted to find out where my bed was and how to get Nicorette. The guard led me down the long, polished hallway, and I took in the scenery.

Holy crap! What am I doing here? I just spent nineteen months as an exemplary prisoner, and now I'm stuck with the craziest of the crazies, I thought to myself, inspecting my buttonless pajamas. I peered into a couple of rooms as I passed by; most of the patients were under the covers sleeping. Others were slouched on the u-shaped pleather couch that was in front of the television.

We arrived at the plexiglass-enclosed nursing station at the far end of the corridor. Peering inside, I saw multiple security monitors. The entire ward, including the bedroom cells and the bathroom were on camera. This was something that I would have to get used to; there were no cameras in regular prison.

The nurse gave me bedding and led me to my room directly across the hall. I stepped inside and reached my hand out to shake my roommate's hand. He was an older man, around fifty-five, medium build with a mustache. Around his bed were pictures that he had taken out of magazines of Mary and Jesus. I sat down on my bed and looked through the barred window out into the back where there was a grassy area a little smaller than a football field. I couldn't see beyond the tall, barbed wire-covered stone fence that surrounded the entire field. I talked to my roommate a little longer, and then I went out to see about a piece of Nicorette, and paper and a pen.

The nurse was hesitant to give me a pen at first, but I talked with her for a couple of minutes, and she decided that it was ok. She told me that I had to keep it in my pocket when I was not using it because other patients would try to eat it. I told her that I would not let anyone eat my pen, and then asked her how I could get a cup of coffee.

"We have the water cooker in here. Only we can use it, and you can only use plastic cups. No glass ever," she explained. "The times that we are going to pour water are posted on the bulletin board. Once we pour it, you must wait about fifteen minutes for it to cool because we've had patients throw boiling water at each other before."

I walked around to get my bearings and met some more people. Leszek, a frail, weak looking man about sixty years old was sitting on the couch in front of the tv with his feet up on the table. He was slouched down as if he had just shot up some heroin; drool was running down the corners of his mouth and his ear was on his shoulder. On the table in front of him was a big plastic green cup with five tea bags. When I approached, he startled to consciousness and yelled, "Smrut, smrut!" at the top of his lungs. The guy standing next to me told me that this meant "stinky." *Alright, that's cool*, I thought. *Let's see what else is in here.*

The hallway ended right after the tv, so I turned around and headed back to the main door that I had entered when I arrived. I looked to the right, and two guards with latex gloves were strapping Timon into his bed with leather straps. He was four pointed, his ankles and wrists secured so that he couldn't move. Except that he could move his head, and he started flailing it around and banging it up and down violently. "Timon, Timon, Timon. My name is Timon. Leave me alone," he bellowed. Another staff member went into the room and fastened a leather helmet to his head.

"How long does he do that for? Shouldn't they give him something to calm him down?" I asked.

"He does this all the time," the nurse replied. "No, in Poland we tend not to give drugs in these situations. He'll be ok."

I spent my time meeting and talking to the nurses and other staff. It was always the same people; it didn't take me very long before I knew who was coming in on the shift changes. I learned that we could not keep razors, shaving cream, shampoo, or belts. One nurse somberly explained, "People drink the shampoo if we let them keep it in their rooms. You can get those things twice a day according to the chart on the wall. Someone will help you to sign them in and out."

Everyone had to get out of bed at 7:00 AM every day, and immediately sweep and clean our rooms and the hallway. Most patients were simply incapable of helping, so the staff did most of the work, but in the other wards only the patients cleaned. After cleaning, everyone lined up to be served breakfast.

The meals were delivered in a catering truck and were better than any menu I would have anywhere else until I was released. After breakfast, everybody had to line up for the drug line, as they did after every meal. Though I didn't have any medication yet, I was pretty sure that it would be difficult to keep it that way. I stood, watched, and kept track of who had how many and which pills.

I watched how the nurses observed the patients, or didn't, and how each patient had to open his mouth to prove that he had swallowed his medicine. This worried me the most; being physically locked up was one thing, but I was not about to let these Polish quacks tamper with my mind. This was my most crucial immediate problem, and I had to figure out how to take care of it so I could remain undrugged. My mind was all I had left, and I knew that I would need it to continue fighting for you.

There were no limits on shower time. This was the first time in a year and a half that I could spend more than five minutes per week in the shower. Though this was a major improvement, I still wasn't able to relax. No matter where I was, I was possibly being watched and evaluated. In prison I was pretty much left to myself, but here there was a constant motion of nurses, assistants, psychiatrists, therapists, and guards, in addition to the twenty prisoner patients. It was like living under a microscope.

On December 11, 2012, I was called in for my second meeting with Dr. Szumska. A woman of about thirty-two, she seemed unsure of herself and afraid of the patients. The good news was that I could get a couple of books and some of my clothes from storage. The bad news was that I would have to stay in this ward for about two weeks under observation before she was willing to move me to one of the other three wards. The worst news was that she informed me that I would be started on the antipsychotic risperidone at 0.5 mg.

"Why do I have to take that?" I asked, feeling like I was standing at the edge of a cliff.

"You don't have signs of mental illness now, but we will treat you because the court has ordered it. Everyone here takes medication; there are no exceptions." She made it clear that if I didn't comply, that I would be put in restraints and given injections in lieu of tablets.

> "A person can have drugs enter his body in two ways, voluntarily by choice, or involuntarily by coercion. (I am disregarding accidental ingestion.) Along with fearing, worshiping, and generally ceremonializing drugs, most Americans have come to view some drugs as satanic destroyers, others as God-like saviors. Accordingly, they have deputized their lawmakers to prohibit and criminalize the voluntary use of the former drugs, and to authorize the forcible medical use of the latter. This has made mental health professionals especially dangerous: in addition to possessing the power to forcibly confine innocent persons, they now also possess the power to forcibly drug healthy persons in the name of psychiatric treatment" (Szasz, 2007, 174).

That evening the door opened and a man was carried in by two guards. He was yelling and singing, but he didn't seem dangerous or violent. "Does the sister (nurse) have hard or soft poop?" he belted out over and over so that it echoed down the entire hallway. Eventually he learned that there was an American in the ward, and he started trying to talk to me through the door, so I talked back and was able to help him calm down.

Because he wanted to come and hang out with me, he eventually convinced the staff that he was going to behave. They let him out, and I made us coffee. He introduced himself as Bronek and told me that his diagnosis was antisocial personality disorder. He spoke a bit of English, which he was excited to show off. He told me about his life and let me read his poetry.

After about a week, I was given the privilege of using the payphone for an hour a week, the internet for research under supervision for about an hour a day, and the small gym for about an hour a day where there was a basketball hoop and a ping pong table. While things were huge improvements over prison, prison was still better.

I began meeting with Jacek Jakimiak, a psychotherapist who was a little older than myself. I liked him, but he made it clear from the beginning that his job was not to evaluate, but to treat according to what the court had already determined. I didn't like that he spoke better English than I did Polish at the time, and yet refused to speak English. His questions and strategies were scripted for the most part; he began trying to explain Cognitive Behavioral Therapy to me with a diagram, and I took the paper and finished his diagram for him. After about ten minutes, he said, "I don't know if psychotherapy will work because of the language barrier."

Of course, it's not going to work, I thought. But I did look forward to talking with him, though it was only for thirty minutes about twice a month. These talks and the notes I took after each meeting helped me to understand what the "experts" were thinking and what their strategies were. I prepared for future meetings and tried to make sure that he was writing the "right" things in my file. I developed a relationship with him, and eventually he brought in pen drives with concerts that he enjoyed so that I could watch them on my laptop, though I couldn't tell for sure if we were friends.

The next morning, a positively charged nurse with long flowing hair came into my room to tell me the director was coming to speak individually to all the patients in the ward today. My heart leapt because the day had turned from ordinary to extremely important. She left, and I got on my knees and prayed to God that he would give me strength and wisdom, and I prayed for you and your mother. When it was my turn, the nurse came back in and touched my shoulder; I thanked her, stood up, grabbed my notebook, and headed down the hall.

The room directly next to the nursing station was used for visits when the director was in the building. Leszek Ciszewski, a Polish Leonard Nimoy, was sitting in the room with his back toward the door. I noticed a button next to where he was sitting that was most likely an alarm. I shook his hand and sat in the chair opposite him. We spoke for a while; his English was quite good, though a bit robotic sounding.

"It is a mistake that you were sent to this special hospital," he began, with a smirk on his face. "It is obvious to me that you shouldn't be here, but there is nothing that I can do about it now. I can send an opinion to court in six months."

In 1887, Elizabeth Jane Cochran concealed her identity, pretending to be indigent and "insane" in order to experience the inside of an insane asylum. Once she was admitted, she stated,

> "'… I made no attempt to keep up the assumed *role* of insanity. I talked and acted just as I do in ordinary life. Yet strange to say, the more sanely I talked and acted the crazier I was thought to be.' [She] quickly discovers that patients cannot possibly convince the doctors to set them free" (Szasz, 2008, 68).

"Aren't you able to send an opinion to the court sooner?" I pled.

"Yes," he replied. "Under Polish law, I could recommend your release tomorrow, but that is not how it works. The court doesn't want to hear from me any sooner. You will have to be here for about six months."

"Ok," I scrambled, "then when you do send in your opinion, can you recommend that I skip going to a medium security facility? Can't I go straight from here to a minimum-security facility given the fact that it was a mistake, as you said, that I was sent here?"

He shifted in his chair, and replied, "Well again, yes that is possible. There is nothing that says that cannot happen. However, that is not the way it works. The court doesn't want that to happen. I think you will have to go from here to medium security, and then to minimum security. My guess is that you will be hospitalized for about 18 months because that is the way that the system is designed to operate."

"Eighteen months!" I had just spent nineteen months in prison, and that seemed like an eternity. The thought of having to do it again was difficult to comprehend and accept. I decided that it wasn't worth pushing the topic further now; I had to go back to the drawing board to reassess and see if I could work on changing his mind.

"How can you treat me for a diagnosis that is over a year old? Don't you think that it might be a good idea to determine my current mental state first? I have also been diagnosed with severe depression, panic disorder, ADHD, and adjustment disorder in the past. Why don't you treat me for one or all of those too?"

He took a moment, and then said, "The court only looks at the diagnosis that it wants to look at. They are only interested in treating the problem that they have identified."

"Do you understand why I have a problem with this? It doesn't make any sense. Please tell me how I am sick now."

"Well, I don't see any obvious signs of mental illness, but that is typical of someone with delusional disorder."

"Yes, and isn't it also typical of someone who is healthy?"

"I see your point, but the Polish system does not."

> "They [Judge Learned Hand and Justice Oliver Wendell Holmes] jogged down to the Capitol together — it was before the justice had a car, and he was bound for the Court. To tease him into a response, as they parted, Hand said: 'Well, sir, goodbye. Do Justice!' The other turned sharply: 'That is not my job. My job is to play the game according to the rules'" (Francis Biddle, 1960, as cited in Szasz, 1974, 109).

> "Attributing a medical diagnosis to a healthy person does not transform him into a bodily-medically ill person, whereas attributing a psychiatric diagnosis to him does indeed transform him into a mentally-psychiatrically ill person. A nephrologist may declare Smith to be suffering from uremia. But if Smith does not, in fact, have kidney failure, then the diagnosis will not make him sick. It will make the diagnosis erroneous. In contrast, a psychiatrist may declare Smith to be suffering from schizophrenia. Regardless of Smith's behavior or mental state, the diagnosis will transform him into a 'schizophrenic,' or at the very least into a 'schizophrenic in remission'" (Szasz, 2008, 15).

Before leaving, I asked him why I was being forced to take risperidone. I left it last to try to downplay how important this topic was to me.

"That's not my choice. The court has ordered that you be treated for delusional disorder" he explained. "If I were to decide that you didn't have to take medication, then the court would not be able to justify detaining you for treatment... that's not what the court wants... At that dose (.5 mg/day), risperidone doesn't act as an antipsychotic. It acts as a sedative," he said with a consoling tone.

The baloney alarm rang in my head, and I pressed into him with more questions. "Why do I need a sedative?... Am I not calm?... Why would I be given an antipsychotic if the only intended effect was sedation?... What is it that you intend to change with this medication?"

He didn't have any answers for me. I was certain that he had used the word "sedative" to make the medication more appealing to me. With my "drug history" in my file, he leapt to the conclusion that sedation would be desirable for me.

> "The widespread acceptance and use of the so-called tranquilizing drugs constitutes one of the most noteworthy events in the recent history of psychiatry... These drugs, in essence, function as chemical straitjackets... When patients had to be restrained by the use of force – for example, by a straitjacket – it was difficult for those in charge of their care to convince themselves that they were acting altogether on behalf of the patient... Restraint by chemical means does not make [the psychiatrist] feel guilty; herein lies the danger to the patient" (Szasz, 2007, 188).

CHAPTER 77

FIGHT FOR YOUR MIND

Though I didn't like being in the "crazy prison," I was beginning to realize that it was by the grace of God that I had been processed through the court the way that I had. I remembered Dawid M. telling me that I would be lucky if my sentence was seven years, and me thinking that his prediction was absurd. However, with the charge of attempted murder, the sentencing range is eight to twenty-five years. The only thing that saved me from such a fate was being deemed insane, because that meant not guilty, but that also meant being locked up indefinitely at the discretion of a court psychiatrist. I also knew that if I played the game right, then they would have no grounds to hold me and would be forced to release me.

The nurses were great to me; while I was in Ward A, there was never a time when I asked for and was denied Nicorette. I was also allowed to stay up until midnight, and everyone else had to go to bed at 10:00. And I could usually get my coffee before the full fifteen-minute cooling period, because they were sure I wasn't going to throw it on anyone. They had pretty much let their guards down with me after getting to know my demeanor and seeing that I had the lowest dose of "treatment" drugs in the entire facility.

The drug line was a game I needed to get good at because I didn't want to ingest their poison. At first, I took the medication if I felt there was a risk of being caught, which would mean six months to a year added onto my stay at that hospital and maybe injections. I saw this as one of my most important jobs: fight to not be forced to use drugs that lessen cognitive abilities, drugs that are no more than chemical lobotomizers.

My journal records show the effects of risperidone at .5 mg/day:

> "*spacey, trouble focusing my eyes, trouble focusing my mind, trouble concentrating, trouble reading, lost in chess to Bronek, heart tightening, sore muscles, tired, dizzy, memory problems, upset stomach, like having those drops in your eyes that dilate your pupils so that you are dazed and cannot focus on anything, can't even watch tv, read a page and then forget immediately, spark plugs not sparking, like someone poured rubber cement into my synapses*" (Journal Entry, December 12, 2012).

I wasn't done addressing the issue with the doctors, but in the meantime, I also wasn't about to let them decide how my brain was going to function. Ward A's drug line was easy because of all the "problem patients" they had to deal with. Only one of the nurses even looked at me after giving me the half a pill that I was to take daily in the evening, but I could tell she only did it out of routine.

One time I went through the motion of swallowing it just to be safe. I was able to catch it in my throat and cough it back up with a little effort after I walked away; this was a good day.

Regular chewing gum that I got at the prison store supplemented Nicorette, and I used it to practice the action of moving something from my tongue to my upper lip. This was pretty much foolproof if I could get the tongue action mastered because I had never seen them check there, but it did take a lot of practice. They inspected the tongue and sometimes under the tongue, but that was it.

For hours a day, I practiced with my piece of gum in front of the mirror, and I always did warmups right before I got into the drug line. I got nervous as the time approached for my performance, the most important moment in my day. But it was a nervousness that was necessary due to the consequences of getting caught.

I always chose my place in line strategically so that I had people behind me. This made it so that the moment my pill was in my hand, I could sidestep just a little, and allow the next guy to put out his hand. When I put the pill in my mouth, the nurse's attention was often on the next guy in line. "Dziękuje" (Thank you), I said, and then I turned and went straight back to my room where there was conveniently a sink. I put the pill in the drain, spit and rinsed out my mouth, and felt a great wave of relief. My job was done for the day, and I could relax a bit for twenty-four hours.

I wasn't immediately an expert at this, and even when I began to feel confident, I remained extremely nervous. But not in the way one might feel if the cops are pulling you over and you know that you are drunk, but in the sense of one who is tiptoeing through a mine field. I knew that I had to remain alert, and that I couldn't take anything for granted – one bad move and I could lose a leg, or my life.

The rumor was that they randomly tested to see if the drug was in our blood, and since I couldn't ask anybody, I had to treat the rumor as possibly true. Therefore, to fully eliminate the possibility of getting caught, I usually took a couple of small pieces of my medication every week, a small piece being about an eighth of the tablet. This tiny bit still had a huge effect on me to the point where I would have considered suicide if I had been forced to do their actual regimen for any length of time.

In the same way that a chemical castration reduces the chance of recidivism in a sex offender, the chemical lobotomy they were forcing on me was supposed to eliminate the possibility that I would again "hurt" your grandfather. Their stated intention was to permanently change my brain, and my intention was to ensure that didn't happen.

It was great to have access to a phone; I hadn't talked to anyone in nearly two years. Brian and I began having conversations at least a couple of times per week, and this would continue until my release. Art made sure that I had money in my account for the things I needed, such as coffee and phone cards. He also began sending me books, which were more valuable than gold, though I had to get to the point where I could actually read them again with the poison that they were making me ingest.

He even started up a blog site that didn't require me to log in, since the rule on computers was "no logging into anything." He wrote to me nearly every day just to put a smile on my face. I was also in contact with Mariusz, who was trying to help me request and obtain visitation with my daughter. These connections to the outside world were a rock for me, an escape from the no man's land that I was in every day, and a reminder that there was a reality beyond what was directly in front of my face.

We could go outside into the area out back for about an hour a day, broken up into a half hour in the morning and a half hour in the afternoon. To qualify to buy things like coffee and sugar, it was mandatory to go at least ten times the previous week, or five out of seven days, morning, and afternoon.

Everyone pretty much walked around the perimeter of the field, around and around, until it was time to go back inside. The field was an improvement on the prison walking cage, but it was just another type of cage. Sometimes Timon took off running, and I would then chase him or get him to chase me. He liked it when I ran around with him on my back. He was ecstatic, bubbling over, like a toddler on a sugar high. "Timon, Timon," he would yell as he thrust a fist above his head. Then he would get down and take off again; I couldn't keep up with him.

I made it a point to spend time with the guy who was always locked in his room and get to know him. His name was Roman, and I thought that he was a pretty good guy. Everyone told me to be careful because he liked to kick people in the head since his hands were restrained just like Krzysiek's. We quickly became friends, so I knew he wasn't going to kick me.

We sat on the couch together whenever he got to come out of his cave. It made me happy when they let him out, and I couldn't imagine what being locked in a tiny room by himself did to his psychological state. He loved coffee, but he wasn't allowed to have any because it energized him. I couldn't give him any without risking both of us getting in trouble, and he knew it. But we found out a way to make it work. After I drank my coffee, I went to my room to wash the coffee grounds out of my plastic cup. He learned to come in just at the right moment. I let him take the cup, and he would eat the coffee grounds and then leave with the evidence in his belly, on top of the world.

Journal Entry, December 14, 2012

"That which I saw in my wife, and in my family as a result of my wife, drove me into a search for the truth, a search for answers and ultimately for 'god.' Death and mental anguish are nothing compared to 'non- change.' There are two choices: find the answers, or die trying"

Journal Entry, December 16, 2012

"Last night, Krzyszek, the guy who was working the day that I was transported here, and Andzej (who is my age) were working. The three of us, and the nurse (a bit) talked about Polish traditions, customs, food, Christmas... One of them was drunk, and I thought that was pretty cool. Andrzej showed me pictures of his 8 year old daughter. Krzyszek told me that he was going to smoke and that he wished that I could go with him. Andrzej told me that Ciszewski is crazy, that he is from 'Matrix,' mimicking how he talks into his little recording device...Andrzej showed me all of the music on his phone, told me that he is a furniture maker by trade, but that it is here, in the hospital, where the jobs are."

The facility employed about five occupational therapists, and there was a schedule of the week's activities they facilitated on the wall. I wanted to research, so access to the internet was the only activity that I was really concerned with. Occasionally they played a movie, though of course it was in Polish, and therefore very difficult to follow.

Sometimes they would play a concert on the movie screen. For example, we watched a Queen show, a Led Zeppelin show, an Eric Clapton show, and a Dave Matthews Band show (at my request). There was also an area for crafts and art, but I never used it.

Despite all the new opportunities for activity that did not exist in prison, this was not summer camp. Movies and concerts were rare. And, even if I participated in all the activities, this would only add up to a maximum of three hours per day. There was a lot of dead time. Each day and week was a carbon copy of the previous one.

Every day was like waking up in a bad dream that I had to do over and over again, with no idea when it would stop. I was stuck in one of the craziest places in Poland, and it was like I had gotten caught in a sticky fly trap. *How long will I have to do this for, and where will I have to go next? Why am I here? When will I be able to leave Poland and start fighting again? When will I get to hold my little girl?*

One of the occupational therapists was Maria (not her real name), a twenty-seven-year-old mother. She taught an English class twice a week from fall to spring when everyone thought it was too cold to go outside, and she asked me if I would come to check it out. When I arrived, she told me that I was now the teacher, and that she would be my student for the duration of my stay there.

I wasn't prepared for that, but I did it, and I was very happy that she asked because it showed that she thought highly of me. After I taught my first lesson, with her as one of the students, she said, "Wow, Iain, you are not anything like what they have written in the court documents. That was amazing!"

My new job made it clear how important it was to eliminate antipsychotics from my diet. I needed to be able to think to prepare and deliver lessons, and I was struggling because of medication-induced cognitive impairments. I felt like a sprinter trying to run a race in shackles.

At the end of the class, she said that she could teach me Polish if I wanted. My Polish was getting better at that point, but I was excited to have a private tutor and to have the opportunity to get to know her without anyone else around. It was nice to get to sit and talk to a beautiful, intelligent woman who was beginning to see through the lies in the court report.

Over the course of a few meetings, I was able to tell Maria some things about my situation and my life, and she was able to gradually get to know me. The difference between her and everybody else in Poland was that she was willing and able to see the holes in the official story about me. I think she saw it as part of her responsibilities as a human to listen to me and make her own judgments. The rest of the people in her position were just punching their timecards, checking their phones, and waiting for their next cigarette break.

Journal Entry, December 17, 2012
"I worked on my English lesson for today last night. I tried to start organizing and planning. I also worked on a letter, but I am not sure how to finish it...I really just want to hug my little girl..."

Journal Entry, December 20, 2012
"She taught me some verb conjugation, and then she asked me what I am doing in Poland...I need to take the question and make it a book. She asked me, and then I thought for a moment or so. Then I began to tell her about Agata's signs of mental disorder, about Adelle's signs of being abused, about me trying to get help, about Agata leaving and telling people that she left because of me, about how I didn't know what to do and how I tried to get help but nobody would listen because I lost my mind when my daughter was taken. I told her that I came to Poland because I thought that getting arrested would lead to an interpreter, a lawyer, and a child abuse investigation."

"No, not in Poland," she said with a sigh. "Yes, but what can I do? What am I supposed to do?" she asked herself out loud. I could see that she was getting upset, that she didn't know what to think, and that she was a bit unsure of the conclusions that she was arriving at since the information in my file was so obviously bogus. I didn't like seeing her burdened by my story; her friendship was enough.

"What can I do? I can teach you Polish," she stated finally, visibly overwhelmed by the things that she was contemplating, the inconsistencies, and her own inability to understand complex child abuse or it's ramifications.

"I know, Maria, and I am just thankful that we can do that. It is good to have you in my life." I returned to the ward, feeling exhilarated. *"Nothing is as beautiful as when she believes"* (Ben Harper lyrics), began playing in my head. Having one person who could see me through the fog made all the difference in the world.

Bronek and I both received word from Dr. Szumska that we would be moving to Ward D. Bronek asked if he could be my roommate, and the doctor agreed. We were both excited to be getting out of Ward A, but the patients and staff in Ward D would take some getting used to. I was most concerned about how this change would impact my success rate with the drug line.

I put my things away in our new room, and then had to go to the English class. I found teaching to be very challenging at first. Some people spoke no English at all, and others spoke some broken English. *How am I supposed to teach one lesson to all these people and make it meaningful? Is it even possible to do so?* To top it off, everyone was on powerful drugs designed to dampen brain activity. I had to constantly adjust my expectations, as well as how I chose to present each lesson. I enjoyed the challenge, and this responsibility helped me to feel a tad more normal, which was difficult to maintain when everything around me was nuts.

That evening, I began meeting some really fantastic people. I was sitting on my bed writing in my notebook when this guy who I had never met before came up to me and introduced himself.

"Hi. My name Cyryl. I think you like this." He looked over his shoulder to see if anyone was watching, and then he gave me an mp3 player with headphones. I hadn't had the pleasure of listening to music with headphones for almost two years. I put them on and was immediately transported to another realm. Cypress Hill's "Hits from the Bong," was playing, and I was lifted, as if Scotty beamed me up into paradise.

Cyryl had blown me away with his generosity and intuitive knowledge that I needed this. I smiled and thanked him, but then a guard came in who I had never seen before. He came right over and took the headphones off my head and walked out, ripping me right back into the terrible reality that surrounded all of us.

"It's forbidden to share music," Cyryl explained. "I'll get it back tomorrow morning and let you have it again."

That first night in Ward D, I decided to take the medication because I hadn't had enough time to observe and determine new risks of the new drug line. In this ward they locked the bathroom for fifteen minutes after each of the three daily medication times to prevent people from making themselves puke their pills up.

Here we were allowed to keep shampoo and soap in our rooms, but still not razors or glass. Everybody took turns cleaning the bathroom, the hallway, and the dining area. The staff woke us up every morning at 7:00 to begin cleaning, except on Sundays. I was up earlier because I didn't like being woken up, and because mornings were a time when I could find a little peace to read or think alone.

After cleaning, we ate breakfast, and then everybody except me had the morning drug line. I was the only one who never had to take medication more than once per day, which made my job of not taking it that much easier. My Nicorette ration was now being monitored closely. Their plan was to gradually taper it down to nothing.

I was assigned a new psychiatrist, Dr. Setua, a fortysomething woman with an air of self-importance. She was the ordynator (head physician), right under the director in the prison hospital hierarchy. She told me that I could get my laptop from storage early because she knew how long I had been without it, and because she felt sorry for me that I was an American in a Polish prison hospital. Normally people had to demonstrate good behavior for two months before being given such a privilege, but she bent the rules for me. I couldn't get an internet connection, but I did have music and pictures of you and your mom. And this allowed me to journal and write more proficiently, instead of by hand. Every night I had to turn it in because they thought I might hang myself with the cord.

Journal Entry, December 20, 2012

"I got my computer back today; I lived for almost twenty months without a computer, without music, without a picture of Adelle, without Adelle in the flesh. Now my head is spinning like a top on acid. Where do I begin? What do I write about? How do I get to the only thing that matters, to my family? How do I trust in the Lord with all of my heart and lean not on my own understanding?

Just evaluate my daughter, thoroughly, for exposure to the severe caregiver inflicted child abuse that I've alleged. I have no more energy. I have nothing. I am nothing. What we know is that Agata and I did conclude that she has a major psychological disorder. We also know that in December 2010, I was trying to get her help. Therefore, it does not make sense to conclude that I was abusing her, holding her hostage...It makes a [expletive] of a lot more sense to conclude that I may be right (since all that I am saying is that she has a major psychological disorder that was caused by major childhood abuse); from there we get to the logical and reasonable conclusion that my daughter must be evaluated."

On December 21, 2012, I got in the drug line after dinner to get my .5 mg of risperidone. The nurse dumped it out of the little plastic cup and into my hand. "This isn't my medicine," I stated, hoping that I was right.

"Yes, the doctor changed it today," she assured me.

"The doctor didn't say anything to me. Why would the doctor not mention doubling my medication?" She understood that I was upset with the medication and not with her, and she went to grab my chart. She showed me the change in my file; I thanked her and took the pill. *No more!* I hated putting that garbage into my body.

Journal Entry, December 22, 2012

"Yesterday evening my Risperdal dose was raised from a half milligram to a full milligram. The doctor didn't say anything to me; she didn't tell me that there was going to be a change. Furthermore, I haven't spoken to anybody. Nobody has asked me how I am doing or what I am thinking about... This situation is ridiculous.

This is not treatment, and what is it that they are supposedly 'treating' me for anyways? For believing that my daughter is being abused? She is, and they do not know otherwise. For believing that the other story is not true, the story that my wife and everybody else believes? It is not true; my wife is a pathological liar. Well, she is not really a pathological liar; in reality, she really does believe her lies, but that is because of a much more complex condition. The result is pathological lying though I do not believe that her intent is to lie. We both concluded that she is suffering from major psychological disorder, and everybody that believes what she has to say is simply following along with the reality of my wife's illness. The only way to know if my daughter is or is not being abused is to evaluate my daughter thoroughly, and that still hasn't been done.

My head hurts. All of my muscles are sore, as if I was hit by a train. It hurts to walk... My memory is shot. I cannot remember things that I thought about five minutes ago. Or rather, I can, but it is difficult. I do not have any ability to plan or to map out issues. I begin the process of thinking, and then I hit a wall. It's like, for example, I think 'I want water,' but then cannot think about the next step. All that I can do is think 'I want water' over and over. Yes, I can change to 'I am going to get water,' but it is not a smooth process. Furthermore, when I change to 'I am going to get water,' then I forget why it is I wanted water. I am trying to write, trying to get this entire story onto paper. It is not easy. I am not sure what to write, first of all. Should it be a non-fiction account of the truth? Should I write logical arguments? Both?

Today we didn't have power for most of the day. The electricity was shut off, and nobody knew why. Towards the end, when it began getting dark, the[y] locked us in our rooms. I didn't get to.....The male nurse, who is bald, came in around 11:10 pm and told me that I had to give him the computer. I said 'not to 11:30?' to see if Odzialowy [the ward boss] had told him that he told me that it was ok to stay up writing until 11:30 without having to tell him 'Oddzialowy told me that I can write until 11:30.' He said no, and I said ok....He then said 'tomorrow is a day too,' and that comment got under my skin a bit; that comment deserved a response. Of course tomorrow is another day, and of course I can write tomorrow. That is surely not the point. Every minute counts, and every minute sleeping is a minute wasted. Anyway, he took the laptop, I said goodnight, and I meditated and prayed a bit, lying in bed and looking at the lone star that I could see through my window."

CHAPTER 78

"HAVE FAITH IN GOD"

In the following journal entries, I desperately cried out to God, though I was still getting to know His nature, and the nature of His promises. Though my understanding of doctrine was progressing, I still had gaps; for example, God does not wish to break us. "Instead of crushing us, He rescues us when we are crushed" (Davis 8). I will deal with this more in chapter 90.

I prayed "In Jesus' name" because Jesus is the "...head over every ruler and authority" (Colossians 2:10 NASB). He promised that "whatever you ask in My name, that I will do, that the Father may be glorified in the Son. If you ask anything in My name, I will do it" (John 14: 13-14 NKJV). I knew that I specifically needed Him, and that no other would do.

Journal Entry, December 23, 2012

"Last night I had a conversation with Tomek about the Bible. He had told me that he believes every gay needs to be killed, that God put that information into his heart and mind. So, last night, I gave him a paper with a couple of verses, such as 'love your enemy...' He then gave me the paper back, and he had written the verse about Jesus not coming to send peace, but a sword. That is one of my favorite verses....Jesus send your sword; divide and conquer...

Anyway, Tomek and I got into a conversation about the old vs. New Testament. Tomek told me that that Old Testament is still in effect and I told him that Jesus is the mediator of God's new covenant, that with a new covenant the old is no more. II Corinthians 3:14; Hebrews 8:13; Hebrews 10:20...He said that he does not believe this. He said that Matthew 5:17 is the answer, where Jesus says that he has come not to destroy, but to fulfill the law of the prophets. I asked him how he reached his conclusion, trying to get him to explain his feelings/beliefs to me. I told him that I believed that Matt 5:17 was an indication that Jesus was the prophet spoken of in the Old Testament, but that I felt that it was clear that the new covenant replaced the old. He said 'no, it just made the old covenant better.' I said 'ok, but when you make something better, you change it, do you not?' He asked me if I was trying to change his mind, and I told him 'no,' that I was just trying to get him to think.

I showed him verses explaining that sin is sin, that there are many who will not enter into the Kingdom of God, showing that God does not differentiate between gay and straight sin. He vehemently disagrees, and he cannot even think that he is wrong for a moment. He has formed a conclusion, and it has solidified. I can only hope to chip away at it, and to not upset him in the process. I also talked to him about judging others, telling him that the Bible tells us not to judge, telling him that our job is to become as perfect as we can in the eyes of God, to worry about ourselves and not about the others, at least not until we get the beam out of our own eye first....

Anyway, Tomek is a good example of how people take a text and mold it into whatever they want it to be, how you can use confirmation bias to support any hypothesis that you have. And, once you reach the point where your hypothesis has been supported, it is almost impossible to then challenge it.

It is now 10:00 pm. My head is aching; it is a headache caused by a lack of Dopamine. I cannot focus. I cannot navigate from one synapse to the next. It is a blockage, and that is painful. My memory is shot; I know I've written this elsewhere, but I've forgotten where and when. It is not good. I think of something, move on to something else briefly, and then when I try to go back to what I had originally thought about, it is gone. The connection has been lost. Yes, I can usually get the connection back, but it is not nice to feel like you have dementia, to not even be able to remember things such as the word 'dementia' until you have to stop and think really hard for a few seconds. And when the thinking pathways are not working properly on this level, it makes deep thinking virtually impossible. Not impossible, but very difficult. Thinking tangentially is just about impossible. Hence the headache; oh my God, please come and get us.

Please Lord; deliver us for thy mercy's sake, so that they know that it is you that did it. Lord, I trust in you, let me not be ashamed. Lord, it has been almost two years without my daughter, two more years of my daughter being abused. Lord, tell me what you need from me so I can do it. I John 3:21-22. Lord, strengthen me; fill me with wisdom, with your Holy Spirit, with the Spirit that is in your Son Christ Jesus. Lord, lead me, direct me, mold me......Lord, Adelle and Agata Bryson. Lord....

Tomorrow I have to attack my outline. I have to go slowly and not try to see the entire picture, because seeing the entire picture just will not work. My brain has been chemically lobotomized. Lord please deliver us before I am no more. You picked me up to the heavens, showed me all that is good, and then you dropped me to the depths of hell. Since then, my head has been held under the surface of hell. It is not my head that I am concerned about, but my little girl's.....In Jesus name. In Jesus name. Thank you Father. Praise God."

Journal Entry, December 24, 2012

"Today was a difficult day. I read the Bible, worked on the computer. I hung out with some of the guys here, played a few games of chess, listened to music....Two years ago I was in the middle of a whirlwind, trying to convince Agata to get help, trying to figure out how to make Adelle's Christmas as wonderful as possible given the state of her mother's psychological health, or rather sickness. I put Adelle's presents under the tree, Agata and I put out milk and a carrot for Santa with Adelle. I remember that Adelle didn't care about any of it; she just wanted her mommy and daddy to be close. I was trying so hard to get Agata to see the harm that she was doing. 'Agata, please get help. You are miserable, and you are making me and your daughter miserable. Can't you try to hold yourself together for your daughter? Agata, we love you, but you are no good in the state that you are in...' She would not listen, and every moment was a moment where her psychological state deteriorated.

And now it is two years later, and I am still trying to get back to my daughter, to shine a light upon this evil that has taken apart my family, stolen two years from us, stolen my daughter's father and mother....Father, please lead me, speak to me, let me know what it is you need me to do, let me know what it is that I should do. I am trampled down to the ground, to below the ground. Every part of my being is in pain. My heart hurts. My head aches and doesn't function anymore. I cry constantly. I am in a Polish psychiatric institution because I believe that Adelle is being abused, and she is being abused. Father, I need you to take over this situation, to guide me with your Spirit, for I cannot do anything.

Tomorrow I am going to work on the computer some more. It should be a pretty quiet day, except that it is always harder to work when people are walking about and making noise. Nighttime is the best, but it is now 11:15 and they only allow me to work until 11:30. My head doesn't want to work, doesn't know what to do. The Risperdal destroys my ability to think, to plot, to remember, to structure complete thoughts. Oh my God, I trust in thee. Give me peace and wisdom. Fill me with your Spirit and lead my family out of this hell. In Jesus' name....."

Journal Entry, December 25, 2012

"'Humble yourself under the mighty hand of God that he may exalt you in due time: casting all of your care upon him, for he cares for you...' (I Peter 5:6–7)

It's Christmas, a day for family, a day for children...I am in a mental hospital, and my child is being abused. Not just abused but ritually abused. I am at a loss for words. I am deflated. I am nothing. God, come and deliver us from this, for I have nothing left. Nothing.

'For I am ready to halt, and my sorrow is continually before me' Psalm 38:17

This afternoon I am going to write. I am not exactly sure what I will write about. I need the internet, so that I can try to get in touch with editors....Get templates, look at plot lines, proposals.....But I have to not make it about what I need, or about what I think that I need. What can I do today with what I have at my disposal? That is what's important. The rest is just procrastination, a waste of time and energy. Thinking 'oh, it would be nice to have the internet' is just a waste of a thought, for the internet is not a possibility today.

I have been trying to put how the Risperdal makes the head feel into words here and there, as it comes to me. It is difficult to describe anything without comparing it to what is known. Hence the reason that analogy works so well as a descriptive tool. I can say that it makes it hard to think, hard to remember, etc..., but you only know what I am talking about in terms of your own thinking and remembering norms. Well, that is all that you will ever know, as there is no way for me to teach you or show you what I feel or have felt, know or have known... Risperdal is like when you come down after a night of Ecstacy. The mind is incredibly tired; there is just nothing left; all of the dopamine has been depleted. This is how they are making my mind feel all of the time, and they do it on purpose, as their 'treatment' because I believe that my daughter is being abused. 'Fools professing themselves to be wise...'

I went to oddzial [ward] 3 today for a visit and sat with some of the guys over there, talking and eating cake. Marcin and Tomek. Marcin is the one who invited me. He told me that he has been in a mental institution for the past eleven years. I was told that he killed his parents, though I do not know. Marcin himself did not tell me, so it is just what I heard. We spoke about music, about Christmas in the U.S. Marcin showed me some of his paintings and lent me a Van Gogh book. I told Marcin that he should come over here and visit tomorrow. I wish that we had a place where we could speak alone; it is difficult when so many people are vying for attention at the same time. When I came back, I ate dinner alone after spacer, because the other guys had eaten while I was visiting. Then I played a couple of games of chess with Jarek; he beat me. I hung out with and spoke to Tomasz [Tomek] about the Bible, trying to plant some seeds in his mind. I took a shower, and now I am working, trying to get some things onto paper. Praise God."

Journal Entry, December 26, 2012

"My heart hurts. I cry frequently. I am desolate. Risperdal has choked my mind. Tomorrow is the two year mark. As of tomorrow, it will have been two years without my family, without my little girl. Two years. I could not before imagine two weeks, two months.....two years. Lord. What is your plan?

Today I hung out with a couple of the guys, went through some Bible verses with Tomek. Tomek is quite lost. His head is filled with lies, he wants to love God, he is fervent, but he is fervent about the wrong things. His zealousness is misdirected towards all that is not God, towards hate, towards intolerance, towards ignorance. 'Do you believe in priests?' 'What do you mean, do I believe in priests?' 'Do you believe that priests are connected to Jesus Christ?' 'No, I believe that priests are people who have been chosen by man, that they have not been chosen by God. I believe that some priests are good men, but that doesn't mean that God has chosen them to be some kind of mediator. There is only one mediator, and that is Jesus Christ. The man Jesus Christ is the only mediator between God and man. All of that other nonsense is just lies, just something that keeps you from knowing the truth. The truth is so simple. Follow the commandments that Christ has given us, and you have a direct relationship with God, who then resides in you via his Holy Spirit.'

Tomek is 22 years old. He says that he is young, stupid, ugly, crazy...He is an interesting psychological specimen to say the least. I am glad that he is in my life. I can tell that he has been hurt, that he is reacting to severe pain. What I can do is show him what I know by living it. I can talk to him and try to plant good seeds in his garden. I can .... Well, that is about all that I can do. He believes that he is being persecuted for his beliefs. He believes that praying to Mary for hours, the same prayer over and over again, is beneficial, that Mary is going to help him. He believes that when the priest speaks to him, that it is Jesus speaking through the priest. His mind has latched onto lies in an attempt to believe something, because he has been dealt a difficult hand. He has no trust in anything or anyone (which is actually wise, though it depends on your reasons and the way that you react to your lack of trust), I don't think that he has known love. He feels betrayed by his parents. I see the fear and hurt in his eyes. He wants to be a hard man, to be tough. He tries to act this way as a defense mechanism to his being hurt.

Anyway, that's enough about Tomek. I just finished a chess game with Jarek, and the nurse came in and told me that it is late. I said 'I talked to Witek (the boss), and he said that I can work until 11:30.' He then said, 'to what time can you work here?' 'Witek said that it is ok until 11:30.' He then looked at his watch and said '11:00.' I replied, 'ok thank you.' I don't understand why he thinks that his boss can say one thing and he another. Or rather, I do understand; his boss is not here, and he is, and so he is calling the shots. What can I do? The answer is not much...Sure I can go to Witek and say, 'I have a problem with the bald nurse'....then Witek will go to the bald nurse and say, 'I told Iain that he can work until 11:30.' And then the bald nurse will have a problem with me, or rather, there is a chance that he will have a problem with me. A couple of nights per week, the bald nurse is in charge. This is his territory, and probably has been for some time. He is used to calling the shots, and I will have a difficult time getting him to change. Patience and more patience.

So anyway, as I was saying before, tomorrow is 2 years...Two years since I sprinted to the police department in The Hague, desperate for help. Two years since my little girl was taken from our home, right out of my grasp. Lord, I trust in you. Show me the way you need me to take. Direct me.

Tomorrow I get to use the internet. I am not sure what to look for; I've got so much research to do, and it is difficult to get any work done at all in here. Not enough time...I've got to work on my two 'books,' and I've got to figure out how to distribute them once they've been written. I've got to look at other books that have been written so I see examples, layouts...I've got so much to do, but then again, I am not supposed to trust in myself, but in God. And, I do not trust in myself, for I know that there is nothing that I can do. However, I still must work. I still must try to put what I can onto paper. Try to get my stories onto the printed page. And it is difficult in here. The Risperdal working on my Dopamine, shutting down my thinking and my memory, my ability to plot and scheme, to dizzle and dazzle. The other patients around during the day. My roommate (Bronek)...

I need the Lord to direct me, to guide me. I need the Lord to step in and take over. I just don't know exactly what that means. I have to quiet my soul and my own desires, like wanting Adelle to be safe, so that I can hear what the Lord wants and needs from me. I have to keep purifying my heart and my mind, keep working towards the goal of righteousness. Only then will I be completely open to the Lord's suggestion. Only then will I be a vessel of the almighty God, a purified vessel. I need nothing but the Holy Ghost running through me. I need to be only the Holy Ghost, with a shell that looks like Iain. I have to be 'crucified with Christ, ...but nevertheless live, yet not I, but Christ living within me...' [Galatians 2:20] I have to be one with God, God in me and me in God. I have to kill the remainder of what remains of Iain so that only the Spirit of the living God remains. Please Lord, help me to get there. Help me to crucify all that you do not want within me. Help me to conform to your will, to the pattern that you have for me, to your plan. Help me to know your will. Help me to stay on a steady and straight course. Help me to overcome. Help me to believe entirely, to know my steps. Give me your words. Give me your wisdom. Give me your Spirit. In Jesus' name I pray. Amen. Praise God."

Journal Entry, December 27, 2012

"Two years. Exactly two years since I last saw my daughter, since I saw my wife. I began writing a letter today, and I believe that it was a great start. I got about 5000 words down. I am writing as if I am writing to Ellen Lacter, who is a ritual abuse specialist in California. And, I will get in touch with Ellen. But, that is not the first priority. The first priority is that I get the story down on paper in a format that is understandable, persuasive,.....

I need to research more about persuasive writing, plot.....

But not really; what I have to do is spend a lot of time on this; I already know how to persuasively write, and I just have to get into the Spirit and execute. I have to do it, to put it together piece by piece and bit by bit. I have to write and rewrite, work and rework until the finished product is a masterpiece. ...Well, God willing. God willing....Praise God. Father help me. Give me strength and direction. Fill me with your Spirit, with your words, direct my mind and my tongue, my steps and my paths.

I am also still working on my book about the path to God, about that path to God that nobody knows about. I am trying to put truth on paper, the truth that has been revealed to me by the Spirit of God, the truth that has to be told to the world.

I played a few games of chess today. I spoke with Tomek, the guy who prays to Mary. He told me that he does not know what real love is. He gave me a piece of paper with Matthew 6:7 on it, which is about praying with vain repetition. He, right away, told me that his praying with his rosary beads is not vain repetition. I looked at him, but I didn't say anything about that. I didn't say anything to him except that I do not pray to Mary. I think that I have the man thinking. Praise God. Lead me, help me to speak to this man, to plant seeds, to plant seeds that will bear fruit. Thank you Father for everything. Thank you Father for delivering my family. Your will be done. In Jesus' name......"

Journal Entry, December 28, 2012

"I woke up at around 6:20 this morning. I got up, prayed and made my bed, made coffee and brushed my teeth. I went to the nurse's station and asked for my computer. I went back to my room, booted up my computer and read the Bible a bit. At 7:15-20, Bronek brought the broom to the room, and I swept the floor, as is the custom every morning except for Sunday. After I was finished sweeping, Bronek mopped the floor. At about 7:40-5 we ate breakfast in the dining room, and then most of the other guys went out for the morning walk. I didn't go. I felt like staying in this morning, enjoying the quiet while the other guys were out, going to the bathroom and drinking my second coffee. I then read a bit of the van Gogh book that I borrowed from Marcin, and a bit more of the Bible. I went to the therapy room from 11 to around 12:30, where I had a chance to get on the internet. I looked at 'confirmation bias,' 'ellen lacter' some more and persuasive writing...I have some articles that I need to print. I think that I will ask Brian to do some printing for me...

I went to the English class at 1:30. Today was much better than the other two times. I started the class with the alphabet, and then I relaxed into the lesson, whereas before I was a bit anxious. Also, before I was pushing the class a bit too much; I didn't take into account the nature of the students, the fact that they are all 'insane' and on a lot of drugs... I tried to deal with the students individually within the context of leading the class in a discussion of the material. I felt good at the end of the class, and I think that [Maria] was happy as well. Praise God.

Tomek started surprising me today with Pawel. He stopped 'hating' him, and he started talking to him and 'loving' him. I was blown away when I first sa[w] this; it is such a huge improvement. Thank you Father. Continue to lead me, to help me to plant the seeds of your word, of your truth into those around me. Continue to tend my garden, to cultivate the fruits of the Spirit within me. Your will be done....Father, please deliver my family unto me. Put us back together. Make us whole once again. Lord please remember that my daughter is being hurt. Father, I trust in you. Show me your path. In Jesus' name.

I wanted to not take Risperdal today, but I am leery of being sneaky. I don't want to get caught first of all. Second of all, I don't want to lie, and I am not sure what I would do if I was asked, for example by the doctor, if I have been taking my pills. Third, though I hate drugs and the effects of Risperdal, I can fight through it, and I can work. Though I would much rather have Concerta or nothing at all, I feel good once I get going, and I feel like I am getting some pretty good stuff onto paper. I could be much more productive under different circumstances, but I have to learn how to fight, how to be productive no matter what the conditions are. I have to learn how to operate under any conditions because it is not always going to be me who is in charge of the conditions. I have to use what I am given, what I am allotted. I have to adjust. I need to hold my daughter in my arms. I need to dance with my wife and our daughter. I need to be a daddy again. In Jesus' name...

Today I got a letter from the prosecutor in Szczecin, the prosecutor who is supposedly supervising the prosecutor in Stargard Szczecinski. She wrote that she received my last letter, that I did not present her with any evidence that changes her mind, that I do not have any evidence to support my child abuse allegations, that there will be no action on the part of the prosecution in response to my allegations."

Paweł was an interesting person, and I enjoyed getting to know him. I thought of him like he was my patient, and I tried to get to the bottom of what was going on with him. He was not given a voice at all, and he was denied attention. Even the Catholic priest who visited from time to time shunned him and wanted nothing to do with him. When he acted out, they force-fed him more medication just to quiet him down. One of my favorite things to do with him was to give him blank paper and a pen and see what he would do (see Appendix 36). To me, he appeared to be just a traumatized child who was now an adult. Nobody was trying to understand him; rather, their only answer was to isolate and medicate him.

Journal Entry, December 29, 2012
"It's almost 11:30 p.m., and at that time I have to give my laptop to the nurse's station for the night. I am listening to 'Spoon' by Dave Matthews, from his 1998 Before these Crowded Streets CD. I just closed my file that is the beginning of my book on my family situation, prison, ...I have about 7000 words on paper. The words are not the problem. I can get hundreds of thousands down. The difficult part is deciding what to put in and what to leave out, deciding how much detail to include. I need some examples; unfortunately, therapy was cancelled today and I had no chance to get on a computer.

I have so much to do. However, today was not a very productive day. I spent a lot of time with Tomek and Pawel this morning. Tomek is really doing well with Pawel; he has switched, like Agata, from hating him to 'loving him.' He sees Pawel as a victim now and not as a gay, and he sees him as a strong man and not just as a lunatic. Lord help me to plant seeds. Help me to see your path, your will....

Anyway, I prayed and I did some thinking today. I tried to relax my brain a bit, in the expectation that it would pay off with writing tonight and tomorrow. And I believe it was necessary. I am totally reliant upon God, for I am already defeated. Two years....Father, I trust in you. Then around dinner time, I started playing Hogs of War, and I got stuck on that mind numbing game for an hour or so. I went out for a walk this morning but not this evening. I went to the sport room and played some volleyball, soccer and shot some hoops. Father lead me.....I am drifting, and I have to get my computer in so I don't have any problems later on. Praise God."

Journal Entry, December 30, 2012
"Today I worked on a letter. I ended up sending it to the Dodd Research Center at UCONN. I wrote all day, first writing a draft, by hand, and then copying it over again, so that it is as perfect as possible. I have the first draft, and I plan on writing a new letter tomorrow off of it. I need to work more on the computer paper, on the book. But it is all working on the book, because writing exercises the process of thinking, of working out problems, of figuring out how to explain things to different people. So, any writing that I do is productive. It's just not productive enough because my girls are still being hurt.

Anyway, I have my work cut out for me for New Year's Eve and New Year's Day. 2013 is around the corner; the last time that I held Adelle in my arms was in late 2010. Oh my God, save us for your mercy's sake, so that they may know that it is your hand. Send me a sign so that I know that you favor me. Deliver my family unto me. ...

Other than working today, I hung out with Tomek and Pawel a bit. But I really didn't have time to do much else other than to write and rewrite the letter. Tomorrow I should have the opportunity to get back on the internet.

'And we know that all things work together for good to them who love God, to them who are called according to his purpose. For whom he did foreknow, he also did predestinate to be conformed to the image of his Son, that he might be the firstborn among many brethren...' Romans 8:28-29

Lord, how am I supposed to do this? How am I supposed to write with my brain on Risperdal? Psalm 38:10 'My heart panteth, my strength faileth me: as for the light of my eyes, it is also gone from me.'

Lead me, direct me, work through me, strengthen and fortify me, fill me with your Spirit, with wisdom, with your words. Lord, I am empty and desolate. I don't know which way to go. I don't know whether to go or not to go. I don't know what 'go' means anymore. I only know that I love the Lord, that the Lord has said that he will direct me and keep me, that he will deliver us, that he will put me and my family back together again. I want to write, but my strength fails me. I feel downtrodden because my strength fails me, because I do not have the energy or the brain waves that are necessary to put a book together.

I have to force my way forward, but I don't even know which way is forward. I don't know what to put down onto paper. I will incorporate the letter that I wrote to Dodd Center tomorrow in the book. I will begin to use the outlines that I have prepared. Lord, settle my heart and my path. Settle my nerves and my mind. Direct my fingers and my tongue. Direct me.

John 10:38 .... the Father is in me, and I in him

John 12:26 ...if any man serve me, him will my Father honor.

MT 21:22 ...and all things that ye shall ask in prayer, believing, ye shall receive

John 14:14 If ye shall ask anything in my name, I will do it

John 16:23 ...whatsoever ye shall ask the Father in my name, he will give it you.

John 17:21 That they all may be one: as thou, Father, art in me, and I in thee, that they also may be one in us: that the world may believe that thou hast sent me.

Mark 11:22 ....HAVE FAITH IN GOD

Father, fill me with the living water. Fill me with your Spirit, the Spirit of your Son. Fill me Father, for I am empty. It is good that I am empty, so that I can be full of only your Spirit, with no filler whatsoever. Father, I trust in you. I trust in you. Deliver my family from this evil. Deliver us Father. Your will be done. In Jesus' name, Amen."

Journal Entry, December 31, 2012

"It is ten minutes until 2013. I am in hell. I haven't seen my family since 2010. And ritual abuse is still destroying everything that I care about. Everything. Oh my God. I don't have any words. What am I supposed to do? I am like a broken record, saying the same [expletive] things over and [expletive] over again, like a fool. A [expletive] fool. A tool. A piece of nothing. A broken, desolate, piece of nothing. A pile of empty flesh and bones. Garbage. Absolutely nothing. Oh my God. What is to become of me? What is to become of my family? Two years. My little girl will be six years old soon. And I am in a maximum security psychiatric hospital, my wife has Dissociative Identity Disorder and Stockholm Syndrome, etc...., you know just the normal, regular [expletive]. And my daughter is being molested and her mind is being tortured. Her mind is being [expletive] wrecked on my watch. I am her father and there is nothing that I can do. I can do nothing and therefore I am nothing. I am nothing.

Father, I hate this life. I hate this life that you've given me. [Expletive] this life that you've given me. I hate this [expletive] life that you've given me. I am just rambling, going on and on. I am obviously broken. I am obviously a bit frustrated. I am obviously just talking to myself, saying the same [expletive] things that I said a [expletive] year ago. A year has passed and nothing has changed except that I moved from prison to an insane asylum. From prison to an insane asylum. Thank you Father. You lifted me up to the heavens. I saw paradise on earth, and then you drop kicked my ass, you took me apart at the seams sent my pieces all over the place, this way and that. And the pieces of me keep getting stretched and spread more and more and more and more. Two years without all that matters to me. Well, that's not true, now what did matter to me doesn't exist. It only exists in memory, which is nothing but a dream because it is not true anymore. Now I care about your will, about the will of the living God, about telling people about the only truth I've known in this life, about all that is real, all that is worth living for.

The fireworks are going off outside the window. I can hear them. Yeah, it is 2013. What are you people celebrating for? Please Father, come and strengthen me. Fill me for I am but a shell. An empty shell that is nothing, can be nothing except it be done by you. Show me your will. Fill me Lord. Deliver my family. I do not ask you for much. Please just get my two girls out of this hell. Praise God. Praise God.

All that is real destroyed. All that is precious taken and trampled, crushed, shat upon. Everything. Adelle Avery Bryson. Father, I surrender. I surrender. Just show me a sign to show me that you favor me. Do you favor me? What is this? It's all gone. All of it. Everything that I hoped for. I am so numb, so dead inside. My girls breathe and I can do nothing. Father, I trust in you with all of my heart. Guide me. Lead me. Beat me into submission. Just deliver those two people. In Jesus' name, amen."

Journal Entry, January 1, 2013

"I was thinking last night about a lot of things. Risperdal was one of those things, probably the least important. It is like pouring rubber cement into your head. You can feel it seizing up, tightening; you can feel the pathways from one segment getting blocked off from the others. It happens rather slowly, so as not to alarm the average person. The average person has no idea what is going on in their head anyway, no reason to be concerned. The average person feels only a little tightness. I feel my brain tightening off. I see my memory fading away, my ability to critical think disappearing. I didn't take Risperdal last night.

The sunrise is right outside of my window every morning. It is beautiful. The sun starts below the horizon, rising slowly until it is completely above the horizon. The panorama outside the window is heavenly, well not quite heavenly, but quite nice. Father, thank you for your promise. Thank you for your Son. Thank you for delivering my family. In Jesus' name.

If I write a book, or something, how are they going to know that God is the cause of saving my family? Not that I can write a book or do much of anything, but what if…? Psalm 50:15 'Call on me in the day of trouble: I will deliver thee, and thou shalt glorify me.' When is the day of trouble? When are you going to deliver me/us? How do I glorify you from in here? How do I glorify you when my family has been so utterly destroyed? How? How??

Do I write with my hand and send off a letter or letters, or do I write on the computer and put together one 'big bomb?' Is writing a letter by hand a waste of time? Is it procrastination, a waste of my limited resources, number one being time? What kind of book do I need to write in order to be persuasive, in order for people to read and understand my situation? Lord lead me.

Tomek said yesterday (he said a lot of things, but for example): 'Mary is all the time virgin. Between me and God is Jesus Christ. Between me and Jesus Christ is Mary.' I said 'but Tomek, there is nothing between you and Jesus Christ. Jesus Christ is your direct connect to God, and all that you have to do is follow his commandments….'

'No,' he replied; 'I do need Mary. She helps me. She has 'revelated.' She is all the time virgin…' 'But Tomek,' I replied, 'she is not a virgin. She was a virgin when she got pregnant with Jesus and when she gave birth to Jesus, but after that she was Joseph's wife, and they had other children, etc. She lived a normal life after she gave birth to Jesus. There is nothing special about her other than that she gave birth to Jesus.' 'What you think that it is impossible for God to make Mary a virgin?' 'No Tomek, nothing is impossible for God.'

He looked at me as if he had won the argument. 'But Tomek, what is the definition of virgin? And why does it matter if Mary remained a virgin for her entire life? Why do you think that God cares? It's also possible for God to make Mary's nose green, for example, but that doesn't mean that he did it. He didn't, just as he didn't make Mary the 'all the time virgin.' Mary was with Joseph, and they had children. They lived 'normal' lives, if there is such a thing, with Jesus as their son.' I can see the lies in Tomek's eyes. I can see his mind locked up, bound with these lies. Lies cause bondage; those who follow lies, even if they believe those lies to be truth are in bondage.

Tomek asked me if I think about death, saying that he thinks about his death all of the time. He said that he would die for Mary. He said that he will die believing that Mary is the 'all the time virgin.' The power of the lie. The power of the delusion. Once you have made a conclusion, it does all that it can to hold on. It is one of the most difficult things to relinquish.

I am now listening to Jack Johnson. It is five after eleven.... 'In Between Dreams'

'If I was in your position, I'd put down all my ammunition and wonder why it'd taken me so long'

I found an audio file with Adelle and Agata singing 'Make me feel....' Oh to hear that little angel's voice is like being in heaven. Except this is not heaven, but rather, this is hell. Two years. Two years.

I am trying to plan tomorrow. I wrote one letter to the family court reminding them of the situation. They will read, maybe, and think or say, 'he is crazy; he is at ROPS, so therefore he is crazy.' I also wrote that I need a visit, or rather visits, with Adelle. It's been two years. Two years. How many times can I write two years?

Tomorrow I am going to finish a couple of letters by hand and continue working on the book. The book. What is the book? Am I supposed to be writing a book, or am I supposed to only be reading The Book? Lord, what is it that you want/need me to do? Once I have the book written, what do I do with it then? I suppose that even asking that question is just an act of procrastination, a complete waste of a thought. Of course the answer is that I will figure that out then. Or rather, God will reveal that answer to me also. What do I do now?

Lord lead my mind, my fingers, my tongue. Lord help me to get this story down onto paper. I just want to die. Why live? Lord you have me. This is a nothing life. I am nothing. Life is nothing. Love is nothing. My family is nothing. You've made me nothing. You've taken that perfect little child, the one who calls me daddy. Two of our years stolen from us, and nothing. Nothing. I don't even think that I have a daughter. It was just a dream a while ago. This is reality. Hell is reality. There is no and was no other reality. Why would there be? I was never a dad. That is just delusion.

Agata was never sick; we never thought that she had Borderline Personality Disorder. Just delusion, of course. I was never trying to get her help. I was beating her like she deserved to be beaten, smackin' her hard like I always did, like every man should. I smacked her and then I smacked her some more. I like smackin' her. It's one of my favorite things to do as a matter of fact. Smack smack. Oh you think it's cause of the [expletive] crack? No, you don't know me. I've always been a beater of the fairer sex. I just love it. My favorite things to do are raise my daughter, read, learn and smack any woman that I can get my hands on. Oh, I like other things like kayaking and teaching. But smackin is the bestest. Thank you Jesus. Praise the Lord. Put us back together. I'm going crazy and it's all because of you."

Journal Entry, January 2, 2013

"It is not for me to worry about what I write, or to worry about how I will 'sell' a book. Yes, I do believe that I need to keep working, but what I really need to do is to make sure that I am right with God, which is my duty. If I am right with God, then he will do the rest, for he will fill me with his Spirit to the brim, without measure. And the Spirit of God can move mountains; the spirit of Iain cannot do anything, which is why I must eradicate that spirit, drive it out into the dark....

It is almost 11:30, so I will have to give my computer to the nurse very soon. I didn't write much today, but I did a lot of planning, meditating and praying. I am going to write a few letters tomorrow. I have to write to a few guys from prison. I also want to finally send a letter to Lacter. And I want to send letters to other people to ask for help, for information....etc., like Orsinger. Today, I had Polish class with [Maria], I walked and talked with James, I went to sport therapy and played some ping pong."

Journal Entry, January 3, 2013

"Today it was difficult to get going. I couldn't work, or rather I couldn't get anything onto paper. When I tried to write letters, I couldn't do more than just stare at the paper and feel impotent. I did get some good meditating done, though it was on the subject of God and not on the subject of my family or ritual abuse. I feel drawn to write about the path to God, and maybe that is God talking to me and telling me that I am not supposed to work on anything else. These working conditions are far from ideal. I can barely get on the internet, so research is not possible. How do I write without research? I suppose that the only book that I really need is the Bible, yet it is always good to know what has been written, what others believe....

The more information that you have, that you can attain, that is available, the better. Information is power. Anyway, I only got onto the computer for about thirty minutes today because there were too many people at therapy. So, I really didn't get anything of substance done. I looked up Orsinger, and he is a family attorney from Texas. I found another ritual abuse website. I am still at the stage of 'what do I do, what do I focus on, what do I write about, who do I write to?'

I have to focus on God, on becoming perfect so that I can have faith in God, so that whatever I ask will be answered. Other than that, I have to take it slow in here, though taking it slow is certainly not my style. I have to write to a few people here and there. I have to put these things that I am writing onto the computer so that I have records, so that my writing is evolving, so that I can make changes here and there rather than having to write and rewrite by hand for everything that I do.

Mark 11:24 '....whatsoever things you desire, when you pray, believe that you will have them, and you will have them.'

Ok, now how do I tell people this or things like this, how do I teach people when I am locked in an insane asylum? I have had my family stolen from me. At the moment, I do not have anything that I desire. Now, granted I do believe that these things will be given to me. Well, I suppose that faith is working toward a goal even though you cannot see it. I have to keep going, keep plugging ahead. I have to keep praying, keep letting the Lord mold me and make me his vessel.

Lord mold me, form me, do it quickly for I cannot do this much longer. Or rather, it is adelle that cannot do this any longer. Lord, for thy mercies sake, so that they know that you did it.....Lord, what is the holdup. Lord, lead me into righteousness, teach me your ways, fill me with wisdom and understanding, keep my steps on the straight and narrow path. ...In Jesus' name I pray.

Tonight I am listening to radiohead 'hail to the thief' and I am a bit frustrated that I didn't get anything written today. I am a bit frustrated by these people's attempts to shut off my brain even though they do not and cannot know if there is anything wrong. They don't talk to me, they have no idea what it is that I am thinking. All that they know is that the court ordered me here, that the court psychiatrists said that I am insane in the membrane because I believe that my daughter is being abused. Oh Lord, this is the definition of Kafkaesque. O Lord, I trust in you, for I see all too clearly how futile my efforts are. Lord, strengthen me and lead me. Prod me and pummel me into shape. Lift me up in the palm of your hand."

Journal Entry, January 4, 2013

"I began writing a letter today on the computer. It is not a book, but a letter. A letter to explain the basics as much as I think is necessary so that those reading will completely understand the situation. We will see how long it is. Now, as of today, I am just starting on the fifth page. I think that I will get five more tomorrow, and maybe that will be the end. We will see. Then I have to figure out how to send it out. I will have to ask about the printer on Monday, and I will have to see what they see here. Either way, that will not work because of how many copies I need. I will have to ask Brian or somebody else to make copies for me. I will cross that hurdle later. For now I just have to write. Thank you Father for putting the words in my mouth, for guiding my fingers on the keyboard with your Spirit.

I got to do some research today, and I found many more experts on ritual abuse, who I am looking forward to contacting. It feels good to see that these people exist, that there are resources out there in the world...

The doctor increased my Risperdal dose today to one and a half milligrams. And I took it because it was too much in my mouth to put into the non-taking position. Or rather, I was nervous. Tomorrow I will have to figure out something else, as there is just no way that I can take that crap. I began teaching Pawel the alphabet today. Lord lead me onto your path. Guide my every step. Deliver my girls. In Jesus' name."

Journal Entry, January 5, 2013

"It is Saturday morning. I am drinking inka and waiting for them to call that breakfast is ready. I am ready to work today, ready to step into the nightmare world of my reality, of my family's reality. Ritual abuse. Something so unthinkable that most people have never heard of it, and when you mention the term, they cannot even begin to comprehend that it exists or can exist. Just saying 'ritual abuse' elicits disbelief. What the hell is that? Did you just make that up? I don't know about 'ritual abuse.' It sounds horrible. I'm sure that it doesn't exist; I've never seen it on tv.

I just finished working on 'letter,' an eleven page letter explaining the situation. I started with the fact that my daughter is being abused, and the fact that I am being 'treated' because I believe that she is being abused. I then went through, step by step, from Agata's signs of psychological disorder and Adelle's signs of serious abuse to December 2010 to April 2011 to present. I am now considering what I should do with this letter. I will continue to revise it over the course of tomorrow. I am thinking that maybe I should send it to David Yalof, though I have not spoken to him in ten years, for revisions. He is one person I know who I believe in his ability to edit, to correct, to point my writing in the right direction.

First I would have to get permission to use e-mail. I am thinking about doing that on Monday. I either have to use e-mail, or I have to send out a lot of letters. My argument on the subject is that I can easily get the same things accomplished with either e-mail or regular mail. However, the financial cost of regular mail would be enormous, and I would have to use a printer. We will see. I am also thinking about writing some handwritten letters to send off on Monday, as I do not think that everybody should be the recipient of the eleven page letter. It is quite difficult for me to describe the situation in less than eleven pages. Sure I could cut it down by a bit, and we will see about that tomorrow. However, there are certain things that have to be said, certain things that people have to understand in order to be able to grasp the nature of the situation in general. I cannot just say 'my daughter is being abused and I am in a psychiatric hospital...' I believe that I have to provide some background and some kind of chain of events.

Anyway, God will provide the answers. I will not worry over things that I have no power to control, and I have no power to control anything, and therefore should not worry about anything. Or rather, I should worry about one thing, and that is to make sure that I am right with God. I should fear him and make certain that I am perfect in his eyes. I should search my heart each and every day to ensure that I am reacting to his direction, to the molding of his hands.

'Beloved, if our heart condemn us not, then have we confidence toward God. And whatever we ask, we receive of him, because we keep his commandments, and do those things that are pleasing in his sight' (I John 3:21-22).

Tomek got tired of Pawel. He doesn't know how to deal with him, and he has separated himself, pushing Pawel away. Pawel is freaking out. The withdrawal of Tomek's love and affection has devastated him. He can hardly take it; yesterday he was talking about suicide. The man has been hurt in ways that are unthinkable. Or rather, I can think of them. I know too well how the man has been hurt. It is not so difficult when you know that for every effect there is a cause or causes. The issue is that Tomek has also been hurt, yet he wants to think that he has not been hurt. He wants to believe that he is hard, that he is tough, that his Mary will answer his prayers...

Lord I pray for my friends. I pray that you shine your light through me, and that you help me to show them you. I pray Father that your will be done, that you guide me and lead me on your path, that you lift me up above and out of the snares of my enemies. I pray that you cradle me in your hand. I pray that you deliver my family unto me, that you reunite us and make us whole once again. I pray Lord and I pray. I trust in you....Thank you Father. All praise to you. In Jesus' name I pray, amen."

Journal Entry, January 7, 2013

"It was snowing for most of the morning, big juicy flakes, the kind that land on your face and make it wet. I went out for a walk this morning. It was quiet and peaceful, the snow falling. Beautiful. I spent the day writing, both on the computer and on paper. I wrote 7 pages of a letter that will be about 8 pages by hand, which I plan on sending tomorrow. I have quite a few letters to send, and I am hoping that I can figure out a way this week to be able to use the computer/printer, or maybe to use e-mail. It doesn't make sense to have to write everything out by hand. It is tedious and time consuming, and really for no reason. I will try to approach the doctor about this tomorrow or the next day.

John S called this evening. It was good to speak to him... he didn't ask what he can do to help. He is busy with his own world and his own depression, barely making it from day to day. What friends I have....Well, they are just people. I love them anyway, and I am just glad and fortunate to have God on my side.

I ended up having to take my pills tonight, one and a half mg of Risperdal. Well, I shouldn't say that I had to take the pills, but that I chose to because the 'hide in the lip' trick did not happen smoothly. I cannot risk any problems. However, I could have easily readjusted today. I am just too nervous about it. I don't need to worry about it anyway, for I am in God's hands. Those drugs are like poison, and I really detest putting them into my body. I pray to God, in Jesus' name that this situation is put to an end, that I am delivered from this, that my family is delivered from the ritual abuse, that I am put into a position to glorify God, to be a light unto the people, unto God's lost children. Praise God.

Father, please guide me and direct me, lift me up into the palm of your hand. Shine your grace upon my face. Deliver me, deliver us for thy mercy's sake. Thank you Father. All praise to you. Thank you for putting little Adelle into my arms, for reuniting my family, for putting the three of us together to dance to 'up up and away.' Thank you Father. Thank you Father for guiding my tongue and my mind, my pen and my fingers. Thank you for everything Father. Thank you for filling me with your wisdom and understanding, the Holy Spirit. Thank you for pouring the Spirit onto me in full force, for filling my empty shell with nothing but the Spirit. Thank you Father.

All praise to you. Thank you for resting my mind tonight as I sleep, for helping me to wake up refreshed, prepared for the day, in fear of you. Thank you for speaking to me, for revealing your plan and your words through dreams and visions. Thank you Father for all of this. Thank you for surrounding Adelle and Agata with your angels. Thank you for empowering them, for strengthening them, for helping them to hold on. Thank you for delivering them unto me, for making us whole again. Father, your will be done. In Jesus' name, Amen."

Journal Entry, January 7, 2013

"Father, I am done. I don't want anything. I don't want anything at all. I am empty and desolate. I spent the day finishing a letter, which I had to write by hand. I fear that it is way too long, eight pages, yet I don't know how to make it any shorter without cutting out vital pieces of information. I will send one of the letters and see what happens. I began writing a shorter version tonight, but I couldn't write. I kept making mistakes; I kept crying. I kept realizing how weak I am, how I am just doing the same screaming into the abyss that I was doing two years ago. I kept realizing how I need God to do this. I kept realizing that I am completely blown away by this, that I do not have a chance. I kept realizing that I have been doing this for more than two years...

English class went well today. I felt good about it. What I did was to keep the class talking the whole time, asking each other questions and answering each other. [Maria] is hard to read, but I think that she was pleased with the class today as well. Doing everything is so difficult nowadays. I have taken the Risperdal for the past two days. Tomorrow I will try to limit my dosage to one half milligram, I think. I don't know the answer to that problem. Father, please guide my steps. Father please deliver my family. Please do so now before I fall into the pit. I am falling into the pit Father. I can do nothing. I am nothing. I am just an empty shell for you to fill up. Father, fill me up with your Spirit. Fill me with your wisdom and understanding. Guide my paths. Make me shine as your light unto this wicked world.

'There's only one road to freedom...'(Ben Harper), and I know the road. Lord, put me in a position to tell others about the road. In Jesus' name. Amen."

Journal Entry, January 8, 2013

"I continued working on my letters today. I am sending a copy of the four page letter that I've drafted to Brian; he is going to read it and tell me what he thinks. He is also going to send it to some places in the U.S. He asked me, or rather, it was his idea. He said that he sent me a box on Friday. I asked him to print out a couple of articles for me today. I did some research on the computer today. I taught James some English. I did some meditating.

Last night I had a dream about tearing down religion. I had a dream about destroying all that is not God, about showing the light to people, showing people the one road to freedom. I woke up energized, like a heretic with a pen. I asked Tomek to ask the priest for a copy of the Catholic catechism for me; I cannot wait to have a copy of all of those lies, all of those lies that people love to believe that they believe that they should believe, all of those lies which keep people from knowing God. I will tear those lies apart, or rather, the Spirit of God that is within me will tear it apart and find a way to shed the Light upon the truth so that people can see what I see, which is the truth, which is God's word, which is Christ in you. Thank you Father.

Then, most of the day I spent in a Risperdal haze, not able to get much going. I did some thinking and some writing, made a couple of diagrams. I ended up taking Risperdal again tonight; I am not sure what to do about it. I really don't like taking it, and I don't like what I have to do in order to not take it. Though taking it is not so bad, it is bad, and it is a form of torture. Depriving my brain of its neurotransmitters. Lord, I trust in you. Lord, my faith is in you."

Journal Entry, January 9, 2013

"Tomorrow I need to write about the conversation that I had with Jacek Jakiniak yesterday and the conversation that I had with Kasia, another therapist, yesterday. Today I got two letters off. One was an eight page letter and one a four page letter. I feel pretty good about the letters that I am writing, but I am thinking more and more that it is the 'book' that is important at this point. The letters are really just a part of the book, so it is good exercise. But what I've got to do is to organize more, to plot a course and then execute that course. I need a finished product. Tomorrow I am sending a letter to Brian and another letter to England. Brian said that he can send out the letter to places in the U.S. I gave him seven addresses.

I had Polish with [Maria] today. We started to read something that she had printed, and then she asked me about my situation again. I think that she just wanted to talk to me, that she used the Polish class as an opportunity to get me alone so that we could talk. We talked and talked some more. Then she started thinking and she said 'I don't know if I should say anything.' I felt bad. She then said 'I don't think that you are crazy. I even talked to my husband about you. I think that your problem has a lot to do with the language problem. People don't understand you. I don't know what I can do for you. I work here. I cannot do much. You have to stay strong. Stay strong Iain.' My eyes started to well up. I got a heavy emotion in my entire being. Those words coming out of her mouth made my day, my week, my year thus far. I will finish writing my journal entries tomorrow.
Lord fill me up. Lord I trust in you."

Journal Entry, January 10, 2013

"I feel like a failure, like a bum when I cannot write. Or is it just that I think that I cannot write? Are my expectations out of line? What do I expect to be able to accomplish in one day, in one week? What is it that I am trying to accomplish? What is it that I need to accomplish? What I need to do is to make myself

perfect in the eyes of God. When that happens, then I John 3:24. My head is so blocked with Risperdal. My dopamine and serotonin levels are depleted. Why do I say the same [expletive] things over and over? Everybody knows that I am taking these drugs. Nobody cares. Just keep plowing ahead. Why do I feel like I can't?

Yesterday [Maria] told me that she thinks that I should ask my parents for help. I asked her what help she had in mind, telling her that I don't want money and I don't need any other support, and she told me that maybe my parents could help to get me out of this country.

I called my mother today, this evening. I think that it was a mistake, but maybe not. I told her that I forgive her. I told her that she doesn't know what she's talking about, that she needs to learn to keep her mouth shut when she doesn't know what she's talking about. She said that she acts based upon her beliefs. I told her that she has no basis upon which to believe anything, that she is just being clamorous. I can see the look on her face, the contorted, tense, lips all scrunched up. 'I don't live in the same reality as you do,' she said. She is such a foolish woman, so lost, so miserable, and she thinks that I would want to be anywhere close to her reality. O my God, deliver us for thy mercy's sake. Father I am in your arms. I am so completely depleted. I am so completely alone. I am so completely nothing."

Journal Entry, January 11, 2013

"Write a narrative like a string of pearls, each pearl being a different situation. Tied together with a narrative, but not just one line, but a bunch of scenes that are linked. My head hurts so [expletive] bad. I didn't get any work done again today. It is the second day on two milligrams of Risperdal, and my head is stuffed like a dead pig. My head hurts like I had a pen jabbed in my nose and my frontal lobe lobotomized. Chemical lobotomy....Legal in 2013 for the government to say that you must have your head turned off because you need 'treatment.' Treatment because I believe that my daughter is being abused and have no evidence, because the 'evidence' is not in my favor, because I say 'ritual abuse' and these people cannot even begin to comprehend what it is that I said. Lord, I am still working, but I don't know what to do or what to write."

Journal Entry, January 12, 2013

"It seems to snow about every other day here in Starogard Gdanski. It is beautiful. It should snow almost every day in the winter. Today I went to the sport room and shot some hoops in the morning. Then I went to bridge, though I didn't want to. I just feel or rather felt today like I had to. I am not sure how to gracefully get out of it. I really hate 'wasting' time playing cards. The only reason to play is for political reasons in that there are only a couple of people that play. If I play, then I can be or would be one of those few people and I get to sit with the people from occupational therapy and talk...etc. I just don't think that sitting and playing cards for hours is my cup of tea, per se.

After lunch, I began writing, thinking, and brainstorming. I rewrote a letter by hand, which I've found to be a great revision exercise though a bit tedious. I have to figure out how to do it all on the computer. I have to figure out how to see the entire work in my head again. I have to figure out how get past the effects of the drug that I am being forced to take. I have to decide whether I will continue to take the drug or whether I will not swallow it.

I am not sure what to do. I think it is better if I can take it, but that I know and keep track of the effects, if I can minimize the effects, if I can work through the effects, if I can be productive, if I can learn from the effects, if I can become stronger from the psychological torture rather than weaker or even completely impotent. Lord, lead me to the rock that is higher than I. Praise God. Pass my family. In Jesus' name. Amen."

Journal Entry, January 13, 2013

"I worked on a handwritten letter today. I am sending two out tomorrow, one to UK and one to Holland. I spent some time organizing the book, though not enough time. Tomorrow I have to spend more time, and I have to plan time daily. Just writing 'write' on my list of things to do is not sufficient. I have to set

specific times for sitting in front of the computer, and I have to stick to those times. I have to work and rework, organize and cut, chop and paste. I have to wheel and deal this story; I have to put this together, and I have to do so now. I have to find a groove. I have to get out of the Risperdal funk. I have to find my memory and my organizing skills. I have to be perfect for the Lord. I have to have the help of God, or I don't have a chance.

'My help cometh from the Lord, which made heaven and earth.' Psalm 121:2

'Help me, O Lord my God: O save me according to thy mercy; That they may know that this is thy hand; that thou Lord hast done it.' Psalm 109:26-27

Today I had an English lesson with James and Tomek and I read some of the Bible. It is quite difficult dealing with Tomek, who I am pretty certain has schizophrenia and 'delusions' of persecution. He thinks that people are listening to him. He thinks that he is being persecuted because he is Catholic. He misinterprets everything to fit into his delusional schematic. I am trying to figure out how I can minister unto him. I am not sure. The best way that I have found so far is to model behavior and thinking.

I talked to Brian for a while this evening. He is still very frustrated with his life, still very stuck. I am trying to give him some advice, but his unresolved issues make it very difficult for him to see good in his life. I need to find a way to get through to him, to show him what it is that I see. He is stuck in a bad trip, in a sense, and it is very difficult to get out of a bad trip. What has to happen is that your/his mode of perception has to be changed. He has to have different values for his inputs so that his outputs can be positive. He has to see all that is good instead of all that is bad. He has to channel his frustration into something positive. He has to get out of the funk that has been holding him back for so long. He has to find God. He needs to know the one living God, the God whose spirit lives inside those who follow his commandments.

Lord help me to know what it is that I can and should do to get through to him. Lord make me a light of your love, to shine upon my friends and family, upon all of your children. Lord, have mercy on me, shed your grace upon me, not for me only but so that I can be a witness of your greatness to all of your people. Lord, my wife and my daughter. I know that you haven't forgotten. Lord, deliver them unto me. In Jesus' name. Amen."

Journal Entry, January 15, 2013

"Today I sent a letter to TAG (Trauma and Abuse Group) in the UK. I worked on organizing some 'scenes' or pearls from the book. I went to occupational therapy and to sport therapy. I went to karaoke. I spoke to Brian for about an hour and a half on the phone. Brian is having trouble with his son, but not with his son. The problem is with Brian, and he knows that it is, which is a good start. He is having problems regulating his emotions, trouble stopping his natural reactions from happening. His automatic responses kick in, and he has no control over them; he cannot figure out how to stop the automated process from taking over, from just happening.

I was trying to explain to him the process that I found, that I discovered when dealing with my wife. I was trying to explain to him that the idea is to stop the cycle, stop the automated process early so that it doesn't play itself out. I talked about the 'bell curve.' I talked about learning to identify the thoughts that lead to the feelings/emotions that lead to the action, or to the response. The difficult part is putting my theory into practice, taking it out of the hypothetical and putting it into a real life situation. Just because something sounds good or even makes sense does not mean that it can be done, or that it will be easy to do it. Of course everything can be done, but 'doability' is another story. Is it 'possible' given the players that are involved who are living and operating in their given environments? The players have to change.

In this case, Brian must change, because it surely doesn't make sense to expect his eight year old son to change. Or rather, his eight year old son will change, but only in response to his changes. He must adapt himself to the situation, learn new ways of resolving the situation that do not lead to unwanted responses. He must learn that the 'path' that he is used to taking does not and will not work, that no matter how it feels or how much he wants to go down that path again, it is not going to work. I need to sit down and write more on this topic, for Brian, for others. I need to write it out, because I do understand it, understanding is only valuable when I can explain what it is that I understand to others, so that they too can understand what it is that I understand.

I need to figure out how to get my family's story onto paper, in the same vein as the other issue above. It doesn't matter what it is that I understand. What matters is that I can make other people understand what it is that I understand. It doesn't do any good to be cooped up inside of my head. I have to lay it down on paper like a coat of smooth paint. I have to 'algebraically' spell it out from the basics to the big picture. I have to paint a portrait with my words.

Lord, please guide my mind and my hand. Lord, please guide me in everything that I do. Lord, please deliver my family. Please fill me with wisdom and understanding, with the wisdom and understanding to know which way to go, to know what to say and to write, to know which steps to take at any given moment in time. Lead me down the path that you have chosen. Shine a light on that path so that I know that it is 'the' path. Help me to stay on that path. Help me to know the difference between that path and the other paths, the other paths that I may tend to wander onto, the other paths that may seem right to me, but in reality they are wrong and just a distraction/diversion from your path. Lord, I pray in Jesus' name. I pray Lord. Father please. Please my Father. In Jesus' name, Amen."

Journal Entry, January 16, 2013

"Today I wrote a letter to Izzy's Promise//RANS (Ritual Abuse Network Scotland). I will be sending the letter out tomorrow. I should be getting responses from a couple of the places that I wrote to in the US. Marshall Center and SMART. That is, if they are going to reply at all. We shall see. I pretty much stayed in today, reading and praying, writing a bit, thinking about the conversation I had with Brian yesterday, thinking about the conversation I had with Jakiniak yesterday, thinking about the conversation that I was going to have with [Maria] today. There was Bridge today, but I didn't want to go; I cannot be spending time with playing cards in my hands, in my mind.

The meeting with [Maria] went well today, though I have a difficult time reading her. I think, or rather I am pretty [expletive] sure, that I am simply thinking too much, that she isn't really thinking that much at all and I try to read too much into her. It is strange having to deal with everybody all the time when they are constantly assessing you to see how crazy you are, or maybe if you are crazy at all in the case of [Maria]. [Maria] didn't have her wedding ring on her finger; I asked her where it was, and she got embarrassed and told me that she left it at home.

I showed her the letter that I got today from Rzczecnik Obywatelskich [social worker] stating that there was nothing that they can do with my case until the court is done with me. I told her about the letter in regards to my wife's divorce petition, told her that I wrote a letter to the court telling them that I need to be in court on January 28. She asked me a couple of questions that make me think that she is not so smart, or that she is thinking that I am crazy now. 'Did you ever consider that your daughter is happier now?'

....And then the other questions that she asked told me that she knows nothing much about my situation, that she doesn't really listen, that she has a lot going on in her own life and doesn't have the time to focus upon mine. 'So, you are saying that your wife is crazy? Your wife should be here.' 'yes' I replied, 'but I wouldn't put her in a place like this. I want her to get help....' I told her that I am talking to Brian almost daily, that he is helping me with some things, that I am trying to help him with some of his situations, that it is easier and probably better for me to stick to his issues and stay away from my own. My issues are too difficult to understand, I explained. If I talk only about his issues, then I can get the point across that I am not crazy, but that I know what I am talking about.

Lord, deliver my family. Make us whole, put us back together again. In Jesus' name, Amen."

Journal Entry, January 17, 2013

"Today I got a call back in response to one of my letters. The woman, Ruth Kerritan from the Willows Center in UK told me that she believes me, that she doesn't think that I am mentally ill. She told me that

I have to convince them that I[am] not bothered by the 'situation' I am espousing. I have to 'act,' she told me. I have to let them think that the Risperdal is working, that my thoughts have been disconnected, and that I am not a danger because I am not dwelling upon delusion. 'I know that you're not mad' she told me. She told me to contact survivorship.org in the US. She said that they have more resources to help in this situation, that her agency is geared towards counseling. She talked about mind control and programming, in reference to my wife. 'Programming' I said. These are the things that I cannot say, because then they just turn around and say that I am crazy. Nobody understands trauma based mind control. She told me to look at Allison Miller's book and to look at a book that Valerie Sinneson wrote that was published by Karmac Publishers....Massey is the editor."

Journal Entry, January 19, 2013

"Today I read Job one and a half times. I was reminded of the similarity between my situation and Job's situation. I am always complaining to God, saying 'what is wrong with me, what is it that I am doing wrong? I have offered my prayer unto you. I do not see you. The evil man prospers while I sit here and rot....' What I need to do is to do for God, not to sit and wallow in the mire in my sorrows. What I need to do is to praise God, to conform to his mold, which is his Son Christ Jesus. Romans 8:29. What I need to do is to be perfect, just like my Father. And I am trying so hard to be perfect. I don't know how to in all situations. For example, I can keep my eyes off of a woman, but how do I not think about her at all when I happen to see her? It is sort of an automatic reaction; it happens incredibly quick, and it is involuntary.

Or, for example, when Bronek says something crazy or gets in one of his attitudes, I sometimes have thoughts like 'you stupid....' Or other things. Sometimes I think that I have acquired tourettes over the past two years in prison/hospital. Two years in a prison/hospital when all that I want is to get my daughter evaluated for exposure to extreme trauma. I had better make myself perfect.

Lord, teach me how to submit to your molding. Search my heart and weed out the tares. Search my mind and eliminate the ungodly. Teach me to steer your course and only your course. Give me a sign Lord. Show me what exactly I can do for you. Show me Father. I want to be perfect in your eyes. I know that I am not. I know that I am not worthy. I know that I am nothing. Fill me with the Spirit of your Son. Fill me with all goodness; there is no room for anything else.

I have been trying to get moving forward with the writing. I don't know how. I don't know what to write. I cannot think. I simply have no brain left. Two milligrams of Risperdal and nothing remains. I cannot remember anything. I cannot even plan an English lesson. I feel like a moron. I feel so depleted, so empty that I don't know what to do. A feeling of absolute worthlessness, helplessness, distress. Distress because my capacity to use my brain has been so greatly diminished that I might as well not have a brain. The only consolation is that taking away the pills will lead to me having my brain back again.

How can these people give such drugs to me on a mandatory basis? How can they keep me physically and psychologically locked up? What is torture if this is not torture? Bad question: the answer is that this is torture. It is control of my mind, dismantling my computer.

Lord, I trust in you to deliver me, to deliver us, my family. Lord, purify me for your will. Your will is the only will that matters. Just let me know what your will is so that I can get there. Praise God."

Journal Entry, January 20, 2013

"I had a dream last night that my mother was driving me to work. My work was to play the saxophone. We were riding in the car, headed to where I was supposed to play the saxophone and I realized that my saxophone was in my car. Because we were riding in my mother's car and not in my car, I did not have my saxophone. However, I do not know if this was true or untrue; I had the feeling the entire time that I just didn't want to go to work, and that I had just thought of a 'good' reason to avoid work. I didn't really know where my saxophone was, or if I could 'work' without it or not. I just decided that I did not have my car and therefore I also did not have my saxophone, and that therefore I couldn't work. I even remember telling my mom that I could only use my saxophone, that there was no way that I could use a different one.

'Turn around and go home mom. There is no reason to take me there when I cannot do anything.' A feeling of dread, anxiety and weakness went through my body, a lot like when I used to have Agata call work for me when I didn't want to go, or when I felt that I could not go. I was off the hook, but at the same time, I was not off of the hook because I knew in my heart that I was just manufacturing excuses.

When I woke up this morning, I had this dream stuck in my head. The first thing that I thought of was how I use Risperdal as an excuse not to write. 'It is so difficult. My head doesn't work......' Blah blah and more blah. Complain complain and get nothing done. Yes, they have given me Risperdal, which is designed and administered to disconnect my thoughts. We all know that. Where should we, or rather I, go from there? The answer is that I have to plow forward; I have to connect my thoughts and put them onto paper. I have to. Anything else is just weakness. Anything else is just ridiculous. A little Risperdal is going to take me out of the game? I don't think so.

Today, I started writing some more. I am working, trying to get things down on paper, trying to see a bigger picture, trying to see how I can fit the pieces of the puzzle together. I also copied a letter by hand, which I am going to send to Jenn W. I don't know why, as I have sent her many letters with no response. I guess I think that this new letter is better, that it is worth trying, that the more people that I can keep talking to the better.

Lord, my trust is in you. Lord, I am waiting on you, I am lying in your hands. Thank you for guiding me, for directing me, for molding me into your Son's image, for filling me with your wisdom and understanding. Thank you Father. Praise your name. All praise and glory to you. Please continue to speak to me, to lead me, to nudge me. Please Father, make me perfect. Your will be done....In Jesus' name. Amen.

Tomorrow is Monday, the beginning of another week. I am going to work on some letters this week. Brian should get the letter that I sent to him, we have to edit it together, I want to get his feedback, and then it has to be sent to places in the US. I have another opportunity to speak to the psychotherapist this week, maybe an opportunity to speak to the director...Father, I am in your hands. In the hands of God."

Journal Entry, January 21, 2013

"Tomorrow is Grandpa day. I don't like grandpa day. I am going to fast tomorrow. Lord how much more of this torture do we have to go through? How much more of this torture does Adelle have to go through? What can I do to become a perfect vessel of your will? The social worker told me today that there are no English books. [Maria] told me today that I have a meeting with the doctor, the psychotherapist, her....on Wednesday, that I need to go over the 'plan,' that....She didn't have much to say except that she didn't understand why I am here, and that she wants to 'help' me. Lord, I need you to help me. I wait on you and on your grace."

Journal Entry, January 22, 2013

"I had a difficult day today. Every day is difficult, but today was especially difficult. I began fasting today. I began writing a letter to nonstatetorture.org and I called Frank Damazio's church in order to get an address for him. I believe that I am honing in on the end. Or rather, I believe that my Father is honing me in on the end, according to his promise and his grace, in accordance to the answer of my prayers. I am going to go to bed, going to try to meditate a bit re: the letter that I will write to Frank Damazio tomorrow. Thank you Father. Praise your name."

Journal Entry, January 24, 2013

"Yesterday I went to watch a Dave Matthews concert in the therapy room. It was quite the spiritual experience. I felt the Spirit flowing through my veins the entire time. I could see the Spirit of God in my brother Dave. The guards came to take everybody back and Gerrard told the guard to wait because he and I were watching the end of the concert. I had a meeting with Jacek Jakiniak yesterday that I did not document. I didn't document anything yesterday. I didn't really get to the computer. Jacek and I pretty much just talked about my family: re: my parents and my brother and sister. He told me that next time *he wants to draw a family tree. I think that he is a good psychotherapist, which is a good thing for me. The language barrier and the fact that I was already diagnosed with a serious mental disorder worry me a bit. Well, I am not worried, per se, but rather my heart aches for my girls.*

Today I had a meeting with Dr. Setua and Jacek Jakiniak together. The doctor asked me if I tried to kill my father-in-law. I explained that I did not try or want to kill him, that I wanted attention, that I thought that I was being pragmatic, that I thought that my arrest would lead to a child abuse investigation. I told her that I did crash a car and I did have a hammer, but that my intention was not to kill him, that I did not try to hit him with the car and I did not hit or try to hit him with the hammer. She asked me if the situation started with a 'conflict' between my wife and I. I was a bit startled by the question, because I know that she is asking Delusional Disorder questions. She is following the cognitive model of Delusional Disorder, looking for a stressor to the 'delusion.'

I told her that I really didn't understand the question, which in fact I did not. She said that I could write the answer, the reasons for 'conflict' according to me versus the reasons for conflict according to my wife. 1. From my wife's point of view. 2. From my point of view. She said that the prosecutor's Akt [case file] is full of information suggesting to prove that it was me who was in fact the problem. So now I have work. The work is not easy work. Well, no work is easy when you want to do your best, when you want to bang it out perfectly, when the stakes 'is' as high as they are as they are in this particular situation."

Journal Entry, January 27, 2013

"I am getting ready to lie down. I just finished handwriting a letter to Frank Damazio. I have some hope that he is actually a real man of God... I need to find somebody who is spiritually alive and awake. I need to find somebody who is righteous, who can pray for me and my family fervently. I need to perfect myself in accordance with God's will. Father, it would be nice to have my family back under my roof and away from ritual abuse.

This morning at around 7:10, Bronek came in, opened the window all the way, turned on the big light, opened the door as wide as it goes and then went back out to sit at the tv. I was trying to meditate, trying to think about my dream and contemplate it's meaning....And then all of the sudden, the tv was blaring into my room. I got up and closed the door and lay back down. Bronek came over and opened the door again, then going back to sit at the tv. This happened about three more times. I told Bronek that I wanted it quiet in the room so that I could think and then he started having a fit.

He said that it was the army, that the 'awake' call had been made. I told him that there was no wake up call, that it was Sunday and that I wanted to relax. He kept going, so I told him to 'close his butt' in Polish. He then went and told the nurse what I told him. He told the nurse that I pray to Satan every morning....He ate breakfast and then he went to sleep for the entire day. I know that he will be up at 6 tomorrow morning to do the same thing, or rather I think that he will.

Romans 8:28

Praise God. Conform me to the image of your Son. Make me a vessel for your will. In Jesus' name."

Journal Entry, January 29, 2013

"Today I was moved into Oddzial [ward] C because of the 'conflict' with Bronek. I looked up Bronek's symptoms today, and I am pretty sure that he has something like Antisocial Personality Disorder. At least, he does fit the diagnostic criteria in my non-expert opinion. I didn't know what to do. What were my choices when the man was being text book passive aggressive towards me, doing everything that he could to make me uncomfortable? How could I stay with him in that situation, especially after he put his hands on me yesterday to push me?

Monday was the court date in divorce court. I completely blocked it out. I had a terrible day yesterday, didn't do anything at all, no English no nothing. But I didn't really know what was wrong at all. Tomorrow is Adelle's sixth birthday. I want to fast, but I don't know if it will be a good idea given the fact that I have not been in this oddzial [ward] for even twenty four hours. Lord, calm my nerves and my thoughts. Lead me and direct me, help me to make the right decisions, the decisions that are in accordance with your will.

Today I had a conversation with Krzyshek from therapy about meditation. He told me that he is Catholic, that he believes everything that is Catholic, that he doesn't believe that it is wise to try meditating on your own or with the help of anyone who teaches anything other than that which is Catholic because being led into the wrong meditation is worse than no meditating at all. He said 'I am Catholic, and it works for me.' Yes, but are you sure that it is 'the way?' How do you know that it is 'the way?' Oh I could/can/should tear his line of argument, the way and reasons that he convinces himself (He is just an example of many people who think like him) apart, and I need to. I need to dismantle his arguments, and make people like him 'find God like a person with their head on fire.' How can you believe something because 'it works for you' or because it is what you are told to believe? How do you know that 'it works?' What signals would you be getting if it didn't work? How would you know if there was something wrong with your belief system? How can you be sure? What is the origin of your beliefs? Can you chase them back to where they originated? Who 'devised' them? Do your beliefs coincide with the word of God? If not, where do they come from? What are they attached to? Who wrote them? Who decided that they are legitimate beliefs to have?

O my Father, please lead me and direct me. Please use me as a tool for your will. Please Lord. Please show me the way, your way. In Jesus' name."

Journal Entry, January 30, 2013

"Adelle Avery Bryson's sixth birthday today. Six years ago, I held her in my arms for the first time. Six years ago, my little baby was brought into this crazy, cruel world. Six years. The last time that I held her was more than two years ago. The last time that I told her that I love her was more than two years ago. The last time that my little girl had her daddy was more than two years ago. So much, all more than two years ago. More than two years ago, I began trying to get help because my little girl is being abused. She was and is being abused. It is ritual abuse. Father, my Father, I trust in you. I have nothing Father. It has all be taken from me. It has all been crushed. Father, please, I am on bended knees. O Father please. Show me the way. Open up my mind, direct me, lead me, destroy me but set my girls free.

Today I got a call from Brian, I had Polish class with [Maria], I went to the classical music and listened to some piano music that I didn't really care for. It was very choppy, not something that moved me emotionally. Good music must be emotionally powerful. It is no good if it isn't. Anyway, Marcin today was asked why he is here. He answered that he killed. Then he said 'I didn't do it. Somebody else did it. Somebody came into my body, took my body over and they did it.' O my God, put me in a position to help him. Lord this man is so messed up inside, so scared, so frazzled, so fried. Lord please help.

It's almost eleven, and in this new oddzial [ward] I have to give back the computer at eleven. For now. I will work on getting that rule changed. Anyway, I need guidance Lord. I need you to calm my mind to focus me, to direct me. You know what it is that I need. Please Father, for the sake of your will, for the sake of your kingdom, for the sake of the Kingdom of God. The Kingdom of God. Amen."

Journal Entry, February 1, 2013

"'When this losin' feels like dyin', I hope you'll be by me then.' [Dave Matthews lyrics] O how I feel like I'm dyin. I tried to write today, and I had no luck. I feel dead. I feel defeated. My mind is shot, fried, seized up. I managed to not take my Risperdal yesterday or today; I am trying to salvage some of my thoughts. So much time is getting wasted. My little girl is six years old.

Tonight I broke off a half of a milligram and took it just to keep some of it in my blood so that I am not completely floored when I have to take two milligrams again. Going from one half to two should be better than going from zero [to] two. I don't know. It doesn't even seem to help. I still cannot think. I am surrounded by chaos and calamity. I am surrounded by hell Lord. I just want my daughter to be evaluated. Does that really make me insane? Tell me once again how it is that you know that she is not being *abused? Oh yeah, you don't know. You cannot know. You foolish people. You leave my daughter to be abused while you hospitalize me for thinking that she is being abused.*

I spoke to Wengelnik the other day. He said 'Oh well Borderline Personality Disorder really isn't that big of a deal.' 'Ok, but it was a big deal in my family,' I replied, though he had tuned me out. 'And, I don't think that it was actually Borderline Personality Disorder. After I got to see it again in December 2010, I reached the conclusion that it looked a lot more like Dissociative Identity Disorder.' He looked at me with his skeptical eyes, certain that I am insane in the membrane. 'Yes, well why do you think that the doctors in Szczecin decided that you are sick? Do you think that doctors make quick decisions? They do not take the decision as to whether or not to diagnose somebody with Delusional Disorder lightly. Surely they had a reason. Do you also think that somebody or something is following you? Do you hear voices? Do you think that there is some conspiracy out to get you?'

'No, I just think that my daughter should've and should be evaluated.'

'What do you mean by evaluated.'

'I think that a good psychologist should take a look at her.'

Wegielnik looked frustrated. He looked a bit upset even. I don't know if he was upset because he thought that I was not being honest with him or maybe he didn't want to be talking to me or maybe he couldn't understand how it was that I was labeled with Delusional Disorder. I hope it is the last option, though I don't think he has come to that conclusion as of yet. Confirmation bias. Respect for his colleagues' opinions. A Polish psychiatrist reached the conclusion that I am seriously mentally ill. Surely the Polish psychiatrist had a good reason for doing so, and surely he was right, for he is a Polish psychiatrist after all.

Father, lead me, calm my mind, direct me, speak to me, direct my mouth and my fingers on this keyboard. Father, I know I have said this to you many times, but I am going to say it again. I am tapped out. I am ready to go down into the grave. I am absolutely nothing. Fill me with your Spirit, for everything that I was is gone. Everything that I was has been destroyed. Praise God. Praise the Lord and pass me my girls. In Jesus' name. Your will Father, not mine. Enlighten me. Keep me going Lord. Show me the way."

Art, Brian, and my mom were sending me packages from time to time. The best gift in the world at this point was new reading material, and no matter what they sent it was never enough. Brian also sent me Nicorette in a Mentos container, but the guards immediately recognized that it was not a sealed container and confiscated it. I did not get into any trouble as I was on good terms with all the guards. Art once sent me a cd/dvd for me to look at on my computer and Dr. Węgielnik inspected it and said that it contained gay porn.

"Is this what you are into?" he inquired suspiciously, thinking he might have found a nugget to write about in his report.

"No," I laughed, "that is just my gay friend doing what he does."

Journal Entry, February 2, 2013

"Lord, lead the way. Shine a light on my paths. Direct me, for I have nothing on my own. Show me the way, for I am lost and ready to go down into the pit, never to return. Deliver us for your mercy's sake. Show your grace. Lord, I am on bended knees.

I spoke to Brian today; he told me that he had read one of the four letters that he had gotten. He said that it was good, but he didn't have it with him, so he was not able to provide any specifics. I asked him to look at the date and to get back to me on the specifics, etc. Father, show me the way."

Journal Entry, February 7, 2013

"I don't know what to do. I don't know what to write, or if to write at all. I am fighting with myself. I am downtrodden. I am defeated. Yet I keep going. I have not given up. I cannot stop thinking about Adelle and her mother. I just don't know what to do. I have been trying to work on a letter for Dr. Setua re: the reasons for the 'conflict' between my wife and I in December 2010, and I don't know what to include and

what to exclude. Do I try to explain something, try to show a glimmer of truth, or do I just remain as vague as possible, doing my best not to even come close to the Delusional Disorder? If I believe that my daughter is being abused, is that delusional? Oh my Lord. O my Lord.

I keep saying the same things over and over and over. I am like a broken record, or rather, I am a broken record. I have to skip out of the groove. I have to skip into a new groove. I have to rise up above all of this. I have to figure out a way to get my family out of this. The Spirit of the living God has to take over my thoughts and my actions, or I have no chance. I am really tired of playing this 'game.' I am really tired. This is real, I am not dreaming. And yet, this is the worst dream that there is. This is hell. My daughter is the victim of sadistic caregiver abuse, of ritual abuse, of satanic ritual abuse. My daughter. Adelle Avery Bryson. Everything. Father, show me what to do. Lead me Father. I know not what to do. I am all done. I am weak, and I do not feel strong. I do not feel like I can do anything through Christ. I do not feel like I can do anything.

Praise God."

CHAPTER 79

"I KNOW NOTHING ELSE"

I wrote the following letter to Dr. Setua as a statement of what I did and did not believe, to pre-empt any questions she may have, and to eliminate any ideas that I was delusional. I knew that nothing I was stating could be legitimately construed as delusional, and I wanted that in black and white. It was much easier for me to communicate on paper than it was with my broken Polish.

"*Iain Avery Bryson*
February 12, 2013
All that I know is the following:
1. *My wife and I reached the conclusion together that she is suffering from major psychological disorder. [Kees de Vries, psychologist, The Hague] This 'major psychological disorder' had a major impact upon our family.*
2. *My wife sought psychological help because of the huge, devastating impact of her 'major psychological disorder' upon our family. [Georgina Saccone, psychologist, The Hague;...]*
3. *I notified Kees de Vries about my wife's 'major psychological disorder,' and I was terrified when I did so.*
4. *Scholarly literature states that the 'major psychological disorder' that we suspected is often the result of childhood trauma.*
5. *My daughter returned from Poland twice in 2010 with multiple signs and symptoms of possible child abuse.*
6. *In December 2010, my wife felt 'empty,' 'out of control,' and like she was 'trapped in a nightmare' [Journal]. I began trying to get help the day after I returned to The Hague after spending three months away from my wife and daughter in the United States. I continued trying to get help for the next seventeen days that we were together under the same roof.*
7. *One of the symptoms of 'major psychological disorder' that both my wife and I identified as a problem was pathological lying/reality distortion; the reality that my wife has presented to the authorities is not accurate.*
I know nothing else."

I also wrote the following letter to Dr. Ciszewski, for the same reasons.

"*My daughter was just under four years old, and the only thing that I could see with my eyes were bruises. What I think you don't understand is that this was my daughter and not just any 3-4 year old child, but my 3-4 year old child. I knew my child. I spent every day with my child. I was teaching my child. I was developing games and curriculum tailored specifically for her age and learning abilities. I was studying my child's development. I was studying child psychology, moral development. I was looking at PhD programs in child psychology because of my interest...*

Child abuse is not seen with the eyes. The effects of child abuse are psychological. The fact that you cannot see it with the eyes surely does not mean that you cannot see it. My child had many symptoms of PTSD: she was having nightmares, throwing tantrums and having panic attacks, she would not go to sleep unless I was in her room, she didn't want me to leave her sight, she had regressed to urinating and defecating in her pants and in her bed. She had bruises, unexplained vaginal pain that my wife would not talk about. She did some things like... asking me to play naked with her and telling me that her grandfather had played naked with her, referencing her grandfather's testicles on several occasions unprompted. She had urination and defecation problems – having to comfort her, hold her hand and help her wipe, urinating and defecating in her pants and bed, regression to baby talk, forgetting the things that I had been teaching her, only wanting to play when role playing her cat – I had to tell her numerous times that I wanted to play with my daughter and not with the cat; she was afraid of her mother, flooding her room with water, dumping potted plants into the carpet and other attention seeking behaviors...

You asked me to give you a percentage of how sure I am that my father-in-law abused my daughter. I can only speculate in regards to him; I do not and cannot know if he did or did not abuse my daughter. What I do know is that I knew my daughter. Based upon what I saw in my daughter, there is a good chance that someone had abused her."

Neither doctor responded directly to any of the issues that were addressed in my written statements.

Journal Entry, February 12, 2013

"I got a letter from Mariusz Wirkus today, a reply from a letter I sent him on Adelle's birthday. He asked me what he can do to help. I am sending him a letter tomorrow. I would like to hear what a lawyer has to say about my situation. I don't know if he will do anything, but we will see. I had a meeting with Jacek Jakimiak –psychotherapist– today. He started trying to explain cognitive behavioral theory to me. I am not sure what he was getting at, what he is leading up to. I gave him a ten page paper that I feel is pretty good, a paper that sticks to the facts and stays away from 'delusional content.' I think. It depends what they decide is delusional content. If delusional content is defined as any version of reality that is not consistent with the prosecutor's version, then I have a problem. No, I think that it was a pretty good letter. We shall see.

Brian hasn't called in a week or so. Last time I spoke to him, he told me that he had received four letters. And now he goes MIA? I wonder what is going on with him. One day I am taking care of my daughter and trying to get help for my wife; the next day I am in hell and all alone, with nowhere and nobody to turn to. Everybody just looks at me and says, 'you are in hell. What do you want me to do? I can't take care of my own hell. Your hell is something that I cannot understand. I have to go back to thinking about my own hell now. When I think or even try to think about your hell, all that I can think of is that you must be crazy.'

Yes, I am crazy. I am so crazy that I am completely crazy. I am in a Polish mental institution because I say that my daughter is being abused. And, she is being abused and there is absolutely nothing that I can do. I should be raising my daughter and I am not. Instead I am in Polish limbo. Life is passing me by. Life is destroying everything that I love and care about. Life is hell. Love is hell. I hate this life. I hate my life. What is the point? Only Adelle. Only Adelle. Your daddy loves you so much little girl. So much. Too much.

I'm a God fearing man. Yes I am. I reach out for my God's hands. ben harper

Father, I reach out for your hands. I reach out for your hands Father. I am lost. I am desolate. I am nothing. I was a man. I was a father. Now I am nothing but a walking shell. Nothing. A shell. Father, deliver us. Show me your grace. Have mercy on my family. Please...Please...Please Father. I beseech you. I...I...I beseech you my Father."

Journal Entry, February 14, 2013

"Today is Slawomir's fifty second birthday. I met with the director of the hospital today. He said that the other doctors told him that I still have 'traces of paranoid thinking.' This means that I still think that my daughter is being abused. I am not allowed to think that my daughter is being abused because the prosecutor claimed to have excluded the possibility. The director also said 'surely the authorities investigated...' No, they didn't investigate. They only spoke to my wife and then went to the psychiatrists who then said that I am delusional because I don't/didn't have any evidence. A big circle of failed reasoning.

The psychotherapist is trying to use cognitive behavioral therapy on me; he doesn't understand that I understand this better than he does, that I understand myself better than he can understand himself. I do see how writing letters, especially to the psychiatrists, did not help my cause. I dug myself deeper into a hole. The director said today that he would recommend that I go to a different hospital or even to the US, but that it is ultimately up to the court. The court says that it is up to him. He said that he thinks it might take until the end of this year to get me to the states.

I am so weak. I am so torn up. I don't care anymore. Oh but I do. But I can't. What can I do? What is there? What is this life? What is this? Father. I don't understand. I don't get it. Why is this still happening to my family? Why is my Adelle still being sadistically abused? Oh my Lord. Oh my Lord. I beg and plead from bended knees. In the name of your Son Christ Jesus, I pray that you deliver my wife and daughter unto me. Save us Father. Save us. Amen."

Journal Entry, February 16, 2013

"Yesterday Margaret Ramsey from the US Embassy in Warsaw came. She was a ridiculous woman. Or rather, she is a ridiculous woman. She was tensed up like a robot, like a board. She was just a talking computer box. 'We are not lawyers. We cannot intervene on your behalf...You say that we haven't helped – what about the translations?' 'Yes, but I told you from the beginning that I needed help because I had no legal representation and because the interpreter that they provided me could not understand me. I think that those things are a bit more important than some translations or magazines. I appreciate the translations, but that is not what I need from you. I really needed an interpreter who understood me. And I told you that I didn't want you talking to my mother. Have you been talking to my mother?'

'Well, I am not going to answer that question because I know that it is against your wishes. Have you been talking to your mother?'

'Yes I spoke to her'

'And what did she say?'

'That is not the point. If I choose to talk to my mother, it has nothing at all to do with whether or not you can talk to my mother. I was specific about you not having permission to talk to my mother. The issue of whether or not I talk to my mother is a completely different issue.'

The woman was a lying psychological manipulator. She would ask me questions and I would answer: 'well, you wrote in your letter that....' She either didn't understand or she didn't want to understand that I was telling her that she had already answered the questions she was asking me, personally, in previous letters. 'Well,' she replied, 'if that is what 'they wrote,' then I suppose that is the way it is.' Speaking to the woman was a waste of my time. She was only there for show, only there to collect information, to tell the Embassy that I am being taken care of....

I told her that I want to get out of this country. She said that she thinks it is not possible without a lawyer. I explained to her that Margorzata Bula-Duane had had me sign releases of information for the US Dept of Health and Human Services and the International Social Services; she specifically told me that I could be transferred to the U.S. I told her that the Director indicated that he would have no problem with it, and that the court indicated that it would be up to the director. She just hemmed and hawed, beat around the bush, flapped her gums with nothing of substance being emitted.

She reminded me a bit of my mother, when my mother gets her tight upper lip, her whole body getting stiff, thinking that she is setting up a good wall. Oh you people are fools. O my God what are you waiting for?

I am having a bit of a difficult time lately. More of a difficult time than 'normal' is more accurate. I don't feel good. I feel horrible. I feel like I am dying. I feel like I am already dead. I feel paralyzed. I cannot write. I cannot think. Even though I don't take Risperdal, I cannot think. I have become pretty good at sticking the 'forced drugs' into my upper lip. I still take a half milligram most of the time in order to keep the crap in my blood stream, but I do not take two milligrams. Anyway, my head hurts all of the time. I don't feel like I have anything to write about. I cannot write at night and it is very hard to write during the daytime. I don't know what to do.

I am trusting in the Lord with all of my heart and leaning not on my own understanding, I suppose. I don't care. I do care, but I don't. I am too tired to care. I am too tired to go on. I am too beaten. I am run into the ground. I am weak, and I do not feel strong. I can do all things through Christ, but I don't feel like I can do anything at all. And I don't even know what to do except that I would like to write a book. However, that is the one thing that I don't feel like I have the ability to do. What do I do? Father? I am here; where are you? I am in ROPS. My daughter, her name is Adelle, she is in intergenerational ritual abuse.

I just looked through my pictures of Adelle, again, and my heart sunk. My heart is sunk. I am sunk. Life has passed me by. All that is good has done left. I am nothing. Lord come now and save us or I am going to turn into a raving lunatic. I am. I just want to be a daddy to that little girl. I just want to read to her, to dance with her, to be her daddy. Lord what do I have to do? Lord open my eyes. Lord guide me. Lord I am in ROPS in Poland and my daughter is in intergenerational ritual abuse. Lord."

Journal Entry, February 17, 2013

"My condition is getting worse. I feel isolated. I feel the de-realization creeping in, enveloping me like a cocoon. I feel despair that I cannot explain, a despair so deep and so ever present. So complete. This Kafkaesque world that I live in. This world which does not work. This world of fakes, of stupid children walking around in adult bodies. I lay in bed this morning, wanting to sleep, but I could not. I could only think, but the thinking was like being in benzodiazepine withdrawal. Swirling thoughts of detachment, fear and pain. Yet it was not my fear, but a subjective, distant fear. I have nowhere to turn, nowhere to run. Vain is the help of man. There is no help from man.

What does it mean to trust in God with all of my heart? Does it mean that I just wait, follow the commandments of Christ, live in as holy a way as I can? Or does it mean that I have to follow the commandments of Christ and then use the Spirit of the living God to bust my way out of this? I Peter 4:1 'For as much then as Christ hath suffered for us in the flesh, arm yourselves with the same mind: for he that hath suffered in the flesh hath ceased from sin: That he no longer should live the rest of his time in the flesh to the lusts of men, but to the will of God.' Is it just that I am suffering? It feels like I am dying. It feels like I am going crazy. It feels like there is no way out of this maze. It feels like hell in here.

What am I supposed to do? Father, I ask you every day. I need a clear answer. I need a lighted path. I need an exit from this hell. My daughter needs an exit from this hell. Adelle Avery Bryson. Everything. I am sorry baby. I am sorry my babies that I am so weak, so useless. I am sorry that I cannot do anything. Father, light my way. Direct me. Show me the way that I am to go. I am on bended knees, begging and pleading. What do I do?

Living but not living. Breathing, but why? Inhabiting space for what purpose? Deliver my family unto me; make us whole again. I believe Father. I believe. I don't know what to do. I don't know how to live in this hell. I don't know how to live. I don't know what of the Lord is against them that do evil (I Peter 3:12).

Lord, if your ears are open to my prayers, then what is going on. I am not claiming to be righteous; I am trying, but that is all that I can do. I can try. I am a man and I am nothing but a sinner. I try and I try. I want to purge myself for you. I want to be pure. I want....Lord I don't know what I want. Adelle Lord. What about Adelle? Father please."

Journal Entry, February 18, 2013

"When you can no longer change a situation, when you have absolutely no chance, then you must change yourself. When you cannot change that what is outside, then you change that what is inside. You can only work on what you have control over, and it is difficult to have control over one's external environment. I realize, well in fact I've realized, that this situation is out of my hands. I realized that back in December 2010. But I spent more than two years trying to get it into my hands. I spent more than two years grasping, groping. I spent more than two years making myself look crazy.

All that I needed to do was to say, 'hey look, my wife is not telling the truth. Can we please evaluate my daughter?' Or something like that. The key is that whatever I said should have been under control, and control should have never been compromised. In compromising my control, I compromised my credibility, and credibility is quite important. Without credibility you are nothing. Without credibility I am nothing. Without credibility I am a lunatic, which is worse than nothing. O Father light my way.

The key now is to not be crazy. My wife and I concluded that she has a major psychological disorder, her version of reality is not the truth, my daughter had signs and symptoms of child abuse....how about we take a look at my child? Thank you and goodnight.

I see how my situation, how dealing with the ritual abuse of my daughter.....how this made me crazy. I see how I went too far in the 'other' direction. What you have to understand is that all that I wanted was help. And then the police would not help me, my parents would not help me. My parents started lying to me, working behind my back, and those things will make a person crazy. Those things made this person crazy. Those things took me and spun me around in circles like a top on LSD. Those things flipped my world upside down and inside out. Those things....

Oh well, you know. I begged Agata to get help, telling her that I didn't want to look at the situation any closer, that I knew enough, that I just wanted her to get help. Then, I had to look at the situation because it hit me square in the face. Then, I needed help and I needed it quick and I was going crazy thinking about getting help, learning about ritual abuse though I didn't know that it was ritual abuse at the time, getting a clear vision of the 'red herring' and its effect upon my parents etc... Oh my God, show me the way. Shine your light on my path. Direct me, lead me. Deliver my family from this incipient evil. Deliver my family, put us back together again. Praise God.

Now how do I deal with this current situation? How do I get out of the 'crazy' house, out of the crazy diagnosis? I don't think that it tries to make an argument to these people that I just had a bad case of Adjustment Disorder. I think that I need to stick to 'My wife ....My daughter....My wife is not telling the truth...I don't know anything....I do see how my ....' In fact I have to work on what it is that I will say because I don't know how it should go. I don't know the best things to say. I am still happy with the letter that I gave to Jakimiak a week ago. I have to remember 'no evidence, firm belief, unfounded, nobody else has the belief...' stick to the basics. Stick to the facts. Stay away from 'delusional content' and stay away from 'psychosis.' Stay away from 'psychosis' and get out of the mental asylum.

Thank you Father. Deliver my wife and my daughter unto me. Your will be done. In Jesus' name."

Journal Entry, February 21, 2013

"I got a letter from a prosecutor in Stargard Szczecinski yesterday saying that my daughter was evaluated and that she is physically and psychologically healthy or 'dobry.' They said that my daughter is emotionally under control. As I've been saying for quite some time, this is severe, caregiver inflicted child abuse. These people who are abusing my daughter are doing so with expertise. This is not random, sloppy child abuse. If you do not look for what I have told you to look for, you will not see it. My daughter must be evaluated for exposure to severe trauma. My daughter .....

My wife has a severe mental illness caused by trauma, and now my daughter is so messed up that I cannot even believe it. I just want to get these girls some help, and I am dealing with the dumbest people that I could possibly have to deal with. Since day one, I've said that this is severe abuse. I told the prosecutor that my wife has a major psychological disorder. I told him that she has Stockholm Syndrome, or severe betrayal trauma. I told him....

And then what do they do? They perform a surface evaluation on my daughter nearly two years after I reported severe child abuse. When their evaluation turns up nothing, they say 'well, it is obviously just a case of Iain's delusions.' This is absolutely ridiculous. I wrote many letters saying 'evaluate my daughter thoroughly for exposure to trauma,' and they do the exact opposite. They don't evaluate her thoroughly, and they don't take into account that I alleged severe, expert child abuse. I wrote a letter to the prosecutor and sent it today asking for the details as to the nature and the extent of the 'evaluation,' asking for a copy of the 'expert' opinions.

Father, I am done. Father, I cannot handle this anymore. Father, I want to die. I want to die. Please take me.

Tomorrow I have to start seriously writing. I have to sit down and bang out scenes or 'pearls.' I have to tell this story. I have to get this down on paper. I have to get my daughter back."

Journal Entry, February 24, 2013

"Another Sunday night. Another Sunday night in ROPS. Another Sunday night without my little girl sleeping in the next room. Another night in hell. I have been working on a short story; it is about twenty five pages long. It is about this situation, from December 2010 to now. I plan on working on it for another day or so and then sending it off to a couple of people using a cd. Father guide me. Shine your light on my path, for I know not what to do or how to do it. Praise God."

Journal Entry, February 25, 2013

"Today I worked on the letter that I am going to send to Jennifer Freyd. I have to write an introduction page and also add my CV, but other than that I think that it is about done. I got a letter from Bogdan bankowy [Mariusz] today. He sent me a zeszyt [notebook] and some stamps. I am not sure if he will 'help' me or not. I wrote him a letter, and I am sending it [to] him tomorrow. For now, I need to work on what I have control over: the way that I am perceived in this hospital and the things that I write and send off. Tomorrow I have a meeting with the psychotherapist, so I need to prepare for that. Praise God. Thank you Father for putting my family back together."

Journal Entry, February 27, 2013

"Today I met with [Maria]. She told me that the director said that I do not belong here. She said that he is not sure that I should be here at all. He said that he thinks somebody might have made a mistake. She said that he wants to explore my beliefs regarding my daughter more, to see if they are real beliefs or not, to see what they are based upon. He says that he doesn't understand why they didn't just take a close look at my daughter instead of labeling me as insane, etc....
Praise God."

Since the United States Embassy continued to refuse to help me with issues such as not having an interpreter who could understand me, and not being able to call witnesses on my behalf, I filed a case with the European Court of Human Rights in Strasbourg, France. Both aforementioned issues were instances of Poland being in violation of international human rights law as far as I could see, but my case was ultimately not accepted.

Journal Entry, February 28, 2013

"I cannot write tonight. I have been trying to tinker with my new letter, the letter that I am planning to send to Freyd, Lacter and Laurel House. I just cannot focus at all. My mind is all over the place. I will have

it ready for Monday. I did work on and finish the Strasbourg application today, and that is a good thing. I had a lot of trouble getting that done as well. I postponed it, I didn't think that I was going to do it at all. Now it is done, and I wonder why I waited so long. Given my experience in Poland, it is necessary to follow up on issues such as the interpreter and the fact that I wasn't permitted to call witnesses on my behalf...

Brian called me today. I spoke to him about Ciszewski and [Maria] and how he told [Maria] and the rest of the staff that I shouldn't be here and that he thinks that the first doctors could have made an error in sending me here. She told me that he said that he is going to look into my situation further, that he wants to figure out what happened, that he believes that something happened along the way, and that a poor decision led to where we are at today. Praise God. Father, clear my head, give me focus, fill me with wisdom and understanding. Fill me with your words, for I do not have my own. I am wasted."

Journal Entry, March 2, 2013

"The line between sanity and insanity is gray and blurry. Elements of both can and do coexist together. They are not mutually exclusive. And, it all lies on a continuum. Nobody is completely sane and nobody is completely insane.

Today I worked on the letter that I've been working on for a week or so. I also worked on my CV. I think that I will be ready to send it off on Monday or Tuesday. I have to send one off first so that I can figure out how much the CD weighs, because I don't know how much the letters are going to cost.

I need to get prepared for Ciszewski, who I will meet with next Friday. As of right now, his stance is that I am not insane, and I need to keep it that way. I need to prepare answers to questions that I expect. I need to try to anticipate all of his questions so that I don't get caught by surprise. I also need to prepare for Jakiniak. The two go together, and I have Jakiniak first on Tuesday, so I can use Jakiniak to get ready for Ciszewski, who is far more important. [Maria] already told me that Ciszewski is going to ask me about my daughter.

I have to have an explanation as to why I believe that she was abused. I need to figure out how I can/should talk about what was obviously (to me) a brief reactive psychosis in December 2010. And, what was going on during my observation? The answers are clear, and so it shouldn't be so hard to get ready for the meetings this week. In December, I was reacting to an extreme stressor and during the observation I was reacting to extreme frustration, another stressor. I need to think about this some more.

I need to get out of this situation. I need to hold my daughter in my arms. I need my daughter to grow up with her father. I need my daughter to grow up in a healthy environment. I need my daughter. Adelle, I love you. I am sorry that this is happening. I love you too much. I am trying. Agata, you know that I love you; I wish that you could have told me so we could've dealt with this together. Our family will be put back together. The house of the wicked will be overthrown. In Jesus' name."

"Reactive psychoses: Here we have a category of illness in which an episode of psychosis is precipitated by stress and then tends to clear up once the stress is removed. The acute picture is often mistaken for schizophrenia or for delusional disorder (DSM III had a separate category of acute paranoid disorder) but rapid resolution of symptoms usually makes the differentiation clear" (Munro 23).

Journal Entry, March 4, 2013

"I am sitting in my room. It is five of eleven. I am just thinking about how ridiculous my situation is, how absolutely crazy this is. I am thinking about what I can do, what I should do, and I just draw a blank. Well, not completely blank, but just nothing pops into mind except the normal. Prove that I am not crazy, write, get out of ROPS...Nothing new. This situation makes me crazy. All that I've wanted since December 2010 is a thorough evaluation of my daughter. I just don't know what to do now. I keep going, I will keep going, I keep trying to grow, I keep trying to move and plan and get things done. But what is it that I am getting done? What should I be getting done? Is what I'm doing sufficient? Obviously not because I am *still in ROPS and Adelle and Agata are still living in ritual abuse. What should I be doing? What do I have to be doing? What could I be doing that I am not doing? What can I do tomorrow that I did not do today?"*

Journal Entry, March 5, 2013

"I sent out the letter that I've been writing especially for Jennifer Freyd to Brian today. I don't know why. I suppose I just want to see what he says, see if he says anything at all. I am going to send it off to Freyd either tomorrow or the next day; I have to finish writing a cover letter. I am also going to send it to Lacter and the Laurel House in Tasmania. Probably other places as well, but I don't know yet.

Jacek Jakimiak, the psychotherapist, didn't come again today. That is now two straight weeks that he hasn't been here to see me. It is a little bit frustrating, but the director will be here on Friday to see me, and that is much more important. I have to get ready for the director. I have to prepare, to look at the psychiatric report from Szczecin, to think about what he will ask me, what he is going to want to talk about. The director is my ticket out of here, I think. And, it is getting out of here that I have to do first. Everything else I can do once I am free, making money and free. However, then again I don't know what I would/will do once I am let out because I have no money to do anything at all, and it is very difficult to survive in this world with no money at all. For example, it takes money to get a job, for clothes for transportation, for transcripts....Father, I trust in you with all of my heart; when is the house of the wicked going to fall?

I am struggling. Well, that is an understatement. I don't know how to put one foot in front of the other. I don't know what I am doing. Every minute of every day is nothing but a mind [expletive]. I am in hell, my family is in hell, I don't see any way of getting out of hell. More importantly, I don't see any way to get my daughter out of this hell. Every minute of every day is a minute that I have to accept that Adelle Avery Bryson is living in ritual abuse. Sadistic caregiver abuse. Child rape and incest and torture: not things that I had in mind for my little girl. O my God, strengthen me and show me the way."

Journal Entry, March 6, 2013

"I just finished putting a letter to Jennifer J. Freyd into an envelope. I hand wrote about two and a half pages (double spaced on graph paper), and I put twenty seven pages on a disc along with my CV. She is an expert in trauma; we'll see if she has anything to say in regards to my situation.
I spoke to Jakimiak today. He started the conversation asking about my parents, again, for the third meeting in a row. I think that he is looking for paranoid thinking, looking for me to say something like my parents planned to do me harm or....I don't know.

We talked about Agata and the situation in December 2010 some more. I cannot tell if he is trapping me in what he believes is a delusional version of reality, or if he is trying to understand the truth. I believe that he doesn't believe my wife's version of events. I believe that he believes that the truth is probably closer to my version of events, but I don't know. This situation has messed with my head so much that I cannot tell anymore. Maybe he is using his psychological skills to trap me. Or rather, the nature of his questioning could go either way.

I am trapped in that I talk about my version of reality; if that is not ok, then I have a problem. I believe that it is ok. The reason that I believe that it is ok is that I am not exhibiting delusional thinking whereby I have firm, steadfast believes that are resistant to change. I am saying 'it looked to me like...,' 'I think that...,' 'I have to speculate, but ...,' 'I don't really know; what I thought in December 2010 was...' In order for my thinking to be 'delusional' thinking, I would have to be saying 'I know, and there is nothing else that it could be. My version is the only version that can exist...' I am not doing that at all. I am flexible. I am listening. I am open to his suggestions.

I compared Agata to an alcoholic today, or rather I compared me trying to get Agata help to trying to get an alcoholic help. He seemed to understand the analogy. I said 'an alcoholic doesn't know that they need help, they don't want help, they don't think that they can be helped, they are afraid of even the idea of help...'

Father, I trust in you. I have nothing left. I am empty. Father, I only want my daughter (and her mother) to be safe. I only wanted to be a daddy to my little girl. Father, please. Father please."

Journal Entry, March 7, 2013

"The director is coming tomorrow, and I get/have to talk to him. I am a little bit nervous. Father, put your words on my tongue; direct me, lead me...

Today I had a conversation with Wegielnik. He asked me questions about my childhood, school, work, the situation with my wife. He asked me if I had thought about hurting my father-in-law again. I told him that I had not, that I am not a stupid man, that I just want to work and get legal representation...I didn't answer his questions perfectly; he caught me by surprise. I didn't know that I was to talk to him today until he came up to me and said 'can you come with me?' Next time we speak, I think that he is going to ask me about my drug use history. He is working a narrative for his report. I have to be focused and directed for the meeting tomorrow with the director. Father please. I am losing my mind. This situation is hell. One day I am trying to get help for my wife and taking care of my daughter, and the next day I am in hell. Lord, Please. Please."

Journal Entry, March 8, 2013

"I am waiting on Ciszewski, the director to come. I have a meeting with him today at 12. I am a bit nervous, and so I thought that it would be a good idea to write a bit. I have been reviewing some things, but I think that the most important factor is ensuring that I am relaxed. I have to realize that some things are not easy to explain, and that the situation did make me crazy. I believe that he is going to ask me about symptoms of abuse in Adelle. I have to be clear that I do not know that she had been abused. What I do know is what I observed. I do know, for example that my daughter had vaginal pain...."

Journal Entry, March 11, 2013

"'What do you see as the future of your marriage? Do you see yourself getting back together with your wife? I believe that understanding how you feel about your marriage is the key to understanding your thinking' (Ciszewski).

'With how much percentage are you sure that your father-in-law abused your daughter?'

'Would you say that you are at a higher or lower economic level than people of your age and education?'

I am going over my meeting with Ciszewski in my head and trying to prepare for the next meeting. I am trying to anticipate questions. I am trying to think of which questions from last time that I need to respond to again. One for sure is that he asked me what I could see with my eyes that led me to the conclusion that my daughter had been abused. I have to be clear that abuse/trauma is not visible with the naked eye. I have to be clear that Adelle was exhibiting signs of PTSD. I have to know more about PTSD. He asked me what percent I am sure that my father in law abused my daughter. In our meeting he said 'fifty' and I said yes. I have to be clear that I do not have a percentage. I do not know who abused my daughter. All that I do know is that she was in Poland twice and both times she came back with multiple signs and symptoms of abuse. I do not know any more than that.

I am sitting in my cell or 'sala' as they call it here in ROPS. I have my headphones on, listening to 'Big eyed Fish.' I am sending out a letter to Lacter tomorrow. Everybody else is sleeping. I will wake up in ROPS tomorrow. My daughter and my wife will wake up in ritual abuse. What can I do? How much longer? Will I ever hold my daughter again? Will I get to be a daddy at all? What is left? O my God..."

CHAPTER 80

"I FEEL DEAD"

Journal Entry, March 12, 2013

"When this losin' feels like dyin', I hope you'll be by me then. [Dave Matthews lyrics]
I have been preparing for my meeting with Ciszewski that I have on Friday. I am figuring out how I should respond to him. I am thinking about what he asked me last time and how I need to clarify my answers for him. I am thinking about 'I believe that your thinking about your marriage is the key to understanding your thinking...' I have to knock this ball out the ballpark. I need Ciszewski on my squad. I cannot alienate him. I've got to convince him that I am not insane in the membrane. I've got to be sane so that I can be free.

I've been also thinking about what I can write in general. One topic that I have been thinking of since before this started is writing to Adelle. I was working on this before I even knew that there was a problem. The idea of writing to my daughter now to give to her when she is older appeals to me. The problem is that things have changed. Now the situation is quite a bit different and I don't know what to write anymore. Before I was going to write about the world that I want for my daughter. Now, I just don't know. I suppose that I could still write about the world that I want for my daughter, but I think that that would be too much thinking about [expletive] that just doesn't matter.

The only thing that does matter right now, Adelle, is being abused. The only thing that does really matter right now, Adelle, is not with me and has not been with me for over two years. (Yes Agata, you do matter too. I love you too much, but others do not understand why or how. You are a little bit crazy you know baby). So how do I get that girl back in my life? How do I get that girl to safety and away from those crazy [expletive]? How? I need to know how and I need to get it done. I need my daughter in my life. I need my family. I need ....oh [expletive], I am nothing."

Journal Entry, March 15, 2013

"Finding a Bible verse is like finding music. Sometimes you just don't feel like looking. Sometimes you feel so down that it doesn't appeal. But, when you find what you are looking for, it feels/sounds good.

'Trust in the Lord with all your heart, and lean not on your own understanding. In all your ways acknowledge him, and he shall direct your paths' (Proverbs 3:5-6)

When you have the verse, the next problem is interpretation, or application to a real life situation. I have dealt with this question before, specifically with this verse. That is part of what comes with being locked up in Poland for nearly two years when all you've wanted is an evaluation of your daughter. Themes seem to repeat themselves; many days are near mirror images of each other. Not much changes because it is still an evaluation of the child that is necessary. Or is it necessary?

So then, let's get to the other questions. How do I trust in the Lord with all of my heart and lean not on my own understanding? What does it mean to trust in the Lord with all of my heart and to not lean on my own understanding? Does it mean that I can or should just forget my own understanding entirely? Is my own understanding irrelevant? Does my own understanding do absolutely nothing? Is not God working through me? If God is working through me, then doesn't my understanding play a role? Should I stop writing? I really don't understand.

Do I do nothing but pray? Do I reject anything that is associated with me understanding? How do I know the difference Lord? How do I know what you mean? Speak to me Father. Tell me. Lead me. Direct me.

I want my paths to be directed. I want God to shine a flood light on the path that I need to take. I want God to funnel me in that direction like a cow being sent to slaughter or like people in the gates waiting to get on a rollercoaster or a ticket line at an airport. I don't want a choice. I want to know the path that I am on is the path that God wants me to be on. I want to believe that the path that I am on has to be the path that God wants me to be on. I don't want there to be any other possibilities. So then, how do I acknowledge God with everything that I do? What exactly does that mean? 'Acknowledge?' That word is very subjective when I think about it. Lord, you have to tell me what it is that you want from me because I don't have a clue. My head is so messed up that I don't know anything anymore except that I am in ROPS and my daughter is still being abused. Lord, Adelle Avery Bryson is still being abused. I pray in Jesus name that you direct my path unto her. Direct my path unto her and do so quickly. I'm begging you Father on bended knee.

'The Lord will not allow the righteous soul to famish, but he casts away the desire of the wicked' (Proverbs 10: 3) My soul feels quite famished. What is your definition of famished Father? When are you going to cast away the desire of the wicked? What is it that you need/want from me?

The director did not come today; he was busy doing something else. It's too bad because I was looking forward to talking to him. I had something prepared to talk to him about, and I believe that talking to him is in my best interest. He has the ability to speed up the process of getting me out of here. He seems to me to be a smart man, a man who thinks and tries to use his brain. I haven't met too many of those types of people during my stay in Poland."

Journal Entry, March 16, 2013

"I am trying to get you Adelle. I am trying. I want nothing else than to dance with you and mommy again.

I have got to get out of this hospital. I have got to stop taking Risperdal, which is stopping my thinking. I have got to be a daddy to my little girl again. O my God. O my God. I am so frustrated because I cannot think. I have no ability to do much of anything. I feel dead."

Journal Entry, March 18, 2013

"I met with Wegielnik today. He has been looking over the psychiatric report from the court, and it has made him very skeptical of me and of my mental health. He said that when he talks to me that he doesn't think that I am mentally ill, but when he looks at what other people say or what they say I have done, then he thinks that maybe I am mentally ill. He is talking about the things that are listed in the psychiatric report, such as the emails that I sent out, me working non stop on trying to get help from December to April, what I did or rather what it is alleged that I did on April 27, 2011...He spoke about the religious references that I made in letters to the psychiatrists in Szczecin, saying 'you know that often those types of things go with mental illness.'

He asked me if he could read my notebooks. At first I told him that they are very private, and then I agreed. Now I have to rescind my invitation to read my notebooks. Why the hell did I ever tell anyone that they could read my notebooks? Nobody can read my notebooks...end of story. My wife cannot read my notebooks, or rather she could not when we were living together. I am anxious about this because I have to let him know soon that I was in error, and I have to do so before he decides to take one to the toilet for some easy reading.

And, I have to tell him that I was in error when I told him that it would be ok. The man makes me feel uncomfortable, always talking about 'diseases' of the brain. 'You must consider the fact that you have a disease.' 'Yes, and you must keep your mind open. What would you base that conclusion on?' Well, the answer is my notebooks, for example. I've got to keep them out of his hands. Why do I allow myself to get stuck in these tight situations?

Other than that, not much happened today. I got a package with some clothes in it from my mom with a couple of Bradbury books. It just shows what she thinks is on my mind. Sorry mom, but the reality I speak about is true. Your granddaughter is being horridly abused in the same way that your daughter-in-law was abused when she was a child, the same ways that led to your daughter-in-law having a serious mental disorder that we both sought help for in Holland. I went and saw a newer Clint Eastwood movie about he and his daughter. It was a good movie that made me cry. All I want is my daughter. Father, please."

Journal Entry, March 19, 2013

"The important thing is that I get out of here and get back into my daughter's life. If I am in my daughter's life, then I can maneuver, I can get things done, I can have her evaluated. If my parental rights are terminated, then my options will be severely limited. I have to fight for Adelle and in order to fight for Adelle, I must be outside. I must still be legally her father. I must have access into her life. Tomorrow I have a meeting with Jakimiak. I have to elaborate on the Brief Reactive Psychosis that I spoke about before. I am not entirely sure what I should tell him, but I feel comfortable talking to him.

To Dr. Wegelnik, I do not feel entirely comfortable. He asked me to read my notebooks. Thursday I have to take care of that and tell him that it is not ok for him to read my notebooks.

To Jakimiak: the level of certainty that I said I had was out of proportion to the level of certainty that I had a right to have. The amount of descriptive detail that I had was out of proportion the amount of descriptive detail that I should have claimed to have. My degree of certainty that my father-in-law abused my daughter was not in line with the degree of certainty that was warranted. I have to make sure that they do not look at my notebooks, and I have to stay on task, to keep my mind focused. I feel good today, not good like I feel good, but good like I feel like I know what I am doing.

Bogdan, Mariusz Wirkus, called me today. He told me that he had looked at the videos I had sent him of Agata. He said that one of them is Agata asking 'How did you beat her' and then the man in the background saying 'No you don't understand' or something like that. I am going to wait for his letter with the explanation or call him again in the next couple of days. I am glad that he called. He said that he is one hundred percent sure that I will be out of here in June. Praise God and pass me my daughter. O my God."

Journal Entry, March 23, 2013

"Another day. Another Saturday. Another day and another Saturday without everything that matters: Adelle Avery Bryson. I am doing everything that I know how to do to get back to you, to get you away from those monsters. I am sorry Adelle. I love you baby.

I spoke to my dad today and he told me that I can stay with him in Florida and that I could also work with him when I get out of here. I told him that I had to get out of here first and told him that I think that it would be a good idea for him to write to the court. Maybe it would be a good idea for him to come to Poland as well, for him to go to the court hearing and be there and say that he is going to take me back to the US, etc. I will talk to him again and I will figure this out. I have to get out of this situation. I have to work. I have to hire an attorney and I have to get back into my daughter's life. I have to get Adelle help. I have to. O my God how much longer will I be fighting this same [expletive] fight? O my God how long will my daughter have to suffer? O my God please."

Journal Entry, March 25, 2013

"I don't want to write. I don't want to do anything. I feel like I cannot do anything. I am filled with apathy, with neuroleptic induced deficit disorder. I am filled with nothing. I spoke to my father again today and he said 'well you have to do what you have to do there.' I think that maybe my mother and father are afraid of what I will do if I get out and that they would prefer me to be locked inside a Polish mental asylum. I have to keep working on my dad. I am sure that my wife is working on my mom, and I have to try to get some sense into them. These people, my parents, are so filled with stupidity, so ignorant of the world, so blown away with lies. They are lie magnets.

Today I called Bogdan again and told him that he should email my dad and tell him what he thinks. I also thanked Bogdan for the money that he sent to me and I told him to look into a J1 visa. If I am going to be working in Florida, he could too. He could think about trying to get his entire family over to the US. What a change that would be for the Wirkus'.

Nothing is new in ROPS. Just more of the same. Waking up at 7 or 7:30 and then praying and hearing the crazy people make noises in the halls. Cleaning the cell, eating, reading and praying some more. Eating at 8, meat and bread and butter. The meeting at 9, which generally lasts a total of 20 seconds. Then spacer at 9:30. Nothing and nothing. I cannot read, I cannot write. I am stuck trying to think when I cannot think, trying to do those things that I cannot do. I pray and I watch tv and I watch the clock tick away. Lunch at 12:30 which was rice and some pieces of pig.

Today was Monday so we had the store at 3 something, then therapy at 5. Therapy is not really therapy, but just a chance to get on the internet for 45 minutes. After that, it was dinner time, a few slices of meat, bread and butter. This week I have to clean the bathroom so me and Skurat, the craziest of them all here cleaned it together. Nothing else, just passing the time, just passing the time. Just waiting until once again your eyes look into mine.

I don't know if it was wise to speak to my mom and dad. I feel like they are too lost to do any good at all. I really get the vibe that they believe that this is where I need to be. I don't know. I have to keep on working on them. I have to figure this out.

Father, help me to figure this out. I have got to get out of here. Father, lead my way out of here. Lead my way back to my family. Reunite us. Make us whole once again. Deliver us from this ritual abuse."

Journal Entry, March 26, 2013

"I try to keep going forward. I try to keep momentum going in the right direction. I don't know which way is forward anymore. I don't know where the momentum should be. All that I know at this point is that I have to get out of here and I have to make some money, hire an attorney and get into Adelle's life. Then I can also hire a private investigator, figure out how to have Adelle evaluated...But first things first. I must get out of here.

I spoke to my mom a bit tonight and we had a good conversation. We argued a bit, but it was healthy arguing, the kind of arguing that we used to do. She is wrong about some things, but that is to be expected and at least we started the process of getting some of those things out into the open. I told her that Agata is a pathological liar. I told her that she has been fooled by my wife, who gave her answers to questions when she needed answers. She didn't really believe me at first, but I think that I got her to start thinking.

I have a meeting with Jakimiak tomorrow. I don't know about preparing. I really don't think that I need to. The important thing is that I am not delusional now and that my father-in-law and everybody else is 'safe.' If those two conditions are met, then there is no reason to hold me in here.
Adelle Avery Bryson"

Journal Entry, March 27, 2013

"Today is twenty three months of being locked up.

The only thing that I can do right now is try to get out of here. I can do nothing else. Get out and then go from there. Being locked up is antithetical to everything. I wish that there was something that I could do now, but I cannot think of anything. I cannot think at all because of the Risperidone, but that is another story. What else can I do while I am here? I always get back to 'don't look crazy and get out of here.' Writing makes me look crazy or obsessed or preoccupied. Writing does not look 'normal,' so I don't think that I should do too much of it. Plus I simply cannot write with the drug that I am given. I can't write, I can't read. What the [expletive] can I do?

I wish I could see the path to Adelle. I wish that I could see any path at all. I wish I could see anything that is worth seeing. It is all nothing. Nothing is out there when my family is in shambles. Nothing is good when my daughter is being hurt. Nothing is good when I am not daddy.

Time. Time is the one thing that you cannot buy. Time is the one thing that you cannot get back once it is lost. Time is precious. Time in a child's life is the most precious. Time in my child's life is priceless. And, I am locked in ROPS and she is being abused in an intergenerational organized child abuse cult. O my God. Show me the way."

Dr. Ellen Lacter's response to my outreach is below. The article she refers to in the letter is in Appendix 37.

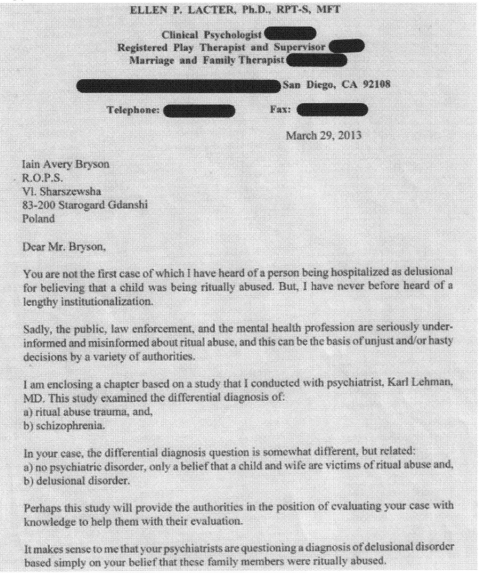

ELLEN P. LACTER, Ph.D., RPT-S, MFT

Clinical Psychologist ▬▬▬
Registered Play Therapist and Supervisor ▬▬▬
Marriage and Family Therapist ▬▬▬

▬▬▬ San Diego, CA 92108

Telephone: ▬▬▬   Fax: ▬▬▬

March 29, 2013

Iain Avery Bryson
R.O.P.S.
Vl. Sharszewsha
83-200 Starogard Gdanshi
Poland

Dear Mr. Bryson,

You are not the first case of which I have heard of a person being hospitalized as delusional for believing that a child was being ritually abused. But, I have never before heard of a lengthy institutionalization.

Sadly, the public, law enforcement, and the mental health profession are seriously under-informed and misinformed about ritual abuse, and this can be the basis of unjust and/or hasty decisions by a variety of authorities.

I am enclosing a chapter based on a study that I conducted with psychiatrist, Karl Lehman, MD. This study examined the differential diagnosis of:
a) ritual abuse trauma, and,
b) schizophrenia.

In your case, the differential diagnosis question is somewhat different, but related:
a) no psychiatric disorder, only a belief that a child and wife are victims of ritual abuse and,
b) delusional disorder.

Perhaps this study will provide the authorities in the position of evaluating your case with knowledge to help them with their evaluation.

It makes sense to me that your psychiatrists are questioning a diagnosis of delusional disorder based simply on your belief that these family members were ritually abused.

2

If people were committed to institutions every time they believed that someone had suffered a crime that could not be proven, we would have no freedom of thought or expression. And if we institutionalized anyone who believed and alleged that a child was being abused without proof, we might as well lock up a large percentage of the populace.

This would include institutionalization of thousands of mental health providers who file mandatory reports of suspected child abuse or ritual abuse. Most cases that clinicians report to the authorities are not provable. Children are afraid to tell anyone when they are being abused, or when they have been abused, and children make easily-discredited witnesses in legal proceedings. So, most cases remain unproven.

I doubt that you would have any success with a private investigator gathering credible evidence of child abuse. Child abuse, including ritual abuse, is done in secret and children are easily silenced.

I know of many cases in which parents have been unable to protect their children in cases of child abuse or ritual abuse. It is very hard to gather credible evidence of any form of child abuse. And in the absence of evidence, the authorities have no grounds upon which to act.

And in many cases in which protective adults continue to press for action in the absence of proof, the systems in place often react against the alleging party. This is a common in child custody disputes. In response to allegations of child abuse or ritual abuse, the family court generally makes a decision to reduce the alleging parent's contact with the child. An organization called California Protective Parents Association is working to address this problem. You may want to correspond with that organization as well. But, I believe that they will tell you the same thing that I have, i.e., that there may be little or nothing that you can do to help your daughter aside from what you have requested already— a thorough evaluation.

I cannot personally advocate for you for a multitude of reasons. This includes the restrictions on my license that prohibit me from taking any position in matters that I have not personally and fully evaluated. I am also not licensed to evaluate or treat anyone outside of California. Furthermore, I am involved in helping many victims and survivors of ritual abuse and cannot devote an inordinate amount of time to any one individual, other than my therapy clients.

I hope the information in the enclosed study will be of help to the mental health professionals evaluating your case.

Sincerely,

Ellen P. Lacter, Ph.D.

Journal Entry, March 30, 2013

"Tomorrow is Easter, and it will be my third Easter in a row without my daughter. I am in hell. On Friday, I had a meeting with the court in regards to divorce. Three people came from the court in Starogard Gdanski to report to the court in Szczecin, one person was an interpreter and another a woman to write down everything. I was asked questions about my marriage; I finally had the opportunity to state my side of the story. I finally had the opportunity to get my opinion on the matter recorded. They seemed to listen; they seemed to care what I had to say.

The woman asked if I agree with the divorce and I said that I do not agree with the divorce as it has been presented to me. I told her that my wife is a liar. She asked me if I agree with the divorce at all and I told her that I do not, but that it is not my choice, that if my wife wants a divorce that there is not much that I can do about it. I told her that the most important thing is my daughter. She told me that I had to write to the court in Szczecin about my daughter, that I had to write about alimony, about visitation, and that I could attempt to terminate my wife's parental rights. I need a lawyer.

I am so tired, so [expletive] empty. I am so low, so spent. I am so sad, so hurt. I am nothing because I am not a father to Adelle Avery Bryson. All that I am, all that I was, all that I want to be, all that I should want to be, all of it taken away from me. I've got nothing. Nothing is what I have. My everything was stolen from me. My daughter…"

Journal Entry, March 31, 2013

"What a day. What a [expletive] [expletive] day. I am going crazy. I am not crazy, but this situation is pushing me. All that I want is to be her daddy. All that I want is to play with my little girl, to hug her and to watch her grow up. All that I want is to be her daddy. O my God.

Where is the light? Which way do I go? How do I get back to my baby? What I see now is that I need to get out of ROPS. I think that that must be my first priority. But then what? What do I do when I am out of ROPS? I have to do one step at a time. Get out of ROPS first. Get out of Poland and then go from there."

Journal Entry, April 2, 2013

"I actually feel alright this evening. I feel like I am living detached from the mess that I am a part of. I feel 'enlightened' in that I am not slammed to the ground in complete despair, in complete agony. I can look at my situation and the situations of others from a bit of a distance; yes I still feel it, but tonight my eyes are open rather than focused on the pain. My head is not spinning around thinking 'this sucks, this is so difficult, when is this going to end…,' but rather, I can think those things and then move on to something else. I am stuck in the funk, but my head doesn't have to be. At least today it doesn't have to be.

As I've said for some time, you cannot let the situation, what others think….you cannot let these things change you or how you think or how you have to think. You have to maintain your ability to navigate your own mind. You have to be able to cycle through your own thoughts using your own will. If your thoughts are controlled or reliant upon what others are thinking, or upon the environment in general, then you have a problem. Of course your thinking and the way that you feel will be changed by others and by your environment, but can you revert back? Can you get your own thinking back, or are you just a pin ball controlled by outside forces?

Oh my God this [expletive] hurts.

Oh my God all that I want is to be a daddy to Adelle.

Oh my God all that I want is for my daughter to have the best things in life.

Oh my God what I want doesn't matter at all. O my God.

I spoke to Brian this evening. He is thinking about quitting his job, but he is afraid because he doesn't know what he will do next. He is terrified of giving up the security. I have to call him back tomorrow and try to convince him to do it. It would be a huge investment in his mental health, which in turn is a huge interest in his children's well being.

Not much new today. Still ROPS. Still Sadistic Ritual Abuse. Still hell."

Journal Entry, April 3, 2013

"All I want is you.

I talked to Brian again about quitting his job. I just think that he might do it. Well, if I had to bet, then I would say no, but I think that he wants to. His problem is that he can't. He doesn't know how."

Journal Entry, April 4, 2013

"I need a miracle. I spoke to the director today and he has now changed his tune to me going to another, less restrictive, hospital in Gozof. He doesn't say that I am crazy. He doesn't say much of anything. I think that he just doesn't want to make any decisions, that it is easier to just pass the buck. I am not sure. His mind is all over the place, and when your mind is all over the place, it is easier to go with the status quo. The status quo is to send me to the next hospital. The next hospital is in Gozof."

Journal Entry, April 8, 2013

"The one guy who I would have picked not to move into my room has just been moved into my room. He is one of the craziest on this floor, and to me is a very frustrating individual. Actually he is ok when he is not in my room, kind of like Bronek, but when he is in the room, things change. When he is in the room I cannot get away from him. He has a computer as well, and he wants to share time because we cannot both use computers at the same time. He says that he doesn't need the computer, but he will. And when he does, he will just say 'hey can I use my computer,' completely forgetting about all of the talk where he said that he doesn't need it. I am going to have to change these arrangements somehow.

Living with crazy people is challenging. I just don't know what to do. The problem is that I cannot do anything. I have no ability to change the situation. And, the situation is changing me. Living in these conditions, without Adelle and with Adelle being harmed daily, is destroying me. I will end up crazy. What can I do?

Karol, one of the people that works here, told me that the only thing that I can do is to make myself perfect for God, to worry about what God wants and let God worry about the rest. I have been saying and thinking the same thing. Yes, I agree with that, yet I do not know what to do. I do not know what I can do to make myself perfect for God. I am falling apart. I am being torn apart at the seams. I am being dismantled. I have been, for all intents and purposes, killed. I am dead. All that I care about is dead. There is nothing. I certainly am nothing. Nothing."

Journal Entry, April 9, 2013

"Lord lift me up in your palm. Direct my paths. Shine light down so that I can see, so that I know which way to go. Deliver my family to me. Put us back together. Allow us to begin healing...

Today was another day in ROPS. That says it all. Tomek was transferred to a lower security hospital today. Brian called me today and we talked for ten minutes or so. I began researching the 'overvalued idea.' I found out that 'Cult and Ritual Trauma Disorder' may be in the DSM V. I don't think so, but it was submitted...My wife and my daughter have Cult and Ritual Trauma Disorder..."

Journal Entry, April 13, 2013

"I cant do this anymore. I don't know how to do this anymore. I don't know what I'm doing. I don't know where to go. I don't have a clue. All that I know is that I have been destroyed. Completely and utterly destroyed. Taken apart at the molecular level. I am dead inside.

I spoke to Art and Bogdan yesterday. It was good to speak to them. It is nice to have communication with people outside of these walls. When I look at the people that are living in this hospital, it is ridiculous. Each one of them is just like 'are you serious?' These people are so entirely messed up, so hopelessly crazy. And here I am, right in the middle of it all. In Poland, in ROPS.

One minute I am taking care of my daughter on my own and desperately trying to get help for my wife and the next minute I am fighting to stay afloat. And that next minute has now lasted almost two years and four months. I was bitten by a black widow. I was destroyed by the one person that I trusted with everything. Agata completely took me the [expletive] out of the picture. Took me out the picture, ripped me from the frame and then made everybody believe that it was me who was and is the problem. Of course I helped her out because I freaked out when I finally got a clear picture of her. When I saw Agata through clear lenses instead of through the foggy ones, the distorted ones that I had been using I was absolutely terrified. I went crazy, as if I had seen a ghost. I had seen a ghost, or rather what I saw was evil, the epitome of evil, and it was in my family and attacking everything that I hold dear.

This place where I am is absolutely ridiculous. Everything in my life right now is absolutely ridiculous. Everything is absolutely [expletive] ridiculous. So completely out of whack. So completely off course. So [expletive] beat. I am so destroyed and so alone. So done for. So nothing. Nothing.

My wife ate me up. She chewed me up and spit me out. She crumpled me in her hands like a piece of scrap paper. She sloughed me off like a queen bee that is done with her sperm donor. She set me up and drilled me into the ground. I am discarded."

CHAPTER 81

"SHE IS THE POINT"

Journal Entry, April 14, 2013

"What do I do? What should I do? What can I do? I need to get out of here, but then what do I do next? What can I do to get my daughter thoroughly evaluated? What do I have to do? I am so battered, so beaten. I don't know what to do. The enemy is too strong for me. Even if I were to be let out of here tomorrow morning, what then would I do? What do I do now in order to get to where I need to be? How do I get my daughter to safety? Get out, work and write simultaneously. Make money and hire a lawyer. Follow up on the Hague Abduction Treaty issue (try to do that now). Get shared custody of Adelle and have her evaluated.

The mornings in this place are absolutely unbearable. The last thing that I want to do is to start a new day. It feels like I am dead, worse than I have ever felt in the morning, or at least equally as bad. Why do I want to get up in ROPS? Why do I want to get up without my daughter in the next room? What the hell can I do to get her out of ritual abuse?"

Journal Entry, April 18, 2013

"There is nothing that I can do, and it kills me. I was just looking at pictures, and it killed me. Sitting here and thinking about my Adelle, my daughter, my everything kills me. The only thing that I want is to be a daddy to that person, to that little child. The only thing. It kills me.

I started looking at PhD programs in Holland the other day and continued today. Holland pays you to go to school; PhD students are employees of the university. That makes getting my PhD very doable for me. I want to get started now. I was looking at child protection law and laws concerning minors today. I have to start thinking about possible research projects."

Journal Entry, April 19, 2013

"Today the director changed his tune. I asked him why he thought that I would be going to the second tier hospital and not the third and he clammed up. He said that the court sees me as a danger because of what I did and that the normal course of events is to go to the three different hospitals before being released to the public again. I asked him if he thought it would be possible to go to the third tier hospital, and he said that he would have to think about it, that he didn't know, that the court would want a reason for straying from the status quo. THE REASON IS THAT IT IS OBVIOUS THAT I DO NOT HAVE DELUSIONAL DISORDER. I think that I have to find a way to suggest this to the director without being so blunt. I do not want to make him feel uncomfortable or too challenged, though I do need to make him think. I do need to make him jump around inside just a little bit.

THE REASON IS THAT IT WAS A MISTAKE PUTTING ME IN ROPS; I SHOULD HAVE BEEN PUT IN THE MOCNIONE [MEDIUM SECURITY] HOSPITAL ORIGINALLY. I said 'so what you are saying is that I will be in Poland for another year,' and he said 'yes, I think so.' I am going crazy inside. My insides churn and burn. My mind just wants to give up, yet it cannot. Everything has been stolen from me. I am in such terrible excruciating pain. I WANT TO REMIND YOU THAT I DO NOT BELIEVE THAT MY FATHER IN LAW ABUSED OR IS ABUSING MY DAUGHTER. WHAT I DO BELIEVE IS THAT MY DAUGHTER HAD MULTIPLE SIGNS AND SYMPTOMS OF POSSIBLE CHILD ABUSE AFTER BOTH RETURNS FROM POLAND IN 2010.

I do not know the way. I am lost. I am so completely and utterly lost. What do I do? How do I tackle this issue?"

Journal Entry, April 21, 2013

"I had a very difficult morning. Nightmarish thoughts swirling through my head, tormenting me. Sweating and tossing and turning. Knowing that I would feel better if I got up, but choosing to lay in agony because getting up is also agony, maybe an agony that is more real. I feel so utterly defeated, so completely done. I have felt this way for quite some time, but now I feel it more deeply. More completely. More often.

Being told by the director that I would probably be here in Poland for another year was not easy to swallow. Another year when I have already been here for two. Another year when the only problem is that I thought that my father-in-law abused my daughter without evidence. As far as they know, I don't even think it anymore. What is the basis for saying that there is anything wrong with my thinking? The answer is that there is no basis. This is just an example of the political/judicial abuse of psychiatry. I did something that was socially unacceptable and now they will use psychiatry to keep me locked up for as long as possible even though psychiatry cannot definitively claim that there is something wrong with me.

Over this weekend, I wrote a letter to the international parental child abduction division of the U.S. Department of State asking for a response to the report that I filed in 2011, updating them on my situation, and telling them that I still need help [see Appendix 38]. I also wrote a letter to Richard Blumenthal's office in CT asking for help getting out of this country. Both of these letters are on the computer in rough draft form."

Journal Entry, April 22, 2013

"Yes, losing my daughter did cause me to go a bit crazy. Or maybe more than a bit. I went [expletive] bananas. One day I was singing to my little girl, trying to comfort her, trying to figure out what was going on with her mother, telling her mother that she was sick and that our daughter had just returned from three months in Poland with multiple signs of child abuse. One day I am rubbing my daughter's forehead so that she can fall asleep, reading her favorite books and the next day an international parental abduction rips my daughter out of my arms. Yes, I did go crazy. Yes, I was desperate. Yes I was and am in so much [expletive] pain that I can barely get a coherent thought across. Yes I love that girl. Yes every [expletive] minute is huge. Yes, I cannot save my daughter because I am absolutely nothing. I am her father and I am nothing.

Yes, on April 27, 2011 I was desperate. I wanted attention and I was not going to wait any longer in order to get it. I was frustrated and I was in a deep pain. I was a wreck. My everything had been taken from me, snatched right out of my hands. My household had been burnt to the ground. My little girl was born into an intergenerational organized child abuse cult.

'It all makes sense when I look in her eyes' Eminem

'I love my daughter more than life itself, but I got a wife who's determined to make my life a living hell...man I should've seen it coming...' Eminem

I didn't see it coming and when it finally slapped me in the face, I went nuts. I literally went nuts looking at the picture that was always right in front of my face. That doesn't mean that I am nuts. What it means is that in reaction to what happened to my family, I went nuts, temporarily. Now how do I get out of ROPS and get back to my girl? How do I get Adelle back into my life? How do I deal with Ciszewski? How do I push him onto my side, onto the side that I need him to be on? Oh my God, lead me. Please Father."

Journal Entry, April 25, 2013
"What do I have to do? What should I do? What can I do?"

Journal Entry, April 28, 2013
"O my God. My blood boils. My heart aches. My head is searching for answers. I look at pictures of my family, of my daughter and I, and my eyes well up with tears. What the [expletive] can I do to get that little girl back? What do I have to do in order to make her safe? That little girl is everything and yet I can do nothing. I am sending a letter to a woman from Survivorship.org tomorrow.

I am waiting to get a letter back from the U.S. Department of State regarding the Hague Abduction Convention report that I filed in 2011. I am waiting to get a letter from the Polish court regarding my request to have visitation with my daughter. Waiting, waiting....time goes by, Adelle's childhood goes by. Everything that matters is going by and everything that matters is completely out of my hands."

Journal Entry, April 29, 2013
"What good is a man who cannot protect his family? What good is a man who can just have his daughter, his little baby girl stolen from him? What good am I? I am no good at all. Just a broken down piece of insanity. A man who had everything torn from his clenched hands, ripped from his closed fist by a force who was much stronger than he."

Journal Entry, May 1, 2013
"Last Friday my medication was lowered from 2 mg to 1 mg. I asked the doctor to lower it, reminding him that I do not have any signs or symptoms of psychosis or mental illness at all, and he agreed. It is amazing how much 'better' I feel. It is as if I have received a breath of fresh oxygen, as if I have been given some of my connections back. Part of my brain was tied up, bound, and now it has been given back to me. It makes me a bit angry to know that I am still taking a milligram.

It frustrates me to no end to think about Adelle, to think about the time that is going by and my inability to do anything at all. It absolutely breaks me. I just want to scream, to [expletive] scream my brains out, to let one rip. But I can't. I have to repress it. I have to press forward. I have to keep moving in the direction towards my little girl. O my God."

Journal Entry, May 3, 2013
"Tonight nurse Beata cut my hair. She did a great job, and I feel much better. I didn't know what to do because none of the patients are able to cut hair. They are all so crazy that they don't even have the ability to cut hair. And it costs fifteen zloty to see the barber, and at the moment I do not have fifteen zloty. Beata is a nice nurse. It feels good to have my hair cut.
Get strong. Get out. Get Adelle."

Journal Entry, May 4, 2013
"I've really got nothing new to say. What is there to say that hasn't already been said? I am in the depths. I am scrounging for purpose, for energy, for anything. I have nothing anymore. Nothing.

I spent some time trying to prepare for my next meeting with Ciszewski. The psychiatric report from the court psychiatrists is quite ridiculous. They just [threw] some [expletive] together and called it a diagnosis. Most of what they put together doesn't make sense or is just plain wrong.

Art says that he wants to hire an attorney and get me out of here. I don't really want him in my life, but he seems eager to help. Even if there is a small chance that he will help, I think that I have to run with it. Dealing with him is like dealing with a hysterical woman. Maybe he can help me to get out of here sooner, and right now that is what matters: getting out of here."

Journal Entry, May 5, 2013
"Just another lonely day..."

Journal Entry, May 6, 2013
"Today one of the guards, Wojciech, gave me thirty zloty for the shop. He said that if we were in 'freedom' that he would buy me a drink, so in here he gives me money for the shop. Karol, one of the workers for this floor gave me a Bible and two chocolate bars. These were two separate occurrences."

Journal Entry, May 6, 2013
"Another guard brought me a Bible and chocolates, realizing that I was a fellow believer in Jesus Christ. We talked about his church and about how rare it was to be a Christian in the Catholic country of Poland. 'God speaks to you, doesn't he?' he asked me. At first, I was hesitant to respond, not knowing for sure that I could trust him, knowing what an affirmative admission to his question could mean if it got back to the psychiatrists. But I looked him in the eyes and decided to tell him, 'Yes, God speaks to all true believers through His Holy Spirit.'

'I know,' he replied, 'but you can't tell them that. You haven't told them that, have you? There was another guy a while back who said that to these psychiatrists, and it didn't turn out well for him.'

'No, I don't get into the details with them, though I do tell them that I believe in God. I know what they are looking for, and I am very careful about what I say to them. I had to stop telling them that I know that my daughter was abused, even though she had bruises and other symptoms. Now I tell them that it appeared that she had been abused, but that I can't be sure, just that my intention was to force them to evaluate her. I know what they would conclude if I were to tell them that I can speak to God, or that He speaks to me, and I would never talk to them about such matters. I need to get out of here...'"

Journal Entry, May 8, 2013
"I feel exhausted. I feel depleted. I feel dead. I don't know what the hell to do. I cannot do anything. I am trapped in a Polish loony bin, and my child is being brought up in the worst family that I could ever imagine, that I couldn't before imagine. Time continues to go by and the situation remains the same. Every day the same. Every day the same except that every day is yet another that is without Adelle, and yet another that Adelle is being hurt."

Journal Entry, May 11, 2013
"I sit here and I stare at the computer screen trying to figure out what to write. I have nothing to say. Everything remains the same. I didn't do much of anything today. I stayed in bed where I just let this bad dream swirl around in my head. There is nowhere for me to go, nothing for me to do here. I am stuck in a complete nightmare. My nightmare is the fact that Adelle is growing up in an intergenerational cult. My nightmare is everything that is happening around me. My nightmare is this life. My baby. My everything. My love. My family. My blood. My hope and my joy. My daughter."

Journal Entry, May 13, 2013
"The more that I think about this situation, the more I realize that I can do nothing. My enemy is too powerful, too entrenched. Just because I can do nothing does not mean that I will or should do nothing. But what should I do? What should I do when I can do nothing, when I am up against an enemy that is way too strong, an enemy that cannot be touched by this one man? What should I do when time is of the essence, when my little girl is getting older every day? I have no idea at the moment. I need to find an idea. I need to get my daughter out of ritual abuse. But how? But how?

Today was just another day in ROPS. Another day in this recurring nightmare. I played some soccer and scored my first goal of the season. I had some time on the internet and I looked and saw that my grandfather died in 2011 at the age of 93. I went to the film, which was about human trafficking for prostitution.
O my God, Adelle Avery Bryson."

Journal Entry, May 15, 2013
"'When this losin' feels like dyin', I hope you'll be by me then' [Dave Matthews lyrics]."

Journal Entry, May 18, 2013
"It still feels like dying. I googled 'Adelle Bryson' on Friday and today, and I saw that she won first prize in an art contest [see Appendix 39]. It also told me what school she is going to. I was looking through the school pictures trying to find her. I cannot tell if it is her or not. I think that she is in there, but I am not sure. I haven't seen her in so long. I stare and I stare and I try to judge whether or not I am looking at my daughter or not. And, I cannot be sure.

O my God. O my God. I stare at the screen and I begin to cry. I begin to feel empty and pointless. This stupid life has destroyed me. Everything that I care about has been destroyed. All that I want is to be that girl's daddy. I'm on my knees, Father please. I am going to carefully look at the pictures again on Monday.

Art is prepared, so he says, to spend up to 200 Euro on an attorney. He has e-mailed the attorney and we should hear something back this coming week. Bogdan may go to see the attorney on Monday since he is in Szczecin. He is going back to Germany to work for the next two weeks, so it would be good if he could get that done on Monday. I am a bit concerned about having Art help me, but I don't really have any other options. He 'loves' me and I need to get out of here. If he can help me to get out, then I think that I have to take the help. I need the help."

Journal Entry, May 19, 2013
"There will never be another May 19, 2013 again. I will never spend May 19, 2013 with Adelle. Adelle will never spend May 19, 2013 in a normal environment. Adelle will never have a healthy childhood. It's not only that she will not have a healthy childhood, but that she is having an unthinkably abusive childhood. Unthinkable but oh so real. O childhood. How important it is and how my own child has been deprived of it so utterly and completely, so horribly. A new week starts tomorrow. Another chance for something to change, for progress to take place. Another chance for letters to arrive, for the attorney situation to progress. Another chance for God to step in and deliver my family from this hell. Another chance."

Journal Entry, May 22, 2013
"Leszek Falkowski died last night. He had been really sick for a few days, and last night he just died. None of the staff said a word about it. They just continued on as if nothing had happened.
We/I didn't take enough pictures because I thought that I had time. I thought that me being a father, a daddy, was a permanent thing. I thought that I had a secure position, that it was the one position that couldn't be taken away from me. Who could take it away from me? Who would want to take it away from me? There are/were many things that we/I just don't/didn't do because the thought is that the times will keep going the same, that such drastic change will not occur. O how I just want to be a daddy again to Adelle. O how I just want to be her daddy."

Journal Entry, May 25, 2013
"Sometimes I feel like I just can't take it, like I just won't make it. Sometimes I feel like I've sunken too far, like I've lost it, like I will never recover. Sometimes I feel so low that I feel like giving up. And then I remember this little girl who is not so little anymore, the one that used to call me daddy. This little girl is living in hell. She is being brought up in an intergenerational cult. I am her father. Lord carry me."

Journal Entry, May 26, 2013

"I was looking over the court opinions again, and I was blown away at all the lies that are in there. Everything from my wife's mouth just transcribed into the court's opinion as truth. And again, I was just floored and overwhelmed at how defeated I am. So easily defeated. There is nothing that I can do except get out of here. But how do I get out of here? How do I get out of here when the court opinion says that I hit a man in the head with a hammer?

The court psychiatric opinion says that I have 'delusions concerning the abuse of my wife and daughter.' Therefore, I have to not believe that my wife and daughter were abused. I have no evidence with which to support such a belief and therefore I do not have the belief. End of story. I don't think anything. I don't have any suspicions whatsoever. What I know is that I need to go back to work and get on my feet so that I can support my daughter and get back into her life."

Journal Entry, May 27, 2013

"Adelle, I saw your picture today on your preschool website. I just knew it was you as I thought that I would when I saw you. The reason that I didn't know if it was you before was because it wasn't you but because I also couldn't figure out why I couldn't find you. I knew that you had to be there somewhere, but I couldn't find your picture anywhere. Now I have seen your picture. O my God. O my daughter. My daughter. Adelle, I don't know what to do. I have to figure out how to get out of here.

Maybe the people at Survivorship will have some ideas about how to proceed, but there is no way to get anything done in regards to you from in here. No matter what I do or how I say or do it, it will always be delusion as far as the Polish authorities are concerned when I talk about you being abused. I tried to change my pitch, my approach, but it didn't work. Once again, daddy is not playing with the smart kids; daddy is up against people who don't know how to think, a system that is broken and ancient.

I cannot convince the Polish authorities. Their ability to listen to me has been turned off. I can only convince the Polish authorities to let me out. Then I have to figure out what to do after that. I have to figure out how to get you, how to get you out of ritual abuse and back under my roof. I love you and I am sorry."

Journal Entry, May 31, 2013

"I feel psychologically stronger than normal today. I don't feel shaky. I feel firmer. I really noticed it when we were playing volleyball because I could block out all of the negative, doubtful thinking. I had more focus and 'strength.' More mental strength that is. I got the report from the doctor today in response to my request for documentation for Strasbourg. It proves a couple of things: that there is no substantive reason for holding me here, that the reason that they are holding me here is because of the court psychiatrist report. And, also that there have been issues with communication.

I think that the primary issues with communication have been with me and the psychotherapist, from what I can see from what had been written in the report. It also appears, though I cannot know for sure, that [Maria] has been revealing things from our conversations. For example, it says 'demands keeps delusional beliefs...' I told [Maria] that I had to stop talking about my wife and daughter. She is the only one that I told. And, I really don't know where else they would have gotten this information, unless they were just guessing. Guessing of course, or just creative narrative are possibilities. However, if I had to guess, I would say that [Maria] had something to do with it. It really doesn't matter; what I've got to do is move forward. She is not my friend; I knew that and know that. She is just some girl that works at this stupid [expletive] institution that is holding me in here for 'delusions' that I do not have.

The report also says that I am aware that Agata has denied the things that I allege. These Polish [expletive] just prove over and over again that the problem is with them. They still don't know what I alleged. They still don't have a clue what ritual abuse is. I told them straight away that Agata would deny the things that I allege, that Agata is seriously mentally ill, that Agata is a participant in the abuse of our daughter. Please lift me up o my Lord for I am low, desolate, and stripped of everything. Keep me strong. Strengthen me and direct me."

Journal Entry, June 3, 2013

"I had a very tough day today. I felt like I was drowning or being burned at the stake. I felt overwhelmed and consumed with agony and grief. I felt utterly helpless. I feel this way now, though now I am a bit better. This bad dream needs to end. Father please."

Journal Entry, June 14, 2013

"My head hurts. I miss my daughter. O how I miss my daughter. Adelle, you were stolen from me. I was trying to get your mother help. I was trying to understand why you had every sign that you had been traumatized. And then you were just stolen from me. My world was flipped upside down and it has been upside down ever since. I don't know how to flip it back. I don't know how to get you back. I don't know how to get you away from those people. I am still trying. I will always be trying. I will never stop trying. I just don't know what to do."

Journal Entry, June 22, 2013

"Still waiting. Still trying to figure this out. I will be transferred soon to the next hospital. The lawyer that Art hired is looking into having me moved to the U.S. I have more to write, but I will have to do it tomorrow. I tend to not write because there is not much to say. I miss my daughter and I am in pain. In pain because I don't want my daughter to be in any pain. In pain because of what was taken away from us, from her. I will put an effort in to make it back here tomorrow."

Journal Entry, June 29, 2013

"All that I can think about is my daughter. She is everything. All that I want is to be her daddy, to give her a home and as wonderful a childhood as I can. I have been thinking a lot about those last two weeks in December 2010 when I was trying to convince Agata to get help, when I was taking care of Adelle on my own and taking her outside to play every day in order to get her away from her mother who was an absolute mess, when I was trying to figure out what the [expletive] happened to my baby when she was in Poland.

I have been thinking a lot about living with Agata in general, about the blindness that I had in regards to who she was, what she was doing, how she made me feel. She lied, cheated and stole. She psychologically abused my daughter right in front of my eyes. She made me feel like I was going to blow up inside. But I couldn't see it. I couldn't see her. I didn't want to see her because she was my wife. It was partly like a courtesy thing; you see something ugly and you avert your eyes or do not focus out of respect, courtesy, fear...
Ritual Abuse.

I am struggling. This situation does not get easier with time. Time only exacerbates the situation. Time means that Adelle is getting older, that her abusers have more time to hurt her, that we have less time to be together. And, I think about how I can help her and I draw a blank. I really don't know what to do except to keep going forward. When I try to think about specifics, I can think of nothing. Nobody believes me, no organization or government agency was or will be willing or able to step in. As I have been saying, my daughter has to be thoroughly evaluated, and from where I am sitting, there is no way to force that to happen. All that I want is to be a daddy to that little girl, that little girl who is less and less little every day.

I love you Adelle. I am sorry I didn't see this sooner. I am sorry I fell apart when I did see it. I am sorry, so sorry, I had different plans for us. God help us. I'm on bended knee."

Journal Entry, July 6, 2013

"What is the point? Another weekend in ROPS... Another weekend without my daughter...Another weekend with my daughter in ritual abuse. I get so down and out sometimes. Sometimes my mind just *runs and runs and I feel like I am in an Edgar Allan Poe book that was laced with acid. Horror. Depression. What do I do? My family... Lord, my family...*

Today I took advantage of the fact that it is Saturday and I stayed in bed for a while. I was in and out of a light, dream sleep. Very light. Nightmarish. Sweating and tossing and turning. Better than reality. Reality is hell. Literally. There is nothing to do in this place anyway. The only thing that I can do is get out. If I could sleep until I got out, I think that I would.

I spoke to Faye a couple of days ago. It was good to talk to her. She is still living off her survivor benefits, with Katie, her health is not well...She told me that I could live with her. I might just do that. I don't know what I will do. I can also live with Art, but I don't really know if I really can. I have to get on my feet, pull myself up by the bootstraps, and I have to surround myself with good people, with educated people, with people who are alive and not so blind. I just want to be Adelle's father. O my God. O my God.

So high, so low. Now not so high and ever lower. The lowest of the lows feel like they will never end, like I will just become absolutely crazy and lose it completely. I know that that is not true, that it is just a cycle, but it feels that way when it is happening. I just want to curl up into a ball and die. And then I remember that my little girl is having a worse time than I am, that she is the only thing that matters, that she is the victim of intergenerational ritual abuse. My little girl. My Adelle Avery. Systematic, organized child abuse. Deliberate dissociation. Terrible trauma.

Pull yourself together. Toughen up. Adelle is six and she does not know or remember me. I have to act and I have to get on track. I have to play my cards smartly. I don't know how to play my cards, but I do know that every card that I play is extremely important. I must learn quickly so that I do not make the same mistake twice.

My head still hurts, not all of the time but enough of the time, a product of having to take Risperadone. I am fairly clear, though not as much as I would like to be and certainly not as much as I am capable of. In the situation that I am in, a certain hit is to be expected. It does not surprise me that everything hurts a bit, that everything has been taken down a notch or two. However, it is time for these things to be restored. It is time for my family to be restored. It is time for....well, the last statement says it all.

There is nothing else that I can say, nothing else to be said. Take me back to just before I was spinning, take me back to just before I got dizzy. One moment I was watching a movie on the couch with Adelle, eating popcorn and drinking tea, the next moment she was taken from me, stripped from me. And I haven't seen her since. It has been about two and a half years. Two and a half years. My God. A lifetime. A [expletive] lifetime. My daughter. Adelle Avery Bryson. The point is Adelle Avery Bryson. She is the point."

CHAPTER 82

MEDIUM SECURITY
"DON'T YOU REALIZE THAT...?"

Journal Entry, July 7, 2013

"Tomorrow starts a new week. I am waiting to be transferred to Choroszczy. I am waiting for Bogdan (Mariusz Wirkus) to call with an update from the lawyer, I am waiting for Adelle to be back under my roof, in my arms, safe from ritual abuse. I am waiting to hear from Strasbourg, I am waiting. That is the bottom line: still waiting. I pray that there will be positive changes this week. I pray for my daughter to be back in my arms, for us to have a chance. I pray for mercy and grace. I pray for Adelle Avery Bryson. Father please."

Journal Entry, July 10, 2013

"Tomorrow I am being transferred to Choroszczy. All of my things are packed, except for the laptop, and I don't remember where I put my stamps. It is kind of bothering me because I need my stamps. However, it is such a small thing when looked at in relation to the other things that are going on in my life. Tomorrow is Agata's birthday. Thirty-one. What is going on? What has happened to my family, to those that I love? What is going on? What the hell can I do? What the hell should I do? I have to get ready for the next round of doctors and be prepared to answer questions, be prepared to set things in motion that will get me out of this situation. I have to stay focused, stay on point, not stray from the 'message,' and emit no risk at all."

Feeling shaky inside of myself and uncertain of what was coming next, I said goodbye to my friends. I met Maria in the hallway, and she wished me good luck. I wanted to give her a hug, but I couldn't. Being a prisoner in the "crazy" ward had caused me to lose my self-esteem, and though I knew she had believed in me, I wasn't certain that she still did. I was tired and depleted, and I knew that I had two more stops before I would be released. How I wished it was only one more stop and not two.

I prepared for transport to Choroszczy, a five-hour drive toward the Russian border, the opposite direction that I wanted to be going. I hoped that the next place would be better in some way, though I doubted it. It seemed that nothing was happening according to my plans, that I wasn't getting any breaks at all, that I was just a bug stuck in a trap. All that I knew was that I had to keep flapping my wings, that I would eventually be released, and that every day was another day that I was losing all that I cared about: my little girl and her wellbeing.

The guard who delivered me to the police assured me that it would be better where I was going. A police van picked me up in the same place that I had been dropped off in late November of the previous year. They drove me about halfway after which I was moved to a larger prison transport bus. As I boarded the bus, I was excited to be able to converse with other normal prisoners, but then I was told that I had to sit in the mental patient isolation chamber up front. The entire rest of the trip I was chained in the Hannibal Lector cage, separated from everyone else by walls of plexiglass and bars.

I prayed and celebrated your mom's birthday in my head, contemplating how strange it was that this was all happening. I dreamt of how I had imagined and wished it would all be, and desired only to hold you both in my arms.

The bus made several stops before arriving at my destination, but I was never allowed to leave the isolation chamber. Once we arrived in Choroszczy, I was led into a waiting room and uncuffed to await my intake processing. The police officer departed, and I was left sitting on a chair in a room with only a couple of secretaries. I considered walking out the door and escaping, realizing that this was the best opportunity that I had seen for escape since my arrest on April 27, 2011. *But where would I go and who would help me to get out of the country? How would it impact my fight for you, which is the only thing that I care about? Maybe this place will be better? Maybe these people will listen to reason and order that you be evaluated?* I stayed put and waited for whatever was coming next.

* * *

July 2013 to May 2014
Samodzielny Publiczny Psychiatryczny Zakład Opieki Zdrowotnej w Choroszczy
(Independent Public Psychiatric Health Care Institution in Choroszczy)
Brodowicza 1
Choroszcz 16-070
Poland

A guard eventually came to get me, and I was relieved that I could stop thinking about escaping. The first thing I did when we got outside was ask him if I could smoke a cigarette. He obliged, and I pulled out the old, stale pack they made me surrender when I arrived at ROPS. Alone with this one unarmed guard in the parking lot, I again considered escaping, or at least recognized that it would be possible to try. *All I would have to do*, I thought, *is knock him out, abandon my things, and Grand Theft Auto a vehicle. But, which way would I go, and where exactly am I anyway?* Thinking about escape was stressful.

A nurse approached me as soon as I walked into the building and handed me a fresh pack of cigarettes, telling me that they were from my friend Łukasz Lelewski, who had also been at ROPS with me previously. I was excited to see him, and knowing that he was thinking about me and my arrival made me feel a sense of welcome. *Maybe this place will be better*, I thought.

My hopes were dashed as soon as I saw the inside of the facility and where I would be staying. My bed was in a room with six or seven other guys, with maybe a total of five of these rooms spaced out over about a one hundred-foot hallway. The doors were all locked at night; to use the bathroom after hours we had to ring a bell and wait for a guard.

I didn't get to see Łukasz right away, because, again, they started me off in the observation/higher security wing. Upstairs was supposedly better, which is where Łukasz was, and where I would be headed in a week or two once they determined that I was not dangerous. How they could have thought I was dangerous after being a model prisoner for more than two years baffled me, but I knew that they were merely following procedure, like when a new chicken is quarantined before being introduced to the rest of the flock.

The meals were worse than they were in either ROPS or prison, and everybody was hungry all the time. We were permitted to have the social worker buy up to four items from the store once per week, but cigarettes, coffee, and sugar for the coffee were always three of these things, so there was basically no extra food available to supplement the meager diet they provided. There was an indoor smoking room, which is where we spent most of our time when we were not sleeping or waiting for food, like zoo animals.

The doctor that I was assigned was Anna Brzozowska, a mid to late 50s woman who I immediately perceived to be miserable. To me she looked more like a truck driver than like a psychiatrist, an alcoholic truck driver from the 1970s.

"I am going to increase your medication," she informed me during our first meeting.

"Why would you do that when I don't have any signs of mental disorder?" I asked, scared, and feeling like I was punched in the solar plexus.

"They were not treating you before. Now I am going to treat you." By "treat," she meant medicate, and by "they were not treating you before," she meant she was going to increase the dosage out of Dr. Ciszewski's "sedative" range, and into his "antipsychotic" range.

"Treating me for what? For thinking that my daughter had signs and symptoms of abuse?"

"Treating you for the disease that the court decided you need to be treated for," she explained. "The dosage that they had you on was not treatment."

"Can't you call Dr. Ciszewski and see what he was thinking?"

"No, I'm not going to do that. I am your doctor now, and I am going to treat you according to what the court has said. Do you realize that nobody has had any idea what you were talking about when you alleged 'ritual abuse?' Nobody in Poland has ever heard of such a thing; don't you realize that?"

"It doesn't matter if they have heard about it or not. This does not take away from the fact that it does exist, nor does it take away from the fact that my suspicion of it was not delusion. Rather, it proves that I was not proven to be mentally ill, because a) they didn't know what it is, and b) they didn't investigate the possibility that it is occurring."

I tried once more to remind her that Dr. Ciszewski had intentionally lowered my dose because of the fact that I didn't have any signs of mental illness, and I told her that when the dose had been higher that it had caused me severe distress. "I couldn't think. It felt like someone was pouring rubber cement into my brain synapses."

She didn't seem concerned about my distress or the fact that I couldn't think. Her mind was set on her need to "treat" me in accordance with the wishes of the court. She did agree to switch medications, and from this point onward I was switched from risperidone to olanzapine. It didn't matter that much to me regardless, as I had no plans of taking anything that they gave me.

"Do you hear voices?" she inquired.

"No, I do not, nor have I ever heard voices. What are you talking about? The only thing that I did was react to my daughter being taken away from me and her mother telling me that her family is a cult. Yes, my reaction was extreme, but so was what I was reacting to."

"Well, when you get out of here," she informed me smugly, "you're going to need to forget about your daughter."

I didn't reply, but just took it all in, realizing that I was going to have to be careful with this woman moving forward.

Journal Entry, July 18, 2013

"I have started writing in a notebook because I do not have as much access to my laptop as I did in ROPS. This new hospital that I am in is a horrible place. It is not a hospital, or rather it is called a hospital, but it is just prison with psychiatrists. I said that about ROPS too, and in a way that is how ROPS is. But this place truly opened my eyes. There is no therapy. There is no sport. There is no nothing except a smoking

room, a tv...the conditions are the same. The difference is that a psychiatrist is in charge. A psychiatrist is in charge, and"

Every morning the doctors and nurses made their rounds to each room, this facility's version of "apel." We had to stand by our made beds and greet them as they entered the room. Every morning, they asked me the same questions: 1) "How do you feel?" and 2) "Do you hear voices?" I always answered that I felt great and that I had never heard voices.

This place was way worse than regular prison or ROPS; it was a true torture chamber. I began to seriously consider escape as a possibility, and I talked to Art about the possibility of him coming to Poland to pick me up on several occasions. Everybody in this place was miserable, and everybody thought about escape and/or suicide.

One man did escape by scaling the brick building and leaping over the razor wire while we were outside for our one-hour walking time. I don't know if they caught him, but I was both proud of him and sorry for him, for if they did catch him, he was not going to get out for a very long time.

I had an mp3 player that I traded tobacco to get, but I no longer wanted to listen to music. Negativity had taken over, and music had lost its strength to lift me out of the hole. All that I could think about was getting out so that I could continue trying to get help for you and your mom. I would have preferred to be put into suspended animation, like in the movie *Minority Report*, rather than live out the time in this place.

I was able to continue teaching English. I did this for the mental challenge as well as to boost my rapport with the staff and the other prisoners, but primarily to show the doctors that I was not the person that I was portrayed to be in the prosecutor's report. *Maybe they will report positive things back to the court.* I prepared lessons twice a week for both the lower and upper floors, about fifty or sixty people in total.

Trips to the dentist provided the best opportunities for escape. The dental office was about a block away from the building, and it was always one unarmed guard who brought me. During the walk to the dentist, one of my wrists was attached to one of the guard's wrists with a leather, buckled on handcuff of sorts. *All I would have to do,* I reasoned, *is knock the guy out and unstrap my wrist. Then I would be in the city alone and somebody could pick me up and get me over to Russia.* I fantasized about this possibility, but I never seriously considered putting it into action.

Another prisoner asked me to kill him because he couldn't take it. One day when I was playing cards, he came up behind me and choked me out. I awoke in a daze, unsure of where I was or what had just happened. When I came to, he said, "Just take me in the bathroom and do the same thing, but don't stop choking off my air or blood supply for a couple of minutes. Please," he begged me, "nobody will know. Please just do that for me."

I explained to him that not only would they know, but that I couldn't help him do this regardless. He was extremely disappointed with me, and he didn't stop asking for a long time.

I became an expert at sleeping, with bedsores to prove it. I arose for my meals and then went immediately back to bed, sleeping from after breakfast until lunch, then after lunch until dinner. I read as much I could, and I kept a journal, but the feelings of depression were overwhelming, and it was very difficult to do either of these things. There was so much dead time that I didn't have enough to read, and while it provided a welcome escape from my surroundings when I had something to read, I usually didn't have new reading materials. I reread what I had and got shipments of books from Art and my mom on occasion.

The Bible was dangerous because it was being used to prove that I was mentally ill, but I still read it. In my journal, I cried out to God, asking him, "How long?" and, "Lord please help Agata and Adelle." I tried to write in my journal daily, and for the most part I did. If it were to be condensed, those are main themes that I was expressing. "Father please!"

I covered myself with my sheets, on my knees in my bed, praying and looking for some sort of reprieve from all the nonsense that was going on around me. From getting attacked, having to repeat daily that I wasn't hearing and never had heard voices, to having people masturbate in their bed a couple of feet from mine, and not getting to hold you or read you a bedtime story... I couldn't imagine how it could possibly be any worse.

My mom agreed to send me pictures of you and your mom after I asked her several times. She was hesitant, as she still sided with your mom and your abductors, thinking that I needed to be "treated," but she did send me two black and white photocopied pictures in one of her packages.

*Pictures sent from my mom. **Left**: You and your mom. **Right**: You at a beach. At the bottom, I wrote "I had hoped you'd see my face, and be reminded that for me, it isn't over" (Adele lyrics).*

I became even better at navigating the drug line, which I had to do given the dose increase and the corresponding effects upon my cognitive abilities. I hardly ever took the medication until I got caught one time. Sometimes they would give normal tablets and sometimes they gave dissolvable tablets. The dissolvable tablets posed the most risk because they couldn't go into the mouth at all, whereas the regular tablets could just be transferred into the upper lip and spit out as I had practiced at ROPS.

The time I got caught I took the dissolvable tablet and pretended to pop it into my mouth but kept it in my hand. The nurse asked me to open my hand, and then she told me that she would have to report me to the doctor.

"I'm sorry," I pled, "do you really have to report me? Can't you let it slide? Please! I haven't ever been in trouble..." She thought about it for a moment, then said that she would let it slide. I was scared at the next "apel," because I didn't know if she would or wouldn't, but she never told on me. From this point on I had to be much more careful, and I never risked it when that nurse was on shift.

One of my friends did hear voices, and one time while we were in the smoking room the voices told him I was Hitler, and he slugged me. I didn't hold it against him. Afterward, he remembered that he had punched me, but he didn't know why anymore; I learned to watch his eyes more carefully.

Another guy in my cell liked to wake up at 5am and play Polish radio so everyone in the cell could hear it. I requested that he not do this, since it immediately woke me up, and because Polish radio at this point was just another form of torture for me. I offered him my ear buds.

In the middle of the night, I awoke to him hitting me in the face. At first, I thought that I was dreaming, and then I just yelled, knowing that defending myself would be construed as an act of violence on my part. The guards came and took him away, and he spent the rest of his time on the observation floor.

When Dr. Brzozowska asked me about it, I told her that it was good that he didn't use a knife or a chair to hit me. Of course, I was speaking in Polish, so maybe I wasn't clear, but her response was, "What would you have done if you had a knife?" implying that I was saying that I would have responded with violence. "No, that is not what I meant," I scrambled to explain in a language I was still struggling to communicate with, "I meant that it is good that he didn't have a knife because then I might not be here anymore."

Dr. Brzozowska informed me that she had diagnosed me with depression, and that she wanted me to take medication to treat it. "I don't have depression," I tried to explain. "This environment can be extremely difficult. I am fine, and I don't want any more medication."

"Well," she countered, "if you don't agree to take the medication, then I will tell the court that you are refusing treatment."

"OK," I answered, defeated again, "can you give me citalopram? This is a medication that I have taken in the past, and for me the side effects were minimal." She agreed, and I had to learn how to do the lip trick with two pills.

Given that the previous mandatory six-month opinion to the court was delivered in May/June 2013, I assumed that the next opinion would be around November/December 2013. I asked to speak to Dr. Brzozowska regarding this, thinking that I would be able to move on to a third tier/minimum security facility sometime in the beginning of 2014.

"I will not be recommending that you are transferred," she informed me. "I don't know you well enough. I need to observe you and treat you for a longer period of time."

"What do you mean, you 'don't know me well enough'? I have been incarcerated for over two years, have had zero issues, and don't have any signs of mental illness. You don't even talk to me except to ask me if I hear voices. What is it that you want to know?"

"I don't know if you are sorry enough for your actions. How do you think the victim feels?"

I had to stop myself from telling her that he was not the victim, but the victimizer of my little girl, and I explained to her that I was sorry for my actions. And, to prove it to her, I drafted a letter to your grandpa apologizing for beating him up. I showed Dr. Brzozowska the letter and asked her to send it for me so that she knew that I was serious about apologizing and admitting fault.

"I still cannot recommend to the court that you be transferred at this time. We can talk about it again in a few months."

Asking to change doctors crossed my mind, but I did not go through with it because I thought this could cause more problems than it would solve. I didn't want to come across as a complainer or seem like I was questioning the decisions of the court "expert" that I was assigned to. I concluded that I would just have to wait it out until Dr. Brzozowska felt that she knew me well enough, whatever that meant.

My mom hired an attorney, Wojciech Bagiński, to look into the possibility of having me transferred to the U.S. I struggled with the idea, not wanting to bring any issues back to the U.S., but also believing that a psychiatrist who spoke my language and was aware of the existence of ritual abuse would be forced to release me. In Poland, there was no telling when I would be released given the absurdity of who they had me dealing with.

The process of considering transfer to the U.S. continued for several months, and I was thankful that my mom had put this plan into motion. We didn't know if it was possible, but I reasoned that it was worth trying in case Dr. Brzozowska decided to play games. Mr. Bagiński informed us that a transfer of this nature had never been done before between the U.S. and Poland.

Dr. Brzozowska eventually agreed to send another opinion to the court after she decided she had asked me enough times if I heard voices. She indicated that she would be recommending that I be transferred to minimum security, the last tier of the big trap I had found myself in. I was learning the true meaning of "the process is the punishment." Did she really think that the attempted forced drugging would make me just forget about you and your mom?

After receiving my transfer orders and date, I prepared to move again, this time a twelve-hour trek to the west, stopping at various facilities along the way to drop off other prisoners at their destinations. I was excited to be closer to you and your mom again, though I had no idea what would be awaiting me when I got there. If medium security was worse than maximum, then could minimum be even worse? I didn't know, but I did know that it was one step closer to being released, one step closer to being able to work on the real problem: you and your mom stuck in a cult family.

I said goodbye to my friends, and I donated most of my books to the facility, unable to keep trekking all my belongings with me. I gave the laundry lady my binoculars and compass that I had brought in case I had decided to try to scope out your great grandfather's place in Sierokowo, and she was ecstatic. "This too shall pass" had finally come to fruition, and I was ready to go, knowing that I had only one more stop before they would have to release me.

CHAPTER 83

MINIMUM SECURITY
"I AM SICK. I WILL ALWAYS BE SICK."

May 2014 to June 2015
Szpital NZOZ MEDiSON
(NZOZ MEDiSON Hospital)
Słoneczna 15
Koszalin 75-642
Poland

Journal Entry, May 20, 2014
"I left Choroszy in the back of a small police van. There was a barrier between me and the two officers in front. The cops seemed alright; I didn't have any problems, and I think that this is because the nurses informed them that I don't pose a threat. One of them was smoking in the van, so I figured that I would as well. I was a little nervous about them getting upset that I was smoking, but I did anyway. I used a banana skin as an ashtray. I don't think that the cops were even aware of this. The back of the van was two plastic benches facing each other, the plastic making it so that you have to brace yourself the entire time to keep from slipping onto the floor.

I had pretty much no view of outside; there were no side windows, and the back window was solid, with bars. They drove me to some central meeting point for prisoner transport a little more than two hours away; I think it was close to Warsaw. When we stopped and parked I asked if I could get out and smoke, but the one in the passenger seat turned slightly so his chin was over his left shoulder, shook his head, and said 'not now.' After about fifteen minutes sitting in the back of the hot van, watching the officers through the front windows open their doors, get out, walk around and smoke, then they came for me.

Now they were all business because their cop buddies were in abundance. I was handcuffed and walked over to the bus where I was going to spend the rest of the day. It was basically a silver school bus cut down the middle, with prisoners in the back, guards and me in the front. When we got to the bus, after putting my bags in the back, the handcuffs were removed; one of the new officers took out his cuffs and secured me. I was handcuffed for the entire ride. I stepped up the two steps into the bus, and the young officer pointed to my seat. I was put in an isolation chamber the size of a port o potty, and my door was locked. When I sat down, I didn't know that I wasn't going to be able to stand up for the next eight or so hours. I was the only one in the isolation chamber out of all of the prisoners, and this was because I was the only psychiatric patient. I kind of felt like Hannibal Lector.

There was another locked gate/door blocking off the front of the bus where my cage was from the back of the bus. In the back of the bus were regular prisoners being transported to other prisons. These people, because they were not psychiatric, could talk to each other. Do the Polish police really believe that the people in the back are less dangerous? Is the guy who killed someone over a cigarette less dangerous than the guy who attacked the man who gave his daughter bruises?

There were three cops, one short pudgy guy who was obviously the boss and sat in the passenger seat with his clipboard and special boss hat and curly tipped moustache. The driver didn't do anything but drive, and drive me crazy because he kept smoking cigarettes. The smoke blew into my chamber, but I could not smoke myself for the entire day, and his smoke only teased me. I had cigarettes and a lighter in my pocket, and I came [expletive] close to lighting up, but I didn't.

The problem was the twenty something crew cut sitting directly across from me. He seemed like a nice enough guy; I didn't think that he was too bright, but he was smart enough in Poland to sit across from me with a Glock 17 on his leg. Of course, he had a much more comfortable chair than mine, and he was distracted by his i phone, sleeping, or eating canned spreadable meat for most of the trip. With him I tried the most of the three to get eye contact with; the [expletive] would not look at me, twelve miserable hours sitting three feet away from this guy and not even a split second of eye contact. But I think that if I lit up one of my Viceroy Red 100's he would have looked at me right away.

They never asked me if I wanted or had to go to the bathroom; we stopped for about an hour to pick up more prisoners, but my door was never opened for the entire trip. Luckily I did have a bottle of water and some sandwiches that two nice guard ladies made for me...also canned spreadable meat, but delicious.

The driver turned off the fan and the light, and I was sweltering. It was a [expletive] hot day. An hour later, he turned on the fan after I asked him three times. The cops wouldn't look at me or talk to me. I was just an item being transported, a court mental patient who needed to remain handcuffed and isolated for everyone's safety. I tried to make eye contact, to establish some sort of human connection, but not one of them took my eye bait. I felt small and insignificant and maybe even like I should be dangerous. Not a person, but like an animal. These people obviously thought I was dangerous.

I was the last to get dropped off, sometime after nine o'clock at night. The young guard finally opened my cage/plexiglass door and beckoned me to step out of my cage and out of the bus. I stepped out and looked around; it was pretty dark, but I could see that the hospital that I was about to be checked into for at least six months was in the woods. And that was a good thing because I love the woods.

I struggled to get all of my bags; I had acquired a lot of things, and I had four bags of various shapes and sizes with a lot of books. And, books are heavy like bricks if you have enough of them. The biggest problem wasn't even the bags or the fact that neither of the police officers who were out of the car and set to deliver me to the hospital even came close to offering to grab a bag. The problem was that I had to do this handcuffed. I looked at the cop, and raised my cuffed hands an inch or so, but he just nodded his head towards my bags and grunted. I figured it out: one bag on each shoulder and one in each hand. Then I just had to waddle like somebody with no knees twenty feet to get inside the door, to the spot where I would meet my first minimum security court psychiatrist.

An average looking, kind of nerdy forty something doctor with short curly brown hair and round horn rimmed glasses met us at the door. He seemed to have a laid back, calm demeanor, but my guard was up. I was tired from the long journey, but I had practiced what I would say for my intake; I knew that I would meet a psychiatrist immediately, because that was how it had been in the first two hospitals. This would be my first contact with a shrink at this facility, and I had to make sure that I made the right impression because one of the psychiatrists at this facility would be deciding whether to let me go or not in six months time. I had to make sure that the right things were written in my file so that I had a good starting point. I knew what the questions would be, and I knew my answers. I knew that I was at the last *of the Polish court hospitals, that the next step was release, and I knew that this guy's first impression of me was important."*

Journal Entry, May 22, 2014

"I arrived in Koszalin on May 20. I left Choroszcz at around eight in the morning with two police in one of the smaller vans. I sat in the back compartment, without handcuffs. We stopped once at a convenience store where I used the bathroom and had a cigarette. We arrived in Bydgosc sometime in the afternoon. I was then moved onto one of the big convoy busses. I was handcuffed and placed in the small, one person compartment near the front. There I stayed, with the door locked until we arrived in Koszalin around 8:30 P.M. There was a psychiatrist waiting for me to arrive.

After I was uncuffed, we went into a little room and he asked me how I was. I told him that I was a little tired from the trip, but otherwise fine. He asked me why I am here, and I told him that the court has ordered that I be here because I attacked my father-in-law. He asked me why I attacked my father-in-law and I told him that I believed that he was abusing my daughter. I told him that I do not now believe that, that that was delusion. He asked me about drugs, and I told him that I smoked marijuana and that I took doctor prescribed morphine and clonazepam for over five years. I was tired and depleted when I was questioned, and unprepared to speak to a psychiatrist, both physically and psychically. I then went upstairs where I was shown the smoking room, and I had my first cigarette in many hours. I was assigned to an observational room with a camera and I checked my bags in.

I have found that the people that I have met have not been here long and will not be here long. They talk in terms of days and weeks rather than months and years. There are a lot of people here because of drugs. I am anxious to get back in to talk to the doctor because I am now prepared, and because I want to state my case. 'I had delusions and I believed that my father-in-law had abused my wife when she was a child and that he had also abused my daughter. Because of those delusions I attacked him.'"

I was put into a temporary room, and I could immediately see and feel that I was in a sort of heaven compared to where I had been. All the people that I had met so far were not prisoners, but just normal people like the ones I had been with during my short stint at the Backus Hospital psychiatric observation ward in Connecticut. Most had no experience with prison whatsoever. This was more of a country club than a prison, but having said that, it also definitely wasn't a country club. I felt liberated, walking the halls and hanging out on the large balcony. I decided right then and there that I was going to take over the place. I didn't know what that meant yet, but this was the feeling that I had.

After one night in the observation room, I was transferred to a regular room. The first night that I was there, people were passing around vodka and marijuana. I hesitated, but not for long. *If they are doing it, then it must be alright,* I reasoned. I knew that they were there under different circumstances than I was, and I flashed back to where I had just been for the previous thirty-seven months, but I also wanted to party. They poured me a tall glass and passed me a joint, and I was able to kick back and relax in my bed for the first time in years.

Overall, my favorite improvement at this facility was the drug line, which I still had to navigate once per day. There were so many people here that I had no trouble at all never taking the olanzapine that they were still trying to make me take. I was able to wait my turn, take the pill and say, "Thank you," then immediately walk away and spit it out. There was no more asking me to open my mouth; nobody was paying attention, and no one seemed to care. I did take a sliver every now and then because I was still worried about the possibility of them testing my blood, but I only did this once or twice a week, and it was an extremely tiny amount.

Journal Entry, May 26, 2014

"On Friday I spoke with Dr. Dorosc, the head psychiatrist of this hospital. The first thing that he said was that he would be deciding when to let me go home. It was good to hear someone talk about going home.

It is the first that that has happened in quite some time. He asked me how long I have been sick, and I told him since December 2010. He asked me what sickness, and I told him Delusional Disorder. He asked me what delusions, and I told him that I had delusions that my father-in-law had been abusing my daughter. I told mom to tell the attorney to put a hold on the transfer, but I am not sure if she will or not. I am worried that I will be transferred now because I believe that I will not be here for too long.

There are many people here, including old people. Many of the people are detoxing. There are only two, including me, who are made to be here by the court. People come and go every day and they talk about being here for days or weeks and not months or years. I met my doctor today, the ordynator, Izabel Ciunczek. My head is still hurting me often. Here they will only give me APAP or ibuprofen. I have to talk to the doctor, but I do not want her to think I am exhibiting drug seeking behavior.

A couple of days ago we had some vodka and pot. I was ripped off, but I am still learning how this place works. I will get my bearings and things will be ok. I was told that I can probably get internet for my cpu. My head hurts now; I am going to go smoke a cig.

Here is the first place that I have been in where they provide toilet paper. This place is in the woods, and it has a good feel to it when I am in my room on my bed. It is like a crazy hostel."

Journal Entry, May 30, 2014

"I tested positive for marijuana and now I am very scared. Will they send me back to mocnione [medium security] because of one mistake? The test was two days ago and I haven't been called in to speak with the doctor. Why are they not talking to me? Did they maybe just send a recommendation to court that I be relocated? Am I worrying excessively? I have to not slip again. I knew that I shouldn't smoke and yet I did it anyway. I was stupid. It was a good lift but it wasn't worth it.

My life is just so incredibly hard at the moment that I gave in, wanting to be able to think clearly just for a little while. Phillip (23) got it through his sister. He was here detoxing from opiates and his sister was bringing him over the counter codeine pills and she brought marijuana that one time. He got tested too, but it doesn't matter for him because he can sign himself out anytime that he wants....and he did today. He told me his doctor said 'don't let Bryson get you caught up in things...,' 'does Bryson have some on him?'...She thinks that I am influencing him when it was really the other way around. I said no and he said 'oh you won't get tested. They have too much else to worry about.'

I am thinking that maybe they are not talking to me because they are just going to wait for me to get transferred. In that case, and that case would suck, I have to be moved to the US. There would then be no other option. I wish I could talk to the doctor and clear this up and move on. I think that I should go in on Monday, ask for a doctor visit, and try to salvage the situation. I need to tell them that I slipped and that I know that it cannot happen again. It is really absolutely ridiculous to even have to be afraid that I could be seriously sidelined because of one positive marijuana urine, but that is reality in Poland – my reality."

Journal Entry, May 31, 2014

"Today I asked to speak to the doctor. I told him that I made a mistake. He said 'yes you made a big mistake. If you do it again, you will probably be sent back to mocnione.' I told him that I was sorry, that it was my first week here, and that it will not happen again. I feel better that I talked with him and that it is not a one strike and you're out policy. I miss my daughter and my wife. Ritual abuse."

Journal Entry, June 1, 2014

"I am now thirty-seven, and I feel horrible. All that I can think about is Adelle and ritual abuse. I am so tired of trying to figure out what to do about this situation. Here I can write what I could not write in my paper journal. Do I kill Slawomir? Should I kill him? If I cannot get help any other way, then it seems as if that is what I should do. I cannot let the ritual abuse of Adelle to continue. That is clear. Of course I cannot. So I have to try to write while I am here in Koszalin, try to piece together a story that is clear and coherent. I think that it will be very difficult to do so, but I must try. My little girl. My everything. I am so dead inside. So incredibly dead."

Journal Entry, June 2, 2014

"Today in the morning I went to the AA/NA meeting from 7:40 to 8:15. It was pretty stupid. Everybody said that they are either an alcoholic or drug addict and then one guy told a story about how he thinks that a nurse is giving him placebos instead of some opiate. I said that I had a problem with medication drugs. After the meeting I had a coffee and then a student, Paulina, who I think is studying to be a psychologist asked to talk to me. She asked about my background, my family, my education, my drug use, why I am here, what I did, about the delusion of believing that my father-in-law abused my daughter. I told her that I tried heroin, cocaine, and ecstasy in college and that I was prescribed oxycodone, hydrocodone, morphine, and clonazepam for chronic pain and panic disorder, respectively.

She asked me if I still believe that my father in law is abusing my daughter and I said no. She asked if I changed my mind and I kind of chuckled because it sounded funny to me phrased like that, but then I said no, the doctors call it delusion. I have to be very careful not to get baited or trapped into talking about ritual abuse. I have to remember that it is not my purpose to convince these people of this. My purpose is to get them to think that I am now healthy and that I can be set free. I have to remind them of things such as the fact that I wrote my father in law an apology. I AM SICK. I WILL ALWAYS BE SICK. I HAVE TO TAKE MEDICATION AND NOT TOUCH DRUGS IN ORDER TO PREVENT A RELAPSE."

I realized that I had to continue to play their games until I was released, which had to be just around the corner. If they wanted me to say that I was a drug addict, so be it. If they wanted me to say that I was mentally ill, I could do that too. These people were not going to and were not able to help me get you, my daughter, evaluated, and I stopped trying. Now my only concern was to get out. I didn't like lying, but if I told them anything else they would never let me go.

Without restrictions on the use of my computer, and the fact that I could now buy internet, I began researching and contacting people again. In addition, I had plenty of time to catching up on tv and movies that I had been unable to watch for the previous three years. It was much easier to burn time with the internet.

I started a cigarette business, which grew exponentially. I began making a couple of packs of cigarettes per day out of black-market tobacco that I was able to purchase from my new contacts on the outside. It wasn't long before I was selling twenty to thirty packs of cigarettes, or more, per day. I was making more money than the guards, and I had to hire people to work for me. I couldn't keep up with the demand, and I also didn't want to spend all my time making cigarettes. And why would I with my newfound wealth?

Because nearly all the other people in my room were transient, only being there for about a week or two at the most, I was able to basically take over the room. I had the best bed, right by the window, and I always knew what was going on in the entire facility. I lent food and money to other people when they arrived, and I kept a tally in my head of who owed me what and how/when they said they would repay me. Everybody knew where the American was, and that it was me that they needed to talk to if they needed anything at all.

There were some people who I never saw again after lending or fronting them something, but that was rare, and the losses didn't impact me at all. Most importantly, I learned to not take it personally, and to give people the benefit of the doubt. I was operating at a level where it was basically all profit, so all I needed to do was keep making cigarettes. This also allowed me to be generous and give a lot away.

One woman who was in her 70s, Jadzia, was a frequent flyer at this hospital, and I got to know her well. The deal that I had with her was that I would loan her as many packs of cigarettes as she needed, but that she had to pay me back with "original" (sealed) cigarettes when her husband visited her. Several times she entered my room and kissed me – just a little peck on the lips – in order to get me to wake up, which I didn't like at all, but I did like having a friend.

From my position I was able to meet everybody that entered the facility, and I met many individuals that I am still friends with today. The staff knew about my business ventures and supported me because I provided a valuable service that many appreciated. People who came and went would later come back just to bring me bags of food, or just to visit.

One of my friends brought me vodka once or twice a week, which I was able to enjoy after everyone else in the room was asleep. I never shared it, as I knew that to do so would exponentially increase my chances of getting caught. After I determined that everyone was down for the night, I would drink either a 100 ml or 200 ml bottle of vodka in one gulp, brush my teeth and get back into bed. Later I would throw the bottle out the window or place it on the floor of the bathroom on the lower level of the building. Drinking was never really my thing, especially not straight vodka, but it made me feel a sense of freedom.

Many of my roommates wanted to help out with my situation. They were ashamed that their country had treated me as it had, and disgusted that your wellbeing wasn't being examined in response to my allegations. I was reminded again and again, "This is not USA, this is Polska." Some younger guys wanted your grandfather's address so that they could kill him themselves, but I didn't give it to them, not wanting him killed and knowing that it would come back to me should they do anything of that nature.

An older roommate claimed to have ties to the Polish mafia. I did consider contacting them once I was released, but again it was too risky for me to be discussing such matters from where I was sitting. People talk, and I had to eliminate all the risk that I could eliminate. It wasn't that I was completely unwilling to take such a route, but I had also come to firmly believe that God had a plan that didn't include me having anyone whacked.

The psychologist that I was assigned, Karolina K, was not known for her skills as a therapist, but for her looks. I was immediately disappointed when I began speaking to her; a bad psychologist can be dangerous when given power. She was dating Dr. Dorosz, the president of the facility, but nobody was supposed to know about this. On Dr. Dorosz's desk was a plaque that read, "Seksuolog," meaning that he was a sex specialist in addition to chief psychiatrist, which only added to the amusement of all who were in the know.

One of the many positives of being in minimum security was that we got to take walks into town with the therapists. It was about a twenty-minute walk to town, where we were permitted to go into shops and grocery stores and sometimes the barber. The level of supervision varied depending upon which therapist was on duty, but I was often allowed to walk a few blocks on my own to a different store and then meet back up with everybody later. This was surely an improvement, though I could never get it out of my head how ridiculous it was that I had to check in with anyone at all.

Journal Entry, June 3, 2014

"I am worried that my mother is lying to me and that she will not stop the transfer to the US from happening. She has lied to me before and thus I have no grounds upon which to trust her."

"Thu, Jul 3, 2014, 10:44 AM
Iain Bryson to John S
Hey John. I am in Koszalin Poland at a minimum security psychiatric hospital. I was transferred here on May 20, a 12 hour drive in a police convoy, handcuffed and in an isolation chamber. This place is much better than where I have been in the past three years. There are women here. I have my computer all of the time and internet as of today. I have a cigarette business. There is much more freedom and visitors can bring in whatever they want without a search. I am doing ok-just ready to be done with this and terribly missing my daughter, the greatest pain that I have ever known. Let me know how you are doing and what is new. I should be out of here within a few months."

"Bryson
Mon, Aug 4, 2014, 5:32 PM
Iain Bryson to Wojciech Baginski [attorney]
Mr. Baginski,

I spoke to my doctor (Dorosz) on Friday. I asked him when he would be writing an opinion to the court. He told me that he would write one soon, but that he would have to say that he has not known me long enough. I asked him if he would be writing another opinion after I have been here for six months (November). He said yes. I asked him if that opinion would be a positive opinion. He said that if everything stays the same as it is now that it will be a positive opinion. The court does not have to follow the recommendation of the doctor, but generally they do. I think that it is in my best interest to stop the transfer process before it is submitted to the court on August 15.
Iain"

"Sun, Aug 10, 2014, 6:20 PM
Iain Bryson to Mom

I think that I am going to stay here. The one thing that I am worried about is my father-in-law's ability to influence the court. His best friend is highly positioned in the local court, and I know (because I read them) that he has written letters asking that they not let me out. As far as the doctors are concerned, I do not believe that they have any reason to keep me locked up. I believe, like my doctor said, that the opinion in November will be positive. There is a gamble staying here and there is a gamble waiting to be transferred to the U.S. I just want this to be over. I really think that it will be this year."

"Fri, Aug 15, 2014, 4:54 PM
Iain Bryson to Mom

I talked to the doctor again today, and he said again that if everything stays the same as it is now- re: that there are no problems-that I will not be here long. The doctor could not check to see if the money was there because today is a holiday. Two guys came to visit me today. Other than that, I've just been catching up on movies and HBO/Showtime series."

"Aug 15, 2014, 9:00 AM
Wojciech Baginski to me
Attachments
Dear Mr. Bryson,
I hope this email finds you well.
Please find attached – as requested – the document with the withdrawal of your motion and consent to transfer to the United States.
If you wish to go forward with the withdrawal of the motion then you should print this document, date it in the highlighted spot, sign it, and together with a copy of the signed document send it to the address indicated in the letter.
Please also send one copy of the signed document to my office.
Before you send this motion to the court I would like to bring to light again some of the potential legal risks that we have previously discussed over the telephone.
1) The time of your release in Poland is not certain. They may want to keep you for an indefinite period of time as they have problems with communicating with you and thus providing proper treatment.
2) They may transfer you in the future, for whatever reasons, to a less favourable institution in Poland.
3) If you now terminate the motion and in the future decide again to file the motion to transfer to the USA you will probably face huge delays in the processing of your motion as it will have to go through all the administrative steps again and there will be evidence that you already dropped one case when it was close to completion.
Ultimately, the choice is yours to make. I understand that this is a hard decision and I as your attorney, having advised you about the pros and cons, will accept any of your choices in this regard.
However, please note that if you decide to file the motion to withdraw the transfer procedure we will be forced to terminate our client – attorney relationship as my office was retained only to handle your transfer to the US.

If it is possible please let me know by Monday what you decide. If you decide to withdraw the transfer request then I will call the court and inform them to expect a letter from you in this regard.
Sincerely,
Wojciech Baginski, Esq."

"Sun, Aug 17, 2014, 8:09 AM
Mom to me
I have emailed the embassy to see if they can track down your money
Mr. Baginski let me know he is filing the papers as you requested. I can't proceed without your consent so I guess it's a done deal
Going to noank today and then back to work tomorrow
Are you watching hell on wheels?"

"Sun, Aug 17, 2014, 12:25 PM
Iain Bryson to Mom
You don't need to check with embassy. I am sure that it is here. The problem was that they couldn't check Friday because the bank was closed. It sounds like you are disappointed that the transfer is not going through. It is a decision that I don't like to make, and it is difficult to make it alone. One thing about going to the U.S. is that I don't know what you will do once I am there.

'I'm not upset that you lied to me, I'm upset that from now on I can't believe you.' Nietzsche
I want to be done with this. I want to be out. I really cannot be certain what you want. I do know that you do not understand the situation, what happened, the situation with my family...This worries me because you don't seem to want to understand, or you think that you already do, which is more concerning. I am supposed to let Baginski know tomorrow so that he can contact the court. I then have to send a letter to the court and to him.

As I think I told you in my last email, I spoke with the doctor on Friday again. Again he said that if everything stays the same, that I will not be here long. Since I arrived at the first Polish hospital in November 2012, the doctors have not detected any signs of mental illness. They have to report this to the court, and this fact gives the court no reason to continue holding me. I think.

Are you going to Noank with uncle Jim? I lost track of time and don't know if he is still there or not. What did you guys do? No, I haven't watched 'Hell on Wheels.' I will google it. I have been watching a few movies, I watched the Showtime series Ray Donovan, which is very good....The next episode is due to air today. That's about it. I had a few people visit me this weekend from the outside. Tomorrow is back to normal; this weekend was a Polish holiday."

"Mon, Aug 18, 2014, 5:26 AM
Iain Bryson to Mom
I checked 'Hell on Wheels' and it looks good. I will have a friend download it for me. I have prepaid internet and cannot download because it sucks up too many GB. The latest episode of Ray Donovan was on Showtime last night, so I got to download it this morning. One episode is not so much GB. I think that you would like Ray Donovan. The head doctor today told me that I can go outside on the hospital grounds, and in her reasoning she said that I am healthy.

You said before that dad locked my room in the school. Are you sure? Do you know the location of my guns? 30-30? shotgun? should be two or three 22's? I know George has my two HK's in the safe. Also, if you get a chance can you tell dad to check on the hope chest. It was in Wendy's room in the school; it would be nice if it could be moved into my room and locked there, but I know that it is difficult to arrange such things with dad.

Dad said that he is going to Turkey. He also said that he is going to send some money, though he said that he doesn't know how. I sent him the account number here and explained how to do it, but he probably won't get to it. I am ok, but if he asks you, can you instruct him on the procedure?
If you have any questions about what happened during the course of this situation, I would be happy to answer them.
love you"

**"Mon, Aug 18, 2014, 5:39 AM
Iain Bryson to Wojciech Baginski**
Mr. Baginski,
Please proceed with stopping the transfer. I will send off the letters the first part of this week. Thank you for all of your help.
All the best,
Iain Bryson"

**"Mon, Aug 18, 2014, 12:49 PM
Wojciech Baginski to me**
Dear Mr. Bryson,
The court clerk is now notified that documents from you stopping the process will be arriving this week. Thank you for working with me over these past [s]everal months and I wish you everything best!
Hopefully they will release you in the upcoming months and it will turn out that stopping the process was a good choice.
Sincerely,
Wojciech Baginski"

**"Mon, Aug 18, 2014, 7:47 PM
Mom to me**
Good news you can go outside.
You can talk to your dad about all of the stuff in storage. I know he has everything packed under lock and key
When you want to tell me what happened I am here to listen
It sounds like the final legal paperwork has been or will be filed with the courts per your request.
I can send your dad the WU instructions again
Love
Mom"

**"Hi
Tue, Aug 26, 2014, 6:30 PM
Mom to me**
Iain
Haven't heard from you in awhile so I'm checking in.
How are you?
Uncle Jim has left and it's back to work"

**"Wed, Aug 27, 2014, 5:06 PM
Iain Bryson to Mom
Attachments**
I am ok. Today I got up and went to a meeting at 7:40. At around 8:15 I got my breakfast and brought it back to my room and made my second coffee. At nine I went to a yoga class. At ten I played monopoly with three guys and two girls. We played pretty much all day. Afterwards we had some tea and cake and just sat and talked a bit. At ten pm me and my friend made our second dinner; we always eat at night. I am going to watch a movie now. My doctor is on vacation until the beginning of September. When he gets back I will have him get the money from the general account so that I have access to it.

I also have to talk to him because I got a tip from an employee who is a friend that they plan to move the court ordered people into a different building. I want to stay where I am, so me and another guy are going to have a chat with him. It is better to stay here because there are normal people and it is always changing. There is always something going on and people to socialize with. The other building is more like prison; there are only about fifteen people there and they are all nuts. So we've got to talk to our doctor to try and prevent that. A friend is coming to visit me tomorrow. I am going to start meeting with another employee's friend because she wants someone to talk to in English. That's about it- keeping busy and looking forward to November."

[My bed in the corner, by the window.]

*[**Middle**: View out the window from my bedroom.*
***Right**: View onto the balcony from my bedroom.]*

The thing that worried me the most about moving into the other building was losing my cigarette business. If I were to be in the other building, I would not have immediate access to the one hundred plus patients in the main building. Furthermore, I was comfortable where I was, and I knew that the rumored change would not be better.

"Fri, Aug 29, 2014, 7:29 PM
Mom to me
Thanks for filling me in on how your day goes. Sounds like you keep busy. And, the pictures were a nice surprise. How about having you in the photos?
Labor Day week end so 3 days off. George is on vacation so maybe a quick trip to New Hampshire"

"Checking in
Sat, Sep 27, 2014, 7:55 AM
Mom to me
Iain
Long time no hear
How are you and how are things progressing?
Has the embassy made contact with you for a visit?
I am heading to watch Emma play soccer. Fall weather has been wonderful.
I am hesitant to mail another box after the ordeal with the last one. Do you need anything?
Ive started my Christmas shopping so let me know
Well , have to run to PQ for the game.
I love you
 Mom"

**"Sat, Sep 27, 2014, 5:19 PM
Iain Bryson to Mom**

Mom,

Things are progressing well. I should not be here much longer. I have a good relationship with all of the people that work here. People from the outside visit me everyday. I am teaching English twice a week for two hours each time to the girlfriend of someone that works here. The embassy has not made contact, but it doesn't matter. I do not need them to visit. Their visits are only for show; there is never anything of substance. They could have helped three years ago when I needed a translator that could understand me. Now the doctors understand me and they know that I am healthy. I don't need you to send anything. I can get everything I need here through my friends if I have money. Nice to hear from you. love Iain"

CHAPTER 84

"AT LEAST HERE I CAN BREATHE"

One of the guards asked me if I could give English lessons to his fiancé, and I was excited to get back into teaching. This would be a paid tutoring job, whereas for the past few years I had just been doing it for practice and something to do. I told him that I would be delighted to teach his fiancé, and I proceeded to draw up lesson plans.

By this point, I was speaking Polish every day, and hardly ever getting to converse in English. I was even thinking in Polish and speaking Polish to myself. I was not fluent, but I could get through most conversations, and I could understand most of what was going on in any situation even if I didn't understand the specifics.

I was in the process of assessing her English mastery during our first meeting in a private room, and right away I was able to feel the tension in the room; it was as if I was on a blind date with someone who had already decided they wanted me. She touched my hand and I figured that this had to be a mistake. After all, she was engaged, and I was a prisoner. I discounted what I was feeling and scheduled our next meeting, accepting payment for the hour that we had just spent together casually talking in English.

At our next meeting we were in a room that was even more private than the first; nobody could see us. We sat next to each other while I started to lay out the plan that I had come up with to teach her English over the next few months. But she wasn't interested in my plan to teach her; she was only interested in hearing about my life and looking at pictures of you and your mom on my laptop. This meeting ended with us kissing and me once again getting paid.

This felt very strange to me given that she was engaged and in a long-term relationship. Furthermore, I was fond of her fiancé, who seemed like a good man to me. I really couldn't understand how this could be happening, but I also felt powerless to stop it. I had been deprived of female contact for years, and now suddenly, I had been given access to a woman who wanted me and a private room. I didn't want to be dishonorable with this guard who was good to me, and all that I wanted was your mother, but the temptation was too great for me. I figured that your mom would understand given the absurdity of the situation, and I wrote off the guard as being foolish to place me in a room with his woman. How could they possibly have a good relationship when it was obvious that she was interested in me in the first five minutes of meeting her?

For the third meeting we were given a different room again, this one with a bed and a lock on the door; it felt like some kind of a setup. I still had an English lesson prepared and ready to go, and I brought us cups of coffee and snacks, hoping in the back of my mind that she would ease off and we could get to work improving her English language skills. *Maybe she and her fiancé reconciled whatever it was that was causing her to desire me*, I considered.

However, this was not the case, and we proceeded to utilize the bed and our privacy. This English lesson lasted for two hours, she paid me cash for the lesson which never happened, and then I went back to my room, knowing that none of my prisoner/patient friends could imagine what had just happened to me. I felt like a homewrecker, but I also felt liberated; at least they didn't have children, I mused.

This went on for a while, with us meeting once or twice per week, always in the locked room with the bed. On one occasion, her fiancé started knocking on the door. We were undressed, and by the time we got dressed he was pounding on the door. Thinking quickly, I gave her headphones, opened the door, and told him that she had been listening to an English lesson through the headphones while I was on my phone in a different part of the room. It seemed that we had gotten away with it, for now.

One evening when the guard was working, he told me that his fiancé, my student, had a surprise for me. He escorted me out of the building where she was waiting in her car. She drove us to a beach about an hour away and we walked in the sand while the waves crashed around us. It was just the two of us, all alone on the beach in the moonlight. *How could this be happening? Is it some kind of a trap? Will the police be waiting to take me back to maximum security upon my return?* Either way, I was powerless to resist, and so I tried to enjoy the excursion and not think about it too much, though I did feel some relief once I was safe in my bed, back in my locked ward.

"Hi
Fri, Nov 14, 2014, 9:00 PM
Mom to me
Dear Iain
Havent heard from you in forever. It's the middle of November. Have you heard any news yet? Has the new Embassy person contacted you?
We had our first snow today. Not much but i guess winter has arrived.
I am hesitant about sending another box after the last fiasco. Are you in need of anything?
Your brother just graduated from the NEAT program! A lineman now. What a great accomplishment.
Well my son, pop your head up once in awhile and let me know how you are.
I love you
Mom"

"**Sat, Nov 15, 2014, 4:42 AM**
Iain Bryson to Mom
Mom, I will be getting out of here in February. I had a little hangup, but now it is certain I am told. No, I haven't heard from the Embassy, but that is not necessary unless they can help me with something such as renewing my expired passport. That was just one box, and many more did make it. I need clothes and money. A couple of shirts, a couple of pairs of Carhartt pants. Do you know where my North Face Coat is? I can get everything else through my friends here if I have some money. I have a phone: 4894570490108. Good to hear from you. love, I"

The "little hangup" that I was referring to was the positive marijuana test. This prevented me from having the chance of being released sometime this winter, and although I was upset about this, I was satisfied that I was not going to be moved back to a higher security facility. Being one step away from release gave me the strength to do the extra time.

"**Sat, Nov 15, 2014, 9:38 PM**
Mom to me
Maybe you could email the embassy and ask them about your passport?
I will put a small box together.

Heading to bed.
Love, mom"

"Mon, Dec 8, 2014, 3:40 PM
Iain Bryson to Mom
I got the package this evening. Thank you. The clothes are small; I weigh 189 pounds.
I got a letter from court. It appears that they considered the transfer even though it was cancelled. They said that they do not agree to the transfer.
love you"

I was gaining weight because my cigarette business was allowing me to eat like a king. Food options were limited before, but at this point they were not, and I stuffed myself. We were allowed to get deliveries, and friends visited me multiple times per week to have a feast.

"Mon, Dec 8, 2014, 4:25 PM
Mom to me
Had no idea. So what size pants are you?
I'll get some more stuff. Do the shirts fit?
Interesting. Wonder why"

"Mon, Dec 8, 2014, 6:27 PM
Mom to me
Ok. New box being mailed this Saturday
Love
Mom"

"Mon, Dec 8, 2014, 6:37 PM
Iain Bryson to Mom
hey, just watching 'sons of anarchy.' good series. size L shirt, and I am not sure about pants.
What were you going to send this Saturday?"

"Pants, shirts, socks
Mon, Dec 8, 2014, 6:52 PM
Mom to me"

"Tue, Dec 9, 2014, 3:03 AM
Iain Bryson to Mom
do they make 35 pants because i think that 36 might be too big. i don't know; it is difficult to know without trying them on. cargo pants; this is not the place for anything too casual. just drinking coffee this morning.
love you"

I brought up my psychologist earlier, Karolina, intimating that she was not the brightest bulb in the bunch. This was not merely due to my intuition, or that of others, but because of several other reasons of which I will provide a few. Through a friendship with another staff member who had access to my records, I was sometimes permitted to read the reports that the psychologist was taking on me. They were comical; it was as if she imagined herself as Sigmund Freud's spiritual granddaughter.

For example, one day when she asked how I was doing I told her that my neck was bothering me. I had previously been treated most of my adult life for cervical stenosis, discogenic disease, and bulging discs in my neck and had multiple MRIs to back up this diagnosis (see Appendix 40). However, when I told her that I was in pain, she reported in her notes that I was probably suffering from a delusion about my neck. Her reasoning was that there was no proof that I had any neck issues.

The similarities between thinking I had a delusion about my neck because I lacked evidence and thinking I had a delusion about my daughter because I lacked evidence astounded me. A new MRI would have settled the matter, just as evaluating you would have settled the other matter. But they didn't want to do either. There hadn't even been, according to Dr. Brzozowska, any understanding of the nature of my allegations. The way that these Polish "experts" were thinking was, in fact, dangerous.

Because of my extra time, my newfound prison wealth, and the fact that I had people working for me, I took up playing the online game *World of Tanks*. I took the game very seriously as it is a game of teamwork and statistics. Others were counting on me, and I was good at my job as an artillery operator with many thousands of battles under my belt. While artillery can see and attack the entire map, other types of tanks are limited to what's in their field of vision in the direct vicinity of their tank.

My psychologist felt that it was necessary to speak to me about this game given that I was spending so much of my time playing. I explained to her how the game worked and that I liked playing an artillery tank because I could have an impact anywhere on the battlefield, shooting other players from far away. She proceeded to analyze the situation in her special way, and to make a claim in her report that I liked having "God vision," because I preferred seeing the entire map, insinuating that this too was a sign of mental illness.

Somehow the guard found out that I had been sleeping with his fiancé. Although I do not know for sure how this happened, it appeared to me by how it all played out that she told him. I made this assumption because he found out shortly after I made it clear to her that I was not going to make her my second wife and bring her back to the United States with me. She suddenly stopped visiting me for lessons, and he began taking me out of the ward to sit in his car with him so that he could berate me about what I had done.

I certainly couldn't defend my actions, nor did I try to with him. I apologized profusely and tried to explain that I hadn't initiated the contact. I did my best to let him know that I was wrong and that I shouldn't have touched his fiancé no matter what. I really did feel quite terrible, and I was not proud of my actions or of myself in any way regarding this matter.

Both he and his fiancé proceeded to try to trip me up so that I would not be released. He gave me random drug tests, peering over my shoulder while I urinated into a cup. They wrote letters to Dr. Dorosz, telling him that I was dangerous and should not be released. The doctor never received these letters because one of my staff friends intercepted them in the mail room, destroyed them, and informed me about what they were trying to do.

My staff friend also told me that the major reason why my release was taking so long was because Dr. Dorosz and the facility were making tons of money by keeping me in one of the beds. The facility received money from the government for each patient, but "at least double" for me because I am an American, she informed me. When I saw Dr. Dorosz arrive at work in any number of his luxury cars, I didn't doubt that this was probably true. But I also knew that he had to let me go, that it was just a matter of time. *At least I'm not in Medium*, I thought. *At least here I can breathe, at least here I feel like I am alive.*

"Wed, Mar 11, 2015, 4:29 PM
Iain Bryson to John S
Hey,
Well, It may be good news. But nothing is certain yet. I am still in Koszalin, where I have been since May 20, 2014. It is a minimum security facility, so it is way better than where I was. I have internet, and a cell phone. I had a cigarette business, and I was making good money for being locked up. I had English lessons, and that turned into conjugal visits though nobody knew about it....But that became a problem because the girl is one of the guard's girlfriends....Lots of stories.

I am very tired of this entire situation. It is tough living this way. It is tough constantly being observed and evaluated, constantly being under the proverbial microscope.

I have a court case at the end of this month or maybe next month, but not much longer for sure. Agata found out about this and petitioned the court to keep me locked up. Yesterday the doctor called me into his office and showed me the letter from Agata. He said that it will not work in my favor, and that even with a positive opinion from his end it may be difficult to get out this time around. If it is not this time around, then it would be another 3-6 months.

Today I was called in to see the second in charge psychiatrist along with the therapist. Now the therapist is a woman that I have become friends with. She is not my therapist, but my friend, but nobody here knows about this. Lucky for me, the doctors think that her opinion is the most important of them all because I have the most contact with her. And she is obviously in favor of setting me free.

So, I sat down with the two of them and the doctor told me that they want [m]e to be set free. She said that she wants to do everything in her power to make this happen, and she went over with me what I need to do. She wants to work with me to prepare the best argument for the court to sway them to the decision to let me go.

My passport is expired, so I am in contact with the embassy about them coming here to begin processing the paperwork for renewal. A year ago they said this would not be a problem, but now they are saying that it is not possible, that I will have to go to Warsaw (six hours away) when I am released and wait there a week for a renewal. They say now that it is too far away for them to come. Anyway, I sent them another email today explaining the situation, reminding them that I had been told that they would be able to come here, telling them that the doctor said that this would be considered by the court in terms of their decision to release me. I should hear back from them tomorrow. If they say no again, then I will get them to write a letter explaining officially what I have to do to get a new passport so that I can submit that to the court, which would be an indication that there is a plan in place.

I need a letter from a psychiatrist saying that he is going to continue 'treatment.' I have put that in motion.

I need a notarized letter from my dad saying that he has a place for me to stay, work for me to do to get me started, that he will support me....He is also going to say that he will come here to get me. And then, he plans on being in court so that in addit[i]on to the letter the court sees that he is actually here to get me.

In addition, I think that I need as many letters as possible to the doctors and to the court on my behalf. This will help counter the efforts of Agata. To the doctors because then they can add this as a positive when they write their opinion, and to the court because they ultimately decide, and without them all they have is me against Agata trying to keep me locked up.

Today I have been thinking about the letters, and I think that the important points are the following:
1. Our relationship, duration, ...
2. That I have been in contact with you and I am sorry about the crime that I committed
3. That I have expressed a desire to get back to work, continue my education towards a doctorate, and continue treatment.
4. That you look forward to having me back in your life once again.

Anyway, if you can do this it would be great. It would be great if Linda could sign it as well. And it would be great if you could send it this week, because this is time sensitive.

Sorry I have been absent for so long. I can't wait to see you guys. I have just been trying to pass the time (now I play World of Tanks). I have been trying to plan what I will do, but is tough to get beyond 'how the hell do I get out of here? When do I get out of here.' I have met a lot of good people in this last place, and that is one positive I will take away. I have also been writing, though it is difficult to do in this environment. I would like to write something of a memoir telling the story of my relationship to Agata, this situation.....

If you can write the letter, here are the addresses:

1. Dr. Stanislaw Dorosz
MEDISON
ul. Sloneczna 15
Koszalin
Poland
75-642

2. Sad Okregowy w Szczecinie

Kaszubska 42
Szczecin
Poland
70-952
Syg. Act. 3K 1/12
Re: Iain Bryson

I see that you are playing a lot. That is great and I cannot wait to see you live again. I can't wait to be out of this and back to normalness....whatever that is."

"Wed, Mar 11, 2015, 4:41 PM
John S to me
I can write you a letter. I may have some questions for you so I know what to say and how to say it. Unfortunately, I can't do this right at the moment, as I'm preparing to go out to do a show. But one thing you didn't make clear in your email I can ask now. What is your plan? Will you be coming back to the US? (hope so!).

I will email you again in the morning. Hope that's cool. Man, it would be so great to see you again.
--John"

"Wed, Mar 11, 2015, 4:46 PM
Iain Bryson to John S
I didn't mean now....just as soon as possible. Ask me....

It is difficult to have plans when in this type of situaiton. It is tough to think beyond 'just get out'
I would like to go to Amsterdam to renew my residence permit, thus allowing me to live in Europe if I so choose. I have a court case in June regarding the terminaiton of my parental rights, and I would like to be there with a lawyer.....so I need to get out and work wherever that is.

I think that I will be in the U.S.; I just don't know the timeframe or where. I am not sure that I want to be in CT, and my dad has a house in Florida that he said I could use. I will wait for your email in the morning."

"Thu, Mar 12, 2015, 10:00 AM
John S to me
Hi,

Actually, re-reading your emails I think I have enough info to write the letter. I quizzed you about your plan because I was trying to determine if you will be stretching the truth a bit concerning your plans, as you mentioned your dad's offer of a job and home but you also seem to think you might stay in Europe -- don't take this the wrong way, I just have to figure out how/what to say truthfully concerning what I believe your post-incarceration life will be.

You know that Linda and I hold you in high esteem. And we miss your company terribly. While we have some concerns about the how and why you are in your present situation, we believe that you have, by now, probably suffered enough justice.

I'm worried about Agata's actions in this situation. She remains so headstrong. You don't have to tell me this, but it might help me write the letter if I understand her motives, her argument, because maybe something I say in the letter could help to counter her concerns.

So, that's where I'm at. I will attempt to draft something over the weekend. I've got some personal problems that I have to pay serious attention to (settling over damage that some drunks did to my car, tax concerns, helping my sister ...). But I will do my damndest to get the letter at least started ASAP.

Stay strong and hopeful. My wish is to play a gig and see you over there by the bar tapping your foot.
-- JS"

"Thu, Mar 12, 2015, 10:52 AM
Iain Bryson to John S
Honestly I just don't know exactly what I am going to do. I have been confined for so long. But the court needs to know that I have a plan, and that plan is to return to the US and work and be with family and friends, continue treatment....

Not really stretching the truth, just that it is not certain, but for the court it needs to be.
If you have questions regarding your concerns, please ask them.

I believe that Agata's motives are to keep me out of the picture. She knows that I will continue to fight for contact with our daughter, and as long as I am locked up I cannot.

It will be great to see you."

"Thu, Mar 12, 2015, 10:57 AM
John S to me
Okay. I'm on it."

"Thu, Mar 12, 2015, 5:17 PM
Iain Bryson to Bob McCoy
Mr. McCoy,

First I would like to offer my condolences for the loss of your son. As you know, I understand the pain of losing a child, and I am sorry for your pain. I have been in a minimum security facility since May 20, 2014. The conditions are much better here. I have internet and a cell phone. I am able to have visitors and pretty much do what I wish with my time. The problem is that I cannot leave; I cannot do the things that I could do if I were not confined.

The doctors are prepared to issue an opinion to the court recommending my release. This is great news, the first time that I have heard such news in nearly four years. However, my wife (ex) and her family caught wind of the fact that I may be getting out, and they have petitioned the court to not let me go.

Now, it is difficult for the court not to go along with the recommendation of the 'expert court psychiatrists,' but in the end the court can do whatever it wants. I am in the process of trying to put together a plan for the court, such as proof that I will be leaving the country, proof that I have a place to live and work, proof that I will continue treatment. In addition, I believe that it would be helpful for the court to hear from people on the other side of my wife and her family, people who are in my corner. Would it be possible for you to write a letter and send it to the doctor here at the hospital and the court? I hope that you are well.
All the best,
Iain"

"Re: Contact Information needed
Fri, Mar 13, 2015, 9:26 AM
Bob McCoy to me
Dear Iain,
So good to hear from you. Would be honored to write a letter...
Could you send the contact information (name address title etc) to which this letter should be forwarded?
Thank you for your condolences regarding Keith... We're trying to keep sight of God's glory amid our grief...

Please write with the above information...
Warmly
Bob McCoy"

"Fri, Mar 13, 2015, 10:56 AM
Iain Bryson to Bob McCoy
Mr. McCoy,
I need one copy to the hospital:
Dr. Stanislaw Dorosz
MEDISON
ul. Sloneczna 15
Koszalin
Poland
75-642

The other copy to the court:
Sad Okregowy w Szczecinie

ul. Kaszubska 42
Szczecin
Poland
70-952

The sooner the better because the psychiatrist (Dorosz) will be writing an opinion soon, and it would be good if he has it prior to that. I had a meeting with the doctor this week and was told that they want to let me out, but that the court needs convincing. The recommendation of the doctor along with a show of support from my family and friends should be enough to finally break free of this trap. Thank you so much. It will be good to see you for coffee :D
All the best,
Iain"

"the letter
Wed, Mar 18, 2015, 10:51 AM
John S to me
The letter is completed. I focused on the points you mentioned, and made it clear that I know you well as a colleague and a true friend. I praised your performance at the AIC, and I also made it clear that my family also considers you a friend, and that Linda and I sorely miss being able to spend time with you. I told them of your plans for the future and that we have to believe, knowing you as we do, that you will be able to turn your life around.

I can probably have both copies in the mail this afternoon, and I will look into the fastest way to get them delivered.
Fingers crossed, Colonel."

"Wed, Mar 18, 2015, 10:56 AM
Iain Bryson to John S
Thank you John. I really appreciate it. I am working on getting things together for the court. Trying to get my passport renewed because the court will want to know that I can leave the country and things like that. Should be ok because I have the 'expert court psychiatrists' on my side, but nothing is certain in this situation. Today I went for a walk to the supermarket. Beautiful day. Would be nice to enjoy the later spring and summer out there and not in here."

"Thu, Mar 19, 2015, 2:23 PM
Bob McCoy to me
Dear Iain,
Letters have been sent... Let me know what I can do next
Text copy below
Warmly
Bob McCoy
Groton Bible Chapel
66 Tollgate Road
Groton, CT
Pastoral Staff

Letter of Reference – Iain Bryson
To Whom It May Concern:
Please receive this letter as a reference for Mr. Iain Bryson in his efforts to gain release and find return to the United States of America. I am a pastor at Groton Bible Chapel and have known Iain for over 20 years. He has frequented our church when in the USA and has been a family friend during his elementary and secondary school years. In high school he and my son played soccer on the same school team.

While I have not had the opportunity to speak with Iain in the last several years we have maintained a correspondence while he has been in prison. It is my deep desire that he be able to return to this area for further care and counseling.

In all of my interactions with Iain he has proven to be articulate and informed. It is my hope that the events of the last several years might prompt him to begin again and to fulfill the potential that I saw in him during his early adult life.

If there is any further help that I can provide, please do not hesitate to call or write.

Sincerely,

Robert C. McCoy

Senior Pastoral Staff

860 ███-███ x 24"

"**Thu, Mar 19, 2015, 3:01 PM**
Iain Bryson to Bob McCoy
Mr. McCoy,
The letter is wonderful. Thank you very much. Did you also send a copy to the hospital?
Dr. Stanislaw Dorosz
MEDISON
ul. Sloneczna 15
Koszalin Poland 75-642
I am really thinking that this might be the end of this chapter of my life.
All the best,
Iain"

"**Fri, Mar 20, 2015, 1:24 PM**
Bob McCoy to me
Dear Iain,
    yes... sent a duplicate to Dr.Dorosz...
    Let me know what's next...
    Praying for you.
Warmly,
Bob McCoy"

"**Fri, Mar 20, 2015, 1:28 PM**
Iain Bryson to Bob McCoy
Mr. McCoy,
Yes, after I sent that email, I noticed that you did say you sent 'letters.'
1. I have the 'expert court psychiatrists' in my corner.
2. I have some letters from family and friends.
3. I will begin my passport renewal next week. This will show the court that I have the ability to leave the country.
It is my hope, and the hope of the doctors here that the court is satisfied and will let me go. I should have a review next month. Thanks again for your help, and thanks for your prayers.
All the best,
Iain"

"**Mon, Mar 30, 2015, 3:10 PM**
Dad to me
I have made an appointment for you April 23rd in Sarasota, 1pm. Waiting for email confirmation."

"**Mon, Mar 30, 2015, 3:33 PM**
Iain Bryson to Dad
and the letter?"

"**Mon, Mar 30, 2015, 4:32 PM**
Dad to me
I am waiting for email for review and will have letter and email to follow."

"Mon, Mar 30, 2015, 5:27 PM
Iain Bryson to Dad

that is excellent news. thanks for working on this. i think i am going to close my eyes for a little while. talk to you tomorrow"

"Iain Bryson court date. April 2
Wed, Apr 1, 2015, 9:11 AM
Dad to Krystyna Holka [public defender], me

Councillor, Two hours ago I received a call from my son saying that his court date is tomorrow. As you may know I had planned on being in court for him and on his release, bring him home with me to America. I can not be present at his hearing, however I want you to assure the court that our plans have not changed. I have paid for his passport update and will pay for his flight back home. I have arranged for him to see a psychologist at home and his first appointment is April 23. I set this date because I had no set date for his return and thought that we would be back by then. I am excited to have my son back and to help him readjust back into society. He has a job with me until he makes new plans to return to school or choose another job more to his liking. Please convey this to the court. I am most dissapointed that I can not be in court. One days notice is not enough considering the distance from the US to Poland. Sincerely, Kirk"

"Wed, Apr 1, 2015, 10:20 AM
Dad to [Office of Dr. Ciunczyk], me
Attachments

Dr. Ciunczk,   attached you will find evidence of my son's appointment with Dr Kinshuk Bose at his clinic on April 23, 2015. Please inform the court of this appointment as proof that he will continue to find help on his return home. We will return to my winter home in Florida where Iain will work with me on a construction project. I think the warm weather will do us both good. This has been a record breaking year for cold and snow. Thank you for all your help, Kirk"

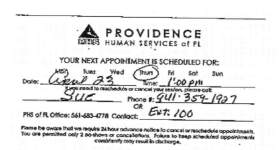

It seemed like all my ducks were in a row; my passport had been sorted out, I had letters of recommendation, and my dad had made the necessary phantom appointment that I knew I would never go to. All I had to do was wait, not get into any trouble, and hope that something crazy didn't happen in court with your mom or grandfather "fearing for their lives" again. But I didn't think their opinions would matter much, because the "experts" were not in their corner anymore.

They did move me to the smaller adjacent building, separating the court-ordered patients from the voluntary patients, but I continued making money when I could. All of the guards, except for my "student's" fiancé, permitted me to go back and forth between buildings in order to sell my cigarettes. My income was greatly reduced after the move, but I was still able to pay my bills.

I was anxious until the very end because I knew something could go wrong, and there were people who wanted just that. I still had an occasional vodka, but I was more careful, and more afraid. Time seemed to slow down even further toward the end, and I was chomping at the bit to get out. At the same time, I was ready to be told "another six months" at any moment.

My anticipation was at its peak when my dad landed, and I knew he was only hours away. I packed my belongings and said goodbye to everybody. It was like a dream come true, but this was a dream that had worn me down and taken my only real dream away – just being your daddy.

"Made it. I am at airport at the gate i exited from. Dont see anyone. Have boston h[a]t on. Old guy in a suit.
Thu, Jun 18, 2015, 1:33 AM
Dad to me"

Roman C., me, my dad, Paweł, Jadzia, Karolina Kluczik (psychologist).
June 18, 2015.

PART 7

JUNE 18, 2015 – PRESENT DAY

"NOT BY MIGHT NOR BY POWER, BUT BY MY SPIRIT"
- ZECHARIAH 4:6B NKJV

CHAPTER 85

"TO THE LORD I MUST GO"

It had felt like I was a child again, playing the game I once played with my brother, or maybe rather he with me, where he pretended to give up and surrender only to reanimate and start fighting again as soon as he was in a better position, out of whatever bind I had him in. "Do you really give up?" I'd ask him, and he'd assure me that he did, even promise me, but he didn't. If I took him at his word, he'd start flailing his arms at me as soon as he had the opportunity to do so; his giving up was merely a ruse to obtain a better position.

What a ridiculous scenario where I was forced to change my official beliefs about you being abused, compelled to recite, "I thought she was being abused, but that was a delusion, and now I must take medication forever... My father-in-law is a good man, and I am very sick...."

I didn't believe any of those things, but if I had not lied, they never would have let me go, in the same way that I only let my brother up when he assured me of his surrender. I knew that lying was not good, but what was I to do? I absolutely had to act resigned to their conclusions, and verbally assure them that their treatment was working. If they had told me that the condition necessary for my release was that I think I'm a chicken, then I would have made it my job to emulate a chicken to the best of my ability.

Fifty months had passed, but my vehemence had not diminished one iota; there was no moment when I considered surrender or defeat. Like my brother, I knew what my plan was: to regain position and restart the fight. Maybe if I had been the younger brother, I would have understood this strategy sooner.

Knowing that you were being hurt multiplied the grief and pain by a magnitude that could not be calculated; no personal torture could measure up to the suffering of knowing you were suffering. I would have chosen any given alternative, even eternity in hell for myself, just not this for you.

When I decided not to go the route of using the Polish mafia, I decided concurrently that I could and would trust in God. It was like a two for one deal, because if I couldn't trust God, then the mafia would've been an excellent option. At that point, the only questions would have been, "How much will it cost?" and, "When can you get her to me?" But because I had nixed all plans to trust in man or myself, I had to figure out what it means to trust in God. The only thing I was sure of anymore was that it was to the Lord I must go, the One who says that "all things are possible to him who believes" (Mark 9:23 NKJV).

CHAPTER 86

"ONE PERCENT TO BLAME"

My dad rented a room for us at Hotel Sport in Koszalin where we stayed for a couple of nights so that I could rest and begin to clear my head. I couldn't even decide what I wanted to do next. Even though I had waited years for this day, it didn't mean that there was celebration when it arrived. It was more like getting a nail out of my foot or a painful tooth out of my mouth, not joyous, but a relief.

I spent the first two nights visiting a friend from Minimum at his workplace, a dance club called Trokadero, just a couple blocks from the hotel. He welcomed me warmly into his office with a stiff drink and an ashtray. As I sank into the leather chair and spoke to my friend, I experienced a feeling I had only previously known vicariously through films: finally out of the slammer after a long bid, sitting in a comfy chair across from a good friend, enjoying my drink and my cigar, soothed solely by the fact that I could do so without being harassed by my jailers, free at last.

After a couple days, my dad and I left the hotel and went to Aniela's (not her real name) house, one of my staff friends from Minimum, where we stayed for the next two nights. We then paid another friend to drive us to Hotel Focus in Szczecin, the same guy who had picked my dad up from the airport. Our plan was to hire an attorney and fight for my parental rights. Rather than shop around, we hired the first guy we found that spoke English – another mistake. I wasn't sharp after having been trodden down for so long, and I was just happy my dad was willing to help with this at all.

Piotr Kotfis, a man my age who seemed nice enough, assured us that he could help us, and my dad subsequently wired him a retainer. "All that we have to do is prove that your wife is at least one percent to blame, and then you will not lose your daughter," he declared confidently, as his assistant delivered me a delicious, professionally made cappuccino. I knew that proving one percent would be easy, and I wanted to believe him. I felt a newfound sense of hope, though it was a doubtful, skeptical hope.

I had already appealed the divorce and custody issues twice from prison, but I still hadn't been heard. I tried to explain over and over in different ways that your mom was not well, and that she had been coerced into abducting you. The family court representatives listened to my side of the story only as a formality. My "insanity" precluded the validity of my testimony.

Having hired a lawyer and started that process, my dad rented a new Mercedes and we drove through Berlin to Prague where we stayed for several days. After, we went up to Hamburg to see Mariusz, who was working there and trying to get situated so that he could move his entire family out of Poland. It felt good to not be in Poland, and that night we had a proper Polish prison graduation celebration, even driving to the mini mart in the middle of the night, wasted, to get another bottle of vodka.

From Hamburg, my dad and I drove to Art's in Amsterdam, where I was going to stay until I figured out what to do next, or until he kicked me out, whichever came first. I had no plans of returning to the United States. I wanted to figure out how to stay in The Netherlands, which I knew could be difficult without your mother. The only reason I had been allowed to work there before was that I was married to a European Union citizen.

My dad left to go back to Connecticut, and I moved into Art's walk-in closet and slept on an air mattress. A slider opened to a balcony, and I liked to sleep with my head outside so I could listen to the birds, or to the neighbors making love, dreaming of the normal days I once knew before my world imploded.

Over the course of the previous four years, I had been unable to yell, scream, or cry. I had been unable to choose when and where I went to bed and woke up. It took me time to get used to the fact that I could just turn off the world, that I could sleep in or decide that nobody was going to interfere with what I was doing from the other side of the door. I could leave when I wanted to leave, I couldn't be moved across the country at a moment's notice, and I didn't have to talk to anyone about how mistaken and mentally ill I was.

Now I was with Art, whose advice to me was, "Just make another baby and forget about that other one." I was extremely grateful to him because he had helped me out more than anyone else during the period of my incarceration. He is my brother, and I love him as such, but his advice was total nonsense. You are irreplaceable.

In *The Handmaid's Tale*, June Osborn lost her eldest daughter to an oppressive regime that simply decided to steal her and make her their own. She made it her life's mission to get her back, stating that she could never be ok as long as her daughter was there. The world didn't seem to care, but she did, and it was obvious she would never and could never stop, no matter the cost. I think June and I would understand each other.

The difference between June and I is that she believed she had to fight only in the physical to save her daughter, while I believe that the real warfare is spiritual. She relied only on herself to save her daughter, but I was coming to believe that I was not on my own, but that the God of the universe was standing by my side, fighting for me and with me.

"...for the LORD your God is the One who is going with you, to fight for you against your enemies, to save you" (Deuteronomy 20:4 NASB).

The existential crisis of losing you made it crystal clear to me that the epitome of good, Jesus Christ, is in fact stronger than the epitome of evil. In June's situation, she had to be the hero. In my situation, there was only a recognition that I can do nothing by myself, and that "with God all things are possible" (Matthew 19:26 NKJV). Once again, I am just a man who really loves his daughter, with a spiritual Father who has guaranteed victory to those who love Him.

In contrast to June's potentially suicidal rescue missions into Gilead, I knew that my path was toward the One who has the power to move mountains (Matthew 17:20) and says that He will.

While it was a blessing to be able to stay in Art's home, life with him was frequently challenging. His desire for me to be gay with him, combined with excessive alcohol consumption, and the fact that my living situation was at his mercy, created an unhealthy power dynamic. The decision to stay or leave was constantly on my mind.

"Wed, Jul 8, 2015, 5:04 AM
Iain Bryson to Art
I really don't have any idea what happened yesterday. The only thing I can say is that I have seen this before in you, and that like before yesterday I was also scared. As far as I can see, I am doing pretty much exactly

what I should be doing. I just got out from having been in a situation that you cannot imagine. I am dealing ok with that, and no I don't need to talk about that. But, I am transitioning, and this will not happen on your schedule. According to you I am on schedule anyways; you told me that I had until July 16th to adjust and find my bearings. I am well on my way there, and in the meantime I am doing all that I can/should be doing.

Yesterday I needed to get away and take a walk by myself. I have had very little time to myself, and I need it. I didn't go to smoke pot. I went to lay down in the grass and be in a place 'in the middle of nowhere' where nobody in the whole world could know where I was. Secondly, you flipped out on me because of my situation with my daughter. You and nobody else is going to persuade me away from what I know needs to happen. I do realize that this is not the priority; this is not what I should be thinking about now, and I am not. I am just looking down the road. I have to send the lawyer a synopsis, and in that synopsis it is inevitable that the truth about my wife and daughter are a key point.

You really scared me. You called my dad. You threatened me and said terrible things. You kicked the table into me a few times and kicked my computer onto the ground. Why couldn't you just let it go so we could talk rationally? Do you really not see that you do this sometimes, and that when you do this you don't make 100% sense, that you can act completely irrational at times?

I knew that this was going to happen if I came here. I knew it, and I feared it because I had seen it before, I dealt with it before on the phone with you. I will look for a hostel. You obviously don't want a real relationship with me."

"Wed, Jul 8, 2015, 11:27 AM
Art to me
I understand now.
I will not support it. I thought I was supporting you. But as I harbor a criminal and risk my family......set a date. I know now.....like I told your father....[Ruben] [Art's husband, not his real name] knows very little. That ends now."

Disagreements sometimes led to full blown attacks, the main problem being that I was adamant that my plan was to keep fighting for you and your mom. Of course, I did consider leaving, but I didn't have anywhere to go, and I figured it would blow over.

"Bryson, Iain
Thu, Jul 9, 2015, 5:06 AM
Iain Bryson to Kees de Vries
Kees,
I hope that you are well. I apologize for bombarding you with crazy letters from prison. I was under a lot of stress with my situation and my family. I was released by Poland on June 18, and now I am in the Netherlands. I need to set up "continuing treatment," and I was wondering if you could help me with that. Thank you.
All the best,
Iain Bryson"

"Thu, Jul 9, 2015, 1:28 PM
Kees de Vries to me
Hi Iain,
Good to hear from you again, and good to hear you're released from Poland. No need to appologize for the letters! How are you now? How is your family?
I can't take you back in treatment myself, since I now work in a different department. The Expat-program no longer exists the way it did back then. To set up a new treatment in the Netherlands, go to a GP (Huisarts) first. He can refer you to a suitable place to get help. If you have documents from Poland, take them with you.
Good luck!
Kind regards, Kees"

"Thu, Jul 9, 2015, 1:40 PM
Iain Bryson to Kees de Vries
Kees,
I am doing alright, though it was a long trip. And it is not over yet; I am now fighting for contact/parental rights/custody. I have a lawyer, and my next case is in October. I have not seen or spoken to either Agata or Adelle since December 27, 2010. I am still fighting.
Thank you for your help. I am going to start looking for huisarts.
All the best,
Iain"

"Thu, Jul 9, 2015, 1:51 PM
Kees de Vries to me
Hi Iain,
I'm sorry to hear you haven't seen Agata and Adelle sinds all these years! That must be horrible. I hope you'll regain contact soon.
Take care!"

"Brian, Jeremiah
Thu, Jul 9, 2015, 4:38 PM
Dad to me
Hi Iain. Tried to call you. I received an email from Brian asking how you are. Not sure how to respond. I'm not giving out any info except that I think you are well and safe. Jeremiah left me a message about the same time Sara called. I was already gone and just picked up my messages today. Not sure what to say to JD [Jeremiah] either. Maybe same as Sara. What do you think?"

"Thu, Jul 9, 2015, 6:40 PM
Iain Bryson to Dad
I think that if they know, then mom or jeremiah will tell agata, and she will tell the court that we lied because we said that we are going back to the US, she will talk about marijuana....it is much better for Agata to not know where I am right now. I don't think that we should tell anyone right now."

"Thu, Jul 9, 2015, 6:54 PM
Dad to me
I agree. Does Brian know or do you think he will talk with your mom or Agata. For sure Jeremiah may talk with Agata?"

"Thu, Jul 9, 2015, 7:02 PM
Iain Bryson to Dad
Brian knows where I am. I talked to him today for a half an hour.
I am not sure about mom. It is not good that she was on Agata's side for court, and it will not be good if she continues to take Agata's side. If we don't tell her, then Agata will probably report to the court that I was released and then my mother couldn't find me or something like that.
Jeremiah no for sure not. I have copies of emails he sent to Agata, one of which says that she needs to take care of the custody issue right away. This is a part of the court record."

"Thu, Jul 9, 2015, 7:04 PM
Dad to me
Glad you told me about JD. I am a little concerned that they may try to make a big deal about your present location."

"Thu, Jul 9, 2015, 7:06 PM
Iain Bryson to Dad
Better they not know for now, I think. Why are specifics so important when you can tell them I am ok."

"**Thu, Jul 9, 2015, 7:08 PM**
Dad to me
Right. I am saying that you are well and in a safe place. That is all."

"**Sat, Jul 11, 2015, 9:39 AM**
Iain Bryson to Dad
the other thing that Agata could try to do is to contact Dutch immigration and tell them that we are in the process of divorcing..."

"**Sat, Jul 11, 2015, 3:05 PM**
Dad to me
Yup. Just have to see what immigration atty says. Jd has not replied to my email. Shows whose side he is on. Hope he stays out of it."

"**Sat, Jul 11, 2015, 3:39 PM**
Iain Bryson to Dad
I hope so too. I sent mom an email just saying that I am doing well."

"**Sat, Jul 11, 2015, 3:40 PM**
Dad to me
Good. Probably not good to tell her where you are."

"**Sat, Jul 11, 2015, 3:42 PM**
Iain Bryson to Dad
no, that is enough. now she can't say 'I didn't even know if you were ok or alive...' What did you say to Jer?"

"**Sat, Jul 11, 2015, 7:40 PM**
Iain Bryson to Piotr Kotfis [Attorney], Dad
Mr. Kotfis,
I failed to include an e-mail that I sent to my wife. Again, I do have the original e-mails. The first quote below you have; I have now included my response to my wife. Does this sound like the reply of a man who was holding his wife and daughter hostage and abusing them? I believe it shows that I was being very calm and level with my wife, as I had been for the entire time that we were together in December 2010 contrary to her allegations. I believe that it also shows that I cared about and loved my daughter; it shows that I was pretty desperate to see her, and that I wanted her to know that I love her. My wife never replied. Never.
'12/31/10
Agata Bryson to me
Hi Iain: I wanted to let you know that Adelle and I are doing OK. We are under professional care in recover

12/31/10
Iain Bryson to Agata Bryson
Agata,
Glad you are well. You told me I could see my daughter in three days. Could you let me know about that because it is pretty high on my priority list. Please tell her I love her'"

Trying to dismantle the red herring was like trying to put out a leaf fire in the woods on a windy day. In order for your mother's "escape" to be legitimate, I had to have been abusing both of you, terrorizing her to the point that she had to leave in fear of your lives. This was obviously not true, but the allegations themselves (as well as my family siding with your abductors) had been enough to allow all of this to happen. *If we can only back it up to the very beginning*, I knew, *if people could see that it wasn't an escape at all, but an abduction...what then?*

"**Thu, Jul 16, 2015, 6:14 AM**
Iain Bryson to Piotr Kotfis, Dad
Mr. Kotfis,

I received a call today from a friend who works at the hospital in Koszalin. She told me that the family court called there looking for me, asking as to my whereabouts. Just letting you know.
Regards,
Iain Bryson"

"Thu, Jul 16, 2015, 6:20 AM
Piotr Kotfis to me
Hello
Thank you for the information.
We are waiting for the files form the court. The criminal court has sent all the documentation to the family court, but they have a renovation right now and all the files are stored in the storehouse, so we cannot get the acces right know. Probably next week it would be possible.
PK"

"Thu, Jul 16, 2015, 12:27 PM
Dad to me
What do you make of this?"

"Thu, Jul 16, 2015, 12:31 PM
Iain Bryson to Dad
He didn't answer my question. I am not sure what he was responding to."

CHAPTER 87

"OPENING A CAN OF WORMS"

One of my priorities was to find a psychiatrist and get a new opinion of me documented for any future court dates in Poland. I needed an expert that would testify that the diagnosis I was tagged with in Poland was erroneous, for vindication, and to show the Polish family court. I believed it was necessary for the attorney to present four arguments to the court: 1) Agata was not stable, 2) Agata did not escape from me in fear of her life, 3) The court did not investigate or disprove the type of child abuse that I alleged, 4) Another expert psychiatrist will testify that I am not insane.

"Fri, Jul 17, 2015, 8:11 AM
Iain Bryson to [Peter Post] [Dutch psychiatrist I found in a Google search]
Hello,
I have recently returned to the Netherlands after living in Poland for about four years. I need a psychiatrist; I have obtained a referral from my huisarts. Thank you,
Iain Byson"

"Fri, Jul 24, 2015, 11:01 PM
Dad to me
Whats going on? Art just sent a message that you were fighting? and he has asked you to leave."

"Sat, Jul 25, 2015, 7:02 AM
Iain Bryson to Dad
he drank 350 ml jack daniels and changed into a different person again, as he does."

"Sat, Jul 25, 2015, 8:44 AM
Dad to me
Hi Iain Phooey. Hope you can work it out. I suggested that you move to the upstairs room and give him more space. Would that help? If not then maybe we shoukd get you back to the US and working and preparing court in Poland. I don't see how you will be able to support yourself there..   hang in there. L, D"

"Sat, Jul 25, 2015, 10:16 AM
Iain Bryson to Dad
yes, now it is ok. he does this frequently. I am trying to deal with it; he can be very difficult. No, I cannot support myself here now. I don't know what to do about that. I am going to call the immigration lawyer Monday. As far as I knew I also could not return to the US. Not CT for sure"

"Sun, Jul 26, 2015, 5:34 AM
Iain Bryson to Dad
Hey dad. So Art apologized and today has been alright. This is a pattern with him.
Art's friend is now here from California. Didn't you say that you were going to talk to Matt [Berger, CT Attorney]? What did he say about the letter that Piotr wrote?"

My dad had arranged for Attorney Matthew Berger to help with the unresolved situation involving Mike from 2010. I didn't want to return to Connecticut, but I especially didn't want to if there was a chance I could be arrested for not appearing in court. Either way, I wanted to clear this up so that I didn't have anything hanging over my head.

"https://bicycledutch.wordpress.com/2011/10/06/nescio-bridge-amsterdam/
Tue, Aug 11, 2015, 11:11 AM
Iain Bryson to Dad
This bridge scares me. I've been a few times, but never over it. I think Art is going to go with me later and maybe..."

"Tue, Aug 11, 2015, 1:33 PM
Dad to me
Hi Iain. My phone is not working for calls. I ordered a replacement. The bridge looks cool. Are bikes ok or just walkers? I think you should get back here and handle this. I can get you a good flight to PVD on the 27 th. I can tell Matt about that date or alittle later and ask him to see Kennedy [Prosecutor] and get a reading. I think its important to have this finushed before Oct. 1st. What do you think? I will try to call you. Maybe skype will work on laptop. L,D"

My dad thought that I should return to CT as soon as possible. I knew that I could resolve the issue by talking to a judge, but I didn't want to get arrested in the airport and spend any more time in jail in the meantime. Furthermore, I simply saw no future in Connecticut; going there seemed like opening a can of worms that didn't require opening, at least not yet.

Even though I had forgiven my family, I still didn't see any need or have any desire to live amongst them or even near them. They had completely dropped the ball, and though I loved them, I was not going to ever trust them with another important ball.

"Fri, Aug 14, 2015, 7:49 AM
Iain Bryson to Dad
... I have nineteen euros.
Yesterday was Art's birthday. [Ruben], Art, and I rode our bikes, stopped to get a beer and then continued on to a restuarant. It was a cool place. [Ruben] says there is a two week waiting list to get in there. Also, they are closed on Saturday nights because they don't want to have to deal with the tourist crowd. Good food, and the bike ride back was nice.
Is Matt on vacation? What did this other guy say?
Why do you want to do this the 27th? It could be done after that as well, up to the middle of September maybe. The important thing is that it is done right. Also, Art is going away on the 27th meaning that that is a nice time to be here.
Strange that attorney Kotfis hasn't responded to my email, no??..."

"Fri, Aug 14, 2015, 11:19 AM
Dad to me
Looking at plane schedule. Could fly in on 20 th and return together on the 27th or 31st. Havent heard fro Matt. Contacted another atty who will get back to me on Monday. Tell Art I said Happy Birthday. Tried to call...will try again later. Doing errands. L,D"

"Fri, Aug 14, 2015, 2:58 PM
Iain Bryson to Dad
why not later after the lawyer situation is taken care of? Art really thinks you should be here for SAIL."

"Sun, Aug 16, 2015, 7:17 AM
Iain Bryson to Dad
1. We have to go talk to the immigration lawyer to:
    a. see if residency here is possible
'Krista Kaptein [immigration attorney]
Aug 11 (5 days ago) to me
Dear mr. Bryson,
If I understand you correctly, you left the Netherlands after 2013 and now you want to return?
It is not possible to extend your old residence permit.
If your ex wife and daugther still live in the Netherlands, and you are (partly) taking care of your daugther, you could consider to apply for a residence permit to stay with your daugther. However, this is not that easy procedure.
If you, yourself, has American nationality, you could also consider to start your own business in the Netherlands. For Americans, it is quite easy to apply for a residence permit as an independent entrepreneur. For more information, you can contact us to plan a consult meeting to discuss your case. The costs for this meeting are 60 euro.
Met vriendelijke groet,
Krista Kaptein'
Once we do this, then we will know the answers about Holland versus Florida, etc. Remember that Kotfis said it may be better to live in Europe.
2. Psychiatrist
A. I saw one and still owe him 80 euro. Our next scheduled appointment is in a week.
B. The guy I really wanted to see I have scheduled for 8/20.
C. I need to get insurance started ASAP
3. Dentist
A. I have to see her one more time, and then it will just be maintenence. I have her 225 euro next week.
B. I told her that you want to see her, and she said that is fine. Tell me when you will be here and I can schedule you and appt.
4. Apartment rentals
Kamernet.nl
funda.nlhe bike riding is amazing. What do I do for money until the card gets here?"

Bicycling around Amsterdam was my new favorite thing to do, and it also got me out of the apartment and into a world where I could go anywhere, freely, and safely. No more guards, no more reports, just the open roads of the biker's paradise that is Amsterdam, the breeze in my face, a new skip in my step.

My teeth, the ones I had left, were an utter mess, and my dad agreed to pay for some trips to the dentist. Most of my Polish dental experiences were not good, but the last one with the eighty something year old woman without gloves giving me root canals without Novocain was on another level. I searched Google for a dentist and settled on a young Dutch woman in West Amsterdam, about a half hour bike ride from Art's. I liked her picture and website, and decided she was who I wanted working on me, even though she was on the other side of town.

"email from Art
Wed, Aug 19, 2015, 9:16 PM
Dad to me
What happened? Can you find us a place to stay? maybe I should not come and get you back here on next plane."

"Thu, Aug 20, 2015, 3:21 AM
Iain Bryson to Dad
he got drunk; that is what happened. he was fighting with [Ruben] and [Ruben] was crying."

"Thu, Aug 20, 2015, 3:28 AM
Iain Bryson to Dad
back where? i will not live in CT. I don't know if he will come back to reality or not, but as I said before the sooner I can leave here the better because this type of thing is recurring. i will see what kind of rooms are available."

"Thu, Aug 20, 2015, 11:09 AM
Iain Bryson to Dad
i am at the airport. i don't see any flights arriving at 5:30 from the us. I am the area of starbucks and train tickets and services"

"Thu, Aug 20, 2015, 12:20 PM
Dad to me
shoot. I leave here today. I forgot...arrive tomorrow...loose a day. sorry."

"Thu, Aug 20, 2015, 1:08 PM
Iain Bryson to Dad
on the train back. i thought something was going on because I couldn't find a reasonable flight on the arrivals board. See you tomorrow. love you"

"Wed, Aug 26, 2015, 6:26 PM
Dad to Matthew Berger [CT Attorney]
Planning ahead for Iain's return. Can you know if he will be stopped at airport and detained or pass through without incident and meet with you and prosecutor on another day? We need to know what to expect. Iain doesn't need more drama."

"Wed, Aug 26, 2015 10:19 PM
Matthew Berger to Dad
Kirk
Rearrest warrant issued on 5/10/11, $15,000 bond.   If he were local I'd say turn yourself in at 7 a.m. at the NLPD and show up in court at 10.   Not sure what would happen on an international flight. The worry is that CT issued an extradition hold and he'll be held in MA or NY (wherever he flies in to) until the hold is released (CT doesn't extradite), which could be a some time (a few days). I'll try to look into this on Friday and see if I can get the warrant recalled or something.
Matt"

"Wed, Sep 2, 2015, 8:16 AM
Iain Bryson to Dad
and if they grab me will it be possible to get me out? until tuesday is ridiculous"

I realized that I wasn't going to be able to support myself in The Netherlands because I couldn't legally get a job. The only other option I saw was to attempt to trust my dad with something small. *I could fly back, take care of the court case, see my dad's farm, and return to Amsterdam if I don't want to be there. I kind of have to because I have no money and can't stay with Art too much longer anyway.* Art did not want me to leave, but my dad assured him that I would return to Amsterdam. With that, I was on my way back to the USA, conflicted and relieved at the same time.

CHAPTER 88

"THE FARM"

I wasn't arrested at the airport, but the police had been by my dad's house looking for me about a week before I got there. Matt, the attorney that my dad hired, informed the judge of my situation of having just returned from Europe after being in prison and losing my daughter. He quashed the re-arrest warrant and set a normal court date. The charges against me stemming from the incident at my dad's school in 2010 were dismissed and my gun was returned to me.

My dad gave me a room in his farmhouse, and I felt extremely fortunate to be there, as if God had decided to send me exactly what I needed. I could close the door, read, work, and pray. I set up my office, and I began to write the initial notes and drafts of this present book. At this point, I still thought that going back to Amsterdam was my best option because of the ongoing custody case in Poland.

"Update
Mon, Sep 21, 2015, 8:20 AM
Iain Bryson to Peter Post
Dr. Post,
I just wanted to update you on my situation. I made contact with the Kaizergracht [street] psychiatrist. I had a problem getting my insurance started, and I am still working on that. I had to return to Connecticut to take care of some things; I should be back in Amsterdam in a couple of weeks, and as of now there is still a custody hearing in Poland in October…
All the best,
Iain"

Aunt Sara met me at a Dunkin Donuts, and I apologized for the mean things I had said to her. Yes, there was part of me that wanted to say, *Well you know I never would have said that if my daughter wasn't literally stolen from me, and if you hadn't been lying to me and working against me.* But that was not the appropriate response, because from my side of things, there was no acceptable time to speak to people in the manner with which I spoke to her in early 2011.

In the back of my mind, I wished she would also apologize for lying to me, or for helping to put me involuntarily into a mental hospital, or for not believing or supporting me as I fought for you. But I knew that this was both unlikely and unnecessary; whatever she chose to do was her journey, and ultimately of no concern to me. My concern was still only you, and for you I had to apologize and forgive.

"For if you forgive men their trespasses, your heavenly Father will also forgive you" (Matthew 6:14 NKJV)

It took me some time before I was willing to sit down and talk to my mom, not that I hadn't forgiven her, but she aggrieved me the most out of anybody. She should have known that the allegations that led to your abduction could not have been true, and that my distress was not due to drugs, mental illness, or being a wife beater, but to losing my child.

I assumed that she was still talking to you and your mom, which I decided was both weird and the best for all involved. Even though it blew my mind that my mom supported and was actively supporting your abduction, I realized that the best thing for you and for my mom, given that I had been eliminated from your life, was that you had contact with each other.

To my cousin, Jer, I sent a text. It read something like this: "Geek [nickname I gave him], I wish that you knew me, and it's hard for me to believe that you don't. I love you and will always love you no matter what. I forgive you, and I'm sorry for anything I did to you that was not right. I have known the loss not only of a child, but also of my brother. Agata, my friend, played you like your trombone. You did not know her, and yet you trusted her..." He never replied.

My dad and I returned to Europe for a hearing in family court. We flew into Berlin and drove to the hotel in Szczecin. It felt strange to be back in Poland, like I had returned to enemy territory. This place was considerably less safe for me than home, and I did not underestimate the power of false testimony. It was possible, I knew, for me to somehow find myself locked up once again.

"We are at Hotel Focus
Thu, Oct 8, 2015, 7:28 PM
Iain Bryson to Piotr Kotfis, Dad
Mr. Kotfis,
I hope that you are well. We just arrived at Hotel Focus not long ago. Please let us know what the plan is for tomorrow. Thanks, Iain"

Your mom and grandmother showed up to court to testify against me, accompanied by several men that appeared to be bodyguards. I was happy just to be in the same building as your mom again and see her face. For me, the trip was worth it just for those few minutes.

She looked miserable and refused eye contact. The way that she was composed let me know that she was barely holding it together, and I felt like crying or screaming out. I knew that I could make her completely unravel if given the opportunity to cross examine her testimony, but I wasn't counting on being victorious in court, or even being given a real chance.

I was willing to go through the motions for the closure and the experience, but I had never before seen or heard of anything close to justice in a Polish court, and I wasn't expecting it now. The act of fooling everybody and convincing them that I was a domestic abuser who deserved to have his daughter taken from him had worked extremely well to date, and I had been interned for a long time for thinking otherwise.

Your mom was staring at the floor, seated next to her mom on a bench directly across from where my dad and I were sitting, maybe thirty feet away, a couple of ruffians next to her. *Could my daughter be nearby?* I thought. *I wonder where she is and who is watching her, I wonder if she would recognize me. I wonder if I would recognize her.*

My dad told me that he was going over to say hi to your mom. He was excited to touch base with your mom, still oblivious to the fact that I had told him she was a cult slave who was an active participant in your abduction. I told him that she wasn't going to talk to him, but I wanted to see him try, which he did. She hardly looked up from the ground, shook her head and acted as if she was afraid, and then redirected her eyes back toward the ground.

Nothing substantive happened in court; I didn't get to speak at all. We essentially flew to Poland for a continuance, but I would've flown to Poland every day even if it was just to see your mom. Attorney Kotfis told me that it was going to be a tough case, that they were saying that you didn't even want to speak English anymore because of all your bad memories of me in our household. My attempt to explain to him that this was impossible and obviously parental alienation went in one ear and out the other.

> "If it has gone on long enough, the programming/brainwashing parent may have to issue few, if any further messages. To the untrained eye 'it's the child's own views.' Judges and professionals often see children at the maintenance stage and incorrectly conclude that the children have formulated their own views. They can find no present external inputs from an adult figure; the damage has been done" (Clawar and Rivlin 26).

To claim that your mom escaped to safety from me was ridiculous, but to claim that a child who had not seen her father for five years, from age 3 to 8, would be so angry as to reject even her father's language is absurd and impossible. The only way this can happen is with parental alienation.

"'psychological, physical abuse....escaped in fear of my and my daughter's lives...'
Wed, Oct 14, 2015, 3:59 PM
Iain Bryson to Piotr Kotfis, Dad
Mr. Kotfis,
I just wanted to be clear on this, as I believe that it is important. The subject line of this email is an example of what Agata alleged.
I believe that Brian and Kees de Vries have testimony which casts serious doubt on these allegations.
It can be proven through witness testimony that :
1. I was very worried about Agata's psychological state and the impact that it had upon our family months before she 'escapes.'
2. I was worried about Agata's psychological state the day after I returned to meet her in Holland in December 2010 after being apart for about three months.
3. I sought help from a psychologist who 'knew' my wife for months the day after returning to meet her in Holland in December 2010. On this day, I told the psychologist that Agata had told me that she was returning to Poland with our daughter. Therefore, the 'escape' was planned. Agata told me and I told the psychologist.
   Does it make sense to say that I was psychologically and physically abusing my wife, that she was in fear of her and our daughter's lives AND I was actively trying to get help (psychologist/police/close friend)? We can prove the second part. The first part is just Agata's word, which is mostly lies most of the time and some pictures which cannot show who gave her those bruises. Again, Agata was away from me for three months. The day after reuniting with her I was trying to get help. We can prove that. I don't think that it makes sense to conclude that I was seeking help and beating my wife at the same time....I wasn't."

"Update Request
Mon, Oct 19, 2015, 10:44 PM
Iain Bryson to Piotr Kotfis, Dad
Mr. Kotfis,
I hope that you are well. Please tell me what you are thinking in regards to the case. This will allow me to direct my efforts towards either getting you what you need and preparing myself for trial and evaluation.
   When we met in June, you said that we needed to prove that Agata is at least one percent to blame. This should be simple: she sought psychological help for mental health issues having 'a large impact' on her family. This is in the documentation, there is a formal record in Holland...
   Or, I wasn't abusing my wife and child and they did not escape from me because I was seeking help within 24 hours of returning to my wife and child after being apart from the[m] for three months. I was seeking help because of Agata's documented mental health issues. (Kees de Vries, psychologist)

Anyway, I don't know if this makes sense to you, if this is something that we can use, if you have other ideas? Have we requested an initial supervised visit with my daughter?
I look forward to hearing from you. Thank you for your help.
All the best,
Iain"

Since 2011, I had been trying to tell the Polish courts that I did not have a criminal history, but they didn't believe me. The "criminal history" part of the red herring had survived even until now, because nobody had ever checked. At this point, I did have the opportunity to put this lie to rest, but it was too late; it had served its purpose.

"Wed, Dec 16, 2015, 10:34 AM
Iain Bryson to Piotr Kotfis, Dad
Attachments
I have attached the document for your review. I have contacted my attorney. Again, I believe that the only documentation we will be able to get will be something like 'no record,' or 'disposed without judgement.'"

"Wed, Dec 16, 2015, 12:30 PM
Iain Bryson to Piotr Kotfis, Dad
My attorney says, 'The case was dismissed and the file is sealed.'
What do I need to get for you?"

"Wed, Dec 16, 2015, 1:31 PM
Piotr Kotfis to me
I have already answered that I do not have any criminal court orders against you. I will inform them that you do not have it also. Did I understand you well that according to US law - you have no criminal sentence in your history?"

"Wed, Dec 16, 2015, 1:35 PM
Iain Bryson to Piotr Kotfis
Yes, I have no criminal history at all in the United States."

"Wed, Dec 16, 2015, 1:48 PM
Piotr Kotfis to me
OK. I will inform the court."

"Thu, Dec 17, 2015, 7:25 PM
Iain Bryson to Piotr Kotfis, Dad
Mr. Kotfis,
Is there any further information on when I will need to be back in Poland? Please let me know as soon as you know anything on this.
Thanks,
Iain"

"Fri, Dec 18, 2015, 2:06 AM
Piotr Kotfis to me
There is no information on the date of the evaluation.
Best regards
Piotr Kotfis"

I printed out all the communication between your mother and I leading up to your abduction/escape, and I spent about a hundred dollars to send it to Attorney Kotfis. "This is the crux of my case," I attempted to convey to him. "This shows that their story is impossible, and that the Polish side of things is where an investigation needed and needs to take place." But Mr. Kotfis never acknowledged the possibility that this could be a strategy, and he never spoke of the hundreds of pages I sent him, not until later when he wanted me to hire him to appeal again.

My dad and I had a large bonfire in the back field, and I fed the fire with most of my past, things like high school yearbooks, prom pictures, and college notes, not everything, but piles and piles of stuff, nonetheless. My world had been shattered; how could I waste time reminiscing? What good were these things if I couldn't show them to you and eventually give them to you?

This act was a statement to myself, and to God, that I wanted something other than what I had once thought I wanted. A sort of sacrifice to the flames, giving up my idea of what I had thought I wanted for something so entirely different that I couldn't even define it. As far as I was concerned, the stakes were so high that it was time to throw it all away except that which was necessary for the mission at hand, and to stop holding onto souvenirs that tied me back to that world that no longer existed, if it ever did.

I had another epiphany moment like I experienced on New Year's Eve and Day 2011. Sitting at my desk, surrounded by pictures of you, thinking about you and your mom and our lives, it hit me again, that sickening but ecstatic feeling of being pulled into deeper understanding about the world and my role in it, given what I had experienced and what we were experiencing as a family. I knew I had to be a mouthpiece not only for you and your mom, but for others suffering under similar conditions as well.

I saw clearly the absurdity and absolute lunacy of a world where evil not only exists, but thrives, where not even my own child is safe in our home. But now it also became clear that our problem was only one example of a much larger, much more insidious problem. Our situation was not unique; so many people were suffering because of an evil that the public had hitherto been unable and unwilling to deal with; unable because it is hidden beneath the surface of "normal" society, and unwilling because they don't believe in what they cannot see with their own eyes. I saw that God did indeed have a plan to turn this terrible situation into good, as He always does.

> "But as for you, you meant evil against me; but God meant it for good, in order to bring it about as it is this day, to save many people alive" (Genesis 50:20 NKJV).

"Sun, Jan 3, 2016, 11:37 PM
Iain Bryson to Piotr Kotfis, Dad
This is an email that I sent to my psychologist two days before she 'escaped.'
Sat, Dec 25, 2010, 5:01 PM
Iain Bryson to Kees de Vries
kees,
i am thinking more and more i am dealing with a psychopath or APD, and wow it is terrifying, especially with all this other [expletive] going on..."

"Sun, Jan 3, 2016, 11:38 PM
Iain Bryson to Piotr Kotfis, Dad
I sent this email to the psychologist three days after the 'escape.'
---------- Forwarded message ----------
Thu, Dec 30, 2010, 3:49 PM
Iain Bryson to Kees de Vries
can you please keep trying to call agata. they wont tell me if they are in the country. i do not like what i see

Thu, Dec 30, 2010 10:44 AM
Kees de Vries to Iain Bryson
I keep trying, Iain.
Regards, Kees"

* * *

It was astonishing to me to leave and be away from the world, and then to return. Things I had never heard of for the first nearly forty years of my life were now the topic of conversation, things like gluten and kale. And while these things had always existed, now the public had taken hold of them, and they were out in the open, a part of the public discourse and general social consciousness. I mused that this is how it will be when the public becomes aware of the incidence and prevalence of ritual abuse; one day it will be as if everybody knew it all along.

> "All truth passes through three stages: First, it is ridiculed; Second, it is violently opposed; Third, it is accepted as self-evident." (Arthur Schopenhauer, from your mom's quote journal).

As I got more settled on the farm, the idea of returning to Amsterdam became more distant. I took the vegetable garden over full time and began planning what to do with thirty fifty-foot rows. In February I started sprouting seeds, and by May I had hundreds of plants that were ready to go into the ground, taking up two rooms in the house. It was a constant process of planting and transplanting and driving to the store to get pots and potting soil. By the time I could get the tomatoes into the ground they were rootbound and nearly two feet tall; I really had no idea what I was doing at first.

To outsiders, it looked like I was a farmer, and while that was partly true, my real job never changed. The only thing I cared about was fighting for you. There was a part of me that could sentimentalize this time of building an idyllic farm with my dad, a blank canvas of sorts that we could do anything with. But as it was, the shadow of your abduction loomed over what would otherwise have been as close to as good as it gets in this life.

Our house was at the beginning of our road, so that everyone coming into the neighborhood had to pass by. There were pros and cons to this in that it was a perfect place for our farmstand, and I got to know all the neighbors, but it was difficult to work outside without being interrupted by someone stopping by to say hello. It was great to be forced to interact with so many different people, and yet there was a part of me that would rather the property had a ten-foot-tall fence around it.

I told everyone that I met the story of losing you to the cult, trying to solve it on my own, ending up locked up, and now continuing that journey with the belief that good does overcome evil. It wasn't that I was looking to tell people, but that it would come up in nearly any introductory conversation: "So, what do you do?" "Why were you in Poland?" "Why don't you get to see your daughter?" etc.

Most people, including those closest to me, simply did not possess the capability to wrap their heads around such a sequence of events. Most people wanted to change the channel as soon as they could, much like when that commercial comes on for starving children in Africa; it's easier just not to think about it. So, I was surprised when a couple up the street knew what I was talking about when I said, "ritual abuse." It was like I was in a foreign country, and I finally found someone who could speak my language.

About twenty years prior, they informed me, they had paid the mafia to get their niece and nephew out of a satanic ritual abuse cult. "Yes," the man said as a matter of fact, "satanists are abusing kids all over the place, and they walk around and look at trees just like we do. We were very fortunate to have gotten them out; it wasn't easy." My mind was blown, and I wanted to hug them as if they were long lost relatives.

In September 2016, my dad and I drove to upstate New York to attend my cousin's wedding. I was excited to see family I hadn't seen in ten years. On the ride, my dad told me that my aunt had hesitated to invite me and had asked him how I was doing, reminding me that my family didn't have a clue.

For the entire time that we were there, about three days, nobody mentioned you, my daughter, almost as if you had never existed. But I was used to it, even though I still found it hard to believe that people could be so blind to the fact that I had lost my child, and that everything I said, wrote, and did after was the direct result of my little girl being stolen from me.

As an aside, later when my cousin and his new bride had a daughter, this child had to fight cancer as an infant. The family flocked in support, providing my cousin and his wife with donations and encouragement, and of course sending their thoughts and prayers. Cancer, I realized, is a less threatening foe than satanic ritual abuse. People can at least wrap their heads around cancer; SRA is so terrible that they can't even try to think about it.

"Evaluation
Thu, Oct 6, 2016, 5:40 AM
Piotr Kotfis to Dad, me
Hello.
Today Dr. Rafal Olszewski - the psychiatrist - has contacted my office, asking Iain to come for the psychiatric evaluation.
The possible dates: 10.17, 11.02, 11.03, 11.16.
Please answer asap which date is the most convenient for you."

"Thu, Oct 6, 2016, 8:34 PM
Dad to Piotr Kotfis, bcc: me
Thank you councillor. I have a busy schedule this fall. The best day for me at this time is 11/17. I am looking into booking a flight for Iain and I. Is there any chance that Iain and will be able to see his daughter while we are there. We could stay a few days longer if that possibility exists. I am in Florida at the moment and will be calling Iain tonight to get his thoughts. Thank you for your efforts. Kirk"

"Fri, Oct 7, 2016, 8:19 AM
Iain Bryson to Dad
I don't think that it makes sense to go. I would have to lie during the evaluation, and if I did, it wouldn't get anything of consequence accomplished."

I knew that I could not continue to lie to get what I wanted and think I was trusting in God, for to trust in God is to not lie. I had lied to get out of Poland, but I was unwilling to continue. It would therefore be impossible to navigate through the Polish psychiatrists.

"Do you believe your daughter was/is being abused?" they would ask right away, and as soon as I responded with anything other than a resounding "No," they would decide that my mental disease had come out of remission.

"Do you take your (anti-thinking) medication that you agreed to take every day for the rest of your life? Are you being treated? Do you think that you are mentally ill? Have you smoked any marijuana since your release? Have you had any alcohol since your release? Do you think that your daughter is being abused? Would you ever try to take your child away from her current family?" There were so many questions that I could not answer truthfully if I were to have a chance. Telling the truth would lead to an even stronger case against me, and maybe they would just lock me up again.

Even if I were to go back to Poland and lie to their "expert" psychiatrist, even if I could somehow jump through all of their hoops and pass all of their tests, even if I lived in Europe and got a job and took my medication as the Polish court deemed necessary; even if I did all of those things, what then?

They weren't ever going to revisit whether you were abducted, or whether you were being abused. They would hold to their original positions, to the "facts" that they had already decided were irrefutable, such as, "Agata had to get away from Iain because she feared for her life and the life of their daughter," "Adelle was not abducted, but rescued from Iain," and "Adelle was not and is not being abused because her Polish family says so, and because Iain is obviously crazy. He is the only one who has ever said Adelle was abused, and therefore, Iain is totally insane; he must be."

Supervised visits, if I could even get that, were not going to cut it for me. If I was given supervised visits, I would attempt to get you out of the country and into an evaluation – no doubt about it. I might as well have had the mafia do it without all this other nonsense, all this asking nicely in this preposterous situation.

I was certain that what I needed was a miracle, an act of God. Anything less would just be a continuation of the nightmare in one form or another. And because this is what I decided I needed, I also concluded that I could not continue to lie for advantage. Lying was not an acceptable means to the end I was seeking, for it is the truth that sets us free, and I knew that my job was to continue to learn how to trust in the Lord with all my heart and lean not on my own understanding (Proverbs 3:5). If I wanted a miracle, I would have to believe in one, and act accordingly.

When it came down to a question of possibly seeing you soon or seeing you later if that was God's will, I was highly tempted do the former and rely on my own understanding again. Part of me wanted to do whatever it would take, even if it was only for one supervised visit. I wanted to look into your eyes and hug you and smell you so badly that part of me would have given my life for that. But what I wanted more than that was what I've always wanted – for you to be evaluated, for you to be delivered, and in my experience, I could not trust in man, but in the God who performs miracles.

"OK, Lord, I believe that Adelle Avery Bryson (and her mother) will be delivered from the cult and brought to safety. I believe that You have a plan to do this, and it is in Your will that I trust," I prayed. "So, what is it you want of me, Lord? What does it mean to pray believing?"

CHAPTER 89

"THE VERDICT OF DECEMBER 7, 2016"

The case that I wanted the attorney to argue was not that I shouldn't have my daughter taken from me because I was "healed," but rather that my daughter should never have been taken from me in the first place. I wanted him to poke holes in the official narrative and bring in other witnesses like Kees and a Dutch or American psychiatrist to testify on my behalf. If he wasn't willing to do this, if we had to keep looking at things only through the lens of the Polish "experts," then I knew I didn't stand a chance.

Why hadn't the attorney attempted to prove that your mom was one percent (or more) to blame? Did he just make that claim to get the sale with false hope? How did I ever believe him when I had all my other Polish court experiences telling me that he was wrong, or lying?

I believed him because I wanted what he was saying to be true. But he just wanted my business, and he used a simple trick to get it, claiming that it would be easy for him to get me exactly what I came to him for. Of course, after that first meeting, after he was hired and paid, he never again mentioned the one percent rule. Nor did he acknowledge, evaluate, or argue any of the evidence or arguments that I presented him.

"Mon, Oct 24, 2016, 7:30 AM
Piotr Kotfis to Dad, me
Dear Sir
The next possible date is 21st of November. The 17th of November is not valid any more. Please confirm 21st!
It you fail to confirm a date - the psychiatrist will set a date without consultation with you.
Best regards,
Piotr Kotfis"

"Mon, Nov 21, 2016, 8:36 AM
Dad to me
---------- Forwarded message ----------
Good morning councillor. Iain and I are struggling with how we should best proceed. He is convinced that the court psychologist will ask him if he thinks his daughter is being abused and is in danger. He believes this and from what he has told me I believe he has solid ground for his opinion. However, should this question come up, he will answer truthfully and believes the court will use this information against him. In this country his doctors think that his situation was mis-diagnosed and outside of making a very bad decision as too how

best get help for his family, he is cognitively very well. A broken heart is quite different from being mentally unstable.

Iain has been living with me and working on the farm and with my business since his return. He is a fine young man, good with his friends and family. No one here has any issues with him. His doctor saw no reason to continue sessions.

Finally Iain and I were concerned at the last court day where we saw some rough looking fellows with Agata and her mom. We are concerned that they may start some trouble and find away to lock Iain up again. This must not happen!

Having this information, what do you suggest we do? Should we change gears and in get visitation rights for his mom and myself or do you think there is a way to unite Iain and his daughter? I will watch for your response and write back asap. Thank you, Kirk

Re: Contact
Nov 21, 2016 5:14 AM
Piotr Kotfis to Kirk
Dear Sir

I cannot give you any other advise than to tell the truth and answer all the question truthfully, both to the court and doctor. I hope the opinion will be professional but of course I cannot promise you that. I do not know the court psychiatrist, all I know his name is Rafał Olszewski. The problem is that the judge asked psychiatrist a controversial question: weather your daughter will be safe with you - it is question not about your mental health but about the future and no one can answer that. It shows the attitude of the judge!
I strongly recommend starting the case re. visitation rights for Iain's mom and yourself - since after last court visit I do not have any good feelings about the judge point of view in this case.
We are now facing he situation, that the next hearing is on the 7th of December and we do not have the evaluation done. Since you didn't contact me for so long - we have no evaluation date. Now I need your answer weather you plan to be present on the hearing and evaluation?!
Best regards,
Piotr Kotfis"

"Wed, Dec 7, 2016, 5:20 AM
Piotr Kotfis to me, Dad
[on Dec. 7, 2016, 12:29 AM, Kirk wrote:
'Please ask for a continuation . I can not get time away from business at this time. I have had a serious injury which makes traveling difficult. The injury has complicated my business and has placed extra femands on my time. Can you set up for early spring? Also I want to talk about grandparent's rights. Thank you, K']

Dear Iain
The court decided to discount your testimony and will announce a verdict today at 1PM. I regret you or your father Kirk didn't contact me earlier about your absence on today's hearing. When we were talking about the case - you and Kirk declared that you will come back to Poland to take part in the procedure. Since you didn't come - the court didn't even want to hear about postponing the case until spring. Now we have a situation where you didn't testify and you wasn't evaluated by a psychiatrist - and the court will make a decision without those two important factors. We were trying to postpone the case and declared objections about going on with the case without the psychological/psychiatric evaluation of your wife - but the court decided to close a case. After the verdict, if it will be not acceptable for you - you will have a possibility to appeal. I will inform you about the verdict as soon as I get it, but please do contact me more regularly!
Best regards
Piotr Kotfis"

"Wed, Dec 7, 2016, 7:51 AM
Piotr Kotfis to me, Dad
Dear Iain
The verdict of 7/12/2016:
1. The divorce without guilt of any of the parties but by the reasons caused by you (Iain).

2. Maintenance for the child: 500 zloty per month to be paid to the mother.

3. Deprivation of your (Iain's) parental authority.

4. The contact with the child is prohibited.

5. You do not have to pay the costs of your wife attorney.

We will apply for the written substantiation and after we obtain it - you have 14 days for appeal. The costs of appeal are 600 zloty (court fee) + 5000zloty (office fee) + 23% vat. All to be paid in advance. Additionally we will send all the e-mails which were not taken into consideration by the district court- this time we should translate it first so I will need money to do it. I will pick just some of e-mails but still it is additional cost of about 1000 zloty - it is up to you...Please contact me asap in this matter. No contact from your side means you agree for such a verdict and do not going to appeal.

Take care

Piotr Kotfis"

"Tue, Dec 13, 2016, 10:13 AM
Piotr Kotfis to Dad, me
Dear Sir

Unfortunately, the court's decision to refuse to postpone the hearing was legal according to Polish law. Our system operates very formal. The law provides very little possibility of delaying the case. In this case, the court found that there has not been any reasons for doing so. The court pointed out in the decision that Iain has not appeared on evaluation - please remember Iain declared he will be present for every court notice and I was trying to set a date for it with you and Iain without any result. I am sorry you feel a disappointment but I must say it was Iain's responsibility and his best interest to be present on the hearing. You knew about the date a month before and informed me about problems with coming few hours before the court date.

As for the cost, our agreement covered only the divorce case (1st instance). I disagree with your opinion about my little effort. You knew, you are paying for the divorce case and you agreed for the fee. The lack of presence of your son on the evaluation and at the court wasn't helpful at all - and I cannot take the responsibility for this!

As for the grandfather's rights - as we speak in Szczecin, Polish law don't literally give the right for contacts for grandparents but it is generally possible to fight in front of the court for it. Of course the circumstances of Iain's case will not help but I hope that the court will agree for contacts for you. The 1st instant case fee is still the same as I offered before: 5000 zloty (+23% VAT) to be paid in advance + court fee.

Best regards

Piotr Kotfis"

"Adelle will probably come looking for you when she turns eighteen, don't you think?" my dad frequently suggested, as if this could be some kind of solace even if what he was saying could be true.

"Dad, first of all, it does nothing for me whatsoever to ponder whether or not my daughter would come looking for me fourteen years after she was abducted from me and raised elsewhere. I am her dad, and it is my duty to fight for her, not to speculate about whatever it is she might do. Secondly, everything that was important to me was taken and destroyed, my daughter's entire childhood, so I find no comfort in looking forward to your hypothetical possibility which you venture 'might' happen in another decade from now. And lastly, you have obviously not been listening to anything I've been trying to tell you about the effects of ritual abuse; no, Adelle would not 'come looking for me,' but will 'hate' me just as her mother does, just as the cult expects of her."

"I don't know about that," he speculated, doubting my reasoning, even though it is what I had been thinking about for many years already, "girls usually go looking for their fathers, I think."

"That could be statistically true," I responded, "but, as I've been saying, this situation is on the extreme end of the spectrum. When you say things like this it tells me you haven't been listening. Why did Agata take Adelle? It had nothing to do with me... Adelle is just a younger version of her mother, and she will be conditioned to hate me as well... and it doesn't matter because I'm not waiting for a hypothetical future. Nothing has changed since that first moment I realized she was gone except more time has gone by and more has been destroyed. I still want the same thing…I'm glad you're my dad and not Adelle's dad…"

I really was glad that he was my dad, and my point was not that he was a bad dad, but that he wouldn't be able to do my job, which is completely normal. What is abnormal is for someone who has never read a book on child abuse to think that their opinion on the subject is valid; this would be like me telling a race car driver how to navigate a tricky course or a golfer how to get out of a tough spot in the rough.

* * *

Getting used to living with my dad seemed to be a smooth and natural process, though it was impossible to trust him entirely, which I believe was prudent given some of his earlier decisions. I had forgiven him and everybody else already for their part in unwittingly assisting in your abduction, and everything that came with that.

I understood how everyone had been fooled, how and why they had fallen for the "red herring" that was served up and delivered to them so skillfully by your grandfather, just as your mom had warned me repeatedly was going to happen. "Iain, I am taking Adelle back to Poland… Stockholm Syndrome… mind control… cult… my dad created a red herring, your drug, psychological, and criminal histories will be used against you, nobody will believe you… your parental rights will be terminated…"

The red herring was designed to make everyone focus on me while the "cult" got away with you, and it really didn't matter too much what people were focusing on as long as they never took their eyes off me. For some people, it was "Iain does drugs," and case closed; they didn't need any more reason or proof that my child had to be taken from me. The fact that I wasn't using drugs had nothing to do with the point; it was enough because I had in the past.

It was nothing more (or less) than a simple sleight of hand, nothing more than, "Hey look over here at this (Iain), don't look there (at whatever Iain is talking about)." This was a classic use of ad hominem fallacy, whereby what I said was discredited based on the assassination of my character, whether true or not. They were duped as soon as they took their eye off the ball, which was my moving child.

The official "truth" in the Polish records, both in my criminal and family court cases, was that your mom "escaped from me to safety, in fear of your and her lives." This was the nonsense that I was up against in court, with zero truth behind it, but backed by those who were on the "Iain does drugs" or "Iain is crazy" bus, in an everybody against me scenario where I had a zero percent chance.

There was nothing I could do once "Iain is abusive and we escaped" became a court "fact" and I had no one testifying on my behalf. The red herring that your mom warned me about was successful, so much so that it fooled even those who it shouldn't have been able to fool.

I was forced to learn firsthand, "When my father and mother forsake me, then the Lord will take care of me" (Psalm 27:10 NKJV) the hard way, the way that demonstrated clearly for me its veracity. I had to learn that life doesn't happen according to how we think it should happen; life just happens, and when there is nobody to turn to, there God is waiting with His arms open wide. This was the best thing I had ever learned, and the most difficult.

CHAPTER 90

"I SURRENDER"

Scripture says, "Draw near to God and He will draw near to you" (James 4:8a NKJV). It does not say "decide that you need God and then you have all of Him immediately." Knowing who He is and what His characteristics are was not automatic for me, and though it was He I was addressing in my Part 6 journal entries, I want to clarify some of the specifics, which I didn't understand until later.

First, as I mentioned in Chapter 78, God does not desire to "beat me into submission." It simply isn't in His nature. He isn't against us in any way, but for us, and He receives no satisfaction in our sufferings; He wants us to choose Him so that He can restore us. Rebecca Davis (2023) put it succinctly when she wrote, "Suffering certainly does test a person's faith and can be instrumental in refining that faith, as Peter described in his second epistle, chapter 1. But that's different from believing that suffering itself will purify a person. We are purified as we look to the Lord Jesus Christ in faith through the power of the Holy Spirit" (Davis 56).

In *You've Got the Wrong Guy* (2021), Lisa Meister writes,

> "When it comes to battles in our own lives, we all have a driving need to understand the whys of conflicts. We think that if we can figure out why God is 'allowing' a person to be attacked or harmed, then our mind can rationalize the conflict and make it okay. We might think the victim deserved it or that God had some ulterior motive for allowing it to happen. An example of this is when we hear a testimony where the Christian explains that God wanted him or her to go through this battle to learn something. This is a justification vainly attempting to explain the why. God does use all things for good and will teach us in every battle, but it does not mean God could not have taught us through His Word or by observing other people in their battle" (10).

God is for me, and He has been equipping me the entire time, but that does not mean that He wanted you to be taken from me, or that he wanted us to suffer in any way at all, because He didn't; it is not possible for Him to want such things. Rather than being the source of any chaos or confusion, He is the One who offers His hand to set us aright.

* * *

With my dad's help we incorporated chickens, ducks, pigs, goats, sheep, and donkeys onto our little farm. For me, farming was work I could do while praying; it was honest, physical labor, and I liked getting my hands dirty. I didn't want money because I knew how easily it could be a distraction from the real "gold" that is promised by God (Proverbs 16:16, James 1:17, Proverbs 2:1-6, Proverbs 4:7). The seeds that I wanted to plant and grow were not in the physical realm, but in the spiritual. Every seed that I planted, every weed that I yanked out, everything that I did was for you.

> "Do not be deceived, God is not mocked; for whatever a man sows, that he will also reap. For he who sows to his flesh will of the flesh reap corruption, but he who sows to the Spirit will of the Spirit reap everlasting life. And let us not grow weary while doing good, for in due season we shall reap if we do not lose heart" (Galatians 6:7-9 NKJV).

I decided to incorporate fasting into my life, doing so because it is a biblical practice that was of vital importance to many men of God (Moses, Elijah, Daniel, Paul), including the Son of God Himself, who said "...follow Me," (Matthew 10:38, Luke 9:23).

Both the Old and New Testaments are full of examples of people fasting to humble themselves before the Lord and to be more effective in their prayer life. They decided to feed only on spiritual food for a given period of time, knowing that His power is made perfect in weakness (2 Corinthians 12:9), and that sowing to the Spirit guarantees reaping in the Spirit.

> "It is written, 'Man shall not live by bread alone, but by every word that proceeds from the mouth of God'" (Matthew 4:4 NKJV).

I tried one day without any calories, just water and sparkling water, then two, then three, then one again, then seven. It took time to increase in faith, for head knowledge to move to my heart, and to see that His grace truly is sufficient. After exercising my confidence in the Lord with shorter fasts I decided on a longer one, from April 27, 2016, to June 6, 2016. I fasted and prayed, eating nothing, and pleading with God to draw near to me as I desired to draw near to Him (James 4:8). I chose this date to begin because it was the five-year anniversary of when I beat up your grandfather in the street and went to Polish prison.

On my knees, I called out to God, and I screamed primally into the fields and into the woods at the top of my lungs with the entirety of my being, as if I was lost deep in the forest and my effort would determine whether I might be heard and rescued, "Father please, Father please! Adelle Avery Bryson!"

I lost about fifty pounds, my muscles were weaker, and I had less endurance. But I was able to continue with the farm work that was on my plate, primarily taking care of the garden and the animals. I moved slower and took more breaks, but I didn't lack energy. I was filled with a new kind of energy that I had never experienced, one that did not fluctuate based upon nutrient intake and normal daily rhythms and habits.

At times, I became distracted by food that I saw on the internet, and by other people around me who were either planning, preparing, or eating their three meals a day. This eventually led to fantasizing about food and different types of foods and what it would be like to be an "eater" again.

I made a folder for new recipes that I wanted to try, a culinary Playboy magazine filled with cheese, greasy meat, and fresh baked bread. I enjoyed shopping even though I knew I would not get to enjoy it for weeks. My favorite thing was cooking for others, preparing things that I would eat if I were eating so that I could enjoy the experience vicariously.

During this time, there was not a morsel of food that touched my mouth. The only flavor I had was in my toothpaste, which I was extra careful not to swallow. I had nightmares involving accidentally eating something or momentarily forgetting that I was fasting long enough to pound a glass of milk. I often awoke in a sweat because of the dreams, and on a couple occasions I pooped my pants as I went through the process of my digestive system shutting down.

Lord, I prayed, *I only want You. You are the only thing I desire. I need You. I cannot do anything on my own. I surrender. It is my desire to take up my cross and follow You, as You said I must do. I pray that You restore my family, that You give us back all that was stolen from us, and not even from us but from our little girl... Deliver those girls and put us back together, please, Lord! Agata is an amazing woman, maybe the most amazing thing that I have ever seen in this life. I am so grateful to You for her... I love her, and I want to do everything that I can for her. For her and for our daughter I would give my life... Lord, I give You my life... and I love them... I know that this is not Your doing, for it was the devil that stole my girls, that it was not Your doing, but its effect was to spin me directly to You. I really had no choice but to come to You, and I do believe in You, but you have to help me. I trust in You, and You know what I want. I want Your plan. You know that I wouldn't be here, on my knees pleading to You, if it weren't for Adelle. You know that she is what makes me so desperate for You. I surrender her to You; I trust her with You, and I know that You are there, even where she is. I want Your will to be done, Father, please, I know You hear me... Adelle... Lord!*

I won't go into the details of what happened when I started eating again, but what I will say is that I don't recommend filling up on Ben and Jerry's ice cream the day after a forty day fast. My flesh was weak, I quickly realized that none of it was as good as when I was lusting after it, and I further realized the emptiness of physical fullness.

God revealed several things to me during this period of intensive prayer and fasting, including reassuring me that He does hear my cries, He does have a plan, and that plan does include setting the captives free. I still didn't know when or how that would happen, but I was reassured that I could and must trust in Him.

My prayers began to shift from, *Lord, I want this specifically,* to something more like *Lord, I trust You, You know what it is that I want, my only hope is in You, I trust in Your will, I just want to serve You, Lord, I believe in Your plan, and I relinquish my own to You, I surrender...* I knew that His will could not include you being in a cult, and it was enough for me to know He would end that however He would.

He was going to take care of the situation with you and your mom, period. But it wasn't going to be because I had a good idea, for it is "...not by might nor by power, but by My Spirit..." (Zechariah 4:6 NKJV) that the Lord gives the kind of victory I was praying for. For me, at this time in my life and in the life of my family, self-reliance wasn't an option.

My attention was drawn to my massive stack of notebooks that I had ferociously guarded for the past five years. For the entire time that I was locked up in Poland, the most constant themes in my journals other than about you, your mom, and God, were "get out" and "write." Even before the abduction, I regarded my journals as some of my most valuable possessions. It was impressed upon me that I was putting too much hope in my writing, and I felt like I needed to get rid of them.

If He wants me to write a book, I reasoned, *He will have to tell me more explicitly.* One by one, I deposited my precious notebooks into our wood burning stove and watched them disappear. The God I was dependent upon did not need my notebooks. Staring at the ashes, I could feel the source of my hope shifting within me. *Alright God*, I said to myself, *now You have to do it because now I can't.*

The next thing He brought to my attention was porn and masturbation. They were so normalized within our culture that it was difficult for me to see how they could be a problem. *What could be negative about porn? Doesn't everybody masturbate?*

At first, I panicked because I didn't really want to kick these things out of my life. But because of the nudging on my conscience, I decided that I would take a break to get a better perspective, trusting that it was God who was doing the nudging, and that I needed to remember not to lean on my own ambiguous understanding.

"And those who are Christ's have crucified the flesh with its passions and desires" (Galatians 5:24 NKJV).

It wasn't long before I could tell that porn was malignant, not benign. It was not the friend I thought it was and nothing more than crack in picture and video form, and so I knew it had to go for good. Once I made this decision, I felt the effects of this invisible addiction wanting to drag me back in. Stopping wasn't easy, and there were relapses; it was like tearing off a persistent little monster.

But what about masturbation without porn? I asked myself. *Surely there is no harm in it, surely it is normal, natural, and maybe even healthy? What about if I think only about my wife when I do it? If not that, what if I can do it while thinking about nothing?* I cried out to God for an answer.

My cries were answered with more questions that weighed on my conscience: *What do you want? What do you really love? Who do you want to serve?*

"And we know that all things work together for good to those who love God, to those who are the called according to His purpose" (Romans 8:28 NKJV).

As I've said, I knew that getting you out of the abusive cult had to be according to God's purpose. So, it seemed that according to scripture there was a lot riding on whether I love God, and I knew that wasn't a matter of wearing a cross around my neck. Jesus said that to love Him is to obey His commandments (John 14:15), and with you on the line, I had the answers to my questions.

CHAPTER 91

"ONLY THIS WAY WILL WORK"

O ne hot summer day when I was reading a book outside, a bug landed on the table in front of me. When I looked closer and focused, I could see that the bug was trying to fly, but it couldn't fly because it had two smaller bugs hanging on its back. I assumed that they were child bugs hanging onto a parent, but I couldn't remember ever seeing anything like it before.

The larger bug tried to fly, flapping its wings with all its might. But it was only able to get a few feet off the ground before it got bogged down. After a few minutes the bugs had worked their way into the road, still the two hanging onto the one, at which point I believed it was highly likely they could all get run over by a car together.

I recall feeling a moment of revelation. It felt like God had sent me a message through part of His creation, the bugs. I couldn't "fly" because I wouldn't let go of you and your mom. I couldn't let go of wanting you back or making you the priority, but God wanted me to make Him the priority, entrusting you to Him, relying on the fact that He can do all things, and realizing that you are His and not mine.

"...For your Father knows the things you have need of before you ask Him..." (Matthew 6:8b NKJV).

He knows that I love you; He knows the entirety of my heart, including the giant aching hole and the excruciating pain. He knows that to me you are more valuable than everything else in the world combined, that I would do anything because of and for you. He knows all of this, and He has given His answer:

"Delight yourself also in the Lord, And He shall give you the desires of your heart. Commit your way to the Lord, Trust also in Him, And He shall bring it to pass" (Psalm 37:4-5 NKJV).

I realized the only way to serve your mom was to serve God, and she knew this before I did. When she had you hand me the little blue Bible in late December 2010, she knew that Almighty God was the only help there was for our family and that belief in the Almighty meant belief in His Son, Jesus Christ (John 14:1). Her certainty was born out of her full immersion in evil, in ritual abuse, in the cult that was forcing her to bring you to them because of mind control. From this perspective, there is only one philosophy that has an answer; there is only one God who both hates evil and promises to intervene on behalf of those who love Him.

When she insisted, "You are like your father," what she was trying to communicate with every fiber of her being was, "Iain, husband, father of our daughter, only this way will work... we have only one option because this evil we're up against is stronger than everything else including you and me. You MUST walk as Jesus walked (1 John 2:6), who is one with the Father (John 10:30) and has overcome the world (John 16:33)."

I knew that she knew that I would never stop trying, that I would fight until my last breath for my girls. She had seen the stubborn, tenacious, hit-the-paperboy-in-the-head-with-the-rock-to-keep-my-word part of me. I think she knew that was how God made me; maybe that was why she married me.

From the onset, nobody could understand how or why I would be fighting for your mom, since she was an adult woman who had just taken our child away from me and said I was to blame. I never stopped fighting for her, but I realized that I could not change people's ignorance from where I was positioned at the time. My pleas changed as needed from, "Please help my daughter and my wife," to "Please help my daughter," to "Please help me, I am sick," but my purpose remained steadfast: to "shut it down" for you and your mother, to end the cycle of intergenerational ritual abuse. The truth was, whether I ever saw her again or not, to me she would always be Agata Avery Bryson.

* * *

Eventually, I was ready to allow my mom back into my life. I had processed through the betrayal and disappointment, and I decided that life was too short to block her out entirely. I couldn't continue being angry with her for having been deceived, and though I didn't trust her, I decided to prioritize forgiveness in being obedient to God.

She never talked about the communication I knew she was continuing to have with you and your mom, but she did randomly give me things like old pictures of you, a ukulele she never got to give you, and CDs that your mom burned and initialed. I thanked her for the CDs and wondered what else she was withholding. No matter what I told my mom, she never budged from the position that she knew your mom well enough to know that she could trust her.

CDs my mom gave to me that your mom burned and initialed.

The red herring was still at work in my family, but I wasn't trying to win over or put my hope in any man or woman; all my hope was in God. I continued working on the farm, researching, and studying the Bible. The scripture says to love God with all of your heart, soul, mind, and strength (Matthew 12:30), and so the farm became my monastery as I sought to live as a monk in full devotion to God, fully set apart, waiting for Him to give me direction.

CHAPTER 92

"UNLESS SHE WAS SENT BY GOD"

2018

When I saw her walking down the middle of the street away from me, it was as if she were my boss, almost out the door on her way home, my paycheck in her pocket. I wanted that check before the weekend, and I dropped everything else that I was doing. If I had been cooking, I'd have left the food to burn.

My vision was blurry, and I couldn't even really see her. I knew that she had long dark hair, and I guessed that she was younger than me, though I couldn't be sure without seeing her from the front. It took her about ten seconds to round the corner just out of my sight, and it took me about twelve seconds to start my Yamaha Enduro 100 and get after her.

Down the street a ways, she was sitting on the steps of one of the abandoned cabins, on the edge of the corn field, across the street from the pond. I rode by her and up the street, trying not to turn my neck toward her, thinking it would be best to look as inconspicuous as possible. I turned the bike around, shut off the gas valve, and headed back in her direction.

I don't remember if I ran out of gas in time, or if I just pretended to run out of gas, but I do remember stalling the bike for the purpose of interacting with this creature. She was barefoot and holding a notebook. It was evident that she had come from the water, as there was a kayak perched on the grassy bank.

She introduced herself as Emily, and then asked me whose goats she had just seen. I explained that they were mine, and then she asked why the corn seeds were blue. "Oh," I replied, "that's not my corn field but those seeds are for GMO corn, that field is covered with poison, you shouldn't walk around barefoot out there." We talked a little while longer, and she told me that she and her mom had moved to the other end of the pond.

"Maybe I'll see you around," she said, and we parted ways.

Inside of myself, I was conflicted, simultaneously wanting to see her again and knowing that my life would be a lot easier if I didn't. I didn't know why I wanted to see her again, but I did know why I didn't want to. I didn't want to waste my time or tempt my flesh; *what would be the purpose of seeing her again? Is this the devil trying to throw me off course with another distraction?*

Around that time, I was having breakfast with a friend when he said something like, "Iain, you are a good man. You deserve to have a wife. You should have a wife. Don't you want a wife?"

"I have a wife," I answered. "I already have one, and I love her. She is the only woman for me. She was taken from me, and what we had was destroyed. I will never let her go. I will never stop loving her and fighting for her. I can't, because if I did, I wouldn't be able to say, 'I love you' or 'I do' to anyone else and have it mean anything at all. If I don't love Agata, then I can't love anyone."

He was impressed with my philosophical exposition of the topic, but I could tell that he wasn't convinced. His certainty that I needed a woman in my life was unsettling because I was certain I would never want or need another woman.

I did not spend any more time thinking about Emily. For all I knew she was gone, and I wouldn't see her again. But when she came back around a month later, "looking to buy eggs" from our farmstand, my heart leapt into my throat, and I hurried over to the door and stepped outside.

"Emily," I said, my focus shifting entirely to her and intensifying.

"Iain," she replied, and without speaking much more, if at all, I led her into the barn, as if we both knew that we had an appointment there, so that we could talk privately. This didn't feel like any of the many times I had met with and spoken to other people who had dropped by the farm; this one felt almost like it was a setup of some kind.

Who is this woman, and why is she here? Don't you know that I cannot be tempted with that anymore? OK, I guess I'll just talk to her and get to the bottom of it, I reasoned; *she doesn't scare me.*

After our brief introductions, I told her about you and your mom, jumping right into ritual abuse and torture-based mind control. I told her that I had dedicated my life to God, because the devil had taken you from me.

"But there is really no devil, right?" she interjected.

"Oh, I can assure you that there is a devil," I corrected. "The truth is that the devil is very real. He stole my daughter, and that's why I need God, that's why I do everything that I do, that's why I am the way I am. I believe that there are answers, and that there is a way to win. I don't believe life is random, and I don't believe my little girl was born to grow up in a cult, without remedy. I believe that the purpose of life is to seek and serve God."

We continued speaking for about an hour, and I knew we weren't done. It wasn't that I didn't notice her legs, but that I was uninterested because I was committed to both your mom and to God. A fright came over me because I didn't know what was happening or what it was about this woman that was piquing my interest. *Why do I want to spend more time with her? I don't need anybody else in my life, do I?*

It was as if my free will was suspended and she was being inserted into my life while I observed from a distance, whether I liked it or not. Over the next couple of weeks, we continued to talk, and we continued to dive deep into our respective searches for God, the need for God because of the evil, and what we wanted to do about it.

She was the most sincere, honest person I had met in maybe my entire life, as if there was no pretense to her whatsoever. Her gentleness, her caring nature, and natural wisdom caught my attention right away. It was almost as if she was an alien, not belonging to this world.

"You're trying to be perfect?" she asked me when we were watching the first movie we ever watched together, *Get Out*, a movie that she chose.

"Yes, that is what I have to try. I, Iain Bryson, can't be perfect, but I have to try, and I have to believe in the One who is perfect, the One who guarantees answers to prayer for he who believes, the One whose will cannot possibly be that my daughter is in a cult being abused. I want everything I do to be in line with believing" (see Matthew 5:48).

I was sweaty and nervous, partially because the film we were watching portrayed a young woman luring a man back to her parent's house under the ruse that they were dating only to be hypnotized by the mother and made into a slave. *Should I "get out" now?* I asked myself. *Should I nip this in the bud, realize I am too weak to be playing around with this fire? What is the purpose of my hanging out with this person?*

I continued wearing my wedding ring, and I continued spending time with Emily. Something was going on, and it had nothing to do with sex or attraction, but just who she was, her makeup, if you will. Sex wasn't something that I was willing to do, nor did it tempt me much. I had finally worked through it, and I felt strong and free, like I had kicked a nasty habit. I also thought that I might be struck by lightning if I were to relapse.

My mind was split in that I couldn't stop thinking about her when I wasn't with her, while I really didn't want to be with her, or anyone (other than your mom) at all. I had been operating on an extremely low cash flow for a long time, and I had no intention of working for money or saving up for anything that could be bought with money. This, I figured, had to be a deal breaker; unless she was sent by God, no woman would stay in this situation.

To make sure that she could see that I had zero spending power, I maxed out the few low limit credit cards that I had been maintaining and using to build my credit. My intention was to make myself as unattractive as possible, though I admit that it was not a wholehearted attempt to drive her off, seeing as some of the things I bought to max out the cards were ice cream and concert tickets for us.

Unless God has some plan that I cannot grasp, which is highly likely, this woman needs to get away from me, I told myself repeatedly; *I cannot be messing around with this.* I did not want to have to face you and your mom in heaven and explain that I gave up because of another woman. I drafted a couple of letters to her, explaining that I could never be with her, that it was simply an impossibility given my situation. *What would be the purpose of starting something with this woman?*

Emily and me. November 29, 2018, Madison Square Garden, New York City—Dave Matthews Band concert

For me, there was no way around the logical argument that I had presented to my friend during breakfast; I couldn't be with anybody else because in doing so I would be proving that I was never dedicated to your mother, and therefore could never be dedicated to the new person. My vows to your mom on our wedding day, July 2, 2005, precluded me from entering into a similar agreement with any other person, I believed.

"Emily," I wrote, "if I won't die for her, if I would leave her, why would you think that I would for you, how could you know I wouldn't leave you? Rather, in leaving her, you would have to know that I would also leave you...," I wrote, as I struggled with this internally as well as on the paper in front of me.

But I never gave these letters to her, nor did I ever really believe that they were for her. Instead, they became a way for me to process and work through what was for me an inordinately difficult and complicated situation. I didn't want or need a girlfriend, and nobody could replace your mom. Nothing in the entire universe could supplant my total steadfast devotion toward ending the slavery of my girls, but Emily wasn't asking this of me. Instead, she agreed with me and wanted to learn more.

There was no way that I would or could ever "leave" your mother. But, at the same time, she was gone. For all intents and purposes as far as my life now, she was deceased. She was taken from me, as you were, and she was now remarried, with another child, information I was privy to as a result of my periodic Google searches. Like a widower, there was nobody else I wanted or thought I could ever want other than my spouse. And, like a widower, my spouse was the one thing that I could never have again. All of that was gone; our nest had been demolished.

But I couldn't be a widower, by definition, because she was still alive. What was I then? I guessed something else entirely, something that hasn't been defined yet and maybe doesn't even have an exact word to describe it. I grieved her every day, but what I lost her to was something far more sinister than death on its own.

Since serving God was serving her, I had to make sure that Emily didn't get in the way of that. There would be no "moving on," no leaving my post, and I would never stop loving your mom, but I had to continue to move forward. The mission could not change, but I still had a lot to learn.

For the entire time that your mom and I were together I was not able or permitted to see her clearly, and it wasn't until after she was gone that her masks fell away, making it possible for me to see and understand all her layers and depths. I was thankful to God for the time I did get with her. But now, I wanted her soul to have freedom, and the same thing for you. Neither of our lives were all that important except insomuch as we could use them to secure that.

Marriage is for now, it is for this life, it is not forever. Nothing here is forever; everything we see will die or disappear. Like wealth, we don't take marriage with us when we go.

"For in the resurrection they neither marry nor are given in marriage, but are like angels of God in heaven" (Matthew 23:30 NKJV).

"Jesus answered and said to them, 'The sons of this age marry and are given in marriage. But those who are counted worthy to attain that age, and the resurrection from the dead, neither marry nor are given in marriage" (Luke 20:34-35 NKJV).

Before, when your mom and I were together, I couldn't fathom the idea of ever being with anyone else. But now she was gone, and in front of me was a woman who, when I told her about you and your mom, decided that both of you were worth fighting for. She never questioned or felt threatened by my loyalty to your mom, nor was she threatened by my love for her. She was about to teach me that loving your mom and loving her were not mutually exclusive, but that it was all just the same thing: serving God.

United in purpose and desire, I knew that two are stronger than one. I also knew that there were areas within myself that I could not work on without the help of a "partner," specifically a wife. Yes, I could simply say "No" to all future possibilities, and that had been my plan until I met Emily. But now it seemed like I wasn't being given that option; this woman wanted to join me in my fight, and she was hungry for the Almighty, Living God.

I got her a Bible right away, and I began reading scripture out loud to her. She had never read one before, so everything that she knew about it was secondhand. I was excited for her to see it with her own eyes, and for us to be able to talk about it together. Up until then, she had been searching for answers in new age teachings, such as *A Course in Miracles* by Helen Schucman, Emmet Fox, Eckhart Tolle, Marianne Williamson, Ram Dass, etc. All of these twist biblical language, diminish Christ, and essentially elevate the ("higher") self to the position of god.

"But even if we, or an angel from heaven, preach any other gospel to you than what we have preached to you, let him be accursed" (Galatians 1:8 NKJV).

It wasn't long before she could see that there were different versions of Jesus being presented: the Truth, and various knockoffs. Having been introduced to the reality of ritual abuse at the same time, it became apparent to her which one was the antithesis of evil and therefore which one we had to run to.

Emily and I holding one of our roosters. 2019.

From the outset, Emily and I believed that the crossing of our paths was not a mere random occurrence. We knew that we were meant to be together for a purpose that was greater than either of us. The reality of ritual abuse and mind control weighed heavily on our hearts, and we embarked on our journey not knowing much more than that, but trusting that God would equip us and show us what to do next.

We knew that commitment was important, and it was early on that we both declared to each other that we were "all in." We thought that our commitment to each other before God was enough, and that we didn't need a paper or ceremony to make it official. This is something God changed our perspective on later when we joined a church and wanted to make it official in everyone's eyes. But before that, Emily moved onto the farm and we joined forces. We did everything together: farming, fasting, working, praying, and eventually working on this book.

* * *

On June 11, 2021, my aunt Sara called to inform me that my stepdad, George, had just collapsed and died while weed whacking. Tears rolled down my face as I was reminded once again just how much everything can and does change in the blink of an eye. We like to think that we are in control, that we have all our bases covered, but we never are, and we never can.

"Just yesterday he rode his bike twenty-five miles in the heat," my mom informed everyone, "he was seeing his doctor regularly for checkups…"

Yes, and I was a dad with a little girl trying to get help for her mom, and then I wasn't, all of a sudden, in the blink of an eye, just like that, I thought to myself. Why couldn't people understand where I was coming from every day of the week? George's death, while difficult because I loved him very much, was also an opportunity for family to gather and realize, even if only for a moment, how precious every drop of this is, and how suddenly it can and will end.

We're all going to fall with the weedwhacker in our hands, and while that is tragic in one sense, in another it is a blessing. It shows us what life is, and what it isn't. It reminds us that we are not in control, that every day could be anybody's last, and that therefore we should live in such a manner as to heed Dave Matthews when he says, "everyday should be a good day to die" ("You Never Know").

I was honored to present the eulogy at the funeral, which was held at Groton Bible Chapel (GBC) because that was and is my mom's church. George was truly an amazing man, and a good man, and I am thankful that he was my stepdad and my friend. Bob McCoy, another amazing man, had also passed away (November 3, 2020), and so GBC had an entirely new pastoral staff.

Emily and I continued going to church with my mom on Sundays, both to give her some company, and because we didn't not like it. As we met the leadership and the community, we were pleasantly surprised to find people who genuinely sought and loved the Lord. Many of them have become family to us.

We began pre-marital counselling as an act of obedience to God. Though we were already committed to each other and to God, we wanted to make sure that we dotted all of our I's and crossed all of our T's, and we wanted to be a good example to others. We met with one of our pastors for about six months, and then we were married on April 16, 2022. Emily was baptized later that year on November 27th.

What has been lost can't be replaced, but the Lord continues to be faithful. By sending such a person as Emily, He has reassured me that He is for us, and that He is working out a plan for good that is beyond what I can conceive.

The Book of Job ends with, "Indeed the Lord gave Job twice as much as he had before" (42:10b), which is great, but I always wondered, *what about those children that he lost? How could a man ever be alright after his children were destroyed because of new children and new wealth?*

Now I think I understand. It was not that Job's pain of losing his original children was assuaged because of new children, because that simply isn't possible. What happened, I believe, is that Job's deeper understanding of God and who He is gave him a peace and hope that surpassed normal human reason. From this standpoint, when one knows with certainty that "[God] can do everything, and that no purpose of [His] can be withheld from [Him]" (Job 42:2 NKJV), everything else falls into line.

CHAPTER 93

I LOVE YOU LIKE ONE

———————————
———————————

The following emails are more recent attempts to elicit a public or governmental response. They were symbolic in nature, as I had no real expectation of receiving any help. I felt it necessary to go through the motions if only to further document the fact that the system is broken.

"S.W. Makowski
Fri, Jun 23, 2023, 12:54 PM
Iain Bryson to [President of Stargard, Rafał Zając]
Dear sir,
I am writing in order to inform you that Slawomir Wojciech Makowski is going to be revealed and outed as a child molester (etc.) very shortly. The world is going to see what has been going on in Stargard. The evidence is overwhelming. I wanted to give you notice, since you are the president of the city.
I am not going to go into further detail now. Please look at my website and youtube page.
iloveyoulikeone.com
All the best,
Iain Avery Bryson"

President Zając did not respond to me.
I saw the movie, *Sound of Freedom,* and thought that Tim Ballard might help in some way, so I wrote him. I received a canned email that explained that the organization was very busy and would not be able to help me. They sent a list of law enforcement contacts for me to try instead.

"My daughter
Sun, Jul 9, 2023, 7:51 PM
Iain Bryson to [Tim Ballard – Operation Underground Railroad (O.U.R.)]
Mr. Ballard,
What do you think about an American child in Poland in an intergenerational SRA family? This is the situation I have been in for the past twelve years. I gave my daughter a hug, thinking she was going to the library, and I haven't seen her since. Ten minutes after she left with my first wife, the words my first wife had been saying to me for the previous three weeks hit me, and I sprinted to the police station. 'I'm taking our daughter back to the cult because of mind control.' 'I have something like Stockholm Syndrome.' 'My dad has created a red herring so that nobody will believe you and you will never see your daughter again.' ... Please read the description on my website - my daughter has not been set free yet. Thank you, sir.
iloveyoulikeone.com

In Christ,
Iain Bryson"

"Tue, July 11, 2023, 1:30 PM
O.U.R. Info to me
Hello,
Thank you for contacting Operation Underground Railroad and for your awareness of the signs of human trafficking and child exploitation.
Due to the overwhelming response we have had from Sound of Freedom, and the limited staff we have, we are sending this automated reply to those needing resources for reporting trafficking or exploitation concerns.
[…]
Again, thank you for reaching out to O.U.R.
Sincerely,
O.U.R. TEAM"

"Adelle Avery Bryson
Tue, Jul 11, 2023, 5:28 PM
Iain Bryson to PreventAbduction1@state.gov, bcc: Melanie Brandt
Dear sir/madam:
On December 27, 2010, my daughter, born in New London, Connecticut, USA, was parentally abducted from where my family was living in The Hague to where my in-laws live in Poland. I immediately went to the Dutch police, but they refused to even take a report. I spoke to a United States Duty Officer in The Netherlands on the phone, and his advice to me was to re-abduct my daughter and get her to the US Embassy, where she would then be evaluated.

I never saw my daughter again, but I have never stopped fighting, and I never will. I am currently finishing a book that will be released this year detailing everything that has happened. For now, I have a website with the basic story: iloveyoulikeone.com

The reason I am contacting the US government again is to reiterate the situation, so that at least, if nothing else, I can say I tried. I am not going to go into too much detail here, but I will say this again: My American citizen daughter was abducted by my first-wife and her dad. My first wife told me that her family is a 'cult.' My first wife told me that she has 'Stockholm Syndrome.' My first wife told me that she was taking our daughter back to Poland because of (trauma/torture based) 'mind control.' She told me that her dad had created a 'red herring' so that nobody would believe me. And then it happened, just as she told me it would.

I have been in contact with numerous United States officials, and I have received no help. I filed under the Hague Convention. I have all of our communications, and it will all be in the book. I have been given many reasons why the US cannot get involved over the years, so I am just writing to say that my abducted US citizen daughter is now sixteen years old, and she is still with the people who stole her from me more than twelve years ago. My tune has not and will not change until she is rescued.

I have plenty of letters from officials stating how concerned they are and how sorry they are that my daughter was abducted. This is not what I'm looking for. My purpose is twofold here: 1., To document my attempt, and 2.) To see one last time if my country might somehow surprise me and help my US citizen daughter. Either way, the story is coming out.

I welcome any sincere questions, and I wish you all the best. Thank you.
Sincerely,
Iain Avery Bryson
father of Adelle Avery Bryson, born in CT, USA on 1/30/2007,
abducted on 12/27/2010,
currently called Adela Soczewska
last known address Stargard, Poland"

"For Erin Nickerson, Consul General
Tue, Aug 1, 2023, 4:26 PM
Iain Bryson to Krakow AIRC [American Information Resource Center], Poland ACS [American Citizen Services]
Ms. Nickerson,
On December 27, 2010, my daughter, born in New London, Connecticut, USA, was parentally abducted from where my family was living in The Hague to where my in-laws live in Poland. I immediately went to the Dutch police, but they refused to even take a report. I spoke to a United States Duty Officer in The Netherlands on the phone, and his advice to me was to re-abduct my daughter and get her to the US Embassy, where she would then be evaluated.

I never saw my daughter again, but I have never stopped fighting, and I never will. I am currently finishing a book that will be released this year detailing everything that has happened. For now, I have a website with the basic story: iloveyoulikeone.com

Of course, if you have any questions, please let me know. My daughter is now sixteen years old, and she is still with the people who stole her from me more than twelve years ago. I am going to continue to fight until she is rescued.
Sincerely,
Iain Avery Bryson
father of Adelle Avery Bryson, born in CT, USA on 1/30/2007,
abducted on 12/27/2010,
currently called Adela Soczewska
last known address Stargard, Poland"

"Tue, Aug 1, 2023, 4:28 PM
Krakow AIRC to me
Thank you for your email.
American Center Krakow is focusing on cultural and educational matters.
If you look:

- For visa related questions, please contact the info-line via phone: 22 307 1361 or via email support-poland@ustraveldocs.com
- For consular issues, please contact the American Citizen Section at KrakowACS@state.gov
- For Information on Immediate Humanitarian Assistance and Visa Information for the People of Ukraine in Poland
  Immediate Humanitarian Assistance and Visa Information for the People of Ukraine in Poland - U.S. Embassy & Consulate in Poland (usembassy.gov)
- For updated information for U.S. Citizens coming from Ukraine
  Updated Information For U.S. Citizens Coming From Ukraine - U.S. Embassy & Consulate in Poland (usembassy.gov)

Regards,
American Center Krakow
U.S. Consulate General Kraków • ul. Stolarska 9 • 31-043 Krakow • Poland
FB Krakow.usconsulate
IG @usakrakow
TT @USConsKrakow"

"Wed, Aug 2, 2023, 9:39 AM
Poland ACS to me
Dear Sir,
Thank you for your update.
Sincerely,
American Citizen Services
U.S. Embassy Warsaw
ul. Piekna 12
00-539 Warsaw, Poland

http://pl.usembassy.gov
tel. +48 22 504 2784
fax +48 22 504 2088
Follow us on Twitter"

"Wed, Aug 2, 2023, 6:42 PM
Iain Bryson to Poland ACS
Dear sir or madam,
Thank you for your prompt reply. My hope was that you would say that you are willing and able to help with the matter. The last time that we communicated on this matter was between 2011-2015, and your position was the following:
  1. You must defer to the criminal and civil courts of Poland and accept their findings and conclusions.
  2. Even though my daughter was born in the United States of America, you cannot leverage an investigation into what has never been investigated - that my first wife's family is a cult family.
Does your position remain the same, or is there a willingness to revisit the 'facts' and help my child? Just to reiterate, what happened was an illegal parental abduction that was predicated on the false claims that I had been abusive, and that they needed to escape from me. In reality, I was trying to get help weeks before because my wife had been telling me repeatedly that she was taking our daughter back to the 'cult.' My daughter is being raised in an abusive cult, and any help you could offer would be greatly appreciated. Thank you.
Sincerely,
Iain A. Bryson
iloveyoulikeone.com"

"Fri, Aug 4, 2023, 2:15 AM
Poland ACS to me
Good morning,
Because the child was taken from the Netherlands to Poland and not from the United States to Poland, or vice versa, the Central Authority in the Netherlands would be the proper venue to handle the abduction case, along with the Central Authority in Poland. We believe this information may have been conveyed to you in 2010 and in 2011.
     We see that colleagues in the Netherlands also told you that you should consider hiring a private attorney to pursue your rights. The U.S. Government cannot provide legal services of the nature you have requested. Should you wish to discuss your case with an attorney in Poland, you may consult the attached list of English-speaking attorneys.
     Additionally, the U.S. Embassy has no investigative authority in Poland. If you believe there are criminal issues involved within the group you mention, this should be referred to the Polish police, if you have not done so already. If you need assistance locating the contact information for the jurisdiction in which you believe your daughter is located, let us know, and we can find that for you. If there is a current criminal case involving your daughter as a victim, please provide us with the details of that case. While we cannot investigate cases ourselves, we can request updates from authorities on the cases, though the amount of information provided to us would be at the discretion of the authorities.
Sincerely,
American Citizen Services
U.S. Embassy Warsaw
ul. Piekna 12
00-539 Warsaw, Poland
http://pl.usembassy.gov
tel. +48 22 504 2784
fax +48 22 504 2088
Follow us on Twitter"

"**international parental child abduction**
Fri, Aug 4, 2023, 12:20 PM
Iain Bryson to kinderontleiding [Central Authority in The Netherlands], Polandchildabduction
Dear sir or madam,

On December 27, 2010, my daughter was illegally abducted to Poland from our home in The Hague under the pretense that they were escaping from me in fear of their lives. I immediately went to the local Dutch police in The Hague, but they wouldn't even take a formal report. I visited the local police several times over the next week, but they continued to refuse to take any action at all.

The United States Embassy informed me that they did not have jurisdiction, and a Duty Officer even recommended that I re-abduct my daughter in order to get her to the Embassy, where she would have then been evaluated. But, I never saw my daughter again, as her abductors were able to get her into Poland.

I attempted to get help for three months, but my efforts were unsuccessful. In April 2011, I decided that I couldn't wait any longer, that as a father I had to take action in order to get attention to my daughter's situation. I had no money or support at all, and so I decided that I would get arrested in Poland for the purpose of obtaining an audience. However, I sat in prison for eleven months before I saw a lawyer, the interpreter didn't understand me, and they never investigated what I had alleged. I ended up spending 50 months locked up in Poland, and I was released in July 2015.

The illegal abduction was predicated on the false claims that I had been abusive. In reality, my wife had been telling me repeatedly for several weeks that she was taking our daughter back to the "cult" because of "Stockholm Syndrome." In reality, I was trying to get help weeks before the "escape." My daughter is being raised by an abusive cult, and I have not seen her or had any contact in over twelve years.

I am in the process of completing a book about this entire ordeal that will be released before the end of the year, and I will not rest until my daughter is rescued. In 2011 I was told that my Hague Abduction report could take up to two years to process, and I went to prison because I wasn't willing to wait for the bureaucracy to get to my daughter. Now, in 2023, I am reiterating that the situation hasn't changed: my child was stolen and she is being abused. Please let me know if you can offer any assistance on this matter.
Sincerely,
Iain A. Bryson
iloveyoulikeone.com
https://www.youtube.com/channel/UCEVbDWXVFJKrZXH3-dATs9g
father of Adelle Avery Bryson, born in CT, USA on 1/30/2007,
abducted on 12/27/2010,
currently called Adela Soczewska
last known address Stargard, Poland"

"**Mon, Aug, 7, 2023 ,6:22 AM**
Info Centrum Internationale Kinderontvoering [Central Authority in The Netherlands] to me
Dear Mr Bryson,

Thank you for your email of August 4th, 2023, we have received it in good order. From your email I understand that you have grave concerns about your daughter who was taken by her mother to Poland, 13 years ago.

The International Child Abduction Center in the Netherlands offers up-to-date information, advice and guidance to everyone who encounters (the threat of) international child abduction, whether as part of their professional or personal lives. There are legal experts working at the Center that have specialized in the specific area of international child abduction.

To answer your question, it is important to have some knowledge about The Hague Convention on International Child Abduction of 1980. According to this Convention a parent is not allowed to move abroad with a minor without the consent of the other parent when the left-behind parent also has the right to decide about the habitual residence of the child (ie. where the child lives). According to Dutch law this falls within the scope of the parental responsibility a parent can exercise over his/her child. From your email I cannot deduct whether you had that responsibility when your daughter was moved. I will assume that you and the mother both have the right to decide about the habitual residence of your child.

However, since the date your daughter was taken to Poland is several years in the past, The Hague Convention cannot provide the same protection as it would have had when you had invoked it within a year after the move to Poland. Moreover, your daughter is now over 16 years old, which means the Convention is no longer applicable in your case.

From my perspective the options you have left are either finding an attorney in Poland to help you re-establish contact with your daughter and create a contact arrangement, or going through child protective services in Poland to make sure your child is safe from abuse. Only the court of the child's country of residence has jurisdiction in requests affecting the child, which means that only a Polish judge can decide about your daughter. I am sorry I have to inform you that we cannot be of any further assistance in this matter.

However, we do have contact details of Polish lawyers who may be of assistance to you: [...]

Hopefully, this information is useful to you.

Kind regards,

Ms H.G. (Pien) Wubbeling LL.M

Centrum Internationale Kinderontvoering

Postbus 2006, 1200 CA Hilversum, Nederland

+31 (0)88 800 90 00

info@kinderontvoering.org

www.kinderontvoering.org"

"**Fri, Aug 11, 2023, 6:30 AM**

Żebrowski Maciej (DSRiN) [Polandchildabduction] to me

Dear Mr. Bryson,

Thank you for your email.

It was received by the unit in the Polish Ministry of Justice that performs the tasks of the Central Authority in 1980 Hague Convention cases.

Therefore we deal with applications for return of a minor to their place of habitual residence or application that are to establish access with a minor living in a differeny country.

Formally an application for return might be submitted anytime as there is no specified deadline to do so. The only thing that an applicant needs to remember is article 12 of HC.

12. Where a child has been wrongfully removed or retained in terms of Article 3 and, at the date of the commencement of the proceedings before the judicial or administrative authority of the Contracting State where the child is, a period of less than one year has elapsed from the date of the wrongful removal or retention, the authority concerned shall order the return of the child forthwith.

The judicial or administrative authority, even where the proceedings have been commenced after the expiration of the period of one year referred to in the preceding paragraph, shall also order the return of the child, unless it is demonstrated that the child is now settled in its new environment.

So an applicant is recommended to take actions as fast as possible.

However you need tp pay attentiopn to article 4 of HC.

4. The Convention shall apply to any child who was habitually resident in a Contracting State immediately before any breach of custody or access rights. The Convention shall cease to apply when the child attains the age of 16 years

I came accross the information that you daughter is almost 17 years now. I am afraid the Polish CA can not proceed the HC application for return and take steps that would help me locate her.

I wish you had submitted the application for return in 2011.

Best regards,

Maciej Żebrowski

Główny Specjalista - Prokurator

Wydział Międzynarodowych Postępowań Rodzinnych

Departament Spraw Rodzinnych i Nieletnich

22 23-90-408

Maciej.Zebrowski@ms.gov.pl

gov.pl/sprawiedliwosc

Al. Ujazdowski 11

00-950 Warszawa

tel: +48 22 52 12 888"

"Fri, Aug 11, 2023, 1:19 PM
Iain Bryson to Żebrowski Maciej
Mr. Zebrowski,
Thank you for your reply. I did submit an application for return in 2011. I was in contact with The Netherlands, Poland, and USA for three months post abduction. There was no indication that anyone was willing and/or able to help.
I appreciate the information you sent. I will continue to fight; my book will be released before the end of the year.
All the best,
Iain Avery Bryson"

"Give us help from trouble, For the help of man is useless" (Psalm 60:11, 108:12 NKJV).

We know from events in the Bible that God uses people to do His work on earth, especially in the face of "impossible" odds. God's children are called and equipped by Him to stand firm against all the schemes of the devil (Ephesians 6:11), including ritual abuse. My hope is that those who "sit together with Christ in heavenly places" (Ephesians 2:6 NKJV) educate themselves and choose to stand with the growing army of ritual abuse survivors and their advocates. Ignorance, apathy, personal comfort, and self-preservation are not Christian virtues. Jesus Christ came "to proclaim liberty to the captives," and "to set at liberty those who are oppressed" (Luke 4:18 NKJV). Therefore, the body of Christ is called to "shut it down."

"Fear not, for I am with you; Be not dismayed, for I am your God. I will strengthen you, Yes, I will help you, I will uphold you with My righteous right hand" (Isaiah 41:10 NKJV).

I know you and your mom are waiting, and we are coming for you.

* * *

In September 2023, Emily and I travelled to The Netherlands. We visited our old home at Newtonplein 25 in The Hague, and we retraced the steps I took with you through the parks and to the farm on our last day together.

The park across from our apartment no longer contained the swing set I used to push you on, but I could still hear your words, "Daddy, higher, Daddy, higher," and I could still feel the joy I felt and the type of smile that involuntarily took over my face as I cherished that you were my daughter. "Ok, Adelle, just hold on. Don't ever let go...," I reminded you. "I love you, Adelle..."

Left: *You on December 27, 2010, the last day we spent together, The Hague.*

Middle: *Me in September 2023 in a similar location.*

Right: *Emily and I standing in front of Newtonplein 25, The Hague, September 2023.*

I LOVE YOU LIKE ONE

APPENDIX I:

RITUAL ABUSE IS NOT AN "URBAN MYTH"

"The term *ritual abuse* is often used broadly to include any organized abusive practice that furthers the abuser group's ideology. However, the term is usually restricted to organized physical or sexual assault, often including homicide and severe psychological abuse, within the context of a spiritual practice or belief. Some definitions encompass any spiritual belief. But, most definitions use the term to refer to practices that involve physical and sexual abuse of children and adults, and human sacrifice to propitiate and empower malevolent deities, such as Satan, but also including many polytheistic gods and goddesses. A substantial body of psychological literature supports that ritualistic abuse is a real phenomenon that must be correctly assessed and treated (Belitz & Schacht, 1992; Bernet & Chang, 1997; Bloom, 1994; Boat, 1991; Boyd, 1991; Brown, 1994; Clark, 1994; Clay, 1996; Coleman, 1994a, 1994b; Comstock, 1991; Comstock & Vickery; Cook, 1991; Coons, 1997; Crabtree, 1993; Cozolino, 1989, 1990; deMause, 1994; Driscoll & Wright, 1991; Edwards, 1991; Ehrensaft, 1992; Faller, 1994; Feldman, 1993; Fine, 1989; Finkelhor, Williams, & Burns, 1988; Fraser, 1990, 1991, 1993a, 1993b, 1997a, 1997b; Friesen, 1991, 1992, 1993; Gallagher, 2001; Golston, 1993; Gonzalez, Waterman, Kelly, McCord, & Oliveri, 1993; Goodman, Quas, Bottoms, Qin, Shaver, Orcutt, & Shapiro, 1997; Goodwin, 1993, 1994; Goodwin, Hill, & Attias, 1990; Gould, 1992, 1995; Gould & Cozolino, 1992; Gould & Graham-Costain, 1994; Gould & Neswald, 1992; Greaves, 1992; Groenendijk & van der Hart, 1995; Hammond, 1992; Harvey, 1993; Hill & Goodwin, 1989; Hornstein, 1991; Hudson, 1990, 1991; Ireland & Ireland, 1994; Johnson, 1994; Jones, 1991; Jonker & Jonker-Bakker, 1991, 1997; Katchen, 1992; Katchen & Sakheim, 1992; Kelley, 1989; King & Yorker, 1996; Kinscherff & Barnum, 1992; Kluft, 1988, 1989a, 1989b, 1994, 1995; Lawrence, Cozolino, & Foy, 1995; Leavitt, 1994, 2000a, 2000b; Leavitt & Labott, 1998a, 1998b, 2000; Lockwood, 1993; Lloyd, 1992; Mandell & Schiff, 1993; Mangen, 1992; Mayer, 1991; McCulley, 1994; McFadyen, Hanks, & James, 1993; McFarland & Lockerbie, 1994; MacHovec, 1992; Moriarty, 1991, 1992; Neswald & Gould, 1993; Neswald, Gould, & Graham-Costain, 1991; Noblitt, 1995; Noblitt & Perskin, 2000; Nurcombe & Unutzer, 1991; Oksana, 1994, 2001; Paley, 1992; Pulling & Cawthorn, 1989; Raschke, 1990; Rockwell, 1994, 1995; Rose, 1996; Ross, 1995; Ryder, 1992; Ryder and Noland, 1992; Sachs, 1990; Sakheim, 1996; Sakheim & Devine, 1992b; Scott, 2001; Sinason, 1994; Smith, C. 1998; Smith, M. 1993; Smith, M.R., 1992; Smith & Pazder, 1981; Snow & Sorenson, 1990; Stafford, 1993; Steele, H., 2003; Steele, K., 1989; Stratford, 1993; Summit, 1994; Tamarkin, 1994a, 1994b; Tate, 1991; Uherek, 1991; Valente, 1992, 2000; Van Benschoten, 1990; van der Hart, 1993; Vesper, 1991; Waterman, Kelly, Olivieri, McCord, 1993; Weir & Wheatcroft, 1995; Wong & McKeen, 1990; Woodsum, 1998; Young, 1992, 1993; Young, Sachs, Braun, & Watkins, 1991; Young & Young, 1997; Youngson, 1993" (Lacter and Lehman, 2008, as cited in Noblitt and Noblitt, 2008, 86).

APPENDIX 2:

MY DEGREES

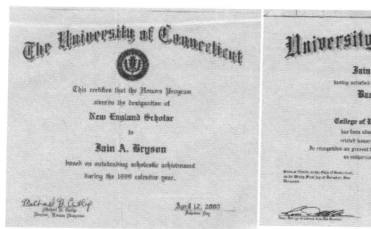

New England Scholar Award (2000)

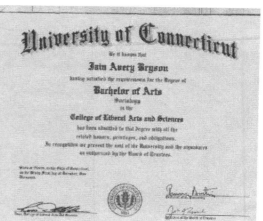

Bachelor of Arts: Sociology (2001)

Minor: Criminal Justice (2001)

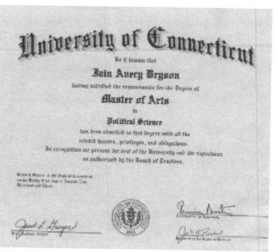

Master of Arts in Political Science (2003)

APPENDIX 3:

LETTER FROM ME TO YOUR MOM SUGGESTING A TRIP TO THE FINGER LAKES IN NEW YORK STATE

"9/25/04 Agatka- I just got finished looking for that address but I couldn't find it. You must have it. I love you. It is not a big deal, but I would just like to drop the box off, especially after the [expletive] today. My brother was very upset, as was I, at how Will approached us. It is not our problem or your problem, and we do not need to deal with and [expletive]. I left a message for the Thursday appointment – they are closed today – and I asked them to call me and let me know if there is anything available on Tuesday afternoon or Wednesday. One thing I thought we could do is go to my Aunt's lake house in up-state New York. We would be on a beautiful lake, by ourselves, and it would not cost a lot of $. Just an idea – I'm not sure what you want to do, but I think that would be a good time. Every time I look at you, you are more beautiful to me. Your eyes, your face, the shapes of your body are like heaven on earth. Your smile makes me smile and your happiness is all that I need to survive. Things will fall into place, and I know that we are supposed to have met. I never believed in love at first sight until I met you. Love, Iain."

APPENDIX 4:

YOUR MOM'S DRAWING OF HER TRIP WITH ME TO THE NEW YORK LAKE HOUSE

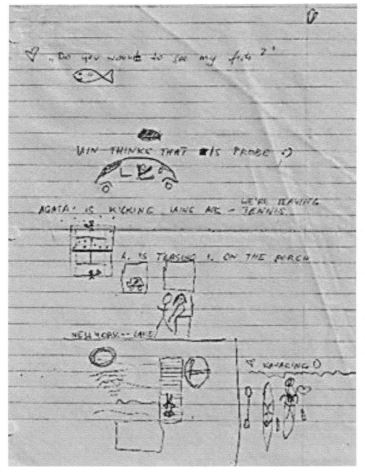

"Do you want to see my fish?"

"IAIN THINKS THAT IS PROBE :D"

"AGATA IS KICKING IAINS ASS – WE'RE PLAYING TENNIS"

"A. IS TEASING I. ON THE PORCH"

"NEW YORK – LAKE"

"KAYAKING"

APPENDIX 5:

YOUR MOM'S NOTE ON GETTTING ENGAGED, OCTOBER 1, 2004

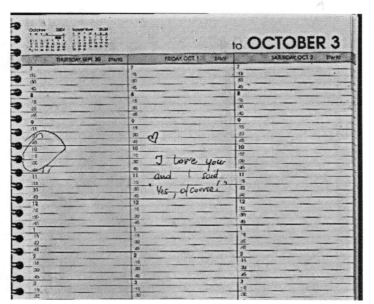

Your mom wrote "I love you and I said 'Yes, of course!'"

APPENDIX 6:

YOUR MOM'S LISTS AND MY COMMENTS

Your mom's writing is in CAPS and blue ink, my comments are lowercase in black ink.

"WHAT I DON'T LIKE ABOUT MYSELF

1■ INSECURITY (you are the most secure you have ever been in your life)

2■ BEING DEFENSIVE (related to outbursts and insecurity)

3■ TOO SENSITIVE (not necessarily bad)

4■ APPEARANCE (you are beautiful and you are working towards being more beautiful)

5■ LOW SELF ESTEEM (why; where did it come from?)

6■ OUTBURSTS (why?; Where did they come from)

7■ VARIABILITY OF MOOD

8■ NOT THINKING ABOUT MYSELF ENOUGH

9■ STUBBORNESS (we are a team)

10■ NERVOUSNESS (about what?; due to what?)

11■ DRAMATIZE (relates to outbursts)

12■ LIES (not acceptable under any circumstances)

13■ NOT AMBITIOUS ENOUGH (you got your BA -> the rest will come)

14■ TAKING OFFENCE

15■ LAZY [I crossed it out]

16■ BEING HYSTERICAL/CRY (- why?)

17■ I CARE TOO MUCH WHAT OTHER PEOPLE THINK (you are an adult and must make your own decisions)

18■ OTHERS ARE EFFECTING MY MOODS AND HOW I FEEL ABOUT MYSELF

19■ I DON'T FEEL THAT I'M NEEDED (-you are more than my legs)

20■ FROM ONE EXTREME TO THE OTHER (same as variability of mood; hormones?; need to stop and think)

21■ FRIGHTEN/STRUGGLE (everybody struggles)

22■ I DON'T KNOW WHAT I WANT TO DO IN MY LIFE (normal; at least you found your 2nd half to help + support you)

23■ I DON'T HAVE HOBBY/DREAMS/GOALS (aerobics, reading. Travelling, paralegal school)"

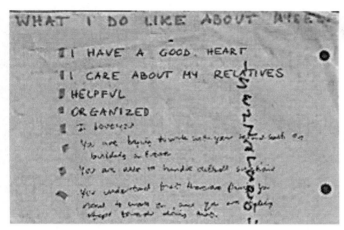

"WHAT I DO LIKE ABOUT MYSELF
- I HAVE A GOOD HEART
- I CARE ABOUT MY RELATIVES
- HELPFUL
- ORGANIZED
- I love you
- You are trying to work with your second half on building a future
- You are able to handle difficult situations
- You understand that there are things you need to work on and you are taking steps towards doing that"

APPENDIX 7:

MY NOTES ON YOUR MOM IN 2004

At-A-Glance 2004

"TX- psychotherapy/meds. Adjustment disorder w/ anxiety. Orgasmic disorder - not a direct effect of substance abuse. Cyclothymia. GAD. Personality disorder. Borderline mostly young women. Repetitive pattern of disorg.[anization] + instability in self image, mood, behavior, and close pers.[onal] relationships. Bright + intelligent. Can sometimes maintain appearance until stressful sit.[uation] like breakup, death, etc. Relationships are intense and stormy. The person may manipulate and have trouble trusting others. Emotional instability. Self damaging actions. Temper tantrums, feelings of desperation and a loss of self control over angry feelings. Maybe difficulty with self identity, sexuality, life goals and values, career, [?]. Deep seated feelings that one is flawed, defective, damaged, or bad in some way – tendency to go to extremes w/ thinking, behavior, and feelings. Under extreme stress -> can be bizarre behavior. Even under less stress can be disturbance in relationships. More frequent in women – connection possible with severe premenstrual tension. Damaged self image from relationships or past experiences."

"Usually relates to self image from earlier relationships. Impulsive behaviors.
-Frantic efforts to avoid real or imagined abandonment
-extremes in personal relationships
-unstable self image
-impulsivity in at least two areas: spending, sex, substance abuse, reckless driving, binge eating
-self mutilating behavior and/or thoughts of suicide
-affective instability due to a marked [?] mood
-irritability or anxiety usually lasting hours, not days
-chronic feelings of emptiness
-inappropriate, intense anger or difficulty controlling anger
-Therapist – relationship to - must be positive and somebody you can relate with
-Meds – to stabilize and help when things are really bad"

APPENDIX 8:

PLANNER NOTES FROM NOVEMBER, 2004

Nov. 11 I wrote: "Logan (evening) Fly to Berlin via Amsterdam to Agatka" Nov. 12 Agata wrote: "Finally I'm gonna see my baby!"

APPENDIX 9:

EMAIL FROM YOUR MOM TO ME

My notes to her are in green ink.

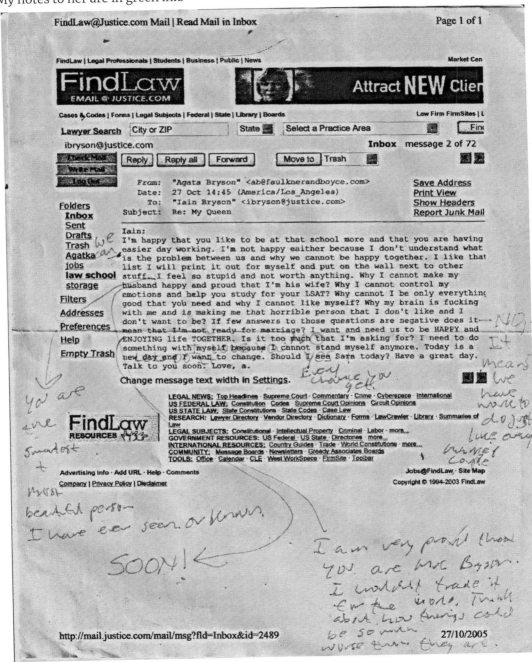

APPENDIX IO:

YOUR MOM'S JOURNAL ENTRIES AND PICTURES 2005-2008

A life spent making mistakes is not only more honorable but more useful than a life spent doing nothing.

In the middle of difficulty lies opportunity

"A life spent making mistakes is not only more honorable but more useful than a life spent doing nothing. In the middle of difficulty lies opportunity."

Polish to English: "The knowledge that somewhere there is someone who will understand you, despite the distance or the thoughts you have expressed, will turn this world into a blooming garden."

Keep love in your heart. A life without it is like a sunless garden when the flowers are dead. The consciousness of loving and being love brings a warmth and richness to life... that nothing else can bring.
— OSCAR WILDE —

"Keep love in your heart. A life without it is like a sunless garden when the flowers are dead. The consciousness of loving and being love brings a warmth and richness to life... that nothing else can bring...-OSCAR WILDE-"

The future belongs to those that believe in the beauty of their dreams.

Life isn't about finding yourself. Life is about creating yourself.

It takes less time to do things right than to explain why you did it wrong.

"The future belongs to those that believe in the beauty of their dreams. Lief isn't about finding yourself. Life is about creating yourself. It takes less time to do things right than to explain why you did it wrong."

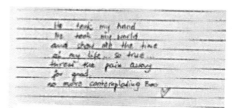

"He took my hand. He took my world and show me the time of my life... so true... threw the pain away for good, no more contemplating Boo"

Your mom in our new car, circa 2006.

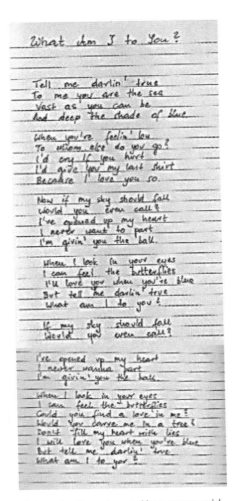

Your mom's 23rd Birthday, July 11, 2005. New London, CT.

Me and you, Connecticut College Arboretum, 2007.

A song by Nora Jones. Your mom said this album, Come Away With Me, *was one of her favorites because Nora Jones wrote it after her husband died.*

APPENDIX II:

YOUR BIRTH RECORDS

January 30, 2007
ADELLE AVERY BRYSON

2:00 a.m.- contractions started and were 5-8 minutes apart.
4:00 a.m.- water broke.
5:00 a.m.- arrived at Lawrence & Memorial Hospital.
5:15 a.m.- 3 cm., 100% effaced, baby high.
Walk for one hour.
6:15 a.m.- 4 cm.
6:35 a.m.- bloodwork taken and I.V. started.
7:00 a.m.- 1 mg. of stadol for pain.
7:10 a.m.- 1 mg. of stadol for pain.
7:30 a.m.- Epidural.
8:25 a.m.- 6 cm. baby about +2.
10:30 a.m.- scalp monitor put onto baby.
Noon- 10 cm.
Noon-12:20 p.m.- baby descended on own.
12:20 p.m.-2:30 p.m. Pushed.
1:40 p.m.- Pitocin to speed up and increase intensity of contractions.
(2:00p.m.)- epidural was out of system.
2:30 p.m.- prep for c-section.
2:51 p.m.- **Adelle Avery Bryson** was born.
8 pounds 9 Ounces
18 and ½ inches long
36 and ½ chest
Apgar was 8&9
Face up at birth

Labor: 0-10 cm. (2:00 a.m.-Noon), 10 hours.
Pushing: (12;20 p.m.-2:30 p.m.), 2 hrs. and 10 minutes.
Total time: 12 hours and 51 minutes.

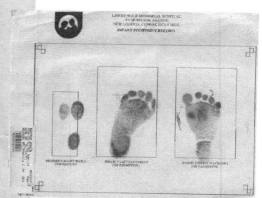

Keep this stub with your personal records. The other side contains important information.

ADELLE AVERY BRYSON
47 BLACKHALL ST
NEW LONDON CT 06320-5015

YOUR SOCIAL SECURITY CARD

Detach the card below and sign it in ink immediately.
Keep your card in a safe place to prevent loss or theft.
DO NOT CARRY IT WITH YOU.
Do not laminate your card.

STATE OF CONNECTICUT
CERTIFICATION OF VITAL RECORD

DEPARTMENT OF PUBLIC HEALTH

CERTIFICATE OF LIVE BIRTH

CHILD'S NAME:
ADELLE AVERY BRYSON

SEX:
FEMALE

TIME OF BIRTH:
02:51 PM

DATE OF BIRTH:
JANUARY 30, 2007

WEIGHT:
8 LBS 9 OZS

BIRTHPLACE:
LAWRENCE & MEMORIAL HOSPITAL

CITY/TOWN:
NEW LONDON

COUNTY:
NEW LONDON

MOTHER'S NAME:
AGATA BRYSON

MAIDEN SURNAME:
MAKOWSKA

MOTHER'S BIRTHPLACE:
POLAND

MOTHER'S DATE OF BIRTH:
JULY 11, 1982

MOTHER'S RESIDENCE:
47 BLACKHALL ST, NEW LONDON, CONNECTICUT 06320

FATHER'S NAME:
IAIN AVERY BRYSON

FATHER'S BIRTHPLACE:
OREGON

FATHER'S DATE OF BIRTH:
JUNE 01, 1977

CERTIFIER'S NAME:
JONATHAN L LEVINE M.D.

DATE CERTIFIED:
JANUARY 30, 2007

ADDRESS:
4 SHAW'S COVE SUITE 101, NEW LONDON, CONNECTICUT 06320

REGISTERED BY:
MICHAEL J TRANCHIDA

TITLE:
REGISTRAR

DATE REGISTERED:
FEBRUARY 09, 2007

CITY/TOWN:
NEW LONDON

I HEREBY CERTIFY THAT THIS IS A TRUE CERTIFICATE OF LIVE BIRTH ISSUED FROM THE OFFICIAL RECORDS ON FILE.

DATE ISSUED:
MARCH 05, 2007

PLACE OF ISSUANCE:
NEW LONDON

SIGNATURE OF ISSUING REGISTRAR

This copy is not a legal document unless displaying raised seal and signature of Registrar

ANY ALTERATION OR ERASURE VOIDS THIS CERTIFICATE

APPENDIX 12:

MY EMAIL TO BRIAN AFTER BREAKING MY JAW

"Thu, Aug 7, 2008, 5:24 PM
Iain Bryson to Brian
So,

I broke my face on Sunday. They didn't take x-rays till the next day, and I had to go home with tylenol suppositories, which is basically like saying take this tylenol and stick it up your [expletive], which the nurse actually did at the ER the first day. My chain fell off when I was going down a hill, and it had just fallen off about 500 meters back, and does occasionally, because it is an old [expletive] bike. But because I was riding on bricks, thrusting forward and off my seat with all my weight on the leg that gave out on the chain leg, I dove headfirst into the bricks. I did not have time to get my hands out; I have many cuts on the backs of my hands, but none on the front, and nothing bad. I remember hitting my chin [expletive] hard, but not caring about that, and just knew I was bleeding anyway, so I had to get home. I just knew there was something wrong when I couldn't close or open my mouth and I had teeth in there...

Eventually the ambulance came. I went, and they sewed my chin and didn't glue it, took no xrays and that is it. The next day they told me I would have to have surgery and teeth removed, but that they didn't know when...hopefully this week. Then they called. and I had it this morning. It was scary as I have never had surgery. They made me come in early and then all of the sudden called to say they were ready because they have a list for cancellations. So, I eventually went up after first giving blood from both arms before and they stuck the IV. I went under and when I woke up, it wasn't so bad. I did not get any postop meds, and they were giving me shots of methadone in the hospital, but have to call the doctor tomorrow. They wanted me to stay the night to keep getting pain shots and there was no way especially since that is the only reason...but I have to get more now. They told me they will look at me Monday and tell me whether or not I have a blood clot in my nose area where they took out a tooth and they would have to have surgery. I have to suck in instead of blow, but it is [expletive] anyway so whatever.

I had to turn down some interviews, but am reconfiguring. I bought some weight gain powder and have to figure out how to gain weight with a jaw closed. I weigh about 135 i think but it is in kilos. I wanted to join the gym this week, but now have to wait. Maybe now, I can find a better job...just have to figure it all out. Hope all is good in AZ. Got some books from my mom including an auto on obama and mccain so that will be ok, along with some other things I like. I would like to try to write, but my plans for stealing back my laptop may be on hold as well. I have gone so far as to make outlines though. Anyway, we are finally going to start putting Adelle on the potty seat I think, but I won't really be taking care of her. Agata's father came yesterday to help. Talk to you soon. I"

I had left my laptop with Wael when we moved out of the West Amsterdam accommodations. The landlord wanted us to pay him more money for the remainder of the month's rent, but we didn't have it to give him. I texted the woman whose dog I had brought over and told her that we needed help getting out of this situation, and she drove over immediately. When packing the car to leave, Wael and the landlord surrounded us and demanded that we pay them. I gave them my laptop just to get them to stop, and to allow us the opportunity to get out of there. I never saw that laptop again and had to get a new one.

APPENDIX 13:

YOUR MOM'S WORK PARTY

APPENDIX 14:

VISIT TO POLAND, EASTER 2010

APPENDIX I5:

PICTURES FROM MY NIGHTTIME WALKS, 2010

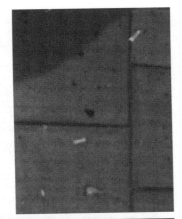

APPENDIX 16:

YOUR MOM'S SCHEMES QUESTIONNAIRE

Name: Agata Bryson

Date of Birth: July 11th, 1982

Highest Educational Level: Bachelor

Today's Date: August 21, 2010

Schemes Questionnaire

INSTRUCTION: Listed below are statements that people might use to describe themselves. Please rate each item based on **how often** you believe or feel each statement **in general** using the frequency scale.

FREQUENCY: In general	
1= Never or Almost Never	4= Frequently
2= Rarely	5= Most of the time
3= Occasionally	6= All of the time

As a child	Now	In general...
5		1. I find myself clinging to people I'm close to because I'm afraid they'll leave me.
2		2. I worry a lot that people I love will find someone else they prefer and leave me.
3		3. I am usually on the look out for people's ulterior motives; I don't trust people easily.
4		4. I feel I cannot let my guard down around other people or they will hurt me.
5		5. I worry more than the average person about danger that I will get sick or that some harm will come to me.
3		6. I worry that I will lose money and become destitute or dependent on others.
5		7. I do not feel I can cope well myself, so I feel I need other people to help me get by.
6		8. My parents and I tend to be overinvolved in each other's lives and problems.
2		9. I have not had someone to nurture me, share with me, or care deeply about what happens to me.
2		10. People have not been there to meet my emotional needs for understanding, guidance, advice and support.

As a Child	Now	In general...
2		11. I feel like I do not belong.
2		12. I'm dull and boring; I don't know what to say socially.
2		13. No one I desire who knew the real me, with all my defects exposed could love me.
2		14. I am ashamed of myself, I'm unworthy of the love, attention, and respect of others.
3		15. I am not as intelligent or capable as most people when it comes to work (or school).
3		16. I often feel inadequate because I do not measure up to others in terms of talent, intelligence and success.
4		17. I feel that I have no choice but to give in to other people's wishes; otherwise they will retaliate or reject me in some way.
6		18. People see me as doing too much for others and not enough for myself.
3		19. I try to do my best, I can't sttle for good enough. I like to be number one at what I do.
2		20. I have too much to accomplish thet there is almost no time to relax and really enjoy myself.
1/3		21. I feel that I shouldn't have to follow the normal rules and conventions other people do. 22.I can't seem to discipline myself to complete routine,boring tasks or to control emotions.

APPENDIX 17:

YOUR MOM'S PATIENT SCREENING QUESTIONNAIRE

<u>Screening Questionnaire Patient version.</u>

1) Reason for consultation
To obtain help in identifying and changing unwanted traits and behavior; help cope with them and stress. Obtain help dealing with and healing over some traumatic experiences in the past and get understanding on how it still effects me and those around me.

2) Referent
Husband

3) Asked for help before? Diagnosis?
Yes-no diagnosis

4) Do you have any physical complains or symptoms? If so, are they still not explained through research?
Migraines, anxiety, stress

5) Present medication
BCP-Yasmin

6) Substance use:

7) Caffeine: YES

8) Alcohol: NO

9) Nicotine: YES

10) Drugs: NO

11) How is your mood? Have you lost interest for things? Changing. Mood swings.

12) How is your sleep? Are you tired? I sleep well. I do often feel tired.

13) How is your appetite? Has your weight been stable? Are you satisfied with it? Good. No it fluctuates. Would like to lose few kilograms.

14) Do you suffer from feelings of guilt/lack of hope? NO

15) Do you have suicidal ideas? NO

16) Do you suffer from concentration problems? Sometimes

17) Do you feel restless? Sometimes.

18) Do you have the need to first do and then think? Often

19) Have you ever experienced anything traumatic? YES

20) Do you suffer from anxiety/or anguish? YES

21) Have you experienced a panic attack in the last weeks? YES

22) How is your social environment? Social support. GOOD

23) How is your work situation? Unemployed

24) Can you generally have trust in people? Not really

25) What is the influence of your symptoms or claims in the people surrounding you?(partner, family) Big influence.

26) Is there any psychopathology in the family? Not diagnosed.

27) Do you ever hear voices? Do some you experience unexplainable events or things in your environment that make you anxious and not at ease. Can you explain? NO

28) <u>Risk factors:</u> Unsure.

29) Do you have children under your care? If so, are you able to properly take care of them? YES. YES

30) If no, go on asking questions oriented to the security of the children (Could you share the care of the children with somebody else, are you the only responsible?) N/A

31) Have you been aggressive for the last weeks, or has there been verbal or physical aggression around you? Explain. NO

32) Did you think of death more frequently than usual during the last weeks? NO

33) Have you ever attempted suicide? NO

34) Has any of your friends or family members attempted suicide. Explain. NO

35) Do you feel very guilty over things: if so, in what measure? If so, and /or very much ask about nihilistic delirium or beliefs and convincement. YES.

APPENDIX 18:

YOUR MOM'S SMI (SERIOUS MENTAL ILLNESS) QUESTIONNAIRE

Name: Agata Bryson

Date of Birth: July 11th, 1982

Highest Educational Level: Bachelor

Today's Date: August 21, 2010

SMI (Version 1.1)

INSTRUCTION: Listed below are statements that people might use to describe themselves. Please rate each item based on **how often** you believe or feel each statement **in general** using the frequency scale.

FREQUENCY: In general	
1= Never or Almost Never	4= Frequently
2= Rarely	5= Most of the time
3= Occasionally	6= All of the time

Frequency	In general...
2	1. I demand respect by not letting other people push me around.
5	2. I feel loved and accepted.
3	3. I deny myself pleasure because I don't deserve it.
4	4. I feel fundamentally inadequate, flawed, or defective.
1	5. I have impulses to punish myself by hurting myself (e.g., cutting myself).
3	6. I feel lost.
4	7. I'm hard on myself.
6	8. I try very hard to please other people in order to avoid conflict, confrontation, or rejection.
3	9. I can't forgive myself.
3	10. I do things to make myself the center of attention.
4	11. I get irritated when people don't do what I ask them to do.
5	12. I have trouble controlling my impulses.
4	13. If I can't reach a goal, I become easily frustrated and give up.
4	14. I have rage outbursts.
5	15. I act impulsively or express emotions that get me into trouble or hurt other people.
Frequency	In general...
4	16. It's my fault when something bad happens.
4	17. I feel content and at ease.

4	18. I change myself depending on the people I'm with, so they'll like me or approve of me.
5	19. I feel connected to other people.
4	20. When there are problems, I try hard to solve them myself.
4	21. I don't discipline myself to complete routine or boring tasks.
3	22. If I don't fight, I will be abused or ignored.
6	23. I have to take care of the people around me.
2	24. If you let other people mock or bully you, you're a loser.
2	25. I physically attack people when I'm angry at them.
5	26. Once I start to feel angry, I often don't control it and lose my temper.
1	27. It's important for me to be Number One (e.g., the most popular, most successful, most wealthy, most powerful).
3	28. I feel indifferent about most things.
2	29. I can solve problems rationally without letting my emotions overwhelm me.
4	30. It's ridiculous to plan how you'll handle situations.
2	31. I won't settle for second best.
4	32. Attacking is the best defense.
1	33. I feel cold and heartless toward other people.
4	34. I feel detached (no contact with myself, my emotions or other people).
6	35. I blindly follow my emotions.
4	36. I feel desperate.
4	37. I allow other people to criticize me or put me down.
6	38. In relationships, I let the other person have the upper hand.
3	39. I feel distant from other people.
4	40. I don't think about what I say, and it gets me into trouble or hurts other people.
2	41. I work or play sports intensively so that I don't have to think about upsetting things.

Frequency	In general...
2	42. I'm angry that people are trying to take away my freedom or independence.
1	43. I feel nothing.
4	44. I do what I want to do, regardless of other people's needs and feelings.
4	45. I don't let myself relax or have fun until I've finished everything I'm supposed to do.
1	46. I throw things around when I'm angry.
3	47. I feel enraged toward other people.
5	48. I feel that I fit in with other people.
3	49. I have a lot of anger built up inside of me that I need to let out.
3	50. I feel lonely.
5	51. I try to do my best at everything.
5	52. I like doing something exciting or soothing to avoid my feelings (e.g., working, gambling, eating, shopping, sexual activities, watching TV).
1	53. Equality doesn't exist, so it's better to be superior to other people.
4	54. When I'm angry, I often lose control and threaten other people.
4	55. I let other people get their own way instead of expressing my own needs.
2	56. If someone is not with me, he or she is against me.
2	57. In order to be bothered less by my annoying thoughts or feelings, I make sure that I'm always busy.
1	58. I'm a bad person if I get angry at other people.
1	59. I don't want to get involved with people.
1	60. I have been so angry that I have hurt someone or killed someone.
4	61. I feel that I have plenty of stability and security in my life.
3	62. I know when to express my emotions and when not to.
3	63. I'm angry with someone for leaving me alone or abandoning me.
2	64. I don't feel connected to other people.
3	65. I can't bring myself to do things that I find unpleasant, even if I know it's for my own good.
1	66. I break rules and regret it later.
2	67. I feel humiliated.
2	68. I trust most other people.
5	69. I act first and think later.
Frequency	In general...

3	70. I get bored easily and lose interest in things.
2	71. Even if there are people around me, I feel lonely.
1	72. I don't allow myself to do pleasurable things that other people do because I'm bad.
2	73. I assert what I need without going overboard.
2	74. I feel special and better than most other people.
1	75. I don't care about anything; nothing matters to me.
4	76. It makes me angry when someone tells me how I should feel or behave.
2	77. If you don't dominate other people, they will dominate you.
5	78. I say what I feel, or do things impulsively, without thinking of the consequences.
3	79. I feel like telling people off for the way they have treated me.
5	80. I'm capable of taking care of myself.
4	81. I'm quite critical of other people.
3	82. I'm under constant pressure to achieve and get things done.
5	83. I'm trying not to make mistakes; otherwise, I'll get down on myself.
2	84. I deserve to be punished.
5	85. I can learn, grow, and change.
2	86. I want to distract myself from upsetting thoughts and feelings.
3	87. I'm angry at myself.
2	88. I feel flat.
2	89. I have to be the best in whatever I do.
1	90. I sacrifice pleasure, health, or happiness to meet my own standards.
3	91. I'm demanding of other people.
1	92. If I get angry, I can get so out of control that I injure other people.
3	93. I am invulnerable.
3	94. I'm a bad person.
5	95. I feel safe.
4	96. I feel listened to, understood, and validated.
4	97. It is impossible for me to control my impulses.
2	98. I destroy things when I'm angry.
Frequency	In general...
2	99. By dominating other people, nothing can happen to you.
4	100. I act in a passive way, even when I don't like the way things are.
3	101. My anger gets out of control.

2	102. I mock or bully other people.
2	103. I feel like lashing out or hurting someone for what he/she did to me.
4	104. I know that there is a 'right' and a 'wrong' way to do things; I try hard to do things the right way, or else I start criticizing myself.
2	105. I often feel alone in the world.
3	106. I feel weak and helpless.
3	107. I'm lazy.
5	108. I can put up with anything from people who are important to me.
4	109. I've been cheated or treated unfairly.
3	110. If I feel the urge to do something, I just do it.
2	111. I feel left out or excluded.
2	112. I belittle others.
4	113. I feel optimistic.
2	114. I feel I shouldn't have to follow the same rules that other people do.
4	115. My life right now revolves around getting things done and doing them 'right'.
4	116. I'm pushing myself to be more responsible than most other people.
3	117. I can stand up for myself when I feel unfairly criticized, abused, or taken advantage of.
3	118. I don't deserve sympathy when something bad happens to me.
2	119. I feel that nobody loves me.
4	120. I feel that I'm basically a good person.
3	121. When necessary, I complete boring and routine tasks in order to accomplish things I value.
4	122. I feel spontaneous and playful.
1	123. I can become so angry that I feel capable of killing someone.
4	124. I have a good sense of who I am and what I need to make myself happy.

APPENDIX 19:

THE "LITTLE DIDDY" I COMPOSED FOR YOUR MOM BASED ON DAVE MATTHEWS LYRICS

"Looking down from here
It's outta my hands for now
Out on my window ledge
It's outta my hands for now
So let me in
Let me in
Confess, your kiss still knocks me off my legs.
The first time I saw you was like a punch right through my chest
and I will forever, 'cause you'll forever be
my one true broken heart, pieces inside of me and you'll forever, my baby be.
If all the things that you are saying love
Were true enough but still
What is all the worrying about?
When you can work it out
You can work it out

Oh I wonder this
AS life billows smoke inside my head
This little game where nothing is sure, oh
Why would you play by the rules?
Who did, you did, you
Who did, you did, you
You say who did, well you did, you
Oh baby it's not easy sometimes
They build these walls ever higher and hide behind them
Seems an odd way to try and make things right
Oh I feel like I go crazy sometimes
Pick me up, love, from the bottom
Up onto the top, love, everyday
Pay no mind to taunts or advances
I'm gonna take my chances on everyday
You make a mess of me here
I dance a thousand steps for you
If you say yes to me
I'll be whatever gets you through
Sometimes I can't move my feet it seems
As if I'm stuck in the ground somehow like a tree
As if I can't even breathe
Oh, and my screams come whispering out

As if nobody can even see me
Like a ghost, sometimes I can't see myself
Sometimes, then again, oh

If I were a king
If I had everything
If I had you then I could give you your dreams
If I were giant-sized, on top of it all
Then tell me what in the world would I sing for
If I had it all

Sometimes I feel lost
As I pull you out like strings of memories
Wish I could weave them into you
Then I could figure the whole [expletive] puzzle out
If I had it all, you know
I'd [expletive] it up

I let you down
Let me pick you up
I let you down
Let me climb up you to the top
So I can see the view from up there
Tangled in your hair
I let you down
I have no lid upon my head
But if I did
You could look inside and see
What's on my mind
I let you down, oh, forgive me
You give me love
Let me walk with you, maybe I could say
Maybe talk with you, open up
And let me through
Don't walk away
Don't walk away
I have no lid upon my head
But if I did
You could look inside and see what's on my mind
You could look inside and see what's on my mind
I let you down
How could I be such a fool like me
I let you down
Tail between my legs
I'm a puppy for you love
I'm a puppy for you love
I have no lid upon my head
but if I did
you could look inside and see
what's on my mind , oh its you
I let you down
I'm a puppy for your love
I'm a puppy for your love
Forgive me
Forgive me
Forgive me
I let you down
It seemed so unnerving
Still somehow deserving
That she could hold my heart so tightly
And still not see me here, oh

Oh, I sleep just to dream her
Beg the night just to see her
That my only love should be her
Just to lie in her
Oh, what I gotta say to you
You got love
Don't turn it down
Turn it loud
Let it build
We got a long way to go
But you, ya gotta start somewhere"

APPENDIX 20:

LYRICS TO "UP AND AWAY" BY DAVE MATTHEWS

"Everyday everyday with you
Every little thing you do the way you do
Little darling in your eyes
Got me up up and away, you get me high
I saw you there since then everyday
Is like I'm lost and thinking of you in every way
Since I fell into your eyes
All i know is that you get me high, you get me high
Like I'm gone, up up and away
You take me baby
Oh you take me baby
And then you walk the way you walk
You blow my mind oh the way you walkin my way
Then i fall into your eyes
Up up and away the way you rise, oh baby, the way you make me high
Before you came you know i never cared
It's just a game i play yea
Up up and away, up up and away, you take me baby
Oh for you I'd give it all, cause when I'm thinking of you and I'm flying above the world
How i wish i was drowning in you i must admit that I'm oh so in love, you know
Please don't ever let me go you've done nothing to me but up up and away you go
Up up and away, you take me baby"

APPENDIX 21:

LEIDEN TRIP

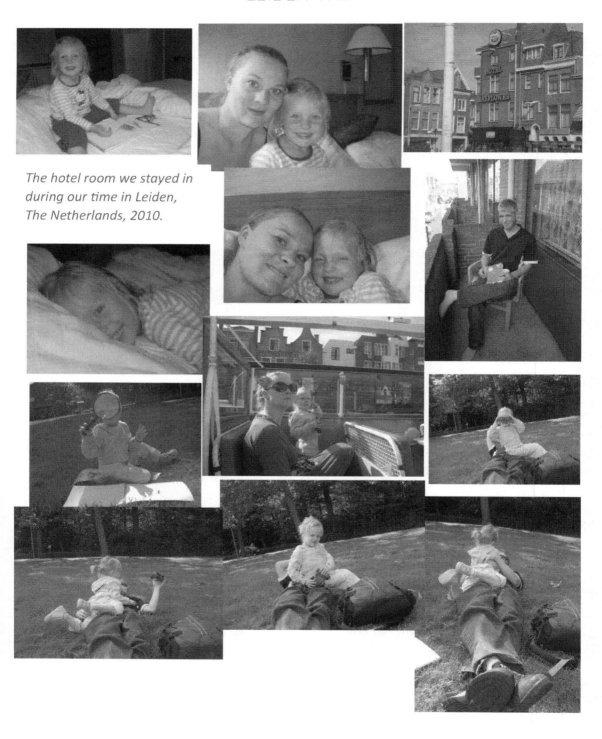

The hotel room we stayed in during our time in Leiden, The Netherlands, 2010.

APPENDIX 22:

DAYS BEFORE MY TRIP TO THE UNITED STATES, AUGUST 2010

APPENDIX 23:

VISA APPLICATION PAPERWORK

Department of Homeland Security
U.S. Citizenship and Immigration Services

I-797, Notice

THE UNITED STATES OF AMERICA

RECEIPT NUMBER		CASE TYPE	I130 IMMIGRANT PETITION FOR RELATIVE
EAC-10-906-82052			FIANCE(E), OR ORPHAN

RECEIPT DATE	PRIORITY DATE	PETITIONER
September 27, 2010	September 23, 2010	BRYSON, IAIN A.

NOTICE DATE	PAGE	BENEFICIARY A096 688 140
March 9, 2011	1 of 1	BRYSON, AGATA

IAIN A. BRYSON
316 GAY HILL ROAD
UNCASVILLE CT 06382

Notice Type: Approval Notice
Section: Husband or wife of U.S.
Citizen, 201(b) INA

The above petition has been approved. We have sent the original visa petition to the Department of State National Visa Center (NVC), 32 Rochester Avenue, Portsmouth, NH 03801-2909. NVC processes all approved immigrant visa petitions that need consular action. It also determines which consular post is the appropriate consulate to complete visa processing. NVC will then forward the approved petition to that consulate.

The NVC will contact the person for whom you are petitioning (beneficiary) concerning further immigrant visa processing steps.

If you have any questions about visa issuance, please contact the NVC directly. However, please allow at least 90 days before calling the NVC if your beneficiary has not received correspondence from the NVC. The telephone number of the NVC is (603) 334-0700.

The approval of this visa petition does not in itself grant any immigration status and does not guarantee that the alien beneficiary will subsequently be found to be eligible for a visa, for admission to the United States, or for an extension, change, or adjustment of status.

THIS FORM IS NOT A VISA NOR MAY IT BE USED IN PLACE OF A VISA.

Please see the additional information on the back. You will be notified separately about any other cases you filed.
U.S. CITIZENSHIP & IMMIGRATION SVCS
VERMONT SERVICE CENTER
75 LOWER WELDEN STREET
SAINT ALBANS VT 05479-0001
Customer Service Telephone: (800) 375-5283

APPENDIX 24:

GREAT GRANDPA WALDEK WITH THE SCARY, FORBIDDEN CAMO HAT. SIERAKOWO, POLAND.

APPENDIX 25:

PHOTOS I TOOK OF YOUR MOM BECAUSE SHE LOOKED LIKE A
"RAPE VICTIM"

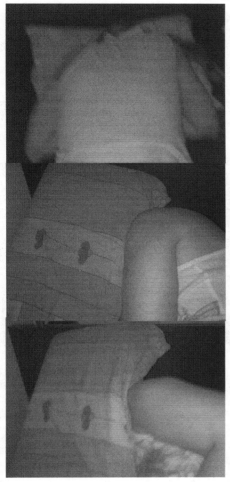
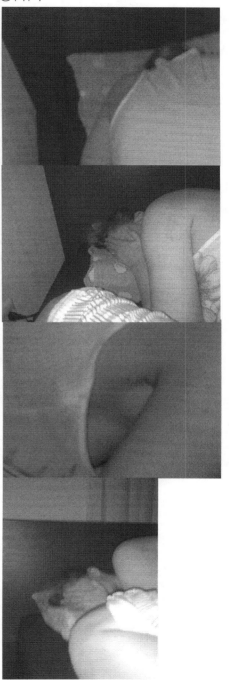

APPENDIX 26:

PICTURES OF YOU AT THE FARM ON OUR LAST DAY TOGETHER

APPENDIX 27:

PICTURES I TOOK OF YOU ON OUR WAY HOME FROM THE FARM
ON OUR LAST DAY TOGETHER. DECEMBER 27, 2010.

APPENDIX 28:

YOUR MOM'S *EAT, PRAY, LOVE* NOTES, DECEMBER 2010

APPENDIX 29:

YOUR MOM'S DECEMBER 2010 NOTES

Translation for this page (above) has not yet been obtained due to difficulty deciphering the handwriting.

Polish to English translation: "Longing. At some point we have to come to terms with what we have received. Take the form you have received and settle into it. Stop interrupting others."

APPENDIX 30:

YOUR MOM'S CV TRANSLATED TO ENGLISH, USING 2024 GOOGLE TRANSLATE

"CURRICULUM VITAE

I was born on July 11, 1982 in Stargard Szczeciński (Poland, West Pomeranian Voivodeship). My parents - Iwona and Sławomir - worked as teachers, later my mother became (and still is) the deputy director of the Construction and Technical School Complex in Stargard Szczeciński, my father was a journalist of the local press and spokesman for the City Management Board, currently he runs his own business. In 1920... I passed my high school final exams at the 1st Secondary School. Adam Mickiewicz in Stargard Szczeciński and I was accepted to study at the Maritime University of Szczecin (now the Maritime University) in Szczecin, majoring in logistics and management in the European transport system. I graduated in 1920... After writing and reviewing my thesis (before its defense), I left for the United States of America and married a US citizen, Iain Avery Bryson, where in 2007 I gave birth to a daughter, Adelle Avery Bryson.

During my stay in New London, Connecticut, I worked as a personal secretary in the law firm of .....(name). In 2008, I came with my whole family to the Netherlands, where I started working at Aramco... (full name) as a legal secretary to the head of the company's branch, first in Leiden, then in The Hague. In the meantime, in 2009, I defended my engineering thesis on logistics in the European transport system at the Maritime University of Szczecin. Until the end of August 2010, I was an employee of Aramco ... (full name).

LETTER OF MOTIVATION

The basis for my application is the fact that I have appropriate education and all the skills required for the position being filled. They are supported by extensive (international) experience in running a secretariat, first in a law firm (USA), recently in the office of one of the heads of a global logistics and transport company. Several years of work in the Netherlands, but in a company from Saudi Arabia, with a cosmopolitan nature of employment, allowed me to learn not only substantive, but also moral and cultural relations with representatives of various components of the European community.

It is not without significance that, despite my multicultural family, my Polish citizenship is not only a formal manifestation, but also an authentic determinant of identity. I am a Pole who adapts perfectly, without intending to assimilate. This also applies to my child (a US citizen), who is raised not only in constant contact with her family in Poland, but also in the Polish linguistic and cultural reality. My contact with the country is not limited to contacts with my family, it consists in constant communication with information about the socio-political situation and following current events in the country.

In the context of the above, a very important motive for my application is the prestige and patriotic motive. The opportunity to work in a Polish diplomatic mission, in such an important place for Europe as The Hague, would be a source of unquestionable pride and an impulse to give literally everything of oneself at work. The possibility of functioning (even at the lowest level) in the structures of the Polish state in a western country is an extraordinary and unique opportunity for a young Polish woman abroad."

APPENDIX 31:

ATTACHMENTS FROM MELANIE BRANDT

United States Department of State

Washington, D.C. 20520

February 28, 2011

Mr. Iain Bryson
25 River View Ave.
New London, CT 06320

Dear Mr. Bryson:

I am writing in response to our telephone conversation of February 25, 2011 regarding your daughter, Adelle, who has been abducted to Poland. I am the officer responsible for cases in Poland for the International Parental Child Abduction Division of the Office Children's Issues. The Department of State places the highest priority on children who have been victimized by parental child abduction. I have already opened a case in the name of Adelle Bryson. The case will remain open until Adelle is returned or you are satisfied that all possible efforts have been exhausted.

To assist you during this difficult time, we offer many services that we hope you will find useful. Please begin by reading our website, www.travel.state.gov/childabduction. There is a great deal of information available on this site specifically for parents in your situation. While I suggest that you familiarize yourself with as much of the material available on the website as possible, I particularly call your attention to the Children's Passport Issuance Alert Program under Prevention. You may also want to look at the A to Z index for other topics.

As I discussed with you, you may file for return under the Hague Convention from the United States. However, since your daughter lived in the Netherlands for more than a year, it may be more productive for you to contact the Dutch Central Authority (DCA) and file the application for return through their office. If you choose to file through the DCA, your case with the Office of Children's Issues will remain open and we will monitor the Dutch case. The contact information for the DCA can be found at http://www.hcch.net/index_en.php?act=conventions.authorities&cid=24.

If you still wish to file the petition through our Office, you will need to submit an original, signed Hague application form (attached and also available on the website). In support of your application, you must submit an Article 28 Power of Attorney form (sample attached and also available on the website), a certified copy of your marriage certificate, a certified copy of Adelle's birth certificate, recent color photographs of Adelle and her mother and evidence of your custodial rights in the form of the state statute, Affidavit of Law, or the court order in effect at the time of Adelle's removal in December 2010. It is important to remember that a foreign court adjudicating a Hague application will look at your custodial rights as they existed at the time of removal. Post-abduction custody orders will not be considered. You will also need to submit Polish translations of all documents, including the Hague application itself.

If you decide that you do not want to file a Hague petition, you may explore our website for other options. You may wish to file for custody, or petition for recognition and enforcement of your U.S. court order in the Polish courts. However, if you decide to pursue either of these two options, your actions could be construed as acquiescence to the jurisdiction of the foreign court and The Hague remedy may no longer be an option.

In the meantime, you may decide to file a missing child report with your local law enforcement agency, and have it follow up with an NCIC (National Crime Information Center) entry. These actions do not necessarily have any criminal implications, but will serve to document your case, and may assist in locating your child should she cross U.S. or international borders at some point. Please take note that, as indicated on our website, pursuing criminal charges against the abducting parent may adversely affect your Hague case.

If the child custody situation cannot be resolved through the Hague Convention or by means of other civil remedies, the U.S. Embassy/Consulate can try to arrange a visit with your child and report on her welfare. You should understand that U.S. Embassy staff cannot act as legal agents, nor can they take custody of U.S. citizen children. Please understand that such a visit can take place only with the permission of the other parent.

If you have any further questions, please do not hesitate to call me at 202-736-9071 or e-mail me at BrandtML@state.gov. I am generally in the office between the hours of 8:15 a.m. and 5:00 p.m., Eastern Standard Time.

Sincerely,

Melanie Brandt

Melanie Brandt
Office of Children's Issues

APPENDIX 32

JURN'S LETTER

"Iain My friend, Many thanks for your Gift of the Bible. That means a lot to me! As you said our paths crossed by the will of God and we'll definitely meet again. You are a real friend of me! You're the first who almost made me cry. And probably you will outside! Stay focused on your fam. My friend as soon as I can I'll assist you. Your everlasting friend, Jurn E. G/G, Ps. When we meet again, I'll introduce you to my fam and daughter!"

APPENDIX 33

PAMPHLET FROM PRISON

English translation: "YOUR DEALER WILL NOT TELL YOU THIS"

The image: Behind bars there are pills, lines of white powder, a gun, and there is marijuana in a spoon.

APPENDIX 34

PORTION OF THE PSYCHIATRIC REPORT

Iain Bryson, sygn. akt Ds 1 Ds. 1018/11

E-mail message from Jan. 7th 2011, sent from Kirk Bryson to Agata Bryson:
"Iain is still convinced that there's a conspiracy to separate you and that you're sending him messages to find you and save you. If we could break his fantasy, he would have much better chance to return to reality and get help".

E-mail message from Jan. 8th 2011, sent from Marianne Stepanik to Agata Bryson:
"In my opinion Iain is having a nervous breakdown. He's convinced that you've been abducted and are in a great danger. I'm sure his mind created that so he doesn't have to cope with reality (...)".

E-mail message from Jan. 9th 2011, sent from Agata Bryson to Marianne Stepanik:
"Judging by your e-mails I think you don't know the whole situation (...) everyday he had outbursts of anger. He caused me physical pain, waking me and Adelle in the middle of the night shouting in my face, strangling me, pulling her out of my arms, locking himself with her in the room, while she was crying for me and changing my life into hell. I do not agree with his ideas for a living (that he will be a writer now, and I will support us again, that he will still take drugs, that we will live in Hague with debts and problems) and I decided that I have to stand for Adelle and my family. Every day he threatened me that if I don't do as he says, he'll kill me or take Adelle from me and I will never see her again. He also told Adelle that I can't play with her or take care of her because I am mentally ill. (...) Adelle is afraid and cries, hides in the corner at every louder noise. She won't allow anyone get nearer if I don't hold her in my arms. (...) I had to let it all out, because I assume that you have no clue what happened during the last three weeks with him under the same roof".

E-mail message from Jan. 9th 2011, sent from Kirk Bryson to Agata Bryson:
"(...) I think I know what he needs and how this fantasy of saving you from bad people developed (...)".

E-mail message from Feb. 13th 2011, sent from Jeremiah D. Wilson to Agata Bryson:
"Since Friday (Feb. 11th) we have received about 115 e-mails from Iain (he sends them to me and other people, family and friends included). The tone of these e-mails is getting worse – borderline with violence and threats".

E-mail message from Apr. 29th 2011, sent from Mickey DeLuca to Agata Bryson contains message sent to him by Iain Bryson:
"It's assassination day, I stalk my enemy like prey. Iain Bryson, I will never lose. Some will"

E-mail message from Apr. 29th 2011, sent from Jackie DeLuca to Agata Bryson:
"We are really worried because his last letters to Mickey threatened with life taking and if he attacked your dad who knows what he'll do to us???..."

E-mail message from May 7th 2011, sent from Agata Bryson to Marianne Stepanik:
"Bad news: the police has visited me yesterday concerning me and Adelle. He contacted some organization in Cambodia and accused my dad of abusing us (...)".

The letters written by Iain Bryson during his stay in Forensic Psychiatry Ward contain numerous references and quotations from the Bible:
"I 'cried out for discernment, and lifted my voice for understanding.' I knocked and the door was opened for me... »many prophets and righteous men have desired to see those things which ye see, and have not seen them... (Matthew 13:17)« When I talk about things like books, movies, music... I am attempting to draw a picture for you; I am attempting to teach the blind. I do not need things like the books, movies and music to know that my wife and child are being abused. I know that they are being abused, because I understand all things. The puzzle of my wife and child is a simple puzzle, but

Tłumaczenie opinii sądowo-psychiatrycznej, strona 2

APPENDIX 35

MY FIRST CELL IN SZCZECIN PRE-TRIAL PRISON

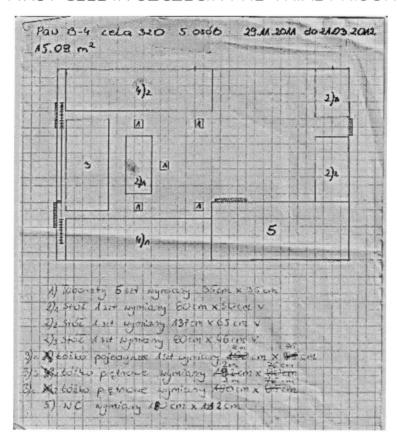

*Diagram of one of the cells I stayed in over the course of
19 months of pretrial detention. Drawn by a cellmate.*

APPENDIX 36

PAWEŁ'S DRAWINGS

APPENDIX 37

ARTICLE SENT FROM DR. ELLEN LACTER

Guidelines to Differential Diagnosis between Schizophrenia and Ritual Abuse/Mind Control Traumatic Stress
by Ellen P. Lacter, Ph.D., and Karl Lehman, M.D.

[Citation: Lacter, E. & Lehman, K. (2008). Guidelines to differential diagnosis between schizophrenia and ritual abuse/mind control traumatic stress. In J.R. Noblitt & P. Perskin (Eds.), *Ritual abuse in the twenty-first century: Psychological, forensic, social and political considerations*, pp. 85-154. Bandon, Oregon: Robert D. Reed Publishers.]

Purpose of these Guidelines

The purpose of this chapter is threefold; 1) to identify the problem of mis-diagnosis of Schizophrenia in adults with trauma-based disorders originating in ritual abuse and trauma-based mind control (we will refer to these hereon as Ritual abuse/mind control traumatic stress), 2) to provide diagnosticians unfamiliar with the clinical presentation of Ritual abuse/mind control traumatic stress with guidelines to facilitate recognition of such cases and to thereby reduce the likelihood of their being mis-diagnosed as Schizophrenia, and 3) to provide diagnosticians experienced with Ritual abuse/mind control traumatic stress with guidelines to facilitate differential diagnosis between such trauma and Schizophrenia in cases with complex clinical features and diagnostic questions.

Mis-diagnosis results in harmful outcomes for ritual abuse and mind control victims in both the mental health and the legal arena. Harmful treatment decisions based on mis-diagnosis include lack of provision of treatment for trauma, incorrect and excessive use of medications, sometimes with severe and irreversible side effects, reinforcement of victims' fears that they are hopelessly crazy and untreatable, long-term hospitalization, and involuntary hospital commitment. Harmful legal outcomes include incorrect findings of insanity, valid reports of abuse being viewed as delusional within law enforcement investigations and judicial proceedings, and forced conservatorship removing victims' basic freedoms.

In order to judge the veracity of victims' reports of these abuses, the clinician must have a basis for understanding what ritual abuse and trauma-based mind control programming are, that they do exist, the kinds of torture endured by victims of these abuses, and familiarity with the most common ritual symbols, artifacts, and holidays utilized by these abuser groups. A general overview of these now follows.

The Existence of Ritual Abuse

The term *ritual abuse* is often used broadly to include any organized abusive practice that furthers the abuser group's ideology. However, the term is usually restricted to organized physical or sexual assault, often including homicide and severe psychological abuse, within the context of a spiritual practice or belief. Some definitions encompass any spiritual belief. But, most definitions use the term to refer to practices that involve physical and sexual abuse of children and adults, and human sacrifice, to propitiate and empower malevolent deities, such as Satan, but also including many polytheistic gods and goddesses.

A substantial body of psychological literature supports that ritualistic abuse is a real phenomenon that must be correctly assessed and treated (Belitz & Schacht, 1992; Bernet & Chang, 1997; Bloom, 1994; Boat, 1991; Boyd, 1991; Brown, 1994; Clark, 1994; Clay, 1996; Coleman, 1994a, 1994b; Comstock, 1991;, Comstock & Vickery, 1992; Cook, 1991; Coons, 1997; Cozolino, 1989, 1990; Crabtree, 1993; deMause, 1994; Driscoll & Wright, 1991; Edwards, 1991; Ehrensaft, 1992; Faller, 1994; Feldman, 1993; Fine, 1989; Finkelhor, Williams, & Burns, 1988; Fraser, 1990, 1991, 1993a, 1993b, 1997a, 1997b; Friesen, 1991, 1992, 1993; Golston, 1993; Gonzalez, Waterman, Kelly, McCord, & Oliveri, 1993; Goodman, Quas, Bottoms, Qin, Shaver, Orcutt, & Shapiro, 1997; Goodwin, 1993, 1994; Goodwin, Hill, & Attias, 1990; Gould, 1992, 1995; Gould & Cozolino, 1992; Gould & Graham-Costain, 1994; Gould & Neswald, 1992; Greaves, 1992; Groenendijk & van der Hart, 1995; Hammond, 1992; Harvey, 1993; Hill & Goodwin, 1989; Hornstein, 1991; Hudson, 1990, 1991; Ireland & Ireland, 1994; Johnson, 1994; Jones, 1991; Jonker & Jonker-Bakker, 1991, 1997; Katchen, 1992; Katchen & Sakheim, 1992; Kelley, 1989; King & Yorker, 1996; Kinscherff & Barnum, 1992; Kluft, 1988, 1989a, 1989b, 1994, 1995; Lawrence, Cozolino, & Foy, 1995; Leavitt, 1994, 2000a, 2000b; Leavitt & Labott, 1998a, 1998b, 2000; Lockwood, 1993; Lloyd, 1992; MacHovec, 1992; Mandell & Schiff, 1993; Mangen, 1992; Mayer, 1991; McCulley, 1994; McFadyen, Hanks, & James, 1993; McFarland & Lockerbie, 1994; Moriarty, 1991, 1992; Neswald & Gould, 1993; Neswald, Gould, & Graham-Costain, 1991; Noblitt, 1995; Noblitt & Perskin, 2000; Nurcombe & Unutzer, 1991; Oksana, 1994, 2001; Paley, 1992; Pulling & Cawthorn, 1989; Raschke, 1990;

Rockwell, 1994, 1995; Rose, 1996; Ross, 1995; Ryder, 1992, 1997; Ryder & Noland, 1992; Sachs, 1990; Sakheim, 1996; Sakheim & Devine, 1992; Scott, 2001; Sinason, 1994; Smith, C. 1998; Smith, M. 1993; Smith, M.R., 1992; Smith & Pazder, 1981; Snow & Sorenson, 1990; Stafford, 1993; Steele, H., 2003; Steele, K, 1989; Stratford, 1993; Summit, 1994; Tamarkin, 1994a, 1994b; Tate, 1991; Uherek, 1991; Valente, 1992, 2000; Van Benschoten, 1990; van der Hart, 1993; Vesper, 1991; Waterman, Kelly, Olivieri, McCord, 1993; Weir & Wheatcroft, 1995; Wong & McKeen, 1990; Woodsum, 1998; Young, 1992, 1993; Young, Sachs, Braun, & Watkins, 1991; Young & Young, 1997; Youngson, 1993.

The publishing arm of the American Psychiatric Association, the American Psychiatric Press, published a text in 1997 explaining the importance of correct assessment and treatment of victims of ritualistic abuse *(The Dilemma of Ritual Abuse: Cautions and Guides for Therapists*, edited by Fraser). One national survey of 2709 clinical psychologists found that 30% claimed to have seen at least one case of "ritualistic or religion-based abuse" and 93% of these psychologists believed the harm actually occurred (Goodman, Qin, Bottoms, & Shaver, 1994).

A review of the empirical evidence of ritual abuse is included in a book by Noblitt and Perskin *(Cult and Ritual Abuse*, 2000, Chapter 6). Noblitt and Perskin (2000) propose that "Cult and Ritual Trauma Disorder" be added as a new diagnosis to the American Psychiatric Association's Diagnostic and Statistical Manual (DSM). Inclusion of this diagnosis in the upcoming DSM would facilitate proper diagnosis and treatment of individuals with Ritual abuse/mind control traumatic stress, and would reduce mis-diagnosis of these individuals as having Schizophrenia and other psychotic or delusional disorders.

Trauma-Based Mind Control Programming

Organizations with a wide range of political and criminal agendas have historically relied on coercive interrogation and brainwashing of various types to force submission and information from enemies and victims, and to indoctrinate and increase cooperation in members and captives. In modern times, these techniques are used by political/military/espionage organizations, race/ethnic hate-groups, criminal groups (e.g., child pornographers and sex rings, and international traffickers of women, children, guns, and drugs) and exploitative and destructive cults with spiritual or other agendas. Methods of "thought reform" used by such groups include intimidation, social isolation, religious indoctrination, threats against victims or their loved ones, torture, torture of co-captives, and brainwashing through social influence or deprivation of basic needs, such as sleep or food (see *Releasing the Bonds: Empowering People to Think for Themselves* (2000), by Steven Hassan).

Trauma-based mind control programming is a term generally used for thought reform that goes beyond the above-described overt torture, intimidation, and brainwashing of the conscious mind, to covert installation of information in the unconscious mind through sophisticated, often technological, Machiavellian means. Mental health and law enforcement professionals working with severe trauma are increasingly seeing victims of such torture (Boyd, 1991; Coleman, 1994b; Hersha, Hersha, Griffis, & Schwarz, 2001; Katchen & Sakheim, 1992; Keith, 1998; Marks, 1979; Neswald & Gould, 1993; Neswald et al., 1991; Noblitt & Perskin, 2000; Oksana, 2001; Ross, 2000; Rutz, 2001; Ryder, 1992; Sheflin & Opton, 1978; Smith, 1993; Weinstein, 1990), and evidence has begun to surface in the legal arena (e.g., Orlikow v. U.S., 682 F.S. 77 (D.D.C. 1988).

Trauma-based mind control programming can be defined as systematic torture that blocks the victim's capacity for conscious processing (through pain, terror, drugs, illusion, sensory deprivation, sensory over-stimulation, oxygen deprivation, cold, heat, spinning, brain stimulation, and often, near-death), and then employs suggestion and/or classical and operant conditioning (consistent with well-established behavioral modification principles) to implant thoughts, directives, and perceptions in the unconscious mind, often in newly-formed trauma-induced dissociated identities, that force the victim to do, feel, think, or perceive things for the purposes of the programmer. The objective is for the victim to follow directives with no conscious awareness, including execution of acts in clear violation of the victim's volition, moral principles, and spiritual convictions.

One common function of trauma-based mind control programming is to cause the victim to physically and psychologically re-experience the torture used to install the programming should the victim consider violating its directives. The most common programs are unidimensional directives communicated during torture and impaired states of consciousness to, "Remember to forget" the abuse, and "Don't tell" about the abuse. Similar to this are pronouncements; claims, curses, covenants, etc., paired with abuse, that convince personalities they are controlled by evil entities, or forever malevolently defined as evil, physically or mentally ill, socially devalued and isolated, sexually enslaved, a murderer, a willing cult member, a coven member, etc.

Much trauma-based mind control programming is significantly more complex, more technological in its methods of installation, and utilizes the individual's dissociated identities (personalities) to effect greater layering of psychological effects. Personalities are usually programmed to take executive control of the body in response to particular cues (hand signals, tones, etc.), and then follow directives, with complete amnesia for these events. Personalities are programmed to become flooded with anxiety or feel acutely suicidal if they defy program directives. Personalities are often programmed to believe that explosives have been surgically implanted in their bodies and that these will detonate if the individual violates orders or begins to recall the programming, the torture used to install it, or the identities of the programmers.

In highly sophisticated mind control, the individual is programmed to perceive inanimate structures in the unconscious inner landscape. "Structures" are mental representations of objects, e.g., buildings, grids, devices of torture, and other containers, that "hold" programmed commands, messages, information, and personalities. In many cases, walls are also installed that serve as barriers to hide deeper levels of programming and structures. Dissociated personalities perceive themselves as trapped within, or attached to, these structures, both visually (in internal imagery), and somatically (in experiences of pain, suffocation, electroshock, etc.).

Structures are mentally installed in early childhood, generally between two and five years of age. Torture, drugs, and even near death, are used in a variety of ways that make it extremely difficult for the child to mentally resist any of the programmer's input, and to ensure that memories of programing sessions remain dissociated. The child may be tortured on a device, and the personalities formed in this process then perceive themselves trapped on these devices. Or an image of an object may be projected on the child's body or on a screen, or in virtual reality goggles, or a physical model of the object is shown. The programmer then tells the child that this object is now within him or her. Because the child is in an altered, disoriented state, and because the mind of the small child does not easily discriminate reality and fantasy (this process relies on the pre-school child's use of magical thinking), the child now perceives the object as a structure within. Then, a code is installed, for the programmer to gain future access to the structure, to erase it, or to input new information.

Immediately after the structure is installed, the programmer will generally command traumatized personalities go to places in the structures, e.g., "Go inside the grid". The programmer will generally also mentally install the perception of wires, bombs, and re-set buttons, to prevent removal of the structure. The child is usually shown something to make him or her perceive these as real, e.g., a button on the belly-button.

Kinds of Torture Endured in Ritual Abuse and Trauma-Based Mind Control

Knowledge of the methods of torture used within ritual abuse and trauma-based mind control provides a basis for recognition of related trauma disorders. Individuals subjected to these forms of torture may experience intense fear, phobic reactions, or physiological symptoms in response to associated stimuli. In some cases, the individual, or particular dissociated identities, experience a preoccupation with, or attraction to, related stimuli.

Victims may be able to describe the torture they have endured, or they may fear doing so. In many cases of ritual abuse and mind control trauma, the abuse remains dissociated when the individual first seeks treatment. Typically, the initial presenting problems are symptoms of anxiety, depression, or trauma derived from childhood sexual abuse, usually by a family member, who is eventually understood as a participant in the abuser group.

The following is a partial list of these forms of torture:

1. Sexual abuse and torture.
2. Confinement in boxes, cages, coffins, etc., or burial (often with an opening or air-tube for oxygen).
3. Restraint; with ropes, chains, cuffs, etc.

4. Near-drowning.

5. Extremes of heat and cold, including submersion in ice water, burning chemicals, and being held over fire.

6. Skinning for sacrifice or for torture. Pain-inducing drugs, chemicals, and/or adhesive tape can create an illusion of being skinned without permanent injury or scars.

7. Spinning.

8. Blinding or flashing light.

9. Electric shock.

10. Forced ingestion of offensive body fluids and matter, such as blood, urine, feces, flesh, etc.

11. Being hung upside down or in painful positions.

12. Hunger and thirst.

13. Sleep deprivation.

14 Compression with weights and devices.

15. Sensory deprivation.

16. Changes in atmospheric pressure (for example, using rapid pressure changes in a hyperbaric chamber to produce the "bends" and intense ear pain).

17. Drugs to create illusion, confusion, and amnesia, often given by injection or intravenously.

18. Oral or intravenous delivery of toxic chemicals to create pain or illness, including chemotherapy agents.

19. Limbs pulled or dislocated.

20. Application of snakes, spiders, maggots, rats, and other animals to induce fear and disgust.

21. Near-death experiences; such as by drowning or suffocation with immediate resuscitation.

22. Forced to perform or witness abuse, torture and sacrifice of people and animals, usually with knives.

23. Forced participation in child pornography and prostitution.

24. Raped to become pregnant; the fetus is then aborted for ritual use, or the baby is taken for sacrifice or enslavement.

25. Spiritual abuse to cause victims to feel possessed, harassed, and controlled internally by spirits or demons.

26. Desecration of Judeo-Christian beliefs and forms of worship; e.g., dedication to Satan or other deities.

27. Abuse and illusion to convince victims that God is evil, such as convincing a child that God has raped her.

28. Surgery to torture, experiment, or cause the perception of physical or spiritual bombs or "implants".

29. Harm or threats of harm to family, friends, loved ones, pets, and other victims, to force compliance.

30. Use of illusion and virtual reality to confuse and create non-credible disclosure.

To illustrate, ritual abuse survivors may experience intense phobic reactions to spiders or maggots (item 20). They may fear water and baths (items 4 and 5). They often fear hypodermic needles (item 18). They become easily too cold, too hot (item 5), or thirsty (item 12). They may have aversive reactions to cameras (item 23). They may become upset upon seeing babies, dolls, or particular animals, or they may strongly identify with abused and abandoned animals and children (items 22, 24, and 29). Sexual aversions are common (items 1, 23, and 24), as is vulnerability to repeated sexual victimization. Sexual compulsions and paraphilias, such as sadism, can also occur (Young et al., 1991).

Food aversions and eating disorders are common. Ritual abuse survivors may not be able to eat food that is brown or red because these remind them of feces and blood. They are often repulsed by meat, are vegetarian, or fast excessively, or regurgitate food, derived from forced ingestion of body matter and fluids (item 10).

Ritual abuse survivors, by and large, believe in the presence and power of spiritually evil forces, and often feel personally plagued by these (items 25, 26, 27, and 28). They may experience anxiety or an aversion to God and religion (items 26 and 27), or may alternatively be devout in their spiritual beliefs and practices.

Art productions, creative writing, and sandtrays, will often reflect their torture; including knives, religious symbols, frightening figures, coffins, burials, etc. Children unconsciously reenact elements of torture they have witnessed or experienced with toys and other objects. For example, a three-year-old boy wrapped a rope three times around his neck and pulled upward, as if to hang himself. A three-year-old girl sang about marrying Satan.

External or internal reminders of torture-related stimuli often precipitate dissociative responses, such as entering a trance state, falling asleep, or an other personality taking executive control of the individual. Torture-associated stimuli may also elicit disturbing impulses to re-enact unprocessed trauma, such as impulses to self-mutilate, or stab or sexually assault an other person.

Somatoform and conversion reactions occur frequently in response to ritual abuse and mind control trauma-reminders. Individuals often experience localized pain, especially genitourinary, musculoskeletal, and gastrointestinal, motor inhibitions, nausea, or even swelling in the affected area, prior to retrieval of any visual or narrative memory of the related torture. These are generally very distressing to the affected individual. Once the trauma is re-associated and processed within the context of psychotherapy or other forms of support, these somatoform and conversion reactions usually dissipate.

Survivors of trauma-based mind control often respond with distress to fluorescent lighting, since so much programming utilizes intense lighting (item 8). They may startle in response to a telephone ringing, related to programming to receive or make calls to abusers. They may believe they have microphones inside their heads that will relay their disclosures to their abusers (item 28). Fears of electronic or spiritual surveillance, and threats to loved ones (item 29), inhibit their ability to defy and escape their abusers or to disclose their abuse.

Victims of trauma-based mind control also usually experience intense or odd reactions to benign stimuli that were used in their programming. For example, they may have been programmed to "remember to forget" every time they see an apple, or to remember they are being watched every time they hear a police or fire siren. Similarly, they may make repetitive, robotic statements that do not make sense in the context of dialogue, e.g., "I want to go home", a common programmed statement intended to keep victims obedient to abuser groups and reporting to their abusers. Specific songs may be compulsively sung for similar programmed purposes.

All of these symptoms can occur prior to the individual having any conscious knowledge of the related abuse. This point is critical. Dissociative and neurobiological responses to overwhelming trauma (van der Kolk, McFarlane, & Weisaeth, 1996) often prevent these experiences from being processed into a coherent narrative memory. The diagnostician cannot rely on the patient to "put the pieces together" of their clinical picture.

Finally, generalized guilt and survivor guilt are strongly associated with ritual abuse, since participation in victimization of others is a mainstay of ritual abuse and mind control torture (items 22 and 29).

For more on recognition of symptoms specific to ritual abuse trauma, see Boyd 1991; Coleman 1994a; Gould 1992; Hudson 1991; Mangen 1992; Oksana 2001; Pulling and Cawthorn, 1989; Ross 1995; Ryder 1992; Young 1992; and Young and Young 1997.

Ritual Symbols, Artifacts, and Holidays Utilized by Groups Practicing Ritual Abuse

Practitioners of ritual abuse observe holidays and employ symbols and artifacts particular to their spiritual practices and beliefs. Victims may describe these, draw them, or be preoccupied with them. Commonly, victims experience increased distress as these dates approach and in relation to these symbols and artifacts. Recognition of ritual symbols, artifacts, and holidays alert the clinician to possible victimization in affected individuals.

Ritual holidays vary between groups, but some of the most common of these include victims' birthdays, many Christian holidays (often in opposition to Christian doctrine and practice), All Hallows Eve through Samhain (October 29 through November 4), Candlemas (February 2), Beltane (May 1, and 10 days prior in preparation), Lammas (August 2), the vernal and autumnal equinoxes (March 21 and September 21), the summer and winter solstices (June 21 and December 21), full moons, new moons, and "Marriage to the Beast" in some practitioners of Satanism (September 5 to 7). Extreme distress, increased self-mutilation, suicidality, and hospitalizations in relation to ritual holidays are a strong indicator of ritual trauma (Ross, 1995).

Symbols and artifacts also vary, but commonly-reported ones include the five-pointed star within a circle (inverted in Satanism, upright in abusive witchcraft), the six-pointed star, the inverted Christian cross, the symmetrical cross in a circle, the letter "A" within a circle (the cross of the "A" extends beyond the circle), the Swastika within a circle (also utilized by Nazi-agenda groups), the circle, the triangle (upright or inverted), the Ankh, the infinity sign, lightening bolts, the Nero cross (peace symbol), the "all-seeing eye" in a triangle atop a pyramid (as on the United States dollar bill), altars upon which people are physically or sexually abused or sacrificed, black candles (often associated with sacrifice), white candles, other-colored candles, chalices, robes (often black, sometimes white and other

APPENDIX 38

FOLLOW-UP LETTER TO U.S. DEPARTMENT OF STATE FROM R.O.P.S. APRIL 22, 2013.

"*U.S. Depatment of state*
Bureau of Consular Affairs
Office of Children's Issues
SA-29
2201 C Street, NW
Washington, DC 20520
April 22, 2013
On December 27, 2010, my wife absconded with our daughter from our residence in The Netherlands to Poland. At the time, our daughter was three years old and a habitual resident of The Netherlands. The act was an international parental abduction, and it was in violation of my parental rights.
On December 27, 2010, I went to the police in The Netherlands, but they refused to help. I contacted the U.S. Embassy in The Netherlands, but they told me that they could not help due to a lack of jurisdiction. In January 2011, I filed a Hague Abduction Convention report through Melonie Brandt with the United States Department of State.
In April 2011, I flew to Poland, assaulted my father-in-law, and I was subsequently arrested. My intention was to force the attention of the Polish authorities to investigate the allegations of child abuse that I had made against my wife and my father-in-law. I believed that getting arrested would guarantee a thorough evaluation of my daughter. I have been in Polish custody since April 2011, and there has been no thorough evaluation of my daughter.
The U.S. Embassy in Poland has told me that they lack jurisdiction to intervene. My daughter is a U.S. citizen who was a resident of The Netherlands from 2008-2010. However, because my daughter's mother is a Polish citizen, the Polish authorities consider my daughter to be a Polish and not an American citizen. The Embassy told me that this precludes them from taking any action on my daughter's behalf.
My wife changed our daughter's residence from The Netherlands to Poland. My wife has filed an application with the family court to have my parental rights terminated. I have not seen my daughter since December 27, 2010.
The Hague Abduction Convention report that I filed in January 2011 is of utmost importance. The removal of my daughter from her residence in The Netherlands to Poland in December 2010 was an international parental abduction. I do not know whether I have received any reply from your office in response to my filed report due to the fact that I have been in Polish custody for nearly two years. Please advise."

APPENDIX 39

YOUR FIRST PLACE PAINTING

I miejsce Adelle Bryson – Przedszkole Miejskie nr 1 z Oddziałami Integracyjnymi w Stargardzie Szczecińskim (w kategorii wiekowej 5, 6 – latki)

Polish: "1 miejsce Adelle Bryson – Przedszkole Miejskie nr 1 z oddziałami integracynymi w stargardzie szczecinskim (w kategorii wiekgowej 5, 6 – latki)"

English: "First place Adelle Bryson - Municipal Kindergarten No. 1 with integrated classes in Stargard Szczecinski (in the age category of 5 and 6-year-olds)"

APPENDIX 40

MY DIAGNOSIS OF CERVICAL STENOSIS

8/6/2020   Patient Portal

CHC OF GROTON MEDICAL

Maria Barros, APRN
Family Practice

Address:
█████████████, Groton, CT 06340

Tel:
860-446-8858

Fax:
860-405-2140

RESULT

Patient
Iain Bryson

DOB
06/01/1977

Address
█████████████████Ledyard, CT 06339

Phone
█████████

Ordered Date
01/13/2016

Test Name
MRI : Cervical Spine without contrast

Assessments
Protrusion of cervical intervertebral disc

Name	Value	Reference Range

Result
multilevel DDD, most severe C5-6 & C6-7, C5-6 disc herniation with cental canal narrrowing b/l

Received Date
02/04/2016

WORKS CITED

1. "Bloodlines." *Criminal Minds*, written by Mark Bruner, season 4, episode 13, ABC Studios and CBS Studios Inc., 21 Jan. 2009.

2. Adele. "Someone Like You." *21.* XL Recordings, Columbia Records, 2011.

3. Aerosmith. "I Don't Want to Miss a Thing." *Armageddon: The Album.* Columbia Records, 1998.

4. American Psychiatric Association. *Diagnostic and Statistical Manual of Mental Disorders, 5th, ed.* American Psychiatric Publishing, 2013. DSM-V, https://repository.poltekkes-kaltim.ac.id/657/1/Diagnostic%20and%20statistical%20manual%20of%20mental%20disorders%20_%20DSM-5%20(%20PDFDrive.com%20).pdf

5. Aquino, Michael A. *Extreme Prejudice: The Presidio "Satanic Abuse" Scam.* 2014.

6. Ball, Alan, creator. *True Blood.* Your Face Goes Here Entertainment and HBO Entertainment, 2008.

7. Barnett, Fiona. *Eyes Wide Open: The Authentic Fiona Barnett book on healing Satanic Ritual Abuse.* 2020.

8. Beastie Boys. "Sabotage." *III Communication.* Grand Royal, 1994.

9. *Bee Movie.* Directed by Simon Smith and Steve Hickner, performances by Jerry Seinfeld, Renee Zellweger, Matthew Broderick, and John Goodman, Paramount Pictures, 2007.

10. Blume, E. Sue. *Secret Survivors: Uncovering Incest and Its Aftereffects in Women.* Ballantine Books, 1990.

11. Breuer, Josef and Sigmund Freud. *Studies on Hysteria.* Basic Nooks, Inc., 2000.

12. Buffett, Jimmy. "Volcano." *Volcano.* MCA Records, 1979. Vinyl.

13. Burgess, Ann Wolbert et al. *Sexual Assault of Children and Adolescents.* Lexington Books, 1978.

14. Calof, David L. with Mary LeLoo. *Multiple Personality and Dissociation: Understanding Incest, Abuse, and MPD.* Hazelden Foundation, 1993.

15. Casey, Patricia. *Adjustment Disorder: From Controversy to Clinical Practice.* Oxford University Press, 2018.

16. Clawar, Stanley S. and Brynne V. Rivlin. *Children Held Hostage: Identifying Brainwashed Children, Presenting a Case, and Crafting Solutions.* 2nd ed., American Bar Association, 2013.

17. Cling, B. J., editor. *Sexualized Violence against Women and Children.* The Guilford Press, 2004.

18. Cypress Hill. "Hits from the Bong." *Black Sunday.* Ruffhouse Records, Columbia Records, 1993.

19. Dave Matthews Band. "Spoon." *Before These Crowded Streets.* RCA Records, 1998.

20. Dave Matthews Band. "You Never Know." *Busted Stuff.* RCA Records, 2002.

21. Davis, Rebecca. *Untwisting Scriptures to find freedom and joy in Jesus Christ: Book 5 Brokenness & Suffering.* New Morning Press, 2023.

22. Depeche Mode. "Policy Of Truth." *Violator.* Mute, 1990.

23. Destiny's Child. "Cater to You." *Destiny Fulfilled.* Columbia Records, 2005.

24. Drake. "Miss Me." *Thank Me Later.* Young Money, Cash Money, Universal Motown, 2010.

25. Drake. "Shut It Down." *Thank Me Later.* Young Money, Cash Money, Universal Motown, 2010.

26. Emery, Carla. *Secret Don't Tell: The Encyclopedia of Hypnotism.* Illustrated by Corey Smigliani, Acorn Hill Publishing, 1997, 1998.

27. Epstein, Orbit Badouk, et al., editors. *Ritual and Mind Control: The Manipulation of Attachment Needs.* Routledge, 2011.

28. Estabrooks, G.H. *Hypnotism.* E.P Dutton & Co., Inc., 1943.

29. *Fantasia.* Directed by Samuel Armstrong, James Algar, Bill Roberts, et.al., starring Leopold Stokowski and Deems Taylor, Walt Disney Productions, 1940.

30. Faulkner, William. *Go Down, Moses.* Vintage Books, 1940.

31. Ford, Julian D. and Christine A. Courtois. "Complex PTSD, affect dysregulation, and borderline personality disorder." *BioMed Central Ltd.,* 9 July 2014.

32. Frankfurter, David. *Evil Incarnate: Rumors of Demonic Conspiracy and Ritual Abuse in History.* Princeton University Press, 2006.

33. Frankl, Viktor. *Man's Search for Meaning.* Pocket Books, 1959, 1962, 1984.

34. Frawley-O'Dea, Mary Gail. *Perversion of Power: Sexual Abuse in the Catholic Church.* Vanderbilt University Press, 2007.

35. *Get Out.* Directed by Jordan Peele, performances by Daniel Kaluuya, Allison Williams, Bradley Whitford, Caleb Landry Jones, and Catherine Keener, Universal Pictures, 2017.

36. Gilbert, Elizabeth. *Eat, Pray, Love: One Woman's Search for Everything Across Italy, India and Indonesia.* Penguin books, 2006.

37. Goodyear-Brown, Paris, editor. *Handbook of Child Sexual Abuse: Identification, Assessment, and Treatment.* John Wiley & Sons, Inc., 2012.

38. Gould, Catherine, and Louis Cozolino. "Ritual Abuse, Multiplicity, and Mind-Control." *Journal of Psychology and Theology* 20.3 (1992): 194-196.

39. Hammond, D. Corydon. "The Greenbaum Speech." *Fourth Annual Eastern Regional Conference on Abuse and Multiple Personality Disorder (MPD),* 25 June 1992, https://pubhtml5.com/rukq/psbx/

40. Harper, Ben. "One Road to Freedom." *Fight for Your Mind.* Virgin Records, 1995.

41. Harper, Ben. "When She Believes." *Diamonds On the Inside.* Virgin Records, 2003.

42. Harris, Sam. "There Is No God (And You Know It)." *Sam Harris.* October 6, 2005. https://www.samharris.org/blog/there-is-no-god-and-you-know-it

43. Hart, Carl L. *Drug Use for Grown-Ups: Chasing Liberty in the Land of Fear.* Penguin Press, 2021.

44. Herman, Judith Lewis with Lisa Hirschman. *Father-Daughter Incest.* Harvard University Press, 1981.

45. Herman, Judith Lewis. *Trauma and Recovery: The aftermath of violence – from domestic abuse to political terror.* BasicBooks, 1992.

46. Hewitt, Sandra K. *Assessing Allegations of Sexual Abuse in Preschool Children: Understanding Small Voices.* Sage Publications, Inc., 1999.

47. Hicks, Robert D. *In Pursuit of Satan: The Police and the Occult.* Prometheus Books, 1991.

48. Jacobs, Janet Liebman. *Victimized Daughters: Incest and the Development of the Female Self.* Routledge, 1994.

49. Jennings, Lyfe. "If Tomorrow Never Comes." *I Still Believe.* Asylum Records, 2010.

50. Johnson, Jack. *In Between Dreams.* Brushfire Records, 2005.

51. Kennedy, William H. *Lucifer's Lodge: Satanic Ritual Abuse in the Catholic Church.* Sophia Perennis, 2004.

52. Kleiger, James H. and Ali Khadivi. *Assessing Psychosis: A Clinician's Guide.* Routledge, 2015.

53. Kluft, Richard P., editor. *Childhood Antecedents of Multiple Personality.* American Psychiatric Press, Inc., 1985.

54. Kreisman, Jerold J. and Hal Straus. *I Hate You – Don't Leave Me: Understanding the Borderline Personality Disorder.* Penguin Group, 2010.

55. Kreisman, Jerold J. and Hal Straus. *Sometimes I Act Crazy: Living with Borderline Personality Disorder.* John Wiley & Sons, Inc., 2004.

56. Krill, William E. *Gentling: A Practical Guide to Treating PTSD in Abused Children.* 2nd ed., Loving Healing Press, 2009, 2011.

57. Lorandos, Demosthenes and William Bernet, editors. *Parental Alienation: Science and Law.* Charles C Thomas, 2020.

58. Marks, John. *The Search for the "Manchurian Candidate": The CIA and Mind Control; The Secret History of the Behavioral Sciences.* W. W. Norton & Company, 1979.

59. Martin, Malachi. *Hostage to the Devil: The Possession and Exorcism of Five Contemporary Americans.* HarperSanFrancisco, 1976.

60. Marx, Karl. *Early Writings.* Translated by Rodney Livingstone and Gregor Benton. Penguin Books, 1992.

61. Matthews, Dave. "Up and Away." *Some Devil.* RCA Records, 2003. CD.

62. McBratney, Sam. *Guess How Much I Love You.* Illustrated by Anita Jeram, Candlewick, 2008.

63. Meister, Lisa. *You've Got the Wrong Guy.* 2021.

64. Michigan State Police. *Occult Criminal Investigation: Reference material.* Child Abuse Unit, Criminal Investigation Division, November 1988. https://www.gvsu.edu/cms4/asset/90 3124DF-BD7F-3286- FE3330AA44F994DE/occult_criminal_investigation_2.pdf

65. Miller, Alice. *Banished Knowledge: Facing Childhood Injuries.* Anchor Books, Doubleday, 1990.

66. Miller, Bruce, creator. *The Handmaid's Tale.* Hulu, 2017.

67. Mullins, Rich. "Awesome God." *Winds of Heaven, Stuff of Earth.* Reunion, 1988.

68. Munro, Alistair. *Delusional Disorder: Paranoia and related illnesses.* Cambridge University Press, 1999.

69. Nathan, Debbie and Michael Snedeker. *Satan's Silence: Ritual Abuse and the Making of a Modern American Witch Hunt.* BasicBooks, 1995.

70. *New American Standard Bible.* The Lockman Foundation, 1960, 1971, 1977, 1995, 2020.

71. Noblitt, James Randall and Pamela Perskin Noblitt. *Cult and Ritual Abuse: Narratives, Evidence, and Healing Approaches.* 3rd ed., Praeger, 2014.

72. Noblitt, Randy and Pamela Perskin Noblitt, editors. *Ritual Abuse in the Twenty-First Century: Psychological, Forensic, Social, and Political Considerations.* Robert D. Reed Publishers, 2008.

73. O'Brien, Cathy with Mark Phillips. *Access Denied: For Reasons of National Security.* Reality Marketing, 2004.

74. O'Brien, Cathy with Mark Phillips. *Trance Formation of America: The True Life Story of a CIA Mind Control Slave.* Reality Marketing, Incorporated, 1995.

75. Ofshe, Richard and Ethan Watters. *Making Monsters: False Memories, Psychotherapy, and Sexual Hysteria.* Charle's Scribner's Sons, 1994.

76. Peck, M. Scott. *People of the Lie: The Hope for Healing Human Evil.* A Touchstone Book, 1983.

77. Peterson, Jordan B. *Beyond Order: 12 More Rules For Life.* Penguin, 2021.

78. Petty, Tom. "Free Fallin'." *Full Moon Forever.* MCA Records, 1989.

79. Philipps, Ina-Maria. *Körper, Liebe, Doktorspiele – Ein Ratgeber für Eltern zur kindlichen Sexualentwicklung. (Body, love, doctor games - A guide for parents on child sexual development).* Edited by the Federal Center for Health Education (BZgA), Volume 1 (1 to 3 years), Volume 2 (4 to 6 years), Cologne, 2000.

80. Piper, August, Jr. *Hoax & Reality: The Bizarre World of Multiple Personality Disorder.* Jason Aronson Inc., 1997.

81. *Reefer Madness.* Directed by Louis J. Gasnier, performances by Dorothy Short, Kenneth Craig, Lillian Miles, Motion Picture Ventures, 1936.

82. Rey, H. A., and Margret Rey. *Curious George.* Houghton Mifflin, 1941.

83. Reynolds, Nathan. *Snatched from the Flames: One man's journey to uncover The Family Secrets buried in his blood-stained past.* 2018.

84. Richardson, James T. et al., editors. *The Satanism Scare.* Walter de Gruyter, Inc., 1991.

85. Rollins Band. "Liar." *Weight.* Imago, 1994.

86. Ross, Colin A. *The Great Psychiatry Scam: One Shrink's Personal Journey.* Manitou Communications, Inc., 2008.

87. Ross, Colin A. *The Osiris Complex: Case-Studies in Multiple Personality Disorder.* University of Toronto Press, 1994. ep

88. Rush, Florence. *The Best-Kept Secret: Sexual Abuse of Children.* Human Services Institute and Tab Books, 1980.

89. Russel, Diana E.H. *The Secret Trauma: Incest in the Lives of Girls and Women.* Basic Books, Inc., Publishers, 1986.

90. Sachs, Adah and Graeme Galton, editors. *Forensic Aspects of Dissociative Identity Disorder.* Karnac Books, 2008.

91. Salter, Michael. *Organised Sexual Abuse.* Routledge, 2013.

92. Sass, Louis A. *The Paradoxes of Delusion: Wittgenstein, Schreber, and the Schizophrenic Mind.* Cornell University Press, 1994.

93. Schwartz, Harvey L. *The Alchemy of Wolves and Sheep: A relational approach to internalized perpetration in complex trauma survivors.* Routledge, 2013.

94. Shengold, Leonard. *Soul Murder: The Effects of Childhood Abuse and Deprivation.* Fawcett Columbine, Ballantine Books, 1989.

95. Solzhenitsyn, Aleksandr. *The Gulag Archipelago Abridged: An Experiment in Literary Investigation.* Harper Perennial Modern Classics, 2007.

96. Spanos, Nicholas P. *Multiple Identities & False Memories: A Sociocognitive Perspective.* American Psychological Association, 1996.

97. Stefani, Gwen. "The Sweet Escape." *The Sweet Escape.* Interscope Records, 2006.

98. Steinbeck, John. *The Winter of Our Discontent.* The Viking Press, 1961.

99. Szasz, Thomas. *Coercion as Cure: A Critical History of Psychiatry.* Transaction Publishers, 2007.

100. Szasz, Thomas. *Insanity: The Idea and Its Consequences.* John Wiley & Sons, 1987, 1990.

101. Szasz, Thomas. *Law, Liberty, and Psychiatry: An Inquiry into the Social Uses of Mental Health Practices.* Routledge & Kegan Paul, 1974.

102. Szasz, Thomas. *Psychiatric Slavery: When Confinement and Coercion Masquerade as Cure.* The Free Press, 1977.

103. Szasz, Thomas. *Psychiatry: The Science of Lies.* Syracuse University Press, 2008.

104. Terr, Lenore. *Too Scared to Cry: How Trauma Affects Children... and Ultimately Us All.* Basic Books, 1990.

105. *The Holy Bible.* King James Version, Holman Bible Publishers, 2000.

106. *The Holy Bible.* New King James Version, Thomas Nelson, Inc., 1982.

107. van der Kolk, Bessel. *The Body Keeps the Score: Brain, Mind, and Body in the Healing of Trauma.* Penguin Books, 2014.

108. Vega, Suzanne. "Luka." *Solitude Standing.* A & M Records, 1987.

109. Victor, Jeffrey S. *Satanic Panic: The Creation of a Contemporary Legend.* Open Court, 1993.

110. Woodsum, Gayle M. *The Ultimate Challenge: A revolutionary, sane, and sensible response to ritualistic and cult-related abuse.* Action Resources International, 1998.

111. Wu-Tang Clan. "Method Man." *Enter The Wu-Tang.* Loud Records, RCA Records, 1993.

112. Zanarini, Mary C., editor. *Role of Sexual Abuse in the Etiology of Borderline Personality Disorder.* American Psychiatric Press, Inc., 1997.

ABOUT THE AUTHOR

Iain Avery Bryson was born in Eugene, Oregon in 1977, and grew up primarily in Oregon and Connecticut. He attended the University of Connecticut from 1995 to 2003, earning a BA in sociology/criminal justice and a MA in political science. He has worked in the fields of criminal justice, social work, education, and organic farming, though his primary job for the past thirteen years has been responding to the abduction of his daughter, Adelle. He is currently living in Connecticut with his wife, Emily.

Made in the USA
Columbia, SC
20 September 2024

42689925R00328